C0-AVE-018

TAX DESK BOOK FOR THE SMALL BUSINESS

by

The IBP Research and Editorial Staff

•

Institute for Business Planning
IBP PLAZA, ENGLEWOOD CLIFFS, N. J. 07632

This publication is designed to provide accurate and authoritative information in regard to the subject matter covered. It is sold with the understanding that the publisher is not engaged in rendering legal, accounting or other professional service. If legal advice or other expert assistance is required, the services of a competent professional person should be sought.

–From a Declaration of Principles jointly adopted by a Committee of the American Bar Association and a Committee of Publishers and Associations.

IBP Plaza, Englewood Cliffs, N. J. 07632

Library of Congress Catalog Card Number: 75-17121

INTRODUCTION

Although there are countless tax reference books available, only a few of these, at most, are addressed to the specific concerns and needs of the small businessman. Yet the small businessman, like the large corporation, faces difficult tax problems; and though his tax problems are often not the same, finding the best tax solution is just as vital to the success of his business as it is to the success of a large corporation.

The purpose of this book, then, is to provide the small businessman with a useful tax reference book designed for his specific needs. In it he will find an up-to-date rundown on most of the major tax factors involved in both the ordinary and extraordinary decisions he will be called on to make in his business career. From the initial setup right through to the final sellout, he will find collected here a thorough explanation of the tax consequences of each decision.

In short, this is a desk book designed to give you, the small businessman, an overview of most of the basic tax problems you are likely to face. Even where you run into especially tough problems, you will find that this book is still valuable—because each paragraph is cross-referenced with other, more comprehensive IBP sources which can give you instant answers on *all* the tax problems you are ever likely to face.

TABLE OF CONTENTS

SECTION I—SHOULD YOU INCORPORATE?

SECTION II—SUBCHAPTER S ELECTION

SECTION III—THE BENEFITS OF A A PROFESSIONAL CORPORATION

SECTION IV—HOW TO MAXIMIZE THE TAX BENEFITS OF DOING BUSINESS AS A PARTNERSHIP

SECTION V— FAMILY PARTNERSHIP FOR LOWER TAXES

SECTION VI—THE BENEFITS OF A SOLE PROPRIETORSHIP

SECTION VII—THE BEST SALARY ARRANGEMENT WITH YOUR CORPORATION

SECTION VIII—MAKING THE MOST OF FRINGE BENEFITS

SECTION IX—USING EXPENSES TO GET BIG TAX BREAKS

SECTION X—DEPRECIATION

SECTION XI—CUTTING TAXES THROUGH BAD DEBTS

SECTION XII—MAKING THE MOST OF BUSINESS LOSSES

SECTION XIII—USING THE BEST ACCOUNTING METHOD

SECTION XIV—INVENTORY METHODS

SECTION XV—EQUIPMENT

SECTION XVI—CAPITAL GAINS OPPORTUNITIES

SECTION XVII—GETTING PROFITS OUT OF THE CORPORATION

SECTION XVIII—BUYING AND SELLING A BUSINESS

SECTION XIX—KEEPING RECORDS TO PROTECT YOU FROM TAX TROUBLE

SECTION XX—THE TAX AUDIT

SECTION XXI—TWELVE TAX KEYS TO WEALTH

APPENDIX

SECTION I
SHOULD YOU INCORPORATE?

Generally speaking, businessmen do not undertake to do anything without having a good reason. In this respect, the decision whether or not to incorporate a business is no different than any other decision. You should have good reasons, and you should be aware of the consequences. In this section, the various advantages and disadvantages of doing business as a corporation are discussed in a general way. Some strategic considerations are also discussed. Most of these will be discussed in much greater detail in subsequent sections. Special attention will be paid to several important tax considerations, however, which are certain to play an important part in your decision.

[¶101] CORPORATE ADVANTAGES

Since the corporate form of doing business has been around considerably longer than the income tax, it obviously has advantages that have nothing to do with the tax law. Among these advantages are limited liability, centralized management, ease of raising capital through the use of stock, and the ability to attract and keep key personnel through various fringe benefit arrangements or through participation in ownership.

Of these advantages, limited liability is probably the most important, since a partnership and even a sole proprietorship can achieve most of the other aims in different ways. Limited liability simply means that the owners of the corporation in most cases cannot be held accountable for losses beyond the value of the stock they hold. For the small business, however, even this factor may not be too important, since when it needs to raise money, as with a loan, the owners will probably have to guarantee the debts anyway. Yet the idea of limited liability has great appeal, even if in practice it does not amount to very much.

Corporations have an additional advantage over other forms of business in that they may have perpetual existence. Again, in practice this may not be a great advantage unless the corporation is spectacularly successful, but the idea associated with it—which is that ownership, through the stock, can be transferred indefinitely—is also appealing. The point is simply that many of the purely corporate advantages of doing business as a corporation are valuable for the most part to a very large corporation, rather than to a small business. This is especially true in light of the fact that a small business that is not a corporation can always choose to operate as a corporation later, if it grows large enough to profit from such a change.

[¶102] TAX ADVANTAGES

As far as a small business is concerned, the tax advantages of operating as a corporation may be much more important than the purely corporate advantages. This is mainly because of the difference in tax rates for corporations and individuals, but there are other reasons as well. Under present law, individuals are taxed "progressively," which means that the more income they make, the higher the percentage of the income they pay as taxes. The top rate is now 70%, which is mitigated in part by the 50% maximum tax on earned income and by the availability of income averaging. (These options are discussed in the Appendix at pp. 408-409.) However, the 50% maximum tax applies only to earned income, which for the most part means salary, and income averaging will be of benefit to a high-bracket taxpayer for only a few years. So, in the end, he will still be left with a 70% rate.

Corporations, by contrast, pay taxes based on a different rate system. The first $25,000 of corporate income is taxed at a flate rate of 22%, and all amounts over $25,000 are taxed at a flat rate of 48%. So, wherever a businessman finds himself in a tax bracket higher than 22% or 48%, doing business in the corporate form presents a potential tax shelter to the extent that its brackets are lower.

Of course, he would ultimately have to pay the piper when the earnings are distributed to him, but even then it usually still works out better overall. What's more, in the meantime, he gets the added benefit of deferring the payment of the tax. In other words, this second tax is not actually due until the earnings are distributed. With a partnership, proprietorship, or Subchapter S corporation, the earnings are taxable to the owners when they are received.

Another tax advantage relates to the 10% minimum tax on tax-preference income. Code §56 allows individuals and corporations a $30,000 exemption from this tax. When an individual operates as a proprietor or as a partner, only one $30,000 exemption is allowed. Where he operates in the corporate form, however, two $30,000 exemptions—a $30,000 exemption at the corporate level and a $30,000 exemption at the individual level—are allowed. Of course, if there is more than one shareholder, they, in effect, share the benefit of the additional $30,000 exemption allowed to the corporation. The total tax savings, assuming that the full exemption is used, comes to about $3,000 per year.

With proper planning, the owners of a closely held business can set things up so that they get two or more $30,000 exemptions.

Take a simple example: You are the sole owner of a corporation that is putting up a new manufacturing plant and warehouse. You will be taking the fastest depreciation you can get on both (150%-declining-balance). The excess of accelerated depreciation over straight line is considered a tax-preference subject to the minimum tax. If you as an individual have no other tax-preference income, it might pay you to hold the warehouse individually and lease it to the corporation. In this way, you'd have another $30,000 of minimum tax exemption plus the amount of your regular personal tax liability as a shield against the tax preference generated by the warehouse. Let's say your total exemptions were $60,000: the tax saving would be 10% of that amount or $6,000 per year. As in the usual lease arrangement, you'd have the problem of working out the rent and the depreciation to produce a good tax result, but this is familiar procedure.

But before you did it, you'd have to consider how the arrangement would work out compared to the 50% maximum tax on earned income. (Tax preferences in excess of $30,000 reduce the earned income eligible for the ceiling).

Another tax advantage of a corporation is that where an individual investor borrows money to carry an investment, he can deduct only 50% of that portion of the interest he pays which exceeds the sum of $25,000 plus the income from his investment (Code §163(d)(1)). The 50% deduction limitation does not apply to the interest incurred by corporations, since the statute specifically excepts corporations from this rule. On the other hand, the limitation applies to partnerships but only at the partners' level. This means that the investment income, interest, and other expenses are passed through to the individual partners. On their individual returns, they would be able to deduct only 50% of the amount in excess of the investment income plus $25,000.

[¶102.1] Checklist of Tax Advantages

The following is a list of the main tax advantages which can result from operating a business in corporate form. Some may not apply in a particular case, but all can potentially result in tax savings.

☐ (1) The corporate form may be used as a tax shelter.

☐ (2) Corporations in foreign trade or in other ventures can get special tax exemptions.

☐ (3) Members of a family may be stockholders without many of the burdens and restrictions of family partnerships.

☐ (4) The corporate form makes it possible for owner-executives to realize better wealth-building advantages under a corporate pension or profit-sharing plan.

☐ (5) Death benefits up to $5,000 can be paid tax free to beneficiaries of a stockholder-employee.

☐ (6) By incorporating, you avoid questions of your right to deduct losses. Individuals can deduct in full only casualty losses or losses incurred in a trade or business or in transactions entered into for profit (§165(c)). Meeting this requirement can sometimes be tough. Corporations are not so restricted. All losses are assumed to be incident to the business of the corporation.

☐ (7) Deferred compensation and stock retirement plans can be utilized to achieve the financial planning purposes of the owner, his family, and his employees.

☐ (8) Only 15% of dividend income is taxed to the corporation—100% is taxed to the partnership or sole proprietorship.

☐ (9) The corporate form may facilitate saving income and estate taxes by gifts to children or to a family foundation.

☐ (10) A new corporation is a new taxpayer. There may be a substantial advantage in choosing new tax elections.

☐ (11) A corporation may be able to carry insurance on the lives of owner-executives at a reduced annual tax cost and then, without any further income tax burden, realize the proceeds and make them available to pay estate taxes. Working stockholders are eligible for $50,000 of tax-free group insurance coverage.

☐ (12) Corporation stockholders can often control the dividend processes. Therefore, unlike partners or sole proprietors, they usually can dictate the year they will get income and can select

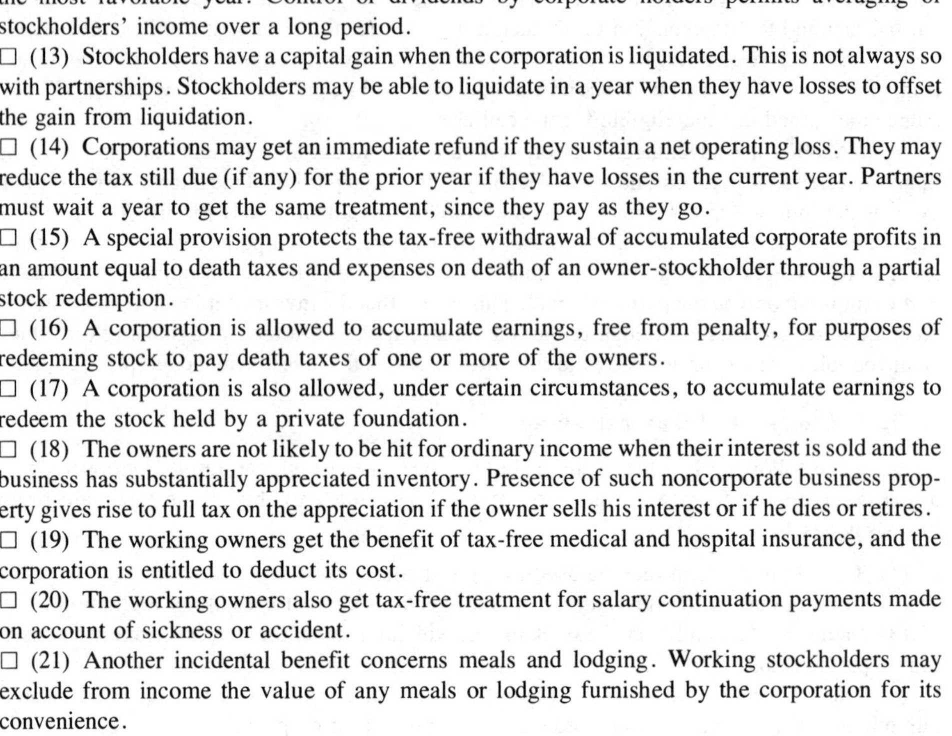

the most favorable year. Control of dividends by corporate holders permits averaging of stockholders' income over a long period.

☐ (13) Stockholders have a capital gain when the corporation is liquidated. This is not always so with partnerships. Stockholders may be able to liquidate in a year when they have losses to offset the gain from liquidation.

☐ (14) Corporations may get an immediate refund if they sustain a net operating loss. They may reduce the tax still due (if any) for the prior year if they have losses in the current year. Partners must wait a year to get the same treatment, since they pay as they go.

☐ (15) A special provision protects the tax-free withdrawal of accumulated corporate profits in an amount equal to death taxes and expenses on death of an owner-stockholder through a partial stock redemption.

☐ (16) A corporation is allowed to accumulate earnings, free from penalty, for purposes of redeeming stock to pay death taxes of one or more of the owners.

☐ (17) A corporation is also allowed, under certain circumstances, to accumulate earnings to redeem the stock held by a private foundation.

☐ (18) The owners are not likely to be hit for ordinary income when their interest is sold and the business has substantially appreciated inventory. Presence of such noncorporate business property gives rise to full tax on the appreciation if the owner sells his interest or if he dies or retires.

☐ (19) The working owners get the benefit of tax-free medical and hospital insurance, and the corporation is entitled to deduct its cost.

☐ (20) The working owners also get tax-free treatment for salary continuation payments made on account of sickness or accident.

☐ (21) Another incidental benefit concerns meals and lodging. Working stockholders may exclude from income the value of any meals or lodging furnished by the corporation for its convenience.

[¶103] AVOIDING TAX PITFALLS

We have pointed out some of the tax and nontax advantages of using the corporate form; now let's take a look at some of the pitfalls and how they can be avoided.

[¶103.1] Changing the Character of Income

Before you choose the corporate form you have to consider how the conversion of income will affect you. When you operate as a proprietorship or partnership, exempt income or capital gains retain their character when either are passed through to you. With the corporate form, they lose their character. In other words, when the corporation distributes to the shareholders income on which it has paid tax, it takes the character of a dividend and is taxable as such. The same is true with capital gains—when they are distributed as current dividends, they are converted into ordinary income.

[¶103.2] Tax Evasion

If the principal purpose of a corporation is tax evasion or avoidance, §269 permits IRS to deny a tax deduction or other allowance otherwise available. But proving such a principal purpose is difficult. Also, under §482 IRS can allocate income of the corporation to the person(s) who produces it and prevent the use of the corporation as a tax shelter.

To avoid the imposition of these statutes, the organization must act as well as look like a corporation. The bylaws, for example, should provide for centralized management, including control of such matters as assignment of personal services; fixing work deadlines, working hours, fees, salaries, and bonuses; termination of employment; and selection and rejection of clients. Corporate formalities must be observed in such matters as meetings, record and minute keeping, adopting and using a corporate seal, etc.

[¶103.3] The PHC Hurdle

Another IRS weapon to fight the tax shelter of the corporate form is the personal holding company. If at any time during the last half of the taxable year a company has five or fewer stockholders who own more than 50% of the outstanding stock, directly or indirectly, IRS can attack it as a personal holding company and subject it to a 70% tax rate on undistributed income. If at least 60% of a corporation's ordinary gross income is "personal holding company income," the corporation will be taxed as a personal holding company.

There are eight separate categories of personal holding company income. They are:

☐ (1) ***Dividends, etc.:*** Dividends, interest, royalties (other than mineral, oil or gas royalties or copyright royalties) and annuities. ("Interest" here doesn't include interest that constitutes rent.)

☐ (2) ***Mineral, Oil, or Gas Royalties:*** The adjusted income from these royalties is phc income unless it constitutes 50% or more of adjusted ordinary gross income. The deductions allowable under §162 for business expenses other than compensation to shareholders constitute 15% or more of adjusted ordinary gross income, and no more than 10% of ordinary gross income is other phc income (§543(a)(3)).

☐ (3) ***Copyright Royalties:*** Copyright royalties are not personal holding company income if: (1) they constitute 50% or more of gross income, (2) other personal holding income for the year is 10% or less of gross income, and (3) business deductions equal 25% or more of the amount by which ordinary gross income exceeds copyright royalties paid plus depreciation on copyrights (§543(a)(4)).

☐ (4) ***Rents:*** The adjusted income from rents is usually phc income unless it constitutes 50% or more of the corporation's adjusted ordinary gross income and the sum of the dividends paid (considered paid or consented to) during the year equals or exceeds the amount by which the personal holding company income exceeds 10% of the ordinary gross income (§543(a)(2)).

In figuring the adjusted income, the following rents are not included: (1) rents for use of corporate property by a 25% stockholder and (2) film rentals (certain film rentals get a treatment similar to these rentals—others are treated as copyright royalties).

☐ (5) ***Film Rentals:*** These are divided into two classes: produced film rentals and all other film rentals. Produced film rentals are phc income unless they constitute at least 50% of ordinary gross income. All other film rentals are treated as copyright royalties.

☐ (6) ***Compensation for Stockholder; Use of Corporate Property:*** Amounts received as compensation for the use of property of the corporation provided that at some time during the taxable year 25% in value of the corporation's stock is owned by the person entitled to use the property. The source or form of the compensation or whether the right is obtained directly from the corporation or indirectly is immaterial.

☐ (7) ***Personal Service Contracts:*** Where a contract with the corporation either calls for the services of a 25%-or-more stockholder (based on value of outstanding stock) or designates the person other than the corporation who is to perform the service, the income from such services is personal holding company income. This rule also applies to amounts received from the sale or other disposition of such contract.
☐ (8) ***Estates and Trusts:*** Income from estates and trusts and gains from the sale or other disposition of interests in such entities.

The phc problem can usually be avoided in any of these ways:

☐ (1) When the corporation has large amounts of personal holding company income (e.g., dividends, royalties, rents) that may put it over the 60% mark, it should try to bring in additional operating income to avoid personal holding company status.
☐ (2) It can consider paying out some of the corporation's income in bonuses and additional compensation to working stockholders. But any such distributions should be made on the basis of services performed by the stockholder-employees, not on the basis of their ownership in the corporation.
☐ (3) Another approach is to increase the number of stockholders. Only those corporations with five or fewer stockholders are subject to this rule. Adding one or more stockholders could do the trick.
☐ (4) Another point is with personal service contracts. Where a contract with the corporation calls for the services of a 25%-or-more stockholder, have the corporation and not the customer designate who is to perform the contract. The income from this contract would, therefore, not be treated as personal holding company income.

[¶103.4] Accumulated Earnings Penalty

Once the corporation has accumulated more than $150,000 of earnings, it may be faced with the penalty tax on accumulated earnings (i.e., 27½% on the first $100,000 and 38½% on the excess) (§531). However, the law says that a corporation may accumulate earnings for purposes of a §303 redemption, i.e., a redemption for purposes of paying estate taxes. It also allows the accumulation of earnings for purposes of redeeming stock from a private foundation under certain circumstances.

Where the corporation has earnings that are subject to the penalty, it is forced to distribute earnings to the shareholders (§535(c)). The distribution is taxable as any other dividend and is subject to the $100 exclusion. An alternative to this ordinary income treatment for dividends lies in the shareholders' selling their stock. Although the sale price will be discounted because of the penalty, the resultant gain will be capital in nature.

The penalty does not present a real problem where the corporation distributes most of its earnings to the working stockholders in the form of compensation because then only a small amount, if any, would be left in the corporation to accumulate, and the $150,000 mark would not be exceeded. However, where the corporation is used as a tax shelter and large amounts are left with it, the penalty does present a problem.

One way the corporation may effectively deal with this problem is to expand its operations. The accumulation of earnings for business reasons, such as expanding operations, is not subject to the penalty.

In order to prove that the accumulation is reasonable, the following steps should be taken:

☐ (1) Annual studies by the corporation to keep track of potential vulnerability to the penalty. This could be conveniently done in conjunction with the review of the annual report. A grace period of 2½ months provided by §563 should give the directors ample time to take action on any distributions necessary to avoid the penalty.
☐ (2) Setting forth in detail in the minutes any plans for expansion or other good reasons for retaining earnings.
☐ (3) Carefully preserving correspondence, estimates, work papers, engineering reports, etc. These will be valuable in supporting your argument that the accumulation was reasonable.

If you anticipate a problem with the accumulated earnings penalty, the following checklist may be useful in helping you to prove that you had a good reason for the accumulation.

☐ Policy considerations and business plans should go into minutes of your directors' meetings or in your files, reports, and records.
☐ Refer to equipment and fixed asset purchase orders if they are placed. Or at least get a complete, written plan showing just why you desire to retain earnings for expansion.
☐ Include a distinterested independent economist's report. That may show whether your business cycle requires your retention of funds to meet the dire forecasts given you by your experts.
☐ Have the directors approve the amount of actual reserves required to meet the possible liability or loss for which you are providing.
☐ Prove through experts that it would be bad business judgment to pay dividends because a shrinkage in the market value of assets offsets the year's earnings. This condition may very properly suggest to good management that dividends should not be paid. This argument may carry some weight if you have an operating company but not if you have a holding or investment company.
☐ Maybe you need a study to show you have impairment of capital to be restored before any earnings are available for distribution to the stockholders. Often, older companies find they do not have the accumulation they assume.
☐ If you do not have the immediate funds, declare a dividend payable in a later year. Several cases (not dealing directly with §531) suggest that the declaration creates a creditor position for a stockholder if surplus is reduced on the books and the debt to stockholders is set up.
☐ Prepare to show that cutting your inventories has produced a high liquid position and reduced borrowing from banks. That does not mean (to avoid risk of a §531 penalty) that you must start paying dividends that would not be essential were you to have large loans outstanding. Minutes should indicate that (anticipating the return of normal times) you are building up your cash resources to avoid borrowing.
☐ You ought to check normal business steps to be taken to keep your cash down. Consider delaying deliveries to your customers; cutting your cash and piling up inventories and receivables; buying all possible inventories or supplies needed for current production to cut your cash; and avoiding advance collections from customers.
☐ Payment of a $25,000 to $32,000 annual premium of life insurance for a nonstockholding officer for the benefit of the company has been held a good business purpose to cut income. It was noted that the payments were not improper accumulations in themselves. You can assume that investments in life insurance will be approved if you insure an important executive at a low cost.

But it is prudent to follow these rules:

(a) Avoid where possible single-premium policies.

(b) Don't tie the insurance to a commitment to buy in shares. Make the corporate retirement of stock a completely separate commitment, backed by the full resources and future earning power of the company.

(c) Keep the insurance in line with the value of the man—proportion it to his compensation, not his stock holdings.

[¶103.5] Unreasonable Compensation

Related to the problem of accumulated earnings is the one dealing with unreasonable compensation. The corporation may deduct only "reasonable" compensation; the excess may be treated as a dividend to an employee-shareholder.

Here, as with the other hurdles, the watchword is caution. One of the steps the parties should take to minimize the impact of a disallowance of compensation is to use a reimbursement agreement ("Oswald By-law"). The working stockholder agrees under such an agreement to reimburse the corporation for any amounts determined by IRS or the courts to be unreasonable. A payment under such an agreement would give employee-shareholder an offsetting deduction and put the money back into the corporation. For a sample reimbursement agreement, see the Appendix at p. 412.

[¶103.6] One-Man Corporation

When a one-man operation incorporates, the first problem he runs into is the personal holding company question. Another is whether the corporate entity is a sham. With a one-man corporation, the owner might find it extremely difficult to operate as a corporation, especially if he has operated as an individual owner. Once he has operated as a proprietor, it's difficult to change to a new approach. His natural inclination is to continue to operate as he has been operating. If he fails to overcome this tendency, he runs the risk of having the corporate entity disregarded and treated as a sham.

With the exception of accountants and attorneys, some tax experts feel that most self-employed individuals would have this problem unless their professional advisors take the time to teach them how to operate a corporation or otherwise supervise the operation. Many state statutes permit a corporation to have one shareholder-director. But some tax experts feel that this classification does not assure immunity from IRS attack. However, K. Martin Worthy, a former IRS chief counsel, has stated, with reference to professional corporations, that "such a provision in itself will not serve to deny corporate classification." The same principle is applicable to other corporations.

[¶104] STOCK AND RELATED MATTERS

Every corporation must have some stock. The purpose of the stock is to establish ownership of the corporation. But it is also used to raise initial capital and, in some cases, capital for expansion or acquisitions. Stock, of course, is not the only way a corporation can raise capital. But for the small corporation, stock or stock plus debt is the most common method. Whether stock or debt is used for corporate financing (after the initial creation, which must employ stock) is a question that depends on many factors. The tax law also plays an important role in this question.

When organizing a corporation, the following tax questions should be carefully considered:

☐ (1) ***Split Up of Business Activities:*** Does the nature of the proposed business lend itself to the division of its activities between two business entities—a corporation and a partnership or a proprietorship? Will the division produce tax savings? What will be the effect on liabilities or financing?

☐ (2) ***Tax-Free Incorporation:*** Property can be transferred on incorporation tax free if the transferors wind up owning stock possessing at least 80% of the total combined voting power of all classes of stock entitled to vote and at least 80% of the total number of shares of all other classes of stock of the corporation (§351; 368(c)). If the property being transferred to the corporation has increased in value and if it is desirable to pay a capital gains tax to step up its value in order to get higher depreciation allowances, it may be desirable to make the incorporation a taxable transaction (§362(a)). There may be a taxable gift for a party who contributes more to the corporation than he receives in order to benefit a member of his family.

☐ (3) ***Advantages of Transfers of Encumbered Property to the Corporation:*** Transfers of encumbered property to the corporation and the assumption of liabilities on the property transferred will not destroy an otherwise tax-free incorporation. The assumption of liabilities lays the groundwork for the accumulation of earnings to pay off the debt and the transferor can use corporate earnings to pay off the debt.

☐ (4) ***Disadvantages of Transfers of Encumbered Property:*** If you transfer encumbered property to the corporation and it assumes the debt, the excess of the liabilities assumed plus liabilities to which the property is subject will be taxed to the transferors to the extent that they exceed the cost or other tax basis of the property (§357(c)).

☐ (5) ***Lease of Assets to Corporation:*** Do the organizers of the corporation intend to transfer buildings or other depreciable property to the corporation for stock? Would a lease arrangement rather than an outright transfer of the property produce more favorable tax results to the corporation and its organizers? The lessor may use depreciation to offset income from the property and the corporation may likewise benefit, since the deduction for rent paid could exceed the depreciation deduction. Bear in mind that accelerated depreciation on real estate generally and on personal property subject to a net lease is considered tax-preference income subject to the minimum tax and also offsetting earned income eligible for the maximum tax on earned income. The 50% limitation on the deductibility of excess investment interest also needs to be considered. This applies to individuals and Subchapter S shareholders but not regular corporations (§163).

☐ (6) ***Promoters' Stock:*** Consider saving the promoters from having stock received by them taxed as compensation by having them buy cheap stock prior to the full financing of the corporation or by having them transfer patents, plans or models in exchange for stock in the corporation transaction. The earlier the promoters acquire their stock, the safer they are.

☐ (7) ***Capital Structure:*** One of the most important decisions to be made will be as to the capital structure to be adopted. How much debt? How much equity capital or stock and what form is it to take? The considerations basically involved are:

(a) Interest paid is deductible but dividends are not;
(b) Debt reduces possibility of tax on improper accumulation of surplus;
(c) Potential tax liability on debt retirement is less than on stock redemption;

(d) Debt imposes fixed obligations of principal and interest, and possibly sinking fund requirements and default may threaten control; and

(e) Choice between par and no-par stock, the latter giving freer hand in fixing considerations that must be paid.

Be sure to observe IRS guidelines on whether securities are debt or equity (§385).

☐ (8) ***Thin Incorporation:*** If the original capital of the corporation is to include both equity and borrowed capital, be careful to avoid the undesirable tax effect of an unrealistic and top-heavy debt structure. The courts have approved a debt to equity ratio of 4 to 1 in some cases. A ratio of better than 2 to 1 is apt to raise questions. Also, the proportions of debt to equity should vary among the individual stockholders to avoid an IRS contention that the loans are in reality capital contributions.

☐ (9) ***Debentures:*** If the corporation's initial capitalization is to include borrowed capital, the debt should be designed in full knowledge of the possibly conflicting "credit" and "tax" positions of the corporation. A debenture that gives the corporation good credit may be viewed as stock and jeopardize the corporation's tax position.

☐ (10) ***Avoiding §306 Preferred Stock:*** If you want to create a preference in equity or earnings, do it with original-issue preferred stock. If you subsequently create or issue preferred stock in order to accomplish this purpose (e.g., by recapitalization or as a dividend on the common), this stock runs the risk of being considered "§306 stock." Such a result would cause a gain on its sale to be treated as ordinary income, at least to the extent of the corporation's earnings. However, if the preferred stock is issued at incorporation, it couldn't be §306 stock. So, in effect, original issue will give the preferred stockholder a way of siphoning off part of his investment without ordinary income treatment.

☐ (11) ***Collapsible Corporations:*** The organizers of a corporation should not overlook the "collapsible corporation" rule if they plan to organize the corporation for a limited period of time or for a specific short-term purpose. This rule converts the capital gains available on liquidation and the sale of corporate stock into ordinary income. If more than 70% of the gain is attributable to appreciated corporate property that has been held for less than three years, the rule may apply (§341).

Finally, the organizers should consider the possibility of electing to be taxed as a partnership under Subchapter S, which will be discussed in detail in the next section, and the possibility of using §1244 stock, which will be discussed in ¶105.

Assuming that there is some stock to be issued, the next question is how much and what kind of stock. The answer to this question depends on the expectations of the business. The following paragraphs may be useful in helping you to decide this question.

[¶104.1] Tax Treatment of Losses

When the transaction is set up as a loan, the lender should seek to have nonpayment of the debt in whole or in part give him an ordinary deduction. Any future adjustment of the debt will raise questions for the borrower as to whether the cancellation or reduction of an outstanding debt must be reported by him as taxable income (or whether it can serve to reduce the basis of property owned by borrower or be treated as a gift to him).

[¶104.2] Equity v. Debt Financing

The use of equity financing (an ownership interest in the enterprise, generally by a stock purchase) or debt financing (such as issuance and acceptance of bonds, notes, etc.) must be viewed in the light of both the business and tax considerations and from the point of view of the borrower and the investor. Check IRS guidelines on whether securities are debt or equity (§385). The holder of debt can always recover the principal tax free, but, in some circumstances, a redemption of stock may be considered a taxable dividend.

Interest on bonds, notes and debentures is deductible from ordinary income by the borrower. Thus, when money is raised, a corporation in the 48% tax bracket must earn about 10% before taxes to carry a 5% preferred stock but can carry a 5% debenture if it earns 5%.

[¶104.3] Certain Interest Not Deductible

Interest on notes, bonds or debentures given by a corporation in order to obtain money to invest in tax-exempt bonds or securities is not deductible by the corporation, nor are interest or loans to purchase or carry certain life insurance, endowment and annuity policies. General working capital borrowing should not be caught in this disallowance where the borrower has assets of this type. See §264 of the Code.

[¶104.4] How Debt Financing Costs Less Than Equity Financing

When a corporation needs money, a prime consideration is the cost of using debt or equity financing. When a company borrows money, all the money earned by the new money carries through to cover interest costs. At a 48% corporate tax rate, a profitable corporation risks 52% of the interest due on its debt. The balance is absorbed by the tax saving on the deduction of the interest.

When equity financing is used, the corporation must earn enough to pay the corporate tax and have enough left over to pay the dividend rate if it is to service the financing. A corporation has to earn 10% before taxes to carry 5% preferred stock. But it needs to earn only 5% to carry a 5% debenture bond. Here is a table that illustrates this comparison:

	4%	*5%*	*6%*	*7%*	*8%*	*9%*	*10%*
Corporate Earnings For Stock	$7,692	$9,615	$11,538	$13,462	$15,385	$17,308	$19,231
Corporate Earnings For Bonds	4,000	5,000	6,000	7,000	8,000	9,000	10,000
Excess Pretax Earnings Needed for Stock	$3,692	$4,615	$ 5,538	$ 6,462	$ 7,385	$ 8,308	$ 9,231

[¶104.5] When It Pays to Use Preferred Stock

Preferred stock is another effective way of getting additional equity capital. Though it is somewhere between debt and equity, for tax purposes it is treated as equity. Distributions are not deductible by the corporation and are considered dividends.

The use of preferred stock is especially useful to small corporations. These companies can use preferred stock as a means of providing key executives with compensatory incentives without giving up any control. It also may be used for purposes of splitting income and bailing out corporate earnings. The stock is issued to members of the owner's family. During the years the business is operated, dividends paid out to them are taxed at lower rates. Corporate earnings may be bailed out by issuing preferred stock to the owner's wife at the time the corporation is formed and redeeming these shares at capital gains rates at a later date.

There are also advantages in disposing of the business. Preferred stock may be used as a means of retaining an investment interest in the business after selling it. It may also be used when the owner wants to transfer the business to his children to save estate taxes but also wants to retain control. This is achieved by a recapitalization under which voting preferred and nonvoting common stock are used. The owner keeps the voting preferred and passes the nonvoting stock on to his children. The appreciation of the business is thereby picked up by the children, while the owner retains control.

[¶104.6] Convertible, Participating Preference Stock

A relatively new type of preference stock that offers maximum flexibility to the investor is illustrated by Litton Industries' issue of "Convertible Preference Stock, Participating Series." The main features of the stock are:

☐ (1) The holder is entitled to cash dividends if cash dividends are declared on the common stock. The rate of dividend is equal to the amount declared on the common multiplied by the number of shares of common stock into which the preference stock is convertible.

☐ (2) Conversion ratio of the preference starts out on the basis of one share of common for each share of preference and increases each year for 24 years until it finally reaches the point where the holder is entitled to 2.0145 shares of common for each share of preference.

☐ (3) As an alternative to converting, the holder may sell up to 3% of his preference shares each year without reducing the number of shares into which the remaining preference stock is convertible.

Litton got a ruling from IRS that §306(a)(1) would not apply to the proceeds of the disposition of the Participating Series. This means that if an investor sells, the gain realized will be treated as capital gain unless such sale is in anticipation of a redemption. Since IRS rules only on pending transactions, a tax ruling as to the effects of future redemptions could not be issued to Litton. However, it was the opinion of independent counsel and also the opinion of Litton's tax counsel when the stock was issued that, under IRS's policy, proceeds from future redemptions would be considered capital gains.

The convertible participating preference stock was issued prior to the Revenue Act of 1969, which contained a number of provisions affecting the tax treatment of stock dividends and conversion rights (§305). Increases in the conversion ratio may result in a taxable distribution under these rules. IRS is authorized to issue regulations governing the extent to which increases in the conversion ratio shall be treated as a taxable distribution. These rules should be considered before using convertible preference stock.

[¶104.7] The Advantages of Using Income Bond Financing

Income bonds have the advantage of reducing the cost of financing through tax deductions while not imposing the fixed commitment usually required with debt obligations.

Although interest is contingent on earnings, it is tax deductible. This benefit is an important advantage. Large corporations paying bond interest can reduce their tax burden by 48% of what they would pay if this amount had been disbursed as dividends on preferred stock.

In the organized exchanges, income bonds are likely to trade "flat." This means that the purchase price of the bond includes all accumulated interest. As a consequence, after the payment is made, the price will tend to drop by the amount of the payment, as in the case of common stock after payment of the expected dividends. Fixed-interest bonds, on the other hand, trade on the basis of "and interest," which means that the seller is entitled to the interest that accumulated during the period he held the bonds. This can have tax advantages for the investor in giving him capital gain rather than fully taxed interest.

Frequently in recapitalizations, preferred stocks—sometimes convertible preferred stocks—are changed into income bonds, which may or may not be convertible. For example, Armour stockholders approved a recapitalization plan providing for the exchange of each share of the company's convertible preferred stock with dividend arrears of $18.50 for $120 principal amount of 5% cumulative income bonds (subordinated to all other debt) plus a warrant to buy common stock. The company estimated that this financing will result in a yearly tax saving of $1.5 million.

[¶104.8] Why Debenture-Warrant Unit Is Better Than Convertible Debentures

Corporations planning the issuance of convertible bonds should consider issuing debentures with warrants instead. Both give the lender equity participation, but even where the two issues may involve identical obligations, substantial tax benefits will often result from issuing debentures with warrants. These benefits stem from the allowable deduction for amortization of the original bond issue discount.

If you used a convertible bond, although bond discount may in fact result from the conversion factor, it is unlikely that you could use the claimed "discount" to sustain a tax deduction (still, a protective refund claim should probably be filed). Let's assume your company issued a 6%, 20-year bond convertible into common stock at a price of approximately 120% of the current market price of the common stock. The company could only deduct the interest expense, plus a small amount of amortized issuance expense. The company in the 48% tax bracket would thus be about $30 per $1,000 bond out of pocket after taxes.

On the other hand, if the company issued 6%, 20-year debentures with warrant to purchase an equivalent number of common shares at 120% of the current market, part of the proceeds received could be allocated to the warrants. The Investment Bankers Association of America made a study of the valuation of warrants, the results of which are set out in the table below headed "Average Values."

On the basis of these figures, the value of the warrants in our example would be roughly $300, so that $700 would be allocable to each $1,000 debenture. The company would thus be able to deduct not only the 6% interest ($60 per year) per debenture, but could also amortize the $300 over the 20-year life of the debenture, thus producing an additional annual deduction of $15. The net annual cash expense, after taxes, would be approximately $22.50 per $1,000 debenture or 25% less than if the convertible debenture route were used. Possibly part of these savings might be lost in the form of a slightly higher interest rate were warrants are used.

Average Values

Ratio of Market Value of Optioned Stock to Exercise Price	*Ratio of Market Value of Option to Exercise Price*
80%	28%
90	34
100	41
110	48
120	55

A special aspect of the problem of debt v. equity is the problem of "thin incorporation," where the shareholders disguise a large amount of equity as debt for the purpose of getting interest deductions on payments that in fact are taxable dividends.

[¶104.9] Debt-Equity Guidelines

The Treasury has the authority to promulgate regulatory guidelines, to the extent necessary or appropriate, for determining whether a corporate obligation constitutes stock or indebtedness (§385). These guidelines are to set forth factors to be taken into account in determining, with respect to a particular factual situation, whether a debtor-creditor relationship exists or whether a corporation-shareholder relationship exists.

Some of the factors that may be taken into account in these guidelines are as follows:

☐ (1) Whether there is a written unconditional promise to pay on demand or on a specified date a sum certain in money in return for an adequate consideration in money or money's worth and to pay a fixed rate of interest;
☐ (2) Whether there is subordination to or preference over any indebtedness of the corporation;
☐ (3) The ratio of debt to equity of the corporation;
☐ (4) Whether there is convertibility into the stock of the corporation; and
☐ (5) The relationship between holdings of stock in the corporation and holdings of the interest in question.

Bearing in mind that the facts in the particular case may change the proper ratio, a 3½-to-1 ratio of debt to equity is considered to be a good rule of thumb as to what the Treasury and the courts will accept. Since both the Treasury and the Tax Court had approved a 3½-to-1 capitalization in a case where there was nothing unusual in the facts, 3½-to-1 ratio of debt to equity soon came to be accepted as a safe ratio. While this may be a useful rule of thumb, there is, of course, nothing final about it.

The courts have also played a major part in this question. Assuming a reasonable ratio of debt-equity, the courts have been influenced by the following factors:

Indicating Debt:

☐ (1) Debt securities have a definite, fixed maturity.
☐ (2) Reasonable interest rate is definitely payable regardless of earnings.
☐ (3) Holders of debt have unrestricted right to sue or enforce payment on default.
☐ (4) Holders of debt do not thereby get voting rights.
☐ (5) Corporation's financial statement reflects advances as debt.
☐ (6) Apart from debt, there is a substantial investment in stock.
☐ (7) There is a bona fide debtor-creditor relationship.
☐ (8) Debentures are not held out as capital.
☐ (9) Loans are disproportionate to shareholding.

Indicating Equity:

☐ (1) Outside creditors would not make loans under similar circumstances.
☐ (2) No business payout for loans.
☐ (3) Shareholders' loans were subordinated to subsequent loans by outside creditors.
☐ (4) No formality of financial records on corporate minutes existed.
☐ (5) No bond or note was issued as evidence of the indebtedness.

[¶105] GETTING ORDINARY LOSS ON STOCK—§1244

The tax law in §1244 recognizes the high risk inherent in a small business. Under this provision, investors in small business corporations can get up to $25,000 in ordinary deductions ($50,000 on a joint return) per year for loss on common stock that is considered to be small business stock (§1244). This rule applies whether the loss was incurred on sale of the stock or on its becoming worthless. It can only be used by the original purchaser of the stock. In order to qualify for this special treatment, the following requisites have to be met:

☐ (1) Such stock cannot be issued in a total amount of more than $500,000; and the entire equity capital of the corporation, including the small business stock, cannot exceed $1,000,000.
☐ (2) A formal plan for the issuance of the small business stock must be adopted during a period of not more than two years. Any previous plan offering "§1244 stock" must first be cancelled.
☐ (3) The stock must be common stock issued for money or property and not for stock or securities.
☐ (4) The corporation issuing the stock must be an operating company. It will qualify if during its most recent five years preceding the loss (or during its entire existence if less), more than 50% of its gross receipts comes from sources other than royalties, rents, dividends, interest, annuities, and capital gains from securities, unless during the period covered, deductions exceeded gross income.

If such stock was acquired for property in a tax-free exchange and the basis for the property was higher than its fair market value, the deductible loss on such stock is reduced by the difference between the basis and that fair market value.

Ordinary losses on small business stock are limited to the basis originally acquired on its issuance. Such losses cannot be increased by increasing basis as a result of subsequent capital contributions. Any such increase must be applied to other stock.

Because of the special benefits of §1244 stock, you may be better off advancing money to a corporation through the purchase of this special stock and be sure of an ordinary loss if business goes bad, than making loans to the corporation and subsequently finding yourself caught in the nebulous area of the bad debt deduction, hoping that it will be considered a business bad debt (deductible as an ordinary deduction) and not a nonbusiness bad debt (deductible as a short-term capital loss).

It may even be possible to establish a loss and still keep the stock in the family by selling it to your in-laws.

[¶105.1] Section 1244 Rules Strictly and Technically Applied

IRC §1244 was obviously adopted by Congress for the purpose of encouraging investment in small business by giving a tax break to such investors. However, IRS and the courts have tended to deny the deduction unless there is a strict and technical compliance with the statute. This means that there must in fact be a written plan, and the stock must be issued in strict compliance with the plan and the statute to a person who is aware that he is purchasing the stock pursuant to §1244 with the intent that he receive §1244 stock. There are, of course, cases that do not apply such a strict standard, but to be safe, all these elements should be provable as a part of the transaction. If you do all these things, your ordinary loss deduction should be safe if your business goes sour.

[¶106] REDUCING CORPORATE TAX

The main way to reduce the corporate tax on the income of a small business is through the use of deductions. And the main deduction used is for salary. The only restrictions on this deduction (which is taken as a business expense under Code §162) are that the salary must be reasonable and that if capital is a material income-producing factor, then some return must be paid upon the capital. In other words, if property was an important income-producing asset of a corporation, it would clearly be unreasonable to pay out all the earnings of the corporation as salary. Some would have to be paid out as nondeductible dividends.

However, in many cases, it is not unreasonable for a small business to pay out a large percentage of its income as salary and thus avoid the corporate tax on that percentage. The only accurate guidelines are the numerous cases on the question, but taxpayers, for the most part, have fared quite well.

Other business deductions include the payment of reasonable rentals or interest to shareholders. However, this is just the reverse of the corporate tax shelter, since the shareholders would have to pick up the income. On the other hand, the shareholders' taxes can be minimized by transfers of the property to lower-bracket members of their families who then pick up the income.

Finally, the corporation is entitled to the 85% dividends-received deduction under Code §243. This means that a corporation in the 22% bracket pays a tax of 3.3% on dividends it receives on the stock of other corporations, and a corporation in the 48% bracket pays only 7.2%. Consequently, if a corporation has surplus funds and puts them into stock that pays dividends, it will receive a much higher net return than an individual, who is entitled to exclude only the first $100 of dividends he receives. This deduction, then, can shield a considerable amount of income from corporate taxes. However, the accumulated earnings penalty and the personal holding company trap must also be considered.

There are, of course, many other corporate deductions, including, in particular, deductions for depreciation and employee benefit plans, but these are discussed at length in subsequent sections. The point here is that all of them can be used to shield corporate income from the corporate tax.

Besides deductions, there are also certain changes of accounting method that may also reduce or eliminate the corporate tax in a given case. The different methods are discussed at length in sections 13 and 14 and need no further comment here.

Finally, perhaps the best way to avoid the corporate tax altogether is by the election of a corporation to be taxed under Subchapter S, which will be discussed in the next section.

SECTION II
SUBCHAPTER S ELECTION

Let's say you have thought it out carefully and decided that operating as a corporation has many advantages. You like the limited liability, want to pass some of the stock to family members, and see other benefits in having your business reorganized as an entity separate from yourself. The only thing that holds you back is that you are afraid you won't be able to get rid of enough of the corporate income, and you don't want to pay a double tax. What can you do?

You can elect to be taxed under Subchapter S. If you qualify, your business will be recognized as a corporation but taxed for the most part as a partnership. That means there is no corporate tax at all. Sound good? It can be. In this section, all the rules and requirements of Subchapter S will be discussed, as well as some important strategic considerations.

[¶201] HOW SUBCHAPTER S WORKS

Basically, Subchapter S (Code §1371-1374) allows certain qualifying corporations to elect to be taxed as partnerships rather than as corporations. Subchapter S corporations are for the most part small business corporations, but they are not necessarily the same small business corporations that qualify for §1244 stock.

A corporation becomes a Subchapter S corporation by election of all of its shareholders. As long as the election is in effect, the earnings of the corporation are taxed directly to the shareholders, as in the case of a partnership, without the incidence of any corporate tax. Losses are also passed through to the shareholders directly, to the extent of their basis in the Subchapter S corporation stock.

As with partnership earnings, the earnings of the Subchapter S corporation are taxed to the shareholders whether distributed or not. This means that they have to pick up the income as earned, whether it is needed in the business or not.

This, of course, is a simplified explanation and will be expanded in the following paragraphs. However, the following list will show some situations in which Subchapter S election may prove beneficial.

☐ (1) The stockholders want to keep earnings in the business and their tax brackets are lower than the effective corporate rate. Where the individual's rates are higher, it is cheaper to pay a salary (assuming it is reasonable) up to the point where the individual's rates reach the corporate rate level and leave the rest in the business. With the availability of an accumulated earnings credit for corporations of $150,000, there is considerable leeway to do this.
☐ (2) The corporation has losses and the individual has profits. By electing to have the individual taxed directly, he can offset the losses of the corporation against his personal profits.
☐ (3) Where the corporation and shareholders are on different tax years, it is possible to defer taxes on undistributed taxable income.
☐ (4) Another positive advantage (and, in many cases, the most important) is the availability of qualified pension or profit-sharing plans. Take a successful partnership whose partners have no desire to accumulate profits in the business and so do not want to incorporate (because incorporation means double taxation). They would like to set up a pension or profit-sharing plan in which they could participate. But as partners, they can't do that. If they incorporate, as corporate employees they can participate in the plan (*Rev. Rul. 66-128*, 1966-1, 339).
☐ (5) Other fringe benefits available are: full tax-free medical reimbursement, health and accident insurance, tax-free sick pay, tax-free meals and lodging, tax-free group term insurance coverage of up to $50,000.
☐ (6) Despite §1378 (which puts a tax on the Subchapter S corporation), there is still leeway to pass through net long-term capital gains by avoiding §1378. Also, a one-shot election may put after-tax proceeds into stockholders' hands.
☐ (7) It is possible for the corporation to make an installment sale of its properties and pass the gains directly through to its shareholders as they are received.
☐ (8) A transfer of Subchapter S stock just before year end can be used to shift income earned by the corporation for the entire year.
☐ (9) Where earnings are substantial and there is a possibility of the accumulated earnings penalty tax, electing Subchapter S eliminates the problem.
☐ (10) In a year when income averaging is available to a shareholder, it may pay to elect Subchapter S to take out ordinary income. The tax cost works out very low when combined with income averaging.
☐ (11) A Subchapter S corporation can also be set up using §1244 stock to insure an ordinary loss deduction rather than capital losses if business goes sour.
☐ (12) Family income can be divided into smaller units taxable at lower rates.

[¶202] REQUIREMENTS OF SUBCHAPTER S ELECTION

There are nine basic requirements that a corporation must meet to qualify for Subchapter S:

☐ (1) It must be a domestic corporation.
☐ (2) It cannot be a member of an "affiliated group" under Code §1504.
☐ (3) It must have only one class of stock.
☐ (4) The stock cannot be held by more than ten shareholders.
☐ (5) All shareholders must be individuals (or estates).
☐ (6) No shareholder can be a nonresident alien.

□ (7) At least 20% of the gross receipts of the corporation must be derived from sources within the United States.
□ (8) No more than 20% of the gross receipts of the corporation may be derived from "passive investment income" sources (which sources include royalties, rents, dividends, interest, annuities, and income from sales or exchanges of stock or securities).
□ (9) The corporation (or any predecessor corporation) has not had a prior Subchapter S election within the last five years.

[¶203] MAKING THE ELECTION

Where all the requirements are met, the corporation elects to be taxed under Subchapter S by filing Form 2553, on which the unanimous consent of all the shareholders is indicated.

A new corporation has one month from the time it begins to elect Subchapter S for its first year. The Regs interpret this to mean that the corporation has until the close of the day preceding the same numerical date of the month following the date it begins to make the election. For instance, if the business starts in the middle of the month, say, January 14, it has to make its election by the day before the corresponding date in the following month—February 13. If there is no such corresponding date in the following month, then the election must be made by the end of the following month. For example, if the corporation begins business on January 30, it must make its election by February 28 (or 29). This requirement of timeliness is strictly construed. The corporation also has the burden of proving that a timely election was filed in the event IRS cannot locate the election.

The first month of its taxable year does not begin until the corporation has shareholders, acquires assets, or begins doing business. This is very helpful because some time usually elapses from the time the corporation is formally organized and officially comes into existence (often the dummy incorporators) until it actually starts operating (Reg. §1.1372-2(b)).

When a new stockholder comes into the corporation he must file his consent within 30 days. An estate becoming a stockholder in a Subchapter S corporation has until 30 days after the appointment of the executor or administrator to make its election. But in no event can the election be made more than 30 days after the close of the corporation's taxable year in which the estate became a stockholder (Reg. §1.1373-2(b)).

The consent filed by a new shareholder should be filed with the District Director with whom the election is filed and should contain this information: name and address of the corporation and the new shareholder; number of shares he owns; date of acquisition of those shares; name and address of each person from whom such shares were acquired. A copy of the consent is also filed with the return of the corporation.

Sometimes it happens that an otherwise valid election is rendered invalid because of the failure (unintentional or unavoidable) to file timely consents. In these cases, IRS will grant extensions of time for filing a consent, thus enabling you to perfect an election or prevent one from terminating involuntarily. However, in order to get an extension, you have to show reasonable cause and that the interests of the government will not be jeopardized. In addition, proper consent must be filed within the extended period, not only by the shareholder who failed to consent, but also by each person who was a shareholder at any time during the taxable year (the taxable year of the corporation for which the election would otherwise have terminated) and thereafter up to the date of the grant of the extension.

[¶203.1] "Cleaning Up" the Corporation to Qualify

If your corporation doesn't meet the qualifications for election, you might start removing the defects so that you can elect in the future. The defects must be removed by the time the election is made (up to the end of the first month of the taxable year) (Reg. §1.1372-1(a)). Here are some of the things you might do:

If you have too many stockholders or stockholders who do not qualify, see if you can get stock transferred by gift, sale, or exchange.

If you have more than one class of stock, recapitalize or redeem all but one class. *Note:* IRS says you cannot recapitalize into one class and accomplish the voting arrangements through a voting trust. Such a trust is considered a trust for tax purposes and, therefore, cannot be a stockholder in a Subchapter S corporation (Reg. §1.1371-1(d)).

Suppose you try to get around IRS's voting trust prohibition via an agreement that couldn't possibly be designated a trust. A limited partnership tried it this way. It incorporated and the limited partners became inactive shareholders. All stock had equal rights, but the shareholders entered into an agreement that required inactive shareholders to grant irrevocable proxies to one or more of the active shareholders. IRS says that, because of this restriction, the rights and interests of the inactive shareholders in the control of the corporation are not identical with those of the other shareholders. This results in two classes of stock (*Rev. Rul. 63-226,* 1963-2 CB 341).

This ruling is a warning that IRS intends to exercise its regulatory authority in the broadest possible manner. Its position is that where the stock is subject to any type of voting control device or arrangement—any pooling or voting agreement or a charter provision granting a veto power to certain shares, which has the effect of modifying the voting rights of any part of the stock so that they are disproportionate—there is more than one class of stock.

[¶203.2] How "Termination Rules" Can Defeat Your Election

The election, once made, is binding for future years. But it can be terminated. Once the election is terminated, you cannot elect to come within these rules again for five years unless IRS permission is given.

After the election is in effect, it can be terminated in one of five ways (except in the first case, the termination takes effect in the taxable year in which the event that causes termination takes place):

☐ (1) All the shareholders consent to a revocation of the election. But if this revocation is made after the first month of the taxable year, it is effective the following year (Reg. §1.1372-4(b)(2)). A statement of revocation on a return, signed by the president, was a valid revocation since it was substantial compliance.

☐ (2) A new person becomes a shareholder and he does not consent to the election within 30 days (Reg. §1.1372-4(b)). The election is revoked as of the year in which he became a shareholder. (Estates have a somewhat longer period.) Advance planning can prevent a change in shareholders terminating the election.

☐ (3) The corporation no longer meets the 10-or-less stockholder requirement, the nonresident alien stockholder requirement, or the one-class-of-stock requirement (Reg. §1.1372-4(b)(3)).

☐ (4) The corporation gets more than 80% of its gross receipts from sources without the U.S. (Reg. §1.1372-4(b)(4)).

□ (5) More than 20% of the corporation's gross receipts are derived from rents, royalties, interest, dividends, annuities, or gains from stocks or securities. Gross receipts from sales or exchanges of stock or securities are taken into account only to the extent of gains (excess of amount realized over adjusted basis). Loss transactions are not counted and do not offset gains from other stock and securities transactions.

By gross receipts is meant the total amount received or accrued by the corporation, depending on the accounting method used for computing its taxable income. Returns or allowances, cost or deductions would not reduce gross receipts. As to nontaxable sales or exchanges, gross receipts would only include that amount equal to any gain recognized by the corporation, except for sales or exchanges made during a 12-month liquidation (§337). In that case, the total amount received or accrued would be included (Reg. §1.1372-4(b)(5)-(ii)). Where timber and patent royalties are treated as capital gains, they are not royalties for Subchapter S purpose (Reg. §1.1372-4(b)(5)(iii)). Constant checking and year-end planning may save a corporation in danger of losing its Subchapter S status through the receipt of passive investment income.

[¶203.3] Second-Class-of-Stock Pitfall

One danger to continued Subchapter S treatment is where the corporation is deemed to have more than one class of stock. Reg. §1.1371-1(g) says, "Obligations which purport to represent debt but which actually represent equity capital will generally constitute a second class of stock. However, if such purported debt obligations are owned solely by the owners of the nominal stock of the corporation in substantially the same proportion as they own such nominal stock, such purported debt obligations will be treated as contributions to capital rather than a second class of stock."

What this means is that as long as advances are made proportionately to stock ownership, even if they should be held not to be debt, there is no second class of stock.

Stock Options, Warrants, and Convertible Debentures: IRS has ruled that neither a stock option, warrant, nor convertible debenture is a second class of stock barring or terminating a Subchapter S election (*Rev. Rul. 67-269*, CB 1967-2, 298).

Great care must be exercised to make sure that the stock subject to the option, warrant, or convertible debenture is in all respects the same as the existing common. Also, of course, care must be exercised to make sure that both the persons to whom the stock options, warrants, or convertible debentures are issued originally and their possible transferees will be committed to maintaining the Subchapter S election if and when they acquire stock.

The consequences of a determination that debt constitutes a second class of stock may be disastrous. The corporation will lose the benefits of the Subchapter S election for the period that the debt existed. It will become liable for the corporate tax and accumulations tax for the period during which the election was invalid. Corporate income previously taxed to the shareholder but retained by the corporation can no longer be withdrawn tax free. Like consequences would follow from a determination that the corporation was ineligible or that the election had been unintentionally terminated.

Disproportionate Voting Rights: IRS's position on disproportionate voting rights and irrevocable proxies has been quite clear. According to IRS, if the outstanding stock of a corporation is subject to any type of voting control device or arrangement, such as a pooling or voting agreement or provisions granting certain shares a veto power so that some shares possess disproportionate voting power, the corporation has been deemed to have more than one class of stock (*Rev. Rul. 63-226*). However, disproportionate voting rights have been held not to constitute a second class of stock (*Parker Oil Co.*, 58 TC No. 95, 1972). In holding that the disproportionate voting power among shareholders did not create more than one class of stock, the Tax Court declared Reg. §1.1371-1(g) and *Rev. Rul. 63-226* invalid as applied in this case by IRS.

It is not clear whether a lack of proportionality is harmless in all cases or whether it is only harmless if achieved through proxies, voting trusts, pooling agreements, or other arrangements between stockholders not involving amendments to the articles of incorporation. This uncertainty is due to the Court's own previous decision (*Pollack,* 47 TC 92) holding that disproportionate voting power can create a second class of stock. The Court distinguished the two cases on the grounds that in *Pollack* an amendment to the articles of incorporation prior to the issuance of any stock established four classes of stock that set up voting power disproportionate to the number of shares in each class.

[¶203.4] Saving Subchapter S Status

The idea behind the limit on passive investment income is to confine the favorable tax treatment of Subchapter S to small corporations engaged in trades or businesses. Those corporations that do receive large amounts of passive income would lose their Subchapter S benefits since they could no longer qualify. Their election would terminate. To avoid this result, it may be necessary to keep a constant check on any of the corporation's income that comes from the disqualifying passive investment sources. This is what to do:

Add together all items of passive investment income. If they total more than 20% of gross receipts, check whether each item is covered by the relevant definition. If not—e.g., income was earned in active business—delete the item and recompute for the 20% test. Careful checking of definitions is one answer to retaining Subchapter S status.

The definitions of items of passive income don't cover all cases, e.g., land held for investment or certain forms of rent and interest. Generally, passive income that may terminate an election is the same type of income that would make the corporation a personal holding company subject to penalty tax. But the tests aren't always parallel, e.g., those for rents and some royalties.

[¶204] TAX TREATMENT OF SUBCHAPTER S INCOME

The profits are passed through by treating each stockholder at year end as the recipient of his pro rata share of the corporation's undistributed taxable income. This undistributed taxable income is the corporation's taxable income computed in the regular manner (except the corporation is not allowed a dividend-received credit for dividends received, a deduction for partially exempt interest, nor a deduction for dividends paid on certain public utility preferred stock) (§1373(d)). Note, too, that the dividend exclusion is not available to stockholders receiving this income (§1375(b)).

The income is passed through after the deduction for compensation and ordinary and necessary business expenses of the corporation. This is very important because it means that the employee-stockholders can receive various fringe benefits.

Since the income passed through to the stockholders is picked up by them in their taxable year in or with which the corporation's taxable year ends, several tax advantages are available.

□ (1) ***Different Tax Years:*** The corporation and the stockholders can have different taxable years. This allows the postponing of some of the tax on the corporation's income for a longer period than is otherwise possible. For example, the corporation's year ends on January 31, 1975. The individual stockholders' taxable years are the calendar years. Although 11/12 of the corporate year occurred in 1974, the entire corporate profit passed through to the stockholders is taxable to them in 1975. Hence, the taxes on that profit will be paid through estimated taxes in 1975 and a final tax in 1976. If the corporation were required to pay the tax, the entire tax would have had to be paid partly in 1974 and partly in 1975, depending on the requirement for paying estimated tax.

□ (2) ***Timing of Income:*** Although the undistributed taxable income of the electing corporation is taxable to its stockholders in their taxable year in which the last day of the corporation's year falls, cash distributions to the stockholders are usually taxable to them whenever received (except for "throwback" rules—see (3)). Thus, in the case above, if the stockholders wanted some of the corporation's income for the year ended January 31, 1975, taxable in their 1974 returns, they could have the corporation make a cash distribution to them in 1974. This would reduce the amount taxable in 1975, since the corporation's undistributed taxable income is reduced by the cash distribution (§1373(c)).

Of course, salaries are also picked up by the stockholder-employees in the year received. So, this is another way of timing the income to the stockholders.

Note this about taxable years, however: When you form a new corporation, you might keep in mind the deferring of income and pick a taxable year for the corporation to give you that result. Or you may already have a corporation that you are contemplating bringing in under Subchapter S. If it has a taxable year different from the individual stockholders, there, too, you can defer income or plan your timing. But, if to get the results you want, you have to change the corporation's taxable year, you'll probably not be able to do it. IRS has made it clear it will not give permission to change taxable years in such cases.

□ (3) ***Two-and-a-Half-Month Throwback Distribution Rule:*** Cash distributions made within 2½ months after the end of a Subchapter S corporation's tax year are treated (this is mandatory, not elective) as having been made out of the corporation's undistributed corporate profits for the prior tax year (§1375(f)).

Example A: Assume that AB, Inc., is a Subchapter S corporation with a fiscal year ending March 31, 1975. Its two shareholders, A and B, each own 50% of its outstanding stock. For its March 31, 1975, tax year, the corporation has made no distributions and has undistributed taxable income of $50,000. On May 1, 1975, the corporation distributes $25,000 in cash each to A and B. AB, Inc., makes no other distributions during calendar year 1975 even though it has profits of $60,000 for its year ending March 31, 1976.

Example B: Y, a Subchapter S corporation on a calendar year, has two shareholders, C and D, each owning 50% of its stock. For 1975, Y has $20,000 of undistributed taxable income. At the beginning of 1976, C and D each have $25,000 as their respective net shares of previously taxed income, including $10,000 as their respective shares of Y's undistributed taxable income for 1975. On February 1, 1976, Y distributes $15,000 in cash to C and $15,000 in cash to D. Y makes no other distributions during 1976 and has $40,000 of taxable income for such year. Of the $15,000 distributions made to C and D on February 1, 1976, $10,000 of each such distribution is treated as a distribution of Y's undistributed taxable income for 1975 and is not a dividend to each shareholder. C's and D's net shares of previously taxed income are reduced by the amounts so treated to $15,000 each (§1375(d)(2)(B)(ii)). The balance of each $15,000 distribution, $5,000, is a dividend to C and D out of Y's earnings and profits for 1976. At the end of 1976, Y has $30,000 of undistributed taxable income, one-half allocated to C and one-half to D as their respective shares to be included in their gross incomes for 1976.

□ (4) ***Transferring Income Already Earned to Another Family Member:*** Just as you might want to transfer part of your partnership interest to a lower tax bracket member of your family, you might want to transfer an interest in the corporation. If you transfer a partnership interest, however, you cannot transfer partnership earnings earned before the transfer (§706(c)(2)(B)). With a Subchapter S corporation, the corporation's taxable income is picked up ratably by the stockholders as of the last day of the corporation's tax year. So, if you transferred stock to a relative a few days before the end of the year, that relative would get his pro rata share of the corporation's income for the entire year, including that part of the year during which he was not a stockholder.

□ (5) ***Tax-Free Income:*** Another problem concerns tax-free income such as municipal bond interest and life insurance proceeds. The nontaxable character does not pass through. And since such amounts are included in earnings and profits, they can be taxed to the shareholders on a current distribution. Furthermore, even if not distributed, such earnings do not increase the stockholders' basis for their stock and thus can be taxed later as ordinary income on distribution as a dividend or at capital gain rates on liquidation.

□ (6) ***Tax-Preference Income:*** Items of so-called tax-preference income are not taxed to the corporation; they, too, are passed through to the stockholders. Items of tax preference are apportioned among the shareholders as losses are apportioned under §1374(c)(1).

However, where capital gains are taxed to both the corporation and the shareholder (under §1378), the capital gains tax preference is subject to the minimum tax at both the corporate and the individual level. In such case, the amount treated as capital gain by the shareholder is reduced by the tax imposed under §1378 and by the 10% minimum tax imposed at the corporate level.

[¶205] TAX TREATMENT OF SUBCHAPTER S LOSSES

If the corporation has net short-term capital gains they are passed through as ordinary income. Normally, this makes no difference because short-term gains are taxable as ordinary income. But it can make a difference if the stockholders had short-term losses and long-term gains. If the short-term gains were passed through as such, the short-term losses would offset them, releasing the long-term gains to be taxable at the preferred capital gain rates. However, when the short-term gains come through as ordinary income, the stockholders' short-term losses will offset their long-term gains.

This point should be borne in mind in tax planning because many taxpayers are under the mistaken impression that all capital gains pass through in the form they take at the corporate level.

Capital losses do not go through the corporation to the stockholders. So here, too, any impression that all capital gains and losses can be used by the stockholders as their own should be dispelled. Since a corporation cannot deduct capital losses except to reduce capital gains, a net capital loss is usually worthless to it and to its stockholders. However, the corporation can carry over the loss for five years to offset capital gains of future years.

[¶205.1] Passing Through Ordinary Losses

An important advantage of the Subchapter S election is that it allows the stockholders to pick up the corporation's loss as if it were their own (Reg. §1.1374-1(b)). This is particularly valuable in a new corporation. Often, the strategy is to operate the new business as a proprietorship or partnership at the beginning, during the time it could be expected to incur losses, so that the losses will be available as offsets against the owners' other income. Then, when the business becomes successful and the rate differentials make it advantageous, the business can be incorporated. You can accomplish the same result, however, using Subchapter S. The corporation can be formed and immediately elect under Subchapter S, so that the losses pass through to the stockholders. Then, when the corporation begins to be so successful that the corporate shelter is desired, the election can be revoked.

Take a cash-basis corporation that is sued and a judgment entered against it. It is now near year end, and the judgment will be paid next year.

Here, the corporation could elect Subchapter S, and when the big judgment is paid in the following year and a corporate loss is created as a result, the stockholders could personally deduct the losses on their own returns. The Subchapter S election in this case should work as long as, under the corporation's accounting method, the deduction became available only when the judgment was paid. There is no business purpose requirement for electing Subchapter S.

Where you can't anticipate the time of the loss (and in any case for that matter), it's a good idea to have §1244 stock (you can have that kind of stock even in a Subchapter S corporation). Then, if the corporation goes sour and you realize a loss on your stock—either on sale or because it becomes worthless—you get an ordinary loss rather than a capital loss.

Losses that occur just prior to liquidation are often used up against capital gains resulting from the sale of property. Proper timing and the use of Subchapter S combined with a §337 liquidation can often overcome this problem. For example, take a corporation operating at a loss that decides to liquidate. If Subchapter S is in effect for that year, the losses will pass through. But before the losses are passed through they can be absorbed in the corporation by gains from the sale of corporate assets that might otherwise be taxable at capital gain rates. By electing a twelve-month liquidation under §337, no gain or loss is recognized on sales within the twelve-month period provided all the assets are distributed within that time. Since no gain is recognized to the corporation, there is nothing against which to offset the losses, and they pass through to the shareholders to be used against their other income.

However, unless the shareholders have substantial ordinary income in the year in which they pick up the loss, make sure that you adopt your plan of liquidation late enough in the corporation's taxable year to permit the liquidation distribution to be made in the following taxable year of the shareholder so that the passthrough loss is picked up one year and the gain on liquidation in the following year. Otherwise, you can have the same problem at the shareholder level; i.e., capital gain on the liquidation distribution offset by the ordinary loss that has been passed through to the shareholder.

There are other ways in which this same strategy can be used. For example, if a real estate corporation is going to have an ordinary loss and its rental income is too high (more than 20% of gross receipts) to qualify it for Subchapter S, it might sell a piece of appreciated property. The selling price of the property can be high enough to boost gross receipts to a point where rents are not more than 20% of receipts. But then the gain (capital gain) on the property sale would be offset by ordinary loss. To avoid that, the corporation first elects to liquidate under §337 (12-month liquidation). That keeps the gain from being taxable at the corporate level, so the loss does not offset it. But the receipts of the sale count as gross receipts under the Regs (Reg. §1.1372-4(b)(5)(ii)(a)). So, the corporation can qualify for Subchapter S (since we assume the rents will not go over the 20% mark if the sales receipts are counted). And the fact that the corporation is about to liquidate does not prevent the corporation from electing Subchapter S.

If the corporation's taxable year ends during the 12-month period following the adoption of the §337 liquidation, here's what happens: The ordinary loss (which we assume will arise by the end of the current taxable year) passes through to the stockholders, and they apply it to reduce ordinary income. In the following taxable year (but within 12 months of the adoption of the plan of liquidation), the corporation liquidates. The gain on the sale of the corporate property passes through at that time as a gain on liquidation. The stockholders pick up their capital gains at that time without offset by ordinary losses.

In addition to these situations, there are situations where potential losses are available in the corporation but have not been realized because taxwise they would have little value. Semidormant corporations, for example, should look over possible realizable losses and elect to be taxable as partnerships in order to pass the losses on to the stockholders. In many cases, this passthrough might eliminate a stockholder's other income altogether, thus having the effect of giving him tax-free income from taxable sources.

Note this about corporate losses: The loss coming down to the stockholders results in a carryback or carryover loss if it exceeds the stockholders' incomes. It might be possible to use the loss to get a refund of previous years' corporate taxes (since losses can be carried back three years) and thus realize the benefits of the loss faster than could the individual stockholders (§172).

[¶205.2] Timing of Losses

Another important tax planning aspect of the use of the corporate loss involves timing. As pointed out above, corporate profits can sometimes be shifted even after they are earned by the corporation. Because the undistributed taxable income of the corporation is allocated among the stockholders as of the end of the corporation's taxable year, it is possible to accomplish this by transferring stock. But the same rule does not apply to losses. So, you cannot shift losses between family members. The losses are allocated to all of the taxpayers who were stockholders at any time during the corporation's taxable year. The corporation's loss is divided by the number of days in its taxable year, and each day's loss is allocated pro rata to the stockholders on that day (§1374(c)).

A stockholder of a Subchapter S corporation deducts his share of the corporate loss in his taxable year during or with which the corporate tax year ended. If he dies before the end of the corporate tax year and such death occurred after 9/23/59, then such loss is deductible for the deceased's final taxable year (Reg. §1374-1(b)(2)). Refund possibilities arise for still open taxable years as a result of a retroactive amendment passed in 1962, which applies this rule where death occurred on or after 9/2/58.

What happens to corporate losses in nonelection years? Of course, a loss arising in a year the election is in effect is passed on directly to the stockholders. But in carrying forward or back a loss arising in a year in which Subchapter S did not apply to the corporation, the Subchapter S years count in figuring the number of years back or forward to which a loss can be carried. But the profits in the Subchapter S years do not reduce the loss available to be carried over to the other years (Reg. §1.1374-1(a)).

Don't Let Loss Years Go By: It is often advisable to distribute previously taxed income in a loss year. In any event, when you see a loss year coming, take a good look at your distribution picture. Here's why:

When you get a distribution of previously taxed income from a Subchapter S corporation, it is reduced by your share of the corporation's losses you picked up for any years after the profit was earned by the corporation. But the previously taxed income is not reduced by the current year's corporate loss that you will pick up currently (Reg. §1.1375-4(d)). So, it becomes important to distribute previously taxed profit in the loss year.

Assume the Subchapter S corporation and the stockholders all report their taxes on a calendar-year basis. In 1975 the corporation had a profit of $20,000. It didn't distribute any of it (it was needed for working capital). Each stockholder picked up his share of the $20,000 on his 1975 return. In 1976, the corporation will end up with a $30,000 loss. If the $20,000 previously taxed 1975 income is distributed in 1976, each stockholder can get his share of that income tax free and still pick up his full share of the 1976 loss. If, however, the 1975 profits are not distributed in 1976, the 1976 loss will wipe out the previously taxed 1975 profit. So, if that profit was distributed in 1977 or later (distributions within 2½ months or 3½ months after 1976 are deemed to be 1976 distributions), it would be a taxable dividend (if the corporation had current earnings or accumulated earnings) or a return of capital and capital gain (to the extent the distribution exceeded the stockholders' bases for their stock).

[¶205.3] Limitations on Losses

Although losses are passed through to the stockholders, each stockholder's loss is limited to his basis for his stock in the corporation and the basis for any indebtedness of the corporation to him. A *guarantee* by a shareholder of a corporate debt does not come within the term "indebtedness of the corporation to the shareholder" (*Perry,* 392 F 2d 458, CA-8, 1968 *aff'g* 47 TC 159). So, if the corporation's loss is going to be so big that a stockholder's share will exceed his basis for his stock, he might consider making a loan to the corporation before year end thus creating a basis for indebtedness that will let him use the corporate loss (§1374(c)(2)).

This limitation on losses operates as follows: Assume that for 1974 the corporation has a $22,000 net operating loss (NOL) after paying $42,000 in salary to B, the sole stockholder. In 1975, it had long-term capital gain of $8,500 and an NOL of $1,800, again after paying B a salary of $42,000. In 1976, it had an NOL of $15,000 after paying a $42,000 salary to B. In 1974, B's basis for his stock was $13,000.

Here's what happens: In 1974, B picks up only $13,000 of the $22,000 NOL. The loss is deductible only to the extent of B's basis. In 1975, B picks up a net capital gain of $6,700 (the long-term gain less NOL). B can't get a long-term gain greater than the corporation's net income. Since the corporation retained the $6,700 in 1975, B's basis is increased from zero to $6,700; and, thus, B in 1976 can deduct $6,700 of the $15,000 NOL. B's basis is increased by the full amount of the long-term gain, rather than the 50% of gain on which he was taxed (*Byrne,* 361 F.2d 939, CA-7, 1966 *aff'g* 45 TC 151).

[¶206] TAX TREATMENT OF SUBCHAPTER S CAPITAL GAINS

The corporation's net long-term capital gains (in excess of net short-term capital losses) retain their nature as long-term capital gains in the hands of the stockholders. This presents a special opportunity for getting them out of the corporation at one capital gains tax. Under prior law, it was possible to make a Subchapter S election just for the purpose of getting the corporation's net long-term capital gains into the hands of stockholders at one capital gains tax. In the next year, the election was terminated (by doing some disqualifying act) to get back to regular corporate tax treatment and the future benefit of the corporate tax shelter (where the corporate rates are lower than the individual stockholders'). This maneuver was aptly termed a "one-shot" election.

[¶206.1] Shine Taken Out of One-Shot Election

Section 1378 imposes a tax on the Subchapter S corporation where: (1) the net long-term capital gains exceed $25,000 and 50% of the corporation's taxable income for the year and (2) the taxable income for the year is more than $25,000. (Note: A Subchapter S corporation's "taxable income" combines ordinary income—or loss—and capital gains.)

Example 1: Jones Corporation has a taxable income of $40,000, including net long-term capital gains of $30,000. Since net long-term capital gains exceed $25,000 and 50% of taxable income (which is over $25,000), §1378 applies.

Under §1378(b), the tax imposed is the lower of: (1) 25% of excess of net long-term capital gains over $25,000 or (2) the ordinary (not Subchapter S) corporate tax. In our example, the tax under (1) would be $1,250 (25% × $30,000 minus $25,000, or $5,000) and under (2), $12,700 (22% × $25,000 plus 48% × $15,000). The tax, therefore, would be $1,250.

Example 2: Assume that Jones Corporation had taxable income of $60,000, including net long-term capital gains of $125,000. In other words, the corporation had an ordinary loss of $65,000. Again, §1378 applies. The ordinary corporate tax on $60,000 is $22,300 (22% × $25,000 plus 48% × $35,000). The tax under the alternate method is $25,000 (25% × $125,000 minus $25,000, or $100,000). Therefore, $22,300 is the amount of tax payable.

[¶206.2] Deduction for Tax Paid Under §1378

Where a Subchapter S corporation is subject to the §1378 tax, the tax paid by the corporation goes to reduce the corporation's undistributed taxable income under §1373(c) and the net long-term capital gains of the corporation and the subsequent passthrough of such gains to the shareholders (§1375(a)(3)).

So, in the first example above, the $1,250 tax paid by Jones Corporation would cut the net long-term capital gains that have to be picked up by Jones from $30,000 to $28,750. He'd still have to pick up $10,000 of ordinary income.

[¶206.3] Exceptions to §1378 Subchapter S Capital Gains Tax

The §1378 capital gains tax does not apply to corporations that have been Subchapter S corporations for three previous tax years. For example, a corporation that has been a Subchapter S corporation for 1973-1975 would not be subject to the §1378 capital gains tax for 1974 on any net long-term capital gains it might pass through.

Another exception is for corporations that have been in existence for less than four taxable years and a Subchapter S corporation for each of those years. A corporation that was created in 1974 and was a Subchapter S corporation in 1974 and 1975 would not be subject to §1378 for 1975 on any passthrough of net long-term capital gains.

Since the §1378 tax is aimed at curing the "misuse" of the one-shot election, it wouldn't apply to any of the above situations in which corporations intend Subchapter S treatment for at least three years (in other words, "operating" Subchapter S corporations).

Under certain circumstances, the §1378(a) capital gains tax can apply to long-term gains of Subchapter S corporations even though they satisfy the three-years-of-operation exception. This might occur where, for example, another non-Subchapter S corporation that doesn't satisfy the three-year exception—King Corporation—is merged into Jones Corporation (an operating Subchapter S corporation) in a transaction in which the basis of property to Jones Corporation is determined by reference to the basis of the property to King Corporation before the merger (or other tax-free exchange).

In such a situation, the basis of such property or any other property for which it may be exchanged tax free is to be determined by its basis in the hands of King Corporation. Also, the property must have been acquired by Jones Corporation in the period three years prior to the beginning of the taxable year or the taxable year in which the property is transferred (§1378(c)(3)).

If §1378(c)(3) applies to a Subchapter S corporation, the capital gains tax imposed can't be larger than 25% of net long-term capital gains attributable to the property.

Example: Jones Corporation, a Subchapter S corporation since 1961, has net long-term capital gains of $100,000 for 1970; its taxable income is $150,000. Included in the $100,000 of capital gains is $10,000 of long-term gain attributable to property it acquired from King Corporation on March 31, 1967, in a tax-free merger. King wasn't a Subchapter S corporation prior to the March 31, 1967, merger. The basis of such property in Jones's hands was determined with reference to its basis in the hands of King. So, even though Jones meets the three-year rule, §1378(c)(3) applies. But the amount of tax on Jones can't exceed $2,500 (25% of $10,000 gain attributable to the property with the carried-over basis acquired by King).

[¶206.4] When the One-Shot Election May Still Be Worthwhile

Since the election must be made in advance (by the end of the first month of the taxable year), it is often too late by the time the sale is imminent. The obvious thing to do, where possible, is to postpone the sale to the following year and then make a timely election for that year. Where that can't be done, try this approach: Make it an installment sale and take back a small down payment in the year of sale, thereby pushing most of the gain into next year—then elect next year.

Where the capital gains are to come from sale of securities, the one-shot election may not be practicable. It may not be possible to accumulate a really considerable amount of capital gains in one year and still keep the corporation eligible to keep alive the Subchapter S election. Where capital gains from securities plus dividends, rents, royalties, annuities, and interest exceed 20% of the corporation's gross receipts, the election terminates.

When the corporation and the stockholders have different taxable years and the corporation makes a cash distribution in one year, the capital gain is treated as if it were distributed ratably in both years, regardless of when it was actually realized. For example, a corporation with a year ending June 30, 1976, distributed $50,000 in 1975 to its stockholders (on a calendar year) and had an additional $50,000 undistributed taxable income at its year end. Of this $100,000 income, $20,000 was long-term capital gain and all of that $20,000 was realized in 1976. Nevertheless, since 20% of the total income was capital gain, the stockholders are required to pick up $10,000 (20% of the $50,000 received that year) as capital gain in 1975 and $10,000 in 1976. Since the stockholders may not have known about the capital gains by the time they filed their 1975 returns, they may have to file claims for refunds to reflect the capital gains that should have been picked up in 1975.

Keep in mind that where the stockholders are dealers in property used by the corporation, you may have a tough time passing through capital gains to the stockholders. IRS says that the sale of that property by the corporation may be treated as ordinary income and passed through to the stockholders as such (Reg. §1.1375-1(d)).

Where you have capital gains, it is important in most cases to make a distribution of these amounts that will apply to the year realized. This is because a distribution in later years usually is deemed first to be out of that year's earnings. This rule may lead to harsh results where you don't distribute capital gains within the prescribed period and the election terminates. If the distribution applies to a later year, even though that income has already been taxed to the stockholders, the distribution is treated as any other ordinary corporate distribution. And if there are enough earnings and profits to cover it, it will be taxable as a dividend.

[¶206.5] Capital Gains "Throwback" Under §1375(e)

Section 1375(f), the automatic 2½-month throwback rule, does not apply to a Subchapter S corporation that has elected to treat distributions of capital gains made within 2½ months after year end as having been made in the year the gains were realized (§1375(e)). Since §1375(f) treats all distributions made within 2½ months after year end as applicable to the previous year, it also includes such capital gains distributions. Section 1375(e) therefore is repealed for distributions made for tax years beginning after April 14, 1966. But it can still apply to tax years ending up to and including March 31, 1967. When it applies, §1375(f) does not.

[¶207] IMPORTANCE OF PROPER TIMING OF DISTRIBUTIONS

The advantages available under Subchapter S can be lost by carelessness in making distributions; and you can, in fact, wind up worse off than you would have been had you not elected. One of these advantages is the postponement of tax to the shareholders by using a fiscal year in the corporation and calendar years for the shareholders. Here's an example that illustrates how such a move can backfire solely because of improper timing of distributions. The result is bunched income. Assume all the stock of Jones Corporation is owned by Jones. The company's fiscal year ends January 31, 1975—its first year under Subchapter S. For prior years, the corporation has accumulated $60,000 in earnings. Its earnings for its first Subchapter S year are $50,000. And Jones expects to pick up that $50,000 in his personal return for the calendar year 1975.

On May 30, 1975, the corporation distributes $50,000 in cash to Jones. Jones believes that this is a distribution of previously taxed income under Subchapter S—so he considers that he owes no tax on this distribution. In other words, Jones expects that his income from his corporation to be reported on his 1975 return will be $50,000. However, it may very well turn out to be $100,000. Here's why:

The $50,000 earned by the corporation in its fiscal year ended January 31, 1975, is included in Jones's 1975 return. But the $50,000 cash distribution is first considered a distribution of the corporation's current year's earnings. So, if the corporation's earnings for the year ending January 31, 1976 turn out to be $10,000, $10,000 is included in Jones's 1975 return (in addition to the $50,000 picked up).

But what of the remaining $40,000 distributed? That, too, may be taxed—in addition to the $50,000 already picked up. It's true that a distribution by a Subchapter S corporation of Subchapter S earnings previously taxed is received tax free to the stockholders. But the definition of previously taxed income refers to income taxable to the stockholder in a previous taxable year *of the stockholder*—not the corporation (see Reg. §1.1375-4(d)). Since the corporation's first year's Subchapter S income is being picked up by Jones in his 1975 return (the same tax year—for him—in which the distribution is made), that $50,000 was not previously taxed. Hence the $40,000 distributed (in excess of the current year's earnings) is a dividend to Jones—a distribution from the corporation's pre-Subchapter S years' earnings. And Jones ends up with $100,000 of income in 1975.

Since the enactment of §1375(f), it is much easier to avoid this type of bunching-of-income pitfall than previously. Had the May 30, 1975, cash distribution been made at any time up to April 15, 1975 (within 2½ months after year end), it would have automatically been considered to have been made out of the corporation's profits for the year ending January 31, 1975, and, assuming the corporation had $50,000, Jones would have had to pick up $50,000 less for 1975.

Another bunching problem can occur where Subchapter S status is lost. Let's assume that Subchapter S status for Jones Corporation ends on June 30, 1975. Once the election ends, the undistributed profit is treated as a contribution to capital (thus increasing Jones's basis for his stock) and can't be distributed tax free unless there are no undistributed earnings.

Here again, the 2½-month throwback rule would relieve the situation by treating any cash payout within 2½ months after January 31, 1975, as a reduction of undistributed earnings for the year ended January 31, 1975.

[¶208] DANGERS OF LEAVING PREVIOUSLY TAXED INCOME IN THE CORPORATION

After shareholders have reported and paid on income earned but not distributed by the corporation, they may withdraw such funds from the corporation tax free (withdrawal can only be in the form of cash). However, there are substantial dangers in permitting the corporation to retain the cash and deferring withdrawals.

☐ (1) Death of a stockholder terminates the right to withdraw previously taxed income—such right does not pass to the estate.

☐ (2) The right to the previously taxed income does not pass with the stock on its transfer to a buyer or donee. While the right of a shareholder to previously taxed income lapses on his transfer of all his stock, the transfer of part leaves his rights unaffected, and the amount that he is entitled to withdraw tax free is not reduced (Reg. §1.1375-4(e)).

☐ (3) Tax-free withdrawal is forfeited if the corporation's election is terminated for any reason, even if the corporation reelects Subchapter S (Reg. §1.1375-4(a)).
☐ (4) Previously taxed income is reduced by the amount of the corporation's net operating loss that is allowable as a deduction to the stockholder. Thus, if previously taxed income is not withdrawn before losses occur, the stockholder loses the benefit of tax-free withdrawal.

Failure to make a cash distribution within 2½ months of the close of its tax year followed by a termination of its status can result in a double tax to the corporation's shareholders. For example: Universal Widgets, Inc., itself made no distributions of cash or other property during its tax year; but, of course, its shareholders were taxable on their respective proportionate share of corporate income. Universal Widgets, through its shareholders, then decided to terminate the Subchapter S election and distribute the income within the 2½-month period following the close of its tax year. That period ended on October 15. On the day before, the accountant gave checks to the shareholders for their respective shares of the total income. Had they promptly cashed their checks, they would have been taxed only on the company's income for its tax year ended July 31. But, unfortunately for them, they didn't cash the checks for a couple of years.

Once the corporation terminated its election, it became tax liable only for its income, with the shareholders taxable only on whatever distributions of money or property Universal Widgets might have made.

At the end of the following tax year, the accountant discovered the uncashed checks in the safe and made an adjustment in the books to reflect the checks as notes payable to the shareholders.

IRS decided the checks were actually promissory notes rather than money, as required by Code §1375(f), and therefore corporate distributions of property taxable as dividends. It was determined that because the corporation failed to distribute its taxable income for the prior taxable year within 2½ months, the shareholders were taxable on its entire undistributed taxable income. In addition, because the checks were distributed on October 14 and Universal Widgets, Inc., was not an electing small business corporation, the checks represented dividend income of that date. The result to the shareholders was to tax them in that year on a substantial amount as undistributed taxable income of the Subchapter S corporation for such taxable year and then *again* tax them on the same amount for the same taxable year as a dividend received from the corporation.

Although the Tax Court noted that the result appeared unjust, the Commissioner nevertheless was sustained. The taxpayers argued that the checks they received were money, thus satisfying the provision of §1375(f). However, the Court held that the parties did not really treat the checks as money, as that term is commonly used, because (1) they held the checks for two years without cashing them; (2) there were not sufficient funds in the bank account to honor the checks at the time they were written; and (3) the checks were not recorded as cash disbursements but rather as notes payable. In this decision, the Court did not imply in any way that checks written on a corporation bank account can not satisfy the requirements of §1375(f), and the universal business custom of paying by check was recognized. Had Universal Widgets and its shareholders treated the checks as cash, negotiating them within a reasonable time, the Court would have been inclined to hold that the distribution satisfied the requirements of §1375(f). However, on the facts, the Court concluded that the checks really represented demand obligation on the corporation, not a distribution of money. On this basis, the checks constituted property and therefore could only be interpreted as a dividend. (See §301(a) and 316(a); *Fountain*, 59 TC 696, 1973.)

[¶208.1] How to Avoid the Problems With Undistributed Income

Before a corporation terminates its election it has to look at its undistributed income situation. That is, it has to determine the amount, if any, of previously taxed income and distribute it before terminating the election. The reason is that if the corporation doesn't do this, the income will be taxed a second time when it is ultimately distributed to the stockholders. The tax-free status stays attached to this income only if the corporation remains a Subchapter S corporation. Once it terminates its election, it gives up this benefit. Here, we'll look at this and some of the other problems you can run into with undistributed taxable income.

As a Subchapter S corporation shareholder, you are taxed on your share of the corporation's undistributed taxable income (UTI). You then have the option of taking it out tax free currently or at some future time. If you opt for the latter, you are, in effect, reinvesting this income in the corporation, whereupon the UTI becomes previously taxed income (PTI) and is available for subsequent distribution as a tax-free return of a capital investment.

All right so far. However, if there is an obstacle that prevents the distribution of the PTI, then the PTI may be converted into buried income (BI) and may either be locked in until other earnings are paid out or be subjected to a second tax.

Let's double back a minute before we get into the BI trap. One of the first things to watch out for is that your PTI doesn't get "buried" beneath an avalanche of current—or accumulated—earnings. Under a LIFO-type technique you are not permitted to distribute last year's PTI until you've first distributed this year's earnings. Thus, you must, in effect, dig out from under the most recent earnings and profits before you can tap the underlying layers of PTI.

Example 1: Assume that your Subchapter S corporation has $20,000 of PTI from calendar year 1974 and that earnings for 1975 are $30,000. You cannot distribute the $20,000 at the end of 1975 and call it 1974 PTI, since any current distribution will be deemed to be out of current earnings. Thus, you must first distribute the entire $30,000 of 1975 earnings before you can have a distribution of the 1974 PTI.

You can avoid the PTI burial by having the corporation distribute the earnings within 2½ months after the close of its taxable year. Thus, if under our example, the corporation had distributed the $20,000 before March 16, 1975, it would be considered 1974 PTI.

Now let's take a look at how the PTI is buried when an election is terminated. Suppose that on January 1, 1976, it was decided to revoke the Subchapter S election. Since the shareholders have not withdrawn their 1974 PTI, the change of the election would bury these 1974 earnings, not only under current earnings as would be the case if it continued as a Subchapter S corporation, but also under all the earnings and profits accumulated before the corporation became a Subchapter S corporation. Here's how it would work:

Example 2: Same as example 1 except that the corporation gives up its election in 1976. If the earnings accumulated by the corporation in its pre-Subchapter S years come to, say, $170,000, the $20,000 of 1974 PTI is buried under $200,000 of earnings ($170,000 plus $30,000 earnings for 1975). In this situation, you could not pull out your 1974 PTI of $20,000 tax free until the corporation has distributed $200,000 of its earnings. What's more, there is also a problem with the $30,000 earned in 1975. The $30,000 will also be buried under accumulated earnings of pre-Subchapter S years. So, you would also have to distribute all the accumulated earnings ($170,000) before you could get at these earnings. The result is that $50,000 of earnings, which if distributed would be tax free to the shareholders, are locked in the corporation.

As we indicated earlier, when a corporation terminates its election, it loses the right to distribute PTI tax free. Once it becomes a regular corporation, the PTI loses its status even though the corporation may later decide to renew its election. Also, a shareholder is not entitled to receive PTI tax free unless he was a shareholder in the year the PTI was earned. In other words, the right to withdraw PTI is personal to the shareholder and cannot be transferred to someone else. Thus, the PTI will be subject to a second tax in the hands of anyone who becomes a transferee of the original stockholder, whether through inheritance, gift, sale, or other disposition of the Subchapter S stock. In fact, where a husband and wife jointly owned all the shares of a Subchapter S corporation and the husband died, the widow could receive, tax free, only her share of the PTI; the withdrawal of her late husband's share of the PTI was deemed to be a taxable distribution (*Rev. Rul. 66-172*, CB 1966-1, 198).

Example 3: Same as Example 1 except that you sell a 50% interest in the Subchapter S corporation to X in January 1975, and a cash distribution of $10,000 each is made to you and X the following month. Since the distribution to you represents a cash payout of 1974 UTI (under the 2½-month rule), it is tax free; but the $10,000 received by X is a taxable dividend. However, if the stock sale had occurred in December 1974, the $20,000 1974 UTI would have been taxed to both you and X; and a distribution prior to March 15, 1975, would thus have been tax free to both you and X.

An intrafamily transfer of Subchapter S stock at year end would be subject to closer scrutiny by IRS to determine whether the transfer was bona fide or merely for purposes of saving tax on the distribution of PTI. See Reg. §1.1373-1(a)(2).

[¶209] DIVIDING FAMILY INCOME; COMPARISON WITH THE FAMILY PARTNERSHIP

A Subchapter S corporation can be used successfully to divide family income into smaller units taxable at lower rates. Large yearly returns to stockholders on minimal investments are possible (*Rocco*, 57 TC 826, 1972). However, family members (and other stockholders) must first be paid the same for services to the corporation that an outsider would be paid for comparable services. In determining the value of a shareholder's services, consideration must be given to all the facts and circumstances of the business, including the managerial responsibilities of the shareholder (Reg. §1.1375-3(a)). This is the traditional standard for determining reasonable compensation (§162(a)(1)). When reasonable compensation is paid for services by a shareholder, generally, the remaining income of the Subchapter S corporation may go as dividends to the shareholders.

It may be desired to keep the business in the family in case of future disagreements. Rights of first refusal on sale or options to repurchase stock where permitted by local law may keep the stock ownership in the family and may be significant as to control where obtained at the time of the original stock transfer to the relative. It can be argued that the option to repurchase would be on stronger legal grounds in the Subchapter S corporation than in the family partnership.

Compare the trust situation that may prevail in a family partnership. To split business income by way of a family partnership, the use of a trust may be indicated. Under the rules of §671-678 the trust must last more than ten years or for the life of the beneficiary. During that time the grantor may have no control over the trust. On the other hand, a corporation is ineligible for Subchapter S status if any of its shares are held by a trust.

[¶210] COMBINING SUBCHAPTER S WITH INCOME AVERAGING

In a year in which income averaging is available to a stockholder, it may pay to elect Subchapter S in order to take out ordinary income (rather than the one-shot election to take out capital gains). The tax cost of taking out of the corporation what would otherwise be after-tax corporate earnings of a regular (non-Subchapter S) corporation can work out to be a very low figure—in our example below, under 14%.

Example: A corporation with income for the current year of $126,000 has two equal stockholders. Each files a joint return with his wife and each has $25,000 of taxable income each year.

When the corporation is operating as a regular corporation, it pays a tax of $54,000 on its $125,000 income and is left with $72,000 after taxes. Each stockholder pays a tax of $6,020 on his $25,000 individual taxable income. Thus, the combined tax of both stockholders and the corporation comes to $66,040. And the $72,000 after-tax corporate income remains in the corporation.

Suppose they elect Subchapter S. The total $126,000 corporate income is divided between the two stockholders and each pays a tax on $88,000 (his regular $25,000 income plus half the corporation's $126,000 income, or $63,000). Each stockholder will pay a tax of $37,980, for a total of $75,960. This is $9,920 more than if they had not chosen to use Subchapter S. But for that additional tax, they have taken that $72,000 out of the corporation. Thus, the effective tax rate paid to get the $72,000 into the hands of the stockholders (via Subchapter S) was only 13.8%—a lot less than if it came out via liquidation at a 25% capital gain rate.

If income averaging is available, the cost of getting those earnings out can be dramatically reduced.

[¶211] MAKING FRINGE BENEFITS AVAILABLE

Probably one of the greatest inducements for presently unincorporated businesses to incorporate and then use the election not to be taxable as a corporation is the availability of the various fringe benefits for its stockholder-employees. As owners of unincorporated businesses they were not eligible for these benefits. As corporate employees, they are. And there is no additional tax because of the incorporation because the double-tax aspect is eliminated by electing to be taxed as a partnership or proprietorship. In addition to pension and profit-sharing plans, here are fringes the owners can now obtain:

□ (1) ***Medical Expenses:*** An employer can set up a health and accident plan for his employees and reimburse an employee for his medical expenses and those of his spouse and dependents. Such reimbursements are tax free (§105(b)). Since the employer's plan apparently can be limited to one or more employees (see Reg. §1.105-5), the medical expense reimbursement might be limited to the employee-stockholders by making it apply only to highly paid employees. The corporation would get a deduction for the payment as an ordinary and necessary expense. The net result is that the owners of the business can get a full deduction for their medical expenses instead of being limited to those in excess of 3% of adjusted gross income and subject to the ceiling limitations of §213.

☐ (2) ***Accident and Health Insurance:*** When a sole proprietor or partner buys health and accident insurance, he cannot deduct the premium. On the other hand, proceeds he may receive under the policy are tax free (§104(a)(3)). As an employee of a corporation, insurance premiums paid by the corporation on his behalf are not included in his income (§106) even though the corporation gets a deduction for them (*Rev. Rul. 58-90,* CB 1958-1, 88). The proceeds of the policy, however, would be taxable to the employee except to the extent they qualify as wage continuation payments. If the proceeds include payment for medical reimbursement, loss of member of body or function or other payment not measured by loss of time from work, those proceeds are tax free, too (§105(c)). Thus, the proprietor or partner is able to get tax-deductible premiums for his health and accident insurance by using the Subchapter S election. But he may be giving up in part possible tax-free proceeds from the policy.

☐ (3) ***Group Life Insurance:*** The Regs (§1.61-2(d)(2)) provide that premiums paid by an employer for a group term life insurance up to $50,000 are not taxable income to the employees even if they name the beneficiaries of their policies. So, this gives the owners of the business an opportunity to acquire life insurance for tax-deductible premiums.

☐ (4) ***Meals and Lodging:*** Section 119 permits the value of meals and lodging furnished to employees for the employer's convenience to be tax free to the employee. Under §162, the corporation gets a deduction for the value of the meals and lodgings furnished. This tax break is also available in the Subchapter S situation.

[¶212] TERMINATING THE ELECTION

Suppose, anticipating a large gain or an ordinary loss, a corporation elects not to be taxable as such. Then, as things turn out, the anticipated gain or loss does not materialize. Without that gain or loss the stockholders don't want the Subchapter S election. Revoking the election wouldn't help because, except for revocations in the first month of the taxable year, the revocation is not effective until the following year. But a disqualifying act before year end would terminate the election for the entire year. So, a recapitalization with a preferred stock dividend might be used; stock might be sold or given to more stockholders to raise the total above 10; stock might be transferred to a new stockholder who fails to consent; property throwing off rent, interest, or dividends might be acquired to boost the disqualifying receipts.

[¶213] TRANSFERRING INTERESTS IN SUBCHAPTER S CORPORATIONS

If your corporation elects Subchapter S, problems will arise if any of the stockholders sell or dispose of any of their stock. So, you ought to take care of the contingencies in advance. Here are some of the considerations to keep in mind.

☐ (1) ***Preventing a Transfer That Will Terminate the Election:*** If one stockholder gives or sells even one share of stock to a trust, partnership, or corporation, the election terminates. Similarly, the election is terminated if stock is transferred to an individual who refuses to agree to the election within 30 days.

Best bet here seems to be to have an agreement requiring any stockholder to give the corporation or the other stockholders first refusal before he sells or transfers any of his stock. This will give the other stockholders a chance to determine whether the proposed transfer will upset the election and to buy the stock if it will. Other types of restrictions—e.g., restricting the sale of stock to only those who can and agree to consent to the election—may not be enforceable. It becomes a question of local law. This may also apply to an option to purchase or repurchase the shares.

A similar first refusal right in the corporation might be given by contract in case the executor of the estate of a deceased stockholder refuses to consent to the election of the corporation. It would also be wise for each stockholder to include a provision in his will authorizing the executor to consent to the election.

□ (2) ***Buying Out a Departing Stockholder:*** If at the time the stockholder is selling out, he has not yet collected his entire share of previous years' undistributed taxable income (upon which he has been taxed), he'll want to get that first. Once he's no longer a stockholder, he can't get that payout tax free. On the other hand, if there are current earnings in the corporation in the year he sells out, he won't get those earnings out because he won't be a stockholder at year end; whoever buys his stock will be entitled to the full share of the earnings (unless they've been previously paid out) for the entire year. So, the departing stockholder will want an adjustment in price. If he gets it, he'll be getting the value of these earnings as part of the price of his stock and he'll get capital gain instead of ordinary income. That fact plus the tax cost to the buyer for picking up a share of the year's earnings might result in further price adjustments the other way.

When the corporation has a loss, the selling stockholder gets his share of the loss passed through to him even though he is not a stockholder on the last day of the corporation's taxable year. Thus, here too, there may very well be a price adjustment to reflect the tax benefit.

□ (3) ***If a Stockholder Dies:*** There are some practical considerations that may cause an executor to hesitate to consent to the election. The accrued earnings of the corporation up to the date of death will be reflected in the value of the stock for estate tax purposes. But when the corporate year ends, the estate's pro rata share of the corporate earnings will be taxable to the estate for income tax purposes. And this type of income does not appear to qualify as income in respect of a decedent. So, income taxes will not be reduced by the estate taxes paid on the accrued earnings. To avoid the double tax, the executor may not want to consent to the election. But the deceased stockholder and his co-stockholders probably agreed to have the election continue. Hence, it might be well to direct in the will that the executor consent to the election.

Problems with an executor can be avoided by having the stock held jointly by the stockholder and his wife. As a joint owner she will have consented to begin with. And the stock will pass directly to her, bypassing the executor.

However, on a distribution of previously taxed, undistributed income to the wife, only half the distribution will be tax free. The other half is taxable as a dividend to the wife. The husband's right to receive this distribution is personal and ended on his death (*Rev. Rul. 66-172*, CB 1966-1, 198).

The executor should also consider the factors set forth above under "Buying Out Departing Stockholders" in valuing the stock for estate tax purposes. His approach might well be, what would a willing buyer with full knowledge require in the way of a discount in order to induce him to purchase the stock?

□ (4) ***How to Avoid Basis Problems on Inheritance of Stock:*** IRS says that the holder of inherited Subchapter S stock is stuck with the estate tax valuation figure for his basis (Regs. §1.1014-3(a)). But the Tax Court has ruled that the estate tax valuation is not conclusive; it merely raises a rebuttable presumption, says the Court (*McIntosh*, TC Memo 1967-230).

In *McIntosh*, Sam and William, Jr., inherited the stock of their father's road construction company. Their father's third wife (not their natural mother) was the executrix of the estate. When she prepared the estate tax return, with the assistance of a CPA, she assigned zero value to the business. The IRS agent went along with this valuation primarily on the grounds of reflected balance sheet deficits and substantial losses suffered by the company.

Some years later the brothers, who were operating the business as a Subchapter S corporation, claimed their pro rata share of $120,000 in net operating losses. IRS disallowed the deduction. The Tax Court sustained IRS but not on the grounds advanced by IRS to the effect that the estate tax valuation is conclusive. The Court said that this valuation can be overcome by the presentation of convincing evidence of a higher value but that, in this case, the stockholders failed to produce such evidence.

It is clear that in making out an estate tax return the person preparing it should look beyond the estate tax consequences to the income tax consequences of the valuations used. The fiduciary should as far as possible consult with and consider the long-range interests of the heirs.

But assuming this is done, you can still run into basis problems. What then? Well, for one thing, in a situation where you have NOL you can help nail down the passthrough by making a capital contribution in the year when the loss occurs. Sam and William, for example, would have avoided all problems if they had contributed the $120,000 to the corporation in the year of the NOL. But that's a sizable contribution, you may say. True; but if they were in a high tax bracket, say the 50% bracket, the net after-tax cost of their contribution would only be half that or $60,000.

Of course, they could also increase their basis by lending the company the $120,000. But this route merely defers the tax. Sam and William would have to pick up $120,000 of income when they are paid back. Under the contribution method, they have no income until the company is actually liquidated, and then the $120,000 comes back via the capital gains route.

SECTION III

THE BENEFITS OF A PROFESSIONAL CORPORATION

In this section, we will consider the nature and relative merits of a professional corporation as compared with a sole proprietorship and provide some basic guidelines to make an effective and intelligent choice as to the form of doing business most suited to the needs of a professional. Keep in mind, however, that this section represents one point of view. To get the whole picture, Section VI, "The Benefits of a Sole Proprietorship" should also be read. An analysis of both chapters will produce the best answer.

[¶301] WHO SHOULD CONSIDER INCORPORATING?

Every professional person performing professional services, e.g., doctors, dentists, lawyers, accountants, architects, engineers, business consultants, or whatever, has the legal right to organize his business activities within the framework of a professional corporation. The only real question is, "Is this an advantage or not?"

The answer, generally speaking, revolves around the question of income and how it relates to the immediate needs of the professional who generates it. Dr. Jones, a bachelor in his late 30s who maintains a small apartment and is too busy to have a very active social life, earns $40,000 per year. This amount is well above his actual needs and he is concerned about putting some of it away for the future. For Dr. Jones, professional incorporation might well be the best answer because it will permit him to accomplish just that, and with some very positive tax benefits. On the other hand, Dr. Smith, in his mid-40s, is married and has several children whose future expenses, particularly for education, must be met. His day-to-day living expenses are not only higher than those of Dr. Jones at this time but will actually increase in the very near future as his children reach maturity. For Dr. Smith, professional incorporation may not serve any advantageous purpose.

Thus the question of who should or should not incorporate largely depends upon the individual. No two cases are exactly alike, and the best that can be done is to establish general guidelines.

[¶302] THE UNINCORPORATED PROFESSIONAL

Does this mean that the professional who does not incorporate will not have any tax advantages or cannot take some positive steps towards financially preparing for his eventual retirement? No, not at all. It does mean, however, that different methods must be used. He can take advantage of various pension and profit-sharing plans, chief of which are the "Keogh Plans," named after Brooklyn Congressman Eugene Keogh, who introduced the legislation known as "HR-10," which permits the establishment of such plans. A full discussion of how a Keogh plan works will be found in Section VI. A detailed comparison of Keogh plans and Qualified Professional Corporation Benefit plans will be found at the end of this chapter. Again, for the full picture, read both chapters and then carefully study the comparison chart.

It should also be pointed out that Keogh plans and corporate plans cannot be objectively measured in terms of "better" or "worse." Because the needs of every professional person will be different, there is no fixed standard to measure good or bad. It just depends on the facts of each particular case.

[¶303] HOW TO AVOID PROBLEMS WITH THE IRS

Corporate status is certainly no panacea for the professional in avoiding problems with the IRS. A corporation, professional or otherwise, comes under the same scrutiny as an individual. Despite this, there are two distinct advantages to professional incorporation:

☐ (a) The very nature of the corporate structure of organization tends to categorize income and allowable expenses, and the corporate taxpayer is usually more aware of such categorization than is the self-employed taxpayer whose only direct contact with the tax requirements comes when his or her return is due.

☐ (b) To create a professional corporation, the services of another professional are usually required, i.e., an attorney, and a certain amount of basic corporate planning is required. This tends to make the taxpayer more planning-conscious and introduces him to the only sure and certain method of avoiding unnecessary taxes and incurring unnecessary tax liability, namely, careful and accurate tax planning.

The truth of this is borne out by an analysis of the cases that eventually reach the courts in regard to tax problems. While a certain percentage do represent attempts at a new or unique approach, the overwhelming majority are situations that could have been resolved often years earlier by competent tax planning. Only too often, a matter is brought before IRS or the courts that should not have been there in the first place. The success of IRS in litigation is not owing to any favored position it may have with the courts, but rather to the fact that many a taxpayer has failed to adequately plan his tax situation and comes to court with untenable defenses.

[¶304] HOW TO SHIELD TAXABLE INCOME UNDER THE CORPORATE UMBRELLA

As a starting point, consider first that the professional corporation is, in and of itself, a tax shelter since it gives professionals all of the tax advantages available to a corporate executive. These can include (but are not restricted to) the following:

☐ (1) A pension or profit-sharing plan to which contributions are made from pre-tax income and on which the professional will pay no tax until withdrawal. When the funds are withdrawn, the tax will usually be at lower rates since the professional will probably be retired with no immediate source of income from his practice. Further, the amount invested will not be subject to tax loss (depletion of capital) and can continue to earn investment profits. For a detailed treatment of this subject, see Section VIII: "Making the Most of Fringe Benefits."

☐ (2) A group term life insurance plan that affords full coverage to the professional without his or her incurring premiums costs but rather letting the cost of those premiums be borne by the corporation as a fully deductible expense.

☐ (3) A wage, salary, or other compensation plan that gives the professional a completely or partially tax-free source of income during periods of extended illness with complete funding by the corporation with pre-tax dollars.

☐ (4) A medical reimbursement or other insurance plan that will cover all such expenses through income on which neither the professional nor the corporation has any tax liability.

☐ (5) The full use of the corporation to shelter, temporarily at least, some of the professional's income. Obviously, this would be used only where the corporation's tax rates are lower than the professional's. While this is not too common, it is not difficult to envision a number of situations where this could be a strong and determining factor. It may well be that, for one reason or another, the corporation has heavy expenses (all tax deductible) and the professional elects, because of his high personal bracket, to make some investments in the corporate name for as long as the "heavy expense" situation prevails. This can materially reduce his personal bracket and means minimal taxes for the corporation.

These, generally, are the income-shielding benefits of professional incorporation, and they will be examined in detail. However, keep in mind that this is not the whole story. One of the most effective ways of shielding income is to have income that would be normally spent by the professional for personal purposes absorbed by the corporation as an intangible part of the professional's compensation. In this manner, expenses that would not be deductible by the individual professional can be fully deducted by the corporation as a business expense. The common name for this approach is "fringe benefits," and there is no reason whatsoever why a professional person, employed by his or her professional corporation, cannot enjoy the same fringe benefits as are extended to executives in industry and other areas. This subject will be treated in this chapter, and it should be weighed as part of the process of shielding income.

Let's now consider some of the specific tax advantages we have outlined in the list above.

[¶304.1] Group Term Life Insurance

One of the very strong considerations taken into account by professionals in the forming of a corporation is the availability of group term life insurance with premiums paid by the corporation in pre-tax dollars. This benefit is not available to a professional who practices alone or in partnership. Furthermore, the tax law places no limits on the amount of group coverage for an individual employee, although it does impose a ceiling of $50,000 on the amount that an employee can receive on a tax-free basis. However, that general rule is subject to a number of exceptions and does not apply in situations where:

☐ (a) The cost of group term life insurance is provided for an employee who has terminated employment and has attained either the employer's normal retirement age or has certain disabilities;
☐ (b) Certain "charitable organizations" are designated as the beneficiaries;
☐ (c) The employer is directly or indirectly the beneficiary; or
☐ (d) The cost of group term life insurance is provided for under certain pension and annuity plans.

As a general rule, most professional corporations involve less than ten employees. This, of course, presents difficulties for insurance carriers, as the risk involved in a group term policy is spread over a small group. As a matter of self-protection, insurance companies usually require medical examinations and medical histories before accepting such a policy.

Initially, IRS ruled that evidence as to insurability could not be used in determining eligibility for group term insurance. IRS has since adopted a more liberal view towards those plans that involve ten or less employees. For these plans, generally associated with professional corporations, evidence of insurability may be used in determining an employee's eligibility or the amount of his or her insurance coverage. This evidence of insurability, however, must be determined only by the use of an appropriate medical questionnaire; an actual physical medical examination cannot be required. Further, IRS also states that the amount of protection must be computed either as a uniform percentage of salary or on the basis of coverage brackets. No bracket in a plan affecting ten or fewer employees may exceed 2½ times the next lower bracket, and the lowest bracket must be at least 10% of the highest bracket. To illustrate this, let's take the following example:

If the lowest bracket is $5,000 of coverage, the highest would be $50,000 and there would be two other qualified brackets, one of $12,500 and another of $31,250. A plan covering four employees would qualify if one employee fitted into each bracket. If the chain is broken, the coverage would be less. For instance, if there are only three employees and the lowest coverage is $5,000, the maximum coverage for the man on top would be $31,250 ($5,000 × 2½ × 2½).

Minimum Employee Coverage: IRS states that a plan will qualify if it covers at least ten full-time employees. Under this rule, a company (i.e., professional corporation) with fifteen employees could limit eligibility as long as the criteria for the covered class are based on factors that preclude arbitrary individual selection and are nondiscriminatory. The key factor here is the number of employees eligible to participate. If at least ten employees *could* be covered, the fact that a certain number of them, for reasons of their own, elect not to participate in the plan will not be sufficient to disqualify it. And this is so even though the number of those actually participating is less than ten.

Allowable Amount of Purchase: The limitation of $50,000 in group term life insurance (apart from the exceptions noted) is a limitation only on the amount that can be provided on a tax-free basis. There is no federal limitation on the actual dollar amount that can be purchased, either except that any amount in excess of $50,000 does not receive the same favorable tax status. However, certain states (and it must be remembered that the creation and existence of any professional corporation is a matter of state law) put a statutory limitation on the amount of group term life insurance that can be purchased. It is thus necessary to consult with an attorney or insurance agent as to the limitation, if any, in any given area.

The Economics of Group Term Life Insurance: Group term life insurance is advantageous to the insurer because the cost of administering a group is substantially less than the cost of administering individual policies. However, most professional corporations constitute small groups and therefore must pay rates that are substantially higher than those applicable to larger groups. In addition, a carrier writing insurance for a small group is frequently incurring a greater liability than in writing insurance for either a large group or an individual. Nevertheless, there is a considerable premium savings in buying insurance for a small group as opposed to the members of that group purchasing it individually on their own account.

As an example, let's take the New York State legal minimum rate, based on the annual cost of a $50,000 group term policy for a 45-year-old professional man. The basic cost will be approximately $400, or about $100 to $150 *more* than the typical annual premium for an individual policy. Of course, some companies provide for a discount after the first year of the policy, but that is a bonus and not included in our example. At first glance, it would seem that the group policy costs more than an individual policy, but is not the case for a very simple reason: A group policy is tax deductible, and hence the real or net cost of the policy will work out to substantially less than any other form of insurance coverage. As a quick indicia of savings, all that the professional shareholder-employees considering group insurance need do is calculate what it will cost to insure the other corporate employees who must be included in the group for tax purposes and measure this against the savings on individual policies.

Don't Be Afraid to Shop Around: A professional corporation should check with several agents before purchasing life insurance. Rates will frequently vary from company to company, and in some instances it will be possible to purchase insurance at substantially reduced rates through an association. However, before committing a professional corporation to purchasing insurance through an association, make sure that the insurance in question is fully tax deductible.

[¶304.2] Health and Accident Benefits

Most professional corporations provide some form of health and accident benefits to their employee-shareholders as well as regular employees. Medical and sickness payments by an employer give the employee the maximum dollar benefit, as they are tax free to the employees. Other forms of benefits may constitute taxable income. If the payments meet the requirements set forth in the Code, they are tax free to the employee and deductible by the employer.

The following table shows how much professionals in various tax brackets who are not part of professional corporations must earn in order to put a premium dollar into a health plan paid for individually or to pay a dollar of nondeductible medical expenses themselves:

Income Tax Bracket	*Employee Must Earn*
22%	$1.28
25%	1.33
32%	1.47
36%	1.56
42%	1.72
50%	2.00
60%	2.50
70%	3.33

Assume a professional in the 25% tax bracket who pays an annual premium of $250 each year for health insurance protection. He would actually have to save $333 before-tax income in order to pay the annual premium ($250 × 1.33 from table = $333).

Most health and accident premiums are deductible, both by the employer who pays the premium and the employee who receives the benefits, if they are provided by a plan that falls in the following categories:

☐ (a) Reimbursement of medical expenses.

☐ (b) Payments unrelated to absence from work; i.e., payments are computed with reference to the nature of the injury without regard to the time of the employee's absence from work—for permanent loss of use of a member or function of the body or permanent disfigurement of the employee, his spouse, or his dependent (§105(c)).

☐ (c) Wage continuation payments; i.e., payments made while an employee is out sick and cannot report to work.

Plans that do not meet the above qualifications are not tax free. However, if a professional corporation contributes to a health and accident plan which is not tax free, the contribution is not taxable to the professional or other employee when made (§106). However, when the employee gets paid from the plan (and this can include direct payments by the professional corporation to the employee under an internally funded plan rather than an insurance-funded one), the employee is taxable on that portion of the proceeds that bears the same ratio to the total proceeds he received as the professional corporation's contribution to the premium bears to the total premium.

For example, suppose the professional corporation pays two-thirds of the premium on a health and accident insurance policy for professionals and other employees. In this situation, two-thirds of the proceeds would be taxable (Reg. §1.105-1(d)(1)). Where a group policy is involved, the determination as to the taxable portion of the proceeds is based on the average of the professional corporation's contribution percentage for the last three known policy years (Reg. §1.105-1(d)(2)).

Medical Expense Reimbursement: If a professional corporation reimburses its employees, including shareholder-employees, for actual medical expenses incurred for themselves, their spouses, or their children, such reimbursements do not constitute taxable income to the employees. The reimbursement can take the form of a payment directly to the employee or to the physician or hospital that provided the medical services. The tax treatment is the same whether the payment comes directly from the professional corporation or from an insurance company, where the professional corporation pays the premiums (§105(b)).

A taxpayer cannot take a medical expense deduction for reimbursed expenses. If the reimbursement comes in the same year as the expense, the taxpayer must reduce his medical expenses by the amount of the reimbursement (§213(a)). If the reimbursement comes in a later year and the taxpayer previously deducted that expense, then the reimbursement is taxable income (§105(b); Reg. §1.105-2). If the reimbursement exceeds the amount that the taxpayer actually deducted, the excess is tax free.

Advantages in a Professional Corporation: In a professional corporation (where frequently the corporation and the employee-shareholders who constitute the corporation are looked upon as one entity), the effect of the medical reimbursement plan for the stockholder-employees and their families is a full deduction for all of the families' medical costs without regard to the limitations on medical deductions for individuals. Furthermore, there's no tax wastage of payments for medical care (due to the 3% floor) or drugs (due to the 1% floor) that occurs when a highly paid professional pays his own doctor bills. Of course, the deduction is at the corporate level and, depending on comparative rates, may be more or less valuable than a deduction at the individual level.

If a professional corporation has elected to be taxed as a Subchapter S corporation, it is not even necessary to be concerned with differences in tax rates. A corporation that has elected under Subchapter S pays no tax; each shareholder picks up his share of the corporation's profits and reports it as his own. In a Subchapter S corporation where medical reimbursements are made, the corporate profits are reduced. Thus, the individual stockholder picking up this reduced profit has the benefit of a full deduction at his or her personal income tax rates.

Payments to reimburse an employee for medical insurance (the employee's spouse and dependents may also be included) are deductible by the professional corporation—if the employee presents proof to the corporation at the time he is reimbursed that the insurance is in force and being paid by the employee.

IRS is satisfied if reimbursement is made by any of the following methods: (1) reimburse each employee of the professional corporation directly once or twice a year for the professional corporation's share of the insurance premiums on proof of prior payment of the premiums by the employee-shareholder; (2) issue to each employee a check payable to the particular employee's insurance agent, the employee being obligated to turn over the check to the insurance company; (3) issue a check made payable to the insured and the insurance company with the understanding that it will be turned over to the insurance company.

Restrictive Reimbursement Plans: Providing medical reimbursement programs for all employees of a professional corporation can be costly. Some professional corporations, therefore, limit these plans to a preferred class of employees, usually the professionals. IRS will go along with such classification as long as it is on the basis of some factor related to employment (e.g., to salaried employees). However, IRS has not gone along where the eligibility is based on stock ownership and participation is limited to stockholder-employees.

If the reimbursement program is only for shareholder-employees, IRS may take the position that the reimbursed medical expenses were in fact dividends.

Although there have been no professional corporation cases dealing with the deductibility or income status of medical reimbursement plans, there have been several cases involving small corporations that provide guidance to steps that should be taken to insure that a medical reimbursement plan will be sustained.

Reasonable Compensation: The benefits that a shareholder-officer of a professional corporation receives by way of medical reimbursement will be weighed on the scale of reasonable compensation. If the benefits bring the officer-director's compensation above the "reasonable" level, the corporation may be denied a deduction (*Sanders*, TC Memo 1967-146).

Plan for Employees: A medical reimbursement plan must be a plan for employees. It cannot be a plan designed merely for shareholders. Where a plan specified that it was for such employees as the officers at their discretion considered should be covered and, in point of fact, only one nonshareholder-employee received any benefits, the courts threw out the medical reimbursement plan (*Larkin*, 48 TC 629, 19).

Note: Medical reimbursement plans are now subject to pension law provisions requiring them to be in writing and to cover stockholders only as employees.

[¶305] VOLUNTARY PAYMENTS TO WIDOWS

It is common for professional corporations to make a payment to a widow or other beneficiaries of a deceased stockholder-professional. These payments are often made even though the professional corporation is under no legal or any other obligation to do so.

Where the total payments do not exceed $5,000, there's no problem. Payments by reason of death up to $5,000 are tax exempt (§101(b)). As a general rule, the excess over $5,000 may be either taxable as compensation or a nontaxable gift (see §102), depending on the dominant motives behind the payment as determined by the facts. If a gift is found, IRS agrees that the exclusion rate of §101(b) doesn't apply and the entire amount is tax free (TIR-371, 1962).

The facts in a typical widow's payment case involved a corporation's resolution to pay the widow of a deceased corporate executive a continuation of his salary (or some other sum) "in recognition" of his past services to the corporation. Before the Supreme Court decided the *Duberstein* case (363 US 278, 1960), the Tax Court found that such payments were nontaxable gifts (*Estate of Hellstrom*, 24 TC 916, 1955; *Est. of Maycann*, 29 TC 81, 1957; *April*, 13 TC 707, 1949).

After *Duberstein*, courts attempted to apply the Supreme Court's gift criteria (proceeds from a detached and disinterested generosity or out of affection, respect, admiration, charity, or like impulses) in their determination of whether these payments are, in fact, gifts. The Tax Court, for example, found compensation where it might earlier have found a gift (e.g., *Pierpont*, 35 TC 65, 1961; *Kuntz*, TC Memo 1960-247). However, both these cases were later reversed (*Pierpont*, 301 F. 2d 287, 1961; CA-4, 1962; *Kuntz*, 300 F. 2d 849, CA-6, 1962). The Fourth Circuit said that the objective is to find the dominant motivation and that *Duberstein* did not destroy any of the earlier cases for purposes of finding motivation. The Fourth Circuit pointed out that factually the *Pierpont* case measures favorably with criteria previously (before *Duberstein*) recognized by the Tax Court as evidencing a gift (rather than a compensation motive).

Although you cannot come up with any hard and fast rules, the outcome of a widow's payment case (i.e., gift or compensation) does depend on the court that hears it. As a rule, the Tax Court usually finds compensation; a district court usually finds a gift. So, if you pay the tax and then sue for a refund in a district court, the cases indicate that you stand a better chance of winning. But there have been exceptions. At the Circuit Court level, the Fourth, Eighth and probably the Sixth Circuits have held such payments to be tax free. Only the Third Circuit has upheld a finding of compensation by the Tax Court (*Smith*, 305 F. 2d 778, 1962; *Martin*, 305 F. 2d 290, CA-3, 1962).

If you are going on the tax-free gift theory, bear in mind that you must have a voluntary payment. If there is a plan—even though cancellable by the corporation—to make death payments, you will not have a gift.

If you want to take the position that the entire payment is tax free, make sure you have a true voluntary payment. For example, although a payment may be technically voluntary, actually it may really not be. Two cases involved payments to widows of deceased executives under a long-standing policy adopted by the corporation. Technically, they were voluntary because the board of directors' resolution establishing the policy could at all times be revoked. But the fact that the policy was a long-standing one and that the other executives' incentive depended, in part, on the continuation of this policy (which made it unlikely that it would be revoked) took the voluntary aspect out of the payments and they were held taxable (*Russek,* TC Memo 1961-28; *Simpson,* 261 F.2d 497, CA-7, 1958).

Keep in mind that where a widow simultaneously receives voluntary payments from her husband's employer and lump-sum payments from a qualified pension or profit-sharing plan, the $5,000 exclusion of §101(b) may be applied against the voluntary payments (which were taxable as ordinary income) rather than against the pension plan payments (taxable as capital gains) (*Olsen,* TC Memo 1961-161, *rev'd* on other grounds).

How to Pay Benefits to Widows: What used to be the more important aspect of this issue—namely, avoiding the tax impact to the widow—has become secondary in importance to the question of deductibility to the professional corporation. The reason, of course, is the limitation on the deductibility of gifts to $25 per year per recipient. Where the widow maintains that the payments represent pure gifts and are entirely nontaxable (§102), the consequences to the professional corporation are unsatisfactory in that, except for the nominal $25 annual deduction, the payments are treated like dividends (i.e., they reduce earnings and profits but not taxable income). How then should companies handle these payments? An analysis of applicable cases involving other than professional corporations reveals that the best tax approach depends largely on the circumstances.

In the nonprofessional corporation situation where the widow is a shareholder and holds enough stock to make her weight felt in corporate policy making, there is a danger that payments will be viewed by IRS as dividends. There have been no cases involving professional corporations, however.

In most instances, state law requires that the shares held by a nonprofessional must be transferred within a limited time. Because of the rule it is unclear what position the Tax Court would take. The Tax Court has accepted IRS's position in the nonprofessional corporate situation (see *Barbourville Brick Co.,* 37 TC 7, 1962, where a widow held 93% of the stock; *Lengsfield,* TC Memo 1955-257, *aff'd* 241 F.2d 508, where a widow held 63% of the stock). For a professional corporation, proper tax planning in this situation calls for setting up contractual obligations to pay a deceased stockholder's widow on the death of her husband. Such an agreement could be made with the professional as an added incentive to accept employment, at the time he becomes a stockholder, or even at some time after he has become a shareholder. To cut the tax impact of these payments to the widow, they should be made over a period of years. Also, it is important to keep in mind that, as noted above, the widow can get $5,000 tax free under §101(b) without bringing into effect the $25 limit on the corporate deduction. That permits payments in the first year to be higher than in succeeding ones.

Payments by professional corporations that are intended to be gifts, however, are deductible only to the extent of $5,025.

[¶305.1] Funding Payment to the Widow

It's quite common to underwrite an obligation to make post-death payment with life insurance. For example, the professional corporation can take out an insurance policy on the life of the professional or other employee, naming itself beneficiary. When the professional-employee dies, the professional corporation will collect the proceeds and use them to pay off its obligation to the widow. The premiums won't be deductible, but proceeds will be received tax free. Then, when the payment is made, the professional corporation will get a deduction.

The Split-Dollar Approach: In a typical split-dollar setup, the professional corporation pays the premium equal to the annual increase in the cash value and the professional pays the rest. The corporation is beneficiary of the policy for an amount equal to the cash value, and the professional's widow is the beneficiary of the balance. Because cash values can increase sharply after the first few years, the professional's cost decreases sharply. Consequently, he can get a lot of insurance for a comparatively small payment. The "fifth" dividend option or term rider (which can provide additional insurance equal to the cash value) can insure the widow's getting the full face value of the policy.

Then, when the professional dies, the widow has no income tax to pay at the time she receives the insurance proceeds. The professional corporation will recover the full amount of its outlay and will not have to make any further payments.

[¶305.2] What About the Professional's Cost of Insurance?

To the extent the professional pays the premiums, the benefits are not really coming from the professional corporation. In the early years of the policy, these payments can be somewhat high for the professional.

One way of handling this, of course, is to give the professional an immediate salary increase that would leave him with enough after-tax money to pay the premium. Since the insurance proceeds can relieve the professional corporation of its obligation to the widow in the future, the current salary increase might be a partial payment in advance of an amount that would otherwise have to be paid later.

Other arrangements could utilize a policy with early high cash values (the kind used in minimum-deposit arrangements) so as to cut down on the professional's early-year contributions. An alternative would be to have the professional corporation pay a higher portion of the premium reflecting the higher cash values in the early years, treating the excess as an additional loan to the professional. In later years, the corporation will pay less than the cash value increase, and the professional will pay back the loan by paying a higher portion of the premium. Thus, overall, the employee's contribution to the policy's annual premium cost is levelled out.

Of course, these latter devices do not relieve the professional of paying a portion of the policy costs as would, in effect, a salary increase.

[¶305.3] Nonstockholder Widows

Where the widows do not own stock or the number of shares is so small that it doesn't amount to participation in corporate affairs, contractual obligations are not essential (but even here, use of a contractual obligation should not be disregarded). In such a situation, the Tax Court has held that voluntary payments were intended (1) as additional compensation to the deceased for services rendered the corporation and (2) to provide the widow with economic security and that they were reasonable and proximately related to business (*Oppenheimer Casing Co.*, TC Memo 1963-216).

Other important points in setting up such an arrangement for nonstockholder-widows include:

☐ (1) Making sure that the payments represent *reasonable* compensation (see *Rev. Rul. 54-625*, CB 1954-2, 85; Reg. §1.404(a)-12; and *Fifth Avenue Coach Lines, Inc.*, 31 TC 1080, 1958, where the widow was paid 31 months' salary over an 11-year period).

☐ (2) Labeling the payments "salary continuation" or some other comparable term and treating them as such on corporate books and tax returns (see *Harry L. Davis Company*, TC Memo 1961-209).

☐ (3) Adopting a corporate resolution to pay the widow of the employee salary continuation as added compensation for past services (reasonable in amount). Where a company had no pension plan or other death benefits and the directors didn't wish the deceased employee's services to go unrecognized, a two years' salary of $55,000 in 24 monthly installments was okayed by the Tax Court. There was also a favorable effect on the morale of the company's executives (*John B. Canepa Company*, TC Memo 1963-337).

☐ (4) Code §404(a)(5) permits an employer to deduct payments to employee's "other plans" (e.g., deferred payment plans). The Regs include in "other plans" death benefits to beneficiaries of an employee (for example, by continuing his salary for a reasonable period) provided the business purpose tests of §162 or 212 are met (see *Loewy Drug Company of Baltimore*, 356 F.2d 928, CA-4, 1966 *aff'd* 232 F. Supp. 143).

[¶305.4] How to Nail Down the Deduction

If you want to nail down the deduction for a professional corporation's payments to a widow or other beneficiary, here are the rules to observe.

☐ (1) Make payments under a contract of employment between the corporation and the employee with provisions for benefits to be paid to his widow on his death.

☐ (2) Make payments under an established pension plan or a program, policy, or custom having the effect of such a plan in effect before the employee's death. Be able to show a benefit related to the employees, such as built-in goodwill, corporate morale, or creating incentive to the employees.

☐ (3) Show that the payments to the widow are in the nature of extra compensation for past services rendered by the deceased employee.

[¶306] THE WONDERFUL WORLD OF FRINGE BENEFITS

One of the major advantages in the professional corporation is that, like any other corporation, it may extend a number of useful and valuable fringe benefits to its employees. In practical terms, this means that the professional corporation can pay out of pre-tax dollars for many of the benefits that the shareholders would have to purchase with after-tax dollars if they used their own personal income. Obviously, this reduces the personal income of the shareholder from corporate distribution (which often has the benefit of putting him or her in a lower tax bracket) but makes that income closer to real net income than if he or she were to receive greater corporate compensation and meet these expenses personally.

Just about all of the fringe benefits presently available to executive employees of business and industrial corporations are applicable with little or no modification to the members of a professional corporation. Let's survey some of the major ones:

□ (1) ***Financial Aid:*** Professional corporations will usually lend their members funds for home building or home improvement on a free or low-interest basis. This is an obvious advantage to the member who otherwise would have to pay the cost of a mortgage loan. The effect is that the member gets tax-free income in an amount equal to the economic value of the benefit (the interest he'd have to pay on an outside loan less the value to him of the interest deduction). In some cases, he ends up paying what amounts to only 2% interest.

The corporation, on the other hand, loses income it could have earned on this money. It has no tax benefit or liability (no taxable income); nor is the member charged with taxable income. To secure the benefits of the arrangement, the loan agreement should be a bona fide loan. There is the danger that the IRS will try to tax the entire amount of the loan as a dividend. It is important, therefore, that the loan be handled in the same manner and under the same terms (except possibly for interest) as it would be handled with an outsider in an arm's-length transaction.

Provision for repayment by offset against future compensation (with the date specified) is important evidence of good-faith negotiations here.

The corporation may also lend the professional money to buy a car, yacht, personal insurance, or to take advantage of capital gains opportunities to invest in real estate, mutual funds, or stocks other than the corporation's. Further, loans may be made for emergency purposes such as illness or death in the family or to meet casualty losses from fire, storm, theft, flood, etc. Such loans are usually made available either without interest or at a very nominal rate and, of course, are tax free. All financial aid programs are quite flexible and there is no limitation on the purposes of such loan, other than the restriction that it cannot be made to purchase corporate stock of the lender corporation.

Remember that when a member borrows from the corporation, he has assumed an obligation that he must pay back regardless of what he makes or doesn't make by investing it. If his investments should turn sour and result in a loss, he still must eventually repay the loan with the agreed rate of interest. If the corporation cancels the debt, he has taxable income. Before a corporation makes a loan of this type, it should have its attorneys check to see if it can legally make such a loan. Also, check the rate of interest, as it might affect the question of whether the loan is, in part, to be considered added compensation. In addition, the corporation may not deem it wise to make an unsecured loan to a member and may wish security.

□ (2) ***Company Automobiles and/or Auto Expense Reimbursement:*** If the members of a professional corporation use cars in the pursuit of their professional and corporate activities, there is no reason why the corporation cannot purchase them (often getting a better price through group or fleet purchase) and simply make them available to the shareholders as a fringe benefit. These cars may also be used for the members' personal and/or family use without affecting the nature of the fringe benefit.

If the members elect to use their own vehicles, that portion of the expense allocated to professional use can be made the subject of full reimbursement and a fringe benefit.

□ (3) ***Company Aircraft:*** The same rules used for automobiles and auto expenses are applicable to aircraft, particularly in the case where one or more of the professionals have an active or consulting practice in different geographic areas. With many professionals, especially those in the medical and legal area, quick transportation is an absolute necessity, and often to areas where commercial air service is less than adequate.

☐ (4) ***Recreation Facilities:*** Recreation facilities can be expensive for the professional and his family, but he can get his professional corporation to provide these benefits in a manner that will not result in a tax. A tax deduction, of course, can nearly cut the corporation's costs in half. There is one sure way to accomplish this, even if the recreation facilities are for pleasure and wholly unrelated to the business of the corporation: Make the facilities available to *all* employees. With the business or industrial corporation, this can present a problem since the great majority of employees are not executives. However, nearly all of the employees in a professional corporation are shareholders. Depending upon its inclination, a professional corporation can own and provide hunting lodges, ski lodges, golf facilities, or facilities for any other activity without regard to whether it is business-related or not.

☐ (5) ***Professional Services:*** As a fringe benefit, a professional corporation can provide free professional services to its members when and where needed. Hence a professional medical corporation can either retain an attorney to handle both the corporate and private affairs of its members or, if the member prefers to choose his own counsel, simply pick up the tab. These services may also be intraprofessional, e.g., if a member of a medical corporation needs certain specialized medical services not available professionally from the other members, the costs of these may be absorbed by the professional corporation.

☐ (6) ***Purchase Discounts:*** Members of a professional corporation, like company executives on their fringe benefit plans, frequently enjoy a considerable benefit in the corporation's being able to get quantity discounts or the like on certain merchandise. For example, in the small professional corporation (2-5 members and their families), group purchasing of meats in freezer quantities can bring meat prices down some 40% from prevailing supermarket prices. For practitioners with larger families, this is a very tangible fringe benefit.

☐ (7) ***Scholarships:*** One way to ease the spiraling cost of a college education is to let the professional corporation provide educational opportunities for the members' children through loans or scholarships. These scholarships may be granted indirectly through a foundation set up for that purpose or through another charitable foundation supported in part by the corporation. This would also include a foundation set up by a number of professional corporations, the members of whom are all familiar to one another professionally or socially. Where policy dictates, such scholarships may be also available to employees of the professional corporations who are not themselves members.

Grants providing scholarship aid for full-time study leading to a degree will ordinarily be deductible by the corporation, within the limitations on corporate charitable contributions; and they will also be excluded from the taxable income of the recipient if: (a) The grant is supported by a contribution to a tax-exempt educational institution or foundation, (b) the grant isn't restricted to named individuals, (c) the class or group of eligible beneficiaries is broad enough to meet IRS standards, and (d) the primary purpose of the grant is to further the education of the recipient as an individual.

Another approach is to establish an educational benefit trust. This device is simply a trust set up by your professional corporation to provide educational benefits to the children of employees designated by the firm. The offspring of every employee do *not* have to be eligible for the trust benefits; eligibility can instead be restricted to the children of key employees. As with other discretionary fringes, though, the selection of a key employee must be based on his value as an employee, not on his possible shareholding in the corporate employer (*Larkin,* 394 F. 2d 494, CA-1, 1968).

The corporation may either earmark payments for the accounts of specific eligible children or create a general fund to which all eligible offspring might apply. In the former case, provision would have to be made for the return to the corporation of any account balance unused by the designated beneficiary before, say, his thirtieth birthday (for graduate students) or, perhaps, twenty-fifth birthday (for eligible beneficiaries not yet enrolled in an undergraduate school). Such repayments would be taxable income to the PC.

Contributions to the educational trust could be made either on a regular basis or infrequently, say when your corporation had enjoyed a highly profitable year.

☐ (8) ***Personal Financial Planning:*** This is becoming one of the most useful and popular of all fringe benefits and is certainly ideal for the professional in any discipline. Through this benefit, the professional corporation picks up the cost for services of professional financial planners who chart out the individual financial future of the individual members focusing on their needs in investment planning, tax planning, and estate planning. Since the members tend to select individual counselors in this area, there is what might be termed a horizontal benefit to the professional corporation in that, as a whole, it will receive the benefit of the collective thinking of these planners and perhaps might adjust some of its own planning and activities to more directly coincide with the needs of the members.

[¶307] COMPARISON CHARTS: KEOGH PLAN VS. PROFESSIONAL CORPORATION

We conclude this section with a comparison of Keogh plans and Professional Corporation plans in terms of both direct benefits and general economics. Go over this material now, and after you have read Section VI for a better understanding of what a Keogh plan is and how it works, you may want to come back to it for quick reference.

[¶307.1] General Comparison

Keogh Plan	Professional Corporation Pension or Profit-Sharing Plan
	Coverage Requirements
Employees with three years' service must be included in the plan. Part-time or seasonal employees, i.e., those with less than 20 hours per week or five months per year service, may be excluded (§401(d)(1)).	The regulations require the plan to be nondiscriminatory. The plan, however, can set rules for determining who may participate. The following factors are used for qualifying employees: employee classification, length of service, minimum age, maximum age. Where a plan provides for a waiting period before employee

Keogh Plan	Professional Corporation Pension or Profit-Sharing Plan
	participation, employees of 25 years of age or older must be admitted to participate in the plan after one year of service. If the employer provides for 100% vesting as soon as an employee is eligible to participate, the employer may amend his plan to require a three-year waiting period.
Contributions	
Owner-employee limited to 15% of earned income or $7,500, whichever is less (§401(d)(5) and §404(e)). However, after 1975 he may elect to participate in a defined-benefit plan. In this event, contributions would be computed with reference to a set percentage based on his age when he begins participation.	Contributions to profit-sharing plans and money-purchase pension plans are limited to 15% of compensation. The Pension Reform Act of 1974 permits unused contributions to be carried over to the extent of 25% of aggregate compensation or $25,000, whichever is less. Benefits under a deferred-benefit pension plan may not exceed $75,000 per year or 100% of the three highest years of compensation.
Credit carryovers where less than the maximum is contributed during any given year are not permitted (§404(a)(B)(iii)).	Credit carryovers are permitted for profit-sharing plans if the contributions for a given year are less than the maximum allowed under the regulations. In addition, extra amounts may be contributed to a pension or profit-sharing plan and deducted in subsequent years.
A definite formula for contributions made by the owner-employee on behalf of employees is required if the plan is of the deferred profit-sharing type (§401(d)(2)(B)).	Professional corporations are not required to follow a definite contribution plan even if the plan is a deferred profit-sharing plan. The board of directors of the corporation may set the contribution each year after the end of the fiscal year.
Excess Contributions	
Excess contributions result in penalties. Willful excess contributions disqualify the plan. Excesses cannot be carried over to subsequent years (*Rev. Rul. 56-366*, 1956-2 CB 976).	Excess contributions can be deducted in a subsequent year if the contributions in that year do not reach maximum permitted level. Excess contributions do not result in a penalty (§401(e)(2)(E)).

Keogh Plan	Professional Corporation Pension or Profit-Sharing Plan
Vesting	
Contributions to a Keogh plan must be fully vested if, as is the case in most plans, owner-employees are participating in the plan. In addition, employee rights must be nonforfeitable (§401(d)(2)(A)).	Professional corporations may choose between the following vesting requirements: (1) The employee's rights must be 100% vested after ten years of covered service. (2) The employee must be 25% vested after five years of service and an additional 5% must vest every year thereafter until 100% is vested after 15 years of service. (3) 50% of the employee's rights must vest where he has at least five years of service when the sum of his years of service and his age total 45. An additional 10% must vest for each year of continued service thereafter.
Distributions	
Distributions by Keogh plans to owner-employees cannot be made before age 59½ without incurring a penalty. If a distribution is made before the owner-employee reaches that age, no further contributions can be made to the plan for the five tax years following the year in which the distributions were made.	A corporate plan does not penalize an owner-employee for withdrawals prior to his reaching age 59½. However, pension plan withdrawals are not permitted prior to retirement or separation from service. Pension plan benefits may begin at a normal or stated retirement age or at disability or death (Reg. §1.401-1(b)(1)(i)).
Distributions to owner-employees must be made by age 70½. They cannot be made for a period greater than the life expectancy of the owner-employee and his spouse, irrespective of the beneficiaries.	Profit-sharing benefits may be paid after a stated period. There is no requirement that they be paid on death or disability (Reg. §1.401-1(b)(1)(ii)).
Taxation of Death Benefits	
Death benefits are taxable when received by the beneficiary. There is no provision for a death benefit exception (§101(B)(3)).	Death benefits distributed by a corporate plan may qualify for the $5,000 death benefit exclusion (§101(b)).

Keogh Plan	Professional Corporation Pension or Profit-Sharing Plan
Federal Estate Taxation of Death Benefits	
An owner-employee's interest in a Keogh plan is includible in his estate and subject to estate tax (§2039(c)).	Distributions attributable to contributions made by a corporate plan are excludable from the decedent's gross estate for federal estate tax purposes unless the distribution is received by the executor or the administrator of the decedent's estate (§2039(c)).

[¶307.2] Economic Comparison

The distinction between a Keogh plan for a self-employed single practitioner and a corporate profit-sharing plan can best be illustrated by the following example:

	Keogh Plan	*Professional Corporation Profit-Sharing Plan*
(1) Net income from practice (gross income less business deductions except contributions to retirement plan)	$75,000	$75,000
(2) Total annual salaries of employees qualified for pension, profit-sharing, or Keogh plan	12,600	12,600
(3) Effective income for professional	66,070	61,860
(4) Annual contribution to retirement plan for professional	7,500	11,250
(5) Annual contribution to plan for employees	1,430	1,890
(6) Income tax exemption for the professional and his dependents (assuming three children)	3,750	3,750
(7) Total of other personal tax deductions	4,750	4,750
(8) Taxable income	57,570	53,360
(9) Federal income tax	20,845	18,740
(10) Annual "take home" pay	36,725	34,620
(11) Total annual net gain [(4) + (10)]	44,225	45,870

The advantages are even more handsome for the higher-income professional with sources of unearned income. The following illustration demonstrates the gain for a professional with double the income and $20,000 in unearned income. The other factors remain constant:

	Keogh Plan	*Professional Corporation Profit-Sharing Plan*
(1) Net income from practice (gross income less business deductions except contributions to retirement plan)	$150,000	$150,000
(2) Total annual salaries of employees qualified for pension, profit-sharing, or Keogh plan	12,600	12,600
(3) Effective income for professional	141,000	125,610
(4) Annual contribution to retirement plan for professional	7,500	22,500
(5) Annual contribution to plan for employees	945	1,890
(6) Income tax exemption for the professional and his dependents (assuming three children)	3,750	3,750
(7) Total of other personal tax deductions	4,750	4,750
(8) Taxable Income	153,055	137,110
(9) Federal income tax	71,506	63,211
(10) Annual "take home" pay	81,549	73,899
(11) Total annual net gain [(4) + (10)]	89,049	96,399

Note: In addition to our professional's immediate annual advantage, his account in the all-important tax-sheltered investment vehicle is significantly greater.

SECTION IV

HOW TO MAXIMIZE THE TAX BENEFITS OF DOING BUSINESS AS A PARTNERSHIP

By way of introduction to partnership tax law, we should note that there are two opposing theories on the nature of a partnership that are operating simultaneously. One theory holds that a partnership is a distinct and separate entity from the partners (entity theory), just as a corporation is a distinct and separate entity from the stockholders. The other, the aggregate theory, holds that partners are co-owners of the firm and the firm property. Under the entity theory, a partner can deal with his firm just as if it were another entity. The aggregate theory views dealings between partner and partnership as a combination of a deal between one partner and his other partners and another deal with himself. As a consequence, a particular transaction may result in different outcomes, from a legal as well as a tax viewpoint. Keep these two theories in mind throughout this section. They explain why tax results in some instances do not conform to the results in others.

Generally, Code §701-771 provide the rules for taxing the creation, operation and termination of partnerships.

[¶401] CHECKLIST OF MAJOR TAX CONSIDERATIONS OF DOING BUSINESS AS A PARTNERSHIP

Here are the basic tax features of doing business as a partnership:

□ (1) Earnings of a partnership are subject to only one tax. There is no double tax on profits where they are distributed as dividends.

□ (2) The tax rate on the individual partners may be less than the corporate 22% or 48% rates.

□ (3) Partners are not taxed on exempt-interest income, like insurance proceeds, received from the firm—while dividends received from a corporation are taxable even if they are out of income that was tax free to the corporation.

□ (4) Partnership losses can be applied against partners' other personal ordinary income. This may also result in a carryover and a return of a prior year's taxes.

However, no loss is recognized on a nonliquidating distribution (§731(a)(2)). Assume, for example, A and B form a partnership. A contributes $75,000 in cash while B contributes property worth $150,000 for which his basis is $200,000. In order for them to have equal interests, B is to receive the $75,000 cash. B's loss is not recognized, but his basis for his partnership interest would be decreased by $75,000.

If B wants to realize a loss before contributing to the partnership, he could sell a half interest in the property to A for $75,000. Then he would have a tax loss of $25,000 (half of $200,000 basis over $75,000 cash received).

☐ (5) If capital gains are realized by the firm, the partners only have to pay one capital gains tax. Stockholders of a corporation realizing capital gain cannot ordinarily get this treatment (exception: 12-month liquidation under §337). Section 1231 gains are taxable as long-term capital gains while §1231 losses reduce ordinary income; but when both occur in one year, they must first be used to offset each other. So, a provision in the partnership agreement that Partner A is to get the gains and Partner B the losses would probably create an overall tax saving. However, the Regs provide that if the principal purpose of any provision is to avoid or evade tax, the provision is to be disregarded and the partners' shares are to be computed according to the general profit ratio (Reg. §1.704-1(b)(2)).

☐ (6) Income splitting on a joint return gives each partner the benefit of lower tax rates on his entire share of partnership income. Stockholders can only split salary and dividend income on their personal tax returns.

☐ (7) You can decide how to divide profits among the partners without regard to investment. You can even do it at the end of the year. However, this division should be spelled out. If no specification is made, long- and short-term capital gains and losses, §1231 gains or losses, foreign tax credit, qualifying dividends, charitable contributions, and each item of income, gain, loss, deduction, or credit will be divided in the same ratio as ordinary income.

☐ (8) Earnings already taxed increase the cost basis of the partner in his company. This is not true of the stockholder. Where a new partner buys an interest in the firm assets at the higher market value, he will want the firm to elect the higher basis for his share of the assets under §754. The result is that the new partner will obtain greater depreciation deductions; while on the sale of the firm's assets, he will have less gain (or more loss, as the case may be) to report.

☐ (9) Where property is contributed to the partnership and the contributing partner's basis for the property is not the same as its fair market value, the partnership will pick up this difference in its income at the time the property is sold. For accounting purposes, the contribution will be credited for the fair market value of the property. Depreciation for nontax purposes will be based on this figure, while tax depreciation must be based on the partner's original basis. However, if the partners have contributed property of equal value to the partnership, the agreement should give the partner contributing the appreciated property a percentage of the depreciation that would equal the amount of depreciation he would have taken had depreciation been based on the fair market value of the property (§704(c)(2)). The result is that each partner obtains depreciation based on the fair market value of the property, not on his share of the profits. If no specific provision is made, this difference between the tax basis and the accounting values will be picked up in the same ratio as ordinary income.

☐ (10) Partners' salaries are not subject to withholding nor do they qualify for sick-pay exemption. Also, payment of these salaries does not create an employer-employee relationship that qualifies for pension or profit-sharing plans.

☐ (11) Capital losses of a partnership reduce capital gains of individual partners. This is not true in corporations.

Where a partner's tax basis is more than the value at which an asset is to be contributed, it is better to sell the asset and contribute the cash to the partnership. In this way, the partner gets a deduction for his loss. Where, however, the partner owning the asset is in a low tax bracket while the other partner is in a high bracket, contributing the property to the partnership could have the effect of switching a loss to the high bracket partner.

Example: A owns property with a basis of $40,000 that is worth $10,000. The property is contributed to the firm, then sold. The $30,000 loss realized by the firm is divided equally between A and B (assuming that is the loss-sharing ratio). So, in effect, this amounts to an assignment of a $15,000 tax loss from A to B, the high bracket partner.

☐ (12) Partners can deduct their share of partnership charitable contributions (up to 50% of adjusted gross income; 30% for certain gifts of appreciated property). Corporations are limited to 5%.

☐ (13) Have the agreement state what the payments to the partner represent: a partner's capital interest, his share of unrealized receivables and fees, his share of the potential gain or loss on the inventory, or mutual insurance among the partners. If nothing is stated, payments (except to the extent they're for unrealized receivables) are treated as payment for his interest in the firm (§736(b)), giving him capital gain and no deduction to the partnership. Such payments do not include amounts paid for goodwill unless specifically provided in the agreement.

☐ (14) For taxable years beginning after 1969, partners are entitled to moving expense deductions. However, because moves of partners or other self-employed persons are more likely to be voluntary than in the case of employees, the period of time the partner is required to work at the new location is 78 weeks instead of the 39 weeks applicable to regular employees.

☐ (15) A partner's sick pay is taxable; the limited exemption provided for employees by §105 doesn't apply (*Rev. Rul. 56-326,* 1956-2 CB 100).

[¶402] CHECKLIST FOR DRAFTING PARTNERSHIP AGREEMENT

Here is a list of items you'll want to cover in your partnership agreements:

☐ (1) Specify how partnership capital gains, foreign tax credit, and charitable contributions are to be divided among partners. If the agreement is silent, these items will be taxed to each partner in accordance with his share of ordinary income.

☐ (2) Specify the allocation of ordinary income and losses.

☐ (3) Spell out guaranteed salary and interest payments.

☐ (4) Specify in the agreement how depletion should be distributed.

☐ (5) Provide for the retirement of partners. Have the agreement state whether there is goodwill and its value. Payments for goodwill are capital gains to the retiring partner and nondeductible by the firm.

☐ (6) Specify how insurance will be used for retirement programs.

☐ (7) Provide a specific method for liquidation and payment of a retiring partner's interest.

☐ (8) Provide a method of valuation to be used in a sale of property by a partner to the partnership.

□ (9) Provide for payments to a partner's wife or estate in case of death of a partner. Such payments are deductible if not for goodwill.
□ (10) Specify how all accounting matters shall be handled.
□ (11) Provide for the assumption of tax liabilities in the case of a transfer of a 50% or more partnership interest.
□ (12) Specify how capital contributions of property other than cash are to be treated.
□ (13) If the agreement is silent, depreciation will be allocated as though the firm purchased the property. However, a special allocation of depreciation in a partnership agreement will be voided by IRS if its principal purpose is the avoidance of tax (*Orrisch,* 55 TC 395, 1971).
□ (14) No gain or loss results to a partnership on the distribution of assets to a partner—but the tax law permits the partnership to elect to increase the basis of its remaining assets by the difference between the basis of the assets distributed and the basis in the hands of the distributee partner.
□ (15) Transfer of a partnership interest will not affect the basis of partnership assets, unless the agreement provides that the partnership may elect to adjust the basis of partnership assets to reflect the difference between the transferee's basis for his partnership interest and the proportionate share of the adjusted basis of all partnership property.
□ (16) Business plans can be formulated so that receivables are collected and inventory absorbed in the year before the retirement of a partner, so that the retiring partner will not have an unnecessary tax burden in one year. Advance notice of retirement will help in planning for this.
□ (17) Provide for condemnation of partnership property. To avoid recognition of the gain, the partnership itself rather than the individual partners must make the election under §1033 (*Mihran Dermirjian,* 54 TC No. 168, 1970).

[¶403] TAXATION OF CAPITAL CONTRIBUTIONS

When a partner contributes property to a partnership in exchange for a partnership interest, there is no gain or loss recognized to the partner or the partnership (§721). This rule applies whether the contribution is made on the formation of a partnership, to an incoming partner for a new interest, or to an existing partner for an increased interest (Reg. §1.721-1). It also applies to cash or noncash contributions (including installment obligations) (Reg. §1.721-1).

Recognition for tax purposes is postponed until the contributed property is disposed of. This may occur by the partner selling his interest, by the partnership selling the property, or by the partner selling after it has been distributed to him.

An increase in a partner's share of partnership liabilities or his assumption of partnership liabilities is treated as a contribution of money (§752(a)) and increases his basis for his partnership interest (Reg. §1.752-1(a)(1)). So, where partnership AB borrows $1,000 and A and B are equal partners, the basis of the partnership interest of each is increased $500. This is also true where one partner increases his individual liabilities because of assumption by him of partnership liabilities, since this is considered a contribution by him to the firm.

Any decrease in a partner's share of liabilities or any decrease in his individual liabilities due to the assumption of these liabilities by the firm is considered a distribution of money to the partner by the partnership (§752(b)). So, for example, where A contributes property with a basis of $1,000 to firm ABC for a one-third partnership interest, and the property is subject to a $150 mortgage, A's basis is $900: $1,000 less $100 (two-thirds of A's original $150 liability now attributed to partners B and C). See Reg. §1.752-1(b)(2). If the amount of decrease for this reason exceeds his basis, there is a capital gains tax (Reg. §1.752-1(c)).

For example, suppose a building was distributed to one partner subject to a $5,000 mortgage; the other partners received assets equal in value to the value of the building but without any offsetting liability. Let's assume there are four partners.

This would be treated as a contribution of $3,750 by the partner who received the building. Before the distribution, his share of the $5,000 liability was one-fourth, or $1,250. Assumption of the entire $5,000 adds $3,750 to his liability. The mechanics would be a reduction of the basis of all partnership interests to the extent of the distributions and then an increase in the basis of the assuming partner's interest by the portion of the liability for which the other partners are no longer liable. See Reg. §1.752-1(a)(2).

Transactions of the above type have to be distinguished from those in which a partner deals with the partnership not as a partner (§707) but as a distinct taxable entity. The distinction between these two types of transactions depends on the substance of the transaction—not the form—and this is gleaned from the facts. See Reg. §1.721-1(a).

[¶403.1] Partnership Interest as Compensation

Normally, a partner is entitled to be repaid his contributions of money or property to the partnership (at the partnership value). However, when a partner gives up his right to be repaid his contributions (but not a share of partnership profits) in favor of another partner as compensation for services (or in satisfaction of an obligation), §721 doesn't apply. The value of an interest in such partnership capital transferred as compensation for services is income to the partner under §61. The amount of income is the fair market value of the capital interest, either at the time the transfer is made for past services or at the time the services have been rendered where the transfer is based upon future services (Reg. §1.721-(b)(1)).

[¶403.2] How to Use Liabilities to Postpone or Avoid Tax

Property contributed to the partnership subject to a liability (e.g., a mortgage) is treated as the assumption of the liability by the firm with the result that the basis of the noncontributing partners is increased for their respective shares. Similarly, the basis of the partner giving the property is decreased by these amounts (§752(b)). Cash may therefore be withdrawn from the firm up to the amount of basis without any immediate tax consequences.

Example: A and B form a partnership. A contributes $5,000 cash and property that cost him $2,000 but is now worth $5,000. B contributes a building worth $20,000 on which there is a $10,000 mortgage. It originally cost B $4,000. As a 50% partner, A is treated as having contributed 50% of the mortgage on B's property, or $5,000. A's basis is therefore $12,000 ($7,000 + $5,000). Assume A and B each draw $11,000 more than the firm earns in the first year. A would have no taxable income due to these drawings because his basis ($12,000) is greater than his drawings. B, on the other hand, would have to report a taxable distribution of $12,000 ($1,000 on the assumption by the firm of $5,000 mortgage and $11,000 in cash distributed to him, since it exceeds his basis, which is reduced, too).

[¶403.3] Adjustments Between Contributing Partners

Sometimes adjustments are made between the contributing partners at the time the firm is organized. A gain on the adjustment will be taxed, but a loss cannot be taken.

Suppose Smith and Jones organize a partnership. Smith contributes property valued at $150,000, for which his basis is $50,000. Jones contributes $75,000 cash. Their interests are to be equal; and in order to start them off on the same footing, it is agreed that Smith is to have Jones's $75,000. Carrying out the plan, the firm distributes the $75,000 to Smith. The result is a gain of $25,000 for Smith (excess of $75,000 over $50,000 basis of contributed property). See §731(a)(1).

However, suppose that instead of receiving cash of $75,000, Smith received cash of $50,000 and other property (not unrealized receivables or inventory) with a market value of $25,000. Smith would seem to have no taxable gain (Reg. §1.731-1(a)(1)). But such a transaction might be treated as a sale or exchange between the partners or between the contributing partner and the firm. In that case, §731 wouldn't apply and the result would be taxable (Reg. §1.731-1(c)(3)).

If the contributed property was a capital asset, Smith's gain will be taxed as capital gain. If the contributed property was noncapital, §751 (see later discussion) may apply, with the gain being taxed as ordinary income (Reg. §1.731-1(a)(3) and (c)(1)).

Suppose Smith's basis for the contributed property was $300,000 instead of only $50,000. In that case, the result of receiving the $75,000 cash would be a loss. He couldn't take the loss. His basis would be reduced to $225,000. See Reg. §1.731-1(a)(2).

Smith could realize a tax loss by selling a half interest in the property to Jones instead of receiving Jones's cash in the roundabout way we have described through a distribution from the partnership. The loss would be $75,000 (excess of half of $300,000 basis over $75,000 cash received from Jones). The two would then contribute their half interests in the property to the firm. The firm's basis for the property would be $225,000 (Smith's half of $300,000 plus the $75,000 Jones paid for his half).

[¶403.4] Basis of Contributed Assets

If the contributions are in cash, there is no problem. The bases of the partners' interests are the amounts they paid in. If the contributions are in property, each partner's interest takes the basis of the property contributed by him (Reg. §1.722-1). The partnership takes the partner's basis (Reg. §1.723-1).

Where the tax basis of contributed property differs from the value at which it is contributed, the deductible depreciation allowed for tax purposes won't accurately reflect the economic depreciation sustained by the firm. For example, if depreciable property with a tax basis of $27,000 and a ten-year estimated life is contributed at its current value of $42,000, the yearly tax deduction will be only $2,700; but the annual economic loss will be $4,200.

If the value was less than cost at the time of contribution, the partnership's depreciation deduction would exceed its economic loss. If, in the above example, the basis was $50,000 instead of $27,000, the annual deduction would be $5,000 as against an economic loss of only $4,200.

To carry this one step further, suppose the partnership sold the property after one year for

$30,000. Reverting to our original basis of $27,000, there would have been a taxable gain of $5,700 ($30,000 less $27,000 basis reduced by one year's depreciation of $2,700). Yet, this tax would be paid on what was actually an economic loss of $7,800 (only $30,000 received for $37,800 economic value remaining after reducing $42,000 value at time of contribution by $4,200 economic depreciation for one year).

[¶403.5] Transfer of Property to a Partnership Converts It to Business Use

Normally, when a partner transfers property to his partnership, the partnership picks up the partner's basis for the contributed property as its basis. However, suppose the partner never used that property as business property—e.g., a car used for personal purposes only. Its basis to the partner is its original cost (he never was permitted to deduct any depreciation) even though its market value is a lot less. Can the partnership pick up this original cost as its own basis for the car that's now to be a business asset in the partnership? The answer is *no*. The partnership gets as its basis the market value of the car at the time it was transferred to it (*Au*, 330 F.2d 1008, CA-9, 1964).

When an individual converts property from personal to business use, his basis for the property as business property is the original basis or the market value at the time of the conversion, whichever is lower. In addition, says the Court, when an individual contributes property that he previously held for nonbusiness use to a partnership, he is at that moment converting it to business use. So, the basis that carries over to the partnership is the basis for the business use that arises at the moment of conversion.

[¶403.6] Method of Handling Partners' Accounts

Unless the partnership agreement so provides, a partner's distributive share of gain, loss, and depreciation with respect to contributed property is allocated as if the property had been bought by the firm (Reg. §1.704-1(c)(1)). This means that gain or loss and depreciation on that property will be based on its basis to the firm—not the fair market value. However, if the firm so elects (see §704(c)(2)), there are other ways in which the above-described discrepancies can be handled in the partners' accounts.

One possible alternate method gives effect to economic depreciation and gain or loss realized by the firm. Another is a combination of this with the regular method. In the first of the alternate methods, the firm's economic depreciation and gain or loss are allocated among the partners in accordance with their respective interests. The result is to take into account an amount that is more or less than is recognized for tax purposes. To reconcile the two, the difference is added to or subtracted from the contributing partner's income. In the second alternate method, tax depreciation is allocated to the partners other than the contributor up to the amount of their shares of economic depreciation, and excess is assigned to the contributor. Tax gain or loss on sale is allocated the same way. If the property was depreciable, gain or loss is increased or decreased by any economic depreciation not allowed as a tax deduction.

To help you decide which method to use, we have prepared a comparison of three methods as they apply to: (1) depreciation, (2) sale of nondepreciable property contributed at a value different than basis, (3) sale of depreciable property contributed at a value different than basis.

[¶403.7] Comparison of Methods of Depreciation

Assume that personal property contributed to the firm by Smith has a fair market value of $42,000, but its basis for tax depreciation is Smith's basis of $27,000. Here is a comparison of the three methods of handling the depreciation. Smith, Jones, and Brown are equal partners. Minus sign denotes a deduction and plus sign denotes income.

Partner	*Regular Method*	*1st Alternative*	*2nd Alternative*
Smith	– $900	+ $ 100	0
Jones	– $900	– $1,400	– $1,350
Brown	– $900	– $1,400	– $1,350

In the regular method, the tax deduction is divided equally among the three.

In the first alternate method, the economic depreciation of $4,200 is first divided among the partners. The difference of $1,500 between economic and tax depreciation has been added to the account of Smith, the contributing partner. Strictly, this would mean a deduction of $1,400 each for Jones and Brown and income of $100 for Smith for a net of $2,700. However, the Regs specifically limit depreciation deductions to the tax depreciation "ceiling" (§1.704-1(c)(2)). The $2,800 total for Jones and Brown would therefore seem to be limited to $2,700 or $1,350 each, and Smith's $100 would accordingly be washed out.

If the economic and tax depreciation were reversed—tax depreciation of $4,200 and economic depreciation of only $2,700—the extra $1,500 would be subtracted from Smith's account instead of added to it. The result would be a tax deduction of $900 each for Jones and Brown and $2,400 for Smith.

In the second alternate method, since the tax depreciation doesn't exceed the economic depreciation Jones and Brown suffered, it is all allocated to them. This leaves nothing for Smith.

If the basis for depreciation had been $36,000 instead of $27,000, so that annual tax depreciation was $3,600, the excess over the economic depreciation suffered by Jones and Brown would go to Smith. The deduction then would be $1,400 each for Jones and Brown and $800 for Smith.

[¶403.8] Sale of Nondepreciable Property

We will assume that Jones's contribution included securities with a tax basis of $100,000 and a market value of $40,000 at the time of contribution. The firm subsequently sells them for $70,000.

Here is the result for the three methods given above:

Partner	*Regular Method*	*1st Alternative*	*2nd Alternative*
Smith	– $10,000	+ $10,000	0
Jones	– $10,000	– $50,000	– $30,000
Brown	– $10,000	+ $10,000	0

The regular method divides the tax loss equally among the three partners.

The first alternative divides the firm's $30,000 economic gain equally among the three partners. However, the fact of the $30,000 tax loss leaves a $60,000 gap between the tax and economic figures. Jones, the contributing partner, gets the benefit of this. Reconciliation of the two figures leaves him with a $50,000 loss.

If the amounts for basis and value at the time of contribution were reversed, basis being $40,000 and value $100,000, the firm would have a $30,000 economic loss on the sale for $70,000 instead of an economic gain. The economic loss would be divided equally among the three partners, leaving Smith and Brown each with a $10,000 loss. However, the addition to Jones's account of the $60,000 difference between the economic and tax figures created by the $30,000 tax gain would leave Jones with a $50,000 gain.

The second alternative assigns the entire tax loss of $30,000 to Jones. This loss would first be assignable to Smith and Brown to the extent of their economic loss. Since they have economic gain rather than a loss, the whole thing goes to Jones. See Reg. §1.704-1(c)(2).

If the basis and value at which contributed were reversed, there would be a tax gain of $30,000, and Smith and Brown would have an economic loss instead of a gain. Without an economic gain, no part of the tax gain would be allocable to them. Jones would bear the burden of the entire tax gain.

[¶403.9] Sale of Depreciable Personal Property

The firm sold depreciable property contributed by Brown for $45,000. Basis and contributed value were $18,000 and $36,000, respectively. The property had a six-year estimated life, and the sale was made one year after contribution. Depreciated basis and economic value at the time of sale are $15,000 and $30,000, respectively.

Here is the allocation for the three methods.

Partner	*Regular Method*	*1st Alternative*	*2nd Alternative*
Smith	+ $10,000	+ $ 5,000	+ $ 4,000
Jones	+ $10,000	+ $ 5,000	+ $ 4,000
Brown	+ $10,000	+ $20,000	+ $22,000

The regular method divides the tax gain equally among the partners.

The first alternative divides the economic gain equally among the partners and assigns the difference between this and the tax gain to Brown, the contributing partner.

If the basis and contributed value were reversed, division of the economic gain would mean $10,000, instead of $5,000, for each partner. The tax gain, $15,000 less than the economic gain, would be allocated to Brown. That means $10,000 gain each for Smith and Jones and $5,000 loss for Brown.

The second alternative allocates the tax gain to Smith and Jones to the extent of their shares of the economic gain. This is $4,000 apiece (one-third of $15,000 economic gain), reduced by excess of $6,000 economic depreciation over $3,000 of tax depreciation allowed as a deduction. The remaining tax gain has been assigned to Brown.

If basis and contributed value were reversed, the tax gain of $15,000 would be allocated to Smith and Jones to the extent of their shares of the economic gain. Since deductible tax depreciation would exceed economic depreciation, there would be no occasion for an adjustment. See Reg. §1.704-1(c)(2).

[¶403.10] Methods Apply Also to Existing Firms

The problem of allocating depreciation and gain or loss on contributed assets among the partners will arise most often upon organization of a new firm. However, the same three methods apply when the contribution is made by a new partner or a continuing partner after the firm is already in existence.

[¶403.11] Tax Savings

When a partner's tax basis is more than the value at which the asset is to be contributed, he can get a tax advantage by selling the assets and giving the cash to the firm. The advantage is the deduction of his loss. On the other hand, if the basis is less than the value for contribution, it would be better to contribute the asset itself. This would save him tax on the gain he would realize by selling the asset and contributing cash.

It is true this would merely defer the tax for payment by the partnership on future disposal; but even this has its advantages for the partnership. Unless the selling partner was expected to pay the tax out of his own pocket rather than out of the proceeds, the firm would have the equivalent of the tax money to use as long as it chose to retain the asset.

By a wise choice of method, we can sometimes shift losses from a low-bracket taxpayer to a high-bracket taxpayer, to whom they will be more useful.

Assume a low-bracket taxpayer contributes property with a basis of $50,000 and current value of only $20,000 while the other man puts in $20,000 cash. The firm sells the property, taking a $30,000 loss, and invests the $20,000 proceeds plus the $20,000 cash in other property with which to operate the partnership.

If nothing is said in the partnership agreement about the allocation of losses, etc., the regular method will apply. As we have seen, this would divide the $30,000 loss between the two partners, which amounts to an assignment of $15,000 of tax loss from a low tax bracket to a high bracket.

[¶403.12] Undivided Interests in Contributed Property

In the absence of any agreement, when two or more people contribute their undivided interests in the same property to a partnership, the bases of all of them are merged, and the total is allocated to the partners in proportion to their interests. Depreciation and gain or loss will be calculated as if the undivided interests had not been contributed but were owned individually by each partner (§704(c)(3); Reg. §1.704-1(c)(3)).

[¶404] OPERATING THE PARTNERSHIP

One of the important basic points in the area of partnership taxation is that the partnership as such is not a taxable entity. It is merely a form of doing business by two or more persons who are liable for any tax in their individual capacities (§701). The tax return filed by a partnership (Form

1065) is really an information return that has as its objective the allocation of the partnership's items of taxable income and deductions. Then, each partner picks up his share of the partnership's income or loss and other separate items (from Schedule K, Form 1065) and reports them as part of his own income or loss on his Form 1040 (see Reg. §1.701-1).

Since partners take the income from the partnership as individuals, they are subject to the special rules concerning earned income and tax-preference income.

The maximum tax on earned income is 50%. This compares with the 70% maximum rate applicable to other types of income. Earned income generally includes wages, salaries, professional fees or compensation for personal services, and, in the case of a taxpayer engaged in a trade or business where both personal services and capital are a material income-producing factor, a reasonable amount but not more than 30% of his share of the net profits of the business.

[¶404.1] What Items Must Be Separately Stated

The partnership return must state separately the firm's long- and short-term capital gains and losses, §1231 gains and losses, §1245 income, §1250 income, dividends from domestic corporations qualifying for the dividend exclusion, partially tax-exempt interests, contributions, foreign tax credit, etc.

The partnership is not allowed personal items such as the personal exemption, the standard deduction, the net operating loss deduction, etc. These items will be factors in the individual computations of the partners. However, the partnership must itemize charitable contributions and taxes paid to foreign countries or possessions of the U.S., although it can't deduct these items. It can be required to itemize other items, too.

Except for the election with respect to foreign tax credit, all elections affecting the computation of partnership income are made by the firm (see §703(b)). These include election to use installment sale reporting, election to reinvest condemnation award to avoid tax on gain, 20% first-year depreciation write-off, election to treat timber cutting as capital gains, treatment of intangible drilling cost, and amortization of bond premiums. The partnership's election doesn't affect an election by an individual partner with respect to his own separate property. Let's say, for example, that the partnership elects to take a 20% first-year write-off on its oil properties. This wouldn't prevent the partners from taking the 20% write -off for their individual holdings.

However, if the partnership fails to elect, a partner cannot do it. Nonelection by the firm can't be compensated for by election by the individual partners, individually or otherwise (see *Beilke*, TC Memo 1963-5; *Cornish*, 348 F. 2d 175, CA-9, 1965).

[¶404.2] Partnership's Losses

The Code limits the partner's deduction of his distributive share of the partnership's losses. He can deduct only to the extent of his adjusted basis for his partnership interest at the end of the partnership year in which the loss occurred. Any excess over his basis becomes deductible at the end of the partnership year or years in which repayment to the partnership is made (§704).

Here's an example: A partner's basis is $2,500; his distributive share of the firm's 1976 loss is $3,500. In 1978, he contributes $1,500. Deductible loss in 1976 is $2,500; basis becomes zero. Remaining $1,000 of loss allowed in 1978 against $1,500 contribution. The $500 excess of contribution becomes the new basis.

If the partner wanted to deduct his full share of the loss in the year sustained, he would have to contribute $1,000 before the close of that year. This would raise his basis to $3,500, enough to cover his share of the loss. Or he could make the contribution in a later year, if he wished, and take the deduction in that year.

[¶404.3] Taxable Year of Partner and Partnership

A partner must include his distributive share of the firm's income or loss in his individual return for the year ending with or after the partnership year during which the firm realized the income or loss (§706(a)).

A partnership must adopt the same taxable year as that of all of its principal partners; it cannot change the year except by establishing a satisfactory business reason for the change (§706(b)(1)). However, a newly formed partnership can adopt a calendar year without prior approval if all of the principal partners are not in the same taxable year (Reg. §1.706-1(b)). The principal partners are those having a 5%-or-more interest in the partnership's profits or capital (§706(b)(3)). A partnership can use a tax year other than that used by its partners if it can show a good business reason and it gets IRS consent. Using a natural business year (i.e., a year that ends with or shortly after the end of the peak period of business) is a good business reason (Reg. §1.706-1(b)).

[¶404.4] Tax Savings Through Partnership Retirement Plans

Traditionally, one big disadvantage of the partnership as opposed to the corporation was the limitation on deductible yearly retirement plan contributions to the lesser of 10% of the employee compensation or $2,500. A corporation can contribute (and deduct) much more to fund a qualified pension or profit-sharing plan (see Section VIII). However, the Pension Reform Act of 1974 greatly increased the maximum deductible contribution that a partnership can make to the so-called retirement Keogh, or HR-10 Plan. The maximum contribution is now the lesser of 15% of compensation or $7,500. While the qualified corporate plan can still provide greater potential benefits for its employees than a partnership's Keogh Plan, the new law makes the Keogh Plan a much more useful tax-sheltered method of deferring a self-employed partner's income.

A Keogh Plan gives the self-employed a chance to boost retirement income without cost and, in some cases, to buy retirement income for his wife and other close relatives with 100%-deductible tax dollars. It can also bring him greater earnings through the greater incentive and improved performance of covered employees.

Here is a checklist of some of the basic advantages and disadvantages of a Keogh Plan:

Advantages:

☐ (1) As we have mentioned, the self-employed can contribute up to $7,500 or 15% of his earned income (whichever is less) each year on his own.

☐ (2) The Pension Reform Act of 1974 provides an alternative to the $7,500/15% contributions limitation. After 1975, the employer may elect to participate in a defined-benefit plan that would provide a straight-life annuity to be purchased at age 65 or five years from the beginning of plan participation, whichever is later. The total fixed benefit would be computed by multiplying the owner-employee's salary (up to $50,000) by a percentage based on the employee's age at participation:

Age at participation	*Percentage*
30 or less	6.5
35	5.4
40	4.4
45	3.6
50	3.0
55	2.5
60 or over	2.0

This provides the amount of yearly annuity income to which the employee will be entitled when he retires. The deductible contribution is the cost of an annuity contract that will provide this fixed benefit. The maximum allowable benefit under this type of plan may not exceed the lesser of $75,000 or 100% of the employee's compensation for his three consecutive highest-paid years.

☐ (3) The self-employed receives an income tax deduction for the full amount he contributes on his own behalf and for the full sum he contributes on behalf of his employees. Thus, for example, if an individual contributes the maximum of $7,500 on his own behalf, he will be allowed the full $7,500 as a deduction. Assuming his is in the 50% tax bracket, he would cut his tax bill by $3,750 each time he contributes that sum. It works the same way with contributions for employees.

☐ (4) If he has any full-time employees, he may include them in the plan and provide retirement benefits for them also. Where the employees have worked for the self-employed for three years or more, he must include them. And he must pay on behalf of his employees the same percentage of their earnings as he does for himself.

☐ (5) A wife who works for her husband may be considered an employee provided she is controlled and directed by the self-employed in the work she performs and that she puts in the required time to be covered by the husband's Keogh Plan—i.e., 20 hours a week.

☐ (6) All realized earnings within the plan are permitted to accumulate tax free. This tax protection permits a tax-free compounding of income increments during the period of their accumulation.

☐ (7) A self-employed individual may also contribute on a voluntary basis an additional 10% of his earned income up to $2,500 maximum where he has one or more nonpartner employees and he extends to them this same benefit on the same voluntary basis. Although neither the self-employed nor the employees are entitled to deductions for these contributions, they still stand to get an important tax benefit by contributing. These funds can be invested and reinvested tax free by the fund, and the accumulation of these tax-free earnings and the contributions themselves help build a substantial retirement fund.

☐ (8) The money in the Keogh Plan can be put into all kinds of investments such as stocks, bonds (including special United States bonds), mutual fund shares, real estate, mortgages, etc. The money in the plan can also go to purchase annuities, endowments, and other retirement income-type contracts.

☐ (9) A self-employed person allocates his lump-sum distribution between capital gain and ordinary income (subject, however, to ten-year averaging) on the basis of service before 1974 and after 1973. The calculation of what part constitutes ordinary income and what part represents capital gain is the same for Keogh plans as it is for pension and profit-sharing plans. This is fully discussed at Section VIII.

Disadvantages

☐ (1) If there is an owner-employee in the plan, then all full-time employees with at least three years' service must be covered by the plan. The employees' rights to contributions made on their behalf must be vested as soon as the contribution is made. Furthermore, there must be no discrimination in the contribution formulas used to determine how much will be contributed for owner-employees and regular employees.

☐ (2) In the case of partnerships, only the firm can set up a Keogh Plan; the individual partners cannot set up plans for themselves alone (Regs. §1.40.-10(e)(1)).

☐ (3) Once money is committed to the plan, it may not be withdrawn prior to age 59½ without severe penalties. So, in effect, the funds are irrevocably committed to the plan once a contribution is made.

[¶405] SELLING A PARTNERSHIP INTEREST

The sale or exchange of a partnership interest results in capital gain except to the extent of unrealized receivables, substantially appreciated inventory items (§741), and depreciation recapture (§1235, §1250).

[¶405.1] Computation of Sale of Interest

Here's how the gain on the sale is computed. Although our example shows ordinary income and capital gain, it is possible that ordinary income and capital loss may arise from this type of action.

Assets	*Adjusted Basis*	*Market Value*	*Capital Accounts*	*Adjusted Basis*	*Market Value*
Cash	$ 6,000	$ 6,000	Smith	$24,000	$ 42,000
Unrealized receivables	. . . .	15,000	Jones	24,000	42,000
			Brown	24,000	42,000
Inventories .	33,000	42,000			
Land & Buildings .	33,000	63,000			
Total	$72,000	$126,000	Total	$72,000	$126,000

Assume Jones sells his interests to Smith for its market value of $42,000. The purchase price will be proportionately allocated to Jones's share of the various assets, as follows:

Cash	$ 2,000
Unrealized Receivables	5,000
Inventories	14,000
Land & Buildings	21,000
Total	$42,000

This gives Jones $8,000 of ordinary income on the receivables and inventory items (which show substantial appreciation) and $10,000 capital gain on capital items.

The $8,000 ordinary income consists of his $5,000 share of the receivables plus the $3,000 gain on inventory ($14,000 received minus $11,000 share of basis). The $10,000 capital gain is arrived at this way: Reduce basis of his interest, $24,000, by his $11,000 inventory basis. Balance of basis is $13,000, which is allocable to capital items; receipts from capital items are $23,000 (cash and land and building); capital gain is excess of $23,000 over $13,000 basis.

If the basis was much higher—say, $15,000 higher—Jones would have a capital loss instead of a capital gain to go with his ordinary income.

[¶405.2] Unrealized Receivables and Substantially Appreciated Inventory

Code §751 (Reg. §1.751-1) taxes the partner at ordinary income rates on amounts received for his share of unrealized receivables and substantially appreciated inventory items. Amounts received with respect to other partnership assets are taxed only at the lesser capital gain rate.

"Unrealized receivables" are defined as: (1) Any rights to payment for goods to the extent amounts received would not be treated as payment for a capital asset, or (2) any right to receive payment for services rendered or to be rendered. In other words, if the payment would be ordinary income to the partnership, the right is an unrealized receivable. If the payments have already been taxed to the partnership, the rule doesn't apply. Unrealized receivables also include the potential ordinary income in depreciable property to which §1245 and 1250 apply (§751(c)).

"Substantially appreciated inventories" covers more than is usually embraced in the term "inventory." For this purpose, inventory includes, in addition to stock-in-trade and other property held primarily for sale to customers in the ordinary course of trade or business, any other property belonging to the partnership that would not be considered a capital asset or real property or depreciable property used in a trade or business. A partnership asset will be considered inventory if its use either by the partnership or by the selling or distributee partner conforms to this definition.

[¶405.3] Inventory Appreciation Not Substantial

Where the inventory of a partnership has appreciated in value but not enough to constitute a "substantial" appreciation, the selling partner will make out better if he sells his interest than he will if the partnership sells its assets and distributes the proceeds or if the assets are sold after a distribution.

Here's an example:

Assets	*Adjusted Basis*	*Market Value*	*Capital Accounts*	*Adjusted Basis*	*Market Value*
Inventory . . .	$ 6,000	$ 9,000	Smith	$22,000	$ 34,000
Land &			Jones	22,000	34,000
Building .	$58,000	91,000	Brown	22,000	34,000
Cash	2,000	2,000			
Total	$66,000	$102,000	Total	$66,000	$102,000

The inventories, with a market value less than 10% of the value of all assets excluding cash, are not "substantially" appreciated. Therefore, the profit on sale of partnership interest will be all capital gain. The gain for each partner in our example would be $12,000 (excess of $34,000 market value at which the sale would be made over $22,000 basis).

If the partnership instead sells all its assets and distributes the proceeds, the $12,000 profit for each partner will be $1,000 ordinary income on the proceeds of inventories and $11,000 capital gain on the sale of land and buildings. The partners would get the same result on a distribution of assets to them first, followed by sales by themselves as individuals.

[¶405.4] How to Get an Ordinary Loss on Partner's Share of Depreciated Inventory

Although the selling partner gets ordinary income for his pro rata share of the substantially appreciated inventory items, he can only get capital loss for his share of substantially depreciated inventory items.

Consequently, it's better to take an in-kind distribution of your share of the depreciated inventory items. Then, on a subsequent sale of these items within a five-year period from the date of their distribution, you get an ordinary loss.

Example: A's basis for his share of the inventory is $8,000. He takes a distribution in kind for his share. When he later (within five years) sells the inventory for $1,000, he gets an ordinary loss of $7,000 (§735).

[¶405.5] Buyer's Basis on Sale of a Partner's Interest

The purchaser's basis for an interest in a partnership generally is his cost (§742). If the partnership assets have appreciated in value, serious problems arise. Thus, if the partnership subsequently sells some of its assets at their appreciated value, the buyer will be taxed for a gain that he never actually realized. Similarly, even though the appreciated assets remain unsold, the buyer will be unable to take the benefit of depreciation on these assets to the full extent of the consideration that he paid.

The Code does provide some relief for the buyer by permitting a write-up of the basis of the appreciated property by the partnership at the time the buyer purchases his interest—but only in respect of the buyer. Section 743 provides for such an adjustment but only if the partnership has filed an election under §754.

[¶405.6] Closing of Partnership Year

Where one of the partners sells his entire interest in the partnership, the taxable year of the partnership closes with respect to him (§706(c)(2)(A)(i)). If the sale results in the partnership being "terminated" within the meaning of §708(b)(i)(B), then the taxable year of the partnership will also close with respect to the other partners (§706(c)(i)). Thus, whenever there is a sale of 50% or more of the partnership interests within a 12-month period, the partnership year will not only close with respect to the selling partner, but also with respect to the others.

[¶405.7] Agreement Should Specify Payment for Goodwill

It is important to have your partnership agreement specify that amounts you receive in payment for your partnership interest constitute goodwill. Otherwise, the amounts you receive over the book value of your interest may come to you as distributive share or guaranteed payments under §736(a) and be taxed at ordinary income rates. In one case, a taxpayer claimed such payments were for his interest in the partnership under §736(b)(1) and therefore eligible for capital gains. However, the Court interpreted §736(b)(2)(B) as requiring that the partnership agreement specify a payment in liquidation of a partner's interest as being for goodwill in order to come under §736(b)(1). Since the agreement did not spell this out, the taxpayer lost. It may be possible to correct this situation with a modification of the partnership agreement.

[¶406] CHECKLIST OF FACTORS TO CONSIDER IN FORMING A LIMITED PARTNERSHIP

In many cases a limited partnership may prove to be a more beneficial form of doing business than a general partnership. The limited partnership gives you the tax advantages of the general partnership without many of the burdens. The two best-known advantages are that the limited partners will not be personally subject to the liabilities of the firm and the general partners, who presumably have more experience in carrying out the partnership's business activities, have complete management control. Here is a list of other factors that you should consider in deciding whether to form a limited partnership.

☐ Wives or children can be limited partners. Each limited partner can be entitled to a fixed percentage of the profits and losses from the operation of the business, or the liability of each limited partner can be expressed not to exceed the value of his capital contribution.

☐ On liquidation, the distributive share of the partners can be in proportion to their partnership interests.

☐ General partners can be given limited authority to determine whether there is a need for additional working capital to be used for improvements, alterations, or additions to the plant or to be withheld for expansion or development.

☐ With the death of a limited partner, his executor or representatives may have all his rights just as if he had survived. This may go on until the termination of the partnership, but the continuation of the partnership after the death of a limited partner should be contingent upon the consent of the general partners.

☐ The agreement should provide either that the partnership terminate upon a general partner's death, bankruptcy, insanity, or inter vivos transfer of his general interest or that the partnership continue in such event only if all the partners agree to a continuation.

☐ There need be no effect on the life of the partnership if a limited partner goes bankrupt or becomes insane.

☐ The agreement may fix the duration of the partnership. At the end of the agreed term, there must be either dissolution or an agreement to go on.

☐ The agreement may state the sole purpose of the partnership (to produce a certain theatrical production, for example).

☐ The plan for financing may provide the right to increase or decrease participations up to the time all contributions originally contemplated have been paid. After that, new limited partners may only get profits from portions of the profit originally allocated to the general partners.

It is usual in a limited partnership that the limited partner does not engage in the management of the business. If he does, he might be subject to liability as a general partner.

[¶406.1] Dangers of the Limited Family Partnership

The limited partnership readily lends itself to the retention of important controls by the general partner; in that case the limited partners may be made more nominal than real. To get IRS approval:

☐ Avoid making the interests of limited partners assignable.
☐ Avoid forcing investments by limited partners to be left in the business for a long term of years, subject only to the right of the limited partner to bring about dissolution of and an accounting for his interest by court decree on proof of wrongdoing or unfitness of the general partners or special circumstances.
☐ Avoid giving the general partners discretion as to distributions of income to limited partners.

IRS has warned that attempts to split family income by using a limited partnership will be scrutinized carefully (*Mim.* 6767, 1952).

When the limited partner buys in or gets an interest in return for services, the IRS attack may be centered on lack of intent to form a partnership; where a gift of an interest is given to a limited partner, IRS may claim that a completed gift was never made. Family partnerships are covered in detail in Section V.

[¶407] WHEN A PARTNERSHIP WILL BE TAXED AS A CORPORATION

When an unincorporated business assumes a sufficient number of corporate characteristics, it can be deemed an association, taxable as a corporation (Reg. §301.7701-2). On the other hand, the fewer corporate characteristics attributable to the unincorporated business, the more apt it is to be considered a partnership; and this can also include groups commonly not called partnerships, such as syndicates, groups, pools, joint ventures, or the like (Reg. §7701-3).

The Regs take the position that there are six corporate characteristics: (1) associates; (2) an objective to carry on a business and divide its profits; (3) continuity of life of the entity despite the death, insanity, bankruptcy, retirement, resignation, or expulsion of any member; (4) centralization of management; (5) limited liability; and (6) free transferability of interests (Reg. §301.7701-2(a)(1)).

Having associates and carrying on a business are ordinarily common to both partnerships and corporations. So, IRS will normally look to the remaining four characteristics (in addition to any other significant factors) to determine whether you have a partnership or an association. Thus, if you want to be treated as a partnership, you have to avoid the corporate characteristics; and if you want an association, you have to get those characteristics into your organization.

This is not, however, a black-or-white proposition. You don't have to have all the characteristics to be an association, and you need not avoid them all to be classified as a partnership. An organization will not be treated as an association unless it has more corporate than noncorporate characteristics. So, if there are no other significant factors aside from the four corporate characteristics (continuity, centralized management, limited liability, and free transferability of interest), the organization will be taxable as a partnership and not as a corporation unless it has more than two of these present (Reg. §301.7701-2(a)(3)).

SECTION V

FAMILY PARTNERSHIP FOR LOWER TAXES

The Federal income tax is a so-called progressive tax as it is applied to individuals. The higher the taxable income, the higher the rate at which that income will be taxed. The rate for the lowest taxable income bracket is 14%. From this low, the taxable income brackets rise progressively to the highest taxable income bracket of 70%. (See the Individual Income Tax Rate Tables on page 405 of the appendix.)

However, there is a 50% ceiling on the rate of tax that may be imposed on an individual's earned taxable income (IRC §1348(a)). Generally, earned income is defined as net income received for the fruits of one's labor, e.g., wages, salaries, professional fees, and other personal service compensation.

[¶501] HOW TO REDUCE TAXES BY BRINGING IN FAMILY MEMBERS AS PARTNERS

Subject to certain requirements that are discussed in this chapter, a family partnership can save income tax by dividing income among family members. This so-called "income-splitting" works as a tax saver because of the progressively arranged tax bracket rates.

Example (1): Mr. Able is married and has two children. He is the sole owner of an unincorporated business in which both personal services and capital are material income-producing factors. The net business profit for the taxable year of the business (which is the same as Mr. Able's taxable year) is $200,000.

For the sake of simplicity, let us assume that all of Mr. Able's business expenses are paid by the company and that the company is the source of all of Mr. Able's income. Let us also assume that Mr. Able files a joint return, his wife and children have no income of their own, and he elects the standard deduction.

As we have pointed out, Mr. Able gets one tax break, according to the Tax Reform Act of 1969 (§1348). He can pay himself a salary of up to 30% of the net business profits (assuming the salary is deemed "reasonable"), and such amount will be considered "earned income." So-called "earned income" (wages, salaries, and the like) is subject to a tax ceiling of 50%.

Result: If Mr. Able pays himself $60,000 as salary (that is, 30% of $200,000), his total income tax for the year will still be a whopping $107,335 because $140,000 of the net business profit ($200,000 less Mr. Able's $60,000 salary) will be taxed as unearned income at a rate of 69%. (In our computations, we have given Mr. Able a $3,000 deduction for four personal exemptions and the $2,000 maximum standard deduction.)

Example (2): Mr. Able can minimize his tax by "splitting" the income with his children. One of many possibilities is for Mr. Able to make a gift of 48% of his business directly to his two children (if they are both adults); that is, each child will receive a 24% interest. (Since income is effectively split between a husband and wife by the filing of a joint return, Mr. Able would gain nothing by making a gift of any interest in his business to his wife.) If his children are minors, Mr. Able could gift them interests in trust.

To facilitate these gifts, a family partnership agreement would be drafted to provide for Mr. Able's salary of $60,000 per year for running the business. The balance of the net business income would be distributed as follows: 24% to each child and 52% to Mr. Able.

Result: Mr. Able would receive his salary of $60,000. In addition, he would receive his share of the net profits of the business, which amounts to $72,800 (52% of $140,000). His tax, giving him the same personal exemptions and maximum standard deduction as in example (1), would be $62,407.

Each of his children would receive income from the family partnership in the amount of $33,600, upon which each of them would pay a tax of $10,715. (Note that each child could take a personal exemption of $750, but, since the Revenue Act of 1971, neither could take advantage of the standard deduction or low-income allowance.)

The aggregate tax that Mr. Able and his two children will have to pay is $88,837 (that is, $62,407 + $10,715 + $10,715). You will recall that Mr. Able's tax in example (1) came to $107,335. Thus, *in one year alone,* Mr. Able's family would save $23,498 through the use of a family partnership. Over a ten-year period, the tax saving would run close to $235,000.

Additional family partners can further reduce the total tax bill. If, in example (2), Able had three children-partners instead of two, his ten-year tax savings would increase to more than $265,000. With six children-partners, the ten-year tax savings would jump to over $315,000.

As you can see, the family partnership is a dollar-saving maneuver well worth exploring.

[¶502] HOW MUCH INCOME CAN YOU SHIFT?

The Code and Regulations require that a family partnership not only render services but be one in which capital is a material income-producing factor. Additionally, there are basic ownership tests that must be met to establish the reality of the transfer of a partnership interest. Here, we discuss this aspect of family partnerships. How to shift the income safely to avoid the possibility that IRS will reallocate it back to the donor of the partnership interest.

[¶502.1] Allocation to Reflect Reasonable Compensation of Donor

In Code §704(e)(2), it is provided that "the distributive share of the donee of a gift under the partnership agreement shall be includible in his gross income, except to the extent that such share is determined without allowance of reasonable compensation for services rendered to the partnership by the donor." It follows that the share of the donor partner in the partnership income includes an allowance for reasonable compensation for the services rendered by him to the partnership. Thus, if necessary, the income of the partnership may be shifted to properly reflect the services rendered by the donor (Reg. §1.704-1(e)(3)(b)).

In calculating a reasonable allowance for services rendered by the partners, consideration is given to all the facts and circumstances of the business, including the fact that some of the partners may have greater managerial responsibility than others. Another factor to be considered is the amount that would ordinarily be paid to obtain comparable services from a person not having an interest in the partnership (Reg. §1.704-1(e)(3)(c)).

Where a limited partnership is concerned, for purposes of allocation, due consideration shall be given to the fact that a general partner, unlike a limited partner, risks his credit in the partnership business (Reg. §1.704-1(e)(3)(ii)(c)).

[¶502.2] Allocation to Reflect Capital Interests

After resolving the problem of what constitutes a reasonable allowance for the services of the donor, the balance of the partnership's income must be allocated between the donor and recipients in accordance with their respective interests in partnership capital. If the correct allocations are not made, IRS can reallocate income among the capital interests (Reg. §1.704-1(e)(3)(i)(a)).

[¶502.3] Special Rules Relating to Indirect Gifts

The provisions affecting reallocations of income with regard to a family partnership are equally applicable where interest in the partnership is created by an indirectly made gift. Thus, where the partnership is created indirectly, a ''donor'' may be construed to include individuals other than the nominal transferor of the interest. The regulations set forth the following illustrations (Reg. §1.704-1(e)(3)(ii)).

Example (1): A father gives property to his son who shortly thereafter conveys the property to a partnership consisting of the father and the son, the partnership interest of the son may be considered created by gift and the father may be considered the donor of the son's partnership interest.

Example (2): A father, the owner of a business conducted as a sole proprietorship, transfers the business to a partnership consisting of his wife and himself. The wife subsequently conveys her interest to their son. In such case, the father, as well as the mother, may be considered as the donor of the son's partnership interest.

Example (3): A father makes a gift to his son of stock in the family corporation. The corporation is subsequently liquidated. The son later contributes the property received in the liquidation of the corporation to a partnership consisting of his father and himself. In such case, the son's partnership interest may be considered created by gift and the father may be considered the donor of his son's partnership interest.

If a purported purchase of a capital interest in a partnership from one family member to another is not considered bona fide, it will be treated as a gift, thereby subjecting the donor and donee to the possible application of the income allocation rules.

A purchase of a capital interest in a partnership, either directly or by means of a loan or credit extended by a member of the family, will be recognized as bona fide if:

(a) It can be shown that the purchase has the usual characteristics of an arm's-length transaction, including the terms of the purchase agreement (price, due date of payment, rate of interest, and security, if any) and the terms of any loan or credit arrangement collateral to the purchase agreement, the credit standing of the purchaser (apart from relationship to the seller), and the capacity of the purchaser to incur a legally binding obligation; or

(b) It can be shown, in the absence of characteristics of an arm's-length transaction, that the purchase was genuinely intended to promote the success of the business by securing participation of the purchaser in the business or by adding his credit to that of the other participants (Reg. §1.704-1(e)(4)).

[¶502.4] Family Partnership Transactions Subjected to Gift Tax

There may be a price extracted from the donor of family partnership interest in the form of a gift tax. Care should be taken in this regard because valuation of the gifted interest may be troublesome.

The Regulations discourage elaborate attempts to establish an artificial valuation, by providing: "For the purposes of Section 704, a capital interest in a partnership purchased by one member of the family from another shall be considered to be created by gift from the seller and the fair market value of the purchased interest shall be considered donated capital" (Reg. §1.704-1(e)(3)(i)(a)).

As a result of the foregoing, it is clear that IRS will treat a gift of cash by the donor to the donee, and the donee's subsequent contribution of that cash to the partnership, as nothing more than a gift by the donor to the donee of the partnership interest. The cash that changed hands will be disregarded for valuation purposes.

Of course, a gift of a partnership interest will reduce the potential estate tax liability of the donor. However, in assessing the income tax savings that may be accomplished by a family partnership, the potential gift tax liability should always be considered.

[¶503] HOW TO ESTABLISH A FAMILY PARTNERSHIP

The family partnership provisions, first added to the Code by the Revenue Act of 1951, are now embodied in IRS §704(3). The Report of the Senate Committee on Finance (Rep. No. 781, 82d Cong., 1st Session, 1951) stated that the purpose of the provisions is "to harmonize the rules governing interests in the so-called family partnership with those generally applicable to other forms of property or business. Two principles governing attribution of income have long been accepted as basic: (1) income from property is attributable to the owner of the property; (2) income from personal services is attributable to the person rendering the services. There is no reason for applying different principles to partnership income. If an individual makes a bona fide gift of real estate, or of a share of corporate stock, the rent or dividend income is taxable to the donee. Your committee's amendment makes it clear that, however the owner of a partnership interest may have acquired such interest, the income is taxable to the owner, if he is the real owner. If the ownership is real, it does not matter what motivated the transfer to him or whether the business benefited from the entrance of the new partner. . . .

"[This will permit IRS] . . . and the courts to inquire in any case whether the donee or purchaser actually owns the interest in the partnership which the transferor purports to have given or sold him. Cases will arise where the gift or sale is a mere sham. Other cases will arise where the transferor retains so many of the incidents of ownership that he will continue to be recognized as a substantial owner of the interest which he purports to have given away, as was held by the Supreme Court in an analogous trust situation involved in the case of *Helvering v. Clifford* (309 U.S. 331, 50 S.Ct. 554). The same standards apply in determining the bona fides of alleged family partnerships as in determining the bona fides of other transactions between family members. Transactions between persons in a close family group, whether or not involving partnership interests, afford much opportunity for deception and should be subject to close scrutiny. All the facts and circumstances at the time of the purported gift and during the periods preceding and following it may be taken into consideration in determining the bona fides or lack of bona fides of a purported gift or sale."

The Code provisions therefore recognize the principles that earnings are taxed to the individual who earns them and that income from capital, however acquired, is attributable to its owner. They eliminate as a factor to be considered in determining the bona fides of a family partnership the fact that the new partner acquired his interest by gift or that he may be an inactive partner. Thus, Code §704(e)(2) provides: "In the case of any partnership created by gift, the distributive share of the donee under the partnership agreement shall be includible in his gross income, except to the extent that such share is determined without allowance of reasonable compensation for services rendered to the partnership by the donor, and except to the extent that the portion of such share attributable to donated capital is proportionately greater than the share of the donor attributable to the donor's capital." This is buttressed by §704(e)(1), which says, "A person shall be recognized as a partner for income tax purposes if he owns a capital interest in a partnership in which capital is a material income-producing factor, whether or not such interest was derived by purchase or gift from any other person."

The determination as to whether capital is a material income-producing factor is made on a case-by-case basis. Capital is a material income-producing factor if a substantial portion of the gross income of the business is attributable to the employment of capital in the business conducted by the partnership. In general, capital is not a material income-producing factor where the income of the business consists principally of fees, commissions, or other compensation for personal services performed by members or employees of the partnership. On the other hand, capital is ordinarily a material income-producing factor if the operation of the business requires substantial inventories or a substantial investment in plant, machinery, or other equipment (Reg. §704.1-(e)(1)(iv)).

Finally, §704(e)(3) lays down the rule that "an interest purchased by one member of a family from another shall be considered to be created by gift from the seller, and the fair market value of the purchased interest shall be considered to be donated capital." (For purposes of §704(e)(3), the "family of any individual shall include only his spouse, ancestors and lineal descendants, and any trusts for the primary benefit of such persons.")

This latter provision is to insure that the tests of §704(e)(1) and (2) are met whether the donor transfers interests in the business to members of his "family" or makes cash gifts to members of his "family" that are either invested in the partnership, used to run the business, or used to purchase their interests in the partnership from the donor.

[¶503.1] Checklist of Family Partnership Ownership Tests

Generally, whether the recipient of a capital interest in a partnership is the real owner of that interest and whether there is the necessary dominion and control over that interest must be ascertained from all the facts and circumstances of the particular case (Reg. §1.704-1(e)(2)(i)). The reality of ownership is to be determined in the light of the transaction as a whole. The execution of legally sufficient and irrevocable instruments of gift under state law is a factor to be taken into account but is not determinative of ownership for the purposes of §704(e). The reality of the transfer and of the recipient's ownership of the property attributed to him are to be ascertained from the actions of the parties to the alleged gift and not by any mechanical or formal test. Some of the more important factors to be considered in determining whether a recipient has acquired ownership of a capital interest in a partnership are the following:

☐ (1) ***Retained Control:*** The donor cannot retain controls of the interest that he has purported to transfer that are sufficient to demonstrate that he is still the owner of the interest for all practical purposes (Reg. §1.704-1(e)(2)(ii)). Controls that will taint the transfer include, for example, the following:

(a) Retention of control of the distribution of amounts of income or restrictions on the distributions of amounts of income (other than amounts retained in the partnership annually with the consent of the partners, including the donee partner, for the reasonable needs of the business). If there is a partnership agreement providing for a managing partner or partners, then amounts of income may be retained in the partnership without the acquiescence of all the partners if such amounts are retained for the reasonable needs of the business.

(b) Any limitation of the right of the recipient to liquidate or sell his interest in the partnership at his discretion.

(c) Retention of control of assets essential to the business (for example, through retention of assets leased to the alleged partnership).

(d) Retention of management powers that are inconsistent with normal relationships among partners. Retention by the donor of control of business management or of voting control, such as is common in ordinary business relationships, is not by itself to be considered inconsistent with normal relationships among partners, provided the recipient is free to liquidate his interest at his discretion without financial detriment. The recipient is not considered free to liquidate his interest unless, considering all the facts, it is evident that he is independent of the donor and has such maturity and understanding of his rights that he is capable of exercising or not exercising his right to withdraw from the partnership.

☐ (2) ***Indirect Controls:*** Where the donor can exercise controls inconsistent with ownership by the recipient indirectly, as, for example, through a separate business organization, estate, trust, individual, or other partnership, the reality of the transfer of the interest will be as tainted as if such controls were exercisable directly (Reg. §1.704-1(e)(2)(iii)).

☐ (3) ***Participation in Management:*** Substantial participation by the recipient in the control and management of the business (including participation in the major policy decisions affecting the business) is strong evidence of his exercise of dominion and control over his interest. This will be indicative of sufficient maturity and experience to deal with the business problems of the partnership (Reg. §1.704-1(e)(2)(iv)).

☐ (4) ***Income Distributions:*** The actual distribution to the recipient of a partnership interest of the entire amount or a major portion of his distributive share of the business income for his sole benefit and use is substantial evidence of the reality of the transfer and ownership, provided the donor has not retained inconsistent controls (Reg. §1.704-1(e)(2)(v)). (Amounts distributed are not considered to be used for the recipient's sole benefit if, for example, they are deposited, loaned, or invested in such manner that the donor can control their use or enjoyment.)

□ (5) ***Conduct of Partnership Business:*** It is important that the recipient is actually treated as a partner in the operation of the business if the reality of his ownership of the partnership interest is to be established (Reg. §1.704-1(e)(2)(vi)). Whether or not the recipient has been held out publicly as a partner in the conduct of the business, in relations with customers, or with creditors or other sources of financing is of primary significance. Other factors of significance in this connection include:

(a) Compliance with local partnership and business registration statutes.

(b) Control of business bank accounts.

(c) Recognition of the recipient's rights in distributions of partnership property and profits.

(d) Recognition of recipient's interest in insurance policies, leases, and other business contracts and in litigation affecting business.

(e) The existence of written agreements, records, or memoranda, contemporaneous with the taxable year or years concerned, establishing the nature of the partnership agreement and the rights and liabilities of the respective partners.

(f) The filing of partnership tax returns as required by law. (However, formal compliance with the above factors may not be sufficient to overcome other circumstances that indicate that the donor has retained substantial ownership of the transferred interest.)

□ (6) ***Trustees as Partners:*** A trustee can be recognized as a partner for income tax purposes depending upon the facts in each case (Reg. §1.704-1(e)(2)(vii)). A trustee who is unrelated to and independent of the grantor, and who participates as a partner and receives distribution of the income distributable to the trust, will ordinarily be recognized as the legal owner of the partnership interest that he holds in trust unless the grantor has retained controls inconsistent with such ownership. However, if the grantor is the trustee, or if the trustee is amenable to the will of the grantor, the provisions of the trust instrument (particularly as to whether the trustee is subject to the responsibilities of a fiduciary), the provisions of the partnership agreement, and the conduct of the parties must all be taken into account in determining whether the trustee in a fiduciary capacity has become the real owner of the partnership interest. Where the grantor (or a "friendly" party) is the trustee, the trust may be recognized as a partner only if the grantor (or such other person) in his participation in the affairs of the partnership actively represents and protects the interests of the beneficiaries in accordance with the obligations of a fiduciary and does not subordinate such interests to the interests of the grantor. Furthermore, if the grantor (or a "friendly" party) is the trustee, the following factors will be given particular consideration:

(a) Whether the trust is recognized as a partner in business dealings with customers and creditors, and

(b) Whether, if any amount of the partnership income is not properly retained for the reasonable needs of the business, the trust's share of such amount is distributed to the trust annually and paid to the beneficiaries or reinvested with the sole interest of the beneficiaries in mind.

□ (7) ***Interests (Not Held in Trust) of Minor Children:*** Except where a minor child is shown to be capable of managing his own property and can participate in the partnership activities in accordance with his interest in the property, a minor generally will not be recognized as a member of a partnership unless control of the property is exercised by another person as fiduciary for the sole benefit of the child under adequate judicial supervision (Reg. §1.704-1(e)(2)(viii)). The use of the child's property or income for support for which a parent is legally responsible will be considered a use for the parent's benefit.

A minor child will be considered competent to manage his own property if he actually has sufficient maturity and experience to be treated by disinterested persons as competent to enter business dealings and otherwise to conduct his affairs on a basis of equality with adult persons, notwithstanding legal disabilities of the minor under state law.

☐ (8) ***Donees as Limited Partners:*** The recognition of a recipient's interest in a limited partnership will depend, as in the case of other donated interests, on whether the transfer of property is real and on whether the donee has acquired dominion and control over the interest purportedly transferred to him (Reg. §1.704-1(e)(2)(ix)). To be recognized for federal income tax purposes, a limited partnership must be organized and conducted in accordance with the requirements of the applicable state limited partnership law. The absence of services and participation in management by a recipient in a limited partnership is immaterial if the limited partnership meets all the other prescribed requirements. If the limited partner's right to transfer or liquidate his interest is subject to substantial restrictions (for example, where the interest of the limited partner is not assignable in a real sense or where such interest may be required to be left in the business for a long term of years), or if the general partner retains any other control that substantially limits any of the rights that would ordinarily be exercisable by unrelated limited partners in normal business relationships, such restrictions on the right to transfer or liquidate or such retention of other control is considered strong evidence of the lack of reality in the ownership of the recipient.

☐ (9) ***Motive:*** If the reality of the transfer of interest is satisfactorily established, the motives for the transaction are generally immaterial. However, the presence or absence of a tax-avoidance motive is one of many factors to be considered in determining the reality of the ownership of a capital interest acquired by gift (Reg. §1.704-1(e)(2)(x)).

SECTION VI
THE BENEFITS OF A SOLE PROPRIETORSHIP

In earlier sections, we discussed the benefits of doing business as a corporation, professional or otherwise, and as a partnership. In this section, we are going to consider the relative merits and drawbacks of a third area—that of sole proprietorship. Although it may lack some of the benefits of other forms of doing business, it is still far and away the most popular form in the country and there has to be a reason for it. In this section, we are going to explore some of those reasons.

[¶601] THE SOLE PROPRIETORSHIP VERSUS THE PARTNERSHIP

The form of business association nearest to the sole proprietorship is the simple partnership of two or more persons, each with an equal say in the management and operation of the business—be it a profession or otherwise. The key distinction here between the sole proprietorship and the partnership is that every member of the partnership has an equal say in how the business is to be run without regard as to how the profits are to be divided. For example, under a partnership, A may receive 75% of the profits and B only 25%, but each will have an equal say in management and operation. This can sometimes create an uncomfortable situation that, while not amounting to a conflict of interests, still puts the majority profit-taker in a position where he or she does not have the scope of authority proportionate to the expected profit yield. Obviously, this situation cannot occur in a sole proprietorship where all management and operational functions are in the sole proprietor.

[¶601.1] The Question of Liability

In a sole proprietorship, the proprietor is wholly and personally liable for all of his debts without regard to whether they may be incurred for personal or business reasons. In short, he or she is a single legal entity and cannot separate business debts or assets from those incurred personally. In a partnership, each partner is wholly liable for any and all debts of the partnership acting as a business entity. He is not, of course, personally liable for the personal or nonbusiness debts of his partner. However, this can lead us to two uncomfortable situations that have occurred time and time again:

☐ (a) The other partner, through his legal right as a member of the partnership, obligates the partnership to a contract that turns sour. *Result:* The partnership is liable, and if it does not have sufficient assets, the personal assets of the individual partners can be reached—including the personal assets of the partner who may not have even known of the deal but is estopped from denying the existence of the partnership. His remedy, so the courts hold, is against his partner, if anyone; but the partner is insolvent, and the unknowing partner has to take the loss.

☐ (b) The other partner incurs private debts of a purely personal nature. His other assets being exhausted, there still remains his partnership interest. Now, while a creditor can't simply take over the partnership interest and become a new partner without the consent of the other partner(s), that creditor can force the liquidation of assets to meet his claim and, in effect, destroy the partnership. The unobligated partner can thus find himself in the uncomfortable position of having to choose between a new partner who may not at all be to his liking or watch a once-productive partnership simply be extinguished. It should be noted in passing that even if the surviving partner weathers out the liquidation of his former partner's assets and interests, there is no guarantee that he will be able to continue or resume the business under the old, familiar partnership name. This depends entirely upon the circumstances and facts of the case and upon the jurisdiction in which the action lies.

As a variant of this question of liability, and one concerned largely with the medical and dental professions, take the situation where two practitioners, each with different specialties and different patient treatment equipment, form a professional partnership. If a malpractice action is brought against one of the professionals for negligent treatment, that action, notwithstanding the fact that it is grounded solely upon the activities of *one* of the partners, is nevertheless a partnership action. The other partner may have had no patient contact whatsoever and be totally unfamiliar with both the equipment and therapy involved. Nevertheless, since it is a partnership, each partner is wholly liable on a personal basis.

While part of the problem can be met with insurance, this spiraling cost of malpractice insurance (especially when more than one specialty is involved) should make the average medical or dental practitioner think twice before forming a professional *partnership* (as opposed to corporation) rather than continuing as a sole proprietor.

[¶601.2] The Question of Credit and Capital

The problem of obtaining credit or securing capital to a sole proprietor rests entirely upon his personal credit standing and reputation. At first glance, it would seem that if he elected to take on a partner, that personal credit would be even more enhanced, since the proposed partner's personal assets would constitute an additional guarantee. However, this is a two-edged sword. If the sources of financing feel that the proposed partner is prone to hasty or ill-advised decisions in business matters, it may very well act as a detriment. Such a partner could conceivably enter into contracts jeopardizing the entire partnership (as we have noted) and convert the financing source's efforts into actions for recovery rather than routine collection.

[¶601.3] The Question of Control

Obviously, the greatest degree of control over a business or professional enterprise is that exerted by the sole proprietor. In a partnership or corporation, that degree of control is diminished. Control often entails decision making, which may become increasingly difficult as the organization itself becomes more complex. Many a venture, initially successful as a sole proprietorship or even small partnership, has faltered when it reached the corporate level where key decisions were made by committee and not by one man.

[¶601.4] The Question of "Doing Business" and Applicable Law

A sole proprietor is free to conduct business in any state, and relatively simple rules apply as to which law is applicable in the event a transaction involves the crossing of state lines. This is not necessarily true in partnerships of any kind and is certainly not true in corporations. If the nature of the business or profession is such that it does cross state lines, be sure to discuss this matter with your attorney as to rights and liabilities *and* with your insurance representative—particularly in regard to malpractice claims. As with the question of control, the question of doing business and the applicable law becomes more complex as the organizational structure of the business becomes more complex.

[¶602] INCORPORATING A SOLE PROPRIETORSHIP

The question of whether or not you should incorporate involves two elements: (1) whether you can legally incorporate, and (2) whether it be advantageous for business and tax purposes to so do.

[¶602.1] Can You Incorporate?

This problem is most commonly encountered in the professional corporation and is strictly controlled by state statutes. These statutes generally prohibit anyone from owning or controlling a professional corporation unless that person is fully qualified and licensed within the particular profession. For example, a medical, dental, or legal corporation may not be formed or have its shares sold to someone who does not meet the state licensing standards for the actual practice of such a profession. Similarly, cross-corporations are also precluded, such as a corporation composed of medical practitioners and attorneys, unless each member is licensed and qualified in both areas.

This is not necessarily the case with partnerships. It is quite possible for a limited partnership to be formed between, say, two dentists and a financial backer. However, this must be a *limited partnership* in which backer has no control or say in the management or operation of the enterprise and his investment is his sole participation. Generally, such a "silent partner" is liable to third parties only to the extent of his financial interest or participation.

While much of the attention in these situations has been focused upon professions and professional organizations, the same is also true in business organizations that must be licensed under applicable state law. The most common of these is perhaps business ventures that retail liquor either by the bottle or by consumption on premises. In some states, all general partners must be either licensed or have no individual disabilities that would preclude their licensing. However, even in these situations, the traditional "silent partners" are usually acceptable.

[¶602.2] Should You Incorporate?

A corporation is solely liable for its own debts, and a creditor may not look personally to any of the shareholders other than to the extent of their interest in the corporation. This is true of business corporations but not necessarily of professional corporations. Since the corporation is a creature of statute, the statute that permitted professionals to incorporate for tax purposes may also permit their liability to exceed conventional corporate limits and the participants in the corporation to be held personally liable for actions such as malpractice. Thus, whether or not the corporate form is the best solution for your situation often depends upon the nature of the business and the limitations of corporate liability.

From the tax standpoint, corporations are subject to an income tax on their net profits and dividends are paid after that tax is calculated. The dividends themselves constitute income to the shareholders and hence corporate earnings are subject to double taxation. To alleviate this burden, Subchapter S was introduced, which permitted smaller and qualifying corporations to pass income directly to the shareholders and elect to be taxed as a partnership. In general, the most advantageous tax situation is still to be taxed as an individual—which itself should say something in favor of the sole proprietorship!

Another element to consider before incorporating is the question of incorporation expenses. By this we mean the costs, fees, and taxes that must be paid to the state in which the corporation is formed. Obviously, these will vary greatly. However, it is safe to say that these costs will be substantially in excess of any occupational or similar licenses required of a partnership or sole proprietorship within the same state. There will also be additional fees and expenses in the preparation of the instruments of incorporation, resident agent certificates, etc., as well as the annual state and federal tax returns. While these may appear to be nominal expenses, they still add up to a lump sum that could sometimes be better spent elsewhere.

[¶603] WHAT ABOUT "FRINGE BENEFITS"?

The sole proprietor of a business venture is not an employee and hence does not qualify for fringe benefits in the strict sense of the word. However, there are certain expenses that, while appearing to be personal, can be absorbed by the business provided that they are for business purposes.

If a car is used in a business, i.e., for business purposes or the production of business income, it is fully deductible. If it is used partly for business and partly for personal use, records must be kept and an allocation of expenses for each use made. Generally speaking, a leased vehicle for business use is wholly deductible.

In addition to automobile expenses, deductions are available for other expenses such as (a) leasehold improvements, (b) capital expenditures and ordinary repairs, (c) travel and entertainment expenses, (d) travel away from home, (e) entertainment expenses, (f) facilities used for entertainment, (g) advertising and promotion expenses, (h) research and development, (i) legal and accounting fees, (j) business gifts, (k) expenses in conjunction with conventions and seminars, and others. All of these, as well as some improper expenses that are not deductible, are treated in detail in Section IX.

[¶604] THE MAGIC OF TAX SHELTERS

If there is one strong tax-motivated reason why the sole proprietorship is favored over the corporate structure, it lies in the area of tax-sheltered investments. This is an area open and available to the sole proprietor concerned with building both his personal wealth and his estate. By judicious use of these tax-shelter opportunities, a sole proprietor can frequently more than offset the immediate gains he might have realized by doing business in the professional partnership or corporate structure.

[¶605] HOW TO TRANSFER A SOLE PROPRIETORSHIP

A sole proprietorship is like any other personal asset and may be sold or conveyed in substantially the same manner. There is no complex procedure, and, for the most part, a simple bill of sale will meet all formal requirements. About the only formal requirement is compliance with Bulk Sales Acts, when and where applicable. The object of such statutes is to prevent transfer of assets by a debtor to the derogation of his creditors, and compliance usually consists of a legal notice inserted in a newspaper and notification of creditors. It should be noted that the same requirements are made of partnerships and, in most instances, of corporations seeking to liquidate the major part of their holdings.

[¶605.1] Transfer by Legacy

Since a sole proprietorship is a personal asset, it can be transferred to heirs by means of a will or other testamentary disposition. Frequently, a sole proprietorship has a value above and beyond the personal services of the proprietor. Such value may be in the form of inventory or simply a good business name. If the value is tangible, such as inventory, it is part of the decedent's estate. If it is intangible, such as ''goodwill'' or a good business name, it is usually not considered a taxable portion of the estate.

Obviously, transfer by legacy or inheritance presupposes that there will be someone left to run the business. If this is not the case, or if the heirs show neither interest nor aptitude in continuing the business, the testator may provide for the orderly liquidation of the business after his death with the proceeds to be turned over to his heirs. This points up one additional advantage of the sole proprietorship over either a partnership or a corporation, in that the principal owner can plan his own estate without concern as to how his plans may affect either a partner or other shareholders in a corporation.

[¶605.2] How to Use Life Insurance to Fund the Sale of a Sole Proprietorship

To a sole proprietor, the ideal situation would be to pass on the business to his children and let them continue to operate it as a source of family income. However, it doesn't always work out that way. Sometimes there just isn't any family member capable of running the business, and the sole proprietor is more or less forced into letting the business become part of his liquid estate, with the proceeds going to his heirs.

There are three disadvantages to this course:

☐ (a) The executor will have to sell or otherwise liquidate the business rather quickly, and the assets will usually not bring what they would have brought through a more orderly or leisurely liquidation. Hence, on the very sale of the assets, the heirs may take a loss.
☐ (b) Goodwill, or a good business name, is usually lost entirely, and a loss of this nature cannot be charged off as a deduction.
☐ (c) The business, now liquidated, no longer exists as a source of income to the family.

A possible alternative is sale to an employee who is interested in buying a business for himself. A common difficulty in this procedure is that the employee may not have money to make the purchase; however, there is a two-part solution to the problem. The first part involves a binding buy-and-sell agreement between the owner and the employee. This agreement obligates the owner or his estate to sell the business as a going concern to the employee on the owner's retirement or death. The purchase price would either be fixed in the agreement and subject to periodic revision or would be determined by a formula set forth in the agreement. This price should include an amount for the value of the tangible assets as well as an amount for goodwill.

The second part involves assurance that cash will be available. To accomplish this, the employee would buy ordinary life insurance on the owner in the required amount, pay the premium, and be named beneficiary. If the employee cannot afford all or part of the premium, the owner can make the premium money available to him in one of two ways:

☐ (a) Increase his salary or give him a bonus in the amount of the premium plus the extra income tax he would have to pay on the increase. This method is not recommended because the owner would be paying for insurance on his own life. Thus, he would, in effect, be giving away all or part of his business.
☐ (b) Have the owner make a personal loan to the employee until the employee is able to pay the premiums from his own earnings (which, hopefully, will increase as time goes by). It is expected that the employee would repay the loan. But the buy-sell agreement should specifically provide for repayment of any unpaid portion of the loan out of the proceeds. The remaining proceeds would be applied to the purchase price, with the balance being paid off in installments.

If the owner retires, the employee can use the cash values (minus the repayment of any loan) as a substantial down payment on the purchase price with the balance to be paid in installments under terms set forth in the agreement.

This agreement benefits the owner (or his beneficiaries) because it assures that, rather than being liquidated, his business will be sold at a fair price on his death or retirement and that all or a substantial part of the purchase price will be available to him or his estate on his retirement or death. The employee benefits because he knows that he'll eventually own the business. The sole proprietor benefits from the loyalty of the employee who should now be eager to do a better job rather than go into business as a competitor!

[¶605.3] Indirect Conveyance to a Prime Creditor

Another way out of the situation in which there are no heirs ready to operate the business is through an indirect conveyance to a prime creditor. This is a technique used when the following elements are present:

☐ (a) There is but one major or principal creditor, and that creditor is a manufacturer or supplier of certain merchandise that is retailed by the sole proprietor and constitutes his largest single line of products in terms of gross volume.
☐ (b) The creditor, for legal or other reasons, does not want to participate in the retailing of his own products. Actually, the creditor would want to, but for various reasons he deems it advisable not to.

Here's how the technique works:

The sole proprietor continues to order merchandise from the prime creditor but does not pay for it. The income he realizes from the sale of the merchandise goes to meet other and lesser creditors and to provide a source of income for his family. The creditor agrees, in lieu of immediate payment, to take an open-end mortgage on the business and waive foreclosure until the death or retirement of the sole proprietor.

Upon that death or retirement, the prime creditor forecloses the business as an entity (charging off and paying off other creditors) and thereby owns the business without actually having gone on the open market to purchase it.

It is essential to note that in such an arrangement, any equity remaining within the sole proprietor's estate may be passed on to heirs as a nonworking interest.

As a result of such an agreement, which is usually reduced to writing in an informal letter agreement between the parties, here is how each side benefits:

The Sole Proprietor:

☐ (a) has provided himself with a lifetime cash flow upon which to base his personal estate planning;
☐ (b) has arranged for the continuation of the business (as operated by the prime creditor or his assignee), which continuation through the nonworking interest will provide funds for the sole proprietor's family and heirs;
☐ (c) has enhanced his own active business by being virtually an exclusive agent of the prime creditor, thus reducing competition for the particular line of merchandise.

The Prime Creditor:

☐ (a) has purchased (in effect) a going and prosperous business with post-profit dollars, since the credits that are building up to the mortgage claim are based on sales of the prime creditor and contain his profit markup;
☐ (b) has not had to lay out any cash for the acquisition of the business other than that reflected in raw materials and labor to make the finished product;
☐ (c) has acquired a proven retail location with built-in goodwill and following;
☐ (d) has entered the highly profitable retail phase of the business without overtly appearing to do so;
☐ (e) has acquired full and complete control of the business in terms of management and operation with no liability other than continuing payments to the nonworking interests, i.e., the heirs.

This simple technique and what it can accomplish for both the sole proprietor and a prime creditor is another one of the many advantages in sole proprietorship. While not impossible to accomplish in the partnership or corporate framework, it is certainly far more difficult. If you ever wonder why, for example, a certain sole proprietor retail store in any given city can offer super special sales at prices that discount stores and chain operations cannot, there is a better than even chance that the little ''Mom and Pop'' store is party to a prime creditor conveyance and the prime creditor is doing a little to help boost the sales!

[¶606] CONCLUSION

As you will have observed from the reading of this and the other sections of this book, there is no cut-and-dried formula to determine which is the best form of business for you. It all depends upon what you want to achieve.

Because of the complexity of our economy, tax is always a strong and dominant consideration. But it is not the only consideration. Keep in mind always that the only *certain* way to avoid all tax problems is to not have any taxable income; tax considerations concern only those who have something which can be taxed. Hence step one is to make a profit and step two is to protect it. In choosing a form of business, you are still in the stages of step one. Your goal should be to make the profit and pick the form of business association that will best insure your profit.

Note: Be sure to go back and review the comparative chart found at the end of Section III.

SECTION VII

THE BEST SALARY ARRANGEMENT WITH YOUR CORPORATION

There are several ways to get money out of a corporation, and the best method in any one case will depend upon the individual's particular financial status and economic needs. By far the most common and tax-favored way of sifting profits through to the shareholder of a small business is through compensation for that individual's services as an employee of his corporation. Funds that are distributed in this way are fully deductible by the corporation as ordinary and necessary business expenses. Also, these funds will be taxed only once—to the individual when earned—and will be subject to the 50% maximum tax on earned income (as opposed to the 70% maximum on dividend income). Thus, under many circumstances, you will want to allocate as much of your corporation's income to the employee-shareholder's compensation and as little to dividends as possible. Unfortunately, this may not be as easy as it looks. Where a shareholder's compensation is unreasonably high, IRS may tax the excess as being the equivalent of a dividend; that is, it will be taxed once to the corporation when earned and again to the shareholder when distributed.

[¶701] SPLITTING INCOME BETWEEN YOURSELF AND YOUR CORPORATION

In addition to the problems involved in determining reasonable compensation, the taxpayer who does business in the corporate form is faced with another dilemma. Businessmen who are the shareholders and employees of the corporation are frequently in high income tax brackets and, in many cases, seek to defer income to years when their rates will be lower. Difficulties arise, however, if a substantial portion of the corporation's income is not distributed, especially where the business is a small one, since IRS is apt to take the position that the income is personal holding company income. If IRS makes such a determination, it can subject the company to a costly accumulated earnings penalty tax. So there are many factors that you are going to have to consider in setting your corporation's pay policy. All of these factors are discussed in detail in the following paragraphs.

[¶701.1] The Accumulated Earnings Penalty Tax

When a corporation accumulates earnings and profits, it runs the risk of a penalty tax under §531-537. The penalty applies to corporations formed or availed of for the purpose of avoiding taxes by accumulating earnings instead of distributing them as dividends (§532).

The tax is imposed on the current year's "accumulated taxable income" at the rate of 27½% on the first $100,000 and 38½% on any excess. This tax, like the personal holding company penalty surtax, is in addition to the regular corporate tax (§532); but you first reduce the current year's income by any amount of corporate tax you've paid. (There are also other technical adjustments.) If your previous accumulations do not total $100,000, you can deduct from your current income the amount required to bring the total up to the $100,000. Then the excess current income (after the other adjustments) is subject to the penalty tax.

If your accumulation exceeds $100,000, you can still avoid the penalty tax by showing that "reasonably anticipated needs of the business" justify the accumulation (§537). It is not necessary to show that earnings and profits will be reinvested in the business immediately; it is enough to show that definite future business needs (not vague or uncertain) will require that these earnings and profits be plowed back (§535(c)).

Where you can't show that an accumulation is for reasonably anticipated business needs, you are going to have to distribute it in order to avoid the penalty tax.

[¶701.2] The Dividend as a Means of Distributing Corporate Earnings

Dividends are taxable as ordinary income to the extent paid out of the corporation's earnings and profits. This means accumulated earnings as well as current earnings (§316). If paid in property, the amount of the dividend is the fair market value of the property (§301).

To the extent that the dividend exceeds the earnings and profits, it is a return of capital that reduces the basis of your stock. Further distributions after the basis has been reduced to zero are capital gain (§301).

Any dividend paid in liquidation of the corporation is subject only to capital gains tax. However, the distribution will not be considered in liquidation if it is "essentially equivalent to a dividend" (§302).

Dividends of stock of the declaring corporation or of stock rights are tax free unless in lieu of money or in reorganization or split-ups (§305). However, sale or redemption of the distributed stock as part of a plan to get earnings out of the corporation at the capital gain rates instead of ordinary income rates will result in tax at the ordinary income rates to the extent the amount realized would have been so taxed if the corporation had distributed cash instead of stock (§306).

Dividends do not constitute earned income and are not subject to the favorable 50% tax ceiling available for compensation payments.

Since the profits are taxed to the corporation when earned, their distribution as dividends taxable to the shareholder when received subjects the earnings to an unfavorable double tax.

[¶701.3] How to Handle Compensation Payments

Just about any payment for services by a corporation is deductible as compensation. Wages, salaries, commissions, compensation on the basis of a percentage of profits, "bargain purchases,'' compensation for injury or sickness, tips, bonuses, severance pay, and other similar payments are deductible as compensation by a corporation.

If the compensation is paid in services or property, the deduction is equal to the value of the property or services. If the firm regulations provide for a stipulated price for services and that employees take property in payment, it can be presumed that the property is worth the stipulated price (Reg. §1.61-2(d)(1)).

When Your Corporation Is Squeezed for Cash: Suppose a corporation that was just formed pays a stockholder an inadequate salary during the first few years and later, when the money begins to roll in, makes it up to him by paying him back pay. The Tax Court has ruled that a corporation may deduct the later payments in full. (See *Weise Winckler Bindery, Inc.*, TC Memo 1967-259.)

To make sure that it gets the deduction, the corporation should fix a reasonable amount of compensation for the stockholder-employees in the year in which the compensation was earned—not years after the stockholders have performed their service, as in *Weise*.

Prepaying Salary–Debtor-Creditor Relationship: Now, let's take a look at the other side of the coin, where the corporation prepays for the stockholder's services. If the professional corporation pays the stockholder compensation with the understanding that it will be paid back by future services, the payments will be considered compensation. However, if a debtor-creditor relationship is created, the corporation does not have a deductible expense nor does the executive have taxable income. (See *Anson Beaver*, 55 TC 85, 1970).

What to do in this situation is to clearly indicate the intentions of the parties. If you want advances from a corporation to an employee-stockholder to stand up as loans, the parties have to indicate an intention that the repayment be made in money, not in future services. If the intention is to prepay compensation, then both the corporation and the stockholder should treat it as such: the corporation taking its deduction for the payment and the stockholder reporting it as income.

Compensation May Be Paid as Notes: Once you have established the amount of compensation, the next thing is to determine how to pay it. Frequently, a new corporation is not in a position to pay salary in cash. As an alternative, it may consider giving the stockholder notes. When a corporation does this it gets a deduction for the notes (assuming the corporation is solvent) if the stockholder treats the notes as income and gives up his claim for salary in trade for his right to sue on the notes.

How to Pay Bonuses to Working Stockholders: Corporations maintaining their bonuses on the accrual basis must establish the liability for bonuses to working stockholders in the taxable year they are to be deducted. The bonus must be paid not later than two-and-a-half months after the end of the taxable year.

Suppose a corporation whose tax year ends on June 30 accrued a bonus to its sole stockholder on its books before June 30, 1976, but it didn't actually pay the money to him until October 1, 1976, three months and one day after the end of the corporation's tax year. The stockholder included the bonus in his 1976 income tax return, just as he would have done if he had received the bonus within the two-and-a-half-month period. IRS has ruled that this fact does not allow the corporation to take its deduction for the tax year ending June 30, 1976. The tax year in which the employee includes the bonus in his income does not affect the tax year in which the corporation may take its deduction (*Rev. Rul. 68-114*, CB 1968-1, 100).

What to Do: If it is important for the corporation to deduct the bonus in the earlier rather than in the later tax year, make sure the corporation either pays the bonus within the two-and-a-half-month period or informs the shareholder-employee within such period that he can draw down the bonus anytime he wishes. If the corporation is temporarily short of money and the difference is only a matter of two or three weeks—as seems to have been the situation in the facts relied on by IRS—it might pay the corporation to arrange a short-term loan so that it can pay the bonus sooner and take the deduction in the earlier tax year.

Caution: Suppose the corporation informs the employee that he may withdraw the money at will, but it has an informal understanding with him that he won't withdraw it for a few months? This is collusion; and, if proved, the corporation will probably lose its deduction until the employee actually withdraws. Proof may be easier if the employee is the sole stockholder of the corporation.

[¶701.4] What Constitutes Reasonable Compensation?

It is impossible to establish one hard-and-fast rule as to what constitutes reasonable compensation. The regulations define reasonable compensation as ''only such amount as would ordinarily be paid for like services by like enterprises under like circumstances.'' Circumstances to be considered are those at the date when the services are contracted rather than those when the contract is questioned (Reg. §1.162-7(b)(3)).

Among the circumstances considered important by the courts are:

☐ (1) The employee's special qualifications and availability of others to fill the job.
☐ (2) The nature, extent, and scope of his work.
☐ (3) The size and complexities of the business.
☐ (4) A comparison of salaries paid with gross and net income.
☐ (5) The prevailing general economic conditions.
☐ (6) Comparison of salaries with distributions to stockholders.
☐ (7) Prevailing rates of compensation for comparable positions, comparably performed in comparable concerns.
☐ (8) The salary policy of the taxpayer as to other similarly situated employees.
☐ (9) The arm's-length element in the compensation deal.
☐ (10) Consideration for past services and compensation in prior years.
☐ (11) Comparison of salaries paid with employees' stock ownership.

No single factor is decisive as to the reasonableness of the salary; the situation must be considered as a whole. For a guide on reasonableness of salary, we must look to the facts of prevailing pay levels and salaries allowed in other situations.

Dividend Equivalency Test: Even where a shareholder's salary is deemed reasonable in light of the aforementioned circumstances, the Court of Claims has ruled that a portion of the compensation paid will be taxed as a dividend where:

☐ (1) No dividends had been declared during the years at issue;
☐ (2) About 50% of the net profits (before taxes and salaries) was paid as compensation; and
☐ (3) Any return on equity capital was so conspicuous by its absence that the ''purported compensation payments necessarily contain a distribution of corporate earnings'' (*Charles McCandless Tile Service Co.*, Ct. Cl., 422 F.2d 1085, 1970).

In other words, where compensation is in proportion to profits and the surrounding circumstances indicate that a portion of the profits was produced by equity capital, that portion of the shareholder's salary will be taxed as the equivalent of a dividend even though it would otherwise be reasonable as compensation.

Obligation to Refund Disallowed Payments; "Oswald Bylaws": Corporations paying salaries in excess of what IRS considers "reasonable" run the risk of having the excess treated as a dividend subject to tax and also of having a portion of their contribution to a profit-sharing plan declared excessive. Most corporations are now writing into their bylaws the requirement that employees be legally obligated to reimburse the corporation for the disallowed compensation. The amounts that are reimbursed are deductible by the employee in the year in which the disallowed compensation is reimbursed. In this way, the additional tax liability that the corporation is required to meet is funded by the reimbursed compensation received from the employee. At the same time, the additional tax that the employee has to pay because of the treatment of the distribution as a dividend is offset by the deduction available through the reimbursement (see *Oswald,* 49 TC 645, 1969; *Rev. Rul. 69-115,* 1969-1 CB 50).

The obligation to repay is imposed by a corporate bylaw adopted when the corporation is formed. A corporate bylaw assented to by the stockholders of a corporation prior to the time reimbursement or repayment is made can help avoid the double tax. Such a bylaw may make clear a duty on the part of the directors to seek reimbursement and, if agreed to by the stockholder to whom payment is later made, will serve to create a binding obligation to repay the corporation. These two obligations should assure that the employee gets a deduction when he repays the corporation and that the amount repaid does not constitute additional income to the corporation. (See sample Oswald bylaw in appendix at page 412.)

If the employee-stockholder fails to repay the disallowed deductions, the bylaw may provide for withholding the excess amount from future compensation or other payments due the officer or employee by the corporation.

IRS has ruled that it will allow the deduction to the executive who repays his corporation provided the payment is made under an agreement legally binding under local law.

Steps for a Corporation to Take in Setting Up Compensation Program: There are several basic steps that a corporation should take in setting up its compensation program to improve the chances of salaries being sustained as reasonable compensation:

☐ *Salaries:* Salaries paid to employees who are also shareholders in the corporation should be made to look like salaries rather than a distribution of profits. Salaries should be on a monthly or weekly basis and should be formally reflected in minutes of the directors' meetings at which they were set. By establishing a fixed monthly salary, the corporation more clearly establishes its intent to pay salary rather than distribute profits.

Monthly compensation should be based on the total compensation expected to be paid to the executive during the year, leaving only small portions of the total annual compensation to be paid in the form of discretionary bonuses. Bonuses are more susceptible to attack than are fixed weekly or monthly salaries.

☐ *Dividends:* Corporations should plan to pay dividends to insure a reasonable return on capital. The payment of reasonable dividends serves to weaken the Government's argument that the compensation is in fact dividends. The amount of dividends can be kept lower if the corporation's invested capital is kept at as low a level as possible. For most service corporations, this is not difficult as the investment generally consists of furniture and fixtures. For a service corporation the principal element of profit is services rather than capital. This reduces the necessity for investment.

Compensation should be based on factors other than stock holdings or profits.

☐ *Changes in Compensation:* Changes in compensation should be avoided wherever possible. If salaries are changed, the changes should be tied to factors other than changes in profit. For example, in the minutes of the meeting setting the salary, the change could be tied to changes in working conditions, responsibilities, or the cost of living.

[¶702] SALARY ARRANGEMENT FOR THE LOWEST OVERALL TAX

The tax advantages of a corporation's retention of income diminished with the adoption of the "maximum tax" as part of the 1969 Reform Act. This feature provides that the marginal rate of tax on earned income shall not exceed 50%.

By today's standards, the income level required to enable a businessman to take advantage of this break is not high—$38,000 for the single individual and $52,000 for the married businessman who files a joint return. The more you make, the greater will be your savings. A married couple with $200,000 in taxable income, all of it earned, realizes about $19,000 in tax savings compared with the ordinary rates.

[¶702.1] Income That Qualifies for Treatment as Earned Income

Earned income generally includes fees, wages, salaries, or compensation for personal services. Where an individual is engaged in a trade or business where both personal services and capital are a material income-producing factor, earned income includes a reasonable amount but not more than 30% of his share of the net profits of the business. Deferred compensation is not considered earned income if it is paid later than the end of the taxable year following the year in which the employee's right to receive such deferred compensation was not subject to a substantial risk of forfeiture.

Profit Sharing: Earned income does not include lump-sum distributions from trusts or employee annuity plans when long-term capital gains treatment is afforded the employer's contribution, nor does it include the employer's contribution if that is eligible for the special averaging rules applicable if the total distribution occurs in one year.

Special Rules Affecting the Earned-Income Ceiling: The 50% limit is not available to taxpayers who use income averaging nor to married taxpayers who file separately. The 50% limit is applicable to earned income reduced by tax preferences in excess of $30,000 in the current year or the average tax preferences in excess of $30,000 for the current year and the prior four years, whichever is greater. Tax preferences for this purpose are the same as those applicable to individuals under the minimum tax.

[¶702.2] How to Compute Taxable Earned Income

For the taxpayer who does business in the corporate form, the 50% tax limit on earned income is available only as to the portion of his income received as salary or bonuses. Any portion attributable to dividends is not eligible.

Corporations that have elected under Subchapter S of the Code distribute their profits tax free. These distributions are not eligible for treatment as earned income. Subchapter S corporations may, however, pay salaries in the same manner as ordinary corporations, and these payments would be eligible for treatment as earned income.

Earned taxable income is defined as that proportion of a taxpayer's total taxable income that is in the same ratio (but not in excess of 100%) as the ratio of earned income to adjusted gross income. Thus, if 40% of a businessman's adjusted gross income is earned income, then 40% of his taxable income is considered earned taxable income.

Basic Computation: If during a taxable year, a businessman has earned taxable income that exceeds the 50% tax bracket he figures his tax as follows:

□ (1) Takes the highest amount of taxable income that is taxed over 50%. Computes the tax on this amount.
□ (2) Takes 50% of the amount by which earned taxable income (as defined above) exceeds the taxable income used in step (1).
□ (3) Computes the regular tax on the entire taxable income and deducts the tax computed on only the earned taxable income.
□ (4) Adds the amounts under steps (1), (2), and (3).

The following example shows how the tax on earned income is calculated.

In 1974, Mr. Jones, married and filing a joint return, has $90,000 in salary and bonus from Jones-Brown, Inc., $10,000 dividends on stock, $5,000 unreimbursed travel expenses, and $10,000 itemized deductions and personal exemptions. He has no capital gains, lump-sum pension distribution, or tax-preferred income. His tax is calculated as follows:

Gross income	$100,000
Unreimbursed travel and entertainment expenses	5,000
Adjusted gross income	$ 95,000
Itemized deductions and personal exemptions	10,000
Taxable income	$ 85,000

The computation is:

(1) Tax on $52,000 (the highest amount on which the tax rate is 50%)		$ 18,060
(2) Determine earned taxable income as follows:		
$90,000 (salary) / $95,000 (adjusted gross income) × $85,000 (taxable income) = $80,526		
Minus income taxed in step (1) 52,000		
Balance $28,526		
50% of balance =		$14,263
(3) Tax on $85,000 of total taxable income	$36,240	
Tax on $80,526 of earned taxable income	33,645	
Balance		$ 2,595
(4) Total tax (sum of (1), (2), and (3))		$34,918

The total tax without the special earned-income tax limit would be $36,240. Thus, there is a $1,322 saving by using the special limit.

[¶702.3] Best Tax Salary

The best tax salary for an officer-stockholder is the one that will cost the least in taxes when the tax cost to employee and corporation are combined. It strikes a balance: Any increase will cost the employee more in taxes than the extra deduction will save the corporation; any decrease will cost the corporation more because of the reduced deduction than the reduction in tax will save the employee.

Suppose a corporation has earnings of $100,000 before salary. It has a sole stockholder who is married. His best salary is between $40,000 and $44,000. If he were paid more than $44,000, the corporation would be saving taxes at a 48% rate, but sole stockholder would be paying taxes at a 50% rate. If he were paid less than $40,000, the corporation would be paying tax at a 48% rate, but the sole stockholder would be saving tax at a 45% rate.

If earnings left in the corporation will not be withdrawn in the near future either as dividends or by liquidation and assuming that the stockholder-employee's other income equals his deductions and exemptions, there can be only one best salary taxwise. Here are the best salary levels for various corporate incomes:

Corporate Income Before Salary	*Single Taxpayer*	*Married Taxpayer*	
		Joint Return	*Separate Return*
Less than $6,000	Full Corporate Income	Full Corporate Income	Full Corporate Income
$6,000 to $12,000	$ 6,000	Full Corporate Income	$ 6,000
$12,000 to $31,000	$ 6,000	$12,000	$ 6,000
$31,000 to $47,000	Full Corporate Income Less $25,000	Full Corporate Income Less $25,000	Full Corporate Income Less $25,000
$47,000 to $57,000	Full Corporate Income Less $25,000	Full Corporate Income Less $25,000	$22,000
$57,000 to $69,000	$32,000	Full Corporate Income Less $25,000	$22,000
Over $69,000	$32,000	$44,000	$22,000

[¶703] HOW TO CONTROL INCOME AND EXPENSES

Tax planning doesn't begin and end with excluding income and gathering up deductions. For one thing, we must consider the tax rates. If the rates are expected to go down it is usually more advantageous to pick up deductions currently and defer income. Provisions for carryovers and accounting techniques for manipulating income and deductions among years enable us to do this. Where the rates are expected to go up, your overall strategy should be to accelerate income and defer expenses.

Even with the favorable capital gains tax, it is less expensive taxwise to defer a tax. Here are some reasons for deferring income:

☐ (1) Spreading payments may facilitate the sale and improve the price. If the tax can't be similarly deferred, we have created a cash liability against a paper profit.
☐ (2) Deferment of a long-term capital gain may provide the opportunity to offset it with a future loss.
☐ (3) If a profitable sale occurs in an operating loss year, we may want to push the gain ahead because we'd rather have it taxed at 25% than used to reduce the amount of loss that can be carried back against a previous year's ordinary income.
☐ (4) An individual will save tax by deferring gain to years when his tax bracket will be less than 50%.
☐ (5) Postponing tax offers a speculation on the rate of tax. If the rate seems likely to be increased, the gain can be accelerated by sale of the installment obligation.

We have three possible methods of deferring tax on profit resulting from a sale: (1) electing the installment method under §453; (2) using a deferred payment sale (any sale in which part or all of the purchase price is payable in the year subsequent to the year of sale); (3) making a contingent sale in which payment is made dependent on future profits or production.

Aside from rate changes, a new tax law may contain structural changes or loophole closers. Where the change is beneficial to the taxpayer, proper strategy may call for postponing a contemplated transaction to come within the effective date for the beneficial change. Where a loophole has been closed, accelerating a transaction to occur before the date that the stricter law is to take effect is also proper strategy.

[¶703.1] How to Accelerate Business Income

If your needs call for pushing more income into this year (for example, where this is the last year to which you can carry a loss carryover or if your corporation's taxable income this year will be less than $25,000), consider using one of these methods:

☐ (1) ***Switch to open account sales,*** if you have been making consignment sales. Title normally passes when delivery is made to a common carrier, and income arises then.
☐ (2) ***Switch from approval sales to outright sales*** with right of return. You have immediate income and if there is a return, you reduce income then.
☐ (3) ***Step up your collection activity*** if you are on a cash basis. Whatever you collect this year is income this year. You might give discounts or other inducements for prepayment.
☐ (4) ***Push out inventory.*** Get it into the hands of a common carrier or the customer before year end.
☐ (5) ***Try for advance rentals, commissions, interest, unrestricted deposits, etc.*** Whatever you receive this year is taxed this year even if you are on an accrual basis—as long as you have unrestricted right to use what you receive. A salesman can get advances on commissions.
☐ (6) ***Sell installment obligations.*** If you have previously reported sales under the installment method, you are spreading the income over the period of collection. If you want to speed up the income now, sell the obligations to a third party.
☐ (7) ***Sell equipment instead of trading it in.*** If you'd have a gain on the sale of equipment, you can avoid it by trading it in. However, if you want to pick up the income this year, make a separate

sale of the equipment and report the gain. Then use the proceeds plus the additional cash or credit needed to buy the new equipment.

If you want a sale—not a trade-in—don't sell to the same dealer from whom you buy your new equipment. Sell to a third party. *Reason:* IRS might say that you have a trade-in, even if you try to set up separate deals with the same party.

[¶703.2] How to Defer Business Income

If you are looking to avoid any more income this year, or to keep it to a minimum, consider using one or more of the following methods:

☐ (1) ***Use consignment sales*** instead of open account sales. Title doesn't pass until the purchaser resells your goods, and income arises then.

☐ (2) ***Sell on approval*** with right of return, instead of outright sale. Income arises only when purchaser approves.

☐ (3) ***Let collection procedures continue without step-up,*** if you are on the cash basis. Possibly, delay billing and offer no inducements for prepayment.

☐ (4) ***Use a sales contract that requires a specific act to be done before title passes.*** If contract requires some additional act, title passage can be postponed until the act is performed.

☐ (5) ***Hold back inventory.*** Delay deliveries to common carriers or customers until after year end, making title pass to customer next year.

☐ (6) ***Use the installment sales method.*** As an installment dealer, you can use this method—it spreads gross profit over the collection period. Expenses of the sale are deducted immediately under the cash or accrual method (whichever you use). You can switch from accrual to installment method without permission.

This method is not limited to installment dealers where you make "casual" sales, but the sale must be for more than $1,000 unless it's a realty sale. Also, make sure you don't receive more than 30% of the purchase price in the year of sale. You can make a separate election as to whether or not to use this method with each sale.

☐ (7) ***Use deferred payment sale.*** This method is often used where the 30% installment sale requirement can't be met. By taking only a bare contractual promise or nonnegotiable note as payment this year, you wouldn't have to pick up any income this year because there is no present value. Negotiable notes, however, constitute present income up to their discounted fair market value. The difference between value picked up and face is not taxable until received.

☐ (8) ***Consider long-term contract reporting.*** If a contract extends over two tax years, the courts say you can use long-term contract reporting. IRS says the contract has to take more than 12 months to complete to use these special accounting methods. If you can use them, you can postpone both income and deductions under the completed contract method. The percentage of completion method picks up the income over the period of the contract; at the end of each year you estimate the percentage of completion and report that percentage of your income.

☐ (9) ***Use escrow arrangements.*** Proceeds put in escrow until "real" conditions are met are not income until released.

☐ (10) ***Sell for a contingent price.*** A sale for a percentage of profits, for example, does not permit calculation of the sale price. So, gain arises only after profit payments received exceed your basis. You may get a fight on this from IRS.

☐ (11) ***Give an option to buy.*** Giving a purchase option postpones gain until option is exercised.

If exercised, cost of option becomes part of sales price; if option expires, seller has ordinary income. Gain can also be postponed by entering into sales contract now, with title-closing date in future (especially for real estate).

[¶703.3] How to Shift Expenses—Checklist

Here are some ways to shift expenses. The approach you choose depends on whether you want to boost the current year's deductions or the deductions of a subsequent year.

☐ (1) ***Prepayments:*** A cash-basis taxpayer can pay all bills by December 31, including limited prepayments of such items as taxes and interest. If he wants to defer expenses, all he has to do is hold off payment until January. There's no immediate deduction for certain prepayments (e.g., insurance premiums, rents), even if you are on the cash basis. Although you can't deduct advance rentals, one way of "shifting" rental expenses to particular years, for example, is to have the payment arranged in this way under the lease. Some of the expenses you can prepay and get an immediate deduction for are: charitable contributions, state income taxes, travel expenses (getting an employee started on a trip before year end and paying his plane fare and other costs this year), advertising, office expenses (supplies, tools, uniforms, equipment, and other noninventoriable items; prepaying for inventory gives you no extra deduction—you are merely changing one asset (cash) for another (inventory)).

☐ (2) ***Large Expenses:*** Rush through repairs, buy substantial amounts of office supplies, pay research and experimental costs and other similarly large expenses if you want the deduction this year. Hold off, if you want them next year.

However, if you anticipate a general remodeling next year, don't postpone repairs until then. Make them now. Standing alone, the repairs are deductible; but even if you have what would otherwise be a repair, it still may not be deductible if the repair costs are included in an overall plan of rehabilitating the property next year.

☐ (3) ***Returns and Allowances:*** Accrual-basis taxpayers can pick up returns and grant allowances by December 31 to get a deduction this year—after December 31 for a deduction next year.

☐ (4) ***Legal and Accounting Fees:*** Have your lawyer and accountant bill you before January 1, if you want to accrue or pay in this year.

☐ (5) ***Junk or Abandon Equipment:*** Do this before the year's end for deduction this year—next year for a deduction next year.

☐ (6) ***Research and Development Costs:*** They can be swung over to future years or deducted now. If you spend money on a research program this year for the first time, you can deduct it all this year. Or if you've been deducting these expenses currently in previous years, you can continue to do so. Or, if you want to push the expenses forward, you can write them off over a period of 60 months or more. Once you switch to amortizing your costs, you have to do so in the future unless you get permission from IRS to switch.

☐ (7) ***Switching From Bad Debt Writeoffs to Reserve Method:*** This switch brings more deductions into this year. Theoretically, this switch can double up your bad debt deduction, but as a practical matter, since you need IRS's permission (within the first 90 days of the tax year) to switch in the first place, IRS will make you spread the additional deduction over a ten-year period. So you can only increase your deduction by 10% this year. Switching the other way pushes deductions into the future. Keep in mind, too, if you switch from reserve to write off, you're going to have immediate income for the amount of the reserve that is being eliminated.

☐ (8) ***Corporate Contribution Deductions:*** They can be accrued this year if paid within 2½ months after the end of the tax year. So where the corporation is short of cash now but wants the deduction this year, make sure you pass the appropriate corporate resolution making the contribution and call for payment no later than 2½ months after the end of your tax year.

☐ (9) ***Items in Dispute—Contested Taxes:*** These items must be deducted when they are paid even though a contest that finally determines the liability is resolved in a later year. This is so for accrual- as well as cash-basis taxpayers. So, if you are anxious to get the deduction this year, pay the liability by year end.

On the other hand, if you'd rather push the deduction into a succeeding year, do not pay the liability, prolong the negotiations, and appeal a decision to a higher court (where permissible) to avoid concluding the dispute before the end of the year.

☐ (10) ***Payment by Check or Note:*** A payment by check on the last day of the year will give you a deduction this year—although the check doesn't clear the bank until next year (as long as it *does* clear and is paid, of course)—even if you are on a cash basis.

Payment by note will not give a cash-basis taxpayer a deduction. If you don't have the cash by year end and want to make a payment in order to get a deduction this year, borrow the money. Then use the cash to make the payment. That will give you the deduction now.

☐ (11) ***Worthless Assets:*** Losses may be realized for worthless assets, but they have to be shown by a complete transaction that fixes the loss by an identifiable event in the year the loss is taken. Where worthlessness may be difficult to prove, sell or dispose of the asset in the year you want the loss.

☐ (12) ***Partnership Losses:*** If you're a partner in a firm that has incurred losses this year and those losses will exceed the basis of your partnership interest, you'd better make a contribution of capital to the firm sufficient to equal this excess. *Reason:* if you don't, you'll get no deduction this year for your share of partnership losses over your basis. Of course, if you don't want the deduction this year, simply don't make the payment; get the deduction in a later year when you do make the payment or your account is credited with undrawn partnership profits.

☐ (13) ***Buying Equipment on Time:*** Even though you lay out little or no cash this year, you are entitled to: (1) a 20% first year writeoff on the full purchase price (up to $20,000 if you file a joint return; that can give you a $4,000 deduction), and (2) depreciation—the guidelines may permit shorter lives for your newly acquired assets.

☐ (14) ***Switch to the LIFO Inventory Method:*** If you see a continued uptrend in costs of inventory, you might switch to this method. You then value your inventories as though you sold the latest acquired items first. That leaves your lower earlier inventory costs as the cost of your closing inventory—cutting down on your profit for tax purposes.

☐ (15) ***Farmers:*** They can buy ahead on feed, seed, or other supplies for a deduction this year. Farmers can also level or grade their property for current deduction.

If clearing brush, trees, stumps, leveling and conditioning land has to be done, farmers have an option to deduct or capitalize such expenses (including depreciation of equipment used). Farmers may also deduct, rather than capitalize, soil and water conservation expenses.

[¶703.4] Year-End Tax Planning Strategy

A good way to start your year-end planning is to adopt some logical procedure. As a suggestion, try the following three steps:

Step One: Determine income to date. Then, check the transactions that may produce income over the balance of the year. Include security holdings and the amount of the potential gain or loss on them. Get the probable amount of income for this year and for next year. Also, figure the expense deductions that you'll be entitled to and arrive at your probable taxable income figure for this year and for next year. Then, calculate how much of this income can be controlled by you to fall into either this year or next year. Remember, accelerating one dollar of expense into this year from next year has the same effect as deferring one dollar of income from this year to next year.

In some instances, despite the probability of lower rates for next year, you may find that your current tax shifting strategy is to accelerate income into this year and postpone deductions until next year. If you're in this boat, you should calculate the amounts of income that can be accelerated and expenses that can be postponed.

Step Two: Where do you fall in the tax brackets for the years involved? That would depend on what income you expect in the next year. Of course, where you know next year will produce an unusual profit or be an exceptionally high income year, then, as we indicated above, your strategy should be to defer deductions into next year and accelerate income into this year.

Step Three: After determining taxable income and the amount of income that can be switched from one year to the next, you're ready to determine how much income you should switch from this year to next or vice versa.

[¶704] YEAR-END STRATEGIES FOR THE CLOSELY HELD CORPORATION

You've seen the basic approach to year-end tax planning. Now we'll get to some of the specific tax-saving moves a closely held corporation can take before its taxable year comes to a close.

[¶704.1] How Companies With Small Earnings Can Cut Their Taxes

As you know, a small corporation pays the 48% tax rate only on income over $25,000. Only a 22% tax applies for the first $25,000. So, if your company's earnings are in this range, in shifting income or expenses, aim to keep taxable income from going over the $25,000 mark.

If this is your first year in business, you have a special opportunity for limiting the corporation's income. As soon as income hits $25,000 (assuming there are no other considerations that make it inadvisable), end your tax year. That immediately starts your corporation on another $25,000, which will be taxed at only the 22% rate. It also means that if next year's income does not run too high, some of the income that would have been piled on top of this year's $25,000 (and be taxed at 48%) may wind up being taxed at 22% next year.

Example: Green Corporation began business in February 1975. By the end of 1975 it will have earned just about $25,000. In January 1976, because of a special order it filled, it will earn $10,000; but in the rest of 1976, it is expected to earn about $20,000. Originally, it was intended to let the first taxable year run 12 months and end on January 31, 1976. If that plan were followed, the corporation would have had income of $35,000—$10,000 of which would have been taxed at 48%. By ending the tax year on December 31, 1975, the corporation's income was only $25,000, all of which was taxable at 22%. For 1976, the taxable income will be $30,000, only $5,000 of which will be taxable at 48%. Net tax saving over the two-year period: $1,300.

[¶704.2] Year-End Dividend Problem

Accumulation of earnings is one of the major purposes for setting up your business operations under the corporate umbrella. However, your corporation cannot go on merrily accumulating earnings indefinitely without a penalty tax. As you know, there is an accumulated earnings penalty tax. The tax starts at 27½% and jumps to 38½% where accumulated taxable income goes over $150,000.

Before paying a dividend to avoid the penalty, consider the consequences of not paying the dividend. There may be a lower tax by paying the penalty instead of having the stockholders pay a tax on the dividends at their tax bracket. Suppose a $1,000 dividend is paid. The stockholder, assuming he's in the 62% bracket, will keep $380 of that. Suppose the corporation pays no dividend and pays a $275 penalty tax for accumulating that $1,000. Eventually, the remaining $725 will come to the stockholder—via a liquidation of the corporation, let us assume. Assuming he pays a tax of 25% on that, or $181, he is still left with $544 after taxes, which is still more than the $380 he would have left if a dividend was paid.

[¶704.3] How to Pay Dividends

If you don't want to pay cash, you can distribute property. Stockholders pick up the property at fair market value and pay a tax on that. If dividends are paid to another corporation, the receiving corporation has a dividend equal to the basis of the property to the distributing corporation (if that's lower) and takes the 85% dividend credit against that.

However, if your corporation distributes this kind of property as a dividend it will be taxed as ordinary income on the lower of: (1) the depreciation taken on that property (after 1961), or (2) the difference between basis and fair market value. Further, if your corporation distributes depreciable real property, it may recapture income under §1250.

[¶704.4] When to Pay the Dividend

The dividend may be declared in one year and paid in the next. So long as you pay it within 2½ months after the close of the tax year, it is treated as having been paid in the year it was declared. The advantage of this move is that the stockholders don't have to pick up the dividend income until the year after it was declared.

If the stockholders would rather have the dividend in the year it was declared, make sure you pay it in that year. If it's a regular policy of the corporation to mail dividend checks on December 31, mailing on that date will postpone the dividend income until next year—when the checks are received. So, if the stockholders want the income that year, make sure the checks are delivered before year end or make it clear they are available for the asking before the last day of the year.

Maybe You Can Shift Dividend Income: You can cut your tax bite by giving stock to children in low tax brackets before the dividend is to be paid.

However, if you have a close corporation, there is a timing precaution that you should observe to make an effective transfer of dividends. Make sure that you transfer the stock before the date the dividend is *declared*. Dividends on stock transferred after the declaration date but before the record date have been taxed to the donor of a close corporation.

[¶704.5] How a Change in Tax Rates Affects Close Corporations' Dividends

Here are the considerations raised by tax rate cuts:

☐ (1) If next year's rates are likely to be lower than this year's, a dividend received by a stockholder next year will be worth more after taxes to him than a dividend received this year.
☐ (2) Where the dividend is very substantial in relation to the stockholder's other normal year-to-year income, putting the dividend income into next year might make the stockholder eligible for income averaging, thus cutting his taxes on the dividend still more (i.e., in addition to the rate reduction he'd enjoy where income averaging is not available).
☐ (3) Where a substantial dividend can be paid either this year or next year, to determine which year is best for the stockholders, determine the tax brackets in which the dividends would fall if received in each year. If there are no other dividends, to be very precise, first deduct the dividend exclusion in each year ($100; $200 if stock is held jointly or by both husband and wife).

[¶704.6] Dividend Paying Policy for the Deficit Corporation

If your corporation has an accumulated deficit from the past few years but is currently making money, you may be in a good position to pick up some tax-free corporate distributions. *Reason:* a corporate distribution is only taxable to the extent of its accumulated earnings and profits (plus its current year's earnings and profits) of the year the payout is made. So, by timing these distributions to occur in a year when earnings and profits are low, any excess over this amount will be treated first as a return of capital, then as capital gains.

[¶704.7] Stockholder-Corporation Relations

Look out for constructive dividends. If there are outstanding loans on the books for a long time, the Treasury may say there's no intention on the stockholder's part to repay and then treat the loans as dividends. Some repayments before the end of the year can help overcome such a Treasury attack.

Also check to see if the corporation made any payments for the stockholders with the understanding that they will repay them. If so, get the repayments in before year end if possible; that will help prove they were always intended as loans.

(1) Timing Stock Redemptions: If you expect a redemption to result in capital gains, time it to fall in a year when your offsetting losses can cut or eliminate it. If there's a chance of your redemption being a dividend, time it to fall in a year of low or no corporate earnings (assuming there's no accumulated income). The redemption occurs at the time you endorse and turn over your stock certificates to the corporation.

(2) Timing 12-month Liquidation Distributions: Look over the stockholders' tax picture before you make distributions. Where the 12-month period after adoption of a plan of liquidation cuts across two taxable years of the stockholders, the corporation can split its distribution. This year, for example, an amount equal to their bases can be distributed without tax. Then, next year, when they get the balance, they'll have capital gains that they may be able to offset with losses.

(3) Income Averaging Can Affect Your Strategy: Keep in mind that deferred compensation when received in the future may be subject to income averaging, which will cut the tax still further when received.

[¶704.8] Do You Expect Unusual Capital Gains or Big Losses Next Year?

If you have a corporation that will have an unusually big capital gain or especially big losses next year, you may want to have it elect to be a Subchapter S corporation—one that is not taxed as a corporation. Then the gain or the loss can be passed on directly to you and your co-stockholders without double tax.

[¶704.9] Where Your Subchapter S Corporation and You Have Different Tax Years, Look Out for Bunched Income

When you elected Subchapter S, you may have seen an opportunity to postpone tax. However, extreme care should be used on timing distributions from Subchapter S corporations, since only distributions that have been taxed to you in your previous taxable years are received tax free.

[¶704.10] Did Your Subchapter S Corporation Have a Profit in Prior Years And a Loss This Year?

When you get a distribution of previously taxed income from a Subchapter S corporation, it is reduced by your share of the corporation's losses that you picked up for any years after the profit was earned by the corporation. However, the previously taxed income is not reduced by the current year's corporate loss that you will pick up currently. So, it becomes important to distribute previously taxed profit this year (the loss year).

[¶704.11] Did You Figure Wrong When You Elected Subchapter S?

Suppose you anticipated a large capital gain or ordinary loss this year and elected to avoid corporate taxation and pass through the gain or loss to the stockholders under Subchapter S. Now it turns out your calculations were wrong and you wish you had never made the election. What can you do before the end of the year to get out of this poor choice? Revoking the election wouldn't help because, except for revocations in the first month of the taxable year, the revocation is not effective until the following year. However, a disqualifying act before year end would terminate the election for the entire year.

[¶704.12] Section 1244 Stock Losses

There is a yearly limit on the amount of ordinary loss deduction that you can take on §1244 losses—$25,000; $50,000 on a joint return. (§1244 stock is special stock allowed in small business corporations, the loss on which is treated as an ordinary, rather than a capital loss.) If near year end you are prepared to sell out and take your loss, sell enough stock this year so that you'll get your maximum deduction; then sell the rest next year and get another ordinary deduction.

In a situation where the stock seems to be approaching worthlessness, sell off enough of the stock to get your maximum ordinary loss this year; if worthlessness occurs next year, you'll get ordinary deduction (within the applicable limits) for the rest.

[¶704.13] Business Gifts at Year End

Since year end is often the season of making business gifts, it's important to check your lists carefully to be aware of whether or not you are making total gifts to one person of more than $25—the ceiling on a business gift deduction. (You may feel you have to do it anyhow for business reasons and give up the deduction; but at least you ought to be aware of the consequences of your acts.) In addition, you ought to be aware of the definitions of business gifts and where you can avoid falling within the definitions.

[¶704.14] "Gift" Can Qualify as Entertainment Expense

There's no ceiling on entertainment costs, but you have to have full substantiation.

Generally, says IRS, where an item might be either entertainment, on the one hand, or a gift or travel cost, on the other, it will be considered entertainment. But packaged food and beverages, for example, given to a customer for use at some other time, is a gift.

As for theatre and similar tickets of admission, if you go along it's entertainment even if you give the tickets to your guest. If you don't go along, you can treat the expense either as entertainment or a business gift.

IRS will treat these expenses (where you don't go along) as gifts unless you treat them as entertainment. Your original choice is not necessarily binding, however, since you can change your treatment later on (as much as three years after you file your return). If you intend to take advantage of this leverage, you had better make sure that you have the substantiation to back up either treatment.

[¶704.15] Net Operating Loss Carryovers

If you have an operating loss this year, watch these points:

☐ (1) You may be able to recover taxes starting from three years back.

☐ (2) Prior years' returns must be able to stand close audit. A carryback claim usually means the revenue agent will look for offsetting adjustments in prior year.

☐ (3) If you are a proprietorship or partnership, avoid long-term capital gains this year. Because they must be counted in full, they can wash out part or all of the carryback.

☐ (4) Increase the loss if the past years' potential tax recovery will stand it. Check possible advantage of selling buildings, machinery, or other depreciable business property at loss. The loss can be included in carryback and newly purchased property can be depreciated at new fast depreciation rates. Also, for machinery, equipment, and similar property you get the investment credit and the extra 20% first-year depreciation write off.

☐ (5) Corporate partial interest exemption, the Western Hemisphere deduction, and nonbusiness and personal deductions cut the amount of operating loss.

☐ (6) An individual's casualty losses can become part of a loss carryback.

☐ (7) Charitable contributions (as well as other deductions limited to a percentage of income) can't be deducted. A corporation can carry over any contributions not deductible this year, but an individual will lose all benefit of a charitable contribution in a loss year.

If you had losses in the last five years, watch these points:

☐ (1) This is the last year to realize on unused losses from five years ago. If necessary, boost income to use it up. Losses from four years ago and later years will apply to next year and later years.

☐ (2) Consider realizing capital gains or selling appreciated machinery, buildings, or other depreciable business property. The gains can be offset by loss carryovers. Newly purchased property can get a higher basis plus new, faster depreciation, the investment credit, and the 20% first-year write off.

[¶704.16] Audit of Pay Set-Up

Wages and salaries are by far the most compelling income and expense factor in any business. The final months of the year provide the last opportunity to arrange compensation policies for the minimum tax cost—both for employer and for employees.

Here are some of the important considerations:

Are Officer-Stockholders Getting the Best "Tax" Salary? That's the amount at which any increase will cost the employee-stockholder more in taxes than the corporation will save by the increase, and at which any decrease would cost the corporation more than the employee saves.

Bonus Declarations: Year-end bonus declarations and payments boost this year's compensation deductions, but you always have to be concerned with the problem of reasonableness. Suppose part of the compensation is disallowed as being unreasonable. The corporation loses the deduction and the employee still has income for what he received—so we have a double tax.

Protect against this result—especially in close corporations—by providing that the employee will have to repay to the corporation so much of the compensation as may finally be ruled to be unreasonable. In the year of repayment, the employee will get a tax deduction. If the repayment involves more than $3,000, the employee has a choice: He can treat the repayment as a deduction in the year of repayment or he can reduce the tax of the year of repayment by the amount of the tax he had to pay on that repaid compensation in the year he received it.

You may get an argument from the Treasury on this type of arrangement, but a court decision has upheld a similar arrangement calling for repayment of rent when a corporation rents property from its stockholder.

Can You Defer Compensation? This will delay tax on the employee or employee-stockholder. Check these points:

☐ (1) Compensation for your lawyer, accountant, or other independent contractor can be accrued though actual payment is deferred.

☐ (2) Bonuses can be accrued though paid next year.

☐ (3) Qualified profit-sharing or pension plans can be used to defer compensation income to employees while getting deduction.

☐ (4) Stock options also defer income, but there is no deduction where you use a qualified option, i.e., option price is at least 100% of market price of stock when option is granted. Qualified options are given special capital gains treatment by the Code. It's a good idea to check on whether any of your employees have disposed of their stock before three years after the stock was acquired. If so, you're entitled to a deduction. You could also use the employee stock purchase plan to defer income. Here, the option and/or stock must be held for at least two years and the stock itself for six months.

☐ (5) Unfunded agreement to pay additional compensation at future time defers both the tax and the deduction.

Accruing Deductions: If the corporation can use more deductions now but doesn't have the cash, it can accrue them (assuming, of course, the corporation uses the accrual method of accounting). It gets the deduction now and the employee has income when he receives it.

If you don't want the employee to have income this year, make sure the income is not available to him now. For example, you can declare a bonus payable due to the valuable services given by him this year to compensate him adequately for this year's services, and you can make the bonus payable next year, so that he has no choice in the matter. Then, he's taxed when he receives it. The employer, having a liability to pay the bonus this year (and being on an accrual basis) is entitled to the deduction now.

However, keep in mind the special rules if the employee is a more-than-50% stockholder, in which case the corporation has to pay the accrued salaries or bonuses within 2½ months after the end of the year. Otherwise, it loses its deduction altogether.

Pension and Profit-Sharing Accruals: If you have a qualified pension or profit-sharing plan, you can get the full deduction for your contribution this year even though you don't pay it until next year. You have to make the contribution no later than the due date of your tax return for this year, including extended due dates where permission is given to file late.

Salesmen's Advances: If you make advances to salesmen that they then must earn, you might lose out on a deduction this year if you require that the advances be paid back should the salesman quit or be fired without having earned his full advance. If there's not much likelihood of the salesman leaving with an unfavorable commission-drawing balance, you might remove the requirement of repayment and pin down your right to deduct the advances as soon as made.

Of course, the other side of the picture is the salesman's tax situation. If you want the salesman to be able to defer some of his income, you can make his advances repayable should he fail to earn them by the time he leaves your employ. That will postpone your deduction, but it will also defer his income.

Payments to Widows: Payments to a deceased employee's dependents (usually the widow) by an employer by reason of the employee's death is tax exempt to the recipient to the extent of $5,000. Where more than $5,000 is to be paid, consider paying the $5,000 tax-exempt portion this year and the balance in later years where tax rates are scheduled to drop. However, you must also take into account the relative tax brackets of the recipient in each of the years.

[¶705] HOW YOU CAN DIVIDE YOUR BUSINESS INTO SEVERAL CORPORATIONS TO YOUR ADVANTAGE

Establishing more than one corporation where possible yields a number of important advantages to the business interests involved:

☐ (1) The sale of property by several smaller corporations rather than by one big corporation results in a smaller tax; the sale of the property can be made through sale of the stock of one of the smaller corporations. Assume the smaller corporations' assets consist entirely of property up for sale. We sell the property by selling the stock; the gain will be taxed only once—to the stockholders, as capital gain.

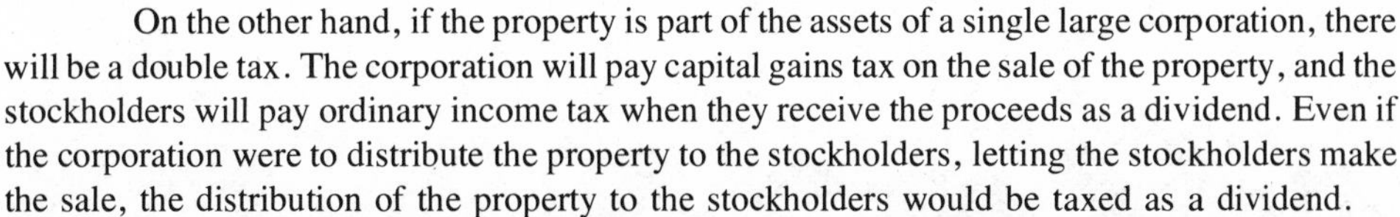

On the other hand, if the property is part of the assets of a single large corporation, there will be a double tax. The corporation will pay capital gains tax on the sale of the property, and the stockholders will pay ordinary income tax when they receive the proceeds as a dividend. Even if the corporation were to distribute the property to the stockholders, letting the stockholders make the sale, the distribution of the property to the stockholders would be taxed as a dividend.

☐ (2) Only the property that gives rise to a claim will be subject to any judgment resulting therefrom. If all the property were in one corporation, all the property would be subject to the judgment. When the judgment is greater than the value of the property involved, we are saved greater losses by spreading our property over several corporations.

☐ (3) By establishing separate corporations for different operations, we may qualify for extra tax benefits peculiar to a particular operation. For instance, one of the corporations may be engaged in foreign trade. If this function was carried out as part of a single corporation engaged in diversified activities, eligibility for tax benefits pertinent only to foreign trade might be denied.

☐ (4) Corporations are taxed at a lower rate on the first $25,000 (the surtax exemption) of taxable income. Thus, it has usually paid off taxwise to spread a business around in separate corporations, thereby spreading the income over as many surtax exemptions as possible. In the past these additional exemptions could be disallowed only where sham was involved or where the corporation was formed or acquired or property transferred to it and a major or principal purpose was to obtain the exemption or to avoid income taxes.

In order to eliminate unintended and substantial tax benefits to large corporations, the law now (beginning in 1975) limits a controlled group of corporations to one $25,000 surtax exemption and one $150,000 accumulated earnings credit.

[¶705.1] Restrictions on Multiple Corporations

Because of the tax advantages that multiple corporate set-ups can offer, many businesses are fragmented into a number of corporations for no other purpose than to save taxes. Of course, IRS bends every effort to upset these arrangements. Actually, there are three ways in which multiple corporation advantages can be removed or modified:

(1) Lumping All The Corporations Into One: Here IRS employs §482 to shift the income and deductions from all of the corporations into one on the theory that that is required to properly reflect income. See *Aldon Homes*, 33 TC 582, 1960.

(2) Disallowance Under §269: Under this section, if you acquired control of a corporation for the principal purpose of securing the benefit of a deduction, credit, or other allowance (including a surtax exemption) which you would not have been able to get otherwise, that credit, deduction, or other allowance is disallowed. See *James Realty Co.*, 280 F.2d 394, CA-8, 1960.

(3) Disallowed Transfers to New Corporations: Under §1551, if a corporation transfers property (other than cash) to another new, or inactive, corporation and a major purpose of the transfer is to get an additional surtax exemption, that surtax exemption can be disallowed. The 1964 tax law made this provision somewhat tougher by applying it to indirect transfers, too—i.e., transfer of money that the transferee corporation uses to buy assets from the transferor corporation or transfers of property to stockholders who, in turn, turn the property over to the other corporation. Also, §1551 can apply to transfers by individuals to a corporation where five or less individuals own at least 80% of the stock.

SECTION VIII

MAKING THE MOST OF FRINGE BENEFITS

One of the main reasons a businessman will want to incorporate is to take advantage of one or more of the various fringe benefits that are available to an employee of a corporation. By far, the most coveted fringe benefit is the tax-exempt qualified benefit plan. These plans provide the employee with enormous potential to build wealth for retirement years. This section discusses the advantages of these pension and profit-sharing plans, along with other money-saving fringe benefit opportunities.

[¶801] ADVANTAGES OF TAX-SHELTERED PENSION AND PROFIT-SHARING PLANS

There two main types of tax-exempt employee trusts generally used by small corporations: profit-sharing plans and pension plans. Each has advantages and disadvantages. Which one will be most desirable in a given situation will depend on the objectives to be accomplished. There are a number of other forms of qualified benefit plans used by larger corporations, many of which are publicly traded. In most instances, however, these plans have little appeal to the small businessman.

Pension and profit-sharing plans that qualify for favorable tax treatment are by far the most economic and advantageous methods for corporate employees to accumulate funds for retirement income and deferred compensation.

Under a qualified plan, the corporation gets a present deduction. The contributions build up by earning a return free of tax. With one minor exception (the term portion of the premium in an insured plan), there is no taxability to the employee until he begins to draw money from the fund. In the case of a profit-sharing plan, the employee's stake may be increased as the result of the reallocation of nonvested amounts left in the accounts of employees whose services have been terminated.

Today's intense activity in forming corporations is in large measure the result of the desire to install a corporate pension or profit-sharing plan. Following are some of the many reasons for this:

☐ High tax rates on corporations make it worthwhile to set up a pension or profit-sharing plan. It costs a corporation only 52 cents to provide $1 of employee benefits under such plans.
☐ High individual tax rates impede a businessman's chance to build his own security out of income—making tax-protected pension and profit-sharing retirement plans attractive vehicles to provide retirement income.
☐ For many corporations, a pension or profit-sharing plan now represents an attractive investment vehicle. Money put into a trust builds up capital values tax free for stockholder-employees. The same money distributed as dividends would be subject to a high tax rate.

[¶801.1] How the Tax Law Favors Pension and Profit-Sharing Plans

The government, by specific design, encourages the adoption of pension and profit-sharing plans by allowing those which qualify under the Internal Revenue Code (§401) certain special tax privileges. Some of the more favorable tax advantages of these plans are:

☐ (1) The corporation can deduct contributions to a qualified plan.
☐ (2) Earnings on funds held by a qualified plan are allowed to appreciate tax free.
☐ (3) Lump-sum distributions on retirement, death, or other termination are taxed under a favorable income-averaging formula. Distribution attributable to pre-Pension Reform Act of 1974 contributions are taxed at a favorable capital gains rate and those attributable to post-1974 are subject to special ten-year income averaging.
☐ (4) Distributions paid out over a long period get the special annuity-tax treatment.
☐ (5) Distributions are exempt from gift tax where the employee designates a beneficiary.
☐ (6) Death benefits attributable to the corporation's contributions are exempt from estate tax provided they are payable to a named beneficiary, not to the employee's estate. Death benefits attributable to contributions made by an employee are subject to estate taxes.
☐ (7) Up to $5,000 of death benefits can be received income-tax free by the employee's beneficiary.
☐ (8) Distributions are usually taxed at a lower rate because the employee receives them at a time (retirement) when he is in a lower tax bracket.
☐ (9) The employee can also use the qualified plan as a tax-sheltered savings account. Participating employees (a professional in a professional corporation qualifies as an employee) may contribute up to 10% of their annual earnings each year. Although the employee gets no deduction for the contribution, the earnings on these savings are allowed to accumulate tax free and at payout time qualify for the same beneficial tax treatment outlined above.

To point up the advantages of a qualified pension or profit-sharing plan in accumulating capital, let's follow through on what happens to dividend dollars, salary and bonus dollars, and dollars going into a tax-exempt trust in the case of a 45-year-old employee in a 50% personal tax bracket. The corporation is subject to a corporate tax rate of 48%.

If his corporation allocates $10,000 to dividends, corporate taxes take $4,800 at the outset. A $5,200 dividend payable to the employee is then subject to a 50% personal income tax, which leaves him a balance of $2,600. Therefore, to provide him with dividend income of $2,600 actually requires earnings of $10,000 for the corporation.

Each year this costly process is repeated. If the employee invests his $2,600 net dividend in tax-free municipal bonds at an average tax-free interest of 5% and repeats this each year for 20 years until he is age 65, he accumulates approximately $90,000.

To save corporate tax, $10,000 of the corporation's earnings could be distributed to our key man as a salary increase or annual bonus. The corporation does not pay a tax on this $10,000 because it is fully deductible as compensation. But the top-bracket employee is still taxed at 50% each year, leaving him with only $5,000 after taxes to invest.

If he invests the $5,000 annually for 20 years in tax-free municipal bonds at an average of 5% interest, his ultimate accumulation through salary increase or bonus will approximate $180,000.

Funds contributed by a corporation on an employee's behalf to a tax-exempt retirement plan escape corporate tax entirely. Also, the employee is not taxed at the time the contributions are made. Moreover, earnings of the retirement fund, including any capital gain in asset values, are also tax exempt. If, therefore, $10,000 of gross pre-tax corporate earnings were put in the employee's credit each year for 20 years in his company's tax-exempt retirement plan and this fund was steadily invested in bonds paying 8%, the fund would accumulate about $495,000 for him by age 65.

Voluntary Contributions: The employee can also use the qualified plan as a tax-sheltered savings account. Participating shareholder-employees may contribute up to 10% of their annual earnings each year. Although the employee gets no deduction for the contribution, the earnings on these savings are allowed to accumulate tax free and at payout time may qualify for capital gain treatment. Here's an example of how this works:

Let's assume the employee is in the 50% tax bracket and deposits $2,500 a year of his after-tax income in the trust. Without the trust he would have earned 4% on his money after taxes (on an 8% corporate bond), assuming the trust puts his money into the same type of investment. The result, after 25 years, is an additional $25,000 by using the trust. The earnings with the tax shelter of the trust would amount to $73,000; and after deducting $17,000 for taxes, he would have $56,000 left. Outside the trust, he would be able to accumulate only $31,000 after taxes.

[¶801.2] Wealth-Injector Factor in Qualified Plans

Two thousand dollars paid annually under a qualified compensation plan and invested at 6% interest can on retirement yield almost four times as much as the same sum paid to a man in the 50% tax bracket without any plan and invested at 6% interest in a conventional non-tax-sheltered investment. Increase the return, and the disparity is even more marked. All this is dramatically demonstrated by the table on the next page.

The table assumes an annual payment of $2,000 under a qualified plan for a person in the 50% tax bracket and the same sum paid to an individual without a plan. The table shows the comparative results when the amount is invested at different rates of interest—6, 8, 10, and 12%—over a span of 35 years. Thus, assuming a return of 12%, the figures in the lower right-hand corner of the table show that at the end of 35 years there will be $966,926 accumulated under a qualified plan as against a mere $118,121 without a plan.

True the amount accumulated under a qualified plan will be subject to tax when paid out to the executive during retirement, but it will escape tax altogether if paid to his widow or named beneficiary. If the executive takes down the whole bundle in a lump sum, it's taxable at favorable tax rates (capital gain and/or a special ten-year income averaging), which makes the actual income tax lower than if he were taxed on the whole bundle as ordinary income in the year of receipt and used regular five-year income averaging.

The amazing thing about this demonstration of the wealth-building power of qualified plans is that it doesn't take into account the full potential. It doesn't take into account additional voluntary contributions on the part of the professional, which, if made, will accumulate within the plan tax free. What's more, it doesn't take into account the great injection of wealth that takes place under a qualified profit-sharing plan when forfeitures are added to the kitty.

Wealth-Injector Chart

	6%		8%		10%		12%	
Number of Years	Under Plan	No Plan	Under Plan	No Plan	Under Plan	No Plan	Under Plan	No Plan
After 1 year	$ 2,120	$1,030	$ 2,160	$1,040	$ 2,200	$1,050	$ 2,240	$ 1,060
2	4,367	2,091	4,493	2,122	4,620	2,153	4,749	2,183
3	6,749	3,184	7,012	3,246	7,282	3,310	7,559	3,375
4	9,274	4,309	9,733	4,416	10,210	4,526	10,706	4,637
5	11,950	5,468	12,672	5,633	13,431	5,802	14,230	5,975
6	14,787	6,662	15,846	6,898	16,974	7,142	18,178	7,394
7	17,794	7,892	19,273	8,214	20,871	8,549	22,593	8,897
8	20,982	9,159	22,975	9,583	25,158	10,027	27,551	10,491
9	24,361	10,464	26,973	11,006	29,874	11,578	33,097	12,181
10	27,943	11,808	31,211	12,486	35,061	13,207	39,309	13,972
11	31,740	13,192	35,868	14,026	40,767	14,917	46,266	15,870
12	35,964	14,618	40,897	15,627	47,044	16,713	54,058	17,882
13	40,242	16,086	46,329	17,292	53,948	18,599	62,785	20,015
14	44,777	17,599	52,195	19,024	61,543	20,579	72,559	22,276
15	49,578	19,157	58,531	20,825	69,897	22,657	83,507	24,673
16	54,673	20,762	65,374	22,698	79,087	24,840	95,767	27,213
17	60,073	22,414	72,763	24,645	89,196	27,132	109,499	29,906
18	65,797	24,117	80,744	26,671	100,316	29,539	124,879	32,760
19	71,865	25,870	89,364	28,778	112,548	32,066	142,105	35,786
20	78,297	27,676	98,673	30,969	126,003	34,719	161,397	38,993
21	85,115	29,537	108,727	33,248	140,803	37,505	183,005	42,392
22	92,342	31,453	118,585	35,618	157,083	40,430	207,206	45,996
23	100,003	33,426	130,232	38,083	174,991	43,502	236,308	49,816
24	108,123	35,459	142,711	40,646	194,680	46,727	264,668	53,865
25	116,730	37,553	156,287	43,312	216,348	50,113	298,668	58,156
26	125,854	39,710	170,950	46,084	240,183	53,669	336,748	62,706
27	135,525	41,931	186,786	48,968	266,401	57,403	379,398	67,528
28	145,757	44,219	203,889	51,966	295,241	61,323	427,166	72,640
29	156,622	46,575	222,361	55,085	326,965	65,439	480,665	78,058
30	168,139	49,003	242,319	58,328	361,862	69,761	540,585	83,802
31	186,347	51,503	263,865	61,701	400,248	74,299	607,695	89,890
32	193,288	54,078	287,134	65,210	442,473	79,064	682,859	96,343
33	207,005	56,730	312,265	68,858	488,920	84,067	767,042	103,184
34	221,545	59,462	339,406	72,652	540,012	89,320	861,327	110,435
35	236,958	62,276	368,720	76,598	596,213	94,336	966,926	118,121

[¶802] WHICH ONE TO CHOOSE IF YOUR COMPANY CAN'T AFFORD BOTH

Profit-sharing plans and money-purchase pension plans are defined-contribution plans. The corporation may make contributions to these plans up to a limit of 15% of the employee's compensation. In any year an employee contributes less than 15% he may carry over the deficit to the extent of 25% of his compensation or $25,000, whichever is less. In a defined-benefit pension plan, there is no limit on contributions. However, benefits are limited to the lesser of $75,000 per year or 100% of the employee's average compensation for his three highest paid years.

A profit-sharing plan does not place a fixed commitment on the corporation. The corporate contributions may be contingent on the existence of profits in excess of a specified amount; the corporation may even reserve its decision and determine at the end of each year whether or not a contribution will be made for that year. The profit-sharing plan need not obligate the corporation in any way until it determines that it wants to make a contribution. A pension plan that provides fixed benefits requires the corporation to contribute enough money to carry the current cost of funding the pensions promised by the plan.

The money that the corporation contributes to a profit-sharing plan must be allocated among the shareholders and other employees of the corporation substantially in relation to their compensation. Only slight additional credit may be allowed for length of service. A pension plan allows the corporation's contribution to be allocated according to salary, length of service, and age. The plan can provide that the amount of pension to be paid to an individual shareholder or other employee is to be geared to his length of service and to his compensation. Then the annual contribution is actuarially allocated to the accounts of the shareholders and other employees so as to fund the individual's pension expectancy. Thus, in the case of a 60-year-old employee who is to retire at 65, the total amount actuarially determined to be needed to fund his pension has to be taken out of the corporation's contribution for the next five years. On the other hand, it would be necessary to allocate a very much smaller amount to a 30-year-old employee because the corporation can take 35 years to build up the amount needed to fund his pension. This means that in a pension plan, a much larger proportion of each year's contributions will be allocated to the account of those shareholders and other employees who are along in years when the plan is inaugurated.

In a profit-sharing plan, participating shareholders and other employees of a corporation get the benefit of appreciation of the assets of the fund. They also carry the risk of loss with respect to any funds credited to their account. Normally, in a corporation's pension plan, the corporation gets the benefit of any appreciation in the value of fund assets in the form of a reduction of the amount that has to be contributed in order to fund pension commitments. Similarly, the corporation, in effect, carries the risk of loss because, to carry on the plan, the professional corporation will have to make increased contributions to offset a loss in the value of the fund's assets.

Many corporations setting up pension plans use the money-purchase form. With money-purchase pension plans, the corporation merely makes annual contributions, usually expressed as a percentage of the employee's salary. The participants get only as much pension as can be purchased with the money that is accumulated. This type of pension plan puts the risk of loss on the employee and gives him the advantage of any appreciation.

Another type of pension plan provides variable benefits by crediting units rather than dollars to the employee's account. When the participant starts drawing down his pension, the number of dollars he receives will depend on the value of the units. The more the fund has appreciated in value, the larger the pension. This kind of pension plan is designed to give protection against inflation. Where the funds are invested in equities, the amount of the pension will depend on the market value of the shares at the time of distribution.

[¶802.1] How to Choose Between Pension and Profit-Sharing Plan

One of the most important questions a corporation is faced with during the initial incorporation procedure is which kind of plan to adopt. The answer most times does not come easily. Both pension and profit-sharing plans have many favorable features that can be applied to a variety of corporate needs.

Both types of plan can be used to make substantial additions to the real income of employees without increasing their current income tax expense. Both provide this advantage at low, net, after-tax cost to the employer-company. Both can include life insurance and annuity features. Both can be combined with an employee savings or thrift plan.

Generally speaking, if the corporation's objective is to provide definite amounts of retirement income and it wishes to make a firm commitment in that respect, a pension plan will best answer the purpose. If the business is cyclical and it wants its payments into the plan to depend directly on profits, and if the remaining period of service of older employees is sufficient to permit worthwhile accumulations on their account, a profit-sharing plan probably will be preferred. A profit-sharing plan may *not* have a contribution formula equal to a percentage of compensation regardless of profits (*Rev. Rul. 70-182*, CB 1970-1, 88).

A diversity of possible provisions can be made as to benefits under both pension and profit-sharing plans. The amount and nature of future benefits to be received by the employees and the extent of prospective administrative, investment, and actuarial expenses are other factors that may influence decisions as to the type of plan to be used.

Here is a list of the salient features of both pension and profit-sharing plans to help you in your choice of a plan:

Profit-Sharing	***Pension***
(1) Generally, favors younger employees.	(1) Generally, favors older employees.
(2) Need not provide retirement benefits.	(2) Must provide retirement benefits.
(3) Contributions can be made only from profits (includes accumulated earnings).	(3) Contributions must be made for profitable as well as for loss years.
(4) Definite contribution formula not necessary; contributions need only be "recurring and substantial."	(4) Must have a definite contribution formula that will provide for definitely determinable benefits.
(5) Contributions cannot exceed 15% of year's payroll.	(5) Contributions to a money-purchase pension plan can't exceed 15% of year's payroll. Benefits under a defined-benefit plan can't exceed the lesser of $75,000 or 100% of compensation.

Profit-Sharing	*Pension*
(6) Forfeitures may be allocated by a fixed formula in favor of remaining participants.	(6) Forfeitures must be used to decrease future cost to employer.
(7) No more than 50% of a participant's account may be invested in life insurance.	(7) May be completely funded by investment in life insurance.
(8) Life insurance on the lives of key employees is allowed and also "incidental" life insurance.	(8) May provide insurance protection of 100 times the employee's monthly pension as a death benefit.
(9) May provide for layoff, accident, and health benefits as "incidental" benefits.	(9) May not provide for benefits not usually included in a pension plan (e.g., layoff, sickness, accident, hospitalization, or medical reimbursement).
(10) Distributions may be made after a fixed number of years (e.g., two) sufficient to indicate that a deferred-compensation plan was contemplated.	(10) Distributions may be made at retirement, disability, death, or other termination of employment.

[¶802.2] Funding Past Services

Although the rules as to forfeitures would seem to give duration of service a strong advantage in a profit-sharing plan, there is a compelling factor pulling the other way, too. This is the factor of benefits provided for past services—years spent with the corporation before any employee benefit plan was in effect. The advantage here is with a pension plan. A common practice in setting up a qualified pension plan is to provide for benefits in the amount of a percentage of compensation for each year of employment after the plan begins and a slightly smaller percentage for each year of employment before the plan was instituted. True, it is possible to obtain Treasury approval also for profit-sharing benefits that take into consideration the relative length of service as well as relative compensation (IT 3685, IT 3686). However, since such a provision may discriminate in favor of highly paid employees, its inclusion is discouraged.

Thus, we might say the employee with long tenure with his corporation has more assurance that his long service will be rewarded under a pension plan, since the reward is part of the plan itself rather than something that depends on forfeitures, as with a profit-sharing plan.

Another and simpler method of funding past services in setting up a pension plan is to provide that benefits shall be a substantial percentage of average compensation over a certain period prior to the inception of the plan—for example, 50% of compensation for the past five years. This makes it possible to give a full pension to highly paid employees who are within a few years of retirement when the plan is begun, just as if the plan had been in effect during all their working years, something you couldn't do with a profit-sharing plan.

[¶802.3] When a Profit-Sharing Plan Might Be Preferred to a Fixed-Benefit Pension Plan

In some cases, a profit-sharing plan might be preferred by a corporation. One such situation might be where the stockholder-employees are young men and other employees are older (see preceding paragraph). Another situation might be where the corporation does not want to be tied down to a fixed annual commitment to a pension fund. For example, the shareholders of a newly formed corporation might want to put in a retirement plan but are cautious about being committed to a fixed payment until they can see how successful the corporation will be. The answer might be a profit-sharing plan, which does not place a fixed commitment on the employer. Contributions can be made contingent on the existence of profits in excess of a specified amount—such as profits above $25,000.

Another situation where a profit-sharing plan might be advantageous involves a corporation that has a rapid turnover of clerical help and other employees. In a profit-sharing plan, participating employees get the benefit of forfeitures resulting from employees who leave the firm before their accounts are fully vested. The amounts the departing employees forfeit are reallocated to the accounts of those who stay on. Since the stockholder-employees are likely to stay on, their accounts can build up rapidly as a result of these forfeitures. In contrast, forfeitures in a pension plan cannot be used to benefit the remaining employees but must be used to reduce the future annual contributions to the plan.

Use of a unit formula can also benefit longer-service employees. One typical formula used is to allocate forfeitures to each employee in proportion to the number of units he has in the plan.

[¶802.4] Tailor Your Plan to Fit Your Needs

The tax law and IRS regulations and procedures fix certain limits within which a pension or profit-sharing plan must be designed in order to receive an advance ruling that the plan is a qualified plan. A plan can't be set up for the exclusive benefit of stockholder-employees, nor can it discriminate in favor of stockholder-employees. There are rules as to who has to be included in the plan, the amount of contributions, and regularity of contributions. The contribution to the employee's pension or profit-sharing account combined with his salary, bonus, or other compensation must be "reasonable" and "permanent." Make sure also that total compensation, including contributions to the pension plan, does not exceed a reasonable level.

[¶803] STOCK BONUS PLANS

Qualified stock bonuses are used where the primary objective is to develop equity and capital values for a broad cross section of employees. This is accomplished by a stock bonus trust in which carryover contributions are made in stock or by a profit-sharing trust in which the contributions are invested carryover stock. These plans are similar to profit-sharing and thrift plans, and similar statutory rules apply (Reg. §1.401(b)(iii)). (See §801.) Thus stock ownership through stock bonuses may permit the employee to build his net worth without tax, to cash it in for himself at capital gains rates, or to hold his stock so that his family can cash it in without tax or at capital gains rates. Also stock ownership avoids the inflationary trends to which other employee benefit plans are susceptible as the value of the stock keeps pace with inflationary tendencies.

Nonqualified plans are similar to bonus and incentive plans. The stock bonus plan may call for immediate issue of stock to the employee or for deferred distribution. The immediate distribution plan has the purpose of getting an immediate deduction for the employer and an immediate benefit (at the cost of a tax liability) for the employee. This is appropriate where there is a business continuation or management succession aim to be served. The deferred stock bonus plan results in a future deduction for the employer and defers taxation to the employee. Such a plan is appropriate where there is a retirement aim, where the employer desires to reduce turnover, and where an objective is to benefit the employee by enabling him to eventually obtain the future appreciation on the stock credited to him without reducing his equity therein by an immediate tax liability.

[¶804] STOCK OPTIONS

Stock options have been in use for some time as a means of providing additional compensation and added incentives to employees. They have also been used to give executives and other highly compensated employees a risk-free ride on the appreciation of a company's stock. However, in order to avoid a current tax on the exercise of the option, you have to comply with the strict requirements of the code (§421-425). Where a nonqualified stock option has a readily ascertainable fair market value at the time it is granted, the employee has taxable income (compensation) at that time in the amount of the excess of such value over the amount paid. The later exercise of the option is not a taxable event. If the option is transferred or the option stock (acquired on exercise) is sold or exchanged, gain or loss is recognized.

[¶804.1] Basic Tax Rules Affecting Qualified Options

No income tax is imposed either at the time the option is granted or at the time the option is exercised and the stock is transferred to the employee. Similarly, no business expense deduction is allowed to the employer corporation (or a parent or subsidiary of that corporation) at any time with respect to these options.

Price: One of the requirements of a qualified option is that the price under the option be not less than the fair market value of the stock at the time the option is granted. Where there is an attempt made in good faith to price the option at the market value of the stock but the market value is underestimated, the option will not be disqualified; but 1½ times the difference between the option price and the fair market value of the stock at the time the option is granted (or the difference between the option price and market value at exercise if smaller) will be taxed as ordinary income when the option is exercised.

Holding Period: Another limitation on a qualified stock option is that the stock must be held for at least three years. The law provides that in those cases where it is not held for this three-year period, the option will still be a qualified option, but the spread between the option price and the value of the stock at the time the option is exercised will be treated as ordinary income at the time the stock is sold. However, in such cases the employee will never be taxed on more than his gain.

Capital Gain: The determination of the type of capital gain, i.e., whether short term or long term, will depend on the length of time the stock has been held. Thus, any gain where the stock has been held beyond the three-year period specified with respect to qualified stock options will result in long-term gain. Where the stock is disposed of in less than three years and, in addition to the amount treated as ordinary income, there is an amount treated as capital gain, this capital gain will be either short term (if the stock is held six months or less) or long term (if it is held more than six months).

Where the employee dies after having purchased the stock but before holding it for the specified period of time, this holding period is waived.

[¶804.2]Small Businesses With Equity Capital Below $2,000,000

Although immediately before the option is granted the employee must not own stock representing more than 5% of the voting power or value of all classes of stock, in the case of certain small businesses, the employee may own up to 10% of voting power or value before being disqualified. For a corporation with equity capital of less than $1 million, this percentage is to be 10%; and for one with equity capital of $2 million, it is to be 5%. Between these two levels of equity capital, the allowable percentage decreases gradually from the 10% to the 5% level as the amount of corporate equity rises. Equity capital for this purpose is the assets of the corporation, adjusted for any change in their basis less any indebtedness of the corporation. Where a parent or subsidiary also is involved, adjustments are made to delete intercorporate ownership. For this purpose, the individual is considered to own stock owned directly or indirectly by his brothers, sisters, wife, ancestors, and lineal descendants. Stock owned directly or indirectly by a corporation, partnership, estate, or trust for this purpose is considered as being owned proportionately by shareholders, partners, or beneficiaries.

[¶804.3] Techniques for Saving Taxes

There are two important provisions that affect qualified stock options, both of which emphasize the need for careful planning in timing the exercise of stock options, taking into account the market price of the stock, the earned income and tax preferences of the holder, and other factors.

(1) ***Minimum Tax:*** The difference between the option price of stock bought under a qualified stock option and the market value of the stock at the time the option is exercised is a tax preference subject to the 10% minimum tax on tax preferences in excess of $30,000 plus regular income taxes payable.

(2) ***Interplay With Earned Income Ceiling:*** There is a special tax rate ceiling on earned income, such as salary, cash bonus, etc. The ceiling is 50% for 1972 and later years.

However, tax preferences over $30,000 reduce, dollar for dollar, the earned income eligible for the special tax ceiling. Tax preferences are the same for this purpose as for the minimum tax and so include the difference between the market price of optioned stock at the time of exercise and the option price.

How the Interplay of Other Tax Rules Affects the Value of the Option: Here's an illustration of how the interplay of the tax preference income and the ceiling on earned income affects the value of the option.

Let's assume the following:

In 1972, Jones, married and filing a joint return, has $90,000 salary and bonus, $10,000 dividends on stock, $5,000 unreimbursed travel expenses, and $10,000 itemized deductions and personal exemptions. During the year, he exercises a qualified stock option to buy 5,000 shares of his company's stock at $10 (at a time when the stock is selling for $30). He has no other tax-preference income. His tax is calculated as follows:

Salary and bonus	$ 90,000
Dividends	10,000
Gross income	$100,000
Unreimbursed travel and entertainment expenses	5,000
Adjusted gross income	$ 95,000
Itemized deductions and personal exemptions	10,000
Taxable income	$ 85,000

Income tax on $85,000 = $36,547

Earned taxable income is:

(a) $90,000 (salary) / $95,000 (adjusted gross income) × $85,000 (taxable income) =		$ 80,530
(b) *Deduct:* Excess of stock value over option price	$100,000	
Less	30,000	$ 70,000
Net earned taxable income		$ 10,530

The top tax bracket on $10,530 is below 50%, so the 50% tax limit is useless to Jones. Thus, Jones cannot use the special tax computation on earned income because of his exercise of the stock option.

Exercising the stock option will also result in an additional tax on his excess tax preferences. This is calculated as follows:

Stock value	$150,000		
Option price	50,000		
Excess		$100,000	
Deduct	$ 30,000		
Regular income tax	36,547	66,547	
Net preference income		$ 33,453	
Tax on $33,453 at 10%			$ 3,345

Adding the tax on preference income to his regular tax of $36,547 puts Jones's total tax at $39,892.

If Jones did not exercise the stock option, he would have been eligible for the special 50% tax on earned income. This would have reduced his tax to $35,177 with no additional tax on preference income. Thus, exercising the stock option costs him an extra tax of $4,715.

Finding the Tax Money: The minimum tax on the supposed value of a stock option at the time of its exercise may create a problem of finding the tax money. If other resources are not available, the executive on exercising the option may be compelled by practical necessity to sell part of the stock acquired to meet his added tax liability, which, as we've indicated, may be quite substantial in future years when we take into account possible loss of the earned-income ceiling due to excess tax-preference income.

This practical situation raises a company policy question of whether or not this added burden should not be taken into account in fixing the number of shares of stock to be optioned. This factor will have to be balanced against the added dilution of ownership that may result. Alternately an additional cash payment to the executive might be considered.

[¶804.4] Qualifying for Favorable Tax Treatment

An option will be eligible for the favorable tax treatment available on eventual disposition of the option stock if it satisfies the following requirements of §422 as a qualified stock option:

☐ (1) The option may be granted to an individual for any reason connected with his employment by a corporation or its parent or subsidiary corporation.
☐ (2) The option must be for purchase of stock of the employer corporation or its parent or subsidiary.
☐ (3) The plan creating the stock must include the aggregate number of shares that may be issued. A plan that includes a percentage of shares that may be issued in the future will not qualify (*Rev. Rul. 71-284*, CB 1971-2, 214).
☐ (4) The plan must spell out the employees or class of employees eligible to receive options.
☐ (5) The plan must be approved by the stockholders of the granting corporation within 12 months before or after the date of adoption.
☐ (6) The option must be granted within 10 years from the date the plan is adopted or the date the plan is approved by the stockholders, whichever date is earlier.
☐ (7) The option, by its terms, must not be exercisable after five years from the date the option is granted.
☐ (8) The option must not be transferable by the optionee except by will or the laws of descent, and during the employee's lifetime it is exercisable only by him.
☐ (9) The option must not be exercisable while there is outstanding any qualified stock option (or restricted stock option) that was granted previously to the same individual to purchase stock in his employer corporation or a parent or subsidiary or predecessor corporation, which prior option is at a price (determined as of the date of granting the new options) higher than the option price of the new option.
☐ (10) The individual optionee immediately after being granted a qualified stock option must not own stock equal to more than 5% of the total combined voting power or value of all classes of stock. If the equity capital of such corporation or corporations is less than $2,000,000, then in addition to the 5% the optionee may own an additional amount that bears the same ratio to 5% as the difference between such equity capital and $2,000,000 bears to $1,000,000.
☐ (11) The option price must be not less than 100% of the fair market value of the stock on the date of grant.
☐ (12) Stock acquired under the option must not be disposed of within three years from the day after the date of transfer of the stock to the optionee who has exercised his option.
☐ (13) From the date of grant of the option to the date three months prior to the date of exercise, the individual must have been an employee of either the corporation granting the option or its

parent or subsidiary or an employee of a corporation issuing or assuming an option in a reorganization or liquidation (§425).

[¶804.5] How to Shortcut the Three-Year Option Holding Period

Normally, an executive who exercises a qualified stock option will hold the optioned stock for the three-year holding period so that the gain on the sale of the stock will qualify for long-term capital gains treatment. However, there are some situations where the executive might want to sell the stock before the three-year period has expired. Say, for example, optioned stock rockets to a new high before the three-year period has expired, and his investment advisor tells him to sell. If he sells, he'll forfeit long-term capital gain treatment because he has not held the stock for three years. On the other hand, if he does not sell, the price of the stock may drop and his large profit would disappear. Is there a solution?

Make a short sale of his optioned stock after holding it for more than six months and deliver the stock after the three-year period has expired.

By selling the stock short, he freezes his investment position in the stock and fixes his profit. By not covering the short sale with the optioned stock until after he has held the stock for three years, he satisfies the three-year holding period and thus qualifies for long-term capital gain treatment.

When This Maneuver Won't Work: If the firm's securities are registered under the Securities and Exchange Act of 1934 and the executive involved is an officer, director, or over-10% stockholder, this gambit won't work except in a very limited way. *Reason:* Section 16(c) of that act makes it unlawful for such persons to sell securities unless they deliver the securities within 20 days of the sale. Bear in mind that this provision applies not only to firms whose securities are listed on national exchanges, but also to firms whose securities are sold over-the-counter and registered with the SEC. Such persons would also have to be alert to the short-swing profits recapture provisions of the Act, §16(b). If the short sale took place within six months of the date of acquisition, any profit they made would be subject to recapture by the corporation in a suit brought by the corporation or by a stockholder on its behalf.

Another Pitfall to Watch Out For: If you or your wife acquire stock substantially identical to your optioned stock before you close out your short sale, your profit on the sale of the optioned stock will be taxed as short-term rather than long-term capital gains (§1233). This method, therefore, limits you with respect to exercising other options during this period. However, it doesn't stop your children or some other close relatives from buying your company's stock. The purchase of stock by someone other than your wife will not be attributable to you (see §1233(e)(2)(c)).

[¶804.6] Convertible Preferred Stock

IRS has ruled that the conversion of optioned preferred stock to common stock is not a prohibited disposition of the stock under §425(c)(1) of the Code (*Rev. Rul. 68-162*, CB 1968-1, 188). This ruling gives the green light to the use of convertible preferred stock in qualified stock option plans.

[¶804.7] Restricted Stock

Suppose the stock acquired by exercising a nonqualified option (or in a direct sale to the employee without a prior option) is subject to restrictions. For example, it may not be resold freely or it has to be resold to the corporation at cost if the employee leaves the employer's employ. It can be argued that the stock's value cannot be determined, and thus no income arises when the stock is acquired.

However, the tax law provides that if an employee receives nonforfeitable restricted stock in exchange for his services, the value of the stock (without considering any reduction in value caused by the restriction) minus the price paid for the stock (if any) is currently taxed as ordinary income to him. If the stock is subject to a substantial risk of forfeiture when he receives it, the value of the stock at the time the risk of forfeiture is lifted (minus the amount he paid, if any) is taxed to the employee as ordinary income when the stock becomes nonforfeitable. The employer can deduct the amount that is taxable to the employee in the year the employee is subject to tax.

[¶805] HOW TO GET DEDUCTIONS FOR THE ENTIRE FAMILY'S MEDICAL EXPENSES

Because of their tax advantages, medical and sickness payments by an employer give the employee the maximum dollar benefit. Where such payments meet the requirements of the Code, they are tax free to the employee and deductible by the employer. This is generally recognized by both employers and employees, as is shown by the fact that more than $5 billion is paid out each year in health insurance covering 121 million people.

[¶805.1] Medical Expense Reimbursement

If a corporation reimburses its employees, including shareholder-employees, for actual medical expenses incurred for themselves, their spouses, or their children, such reimbursements do not constitute taxable income to the employees. The reimbursement can take the form of a payment directly to the employee or to the physician or hospital that provided the medical services. The tax treatment is the same whether the payment comes directly from the corporation or from an insurance company (to which the corporation pays the premiums (§105(b)).

A taxpayer cannot take a medical expense deduction for reimbursed expenses. If the reimbursement comes in the same year as the expense, the taxpayer must reduce his medical expenses by the amount of the reimbursement (§213(a)). If the reimbursement comes in a later year and the taxpayer previously deducted that expense, then the reimbursement is taxable income (§105(b); Reg. §1.105-2). If the reimbursement exceeds the amount that the taxpayer actually deducted, the excess is tax free.

Advantages in a Small Corporation: In a small corporation (where frequently the corporation and the employee-shareholders who constitute the corporation are looked upon as one entity), the effect of the medical reimbursement plan for the stockholder-employees and their families is a full deduction for all of the families' medical costs without regard to the limitations on medical deductions for individuals. Furthermore, there's no tax wastage of payments for medical care (due to the 3% floor) or drugs (due to the 1% floor) that occurs when a highly paid shareholder-employee pays his own doctor bills. Of course, the deduction is at the corporate level and, depending on comparative rates, may be more or less valuable than a deduction at the individual level.

If a corporation has elected to be taxed as a Subchapter S corporation, it is not even necessary to be concerned with differences in tax rates. A corporation that has elected under Subchapter S pays no tax; each shareholder picks up his share of the corporation's profits and reports it as his own. In a Subchapter S corporation where medical reimbursements are made, the corporate profits are reduced. Thus, the individual stockholder picking up this reduced profit has the benefit of a full deduction at his or her personal income tax rates.

Payments to reimburse an employee for medical insurance (the employee's spouse and dependents may also be included) are deductible by the corporation—if the employee presents proof to the corporation at the time he is reimbursed that the insurance is in force and being paid by the employee.

IRS is satisfied if reimbursement is made by any of the following methods: (1) reimburse each employee of the corporation directly once or twice a year for the corporation's share of the insurance premiums on proof of prior payment of the premiums by the employee-shareholder; (2) issue to each employee a check payable to the particular employee's insurance agent, the employee being obligated to turn over the check to the insurance company; (3) issue a check made payable to the insured and the insurance company with the understanding that it will be turned over to the insurance company.

[¶805.2] Restrictive Reimbursement Plans

Providing medical reimbursement programs for all employees of a corporation can be costly. Some corporations, therefore, limit these plans to a preferred class of employees. IRS will go along with such classification as long as it is on the basis of some factor related to employment (e.g., to salaried employees). However, IRS has not gone along where the eligibility is based on stock ownership and participation is limited to stockholder-employees.

If the reimbursement program is only for shareholder-employees, IRS will take the position that the reimbursed medical expenses were in fact dividends.

There have been several cases involving small corporations that provide guidance to steps that should be taken to insure that a medical reimbursement plan will be sustained.

Reasonable Compensation: The benefits that a shareholder-officer of a corporation receives by way of medical reimbursement will be weighed on the scale of reasonable compensation. If the benefits bring the officer-director's compensation above the "reasonable" level, the corporation may be denied a deduction (*Sanders,* TC Memo 1967-146).

Plan for Employees: A medical reimbursement plan must be a plan for employees. It cannot be a plan designed merely for shareholders. A company that adopts a plan that in its terms or in its practical application operates in favor of working stockholders has the burden of showing that the plan is intended to benefit working stockholders, not because they are stockholders, but because they are employees of the company. The line of demarcation may sometimes be very thin.

[¶805.3] Checklist for Setting Up the Plan

Here's what a corporation that contemplates adopting a medical reimbursement plan for stockholder-employees should do:

□ (1) ***Adopt a Written Plan:*** Although the Regs (Reg. §1.105-5(a)) do not require that the plan be in writing, a writing is essential for stockholder plans because it may be used to support the company's position that the plan is for the benefit of employees.

□ (2) ***Make Formal Announcement of Plan:*** This, too, is not required; but it may help in establishing your claim.

□ (3) ***Avoid Discretion in Plan:*** In *Larkin* (394 F.2d 494, CA-1, 1968) IRS contended that there was really no plan, apparently because of the provision giving the officers discretion to choose eligible employees. The plan should spell out the class of employees to be covered.

☐ (4) ***Place Maximum Limitation on Benefits:*** In *Larkin,* the fact that there was no limit on benefits was viewed as negating an intention to provide benefits for employees.

☐ (5) ***Avoid Discrimination in Favor of Stockholders:*** It is important that the plan in its provisions and in its actual operation does not discriminate in favor of stockholder-employees as such. (See also, *Smith,* TC Memo 1970-243; *Seidel,* TC Memo 1971-238; *Epstein,* TC Memo 1972-53.)

☐ (6) ***Gear Benefits to Compensation and Services Performed:*** Avoid discrepancy in compensation and benefits. Benefits for employees should be in relation to the services rendered by them.

☐ (7) ***When You Cover Dependents, Treat Them Equally:*** If the plan is intended to cover dependents of employees, it should say so; and the plan should be operated according to its provisions. Dependents of stockholder-employees should not be favored.

☐ (8) ***Reasonable Compensation Test:*** The board of directors or an advisory committee should be given authority to reduce benefits where there is danger that they may be considered excessive compensation (see *Sanders, supra*). Of course, inserting a maximum figure might avoid this problem. Another way to avoid this problem is through an insured plan. The payment of premiums rather than benefits minimizes the danger of the company being attacked for paying "excessive compensation." With an insured plan, the insurance company pays the benefits, not the company.

☐ (9) ***Reimbursement Agreement:*** In any event, a company should make provisions against the double taxation that will result if the payment is held not deductible by the corporation and also taxable income to the recipient. There should be an express agreement by all concerned entered into the minutes of the corporation that, in view of the legal uncertainty, payments are made and received under an express obligation to refund them to the corporation if they are determined to be nondeductible. While such an agreement will be of no avail if made after the deduction is disallowed (*Blanton,* CA-5, 379 F.2d 558, 1967, *aff'g* 46 TC 527), it should hold up if entered into before any medical payments are made.

[¶806] HOW TO CUT FAMILY INSURANCE COSTS

By establishing a corporation, the cost-conscious businessman can realize new money-saving insurance opportunities in three broad forms:

☐ (1) By providing group term life insurance for corporate employees, the stockholder-employee can take advantage of the lower insurance rates available under group coverage.

☐ (2) Under a group term policy, otherwise uninsurable individuals can obtain life insurance coverage.

☐ (3) Both group term life insurance and ordinary individual life insurance policies (provided for under a qualified corporate benefit plan) are paid for with pre-tax dollars. This favorable tax treatment is not available to the individual who does business as a sole proprietor or partner.

Let's take a closer look at these cost-cutting insurance arrangements.

[¶806.1] Group Term Life Insurance

One consideration that many businessmen take into account when choosing a form of business is the availability of group term life insurance paid for with pre-tax dollars. Neither a sole proprietorship nor a partnership can provide group term life insurance on a tax-free basis, while a corporation can. The tax law places no limits on the amount of group coverage for an individual employee, although it does impose a ceiling on the amount that the employee can receive tax free. That ceiling is $50,000 (§79).

There are exceptions to the rule that there is no limit on the amount of group coverage. The general rule does not apply where

☐ (a) The cost of group term life insurance is provided for an employee who has terminated employment and has attained either the employer's normal retirement age or has certain disabilities;
☐ (b) Certain "charitable organizations" are designated as the beneficiaries;
☐ (c) The employer is directly or indirectly the beneficiary;
☐ (d) The cost of group term life insurance is provided under certain pension and annuity plans.

Many corporation plans involve less than ten employees. Small plans present difficulties for insurance carriers, as the risk inherent in a group term life policy is spread over a much smaller group. Insurance companies look for medical examinations and medical histories as a means of reducing their risk.

The Internal Revenue Service initially ruled that evidence as to insurability could not be used in determining eligibility for group term insurance. However, the Service has since adopted a more liberal attitude toward plans where less than ten employees are involved. For these plans, IRS now says that evidence of insurability may be used in determining an employee's eligibility or the amount of his insurance coverage. This evidence of insurability, however, must be determined only by the use of a medical questionnaire; a medical examination cannot be required. IRS also says that the amount of protection must be computed either as a uniform percentage of salary or on the basis of coverage brackets. No bracket in a plan affecting ten or fewer employees may exceed two-and-a-half times the next lower bracket, and the lowest bracket must be at least 10% of the highest bracket. These rules can be best illustrated by an example:

If the lowest bracket is $5,000 of coverage, the highest would be $50,000, and there would be two other qualified brackets—one, $15,000; and the other, $37,500. A plan covering four employees would qualify if one employee fitted into each bracket. If the chain is broken, the coverage would be less. For example, if there are only three employees and the lowest coverage is $5,000, the maximum coverage for the man on top would be $37,500.

Minimum Employee Coverage: IRS says that a plan will qualify if it covers only ten full-time employees. Under this rule, a company with fifteen employees could limit eligibility to ten as long as the covered class is selected on the basis of factors that preclude individual selection. What's more, a plan will not be disqualified merely because an eligible employee elects not to participate in the program.

[¶806.2] Profiting From Life Insurance via a Qualified Plan

Businessmen may benefit from many life insurance tax breaks in the context of a corporation's qualified retirement plan. You may advantageously use ordinary life insurance you already own or that has been bought for you or, if you don't own insurance, there may still be an opportunity to benefit from insurance via your corporation's qualified retirement plan. So you should examine your insurance portfolio in the light of the facts we discuss here to determine whether you are taking full advantage of the opportunities the law allows an informed individual.

How Much May a Qualified Plan Pay for Life Insurance? A qualified pension or profit-sharing plan may buy ordinary life insurance "incidental to the plan's primary benefit." There are generous limits (Reg. §1.401-1(b)(1)(i) and (ii)).

☐ (1) Pension and annuity plans can buy life insurance equal to 100 times the monthly benefit the insured participant will receive on retirement. This is true even though the pension plan is of the money-purchase type.

☐ (2) Profit-sharing plans can buy life insurance as long as the premiums for each participant are less than 50% of the aggregate contributions allocated to the participant's credit. This is also true of a money-purchase pension plan.

The result is that the corporation pays the premiums with pre-tax dollars and the insured participant pays tax on only the cost of current life insurance protection each year (§72(m)(3)(B)), which is relatively little. The cost computation makes this a sizable tax break (*Rev. Rul. 55-747,* CB 1955-2, 228) especially since the businessman would otherwise pay for his insurance with after-tax dollars.

If the insured dies before retirement, his beneficiary gets three tax benefits. First, life insurance proceeds are excluded from the beneficiary's taxable income (§101(a)). Second, the beneficiary or estate may exclude from gross income up to $5,000 of death benefits paid by or for the corporation (§101(b)). Third, insurance proceeds are exempt from estate tax to the extent the retirement plan is noncontributory (§2039(c)).

How to Transfer Life Insurance to a Qualified Retirement Plan: A plan participant may transfer an existing life insurance policy to his qualified plan from three sources: (1) preincorporation personally owned life insurance and present personally owned life insurance; (2) preincorporation Keogh plan life insurance; and (3) life insurance from another corporate plan.

(1) *Transfer of Personally Owned Life Insurance:* For top dollar benefits, an employee may transfer his life insurance policy directly or indirectly to his qualified retirement plan.

(a) An indirect transfer takes place where the corporation buys the policy from the employee for its cash surrender value and transfers the policy to the plan. The sale frees the employee from the obligation of paying further premiums from his after-tax dollars. The corporation may thereupon deduct from its income the sum it paid the employee and transfer the policy as its contribution to the qualified retirement plan. Thereafter the corporation's contributions will pay for the premiums with pre-tax dollars. The qualified plan can, generally, buy enough additional insurance to cover the employee's needs. Policies transferred to the trust by the employee will continue at the same premium that he paid. This method of transfer presupposes that the corporation drafted or amended its qualified plan to provide for incidental death benefits (*Rev. Rul. 73-338,* CB 1973-2, 20). It's safest to extend this privilege of transfer of life insurance to all plan participants.

(b) A direct transfer takes place where the participant contributes his policy directly to the qualified retirement plan. However, the plan must be suitably drafted or amended to allow for: (i) voluntary contributions by participants; (ii) assignment by participants of life insurance contracts having cash surrender values; and (iii) the aggregation or making up of voluntary contributions in a good year, where not contributed by the participant in a lean year (*Rev. Rul. 74-76*). You would use this third method where the cash surrender value of the policy is much greater than the permissible corporate contribution for the year (see above). Normally, corporations want a current deduction for their contributions instead of carrying it over to future years. So, this is how the direct transfer method works: The voluntary contribution limit is 10% of compensation per year. But aggregation allows a participant to make up voluntary contributions in one year if he contributed less than the 10% in a prior year (*Rev. Rul. 69-217*, CB 1969-1, 115). Thus, if accumulated missed contributions exceed the cash value of the policy, the participant can contribute the entire policy directly to the qualified plan in one year. Make sure, though, that the cash value is payable to the participant upon retirement or termination of employment and that upon his death, if earlier, proceeds will go to his beneficiary.

(2) *Transfer of Insurance Bought by Keogh Plan:* The transfer of life insurance bought under a Keogh plan to a corporation's qualified retirement plan can be accomplished in one of two ways:

(a) All Keogh fund assets (including life insurance) may be transferred to the qualified plan of a new corporation (*Rev. Rul. 71-541*, CB 1971-2, 209). The Keogh trustee would transfer the funds directly to the corporate qualified plan trustee and then terminate the Keogh plan. However, you have to make sure that the corporate plan has the same restrictions as the Keogh plan.

(b) The insurance part only of Keogh assets can be transferred to a corporate qualified plan (*Rev. Rul. 73-503*, CB 1973-2, 502). The balance of the Keogh assets will then remain frozen in the Keogh trust until the originally planned retirement age, when all the Keogh assets will be paid out. In the meantime the corporate qualified plan can buy additional insurance.

(3) *Transferring Life Insurance From Another Corporate Plan:* An employee may decide to join another corporation or even form his own corporation. In such instances he might like to transfer his life insurance and other vested interests in his present-qualified plan tax free to the qualified plan of the new corporation. Provided both qualified plans are suitably drafted or amended, the trustee of the new qualified plan can purchase the life insurance directly from the trustee of the former qualified plan. The former plan should not allow participants to elect a lump-sum payout on termination of the plan or separation from service (see *Rev. Rul. 67-213*, CB 1967-2, 149). If the plan permits, then in case of one corporation merging into another, vested interests can be transferred tax free.

Transferring Insurability and Premium Rates: What should an uninsurable businessman do? It's true he can transfer insurance with cash surrender value to a corporate qualified plan, but that may not give him enough coverage. Or maybe his health is such that the premium rates would be too high. If he owns convertible term insurance, he should surrender the policy to the insurance company, so that the company can issue the plan trustee a life policy (without further evidence of insurability). Thus all that's transferred to the trustee is insurability.

Any refund of premiums on the old policy will go to the employee who'll be allowed to name a beneficiary. This was the import of a private IRS letter ruling signed by William W. Wharton, Chief, Review Staff, IRS, 2/10/71.

SECTION IX
USING EXPENSES TO GET BIG TAX BREAKS

A great variety of expenses, carefully used, can generate substantial tax breaks for the small businessman. In this chapter, we will discuss a number of them, starting out with deductions generated from leasehold improvements and repairs.

This area of improvements and repairs is common to almost every business activity. Few small businesses own their own real estate; most either lease or rent, which raises the question of who gets the benefit of the deduction for improvements and repairs. Most of this question should be answered by the lease instrument itself. In a nutshell, here is an outline of the situation:

[¶901] LEASEHOLD IMPROVEMENTS

If improvements are to be made by either the lessor or the lessee in conjunction with the lease of the property, the possible tax consequences should be carefully noted before the lease is committed to final form. The most important tax questions in this area relate to the following points:

☐ (1) The tax effect on the lessor. Tax liability may be completely avoided by careful drafting;
☐ (2) The deduction for the depreciation of the improvements, i.e., whether either party or neither party will be entitled to the deduction.

[¶901.1] Where the Lessor Makes Improvements

Where improvements are on the property at the commencement of the lease or where lessor places improvements on the property, the lessor is entitled to deductions for depreciation of the improvements in computing his taxable income. However, if the lease provides that the lessee will, at the end of the term, return the premises in as good condition as at the commencement of the lease, the lessor will not be entitled to depreciation deductions, since the lessor will have suffered no economic loss during the lease term. The lessee is likewise not permitted any deductions for depreciation during the term; he may only take deductions for the cost of restoring the property to its original state in the year of such restoration. Such a provision may, in view of all the circumstances, be deemed advisable; but before adopting it, bear in mind that neither lessor nor lessee will be entitled to deduct depreciation under this type of provision.

[¶901.2] Where Lessee Makes Improvements

Many long-term leases of unimproved property or property improved by buildings that do not economically utilize the land provide that the lessee shall erect and place upon the land substantial buildings and structures. The lessee may not deduct the cost of construction in the year of completion. He is, however, permitted to amortize these improvements over the term of the lease or, if the useful life of the improvement is less than the remaining term of the lease, to depreciate the improvement over such useful life.

Many long-term leases calling for improvements by the lessee provide that the improvements shall become the property of the lessor at the termination of the lease. Although the improvements may increase the value of the leased property, the increased value is not taxable income of the lessor either at the time of construction or at the termination of the lease; nor is the lessor's basis for the property increased. Neither gain nor loss is recognized until the property is sold or disposed of in some taxable transaction, and then the increase in value will usually be considered capital gains income, taxable at favorable rates.

The lessor should therefore determine whether he will be better off from both a tax and business point of view if he makes the improvements himself and realizes additional income net after depreciation and other expenses, taxable at ordinary income rates, or if he has the lessee make the improvements, receives a lower rental, and realizes any gain inherent in the improvements at capital gain rates when he disposes of the property.

Note: If the lessee makes improvements as a substitute for the payment of rent, the fair market value of the improvement is income to the lessor when the improvement is placed on the leased property.

In addition, if the lease requires the lessee to remove the improvements prior to the termination of the lease, the cost of removal is deductible by the lessee in the year of removal.

Code §1250, which provides for the recapture of excessive depreciation on real estate, including leasehold improvements, introduces a new factor that needs to be taken into consideration by both parties.

Here is a summary of the advantages and disadvantages—from both the lessor's and lessee's viewpoint—of improvements by either of them:

Improvements by Lessor

From Lessor's Point of View:

☐ (1) Higher rental obtainable.

☐ (2) Lessor bears cost of construction.

☐ (3) Rental taxable at ordinary income rates.

☐ (4) Lessor may deduct for depreciation. Basis may be increased. Possible recapture of excessive depreciation.

From Lessee's Point of View:

☐ (1) Lessee pays more rent.

☐ (2) No cost of construction.

Improvements by Lessee

From Lessor's Point of View:

☐ (1) Lower rental obtainable.
☐ (2) No cost of construction.
☐ (3) Increase in value recognized only on disposition of property, and usually treated as capital gain taxable at favorable rates.
☐ (4) No deduction for depreciation.

From Lessee's Point of View:

☐ (1) Lessee pays less rent.
☐ (2) Lessee bears cost of construction, but is entitled to depreciation deductions or amortization. Possible recapture on disposition.

[¶901.3] How to Amortize or Depreciate Leasehold and Improvements for Tax Purposes

A lessee can amortize the cost of acquiring a leasehold interest over the remaining term of the lease. He is limited to the use of straight-line amortization. Leasehold improvements made by the lessee, on the other hand, in cases where the remaining term of the lease is longer than the useful life of the improvements, may be written off by any of the different methods of depreciation available for the type of property under Code §167(b). If the remaining term of the lease is shorter than the useful life of the improvement, the lessee must use straight-line depreciation. For the purposes of getting the amortization or depreciation deductions, the lessee can generally ignore the renewal periods provided for in the lease where (a) in the case of a leasehold deduction, at least 75% of the cost of the lease is attributable to the initial term, and (b) in the case of a leasehold improvement, the remaining initial term is at least 60% of the useful life of the improvement.

If the lessee disposes of his lease, excess amortization or depreciation is subject to recapture under Code §1250. For the purposes of §1250, renewal periods up to two-thirds of the original period on which depreciation was based are considered, even though they might have been ignored for the purposes of determining the propriety of the deduction in the first place. For example, suppose you pay $9,000 to acquire a lease that has a remaining term of nine years and is renewable for another nine years. You dispose of the lease when it has another three years to run on the original term after having amortized the leasehold to the extent of $6,000. On this basis, $2,400 would be subject to recapture under §1250. Two-thirds of the renewal term or six years would be added to the original term of nine for a total of 15 years as a basis for straight-line amortization of the cost of acquisition. This works out to $600 per year for six years or $3,600 instead of the $6,000 taken. The same approach is used for leasehold improvements.

[¶901.4] Tax Consequences of Renewal Options

If you buy a lease that has renewal options or, as lessee, construct improvements on a leasehold that has renewal options, §178 sets forth rules for determining whether or not to take the renewal terms into consideration in computing depreciation or amortization.

If, as lessee, you construct an improvement on a lease containing an option to renew, you should take the renewal option into consideration if the remaining term of the lease (without renewal periods) is at least 60% of the life of the improvement. So, you can still depreciate the improvement over the life of the lease (in slightly more than half the time you would depreciate it if you used its useful life). Treasury can, however, make you use the renewal term in the computation if there is a reasonable certainty that you will renew.

Example 1: You put up a building on property you lease. The building has a 35-year life. The lease has 21 years to run, with a renewal option of 10 years. Since the 21-year original term is 60% of the 35-year life of the building, you can write off your building cost over 21 years, unless there is a reasonable certainty you'll renew the lease.

Example 2: You put up an improvement with a 30-year life on a leasehold having a remaining term of 15 years with a 20-year renewal period. The 15-year remaining term is only 50% of the life of the improvement. So, you have to use the combined terms of the lease (35 years) in your computation. Since the building's life of 30 years is less than the combined term, you depreciate over the 30-year period. But you can still use the 15-year period if you can prove that there is a greater probability that you will not renew the lease than that you will renew the lease.

Special rules for related lessees and lessors require that the cost of improvements put up by the lessee be written off over their useful lives, regardless of the term of the lease. "Related persons" in this context include corporations that file consolidated returns and all those between whom losses are disallowed (§267), e.g., brothers, sisters, spouses, lineal descendants, and ancestors; stockholders and their corporations; trusts and their grantors and beneficiaries; etc.

[¶901.5] How to Get Tax Deductions for Capital Expenditures and Ordinary Repairs

Both the lessor and the lessee should be alert to the distinction between ordinary repair to the leased property and an improvement or other type of capital expenditure. While the expenses incurred for repairs are full deductible, capital expenditure outlays must be written off in depreciation or amortization deductions.

Normally, it is not difficult to distinguish between an ordinary and fully deductible repair expenditure and an improvement, alteration, or other capital expenditure. Situations will arise, however, in which the problem of identification will be difficult. In this context, the definitions that are set forth in tax cases may prove helpful:

□ (1) ***A repair*** is work done on the property whose purpose is to keep the property in an ordinarily efficient operating condition. It does not add to the value of the property, nor does it appreciably prolong its life; it merely keeps the property in an operating condition over its probable useful life for the uses for which it was acquired.

□ (2) ***A capital expenditure*** is made for a replacement, an alteration, an improvement, or additions that prolong the life of the property, increase its value, or make it adaptable to a different use.

If repairs are made in connection with a general plan of improving the property, great care should be taken to differentiate between repairs and improvements. Otherwise, all the expenditures, regardless of their nature, may be merged with the improvement expenditures and the current "repairs" deduction will be lost. Two suggestions are in order: (a) Separate breakdowns of the repair and improvement expenditures should be made. (b) Separate, itemized invoices should be obtained for each type of expenditure.

[¶902] BUSINESS EXPENSES

Let us turn our attention now to probably the largest single source of deductions—business expenses. In dealing with business expenses, we may have one or more combinations of the following objectives:

☐ (1) To get full tax benefits for the expense to avoid having it cut into our capital.
☐ (2) To build future capital values with dollars that would otherwise be substantially taken away. Research and development expenses that produce new products or income-producing machinery; advertising and promotion expenses that produce goodwill, trade names, and public acceptance; salaries paid to men who develop new markets—these are some examples.
☐ (3) To conserve cash by doubling up on or accelerating the charge-off of certain expenses, e.g., switching to the reserve method of taking bad debts, switching to the accrual for next year's vacation pay, accelerating depreciation.
☐ (4) To conserve cash by charging off certain noncash expenses outlays such as compensation paid in company stock, settlement of obligations or liabilities with other property, and depreciation.
☐ (5) To get more mileage on certain expenses by setting them up so that they constitute capital gain to the recipient; examples are: pension and profit-sharing contributions, stock options, and bonus arrangements.
☐ (6) On certain expenditures, to make the best choice between capitalizing or expensing, e.g., repair and maintenance expenditures and some financing charges.
☐ (7) To offset income by the realization of losses on property that has depreciated in value, either by selling or by scrapping the property. By marking down inventory to a current value that is less than cost, we can offset income with loss that has not yet been realized.

[¶902.1] What Constitutes a Trade or Business Expense

Any expense that is (1) "ordinary and necessary"; (2) paid or incurred during the taxable year; and (3) connected with the carrying on of a trade or business qualifies. Let's look at the cost first:

The Regulations (§1.162-1(a)) specifically require that a business expense be "directly connected with or pertaining to the taxpayer's trade or business." Unfortunately, an exact definition of this phrase goes much further than the Regulations and involves knowing the judicial interpretations of many cases. Basically, the important points are that the activity be entered into with the expectation of making a profit and that there be some regularity and continuity in the activity. As to the profit motive, it is important to distinguish those activities that are primarily entered into for pleasure, for example, a hobby. The actuality of profits from the activity is not all-important. Devoting time and money in the belief that eventually there will be profits may spell out a business.

[¶902.2] Ordinary and Necessary

The requirements that an expense be "ordinary and necessary" and "paid or incurred during the taxable year" must be satisfied to qualify a particular expense either as business expense (§162) or investment type, nonbusiness expense (§212).

Even though there have been many cases on what is an ordinary and necessary expense, there is no rule of thumb. What is ordinary and necessary depends on the taxpayer's business and business customs in taxpayer's locale. In a leading case on this point it was stated by the Supreme Court that an ordinary expense is not one that recurs frequently, but must be one that most businessmen in the same situation would make (*Welch*, 290 US 111, 1933). However, in arriving at a working definition of "ordinary and necessary" it may be more meaningful to attack it from the viewpoint of the exceptions to the general rule.

Looking at it this way, all expenses are ordinary and necessary except the following:

☐ (1) Personal expenses (food, clothing, rent for you and your family) or expenses that fail to meet the business requirement of §162 or the nonbusiness requirement of §212.
☐ (2) Expenses that are extraordinary and must be capitalized (§263). If an expenditure adds materially to the value of a capital asset or appreciably prolongs its life, the deduction must be capitalized and spread over the life of the asset. If the asset has no determinable life; recovery of the capitalized expenditure may be delayed until the asset is sold; having become part of the basis of the asset, it would reduce any taxable gain on the sale.
☐ (3) Expenses that violate public policy. Section 162 as revised by the Tax Reform Act of 1969 and the Revenue Act of 1971 denies deductions for (a) fines paid for any violation, (b) kickbacks by doctors and others who provide services under Medicare and Medicaid, (c) two-thirds of treble damages paid after conviction or a plea of guilty or nolo contendere in an anti-trust case, (d) illegal payments to government officials. Deduction for other unethical expenditures will be denied only if they violate a clearly defined public policy. Note that legitimate expenses incurred for an illegal business may be deductible, for example, cost of lottery tickets (*Cohen*, TC Memo 1958-55); rent and wages paid by a bookmaker (*Sullivan*, 356 US 27, 1958); salaries and miscellaneous expenses of bookmaking (*Comeaux*, 176 F.2d 394, CA-10, 1949). If a state's actions are inconsistent with its stated public policy (for example, taxing and issuing licenses to a prohibited business), the policy will not bar a deduction.
☐ (4) Expenses disallowed specifically by one of the Code sections that prevent unintended benefits. Examples are expenses relative to tax-exempt income (§265), certain unpaid expenses and interest between certain related parties (§267), acquisitions to evade or avoid tax (§269), etc.
☐ (5) Expenses that can be deducted under another category of deductions, or are included in cost of goods sold and so will decrease gross income.

Special Situations: An expense can be ordinary and necessary even though it is unusual. Attorneys who had recommended a business venture to clients that (through no fault of theirs) turned out to be fraudulent, reimbursed their clients for the amount of their loss. The Tax Court approved their deduction of this amount as an ordinary and necessary (although unusual) expense to protect their legal business (*Pepper*, 36 TC 886, 1961).

A corporation's payments to depositors and creditors of its insolvent foreign subsidiary to protect the corporation's reputation and goodwill are deductible business expenses. Ordinarily, the debts and expenses of one company are not those of another. If, however, the primary motive of the payer of another company's debts is to preserve its own goodwill and credit rating, rather than to keep the debtor company in business, the payments are deductible. This rule is particularly applicable where the creditors are important customers of the payer. (See, e.g., *Rev. Rul. 73-226*, CB 1973-1, 62; *Scruggs- Vandervoort-Barney, Inc.*, 7 TC 799, 1946; *L. Heller & Sons*, 12 TC 1109, 1949).

Reasonableness: Another aspect of ordinary and necessary is reasonableness. Expenses like salaries and rents that are excessive are usually disallowed (see Reg. §1.162-8). Even though you can lease property to your family or corporation, if the rent is excessive, that part that is excessive will be disallowed (*Jolly's Motor Livery Co.*, TC Memo 1957-231). Sometimes, reasonableness can be determined by comparing the rental to those of similar property in the area.

In setting up your proof to justify either a business or nonbusiness expense as ordinary and necessary, don't overlook the importance of custom. A Treasury ruling, denying a deduction, brings this out. A man in the business of managing entertainers for a percentage of the receipts insured his client, naming himself as beneficiary, to protect his interest in the client's income. He asked the Treasury whether he could deduct the premiums, and the Treasury said, No (*Rev. Rul. 55-714,* CB 1955-2, 51).

Quoting the Supreme Court (*Lilly,* 343 US 90, 1952), the Treasury conceded that customs and actions of professional organizations have a part in determining what are ordinary and necessary expenses at a given time and place. However, the Treasury pointed out, there are no customs prevalent in the business of managing entertainers by which the expense of insuring the client might be considered ordinary and necessary to the business.

Let's carry the Treasury's point one step further. Suppose managers as a class, recognizing the wisdom of having protection against the hazards of fleeting fame and occupational disability, started insuring their clients as a regular thing. In time, such insuring would achieve the status of a custom. At that point, assuming no other provision of the law interfered, the premiums should become a deductible expense.

You may be able to increase your deductions by running down all the doubtful ones to find out whether you can tie them to a custom.

[¶903] TRAVEL AND ENTERTAINMENT EXPENSES

There are four sets of rules at work in this area. First, the general rule is that expenses, entertainment or otherwise, have to be ordinary and necessary at the corporate level. Secondly, at the individual level, they cannot be personal expenses; they have to be business expenses.

Section 274 adds two other tests. One relates to the type of expense that is allowable for entertainment and the second relates to substantiation. Section 274 says, in effect, that a rule of substantiation as to the type of expense either at the corporate level or at the employee level, not at both, will be imposed; but a rule of record keeping at both levels will be imposed.

The section says that the corporation can impose the type-of-expense burden on the employee if the corporation treats the amount paid as compensation. For example, if a corporation pays a salesman a flat amount to cover expenses to entertain customers, treats it as compensation and withholds on it, then the burden to show that the expense was incurred for a proper purpose and, therefore, is deductible under §274 is on the salesman. The salesman has to pass the type-of-expense test *and* also the record-keeping test.

Now, alternatively, if the corporation does not treat the payment to the salesman as compensation and does not withhold on the amounts paid, then the burden of showing whether the salesman spent the money for the right purpose under §274 is at the corporate level and may result in a disallowance to the corporation if the funds were not spent for the right purpose. Assuming there is a business purpose, all the salesman has to do then is to show that he spent the money; that is, meet the record-keeping requirement.

Where the corporation treats the payment as compensation and the employee fails to show that the expense was for a business purpose, the corporation would get a deduction for the payment, but the employee would be taxed on the amount.

If an employee does not have the proper accounting for the expenditures, he is taxed on such expenditures. The record-keeping requirement, as indicated earlier, is imposed on both the corporation *and* the employee.

There are three possible tax results you can have with travel and entertainment expenses. The expenditure may be allowed at both levels, disallowed at the corporate level and not taxable to the employee, or disallowed at the corporate level and taxed to the employee.

[¶903.1] Travel Away From Home

Expenses of business travel away from home are deductible as ordinary and necessary business expenses. Thus, it is first necessary to show that the travel was for business reasons. Usually this means that you would not have gone but for the business reason. In addition, there are two requirements for travel away from home expense deductions that are imposed by §274. Both involve keeping good records.

☐ (1) You get no deduction for any expense for travel away from home unless you comply with the substantiation rules. No substantiation, no deduction.

☐ (2) If your trip takes you outside the United States, exceeds a week in length, and 25% of the trip is occupied with nonbusiness activities, you may have to allocate your travel expenses between the business and nonbusiness portions. Your deduction is then limited to the portion of the total expenses allocable to the business portion of the trip.

In addition to transportation expenses and the cost of meals and lodging, travel away from home expenses include those that are incidental to the travel such as sample rooms, telephone and telegraph service, public stenographers, etc. Also included are taxi, bus and baggage fares, cleaning and laundry expenses, and the expenses of traveling from your hotel to your first call and back. This last expense would be a nondeductible commuting expense except for the fact that it is incurred while in travel away from home status.

Entertainment expenses do not become travel expenses, however, just because you happen to be on the road. They are still entertainment and must meet the stiffer entertainment deduction and substantiation rules.

Away From Home: The term "home" to the individual, ordinarily means the place where he and his family live. The term has a different meaning, however, for the purpose of deducting traveling expenses. Your "home," for this purpose, is your principal place of business, employment, station, or post of duty, regardless of where you maintain your family residence. Thus, there may be instances in which you are "traveling away from home" even while working in the same city in which you and your family live. "Home" is not limited to a particular building or property, but includes the entire city or general area around your business premises or place of employment.

In the typical case of travel away from home, you make a trip on business away from the city in which you work and live. However, suppose you and your family live in one city and you work in another (perhaps living in the city in which you work during the work days and returning home on weekends). Your travel to the other city and your expenses of living there during the workdays are normally not deductible. *Reason:* You're not away from home. For tax purposes, the usual rule is that your home is at your principal place of employment.

To get the travel deduction you have to show your travel is a business necessity. Merely living in one city and traveling to the other to work has nothing to do with the needs of the business; but if your employer sends you to the other location, you have a different situation. Take the case of an employee of a harness racing promoter. He lived in New York and worked there, but he was sent to other cities by his employer to investigate the possibilities of expanding his employer's activities there. Here, New York City was his tax home (where he usually worked) and his travel to other cities was away from home (*Schoenbaum,* TC Memo 1957-137).

Sometimes the job itself—although you spend all your time in one place—requires that you be away from home. That can happen where state law, for example, requires judges to live in the districts from which they are elected although they sit on the state's highest court in the state capital. However, where custom, rather than law, requires judges to live in their districts, they are not considered away from home while on the job. See *Rev. Rul. 63-82*, CB 1963-1, 33, for IRS's view.

The distance you travel also goes into determining whether you've traveled away from home. Travel within the same city or county usually does not qualify as being away from home (*Kershner,* 14 TC 168, 1950; *Smith,* 21 TC 991, 1954; *Jacquemot,* TC Memo 1956-198). Travel into another city only ten miles away did not qualify as away from home (*Amoroso,* 193 F.2d 583, CA-1, 1952).

Here's a case that illustrates how the distance factor can be applied to determine whether travel is away from home. A supervisory employee on two Texas mineral leases was required to travel daily between the leases which were five miles apart, weekly to a town 25 miles from his home to test the content of the water from wells, monthly to buy supplies in a town seven miles away, and monthly to his employer in Louisiana, 84 miles away. He could not deduct the Texas travel up to 25 miles away as being away from home. The monthly 84-mile trip qualified as being away from home (*Winn,* 32 TC 220, 1959).

[¶903.2] You Can't Be Away From Home If You Have No Home

To be on travel status away from home, some place must be pinpointed as your tax home. But suppose you are a traveling salesman, an entertainer, or an itinerant worker—practically always on the road, living most of the time in hotels near where you happen to be working. Then you have a tough time showing you have a permanent home and you'll be denied any away from home costs. Transportation, telephone, telegraph, entertainment, and similar items connected with your business are deductible whether or not you're away from home; but if you can't establish travel status, you'll get no deduction for meals and lodging.

To prove you have a permanent home, you should show a place you normally return to when you come to your "home" city. Using a relative's home as a mailing address is not enough. It helps to show you contribute to the upkeep of the home even when you're not there, that you keep your clothes there, that you lived there before you went on the road, and that you return more often than for occasional visits. See *Duncan,* 17 BTA 1088, 1929, and *Gustafson,* 3 TC 998.

Itinerant workers living in trailers at their job sites usually cannot deduct their living expenses or cost of maintaining their trailers because the trailer itself is their tax home (*Lewis,* TC Memo 1954-233; *Wood,* TC Memo 1958-198; *Ullom,* TC Memo 1958-201).

[¶903.3] Temporary Employment

Although the place where you usually work is your tax home, the courts have engrafted an exception to this rule. That's the temporary job rule. If you leave the city where you usually live to take a job in another location, you are considered to be away from your tax home if the job you take is temporary; but not so if it is for an indefinite period of time.

The courts and the Treasury recognize that you are away from home for tax purposes while you are on a temporary job if you continue to maintain your permanent residence where it was before you got the temporary job.

The Supreme Court, in considering this question, noted that it had previously said that travel expenses away from home required that the travel be to somewhere other than where the principal job was. However, the lower courts had added an exception to this rule involving temporary jobs. Since IRS was not challenging the temporary job exception in the case before the Supreme Court (it was merely arguing that the lower court was correct in this case in saying the job in question was not temporary), the Supreme Court did not rule on the temporary job exception (*Peurifoy*, 358 US 59, 1958). So, unless IRS decides to change its mind, the temporary job exception applies. If you can show your job is temporary, you can deduct your travel and living costs while on temporary work away from home.

[¶903.4] If You Have Two Jobs or Businesses

If you have two jobs or businesses, you are usually entitled to deduct the expenses of traveling between the two and the living expenses at the job away from home. The tax home is the place of the principal place of business or employment. ''Away from home'' is the minor place of business or employment.

Again we're thrown to the facts in each case to find which place is the principal place of employment and which is minor. Important factors are: (1) total time ordinarily spent at each place, (2) degree of business activity at each place, and (3) significance of financial return from each place. It's possible for the city in which you live to be the minor place of employment and the city away from where you make your residence to be your principal place of employment. Then, you deduct your expenses arising in the city in which you live—which for tax purposes is away from home—but you're limited to such expenses as are attributable to your duties as employee or businessman.

[¶903.5] Wife's Travel Expenses

Some time ago, a Tennessee district court allowed an employer to deduct the costs of an employee's wife's travel expenses for accompanying her husband on business trips (*Allenberg Cotton Co.*, D. Ct., Tenn., 1961). The husband was diabetic and required a trained companion to accompany him and administer insulin. The wife was qualified to do so. The Tax Court, which takes a much tougher view of such expenses, has refused to follow Allenberg in a case involving a U.S. Department of Labor employee who has suffered several strokes. He'd been a diabetic for 39 years and his doctor had advised him not to travel alone. His wife accompanied him on the many trips his job required him to make, helped take care of him, and did much of the driving. The Department of Labor did not authorize the wife's trips as official business. The taxpayers claimed a business deduction for the costs of the wife's trips, but the court held that the expenses were not business expenses and so were not deductible (*Rieley*, TC Memo 1964-66). The court left open the question of whether the expenses should be allowed as medical expenses because the taxpayers did not raise it.

In another case, a district court allowed a deduction for the wife's travel expenses because the employer considered the wife also as an employee who was actively helping her husband to succeed and *required* that wives accompany their husbands to company conventions. The court said that that spelled out a business purpose. However, taxpayer's victory was short-lived. The Fifth Circuit reversed the district court and denied the wife's travel deduction. *Reason:* The facts (relatively small amount of time devoted to business, convention held at resort hotel, employer's sponsoring the convention, which was limited to employees) indicated that the primary purpose of the trip was pleasure (*Thomas,* 289 F.2d 108, 1961; *Rudolph,* 291 F.2d 841, 1961).

Necessity is the clue to the deductibility of a wife's travel as a business expense. When is a wife's presence sufficiently necessary to warrant a deduction for her expenses? Here, again, we are thrown to the rule that says we must look to the facts in each case. In the usual case, it is claimed the wife was a necessary secretary and valuable aide in entertaining customers. The president of two California corporations got the deduction for his companies for his wife's travel expenses on that basis. And singer John Charles Thomas's wife's travel costs were allowed because, in addition to being his secretary, she was able to act as voice coach, help him with pronunciation of foreign languages, help in getting publicity for him, and plan his itineraries (*Thomas,* BTA Memo 1939). Still another helpful wife's expenses were allowed, this time a writer's spouse: She went to Australia to collect background material for an article he wanted to write (*Kluckhohn,* 18 TC 892).

On the other hand, we have many cases that have disallowed the expense deduction for the wife's travel costs. In most of these cases, even if it is shown the wife did some secretarial work or aided in entertainment, the courts found that such services were not necessary for the business. (See Reg. §1.162-2(c); *Rev. Rul. 55-57,* CB 1955-1, 315).

It won't be easy to pass IRS's muster when you claim a deduction for the travel expenses of an executive's wife, but the tax planner can counsel certain steps to help sew up the deduction. Here are five steps to consider.

☐ (1) ***Have a Written Plan:*** Have the company adopt a formal policy and plan encouraging executives to take their wives on business trips by providing reimbursement of the wife's travel expenses. The plan should include a provision for management approval of the trip as serving a valid business purpose.

☐ (2) ***Reflect Basis of Policy in Minutes:*** Have the minutes adopting the plan reflect discussion of the reasons for the adoption of the policy and plan. Thus, instead of having a director come in and testify in the Tax Court that a wife's presence is "essential to present a family picture to the world," have remarks such as this and similar remarks read into the corporate minutes.

☐ (3) ***Have Wife Handle Business Chores:*** Try to have the wife take on secretarial chores, traveling chores, publicity, and other business items.

☐ (4) ***Keep Detailed Records:*** IRS will most likely ask for a detailed report of the places and things done on the trip, the business connection, and how the wife's presence served a business purpose. An accurate, detailed diary will go a long way in establishing your case.

☐ (5) ***Wife Essential to Trip:*** You should be ready to show IRS that in the wife's absence the executive would have hired someone else to perform business services on the trip. Establishing this will at least give you a partial deduction for the wife's expenses.

[¶904] AUTOMOBILE EXPENSES

Automobile expenses incurred in business travel are deductible either as a travel expense (if away from home on business) or as a transportation expense (even if not away from home). However, to get any deduction there must be a connection between the use of the car and your trade or business or some income-producing activity. Only the portion of your car expenses directly attributable to business use is deductible; the portion attributable to nonbusiness or personal use is not deductible.

To the extent your car expenses are incurred in business use, the following items are deductible:

☐ (1) ***Cost of Operation.*** This includes gas and oil, maintenance, lubrication, repairs, antifreeze, car waxing and polishing, car washes, garage parking charges, tolls, motor club memberships, etc.
☐ (2) ***State and Local Taxes.*** This includes registration fees, plates, car inspection fees, special use taxes, gas and oil taxes, sales taxes, operator's license fees, etc. The nonbusiness portion of gas, oil, and sales taxes may also be deductible if you itemize deductions.
☐ (3) ***Insurance.*** This includes all forms of car insurance.
☐ (4) ***Depreciation.*** The cost of the car, as well as repairs and replacements that prolong the useful life of the car for more than a year, may be recouped through depreciation chargeoffs.
☐ (5) ***Casualty and Theft Losses.*** You can deduct losses to your car due to auto accidents, fire, theft, etc., to the extent not compensated by insurance or otherwise. Here, there is no business-use limitation.
☐ (6) ***Chauffeur's Salaries.*** There must, of course, be a business connection.

[¶904.1] Allocating Expenses Between Business and Personal Use

In allocating your car expenses between business and personal use, there are several methods you can use: One way is to find the mileage percentage of business use. You simply divide your business mileage by your total mileage, and take that percentage of your total expenses as a deduction. Another method is to base the deduction on the weekly percentage of business use. If you use your car, say, five days a week on business, you may deduct $^5/_7$ of your total expenses.

The first method is approved by IRS, but you can use any other reasonable method in making the allocation. In a typical example, a court allowed a deduction for a business use of a car based on an allocation of ⅔ use for business and 8 cents a mile (*Lovelady*, TC Memo 1956-288). Another case allowed a deduction based on an allocation of ⅞ for business use (*McWilliams*, TC Memo 1950). Whichever method you use, bear in mind the deduction must be a fair and reasonable representation of your business expenses. Thus you should keep accurate records of your actual expenses.

[¶904.2] Standard Mileage Allowance

IRS has approved a flat mileage allowance deduction for business and professional persons and most employees of 15¢ per mile for the first 15,000 miles and 10¢ per mile thereafter.

Previously only 12¢ and 9¢ were allowed. The new rates are retroactive to taxable years beginning after 12/31/73. This simplified method will go a long way toward eliminating the burdensome task of allocating most automobile expenses between business and nonbusiness use, since all it requires is a speedometer reading. It does not, however, eliminate the need to substantiate the other elements of an expense (Reg. §1.162-17 for local transportation; Reg. §1.274-5 for travel away from home).

The standard mileage rate, as it's called, is in lieu of operating and fixed costs of your automobile. Included in that category are such items as gasoline (including all taxes thereon), oil, repairs, license tags, insurance, and depreciation. Thus, if you use the standard mileage rate, you have to give up separate deductions for these amounts.

However, even if you use the standard mileage allowance, you can still deduct parking fees and tolls that are attributable to business use. Deductible also are gasoline taxes allocable to use for nonbusiness purposes (allowable under §164), interest relating to the automobile's purchase (allowable under §163), and state and local taxes, other than those included in the cost of gasoline (otherwise allowable under §164) (*Rev. Proc. 74-23*).

All self-employed persons and nonreimbursed employees using an automobile or truck in a business or profession may elect to figure mileage expenses by way of the standard mileage allowance rather than by way of the actual expense method. This standard mileage allowance is available also to reimbursed employees who want to claim the difference between the actual allowance and a lesser reimbursement. *Note:* The flat mileage allowance for moving expenses, charitable work, and medical travel is figured at 7¢ a mile.

Which Way Is Better? Although the standard mileage rate will simplify your record-keeping chore, it won't necessarily provide the greater overall deduction. You'll have to make your own comparisons. Accordingly, if you want to keep your options open, you have to be prepared to make your move either way. You can only do so if you keep timely records to substantiate a deduction under both methods. This means the burden of additional record keeping to be weighed against tax savings.

Where you use your car partly for business and partly for pleasure driving, you would still have to allocate expenses in order to determine which method is better. Often, because of the decrease in both the depreciation deduction and the business portion of the actual expenses, the standard mileage rate will likely work out better.

[¶904.3] Tax Strategy: Depreciation and the Standard Mileage Allowance

You may alternate by taking the standard mileage allowance one year and the item-by-item actual expense deduction the next year. For instance, say depreciation has allowed you to recover the cost of your car (less salvage value) over a three-year useful life. Since there is no further depreciation to recover, if you continue to use your car after the three years, the standard mileage allowance rather than the item-by-item deduction may save you many tax dollars.

However, you won't qualify for the standard mileage allowance if you depreciated your automobile under an accelerated depreciation method for an earlier year or claimed the additional 20% first-year depreciation allowance (where the use of your car allows a useful life of at least six years).

In any year in which the standard mileage allowance has been used, straight-line depreciation will be considered to have been allowed. The allowable depreciation will reduce the basis of the car in determining adjusted basis. *Note:* The trade-in values of the large luxury cars may have dropped in recent times. If you drive such a vehicle, you can readjust your salvage value downwards to get a bigger depreciation deduction under the item-by-item method of deduction. Moreover, you may disregard salvage value that's less than 10% (§167(f)).

You can claim the mileage deduction by preparing your own statement, but it's easier to use IRS Form 2106, "Statement of Employee Business Expenses," whether you take the automatic deduction or the item-by-item deduction. Also, you can use Form 2106 whether you're an outside salesman, traveling employee, businessman, or professional. This form is also useful in the trade-in of your business car because it simplifies computations.

[¶905] ENTERTAINMENT EXPENSES

In order to deduct an expense incurred for business entertainment, you have to show that it meets each of these tests from Code §274: (1) It must be an ordinary and necessary business expense. Section 274 is strictly a disallowance provision; it doesn't make deductible anything not otherwise deductible. (2) It must not be lavish and extravagant under the circumstances. (3) It must not violate public policy or local law (e.g., serving liquor where it's against local law or providing "call girls"). (4) It must be either directly related or associated with your trade or business or come within one of the specific exceptions to this requirement such as business meals. (5) It must be substantiated in accordance with IRS requirements. Estimates won't do. If you don't substantiate properly, you lose the deduction even though the expense was otherwise a proper one.

[¶905.1] What Is Entertainment?

Entertainment includes such activities as entertaining at night clubs, sporting events, or on hunting, fishing, and similar trips. Certain items, says IRS, are clearly *not* regarded as entertainment, e.g., supper money to an employee for working overtime, a hotel room furnished by an employer to an employee while on business travel, an automobile used in business even though used for commuting, too.

If an activity is generally considered entertainment, the following arguments won't change things, says the Treasury: (1) that the expense is for the taxpayer himself only; (2) that it is really an advertising or public relations expense.

The taxpayer's trade or business also enters into the determination if entertainment is involved. For example, if a dress manufacturer runs a fashion show to introduce his spring line to the buyers, that would not be entertainment. But if an appliance distributor runs a fashion show for his retailers' wives, that would be entertainment.

[¶905.2] Gifts or Entertainment?

Some expenses might fall on the borderline, and whether they are gifts or entertainment might make a big difference—business gifts are deductible only to the extent of $25 per year per donee. So, where possible, you're going to want to have an item called entertainment (assuming, of course, that the expense will meet the rules for deducting entertainment costs).

Generally, says IRS, where an item might be either entertainment, on the one hand, or a gift or travel cost, on the other, it will be considered entertainment. However, packaged food and beverages given to a customer, for example, for use at some other time, is a gift.

As for theatre and similar tickets of admission, if you go along it's entertainment even if you give the tickets to your guest. If you don't go along, you can treat the expense either as entertainment or a business gift.

Advantage of treating it as a gift is that you don't have to meet the entertainment rules for deductibility. Disadvantage is that business gifts to one recipient in one year are deductible only to the maximum extent of $25 per year. So, if you go above that mark, you have to use the entertainment route to get your deduction.

IRS will treat these expenses (where you don't go along) as gifts unless you treat them as entertainment. Your original choice is not necessarily binding, however, since you can change your treatment later on (as much as three years after you file your return); but if you intend to take advantage of this leverage, you had better make sure that you have the substantiation to back up either treatment.

An automobile or airplane can be considered a facility for entertainment, and then you have to meet the special tests in order to deduct expenses connected with it. To the extent an automobile or airplane is used for business transportation, the special facilities rules don't apply.

[¶905.3] Directly Related Entertainment

The Regulations set up four categories of entertainment costs that meet the directly related requirement: (1) general, (2) clear business setting, (3) services performed, and (4) allocable club dues and expenses. If your entertainment expense meets the requirements of any one of these categories, say the Regulations, you meet the directly related test.

☐ (1) ***The General Test:*** To qualify an expense as directly related under this test, the expense must meet all of the following four requirements (even then, it can be knocked out if it falls within those situations IRS has labeled as generally considered not directly related—discussed below):

(a) At the time you made the entertainment expenditure (or committed yourself to it) you had more than a general expectation of deriving some income or other specific trade or business benefit (other than the goodwill of the person entertained) at some indefinite future time from the making of the expenditure. But you won't have to show that you actually got the income or other business benefit for each deduction claimed.

(b) During the entertainment, you actively engaged in business meeting, negotiation, discussion, or other bona fide business transaction, other than entertainment, for the purpose of obtaining such income or other business benefit—or it was reasonable for you to expect to do so although circumstances beyond your control prevented you from doing so.

(c) All things considered, the principal character or aspect of the combined business and entertainment was the active conduct of your business (or you could have expected it would be, although circumstances beyond your control prevented it from coming about). It's not necessary that you spend more time on business than on entertainment. However, if the entertainment takes place on hunting or fishing trips or on yachts or other pleasure boats, IRS says that you won't meet this requirement unless you can clearly establish that the active conduct of business was foremost.

(d) The expenditure for entertainment was allocable to you and a person with whom you engaged in active conduct of trade or business (or would have, but for circumstances beyond your control). If any portion of an expense satisfies this general test, the remaining portion of the expense (to the extent allocable to a person closely connected with either you or someone else with whom you engaged in the active conduct of business) is presumed to meet the test for deductible goodwill and associated entertainment (Reg. §1.274-2(d)(3)(ii)). Thus, if you entertain a customer under circumstances that meet the above test, your wife and his wife can also be present and the expenses attributable to them are also deductible. That's because a spouse is considered closely connected for this purpose.

□ (2) ***Clear Business Setting:*** To qualify an expenditure as directly related under this category, the expense has to occur in a clear business setting directly in furtherance of your business—one in which the recipient would have reasonably known that you had no significant motive in furnishing the entertainment other than furthering your trade or business. An example of this is a "hospitality room" at a convention where your products are displayed or discussed.

Entertainment of this nature will meet the requirement if there was no meaningful personal or social relationship between you and the recipients of the entertainment. For example, you'd have a directly related situation where business representatives and civic leaders are entertained at the opening of a new hotel or theatrical production, where your clear purpose for entertaining them is to get business publicity rather than the goodwill of the guests.

Also, you meet the clear business setting rule where the entertainment has the effect of a price rebate—e.g., a hotel provides a free meal to a good customer. Note that you can lose out under this test if the entertainment falls within a category IRS considers generally not directly related—see below.

□ (3) ***Services Performed:*** You have a directly related entertainment expense if it is really compensation to an individual (other than an employee) for services rendered or was paid as a prize or award that is required to be included in the recipient's income. IRS gives the example of a manufacturer of products who provides a vacation trip for retailers who exceed certain sales quotas.

□ (4) ***Allocable Club Dues and Expenses:*** If you use your club or other facility under circumstances that qualify under the business meal exception, a pro rata portion of club dues, depreciation, and general operating expenses equal to the business meal use is deemed to be directly related. Thus, if a club or other facility is used 20% for business meals and 40% for other directly related entertainment, 60% of the dues, depreciation, and general operating expenses will be deductible (Reg. §1.274-2(c)(6)).

Expenses IRS Considers Generally Not Directly Related: If the entertainment occurred under certain circumstances, IRS says it's not directly related unless you can clearly establish the contrary. There is little or no possibility of engaging actively in business, says IRS, either if you were not present or if the distractions were substantial. Here are some examples where distractions are considered to be substantial: (a) a meeting or discussion at night clubs, theatres, and sporting events, or during essentially social gatherings such as cocktail parties; (b) a meeting or discussion, if the group includes persons other than business associates, at places such as cocktail lounges, country clubs, golf and athletic clubs, or at vacation resorts. A business associate is anyone you could reasonably expect to deal with in your business such as a customer, client, supplier, employee, agent, partner, or professional advisor (whether established or prospective).

[¶905.4] Facilities Used for Entertainment

Expenses incurred for maintaining facilities that are used for, or in connection with, entertainment, such as yachts, hunting lodges, fishing camps, swimming pools, tennis courts, bowling alleys, automobiles, airplanes, hotel suites, apartments, and homes in vacation resorts are deductible only to the extent they meet certain rules. Dues paid to social, athletic, or sporting clubs are also subject to these rules.

No part of the cost of maintaining a facility or the club dues is deductible until you first establish that the "primary" use of the facility was to further your trade or business. Then, if you've met this first test, only so much of the expenses in question that meet the test of "directly related" entertainment are deductible.

For this purpose, business meals are considered to be directly related. The portion of the total expenses allocable to this type of entertainment, therefore, is deductible just as if it were allocable to entertainment that met the general test for directly related entertainment.

To deduct an expense subject to the facilities rule, you have to show the facility was used primarily for business purposes. The test of primary use will depend on the actual use of the facility, not its availability for use or the intention lying behind its acquisition. Objective standards will apply. Factors to be considered are nature of each use, frequency and duration of each use for business purposes as compared with other purposes, amount spent for business purposes compared with expenditures for other purposes. However, no single standard will necessarily apply to each type of facility to determine the primary use, nor will IRS necessarily depend on a quantitative measurement.

[¶906] ADVERTISING AND PROMOTION EXPENSES

We can spend before-tax dollars in advertising and promotion and in building distribution channels. Whether these dollars produce additional sales currently or in the future, they can be translated into additional capital value, not taxed until realized and then at the 25% capital gain rate.

Each advertising commitment should be appraised in these tax terms:

☐ (1) It may bring profits into a higher or lower rate bracket, depending upon whether tax rates rise or fall.

☐ (2) It may bring sales that, after fixed costs have been met, show an additional margin. Because of the additional margin, the advertising risks may be covered very quickly.

☐ (3) It may give us the equivalent of a cash reserve. A reserve of additional volume may be built up by deductible advertising expenditure. Cash reserves are not deductible and must be built from profits after taxes.

☐ (4) By building customers, it may insure stability of earnings. That gives a stockholder a chance at an improved net return—since he is taxed at capital gain rates if the business or his stock is sold.

To act on a proposed advertising appropriation, we must compare it with other uses to which the funds might be applied. Tax factors will influence such choices as:

☐ (1) Building capital value by nondeductible plant expansion or by deductible advertising.

☐ (2) Increasing current dividends to stockholders or using the funds in advertising to underpin the value of their stocks. How does the tax increase in stockholder income from dividends compare to the possible loss in capital value if reduced promotion results in a loss of sales volume?

[¶906.1] Relating Activities to Business

Advertising expenses are deductible if reasonable in amount and reasonably related to the activities of the business. They needn't be for direct or immediate effect; an aim to develop goodwill or to influence the buying habits of the public is all right. However, a purchase of goodwill or the development of a trademark involves a capital expenditure rather than a current expense (*Richmond Hosiery Mills*, 6 BTA 1247, 1927). Payments to gain political influence or influence public officials are nondeductible as against public policy (*Stover*, 27 TC 48, 1956).

The nature of the advertising usually isn't material so long as it meets the above requirements. Deduction has been allowed for such quasi-personal items as the cost of maintaining show horses acquired to publicize a restaurant chain (*Rodgers Dairy Co.*, 14 TC 66, 1950). But be careful with this: Cost of showing horses was disallowed where the only tie-in was to give the horse a name similar to the owner's, with an inferential reference to the owner's business of wholesaling (*Schulz*, 16 TC 401, 1951); as was the cost of maintaining and racing speedboats where the corporation was practically never mentioned and the racing association did not allow registration in the name of the corporation (*Gale*, 297 F.2d 701, CA-6, 1962). However, the Tax Court has approved an equipment and machinery company's deduction of all its expenses (including depreciation) in connection with operating a power boat for advertising purposes. The program was undertaken for the sole purpose of publicizing the business (*U.S. Equipment Company*, TC Memo 1963-261).

The cost of installing products in residences for demonstration purposes is a deductible advertising expense (*Rev. Rul. 56-181*, CB 1956-1, 96). Similarly deductible are a doctor's cost of sending postcards to patients, referring doctors, and business contacts while touring Europe (*Duncan*, 30 TC 386, 1958).

Expenditures for contests and prizes must be reasonable in amount and relationship to the business (*Citizens Trust Co.*, 2 BTA 1239, 1925). IRS has allowed cost of an automobile given away by a restaurant owner to the patron holding the winning ticket in a drawing, and the cost of outfitting a baseball team.

[¶907] RESEARCH AND DEVELOPMENT

U.S. industry is spending billions of dollars on research programs. These figures and the story they tell were an important reason for the adoption of Code §174, which governs the handling of research and development costs. Generally, these expenditures are deductible if incurred "in connection with" the taxpayer's trade or business. They include experimental or laboratory costs incident to developing new or improving existing experimental or pilot models, plant processes, products, formulas, and inventions (costs of obtaining a patent, including attorneys' fees). Expenses for testing, inspection, quality control, management, or efficiency studies and advertising promotion are not included (Reg. §1.174-2(a)(1)).

Even without being engaged in an existing trade or business, an entrepreneur, such as an independent researcher, can obtain a double-barrelled tax benefit: He can get an immediate deduction for his research investment; and, generally, if he is successful, he will later enjoy favorable capital gain treatment. This result flows from a recent taxpayer victory in the Supreme Court (*Snow*, Sup. Co., 5/13/74).

When §174 was enacted in 1954, the aim was to equalize somewhat the tax benefits of established companies and those of small upcoming concerns. Large corporations with continuous research programs routinely deducted the costs of experimental work under §162 as ordinary and necessary in carrying on a trade or business. On the other hand, a venture not yet carrying on a business was denied a similar deduction. To equalize treatment for both rich and poor taxpayers, §174 was enacted giving small emerging businesses a deduction for these expenses.

Under §174, a taxpayer takes a deduction for "experimental expenditures which are paid or incurred by him during the taxable year 'in connection with' his trade or business as expenses which are not chargeable to capital account." This contrasts with §162, which allows a deduction only for expenses "in carrying on" a trade or business. Here's what happened to Snow.

In 1966, Snow invested $10,000 for a 4% interest in a partnership formed to develop a trash burner. Several prototypes had been developed, but it wasn't until 1970 that the trash burner was patented and marketed. Snow claimed deductions for his proportion of the losses during the research and development stages of the venture. The Supreme Court rejected the lower courts' reasoning that Snow's deduction wasn't "in connection with" a trade or business, because the venture wasn't in business or production and didn't even have a patent at the time. However, there has to be a profit motive underlying the venture; someone puttering around with a hobby will merely be subject to §183 (covering "hobby losses") if the venture is abandoned later.

Note: A person may be in the business of being an inventor if his activities are of a sufficiently sustained character. Such an inventor was allowed to deduct his outlays for attorney's fees, technical books, and copies of patents (*Louw,* TC Memo 1971-326). Where an investor decides to back an inventor by advancing funds to him, the only safe way to establish the business requirement is with a written agreement of partnership or joint venture (*Cleveland,* 297 F.2d 169, 1961). Otherwise, the advances will be loans and not research and development expenses.

[¶907.1] Deduction v. Capitalization

Here are your alternatives for writing off the cost of research and development. You can elect either to:

□ (1) Deduct currently all research expenses paid or incurred during the year even if spent for a patent or other technological property. Only exclusions are cost of new land or improvements, cost of new depreciable or depletable property, and cost of locating oil, gas, and other minerals after the beginning of the development stage. Oil and gas drilling and development costs can be capitalized or expensed, at the operator's option (Reg. §1.612-4).

□ (2) Capitalize the expenses, amortizing them over a period of time not less than 60 months. Exluded again are expenditures applicable to depreciable or depletable property. Only drawback is that you get no amortization deduction until the first month the expense benefits you.

If you don't elect either method, the expenses must be capitalized and charged off over the useful life of the property created by the research activity. But if you abandon the project, research and development expenses can be deducted as a loss.

The election to deduct currently is available even if you capitalize the expenses for accounting purposes (*Rev. Rul. 58-78,* CB 1955-1, 357). If you made such an election and failed to deduct all the costs currently, file an immediate claim for refund for any open years. Otherwise, should those years be closed by the statute of limitations, you will lose the deductions forever (*Rev. Rul. 58-74,* CB 1955-1, 230).

Making the election to amortize research costs over 60 months or more is a simple matter. All you have to do is attach a statement to your tax return for the first year the expenditures are made. The statement must include the following information: (a) the amounts of each type of such expenditures, (b) detailed information describing the nature of such expenditures, and (c) the period over which such expenditures are to be ratably deducted. (See Reg. §1.174-4(b)(1).)

The current expense method requires no information statement if properly adopted (Reg. §1.174-3(b)(1)).

[¶907.2] Benefits of Deducting Currently

The sensible thing seems to be to deduct currently. If your business is losing money at the moment, there is something to be said for electing to defer deductions until future years when you have income they can offset. The trouble with this is that you will need permission to change to current deducting when the profitable days arrive. Furthermore, deferral of depreciation deductions distorts the relationship between economic and tax depreciation.

Anyway, you won't lose the tax benefits of current deducting even in a losing period as your increased loss can be used as a carryover loss for the next five years.

If you already own depreciable property used in research, you have an incentive for spending money on research now. Spending the money will give you the right to make an election to deduct currently and deprive the Treasury of an excuse to throw depreciation into a deferred account so as to postpone the deductions.

Machinery costs are generally recovered by taking depreciation deductions over the life of the machine (except for the 7% investment credit and the 20% first-year writeoff). Generally overlooked is a provision in the regulations that may entitle you to an immediate writeoff for part of your cost.

If you pay someone for research or development work, you can deduct or capitalize the cost as your own. If you order a machine to your specifications and the manufacturer has to undertake research and experimentation to fill your order, you can deduct the part of the cost of your machine that covers these costs, provided the product you are buying is on your order and at your risk. In other words, there can't be a guarantee as to how the machine will perform (but you can get a guarantee as to engineering specifications). Of course, you can't include the manufacturer's costs of material, labor, and the like (Reg. §1.174-2(b)(3)).

[¶908] LEGAL AND ACCOUNTING FEES

To be deductible, legal and accounting fees must be "trade or business expenses" or "non-trade or non-business expenses." A nonbusiness expense is one incurred "for the production or collection of income; for the management, conservation or maintenance of property held for the production of income; or in connection with the determination, collection, or refund of any tax" (§212).

The fees must be established as expenses rather than capital expenditures; they must be ordinary and necessary, and they must be reasonable in amount (*Welch,* 290 US 111, 1933; *Kornhauser,* 276 US 145, 1928).

Broadly speaking, an attorney's or accountant's fee based on services tending to increase or protect taxable business income is deductible (e.g., defending inherited stock, *Sergievsky,* 135

F.Supp. 233, DC N.Y., 1955; investigation by SEC of taxpayer's relations with an associated corporation, *Lomas & Nettleton Co.*, 79 F.Supp. 886, DC Conn., 1948), while fees based on services tending to establish or defend title to property can't be deducted at once, but must be added to the cost of such property (e.g., legal expenses on the purchase of a home; revoking a trust and redistributing trust property). Ordinarily, if the expense is incurred to accomplish both purposes—protect and defend title—apportionment has been the method used. In *Galewitz,* 50 TC 104, 1968, the Tax Court said it would look to the primary purpose.

Legal fees for services performed in drafting a corporate merger agreement are to be capitalized as incident to the reorganization. Legal fees for tax advice as to a merger or reorganization, a split of the stock of the surviving corporation, and a proposed redemption of a portion of its stock are also to be capitalized. However, if the proposed redemption of stock is abandoned, the capitalized fee attributable to it is deductible in the taxable year of abandonment (*Rev. Rul. 67-125*, CB 1967-1, 31). Legal expenses incurred in defense of a proposed deficiency in income taxes attributable to business income are deductible for adjusted gross income, so you can deduct them even though you take the standard deduction (*Thomas,* 41 TC 614, 1964).

A legal or accounting fee incurred in connection with the purchase of a capital asset and properly capitalized may be recovered through depreciation or amortization. Fees incurred by the seller of real property are offset against the proceeds of the sale. If both types of property are involved, fees are allocated according to how much of the fee was necessitated by the various interests (*Arnett Estate,* 31 TC 320, 1958).

The taxpayer must prove the allocation. (The attorney or accountant can show the allocation on the bill on the basis of time spent, the complexity of the matters involved, or some other charge method that can be justified.) It is usually safe to say the Tax Court will allow a full deduction for legal expense incurred to defend a non bona fide claim and make sure the attorney's billing properly reflects the services performed by him.

[¶909] INDIRECT POLITICAL CONTRIBUTIONS

The general rule is that contributions to political organizations are not deductible. However, some business firms have been able to avoid this rule and get a tax deduction for political contributions, merely by distinguishing the contribution as a business expense (see *Rev. Rul. 56-343*, CB 1956-2, 115). One of the most common ways that this was done was by advertising in political convention programs or in some other political publications. Under existing law, these firms were able to get the deduction on the basis that their intent in advertising in these various political publications was to sell the product that was being advertised rather than to benefit the political aspirant. In one case, cost of advertising that actually extolled a political party rather than taxpayer's product was held deductible on the grounds that it created goodwill (*Denise Coal Co.*, 29 TC 528, 1957).

Code §276 plugs this hole. Now, no deduction will be allowed for advertising in any publication—political or nonpolitical—where any part of the net proceeds of the publication directly or indirectly inures to the use of a political party (including any committee, association, or organization that attempts to influence elections) or to a political candidate.

Code §276 also reaches various other indirect political contributions and disallows a deduction for these items where the proceeds from the event directly or indirectly inure to or for the use of a political party or a political candidate. Here are some items that are specifically disallowed:

☐ (1) Payments for admission to a political fund-raising dinner or program (which includes any separate charges for food or drink).
☐ (2) Admission charges for such events as galas, dances, theatrical or film presentations, cocktail parties, picnics, sporting events.
☐ (3) Admission charges to an inaugural ball, gala, parade, cocktail party, concert, or similar event.

[¶910] LOBBYING EXPENSES

Certain types of lobbying expenses are deductible if they are incurred in taxable years beginning after December 31, 1962 (§162(e)). Lobbying expenses incurred in prior taxable years were not deductible (*Cammarano and Strauss & Son, Inc.*, 358 US 498, 1959), and lobbying expenses that do not come within §162(e) are still not deductible.

For lobbying expenses to be deductible under §162(e), they must be ordinary and necessary expenses of carrying on a trade or business (including travel expenses and the cost of preparing testimony). In addition, the expenses must be incurred in either of the following two situations:

☐ (1) In direct connection with appearances before, submission of statements to, or sending communications to the committees or individual members of Congress or of any legislative body of a state, a possession of the United States, or a political subdivision of any of the foregoing with respect to legislation or proposed legislation of direct interest to the taxpayer.
☐ (2) In direct connection with communication of information between the taxpayer and an organization of which he is a member, with respect to legislation or proposed legislation of direct interest to the taxpayer and to such organization.

If you are a member of any organization that carries on the activities described above, you can deduct the portion of your dues paid to that organization that is attributable to the cost of deductible lobbying activities.

However, gifts, contributions, or other expenditures to, or on behalf of, political parties or candidates for public office or that attempt to influence the general public with respect to legislative matters, elections, or referendums, are specifically excepted. These expenses remain nondeductible.

[¶911] IMPROPER PAYMENTS—BRIBES AND KICKBACKS

Kickbacks, bribes, and similar payments that businesses are sometimes forced to make are not specifically prohibited as business deductions unless they fall into a special category. That is, they are not deductible (1) if they are made to government officials or employees or (2) the taxpayer is convicted in a criminal proceeding of making an illegal payment (§162(c)).

Payments that do not come under this category generally are barred by IRS on the broad ground that they violate "public policy." The Supreme Court, however, has severely limited the disallowance of deductions on "public policy" grounds.

In *Heininger,* 320 US 467, 1944, the Supreme Court held that the deduction should not be allowed only when it would "frustrate sharply defined national or state policies proscribing particular forms of conduct." The mere fact that an expenditure bears a remote relation to an illegal act is not enough.

In *Lilly,* 343 US 90, 1952, the court allowed deductions for kickbacks by owners of an optical business to doctors who prescribed glasses. In doing so, the court expanded on *Heininger* by including the further requirement that the "sharply defined national or state policies" alleged to be frustrated must be evidenced by some specific "governmental declaration of such policies." In *Tellier,* 383 US 687, 1966, the High Court reemphasized the guidelines of *Heininger* and *Lilly*. In a rebuke to IRS, they declared that IRS would not be allowed to raise the "public policy" bar except in "extremely limited circumstances."

When the rule (§162(c)) denying a deduction for payments where there is a criminal conviction was enacted, a journal of national circulation had this to say: "Whatever the ethical implications, fee-splitting payments are now a perfectly legal income tax deduction. That's the result of an obscure change in the [1969] tax law. It provides that such payments must be allowed unless the taxpayer is convicted in criminal proceedings."

We beg to differ: Section 162(c) doesn't expressly require that the deduction be allowed unless the taxpayer is convicted in a criminal proceeding. What it really says is that if he's convicted or pleads guilty to having made an illegal bribe or kickback, the deduction is not allowable. Now, you can argue from this that if you're not guilty, the deduction should be allowed, but we wouldn't bank on your winning the argument. Certainly, don't count on IRS yielding the point.

What to Do: Play it safe. Be prepared to show that the fee-splitting arrangement is made in proportion to the services performed and the responsibilities assumed by each party.

Where the payments are for specialized services, the customer (or client) should be told that a specialist is being used and he should be billed separately by the specialist.

Tell the client (or customer) that you will be working with the specialist on the matter and that each of you will bill him separately for the professional services rendered. With this approach there can be no question of illegal fee splitting or kickbacks, no chance of criminal involvement, no question of improper fee splitting under a professional code of ethics, and no tax problem.

Proper business expenses of an illegal business are deductible as long as no law or regulation prohibits the deduction (*Sullivan,* 356 US 27). In the *Sullivan* case, the Supreme Court allowed the deduction of wages and rents incurred by a bookmaker whose operations were illegal in Illinois. It held that costs connected with condemned activities can be disallowed if there is a clear policy for such disallowance.

In general, the expenses of an illegal business will be treated in the same manner as the illegal expenses of a legal business. In *Tellier,* the court considered its decision in *Sullivan,* in reviewing and setting forth the general principles in this area.

[¶912] BUSINESS GIFTS

Deduction of business gifts is for the most part limited to $25 per year per donee. To the extent that the total amount of gifts to any one person in any one taxable year exceeds that amount, it is not deductible.

Incidental costs, such as custom engraving on jewelry and for packaging, insurance, and delivery are not taken into account in applying the $25 limitation.

Where gifts are made by a partnership, the $25 limitation is applied at the partnership level *and* at the individual partner's level.

Husband and wife are treated as one donor. This is the rule even though they may be engaged in separate businesses and even though they do not file a joint return.

Any item that is excludable from the gross income of the recipient as a gift (§102) that is not also excluded under some other provision of the code is a gift for this purpose. Thus a scholarship that is excludable under §117 and a prize or award that is excludable under §74 are not subject to the $25 limitation.

Payments to widows of key employees usually qualify for the $5,000 death benefit exclusion from gross income of §101(b). If they don't qualify, or even if they do, to the extent that they exceed $5,000 they are taxable to the widow unless it can be shown that the payment was in fact a gift. If such amounts do qualify as gifts, the deduction to the employer making the payment will be limited to $25. The $5,000 death benefit under §101(b) is not subject to the rule, however, since that amount is excludable from gross income under another code provision.

[¶912.1] Exceptions to the $25 Rule

The following items are not subject to the $25 limitation:

☐ (1) Items of a clear advertising nature that cost $4 or less and (a) on which the taxpayer's name is permanently printed and (b) are one of a number of identical items generally distributed by the taxpayer. So, if a number of these advertising specialties were given to one customer or prospect during the year, the $25 limit would not apply.

☐ (2) Signs, display racks, or other promotional material given to a retailer by a producer or wholesaler for use on the business premises of the retailer.

☐ (3) Watches and other similar gifts awarded to employees because of length of service or for some safety achievement, if they cost $100 or less.

[¶912.2] Indirect Gifts

A gift made to the wife of someone with whom you have a business connection is treated as an indirect gift to the husband, says IRS. So, you can't double up on the $25 figure by making a $25 gift to each spouse. Of course, if both husband and wife are active in the business, you can make a deductible $25 gift to each.

The $25 limit applies to gifts to individuals. If you give to a corporation with the intent that a particular individual is to benefit from it, then it's considered you gave the gift to that individual. On the other hand, where one or several of many persons can make use of the gift and you don't know which ones will ultimately benefit, then it will not be considered that you gave it to any one individual. So, if you provide several baseball tickets to a corporation for eventual use by any one of a large number of employees or customers of the corporation, they will not be considered gifts given to any one individual indirectly (Reg. §1.274-3(d)).

SECTION X
DEPRECIATION

One of the most important sections of the Code to any businessman is §167, which provides for an "allowance" for depreciation. This deduction is useful because it requires no cash outlay: If you own depreciable property, you get the deduction.

In this section, the various tax rules governing this key deduction are discussed. The various methods of depreciation are covered, as well as the pitfalls, like recapture.

[¶1001] WHAT IS DEPRECIATION?

Basically, depreciation is the way that the tax law recognizes that things wear out. When a businessman buys a machine, he knows it will not last forever and that someday he will have to replace it. So, as he uses it, it becomes less and less valuable. At the same time, it is earning money for him; and since a part of the money the machine earns is a return of the original investment capital, and not income, it would be unfair to tax this part of the earnings of the machine. So, the tax law allows a deduction for depreciation.

However, this deduction is not granted to all property—only property "used in the trade or business" or "held for the production of income." Only these types of property—called "depreciable property"—return any income, and so only in these cases is there any possibility that a return of capital could be taxed.

This, then, is the theory behind depreciation—to insure that the user of depreciable property will recover his capital investment in the property tax free. It is the same idea as allowing him to deduct the whole cost in the year of purchase; but if he did that, his income would be distorted whenever the worn-out property had to be replaced. To prevent this kind of distortion of income, the tax law requires all taxpayers to use one of several types of averaging methods to spread the cost of the property over its useful life. The amount you can deduct in any year depends on three factors: (1) The cost or other basis of the depreciable property; (2) the useful life of that property to you; and (3) the method of depreciation you use.

[¶1002] BASIS AND SALVAGE VALUE

Normally, your basis in depreciable property is your cost of the property. This cost is adjusted upward for installation charges, transportation charges, substantial improvements, etc., and adjusted downwards for any depreciation you subsequently take. In practice, this may not work out to be as simple as it sounds. For example, where you replace a depreciable asset by trading in an old asset, your basis in the new asset will be your adjusted basis in the old asset (regardless of what it may really be worth) plus any additional amounts paid for the new asset.

[¶1002.1] Allocation of Basis

When property is acquired, it is often necessary to allocate basis. Here are the instances when allocation is necessary:

☐ (1) ***Acquisition of Improved Real Estate:*** Whenever you acquire a piece of improved real property, you have an immediate need for an allocation. Land is not depreciable; and in order to determine your basis for depreciating the building, you have to reduce your overall basis by an amount that represents a reasonable basis for the land. The usual method of making the allocation is in proportion to the respective fair market values.

If you have in fact paid proportionately more for the building for some special reason and can establish the fact, you can use the higher amount as your depreciation basis. The best way to secure such an advantage, however, is by a specific allocation in the contract that spells it out in detail.

If any of the contents of the building are included in the purchase transaction, you need a further allocation between the structure and the contents. Then the amount allocated to the contents must be further broken down among the various items included in the sale.

This latter allocation will require all parties to consider the investment credit and depreciation recapture provisions of the Code.

☐ (2) ***Acquisition of More Than One Asset:*** The purchase of more than one asset (mixed assets) calls into play the same rules discussed above. The cost of a group of assets that is stated as a single sum must be broken down and allocated among the separate items or groups. This permits the proper allocation of useful lives to different assets or groups and separates depreciable from nondepreciable assets. Again, the possible effects of the investment credit and depreciation recapture provisions must be watched.

☐ (3) ***Acquisition of a Going Business:*** Where a business is acquired by a purchase of its stock, there is no need for an allocation as far as the seller is concerned. He has sold stock. If the buyer continues to operate the business in the corporation, the basis of the assets is unchanged. However, if the buyer is a corporation and liquidates the acquired corporation within two years in order to obtain a stepped-up basis, he's got the same problem as the purchaser of a sole proprietorship. The cost of the stock must be allocated to the various items that make up the business (§334(b)(2)). You can have the same result even where the purchaser is not a corporation.

Other ways in which this question can arise include the purchase of assets or of a business by buying assets either from a partnership or corporation, or by a purchase from stockholders who have received property in a liquidation.

Allocation in the Purchase Agreement: An allocation made at the time of the agreement and reduced to writing will ordinarily be accepted for tax purposes where it was bargained for at arm's length and in good faith. A self-serving allocation, however, that has been created with tax consequences in mind will not be binding on IRS.

Goodwill and Noncompete Covenants: From a tax viewpoint, here is an area where the interests of the buyer and seller are directly opposed. The seller wants to allocate as much as possible to goodwill so as to obtain capital gain treatment. The buyer wants to avoid nondepreciable goodwill and to categorize any payment of this nature as a covenant not to compete, which is subject to depreciation. Where these factors are contemplated at the time of the sale, it becomes a matter of negotiation.

[¶1002.2] Salvage Value

Before applying depreciation rates to basis to determine how much we can deduct, we first have to consider salvage.

Salvage value is the amount that it is estimated will be realized upon sale or other disposition of an asset when it is no longer useful in your trade or business or in the production of your income and is to be retired. Salvage value must be taken into account in determining your depreciation deductions unless an election to use the Asset Depreciation Range System is in effect. Under this system, salvage value is not taken into account in establishing annual depreciation deductions for an asset or a class of assets, but the asset or class of assets may not be depreciated below salvage value. We cover this subject under our discussion of useful lives.

Where the determination of salvage value is required, you may determine it either by reducing the basis of the asset or by reducing the rate used to depreciate the asset.

Where the 200%- or the 150%-declining-balance method of depreciation is used, salvage value is disregarded in determining the annual allowance. But the asset cannot be depreciated below a reasonable salvage value (Reg. §1.167(b)-2).

What the salvage value will be depends on the asset and the way you handle such an asset. If it is your policy to dispose of assets while they are still in good shape, your salvage value will be a relatively large proportion of your basis. On the other hand, you may customarily use assets until their inherent useful life has been substantially exhausted, and the salvage value may represent no more than junk value. Salvage has been held to be what you reasonably expect to sell the asset for at the time you normally dispose of it.

Depreciation Deduction in Year of Sale: The Supreme Court ruled that IRS cannot disallow a depreciation deduction in the year of sale of depreciable property just because its sale price is higher than its adjusted basis at the start of the year (*Fribourg Navigation Company, Inc.*, 383 US 272, 1966).

[¶1003] DEPRECIATION METHODS

Depreciation methods permitted by the tax law include: (1) straight-line method (equal annual installments), (2) declining-balance method (up to double the straight-line rate), (3) sum-of-the-years-digits method (rate is a fraction, the numerator being the property's remaining useful life at the start of the tax year and the denominator being the sum of all the years' digits corresponding to the estimated useful life at acquisition), and (4) any other consistent method that during the first two-thirds of the property's useful life does not give greater depreciation than under the declining-balance method (§167(b)).

Method number (4) embraces use of a sinking fund, writeoffs on the basis of periodic appraisal, unit of production, etc. However, most taxpayers who do not use the classic straight-line method employ instead one of the acceleration methods, either the 200%-declining-balance method or the sum-of-the-years-digits method.

Another possibility that should be mentioned is a combination of the straight-line method and the 200%-declining-balance method. With this method, you use the 200%-declining-balance method, which gives you extra large deductions in the early years. At the point where this starts to peter out, you switch to straight line, which can be accomplished without consent of the Commissioner (Reg. §1.167(e)-1).

The applicable allowable depreciation (or amortization in lieu of depreciation) methods and rates may be summarized as follows:

☐ ***Declining-balance method, 200% rate*** is allowed for new tangible personal property with a useful life of three years or more; all types of newly constructed real estate structures acquired before July 25, 1969; only to residential rental property if acquired after July 24, 1969.
☐ ***Declining-balance method, 150% rate*** is allowed for new tangible personal property; newly constructed rental property acquired after July 24, 1969.
☐ ***Declining-balance method, 125% rate*** is allowed only for used residential rental property acquired after July 24, 1969, and having a useful life of 20 years or more.
☐ ***Sum-of-the-years-digits method*** is allowed only for new tangible personal property and new residential rental property.
☐ ***Straight-line (useful life) method*** is allowed for all property, new or used, personal or real.
☐ ***Straight-line method (no salvage value), 60 months*** applies to low-income rental housing rehabilitation expenditures, certified pollution control facilities, and certain railroad rolling stock.

The use of the 200%-declining-balance and the sum-of-the-years-digits methods was suspended during the period beginning October 9, 1966, and ending March 9, 1967. But there are a number of exceptions to the rule that can take you off the hook.

[¶1003.1] Straight-Line Method

The depreciation expense is the same from period to period. The formula followed for this method is:

$$\text{Depreciation expense} = \frac{(\text{Cost} - \text{Salvage Value})}{\text{Estimated Life}}$$

For example, if the asset costs $10,000, has a salvage value of $100, and an estimated life of ten years, the depreciation expense for the year would be computed as follows:

$$\frac{(\$10{,}000 - \$100)}{10} = \$990$$

The straight-line method depends upon the hypothesis that depreciation will be at a constant rate throughout the estimated life.

[¶1003.2] 200%-Declining-Balance Method

Under this method (also called the double-declining-balance method), the amount of depreciation expense decreases from period to period. The largest depreciation deduction is taken in the first year. The amount then declines steeply over succeeding years until the final years of estimated useful life when the depreciation charge becomes relatively small. Code §167 restricts the taxpayer to a rate not in excess of twice the straight-line rate if the straight-line method had been employed.

While true declining-balance method requires the application of a complex formula, if you are going to use the maximum declining-balance depreciation—i.e., the 200% method—you need not go through these mathematical computations. Just do this: (1) determine the straight-line percentage rate; (2) double it; (3) apply it against your full basis (undiminished by salvage value) to get your first year's deduction. In the second year, (1) reduce your basis by the previous year's depreciation deduction; (2) apply the same percentage rate to the new basis you arrived at in step (1). In the third year and later years, repeat the same process.

Example: You buy a truck for the business. It costs $5,500 and has a five-year useful life. We'll assume you bought it January 1, 1973. Since it has a five-year life, the percentage of depreciation by the straight-line method is 20%. Using 200%-declining-balance, you'll use a 40% rate. So, for 1973, you'd deduct $2,200 (40% of $5,500). For 1974, you'd reduce your $5,500 basis (original cost) by the $2,200 1973 depreciation deduction. That gives you a basis for 1973 of $3,300. For 1974, your depreciation deduction would be 40% of that $3,300, or $1,320. That cuts your basis for 1975 to $1,980 and your depreciation deduction for that year becomes $792 (40% of $1,980). This process continues on for the future years you continue to hold this truck.

[¶1003.3] Sum-of-Years-Digits Method

Here, diminishing rates, expressed fractionally, are applied to the total depreciable value (cost − salvage).

Under sum-of-the-years-digits, the annual depreciation charge decreases rapidly; since maintenance charges, on the other hand, increase rapidly, the effect is to level off the annual costs of depreciation and maintenance.

To use sum-of-the-years-digits, you proceed as follows. Using, for purposes of illustration, a depreciation account of $5,500 with a ten-year life and ignoring salvage, add the numbers of the years: 10 + 9 + 8 + 7 + 6 + 5 + 4 + 3 + 2 + 1 = 55. Depreciation the first year will be 10/55 of $5,500, or $1,000. For the remaining years, you can follow one of two practices. Either you continue to base depreciation on original cost, using 55 as the denominator of your fraction and the number of the year as the numerator—9/55 of $5,500, 8/55 of $5,500, and so on (Reg. §1.167(b)-3(a)(1)), or you apply a fraction with a diminishing denominator to unrecovered cost—9/45 of $4,500, 8/36 of $3,600, and so on (Reg. §1.167(b)-3(a)(2)).

Note that in the second method, the amount by which the denominator for a given year diminishes is always the amount of the numerator for the preceding year. Denominator 45 in the second year is denominator 55 for the first year, less numerator 10 for the first year; denominator 36 for year 3 is denominator 45 for year 2, less numerator 9 for year 2.

Regardless of which method is used, annual depreciation will be the same: 9/55 of \$5,500 and 9/45 of \$4,500 both give \$900 of depreciation; 8/55 of \$5,500 and 8/36 of \$3,600 both give depreciation of \$800.

[¶1003.4] Sinking-Fund Method

The sinking-fund method of computing depreciation has been generally preferred by independent businessmen. An imaginary sinking fund is established by a uniform end-of-year annual deposit throughout the useful life of the asset. The assets are assumed to draw interest at some stated rate, e.g., 6%, sufficient to balance the fund with the cost of the asset minus estimated salvage value. The amount charged to depreciation expense in any year consists of sinking fund plus the interest on the imaginary accumulated fund. The book value of the asset at any time is the initial cost of the asset minus the amount accumulated in the imaginary fund.

Assume that an asset cost \$1,000 and has no salvage value but has an estimated life of 25 years. The interest rate is assumed to be 6%. By using conversion tables, the sinking fund deposit is \$1,000 × .01823 or \$18.23. In the second year, the depreciation charge will be \$18.23 + (\$18.23 × .06) = \$19.32; in the third year, it will be \$18.23 + (\$18.23 + \$19.32) × .06 = \$20.48, and so forth. The \$18.23 represents the sinking-fund deposit and remains the same for the period of depreciation. In other words, under this method the businessman anticipates earnings and profits on his capital investment and thus increases his capital.

This method is permissible for federal income tax purposes provided it does not exceed the rate as computed under the declining-balance method.

[¶1003.5] Unit-of-Production Method

This is a method used for the depreciation of assets used in production. Under this method, an estimate is made of the total number of units the machine may be expected to produce during its life. Cost less salvage value, if any, is then divided by the estimated total production to determine a depreciation charge for each unit of production. The depreciation for each year is obtained by multiplying the depreciation charge per unit by the number of units produced. Here's how it works on a \$10,600 machine good for 300,000 units of output:

$$R = \frac{\text{Cost} - \text{Salvage Value}}{\text{Estimated Units}}$$

$$R = \frac{\$10{,}600 - \$600}{300{,}000}$$

$$R = \$.03\tfrac{1}{3}$$

Units produced for 1 year = 24,000
Depreciation = 24,000 × \$.03⅓ = \$800

A severe obstacle to the use of this method is the difficulty of ascertaining the total number of units that the asset will produce. The production method is most applicable to fixed assets like airplane engines, automobiles, and machinery where wear is such an important factor. It is useful for fixed assets that are likely to be exhausted prematurely by accelerated or abnormal use.

[¶1004] USEFUL LIFE

There are two basic methods for determining useful life of an asset. You can determine the useful life by reference to the facts and circumstances surrounding the use of the asset or you may elect the "Class Life System," which is referred to as the Asset Depreciation Range (ADR). We'll discuss the "facts and circumstances" standard first.

Estimated useful life for purposes of this standard isn't necessarily the useful life inherent in the asset; rather, it is the period over which the asset may reasonably be expected to be useful in *your* trade or business or for production of *your* income (Reg. §1.167(a)-1(b)). Determine the period by reference to your experience with similar property, taking into account present conditions and probable future developments.

Factors to be considered in determining the period are:

☐ (1) Wear and tear and decay or decline from natural causes;
☐ (2) The normal progress of the art, economic changes, and inventions and current developments within the industry and your trade or business;
☐ (3) The climatic and other local conditions peculiar to your trade or business; and
☐ (4) Your policy regarding repairs, renewals, and replacements. If your own experience is inadequate for determining the useful life of some items, you can use the general experience in the industry.

Estimated useful life may be modified by reason of conditions known to exist at the end of the taxable year. However, the change in useful life must be significant, and there must be a clear and convincing basis for the redetermination.

[¶1004.1] Asset Depreciation Range (ADR)

The Revenue Act of 1971 incorporated liberal depreciation rules with the Guideline lives fixed by IRS back in 1962 and established an Asset Depreciation Range (ADR) System. This system may be elected for assets placed in service in 1971 and thereafter.

Briefly, the ADR System does five things:

☐ (1) Authorizes IRS to accept depreciation based on lives for business equipment that are 20% shorter or 20% longer than the "guideline lives" (discussed below).
☐ (2) Provides for a half-year averaging convention as exemplified by the following two alternative methods: (a) All eligible property placed in service obtained during the taxable year is deemed to be acquired at midyear, or (b) each asset placed in service during the first half of the taxable year is deemed to be acquired on the first day of the same year, while each asset placed in service in the second half of the year is deemed to be acquired on the first day of the next taxable year.
☐ (3) Permits a deduction for expenditures for repair and maintenance based on a percentage of the assets in a guideline class on which depreciation under the ADR System is elected. It will not be necessary to prove that such expenditures do not have to be capitalized.
☐ (4) Sets up a new Office of Industrial Economics that will analyze the annual information

submitted by taxpayers using the ADR System; constantly revise the guideline classes, guideline lives, and repair allowances; and set up new guidelines and allowances where appropriate.
☐ (5) Eliminates reserve ratio test. Deductions for depreciation no longer need to be justified under this test.

[¶1004.2] Guideline Lives

Back in 1962, the Treasury issued depreciation Guidelines (*Rev. Proc. 62-21*, CB 1962-2, 418) with more liberal (i.e., shorter) useful lives than the outmoded *Bulletin F*. These guidelines are the basis of the useful life used under the ADR System. (See ¶1004.8.)

Rev. Proc. 62-21 grouped all business assets into four groups with 75 classes of assets and showed a useful life for each broad class. The first group deals with assets used by business in general—office furniture, fixtures, machines; automobiles and trucks; land improvements; buildings. The next three groups deal with types of businesses: Group Two deals with nonmanufacturing activities; Group Three, with manufacturing activities; and Group Four, with transportation, communications, and public utilities.

To use the Guidelines, you find the useful lives of the groups of assets that fall into Group One. Then, usually all the rest of your assets will fall into one classification of one of the other three groups into which your business falls. For example, a plastics products manufacturer would find that he falls into classification 18 (plastic products) of Group Three. So, his office furniture, cars, etc., would use the appropriate useful lives in Group One and all the remainder of his assets would use the 11-year useful life assigned to subcategory 18 of Group Three.

If your activities cut across more than one group, then segregate the assets into the proper Guideline classifications within each of the appropriate groups.

[¶1004.3] How to Decide Whether to Adopt ADR System

In order to make an evaluation of whether it pays you to sell or trade in your old equipment and buy new in order to get the higher or lower depreciation under the ADR System, you have to take a careful look at the arithmetic. How much depreciation are you getting out of the old equipment? How much will you get with the new? How much is any loss on the sale of the old worth? What are the estimated expenses with the old? With the new? What are the estimated cost savings, if any, through the higher efficiency of the new, etc.?

In some situations it may be worthwhile for a businessman to trade in old equipment and start out with new equipment that is subject to lower depreciation deductions.

The approach he takes depends on whether or not the tax basis of the old equipment is higher than its present value. If it's not and he trades it in on the new equipment, he avoids the recapture of the gain as ordinary income under §1245. The gain carries over to the new equipment and is not realized until the new property is sold.

On the other hand, if the basis is higher than the present value and he trades in the old property, he can't claim the loss, so that he will be looking to sell the property in order to realize the loss (and to avoid having IRS look on it as a trade-in anyhow, the sale should be to a third party).

Tax Savings and Insured Cash Flow: Assume that on May 1, 1971, a calendar-year corporation that purchases equipment at various times throughout the year acquires equipment costing $1,000 and having a depreciable life under the existing guidelines of 5 years:

□ (a) *Earlier Rules:* Under the double-declining-balance method of depreciation the taxpayer's deduction for a full year would be 40% (2 × 20%) of the cost of the equipment, or $400; but under the half-year convention the taxpayer's first-year deduction is $200. The tax saving in the first year was $96 (48% tax rate × $200).
□ (b) *Shorter Depreciable Period:* Under the ADR System, the depreciable period is shortened from 5 to 4 years. Thus, the taxpayer's double-declining-balance depreciation increases to 50% (2 × 25%) for a full year, or $500. Under the half-year convention, its deduction is now $250 (½ of $500). The tax savings in the first year is $120 (48% × $250).

Life of Ten Years: If the equipment in the above example had a depreciable life of ten years under the earlier guidelines, the results would be as follows:

□ (a) *Earlier Rules:*
Full year's depreciation 20% (2 × 10%) $200
Depreciation under the half-year convention 100
Tax savings 48
□ (b) *Shorter Depreciable Period:* Under the ADR System, the depreciable period can be shortened from 10 to 8 years.
Full year's depreciation 25% (2 × 12.5%) $250
Depreciation under the half-year convention 125
Tax savings 59

Special Repair Allowance: If the repair expenditures have the character of capital additions and might not ordinarily be deductible, election of the ADR System may get you a current deduction for a percentage of the expenditures. This is illustrated as follows:

□ (a) *Earlier Rules:* Let's say the property to which you have made repairs is in a vintage account (see ¶1004.5) with an unadjusted basis of $200,000. The repairs, all at the beginning of the year, total $10,000. Ordinarily you would get an annual depreciation deduction of $1,000 on a straight-line basis ($10,000 total deductible over 10 years). The tax reduction is $480 ($1,000 × 48%).
□ (b) *ADR Repair Allowance:* An amount equal to 6.5% of $200,000 or $1,300 may be allowable on the guideline class property as the repair allowance for the year plus depreciation on $8,700 ($10,000 − $1,300) under the ADR System that permits a life smaller by 20% or $1,087.50 ($8,700 over 8 years). The total deduction for the year would be $2,387.50.

On the difference of $1,387.50, the amount of tax saved would be $666 ($1,146 − $480). The year's cash outlay would be reduced by the amount saved.

Even under the ADR System, if all your expenditures are clearly deductible repairs, you may choose not to apply the repair allowance and so be free to deduct all expenditures currently.

[¶1004.4] Checklist of Basic Rules

Generally, the ADR System applies to all types of assets for which guideline lives are provided. This includes tangible personal property as well as tangible assets (including research or storage facilities) that are used as an integral part of manufacturing, production, or mineral extraction or the furnishing of transportation, communications, electricity, gas, water, and sewage disposal. (Special rules apply to public utilities.)

Real property (buildings, realty improvements, etc.) and so-called subsidiary assets (jigs, dies, textile mill cam assemblies, returnable containers, glassware, and silverware) are also eligible for class life treatment. To give the Treasury Department time to establish separate class lives for real property and subsidiary assets, transitional rules will apply to them. Taxpayers placing such assets in service in the period beginning on January 1, 1971, and ending on either December 31, 1973, or such earlier date on which the Treasury establishes the appropriate class lives may continue to use shorter lives where such lives can be justified.

□ ***Range of Asset Life:*** In general, the ADR System is from 20% shorter to 20% longer than the guideline class life for the asset or class of assets.

□ ***ADR System Assures Acceptance of Deductions:*** The ADR System establishes ranges of depreciation periods. The deduction based on the depreciation period that the taxpayer has chosen within the applicable range will be accepted for all assets to which he has elected to apply the ADR System.

□ ***System is Optional:*** Unless a taxpayer elects the ADR System for the taxable year, it will not apply. However, if elected for the taxable year with respect to a trade or business, all assets placed in service in that trade or business during that taxable year must be depreciated under the ADR System.

□ ***Methods of Depreciation Allowable Under the ADR System:*** To figure out the amount of depreciation either (a) the declining-balance, (b) sum-of-the-years-digits, or (c) straight-line method may be used. A choice is made as to each vintage account. To use (a) or (b) the depreciation period must be at least three years.

For new property, you can figure depreciation on a 200%-declining-balance rate; on used property you may use 150% of the straight-line rate. Do not use any depreciation method not listed above for any vintage account, because all the assets in the vintage account will be barred from the ADR System unless you can prove you made a mistake.

Should you find it advantageous, you can change your method of depreciation for a vintage account from the declining-balance to either the sum-of-the-years-digits or straight-line method and can change sum-of-the-years-digits to straight-line without the consent of IRS. Any other change requires the consent of IRS.

Don't overlook the additional first-year depreciation of 20% of the cost of the property. This is allowed in addition to the ADR System on the balance of the cost. The 20% is deductible in full without proration based on when acquired during the year. The allowance is limited to 20% of no more than $10,000 ($2,000) per taxpayer, whether corporation or individual. In a partnership the allowance is to each individual partner, not the partnership. A husband and wife can each take up to $2,000 for a total of $4,000.

□ ***How and When to Make Election:*** Once you have decided to use the ADR System, make sure that you make a proper election. Your business has until the time for filing its income tax return (including extensions) to make this decision. The election is filed with the income tax return for the year the election is to go into effect.

IRS will make available forms (revised Form 4832) on which the election may be made; but the election can be made by attaching a statement to the tax return indicating that the election is being made. The statement should be as detailed as possible, indicating that an election to use the ADR System is being made and giving all the required information relating to the equipment that qualifies under the System.

□ ***Placing Equipment in Service:*** The equipment has to be "placed in service" in the taxable year for which the election is made. This doesn't necessarily mean that it has to be put in actual use; the equipment qualifies if it is "ready or available" for the function it is expected to perform.

Also, the "placing in service" rule refers to the year in which the property is placed in service by the taxpayer. So, if the property was purchased from another taxpayer who did not use the System, the purchaser can still use it for the first year in which the property is placed in service.

[¶1004.5] First-Year Convention

A half-year convention applies to all item and multiple-asset vintage accounts under the System. A taxpayer who elects to apply the ADR System must elect to apply either the half-year convention (treating all assets placed in service during the taxable year as placed in service at the midpoint of the year) or the modified half-year convention, (treating all assets placed in service during the first half of the year as placed in service at the beginning of the year and all assets placed in service during the second half of the year as placed in service at the beginning of the following year).

□ (1) ***Vintage Accounts Retirements:*** Assets subject to the election are required to be accounted for in accounts by the year placed in service (vintage accounts). Normal retirements from such accounts are ignored—the deduction for depreciation is computed as if all assets in the account survived for as long as the period selected. Also, no gain or loss is recognized on such a retirement.

In the case of abnormal retirements (resulting from casualty, curtailment of business, etc.), the unrecovered basis of the asset is removed from the vintage account and the allowable depreciation from the reserve for depreciation. Also, gain or loss is recognized on abnormal retirements.

□ (2) ***Used Assets:*** If the ADR System is elected, it applies to used as well as new assets. The depreciation period of the used as well as the new assets must be within the System for such assets or classes of assets. Be sure to put used assets into a separate vintage account. New and used assets may not be in the same vintage account.

An exception is made where the basis of used assets exceeds 10% of the total basis of all assets placed in service in the year. In such case, lives for used assets may be determined without regard to the System. It may even be possible for you to depreciate such used assets more rapidly. But be sure to make use of the exception only if it works out favorably for you, because all the used property acquired that year will be kept out of the System.

Similarly, the costs of rebuilding, rehabilitating, or repairing an asset to the extent such costs must be capitalized are known as "excluded additions" to which the repair allowance can in no event apply. Such "excluded additions" must be accounted for in separate vintage accounts and treated in the same manner as used assets.

□ (3) ***Salvage Value:*** Salvage value is not taken into account under the ADR System in establishing the annual depreciation deduction for an asset or class of assets. Thus, the annual depreciation deduction is determined by applying the appropriate fraction or percentage based on the period selected to the original cost or unadjusted basis of the asset. But no asset or class of assets may be depreciated below the salvage value after application of §167(f) of the Code. However, for new equipment with a useful life of at least three years, salvage value of up to 10%

of cost can be disregarded. In addition, IRS won't disturb the salvage value estimate unless it's out of line by yet another 10% of cost. In other words, there's a leeway of up to 20% of cost in estimating salvage value.

[¶1004.6] Checklist of ADR Benefits

The ADR System is complex and highly detailed, but it does have many tax benefits. Here are some ways in which the annual election to use the System can reduce taxes:

☐ (1) ***Shorter Useful Life:*** By selecting a useful life for newly acquired equipment that is approximately 20% shorter than the usual straight-line period (e.g., 8 years instead of 10).
☐ (2) ***Convention Depreciation:*** By adopting a first-year "convention" that permits depreciation to start as of the first day of the taxable year for all property acquired during the first half of the year and as of the first day of the following year for all property acquired during the last half of the year.
☐ (3) ***Lower Salvage Values:*** By setting a salvage value that can be an amount lower than previously deemed necessary by anywhere from 10 to 20% of the unadjusted cost of the property and so increasing the amount that can be fully deducted over the life of the property.
☐ (4) ***Flexibility:*** If the amount of "used property" placed in service during the year exceeds 10% of all eligible property placed in service during the year, all the "used property" placed in service may be excluded from the election. This might permit even shorter writeoff lives for such property or the use of depreciation methods not otherwise allowable while keeping ADR System benefits for all other eligible property.
☐ (5) ***Repair Allowances:*** By omitting an annual election that can result in maximum deductions for repair expenditures. Election of the ADR System repair allowance allows a percentage repair deduction even where it is clear that the expenditures would otherwise be treated as capital additions.
☐ (6) ***Additional First-Year Depreciation:*** By permitting the deduction in the first year of 20% of the cost of eligible property and still having the benefits of the System as to the remainder of the cost. (See ¶1005.)
☐ (7) ***Continuing Use of the System:*** By permitting the acquiring corporation in a reorganization to use the benefits of the ADR System if the transferor corporation has elected to apply the System to the eligible property being transferred.
☐ (8) ***Flexible Election:*** By permitting depreciation to start in some instances even if the eligible property has not yet been put in use. The definition of year "first placed in service" applies to permit this.
☐ (9) ***Postponement of Gain on Disposition:*** By postponing the reporting of gain on certain dispositions of eligible property.
☐ (10) ***Additional Investment Credit:*** By permitting the use of the 7% investment credit for eligible property and still having the benefits of the ADR System without the credit reducing cost or basis.

[¶1004.7] How to Make ADR Election

An election is made for a particular taxable year by including in the return substantially all the information set forth as required in the regulations:

☐ (1) ***Consent:*** Your consent and agreement to apply all the provisions of the ADR System.
☐ (2) ***Guideline Class:*** The asset guideline class under which you plan to depreciate each vintage account set up for the taxable year.
☐ (3) ***Vintage Account Depreciation:*** For each vintage account you must designate the asset depreciation period you will use. The period must be within the range set up in the asset guideline class.
☐ (4) ***First-Year Convention:*** The first-year convention that you adopt for the taxable year of this election.
☐ (5) ***Unadjusted Basis and Salvage Value:*** The total unadjusted basis (cost in most cases) and total salvage value for all the assets in each vintage account. (You will undoubtedly have a record of all the assets that you put into each of the vintage accounts for the particular year with the applicable salvage value.) Also, you must state the amount, if any, by which you decreased the salvage value from what it perhaps should have been.
☐ (6) ***Used Property Exception:*** Whether you applied the 10% used property exception and intend to exclude from the election all used property acquired during the year; also, state the unadjusted basis of all used property placed in service during the year and the unadjusted basis of all property (new and used) first placed in service during the year.
☐ (7) ***Repair Allowance:*** As to each asset guideline class for which the repair allowance is to be used, state the amount of property improvements, how much the repair allowance deduction will be, and how much (the balance) will be set up as a "special basis vintage account" for the year.
☐ (8) ***Excepted Eligible Property:*** A reasonably clear description must be included of the eligible property acquired during the year for which no election is to be made because of special rules. (*Note:* The ADR System cannot be elected for property subject to special speedy amortization or depreciation provisions; e.g., railroad rolling stock, coal mine safety equipment, pollution control facilities, etc.)
☐ (9) ***Investment Credit Exclusions:*** A reasonably clear description must be included of all property that is to be excluded because it is to your advantage to use a longer useful life for the investment credit.

While IRS is insisting that the information submitted as part of the election be complete, the election will not be invalid if you have substantially complied with the regulations in supplying the information requested.

[¶1004.8] Class Lives Under ADR

As has been pointed out, the class lives for various assets are based, for the most part, on the earlier guideline lives of *Rev. Proc. 62-21*. The specific limits, however, were set out in *Rev. Proc. 72-10,* CB 1972-1, 721, which has been regularly supplemented.

These tables of class lives under ADR are quite comprehensive, although they do not cover every possible depreciable asset. They are reproduced on page 414 of the appendix for your reference.

[¶1004.9] Information as to Each Guideline Class

The election will not be considered complete unless the following actions have been taken as to *each asset guideline class* selected for assets acquired during the year:

☐ (1) State the total unadjusted basis (original cost in most cases) of all property retired from each vintage account in the asset guideline class and how much you received for the property.
☐ (2) Include a reasonably clear description of the retired property identifying the separate vintage accounts by year in each asset guideline class from which the property was retired during the taxable year.
☐ (3) State clearly how and why the retirement took place. Indicate whether the asset was sold, exchanged, abandoned, subject to a casualty or whether there was some form of curtailment of the operation of the business.
☐ (4) Submit the amount and identify the property for which there were expenditures for repairs, maintenance, rehabilitation, or improvements and state the vintage accounts and asset guideline classes in which the property was placed.
☐ (5) If you have entered into an agreement with the Commissioner of Internal Revenue on how you are to depreciate certain types of property as you acquire it and now find you can benefit by applying the ADR System to similar newly acquired property, include information as to such property and state your intent to withdraw the property from the agreement so that you can apply the ADR System.

If you happen to put property into the wrong asset guideline class, your election will not be revoked provided the classification is corrected and all the necessary adjustments to the accounts are made.

[¶1004.10] Multiple-Asset Accounts

This is the grouping of depreciable assets into one or more accounts, based on types of assets, method of depreciation, or any other grouping that makes sense for that business. Assets subject to the ADR election are put into a vintage account for the year of election.

Before we get into a discussion of multiple-asset accounts, let's get our terms straight. Here, as a guide, are some Treasury definitions:

☐ (1) ***Group Account:*** Assets similar in kind with approximately the same useful lives.
☐ (2) ***Classified Account:*** Assets segregated according to use without regard to useful life; e.g., machinery and equipment, furniture and fixtures, or transportation equipment.
☐ (3) ***Composite Account:*** Assets are included regardless of their character or useful lives; e.g., all assets used in a business. This is broader than classified account.

Group, classified, or composite accounts may be further broken down on the basis of location, dates of acquisition, cost, character, use, etc. (Reg. §1.167(a)-7(a)).

A component account is one in which assets are segregated according to their function; e.g., electrical wiring, plumbing, floors, roofing, appliances, etc. (*Shainberg,* 33 TC 241, 1959). Component accounts can be segregated and used to form one part of a composite account. So, where we want to depreciate a complete factory and everything in it, we might segregate the furniture and fixtures into one component account, machinery and equipment into another component account, etc. Then, the composite account would be the total of each component account.

Assets may be grouped on any logical basis for some benefit, not only tax reasons. Among the reasons for these types of accounts are: (1) taxes, (2) ease of bookkeeping, (3) companies in interstate operations may need to group assets located in each state separately for local tax purposes, (4) cost accounting purposes. There may be some drawbacks in group accounts; for example, lack of data on the cost of operation of some particular assets, lower depreciation deductions than on item-by-item basis, and recalculation of group rate when assets sufficient to affect the rate are acquired.

Another consideration is that the grouping of assets for tax purposes doesn't necessarily have to be the same as for financial statement purposes or for management's cost-type information. Dual sets of books may be kept.

The Treasury's guideline rules suggest the possibility of combining all assets falling within a guideline class into one account to be used for financial as well as tax purposes. This would simplify the calculation of depreciation and minimize your bookkeeping cost. But you might get larger depreciation deductions by using itemized accounting.

[¶1005] ADDITIONAL FIRST-YEAR DEPRECIATION (§179)

Under Code §179, a special, one-shot depreciation deduction is allowed on certain kinds of depreciable property. The deduction is 20% of the cost of the property (but limited to $2,000, or $4,000 if a joint return is filed) if

☐ (1) The property is tangible depreciable property; and

☐ (2) The property is acquired by purchase for use in a trade or business, or for production of income; and

☐ (3) The property has a useful life of six or more years (as of the date of purchase).

Section 179 depreciation is not available to trusts. However, it can be taken in addition to the investment credit, if the property purchased otherwise qualifies for the investment credit. It is also taken in addition to any other depreciation allowable on the property for the year of purchase. The taxpayer need not take the full deduction to which he is entitled. Finally, the deduction is not prorated over the year—in other words, if you buy qualified §179 property in December, you get the full deduction, not just one-twelfth.

[¶1006] DEPRECIATION RECAPTURE

So far, we have discussed the plus side of depreciation, which is computing the deduction. As we said, this deduction is a noncash expenditure—you can shelter other income with it, since you don't pay anything out. But what if you later sold the property? Let's say that it had gone up in value over the years. You paid $10,000 for it in 1960, and now it is worth $25,000. So you sell it for $25,000. You report a gain of $22,000, because you have an adjusted basis of $3,000 after deducting $7,000 worth of depreciation on the straight-line basis. Is the gain a capital gain?

The answer depends on the kind of property you sold. If it was personal property, $7,000 of your $22,000 gain is ordinary income (§1245). If it was real property, all $22,000 is capital gain (§1250). The difference in the treatment is the result of two depreciation recapture sections, each with its own rules.

[¶1006.1] Personal Property (§1245)

The recapture section for personal property is §1245, and its rule is simply that any gain attributable to depreciation deductions taken after June 30, 1963, will be recaptured. When gain is recaptured, it is treated as ordinary income, even though it would otherwise be a capital gain.

What this means is that you can't use the depreciation deduction on personal property as a tax-shelter device to convert ordinary income into capital gains. Any time your adjusted basis (which is adjusted for depreciation) is less than the price you get when you sell the property, the gain will be ordinary income up to the amount of your accumulated depreciation deductions. Just to make sure, §1245 provides that this gain shall be ordinary income "notwithstanding any other provision of this subtitle" (§1245(a)(1)).

However, §1245 itself does contain six fairly limited exceptions. They are:

☐ (1) Gifts.
☐ (2) Transfers at death.
☐ (3) Tax-free transactions under §332, 351, 361, 371(a), 374(a), 721, and 731.
☐ (4) Like-kind exchanges and conversions under §1031 and 1033.
☐ (5) Regulated transactions under §1071 and 1081.
☐ (6) Distributions by partnership to partner.

Except for these few special cases, the rule of §1245 is unavoidable: The gain attributable to depreciation deductions will be taxed as ordinary income.

[¶1006.2] Real Property (§1250)

Where real property is involved, the appropriate recapture provision is §1250. As will be seen, §1250 is considerably milder in its effect than §1245, and some tax-shelter potential (conversion of ordinary income into capital gains) is still possible.

Like §1245, §1250 applies "notwithstanding any other provision of this subtitle." However, unlike §1245, §1250 recapture applies only to gain attributable to additional depreciation, which is defined as depreciation deductions taken that exceed those that would have been allowed using the straight-line method. So, for starters, you can convert all the straight-line depreciation you take on real property into capital gains, if you hold the property for one year before you sell it. This depreciation will never be recaptured under any circumstances.

As long as you hold real property for one year, the only thing §1250 will recapture—and the only thing you have to worry about—is excess depreciation, which comes from using one of the accelerated methods of depreciation, like declining-balance or sum-of-the-years-digits. However, §1250 will not even necessarily recapture this depreciation, since it contains a tax incentive for low-income housing and a lesser incentive for housing generally. (There is no incentive for commercial real estate.) The incentive comes in the form of a phaseout, so that recapture phases out at a rate of 1% per month for each month over 20 months (low-income housing) or 100 months (other housing) that you hold the property.

For example, if you owned regular (as opposed to low-income) residential rental property that you had held for a period of 15 years, and depreciated under the 200%-declining-balance method, the amount of additional depreciation recaptured would be 20%. (Fifteen years equals 180 months, or 80 months longer than 100 months. Since the phaseout is 1% per month, 80% of the recapture is phased out, leaving only 20%).

In the actual calculation, you would subtract the amount of straight-line depreciation you could have taken from the actual amount of depreciation you deducted over the 15 years. The difference would be the additional depreciation, and 20% would be taxed as ordinary income, while 80% would be capital gains.

If, in the same example, the property had been low-income housing, there would be no recapture, since you held the property more than ten years. However, this special rule for low-income property (§1250(a)(1)(C)(ii)) applies only to property constructed, reconstructed, or acquired before 1976 (unless extended by law).

Also note that unless real property is residential rental property, the fastest depreciation method that may be used is the 150%-declining-balance method (§167(j)(1)(B)). This is the other tax incentive Congress inserted in the Code to favor low-income housing in particular, and housing in general. This is an important incentive, too, in spite of recapture, because accelerated depreciation, even if recaptured, still amounts to an interest-free loan from the time you take the deduction up to the time you have to pay the tax.

Section 1250, like §1245, contains some exceptions to recapture. These are basically the same as those contained in §1245 (see ¶1006.1) with somewhat different rules of application (see §1250(d)(1)-(6)). In addition, §1250 contains an exception for the sale of a principal residence under §1034 and §121 by a person over 65 and for the sale of qualified low-income housing where gain is not recognized under §1039.

SECTION XI

CUTTING TAXES THROUGH BAD DEBTS

Two major problems arise with the deduction for bad debts:

☐ (1) Proving worthlessness. You don't get the deduction until you show the debt is worthless. (With business bad debts, you *can* deduct for partial worthlessness.)
☐ (2) Distinguishing between business and nonbusiness bad debts. Business bad debts are fully deductible; nonbusiness bad debts are deductible as short-term capital losses only.

[¶1101] BUSINESS V. NONBUSINESS LOSSES

The distinction between business and nonbusiness losses is only of concern to the individual taxpayer. To a corporation, all losses are deductible. However, individuals' losses are limited to certain types: (1) losses incurred in a trade or business; (2) losses incurred in a transaction entered into for profit; and (3) casualty and theft losses (§165(c)). All losses are only deductible to the extent not compensated for by insurance or otherwise (§165(a)). And they must be evidenced by closed and completed transactions and fixed by identifiable events (Reg. §1.165-1(b)). Losses from a trade or business (including property held for the production of rents and royalties and from the sale or exchange of property) reduce adjusted gross income. That means that in addition to being fully deductible, the standard deduction may also be used. Nonbusiness losses from transactions entered into for profit (not connected with business) are only deductible if the individual itemizes his deduction and in lieu of the standard deduction.

Where you have a nonbusiness loss involving a capital asset (e.g., where you invest in the stock of a corporation in the expectation of capital appreciation), §1211 and 1212 limit the deduction to the extent of capital gains plus $1,000 of ordinary income for the current year. Any amount not deductible in the year of the loss may be carried forward indefinitely and deducted in the same way against future capital gains and ordinary income. Business bad debts are business losses; nonbusiness bad debts are treated like capital losses (§166(d)). For these reasons, a taxpayer would like to have a business loss rather than a nonbusiness loss.

[¶1101.1] Guarantors

When you are obliged to pay someone else's loan you guaranteed or endorsed, and you can't collect from the original borrower, you have a bad debt. As an individual, you can take a full deduction, regardless of whether the debt is business or nonbusiness, provided you can show that a noncorporate borrower used the money for business and the original debt is worthless (§166(f)). However, you cannot get a business bad debt deduction if you must make good on your guarantee of a noncorporate loan used to buy an interest in a business. Other types of guarantees are treated as bad debts—business or nonbusiness, as the case may be (*Putnam*, 352 US 82, 1957; also see §166(g) on reserve for guaranteed accounts).

How to Get an Ordinary Loss on Advances on Behalf of a Corporation: Instead of guaranteeing the corporation's credit, buy the merchandise the corporation would have bought on its credit. Arrange for a set-up where you are billed for the goods but the corporation receives and uses them and pays for them. If the corporation cannot pay, you (the primary debtor) will have to pay. But it's your primary debt, not a guarantee of the corporate debt that's being paid. If this debt is incurred in your business or in a profit-seeking transaction, it's a business payment and fully deductible.

[¶1101.2] Advances to Your Corporation

Loans to a corporation by its officers, principal stockholders, or by an investor or a promoter are in a twilight zone that is neither clearly business nor clearly nonbusiness. Unless the lender's activities in organizing, promoting, managing, and financing various business enterprises are sufficiently extensive and continuous to constitute them a business, the Government doesn't consider them business loans. Therefore, if they become worthless, they are capital losses just like any other nonbusiness bad debt.

The business v. nonbusiness bad debt contest is especially acute in the area of loans or guarantees of debts by a taxpayer to an enterprise in which he has an interest. The key to the nature of the bad debt deduction is whether or not the loan arose in connection with activities that the tax law recognizes as a trade or business.

Here are the facts in a Supreme Court decision: Whipple furnished management and other services to many corporations in diverse fields that he controlled or had an interest in. When a sizeable advance to one of these companies (a soda bottling corporation) became worthless, he deducted it as a business bad debt. The Tax Court disallowed the full deduction after finding that Whipple was not in the business of organizing, promoting, managing or financing corporations, of bottling soda or of financing or lending money. The Supreme Court agreed (*Whipple*, 373 US 193, 1963).

Here's when the Supreme Court indicates you may get a business bad debt on loans to your corporation:

(1) When you're in the business of lending money or financing;

(2) When you're in the business of organizing or promoting companies for a fee or commission or make profits on the sale of such businesses;

(3) When you furnish management or other services to a corporation for more than the rewards of a normal investor (e.g., income in the form of dividends or enhancement in value);

(4) When you work as a corporate executive for a salary and the loan is necessary to keep your job or otherwise proximately related to maintaining your trade or business as an employee.

Whipple came close to (3)—but he didn't quite make it because his management services were furnished for nothing more than the rewards of a normal investor.

Since what may be an investment-type deal to some taxpayers is a business-type deal to others, the final decision of whether a particular loss is business or nonbusiness is dependent upon the facts. The determination of a business bad debt, like a business loss, is essentially the same.

Three Cases Highlight Problem: Two brothers organized a corporation to make aluminum sash windows and glass doors. The business did well the first year but then ran into trouble and finally wound up in bankruptcy. But before that, the brothers, struggling to keep the business alive, were forced to personally guarantee their corporation's bank loans and obligations to its main supplier.

The brothers argued that the guarantees were given to protect their business interests as employees and landlords of the corporation. However, the Tax Court in refusing to buy the argument pointed out that they took salary cuts when the business got into trouble and failed to show that they could not secure more lucrative employment elsewhere. Likewise, they reduced the corporation's rent and did not show that they could not secure another tenant for the space (*Ninberg,* TC Memo 1967-109).

However, in another case, similar considerations were held to warrant business bad debt deductions.

In *Lundgren* (376 F.2d 623, CA-9, 1967), the Court of Appeals reversed the Tax Court and allowed a business bad debt. Lundgren was able to get a substantial Small Business Administration loan for his corporation on condition that he lend a similar sum to the corporation, that he draw no salary from the corporation for his services, and that he sell timber to it at cost. His interest in future remunerative employment and business with the corporation was held sufficient to support a business bad debt deduction when his loan to the corporation became worthless.

Advances made by an employee to his company were allowed as a business bad debt because the advances were made to maintain his business reputation, not as an investor. The employee made the advances to protect his reputation and employability as a designer and a salesman of shoes, thus assuring his continued ability to obtain employment elsewhere even though the company went bankrupt (*Artstein,* TC Memo 1970-220).

[¶1101.3] Subchapter S Offers Solution

An election to be taxed as a Subchapter S corporation is a method of salvaging the full loss deduction where it appears that the corporate venture is going sour and that there is a danger that losses may be incurred.

Where a corporation elects Subchapter S treatment, its net operating loss passes through to the stockholders and is deductible by them against ordinary income.

The stockholder's loss deduction is limited to the basis of his stock in the corporation and any debt the corporation owes him (IRC §1374). However, if the stockholder has to make good on a guarantee of the corporation's obligations, the corporation immediately becomes indebted to him in a like amount.

The fine technical distinction between the business and nonbusiness bad debt rules and the passthrough of the corporation's operating loss must be kept in mind. Thus, where the stockholder gets stuck on his guarantee of the corporation's obligation, it is a nonbusiness debt as far as he is concerned. However, it increases his basis in the corporation, so as to increase by a like amount the extent to which he can charge off against other income his share of the corporation's net operating loss.

The use of a Subchapter S election to obtain the benefit of a loss passthrough may involve timing problems. The election must be made in the first month or the month preceding the first month of the corporation's taxable year. On the other hand, the limits to which an operating loss can be charged off cannot be increased by an increase of investment or corporate debt to the stockholder in a year subsequent to the taxable year in which the corporate operating loss occurs. Thus, it is important that the election be made as soon as it appears that the corporation is in trouble and that the advances to the corporation and the obligations on the guarantee of its debts be called during the year the operating loss is incurred.

[¶1101.4] Employee Can Get Fully Deductible Bad Debt on Advances to Employer

If you make your livelihood as an employee, you are engaged in a trade or business. When you make a loan to your employer in order to hold your job, you are making a loan in connection with that trade or business. So, if the loan becomes worthless, you are entitled to a fully deductible business bad debt (*Trent,* 291 F.2d 669, CA-2, 1961; *Fitzpatrick,* TC Memo 1967-1).

[¶1102] RESERVE FOR BAD DEBTS

In lieu of deducting a business bad debt in the year in which it becomes worthless, you can deduct it under the reserve method. What this means is that you can deduct an estimated amount of your bad debt losses each year instead of deducting them as they occur (when they become worthless). The deducted amount is then held in reserve to cover the actual losses. That is, as a debt becomes worthless it is charged against the reserve. The reserve is then replenished by annual additions. The rule is, however, that these additions must be reasonable. What is a "reasonable addition" to a reserve for bad debts depends on all the facts and will vary as between classes of business and with conditions of business prosperity. The reasonableness will depend primarily upon the total amount of debts outstanding and the total amount of existing reserve (Reg. §1.166-4(b)).

Although debts may not be charged off against the reserve until they have become worthless, it does not follow that the circumstances particularly affecting a specific debt must be completely disregarded in determining the reasonableness of additions to reserve.

Use of the reserve method is predominantly for accrual-basis taxpayers. However, banks, and other finance companies on the cash basis have been permitted to use it (*First National Bank of Omaha,* 17 BTA1358, 1930).

When it becomes evident that a big account can't pay, an increased addition to the bad debt reserve is justified.

A district court permitted a finance company to base its year-end bad debt reserve on outstanding loans on the national average of 2.25% (deemed fair to taxpayer and IRS). This was so even though actual losses only came to .25%. The court reasoned that economic conditions may get worse at any time; in fixing a reserve, taxpayer must look to the future (*Reeves,* DC N.M., 1966).

The best way is to base your addition on past experience over a reasonable period of time. Since the reserve is the uncollectible part of the receivables, a common method is one that uses the ratio of net chargeoffs (chargeoffs less recoveries) to total receivables. However, failure to use a formula isn't fatal.

Year	*Net Chargeoffs*	*Receivables, Dec. 31*
1968	. . . .	$ 350,000
1969	$ 18,155	400,000
1970	22,400	475,000
1971	25,445	600,000
1972	28,350	675,000
1973	30,650	. . . .
Totals	$125,000	$2,500,000

Percentage of net chargeoffs to receivables	5%
Accounts receivable as of Dec. 31, 1973	$750,000
Reasonable reserve (5% × $750,000)	37,500
Reserve at beginning of 1973	$ 33,750
Less net chargeoffs during 1973	30,650
Reserve at end of 1973	$ 3,100
Reasonable addition to reserve	34,400
Reserve to start 1974	$ 37,500

The addition is sometimes based on either credit sales or total sales. The computation is the same except that the applicable sales figures are substituted for the receivables.

A moving five-year average is generally acceptable to the Government. If the accounts are relatively short-term, a shorter period may suffice; and if the accounts are long or the business has a longer than normal cycle, a longer period may be required. A substitute method for the past experience ratios is merely to make a careful evaluation of current receivables and base the addition to the reserve on a reasonable estimate as to their collectibility.

Of course, none of this is binding on the Government, and by the time the revenue agent comes to examine the books many doubtful accounts will have been resolved one way or another. That will change the allowable addition to the reserve, and consequently the allowable deduction.

In the interest of coming as close as you can to the amount finally allowable, it is a good idea to make trial computations using both the past experience and current evaluation methods and weigh the two.

In any case, if subsequent events show that the reserve for a particular year was either excessive or insufficient, the correction will be made in the current year's reserve. The reserve for the earlier year will stand, provided the addition to it was reasonable in the light of circumstances at the time.

To prevent distortion of the past experience ratios, a regular method of handling charges and recoveries should be established.

[¶1102.1] When Must Bad Debt Reserve Be Picked Up as Income?

If the accounts turn out better than anticipated, a reserve can build up to a point where it is much larger than is reasonably required. At this point, the action or nonaction of the taxpayer will determine whether any of this excess reserve will become taxable income.

If you want to create income—perhaps you have a loss to offset it—you can reduce the reserve (*Lutz*, 29 TC 469, 1957). If you want to avoid income, do nothing. Leaving the reserve alone will not create income (*Gsell*, 34 TC 41, 1960). However, one case points out, if the time comes when you sell off your assets or discontinue your credit sales—so there's no longer any need for the bad debt reserve—the amount of reserve must be restored to income (*Arcadia Savings & Loan Assoc.*, 300 F.2d 247, CA-9, 1962).

[¶1102.2] Treatment of Bad Debt Reserve When Liquidating Your Company

The answer to whether or not a bad debt reserve must be included in income is dependent upon the type of liquidation or merger involved. So, for example, if there is a complete liquidation where the corporation goes out of existence under §337 (12-month liquidation) and a sale of the corporation's assets, including its receivables, the reserve must be taken into income. However, if there is a liquidation of a subsidiary (for example, in a §332 liquidation by a parent of its wholly owned subsidiary, with the parent continuing intact the subsidiary's business) or an exchange of stock under a corporate reorganization, where the holder of the receivable continues in existence (even though in altered form), the risk of bad debt loss continues and the necessity for the reserve remains. This is what happened in *Home S & L*, 223 F. Supp. 134, DC Ca., 1963. Home S & L bought all the outstanding stock of Hollywood S & L; then Hollywood merged into Home. The corporate existence of Hollywood ended, but its entire business was continued as part of Home.

[¶1103] HOW TO SHOW A DEBT IS WORTHLESS

In order to get a deduction for a debt or for securities that have lost all their value, it is necessary to show a condition of worthlessness (except that business bad debts are deductible in part if partial worthlessness is shown—Reg. §1.166-3). The Regulations require that the loss be linked to an identifiable event occurring during the year for which the loss is deducted (Reg. §1.165-1(d)(1)).

Where the year of worthlessness is difficult or ambiguous, from a practical angle, it may pay the taxpayer to take the deduction in the *first year* in which he objectively determines the worthlessness to exist. If IRS challenges his determination, it may be deducted in subsequent years.

[¶1104] ELECTING TO REDUCE BASIS FOR BAD DEBT

A corporate debtor can elect to reduce his basis for gain or loss, instead of reporting the cancellation of a debt as income (§108 and 1017). The election is made by filing Form 982, in duplicate, with your tax return for the taxable year when this cancellation occurred. The rules for reducing basis are spelled out in the Regulations (Reg. §1.1017-1).

What to Do: Don't make an election unless you are absolutely sure that you have cancellation-of-indebtedness income. The election only applies where the cancellation results in income. If the cancellation does not result in income, you would be in effect conceding that it is income by electing to reduce your basis.

Since there is uncertainty in this area, you would do better when faced with a questionable transaction to contest the taxability of the cancellation rather than accept the benefits of reducing your basis. The difference between taking and not taking the election is the time when you will be taxed. If you take the election, you will be taxed when you dispose of the property; if you don't take the election, you will be taxed in the year the cancellation occurred. However, you may be able to contest the cancellation and then take the election to reduce your basis in the event you lose.

The regulations provide that a taxpayer who wants to take advantage of the election "must file with his return for the taxable year a consent to have the basis of his property adjusted. . . ." This would mean that you would have to make the election in the year of the cancellation, and in effect concede that you have cancellation-of-indebtedness income. (Unless, of course, you could file a conditional consent; but there is no rule on this matter, and it could be successfully argued that a conditional consent is no consent.) But the regulations also provide that if you fail to file the consent with your original return, you may file the consent with an amended return upon establishing to the satisfaction of the Commissioner "reasonable cause" for the failure.

Although there are no cases on this specific issue, it would seem that failure to file because you are contesting liability under competent advice from a tax specialist would constitute "reasonable cause." Therefore, if you contest liability and lose, you may be able to file an amended return for the year of cancellation to include your election to adjust your basis, rather than have the cancellation-of-indebtedness treated as income for that year. (However, you must be careful to watch that the time for filing an amended return does not expire before you settle the question.)

The bad debt deduction is taken in the year the debt becomes worthless. In determining when a debt becomes worthless, you must consider all the surrounding circumstances including the value of the collateral, if any, securing the debt and the financial conditions of the debtor. Where it is indicated that the debt is uncollectible and that a legal action to collect the debt will not in all probability result in a recovery of the debt, then the debt is considered to be worthless (Reg. §1.166-(2)).

A debt may become worthless before it matures. Thus, where you are holding a note that matures in 1981 and you learn in 1978 that the maker of the note is in bankruptcy (a general indication of worthlessness of a debt), you do not have to wait until 1978 to claim your loss. Indeed, the debt may become worthless before maturity. Note that if there are joint obligors, failure to collect from one of them does not mean that the debt is bad and does not even justify a proportionate deduction.

[¶1105] UNCOLLECTIBLE DEFICIENCY ON SALE OF MORTGAGED PROPERTY

A debtor sometimes accepts property in compromise of a debt. This occurs usually with mortgages or pledges. Under these types of financing the property stands behind the debt and secures its payment: If the debt is unpaid you can sell the property to satisfy the debt.

If mortgaged or pledged property is sold for less than the amount of the debt and portion of the indebtedness remaining unsatisfied after such sale is wholly or partially uncollectible, the mortgagee or pledgee may deduct such amount as a bad debt for the taxable year in which it becomes worthless (Reg. §1.166-6(a)(1)). If the mortgagee forecloses and gets property worth less than the mortgage, the mortgagee will get a bad debt deduction in the amount of the difference between the amount of the debt and the net proceeds of the sale provided that the difference is uncollectible. If the mortgagee buys in pledged property, he may also realize loss or gain measured by the difference between the amount of the obligation to the debtor that is applied to the bid price and the fair market value of the property. Generally, this will not occur. The bid price and the fair market value are presumed to be the same (Reg. §1.166-6(b)(2)); occasionally you will find a situation where they differ. See also Reg. §1.166-6(a)(2).

If you compromise a debt because of the inability of the debtor to pay, your loss will be a bad debt deduction (IT 3121). If you compromise the debt voluntarily or simply forgive the indebtedness, you have no deduction because there is no worthlessness of the debt. However, a taxpayer has been allowed a deduction where it forgave past due rent to prevent the tenants from moving (*Lab Estates*, 13 TC 811, 1949). You cannot compromise simply because you are faced with litigation and take a bad debt deduction. If debtor is solvent, you cannot deduct your loss on a compromise. When you settle a debt for less than face value, the balance is a bad debt only if the debtor is insolvent. Renegotiation of the sale of a business, resulting in reduced sales price, is not a compromise settlement entitling seller to fully deductible ordinary loss; the character of the loss is determined by reference to original transaction.

[¶1106] CANCELLATION OF INDEBTEDNESS

When you borrow money or property and subsequently return to your creditor less than what you initially received, have you realized a taxable gain? Generally, the answer is yes. The theory behind taxing this type of transaction is that you realize an economic benefit and thereby increase your net worth just as effectively by the reduction of your liabilities at a profit as you do by disposing of assets at a profit. Since the gain on the disposition of your assets is taxable, it logically follows that a gain on the disposition of your liabilities should be taxable.

Example: Assume you owe $100,000 and you settle the debt for $50,000. Generally, you have $50,000 of cancellation-of-indebtedness income. As a result of the cancellation, you freed $50,000 of assets that were previously offset by the $50,000 liability. There is a clear economic gain that is taxable (*Kirby Lumber Co.*, 248 US 1, 1931).

There are numerous exceptions to this rule, more so because of emotional rather than logical reasons. Under the ordinary taxing transaction, the taxpayer *receives* something. In a debt cancellation transaction, the debtor received the property underlying the debt before the taxable event (the cancellation) and is usually paying out—rather than receiving—property. Although the cancellation results in an economic gain, there is still no apparent receipt of anything tangible at the time of cancellation. Since the creditor received the benefits (e.g., cash) of the cancellation before the actual cancellation and gets "nothing" (no tangible property) when the creditor cancels, it seems equitable not to tax the gain resulting from the cancellation.

Another emotional argument could go like this: The cancellation of an indebtedness is an attempt by a creditor to assist the debtor out of his financial embarrassment. To tax the debtor because of this cancellation frustrates to some extent the creditor's purpose and also further weakens the debtor's financial position.

The emotional "thinking" and the variance of factual situations under which cancellation-of-indebtedness income can arise have resulted in a mass of confusion in this area.

Decisions are hard to reconcile; and, consequently, it is a monumental task to determine the taxability of a particular transaction.

Whether some type of debt adjustments can be accomplished tax free is an uncertainty and can only be determined after judicial review; or, to put it another way, it can be determined only on a case-by-case basis. However, when you are faced with a cancellation-of-indebtedness situation, the courts will generally consider the following important factors (of course, you should also remember the emotional factors):

☐ (1) ***The Nature of the Debt Discharged.*** Is the debt an unconditional, uncontested, liquidated, obligation (see Reg. §1.108(b)-(1)(c)); is the debt a personal obligation of the taxpayer or a lien on property?

☐ (2) ***How the Debtor Used the Borrowed Funds.*** If the debtor wastes the money or loses it, the cancellation of the debt might be considered to be a "reduction of the loss," rather than a realization of income.

☐ (3) ***Financial Condition of Debtor.*** If the debtor is insolvent before and after the cancellation, no income is realized (Reg. §1.61-12(b)). The theory is that no asset has been freed by the cancellation.

☐ (4) ***Intention of the Parties.*** Did the creditor intend to make a gift? Gratuitous forgiveness is not taxable (*American Dental Co.*, 318 US 322, 1943; but see *Jacobson*, 336 US 28, 1949).

☐ (5) ***Method of Discharge of Debtor's Obligation.*** This factor usually determines the type of income you have because of the cancellation. For example, if you discharge the debt by services, you have compensation income; if the debtor is a stockholder of the creditor corporation, the cancellation may be the equivalent of a dividend.

[¶1107] WHAT KIND OF INCOME ARISES ON CANCELLATION OF DEBT?

If a cancellation results in income, the type of income you have is significant; clearly you would rather have capital gains than ordinary income. The type of income depends largely upon the method the debtor uses to discharge the obligation. Thus, for example, if you discharged the obligation by a payment of cash, you have ordinary income. There is no "sale or exchange" of an asset to come within capital gains. On the other hand, a foreclosure of mortgaged property does constitute a "sale or exchange" by the mortgagor even though it is an involuntary conveyance. The gain as a result of such foreclosure would be a capital gain so long as the asset sold is a capital asset.

[¶1108] HOW LONG DO YOU HAVE TO CLAIM A BAD DEBT DEDUCTION?

You can claim a bad debt deduction over a period of seven years, beginning with the due date of the return for the year in which the deduction was allowable. This protects you from losing your deduction entirely, simply because you claimed it in the wrong year and didn't learn about your mistake quickly enough. Three years (and two years in some cases) is the usual statutory period for refund claims.

SECTION XII
MAKING THE MOST OF BUSINESS LOSSES

Naturally, the ordinary business is entered into to make a profit. However, every business venture is subject to certain risks that cannot be ignored. Losses can result from a variety of causes—anything from a general downturn of a nation's economy to the unexpected illness or death of a business associate. Even where a business has done well in the past, unexpected events in any one or two years can result in net operating losses. While losses cannot be ignored, they need not be as devastating as they might at first seem, since the tax law provides a cushion by which you may apply your loss against several years' gains.

[¶1201] NET OPERATING LOSSES

A net operating loss can be carried back three years and ahead five years and used to reduce taxable income. The loss is applied to offset income of the earliest carryback year first; any excess offsets income of the succeeding years in order. Here's an illustration:

Producers, Inc., had a terrible year in 1969; it lost $250,000. However, the business is relatively new; it didn't do badly in 1966, 1967, and 1968 ($30,000 profit each year), and the owners decided to expand.

Suppose they make headway during the next five years—$20,000 profit in 1970, $30,000 in 1971, $40,000 in 1972, $50,000 in 1973; finally, in 1974, $125,000. But that $250,000 loss still hurts.

The net operating loss carryback and carryover saves them; it lets Producers, Inc., offset the $250,000 loss against the income of the other years.

Here's the tabulation:

1966	$250,000 −	$30,000 =	$220,000
1967	$220,000 −	$30,000 =	$190,000
1968	$190,000 −	$30,000 =	$160,000
1970	$160,000 −	$20,000 =	$140,000
1971	$140,000 −	$30,000 =	$110,000
1972	$110,000 −	$40,000 =	$ 70,000
1973	$ 70,000 −	$50,000 =	$ 20,000

1974	The remaining $20,000 is offset against the $125,000 profit that year, leaving only $105,000 subject to tax.

[¶1202] WHO CAN BENEFIT FROM CARRYOVERS AND CARRYBACKS?

Individual taxpayers (joint or single returns) and corporations (except for regulated investment and mutual insurance companies other than marine) can benefit.

A partnership return (Form 1065) is really just an information return with allocation of the income and expenses to the individual taxpayers. So, the partnership loss is carried over or back in the returns of the individual partners.

The net operating loss of an electing small business (Subchapter S) corporation is allowed to its shareholders, but the deduction is limited to the extent of the shareholder's basis in the stock plus his indebtedness to the corporation. (§1374). However, net operating losses from non-Subchapter S years cannot be carried to Subchapter S years and vice versa.

Real estate investment trusts are not allowed the net operating loss deduction, and personal holding companies are subject to limitations.

If, on the termination of an estate or trust, the estate or trust has either a net operating loss or any unused net operating loss carryover, the beneficiary succeeding to the property of the estate or trust can take advantage of the carryover or the net operating loss (§642(h)).

Based upon a recent IRS ruling, trust beneficiaries may take advantage of net operating loss carrybacks. Actually, there has been no change in the 1954 Code to bring about this result. Section 642(d) has always allowed trusts to deduct net operating losses. However, that alone had no effect on a beneficiary because it wasn't clear that the net operating loss had any effect upon the trust's distributable income (§643(a)). Although §642(h) specifically provides that a beneficiary may receive a direct benefit from a net operating loss carryover of a terminating trust, nothing is said in the Code about net operating loss carrybacks. Now, however, IRS says that the net operating loss of a trust reduces the distributable net income of the trust for the prior taxable year. Based upon that reduction, a trust beneficiary can recompute his prior years' taxable income and recover any overpayment of tax (*Rev. Rul. 61-20,* CB 1961-1, 248).

[¶1203] SHORT TAXABLE YEARS

In case of a return filed for a period of less than 12 months due to a change in the taxpayer's accounting period, there is nothing in the Code to allow the annualizing of net operating loss for that year for carryback and carryover purposes (*Rev. Rul. 56-463,* CB 1956-2, 297). A short taxable year is counted as a full taxable year for the purpose of the carryback or carryover (*Pennsylvania Electric Steel Casting Co.,* 20 BTA 602, 1930).

[¶1204] MORE THAN ONE LOSS

Let's assume Producers, Inc., has a relapse in 1971. Instead of making $30,000 that year, it loses $30,000. That would leave it with two carryovers working at the same time, $250,000 from 1969 and $30,000 from 1971.

They will be aggregated and used up in order of their occurrence. Here's the table, using + and − signs for profit and loss.

Year	*Profit or Loss*	*Carryover Balance*
1966	+ $ 30,000	$220,000
1967	+ 30,000	190,000
1968	+ 30,000	160,000
1969	− 250,000	160,000
1970	+ 20,000	140,000
1971	− 30,000	170,000
1972	+ 40,000	130,000
1973	+ 50,000	80,000
1974	+ 125,000	0

The carryover period for the 1971 loss is 1968-74. If the 1971 loss was $130,000 instead of just $30,000, the available carryover after 1971 would be $180,000 instead of $80,000. The $125,000 profit in 1973 would use up $125,000 of that, leaving $55,000 to offset 1975 and 1976 profits.

[¶1205] REFUND OF PAST TAXES

If you have a net operating loss and a carryback, you will want to get either a refund or a credit for the year to which the loss is carried back. Normally, a claim of this sort must be made within three years. However, in the case of net operating loss carrybacks the time limit is the fifteenth day of the 40th month (39, for corporations) following the end of the taxable year in which the loss originated (§6511(d)(2)).

[¶1206] SPECIAL PROCEDURE FOR REFUNDS BASED ON CARRYBACKS

You can get a quick refund on a net operating loss carryback by filing Form 1045. Corporations will use Form 1139.

The claim for refund or credit must be filed within 12 months of the end of the taxable year of the net operating loss from which the carryback results. Your refund or credit will then be determined within 90 days.

A corporation that expects to have a net operating loss during the current year can file a Form 1138 and get a reduction or a deferment of any installments still payable on the tax for the preceding year. (See Code §6164.)

Let's assume that your company has consistently been in the black. Now, the picture is not so rosy. You can logically anticipate a loss for the current year, early in the year. If there are any unpaid installments or any balance due on the taxable income earned in the prior year, you increase your working capital to the extent you reduce or defer the installments.

[¶1205.1] What About Postponing Return Due Date?

If your corporation files Form 7004 (Application for Automatic Extension of Time to File U.S. Corporation Income Tax Return), it could get an automatic extension to file the return for the preceding year. That would seem to mean that the balance of tax due for the prior year would be due and payable June 15 of the current year. However, you can't get away that easily.

To begin with, you've already made estimated tax installment payments. Also, the regulations require you to pay any balance due in two installments, one-half on March 15 and one-half on June 15. (Under Reg. §1.6152-1(a), filing Form 7004 is also an election to pay the balance of any tax due after estimated payments during the year in two installments, one on March 15 and one on June 15.) So, the three-month extension doesn't save much working capital. Isn't there anything else that can be done? Answer: Yes, according to an IRS ruling.

Have the corporation file a timely Form 7004. In addition, it should file Form 1138, on which it may apply to reduce the balance of tax due for the prior year by the amount of tax that would be refunded due to the anticipated net operating loss carryback. So, for example, if the anticipated refund is $15,000 and the installment due March 15 is $18,000, the payment need only be $10,500. In other words, the payment can be reduced by 50% of the expected carryback refund of $15,000 (*Rev. Rul. 63-222*, CB 1963-2, 605). The June 15 installment will also be reduced from $18,000 to $10,500.

[¶1206] RECOMPUTATIONS

In redetermining taxable income (for an individual) to compute the lower tax on which the refund is made, you must make certain recomputations in relation to the standard deduction and the medical deduction. Since the adjusted gross income is changed (decreased) by a net operating loss carryback, the amount of the standard deduction taken or the amount of medical expenses allowed as a deduction changes. The lower the adjusted gross, the higher the medical expense allowance. If the adjusted gross is lower, the standard deduction may likewise become lower, depending upon the amount of adjusted gross. Note that it is not necessary to recompute the charitable deduction since §170 specifically excludes this percentage deduction from recomputation.

[¶1207] RECOMPUTATION TO REFLECT ECONOMIC LOSS

The net operating loss carryover is more a matter of economic relief than of tax relief. The object is to avoid economic injustice by putting profits and losses on the same tax plane. For instance, the individual in computing his capital gains for the purpose of net operating loss does not consider the 50% deduction provided for by §1202. This 50% deduction is part of the tax law, designed to give preferential treatment to capital gains. Yet from the economic practical point of view, if you get a gain of $100 on the sale of stock, you are $100 ahead and not $50 ahead. Therefore, for the purposes of net operating loss that eventually becomes a deduction for earlier and later years, it would be inequitable to consider that you have gained only $50. The idea is to limit your net operating loss to your economic loss.

[¶1208] HOW THE CORPORATION COMPUTES ITS NET OPERATING LOSS

The recomputations for an individual and a corporation are different. We have already looked at the adjustments for an individual's return. Now, let's look at the corporation.

To arrive at the proper carryover, these deductions on the tax return must be eliminated:

☐ (1) Net operating loss;
☐ (2) Partially tax-exempt interest under §242 (§172(d)(5)).
☐ (3) Allowance to Western Hemisphere trade corporation under §922 (§172(d)(5)).

Assume Producers, Inc., has a net operating loss of $160,000 carried over from a prior year. This will appear on the company's returns until it is used up.

Producers also had a $1,000 deduction for partially tax-exempt interest. It was not a Western Hemisphere trade corporation.

The additions relate to a limited deduction (roughly 85%) allowed to a domestic corporation for certain types of dividends paid to or received from other corporations. Enough is added to give Producers the full deduction for these dividends instead of only a partial one (§172(d)(6)). The dividends involved are:

☐ (1) Dividends received from other domestic corporations under §243;
☐ (2) Dividends received on public utility preferred stock under §244;
☐ (3) Dividends received from certain foreign corporations under §245; and
☐ (4) Dividends paid on preferred stock of public utilities under §247.

Producers didn't pay any dividends to corporations, but it did receive a total of $5,000 that falls into the first three classifications above. Assuming it deducted 85% of this on its tax return, it does not follow because of the dividend credit limitation that in a losing year 15% of the amount of dividends received must be added to its tax loss to give it the full 100% deduction.

Here is the complete recomputation:

Loss shown on tax return		$190,250
Less: Net operating loss deduction	$160,000	
Deduction for partially tax-exempt interest	1,000	
Allowance to Western Hemisphere trade corporation		161,000
Amount to be carried forward		$ 29,250

Now for some explanation:

The reason for eliminating old carryovers was explained in connection with the individual's computation.

The deduction for partially tax-exempt interest is a form of income tax relief. There is no economic loss in connection with the receipt of this interest, so it can't be part of the carryover.

As for the special dividends received, the purpose of the 85% deduction is the prevention of double taxation, these dividends having already been taxed to the distributing corporation. The law limits the deduction to "85% of the taxable income" but says the limitation doesn't apply in a loss year. The reason is obvious; in a loss year, there is no taxable income, and 85% of 0 would be 0. The limitation only *limits* the 85% dividends received deduction and does not change or vary the percentage to be applied. Since the limitation does not apply in our case, Producers is entitled to the full 85% (not 100%) dividends deduction not limited to 85% of the taxable income in figuring its carryover (§246(b)(1); 172(d)(6); *Rev. Rul. 57-585*, CB 1957-2, 249).

[¶1209] CONTROLLING THE CARRYOVER

The net operating loss carryover, like other tax deductions, can be controlled to a degree. If income was high in 1972 but a net loss is coming up in 1975, expenditures that are necessary but not urgent can be made now to increase the loss and build up the refund from 1972. However, if 1972 was a mediocre year and you expect 1978 will be good, you might decide it would work out better if you passed up the opportunity for a bigger carryback to 1972 and saved the deduction for 1978. In that case, you would defer making the expenditure until 1978.

Or you might have a choice of realizing some income either in 1975 or in 1976. Would it be better to realize the income now and reduce the carryback to 1972, or wait until next year and increase the income for 1976? Not only would you have to weigh the tax effects, but you would have to consider the possible advantages of having the extra cash now.

These things are a matter of the judgment of whoever does the accounting, applied to the circumstances of the business he's dealing with. He might try a special system that would treat the carryover each year as a new nine-year problem.

The nine years are of course the present year, the past three, and the five coming next. The work is done in the present year. The accountant considers: (1) Whether the year will result in profit or loss; (2) what income and deductions are available for legitimate manipulation among the years; (3) the tax rates for different years; (4) allocation to which year will produce the best tax result (for this, he will make a test for each year and three carrybacks and five carryovers).

In testing years, the adjustments to change a tax loss into an economic loss will have to be made. All this involves is regularly making the adjustment for the current year, regardless of whether there has been a profit or loss. The current year eventually becomes a carryback year. After four years, the accountant has the adjustment he has just made for the current year, plus the adjustments he saved for the three carryback years. As for the five carryover years, he can't adjust future years anyway.

[¶1210] PURCHASE OF BUSINESS TO ACQUIRE LOSS CARRYOVER

Suppose that after 1976, the owners of Producers, Inc., decide that they'd had enough and sell out. Could the new owners use the remaining $160,000 of carryover?

☐ They couldn't if the principal purpose of the acquisition by the new owners was to acquire the loss carryover. The new owners would probably be denied the carryover loss under §269 as having made an acquisition to evade or avoid income tax. The motive for acquisition of stock is a question of fact. It has to be determined whether or not the principal purpose of the acquisition was to acquire the loss carryover.

For instance, what was the price paid for the stock? If it is "substantially disproportionate" to the property acquired plus the tax benefits, then the burden falls on the taxpayer to prove that the corporation was not acquired principally to avoid tax. This rule would apply even if the acquirers came within §382, which sets up the rules governing the allowance of the carryover.

☐ Even if the acquisition was not to avoid taxes, where there is the required change of ownership either as a result of a purchase from unrelated parties or by redemption of stock (other than to pay estate taxes (§303)) and the corporation changes its trade or business, no net operating loss carryover is to be allowed even in the same corporation (§382).

The required change of ownership test is this is not a reference to the total of all stock outstanding but rather to the percentage of ownership of each of those ten persons who own the greatest percentage of the fair market value of the stock of the loss corporation at the end of the taxable year. (Note: If there are less than ten stockholders, all are considered.)

If these persons own 50 percentage points more at the end of the taxable year than they owned at the beginning of the taxable year or at the beginning of the prior taxable year, then the required change of ownership has occurred. Note: A stockholder who owns 20% of the stock at the beginning of the year and 40% at end of the year has had a 100% increase in his holding, but for this section his increase is taken into consideration as a 20 percentage point increase.

In selecting the ten persons, you follow these rules:

(1) List all persons who own, actually or constructively, the stock of the loss corporation and determine the fair market value of the stock owned by such persons.

(2) Select those ten stockholders (after giving effect to the attribution rules) who own the greatest percentage of the fair market value of the outstanding stock of the loss corporation at the end of the taxable year.

(3) Compare the holdings of these ten listed stockholders at the end of the taxable year with their holdings at the beginning of the taxable year. If the stockholdings of these stockholders has increased by 50 percentage points during the year as a result of purchase then the required change of ownership has occurred. If the increase did not amount to 50 percentage points, another comparison is made with the holdings of these stockholders as of the beginning of the prior taxable year to see if there has been an increase of 50 percentage points since then. If the answer is yes, then the required change of ownership has occurred.

Remember the increase in percentage of outstanding stock held may also occur as a result of a decrease in the amount of outstanding stock by redemption.

☐ If the trade or business of the loss corporation has remained substantially the same as it was before the required percentage change in ownership occurred, then the net operating loss deduction is not affected.

If the trade or business has changed at any time on or after the date of the earliest purchase includible in the 50 percentage point change, then the provisions denying the net operating loss carryover deduction apply.

Where IRS can show that a change in the trade or business was made prior to the required change in ownership but it was all part of the plan for prospective purchasers who wish to avoid the effects of §382, the change in business will be treated as if it had occurred after the sale of stock (Reg. 1.382(a)-1(h)(3)).

IRS will check changes in employees, plant, equipment, product, location, customers, and any other items significant to the operation of the business to determine if a change of business has occurred.

Inactivity: A corporation is not carrying on substantially the same trade or business as that conducted before the required change in ownership if the corporation is not carrying on an active trade or business at the time of the change in ownership. This rule applies even if the corporation is reactivated and then carries on its original line of business.

However, if the inactivity is due to a fire or similar casualty and there is a change in ownership during the temporary suspension of activities, IRS will not consider the corporation to have been inactive.

Addition of a New Trade or Business: If the trade or business of the corporation is carried on substantially undiminished after a change of ownership, the addition of a new trade or business does not constitute a change in the trade or business that would deny the right to carry over a net operating loss. *Caution:* If the purpose of the acquisition was principally to be able to apply the carryover losses against the very profitable newly added business, §269 might apply (see above).

Major Change in Location: IRS will take the position that there has been a change in the trade or business if the corporation changes the location of a major portion of its activities. *Example:* A corporation disposes of its plant, terminates the employment of a majority of its employees, and sells off most of its equipment in State A. In State B, the corporation resumes the same manufacturing activities, makes the same product, and serves substantially the same customers. However, the plant, equipment, and substantially all the employees are different. Under the Regs, the corporation is not carrying on the same business.

Change in Individuals Rendering Services: Where a corporation is in the business of rendering services by a particular individual and after the change in ownership, the services are rendered by another individual, the trade or business will not be considered the same. *Example:* A real estate brokerage firm is owned by A, and A is the individual who renders the real estate services for that corporation. B buys the corporation and thereafter B renders the services. IRS will consider the trade or business to have changed and will disallow any carryover losses.

[¶1211] LOSS CARRYBACKS OF A CONSOLIDATED GROUP

Affiliated corporations can report their income on consolidated returns and offset losses of one company against the gains of another. But how does the affiliated group handle the situation where a corporation that is a member of the group during the year it has operating losses had filed separate returns (or a consolidated return with another group) in a prior year in which it showed a profit? Can so much of the operating loss that is attributable to it be carried back to the profitable year? Yes, it can (*Trinco Industries Inc.*, 22 TC 959, Regs §1.1502-31A(d)). What's more, the balance of the unused loss is available to the affiliated group as a carryover or carryback.

Where a member corporation was not in existence in the deduction year, according to IRS, the operating losses attributable to the corporation will still be allowed. IRS says that it will not follow those cases that hold to the contrary (e.g., *Midland Management Co.*, 38 TC 211, 1962; *Houston Oil Field Material Company*, 252 F.2d 357, CA-5, 1958; (*Rev. Rul. 64-93*, CB 1964-1, 325).

[¶1212] FOREIGN EXPROPRIATION LOSSES

Generally, a net operating loss can be carried back to each of the three years preceding the year of loss and carried forward to each of the five succeeding years. Taxpayers who incur foreign expropriation losses can elect to take a ten-year carryforward instead (§172). To qualify, the expropriation loss must be at least 50% of taxpayer's net operating loss for the year. Thus, this extra carryforward period will not be available unless the major portion of a company's operating loss is attributable to expropriation losses.

Types of Losses That Qualify: The types of losses involved are trade or business, or production-of-income losses that are sustained by reason of the expropriation, intervention, seizure, or similar taking of property by the government of any foreign country, or its political subdivision, agency, or instrumentality.

[¶1213] USING SUBCHAPTER S TO PASS LOSSES THROUGH TO STOCKHOLDERS

Generally, the owners of a corporation cannot use the carryover provisions to offset corporate losses against their personal incomes in prior or subsequent years. Corporate losses may only be applied against corporate (as opposed to personal) income. However, this is not true if you elect to be taxed as a Subchapter S corporation. The advantage of the Subchapter S election is that it allows the stockholders to pick up the corporation's loss as if it were their own (Reg. §1.1374-1(b)). This is particularly valuable in a new corporation. Often, the strategy is to operate the new business as a proprietorship or partnership at the beginning, during the time it could be expected to incur losses, so that the losses will be available as offsets against the owners' other income. Then, when the business becomes successful and the rate differentials make it advantageous, the business can be incorporated. You can accomplish the same result, however, using Subchapter S. The corporation can be formed and immediately elect under Subchapter S, so that the losses pass through to the stockholders. Then, when the corporation begins to be so successful that the corporate shelter is desired, the election can be revoked.

Take a cash-basis corporation that is sued and a judgment is entered against it. It is now near year end, and the judgment will be paid next year. The corporation could elect Subchapter S; and, when the big judgment is paid in the following year and a corporate loss is created as a result, the stockholders could personally deduct the losses on their own returns. The Subchapter S election in this case should work as long as, under the corporation's accounting method, the deduction became available only when the judgment was paid. There is no business purpose requirement for electing Subchapter S.

[¶1213.1] Limitations on Losses

Although losses are passed through to the stockholders, each stockholder's loss is limited to his basis for his stock in the corporation and the basis for any indebtedness of the corporation to him. A *guarantee* by a shareholder of a corporate debt does not come within the term "indebtedness of the corporation to the shareholder" (*Perry,* 392 F.2d 458, CA-8, 1947, *aff'g* 47 TC 159, 1946). So, if the corporation's loss is going to be so big that a stockholder's share will exceed his basis for his stock, he might consider making a loan to the corporation before year end and thus create a basis for indebtedness that will let him use the corporate loss (§1374(c)(2)).

SECTION XIII

USING THE BEST ACCOUNTING METHOD

There are several basic methods that a taxpayer may use to report income. The cash and the accrual methods of accounting are the most well known; however, other ways are available to fit specific transactions. Before you can make an intelligent decision as to which alternative is best, you must know two things:

□ (1) How are income and deduction items handled under each method of accounting?
□ (2) What are the advantages and disadvantages inherent in each method of accounting?

[¶1301] THE BEST ACCOUNTING METHOD FOR YOUR TYPE OF BUSINESS

There are no broad and all-inclusive standards to use in determining which accounting method is best for you. Every businessman has his own unique financial needs and obligations. So, in the end, you are going to have to make the final decision for yourself.

To aid you in making this important decision, we include the following table, which summarizes the various accounting methods, their advantages and disadvantages.

A Bird's Eye View of the Various Accounting Methods

Who May Use	When Income Is Taxed	When Expenses Are Deductible	Advantages	Disadvantages
		Cash Method		
Any taxpayer unless inventories necessary to reflect income. Must be used if have no records or incomplete ones.	In year cash or property is received. For property, use fair market value.	Year in which payment is made in cash or property. Giving note is not payment; payment can be made with borrowed funds.	You don't pay taxes until you get the income. You can control each year's receipts and payouts and even out income over the years.	You don't always match related income and expenses in one year, thus creating distortions.

Who May Use	When Income Is Taxed	When Expenses Are Deductible	Advantages	Disadvantages
Can use in one business although other method is used in other business.	Taxed in year of *constructive receipt* even if there's no actual receipt (i.e., year income was available to you although you didn't take it).	Certain prepaid expenses must be spread over periods to which they apply even though full amount has been paid, e.g., insurance premiums, rent, fees to negotiate long-term lease. But payment for supplies bought in advance is currently deductible (Ernst 32 TC 181, 1959).	You can keep simple records.	You may not have full control over receipts, and income may pile up in one year. Liquidation or sale of business may create income bunching—all accounts receivable may have to be picked up at one time.
		Accrual Method		
Anyone except those with no or incomplete books or records. You must use if inventories are necessary clearly to reflect income unless you can use one of methods discussed below.	In year income is earned—i.e., year in which right to income becomes fixed, regardless of year of receipt. You do not accrue contingent, contested or uncollectible items. Prepaid amounts are income when received even if not yet earned.	In the year all events have occurred which fix the fact and the amount of your liability, regardless of the year of payment. You do not accrue contingent or contested liabilities. But if you pay a liability and still contest it, you deduct it when you pay it. If you get a recovery later, it's income when received. *Special Rule:* Accruals to certain related taxpayers must be paid within 2½ months of close of taxable year of accrual or deduction is lost.	It matches income and related expenses and tends to even out your income over the years.	Have less leeway than cash-basis taxpayer to defer or accelerate income or deductions. Can still accelerate deductions, however, by advancing repairs and advertising expenditures within desired period, purchasing supplies, getting bills for professional services before year-end.
		"Hybrid" Method (see Reg. §1.446-1(c)(1)(iv))		
Any taxpayer if method clearly reflects income and is consistently used.	Accrual method is used in respect of purchases and sales, while cash method is used for all other items of income and expense.		Method is simple; It's not necessary to accrue income items such as interest, dividends. And the bother of accruing small expenses is removed. Chief benefit is to small	Method is not entirely accurate. Since it is a "hybrid," it does not reflect *true* income. However, if consistently used (and absent any unused nonrecurring income or expense items), it gives a

Who May Use	When Income Is Taxed	When Expenses Are Deductible	Advantages	Disadvantages
			businessman, such as retail store.	fairly good comparison of how business is doing from year to year.
		Installment Method		
Installment dealers who elect this method. Seller in casual sale of personal property of more than $1,000 or of real property provided, in either case, no more than 30% of selling price is received in year of sale.	Each year that collections are made, a proportionate amount of each collection (equal to percentage of gross profit on entire sale) is picked up as gross income in the year of collection.	Dealer deducts expenses when paid (if he's on cash basis) or incurred (on accrual basis). On casual sales, expense of sale reduces sales price, thereby having effect of spreading deduction over period of reporting income.	Income is spread over period of collection—so you do not pay taxes on amounts not yet received. If tax rates decline in future, part of profits will bear a lower tax.	Dealers who switch from accrual to installment basis may have to pay a double tax on some receivables—unless they sell off all receivables before the switch. Tax rates may go up; in which case, some profits will bear a higher tax.
		Deferred Payment Sales Method		
Any cash-basis taxpayer on sale of personal property. Any cash- or accrual-basis taxpayer on sale of real estate.	At time of sale, seller picks up cash and *fair market value* of buyer's obligations. If total exceeds basis of sold property, difference is taxable. In later years, as obligations are collected, difference between amount received and value at which obligations were picked up originally is taxable at time of collection.	Used generally with casual sales, so expense of sale reduces sales price and is thus spread over period of collection.	Can use where installment sale reporting is not possible—i.e., where more than 30% of sales price is received in year of sale. Useful in somewhat speculative deals where value of buyer's obligations are contingent on future operations and have little or no ascertainable present value.	You may be in for a long and costly argument with IRS as to value of obligations. Even though original sale gave capital gain, gain on collection of the obligations in future years will be taxable as an ordinary income.
		Long-Term Contract Method—Percentage of Completion		
Taxpayers who have contracts that take more than a year to complete, usually construction contracts. IRS permission is needed to switch to or from this method.	A portion of the total contract price is taken into account each year according to the percentage of the contract completed that year. Architects' or engineers' certificates are required.	All expenses made during the year allocable to that contract are deducted, with adjustments made for inventories and supplies on hand at the beginning and end of the year.	Income from long-term contract is reflected as earned. Income bunching in one year is avoided.	Accurate estimates of completion are difficult to make in some cases. If expenses are irregular as compared to income, there may be distortion of income in the interim years, although the final total will work out accurately.

Who May Use	When Income Is Taxed	When Expenses Are Deductible	Advantages	Disadvantages
		Long-Term Contract—Completed Contract		
Taxpayers who have contracts that take more than a year to complete, usually construction contracts. IRS permission is needed to switch to or from this method.	The entire contract price is picked up as income in the year the contract is completed and accepted.	Expenses allocable to specific contracts (that would exclude general administrative costs) are not deductible until year of completion—when income is picked up.	Income can be reflected more accurately—all the figures are in when the computation is made. Avoids estimates in interim years that may turn out to be wrong.	Bunching of income or losses in one year is possible if a number of profitable or unprofitable contracts are all finished in one year. A steady flow of completed contracts from year to year overcomes this problem. (There may be some argument with IRS as to proper year of completion in some cases.)

[¶1302] CASH METHOD

The cash receipts and disbursements method is used largely by individuals whose income is derived principally from salaries and wages; by retail merchants, shopkeepers, and professional men; and also by many large business enterprises in the service, financial, and real estate fields, where merchandise inventories are not a material income factor.

[¶1302.1] Basic Principles of Cash Method

Under this method, a taxpayer has income to the extent of cash or property actually or ''constructively'' (see below) received during the tax year; it makes no difference how much he actually earned during the year—it is the amount that he receives that is important under this method. See *Edelman,* 329 F.2d 950, Ct. Cl., 1964.

Where payment is made in the form of property, you have income to the extent of the fair market value of such property. Therefore, for example, if you received a note for your services, you would have income to the extent of its fair market value (*Pinellas Ice Co.*, 287 US 462, 1932). The same would be true if you received stock or other like property.

[¶1302.2] Deductions Under Cash Method

Generally, your deductions will be allowed in the year paid, even though they were incurred or relate to another year. Thus, prepayment of interest on a loan is deductible in the year of payment. (*Fackler,* 39 BTA 395, 1939). Similarly, prepayment of supplies that are to be delivered the following year is deductible in the year of payment (*Ernst,* 32 TC 181, 1959).

Where the prepayment results in the acquisition of a ''capital asset,'' the deduction will be prorated over the related years. Thus, for example, commissions, legal fees, and other expenses incurred in negotiating a long-term lease or mortgage loan must be spread over the term of the lease or loan (*Spring City Foundry Co.*, 292 US 182, 1935).

[¶1302.3] "Constructive Receipt"

Under this doctrine a taxpayer is taxed on income even before it is actually received, if it is his for the asking. The most common examples are: matured interest coupons on bonds that have not been cashed, declared dividends unqualifiedly subject to the stockholder's demand, and interest credited on savings bank deposits although not withdrawn (Reg. §1.451-2).

[¶1302.4] Who May Use the Cash Method?

It *may* be used by any taxpayer who does not use inventories to determine income or who does not keep books of account (*Greengard,* 8 BTA 734, 1927). Stockpiling of items used in your business can be construed to be an inventory. *Wilkinson-Bean, Inc.,* TC Memo 1969-79, involved a funeral director who kept a substantial supply of caskets because his supplier was far from his place of business. The Tax Court forced the funeral director to use the accrual method because it found that the income (about 14% of the gross income) from the sale of caskets was a significant income factor requiring the use of an inventory.

[¶1302.5] Advantages of the Cash Method

☐ (1) You don't pay any taxes until you have received the income.
☐ (2) You can control receipts and disbursements for each year, so as to avoid higher tax rates on income piled up in a single year.
☐ (3) You don't have to maintain complicated records or books of account. In most cases, a checkbook or simple cashbook showing receipts and disbursements will suffice. There is no need for accruals.

[¶1302.6] Disadvantages of the Cash Method

☐ (1) The chief defect of the cash method is that it does not truly reflect annual net income. It produces "peaks" and "valleys."
☐ (2) Income may pile up in a single year despite meticulous efforts to regulate income and outgo. For example, advance payments of rents, salaries, royalties, interest, etc.
☐ (3) If the business is liquidated or sold, income may be "bunched" into one year and deductions forever lost. *Examples:* Where a cash-basis corporation liquidated and transferred its accounts receivable to its stockholders, the court held that the receivables were taxable to the corporation as income realized prior to dissolution (*Floyd,* 193 F.2d 594, CA-5, 1952; *Williamson,* 292 F.2d 524, Ct. Cl., 1961).

The best way to avoid this tax trap is to continue the corporation in existence for a reasonable period until the outstanding receivables are collected and the debts paid off. In any event, prepay all deductible items before dissolution.

[¶1303] ACCRUAL METHOD

This method is used by businesses with numerous and complex transactions because it is a more scientific and accurate method for determining true income for any given period of time. It is used in practically all manufacturing, wholesale, or retail businesses, and service establishments where the production, purchase, or sale of merchandise is an "income-producing" factor.

[¶1303.1] Basic Principles of Accrual Method

The accrual of income depends on the right to receive it, rather than actual receipt. But in *Schlude,* 372 US 128, 1963, the Supreme Court seems to have applied an actual receipt test in holding that negotiable notes not yet due were taxable when received.

There are three basic rules as to when the right to receive income becomes fixed and accruable. They are: (1) The taxpayer must have a valid, unconditional and enforceable right to receive the income within the taxable year (*Spring City Foundry Co. v. Com'r,* 292 US 182), 1935; (2) The amount due must be determinable or susceptible of reasonable estimate (*Brown,* 8 BTA 112, 1927); (3) There must be a reasonable expectancy that the amount due will be paid and collected in due course (*Georgia School Book Depository, Inc.,* 1 TC 463, 1942).

The same rules apply to the deduction of expenses on the accrual basis. Where all the events have occurred within the taxable year that fix the amount and the fact of the taxpayer's liability, such expenses are properly accruable and deductible for tax purposes, even though paid in a subsequent year (*Anderson,* 269 US 422, 1929). Amount accruing is the known liability at the year end, without alteration for events and transactions of later years (*Lewyt Corp.,* 349 US 237, 1955). It may be used by any taxpayer who maintains records or books of account; it must be used by a taxpayer who uses inventories to determine income.

[¶1303.2] Accrued Expenses in Family Business

In closely held corporations, or between members of a family, when the taxpayers use different accounting methods, care should be exercised in accruing expenses.

The deduction will be lost if:

☐ (1) The expense (e.g., officer's year-end bonus) is not paid within 2½ months after the close of the taxable year; and

☐ (2) The method of accounting of the person to whom the payment is to be made does not require inclusion of the item in gross income unless paid. In other words, payor on the accrual basis, payee on the cash; and

☐ (3) Related taxpayers are involved. Related taxpayers include brothers, sisters, spouses, parents, grandparents, children, grandchildren, individuals and their more-than-50%-owned corporations, and two corporations in which more than 50% of the value is owned by the same individual.

[¶1303.3] Adjustment of Accrued Liabilities

If the amount actually paid turns out to be more or less than the amount of expense accrued and deducted, it becomes necessary to reflect the difference in the tax return for the year of accrual or the year of payment.

When a dispute as to liability has been settled or finally adjudicated, you can deduct the amount determined to be due in the year of final determination, but you have to make the deduction in the year of actual payment if that occurs before the contest is settled.

[¶1304] HYBRID ACCOUNTING

The Code permits hybrid accounting when it is approved by the Regulations (see Reg. §1.446-1) as clearly reflecting income (§446(c)(4)). A hybrid method of accounting combines the principles of several recognized accounting methods. For example, many small retail stores use a combination of the cash and accrual methods. By this system, they are permitted to report gross income (gross receipts less cost of goods sold) on the accrual basis and deduct selling and administration expenses on the cash basis. This combination of accounting methods simply removes the bother of accruing small expenses and can be of substantial benefit in small business operations.

Nonapproved Hybrid Methods Are Dangerous: The law gives the Commissioner broad authority to determine whether or not a particular method of accounting clearly reflects income (IRC §446(b)). The courts are reluctant to get involved in the niceties and refinements of different accounting methods, and they won't disturb the Commissioner's determination in the absence of a clear abuse of discretion (*Niles Bement Pond Co.*, 281 US 357, 1930).

If you use a nonrecognized hybrid system, the Commissioner may follow one of two courses: (1) he may insist on immediate correction of the accounts to conform to a uniformly acceptable method of accounting; or (2) he may ignore the incorrect handling of the accounts until such time as a required change will result in increased taxes. The decided cases leave no doubt of the danger in using hybrid accounting without approval (see *Moody Cotton Co.*, 2 TC 347, 1943; *Schuman Carriage Co.*, 43 BTA 880, 1941).

[¶1305] INSTALLMENT SALES

If you're to be paid in installments, you're taxed pro rata as proceeds are received. Deferred and contingent sales are different in that they can postpone all tax until cost is fully recovered. The installment sale is available only to a dealer in personal property who regularly sells on the installment plan, a person who sells real property, or a person who makes a casual sale of personal property (other than merchandise) for a price exceeding $1,000.

For a sale of real property or a casual sale of personal property to qualify, payments in the year of sale can't be more than 30% of the purchase price.

Payments in the year of sale are called "initial payments." The term embraces not only cash payments but also payments with property, including the notes or other obligations of a third party. If there is no initial payment at all, the 30% requirement is of course met. However, the contract should provide for payment of fixed amounts at stated intervals (*Rev. Rul. 56-587*, CB 1956-2, 303).

"Installment dealer" isn't defined either, and no minimum percentage of installment sales is prescribed (*Marshall Brothers Lumber Co.*, 13 BTA 1111, 1928). Nor is frequency the decisive factor; eleven installment sales over a thirteen-year period were considered enough, when the item was so large that it wasn't sold very often (*Davenport Machine & Foundry Co.*, 18 TC 39, 1952). Regularly engaging in installment selling is the important thing; number and frequency of installment sales, and the holding out to the public as an installment dealer, are factors only in determining regularity.

The installment method is really a combination of the cash and accrual methods of accounting. Income arising from an installment sale of real or personal property is reported for tax purposes proportionately when the income is actually collected. The theory is that each dollar collected includes a pro rata recovery of cost (nontaxable) and a pro rata receipt of profit. If there's no profit, you can't use installment reporting (*Rev. Rul. 70-430*).

Cash sales and costs of a dealer who elects installment reporting should be segregated from installment sales and costs. Failure to do so may force the dealer to resort to a composite computation based on combined sales applied to total cash receipts in order to determine his tax (*Blum's, Inc.*, 7 BTA 737, 1927). Although this may give an advantage in certain cases (see *Rev. Rul. 54-367,* CB 1954-2, 109), it can prove costly taxwise. For instance, note that failure to segregate proved costly to a furniture business selling on both the installment and cash basis. Profit rate was greater on installment sales than on cash sales; since the composite rate was 40%, as against a 20% rate on the cash sales alone, use of the composite rate resulted in a higher tax on the cash sales than would have been the case if they had been taxed separately (*Kay-Jones Furniture Co.*, TC Memo 1955-235). If the court isn't satisfied with a substitute the dealer offers in place of accurate bookkeeping, use of the installment method will be denied altogether (*Tillman,* 10 BTA 4, 1928).

[¶1305.1] Financial Reporting

You can't usually report revenues on the installment basis for purposes of financial reporting unless there are exceptional circumstances. Profit is deemed to be realized when you make a sale in the ordinary course of business, unless circumstances are such that the collection of the sale price is not reasonably assured, says the Accounting Principle Board. (See Chapter 1A of APB No. 43; APB Opinion No. 10.)

[¶1305.2] Retroactive Revocation of Election

A taxpayer has the right to retroactively revoke an election to report on the installment basis. The election is given to taxpayers ostensibly as a relief measure for firms that are caught in an accounting bind because of the maintenance of records to satisfy two methods of reporting —financial and tax.

To revoke an election, the taxpayer must file a notice of revocation within three years following the date of the filing of the tax return for the year the installment method was elected. The revocation applies to the year installment reporting was elected and subsequent years. Interest is not allowed, however, on any refunds or credits resulting from a revocation (§453(c)(4)).

[¶1305.3] Trust Device Not Available To Convert Ordinary Sale Into Installment Sale

In the following situation, the trust device was not available to the taxpayer as a method of reporting his sale gain. Here are the facts:

The taxpayer sold real property in a year, realizing gain. The total selling price on delivery of the deed was to be paid as follows: 20% to the taxpayer; the balance of 80% to a bank in trust for the taxpayer who was the beneficiary of the trust. Under the trust indenture, the trust agreement provided that the bank was to pay the taxpayer not more than 20% of the trust principal annually, plus any income earned by the trust. The taxpayer could not elect to report the gain on the installment basis, although payments did not exceed 30% of the selling price because, in effect, the entire purchase price was received in the year of sale by the taxpayer when the 80% of the purchase price was paid to the bank for the taxpayer's benefit. The entire gain was therefore taxable in the year of sale (*Rev. Rul. 71-352*, CB 1971, 2-221).

[¶1305.4] Prearranged Plan Voids Installment Sale

Where a taxpayer, in order to avail himself of the installment provisions, arranges an intermediary sale whereby a related party consummates the prearranged transaction, receives the full payment from the purchaser, and dispenses the proceeds from the sale to him in installments, the courts have ruled that installment reporting is not available. A sale by one person cannot be transformed, for tax purposes, into a sale by another by using the latter as a conduit through which to pass title.

[¶1305.5] How to Handle Selling Expenses

The treatment of selling expenses under the installment method depends on whether or not the taxpayer is a "dealer." Here are the rules:

☐ (1) If he is a dealer, then he must deduct the expenses in the year when paid (on the cash basis) or when incurred (on the accrual basis). In other words, he cannot apportion or spread the expenses over the years when the income from the installment sale is reported as collected.

☐ (2) If he is not a dealer, commissions and other expenses incurred in connection with the sale of the property are deducted pro rata over the period in which the installment payments are collected. This result is accomplished by offsetting the commissions and selling expenses against the selling price in determining the amount of profit realized from the sale of the property and the percentage of profit in each installment payment that is to be reported as taxable income. This rule is applicable to casual sales of personal property and to sales of real property, on the installment plan, by a taxpayer who is not a dealer in such property.

[¶1305.6] Handling Installment Receivables

There are two types of arrangements a dealer can make with banks or factors to obtain advances on his installment receivables. He can: (1) Pledge them; that is, borrow against the receivables as collateral; or (2) Discount them; that is, sell them at less than face value.

Under a pledge, the dealer receives a loan of about 85% of the balance due on the installment sales contracts and pays interest on the loan monthly. By discounting, he receives about 85% of the balance due, less a service charge; the remaining 15%, known as a holdback, is placed in a reserve account to secure the dealer's contingent liability as guarantor that the installment balances will be paid.

The installment method of reporting is available to the dealer only if he uses the pledging arrangement. If he discounts, he must report all of the income in the year of sale, even though the bank or factor has full recourse against him in the event the purchasers don't pay off their installment liabilities.

[¶1305.7] Record Keeping

It should be possible to ascertain the different years of sale from your accounting records. One way of doing this is to break down the receivables ledger into the different years of sale. However, a simpler way of doing this (also acceptable by IRS) is to have different colored accounts receivable cards for different sale years. At year end, it then becomes relatively simple to ascertain the remaining receivables of a particular year. The gross profit percentage for each year is then applied to the remaining receivables of that year, and the total unrealized profit is determined. This is then compared with the unrealized profit reserve at the beginning of the year. If there is a decrease, it is added to accrual-basis income. If an increase, it is subtracted from the accrual-basis income.

[¶1305.8] Calculated Risks

There are risks in adopting installment selling. Expenses are larger than in cash selling, not only because of the extra bookkeeping, but also because of the capital outlay required and because collecting accounts costs money. In addition, collections become more uncertain as the period of payment is extended. This means more losses than in cash selling. Even if the property is repossessed, wear and tear may have rendered it valueless.

The question will always be: Are the probabilities of a greater volume of sales and the tax advantages of installment reporting worth these risks? In a business such as the appliance field, where annual sales volume is subject to more than normal fluctuation, the advantage of being able to level income over the years may weigh heavily.

[¶1306] DEFERRED PAYMENT SALES

Here we're dealing with a sale where the value of the consideration (usually notes) given to the seller is unascertainable. Because the value is unascertainable the transaction is considered ''open'' and gain realized is not taxed until the seller has first recovered his costs (*Ennis,* 17 TC 465, 1951; cf. *Osenbach,* 198 F.2d 235, CA-4, 1955). Where the underlying asset is a capital asset, the amounts recovered received after the recovery of basis are taxed as capital gains so long as the transaction does not ''close.'' Payments made after the transaction is closed are taxed as ordinary income because we don't have a ''sale or exchange.'' (See *Culbertson,* 14 TC 1421, 1950.) But there is one exception. If the payment is made in redemption of a corporate note, the proceeds should qualify for capital gains treatment if it was held for more than six months even though the transaction is closed. See §1232(a)(1).

[¶1306.1] When Value Is Unascertainable

Generally, the value of the consideration given by a purchaser is unascertainable if (1) the property is not salable, and (2) if its receipt is subject to substantial contingencies so as to make it impossible to determine how much the seller will actually receive.

Executory Contract Can Create Taxable Income: Although many courts have said a bare contract has no ascertainable value, IRS does not agree, and some courts have supported the IRS position. A contractual right may be held to have value where the following factors are present:

☐ (1) The obligor was solvent;
☐ (2) The promise to pay was unconditional and assignable;
☐ (3) The obligation was not subject to set-offs; and
☐ (4) The note was of a kind that is frequently transferred to lenders or investors at a discount not

substantially greater than the generally prevailing premium for the use of money (*Cowden*, 289 F.2d 20, CA-5, 1961).

Inserting conditions into your agreement can probably help avoid the impact of the *Cowden* case. Where the contingencies are substantial and the amount to be paid (as in a royalty set-up) are uncertain, the *Cowden* doctrine would not seem to apply. Nor would it apply where the buyer's agreement to pay is not subject to discount at rates that compare with the going "price of money." Further, where the obligation is not of the type that is usually discounted in normal financial channels, the *Cowden* rule may not apply.

[¶1306.2] Sales at a Contingent Price

This is a sale where the consideration received by the seller is incapable of valuation with the result that the transaction is not considered closed and no income is realized until the seller recovers his basis for the property. Any excess over basis is capital gain if the property qualifies as a capital asset. The classic case involved a consideration of 60¢ a ton on all iron ore mined by a corporation (*Burnet v. Logan*, 283 US 404, 1930). The Court held that no valuation could be attached to this agreement since there were no maximum and minimum requirements as to the amount of ore to be mined set forth in the contract.

Similarly, the promise of a corporation to pay a percentage of its profits for a number of years was held to be indeterminate, with the result that the transaction was not considered closed (*Yerger*, 55 F. Supp. 521, DC Pa., 1944). The same result should follow where the consideration is contingent upon net profits to be received from real property that is the subject of the sale. No gain will be realized until the seller's basis is recovered.

You'll get an argument from the Treasury on this, though. It insists there rarely is a situation where value is indeterminable (*Rev. Rul. 58-402*, CB 1958, 15).

[¶1306.3] Switching to Installment Reporting

Where the notes given by the purchaser do not have an ascertainable value, the taxpayer cannot use the installment sale method (*Pacific National Co.*, 304 US 191, 1938). But where the buyer's notes do have an ascertainable value and the taxpayer erroneously uses the deferred payment method, believing that the value of the notes cannot be ascertained, he may switch to the installment method on a timely filed amended return (*Mamula*, 346 F.2d 1016, CA-9, 1964, *rev'g* 41 TC 572, 1964).

[¶1307] LONG-TERM CONTRACTS

Taxpayers engaged in heavy construction work meet special accounting problems. Usually building, installation, and construction projects require a considerable length of time to complete. Frequently, unforeseen difficulties are encountered before the contract is completed, such as price changes in materials used; losses and increased expenses due to strikes, weather conditions and work stoppages; penalties for delay; and unexpected difficulties in laying foundations.

These conditions make it impossible for a construction contractor, no matter how carefully he may estimate, to tell with any certainty whether he will make a profit or sustain a loss on a particular contract until it is completed.

Because of these problems, contractors are permitted to use special methods of reporting their income from long-term contracts—the percentage of completion method and the completed contract method (Reg. §1.451-3).

What Is a Long-Term Contract? This is a building, installation, or construction contract covering a period of *more than one year* from the date of execution to the date on which the contract is finally completed and accepted (Reg. §1.451-3). The courts have allowed the use of the "completed contract method" for contracts taking less than 12 months to complete but begun in one tax year and completed in the following tax year (*L.A. Wells Construction Co.*, 46 BTA 302, 1942).

Long-term contracts include contracts for engineering work and contracts to construct large machines (*Rice, Barton & Fales, Inc.*, 41 F.2d 339, CA-1, 1930). Excluded are: architect's services in connection with construction projects (GCM 7998), merchandise purchased for resale covering operations of more than one taxable year (*C. H. Swift & Sons, Inc.*, 13 BTA 138, 1928), and fixed-fee contracts with the U.S. Government (IT 3459).

[¶1307.1] Percentage of Completion Method

Under this method a portion of the total contract price is taken into gross income each year according to the percentage of the contract completed in that year. For example, if the contract price is $100,000 and 30% of the work was completed in 1976, the contractor would include $30,000 in his gross income for that year (regardless of the time when payments were actually received).

From this amount are deducted all expenditures made during the year on account of the contract. However, adjustment must be made for inventories of materials and supplies on hand at the beginning and end of the taxable year for use in connection with the work under the contract (Reg. §1.451-3).

The Regulations provide that if this method of accounting is used, certificates of architects and engineers showing the percentage of completion of the entire work should be attached to the tax return. However, where a taxpayer has consistently followed this method without attaching the certificates, he has not been required to change his method of reporting income (*W. F. Trimble & Sons Co.*, 1 TC 482, 1943).

The percentage of completion method, in a general sense, corresponds to the accrual method of accounting. Income from the contract is reported as it is earned each year. Expenditures during the year are deductible currently, with appropriate adjustments for inventories of materials and supplies on hand at the beginning and close.

Interim estimates of the work completed by the end of each year are essential. The validity of the method therefore depends to a large degree on the reliability of the progress-of-work estimates made by the architects and engineers and of the cost records for each construction job maintained by the contractor.

Advantages: The percentage of completion method is gaining increased acceptance among contractors because of the following advantages:

☐ (1) It reflects the income from long-term contracts as it is earned up to each stage of completion more accurately than perhaps any other method of accounting.

☐ (2) It avoids the "bunching" of income from a long-term contract all in one year, as under the completed contract method, which exposes the contractor to the twin dangers of progressively higher surtax brackets and possibly increased tax rates.

Disadvantages: On the other hand, the following disadvantages are ascribed to the percentage of completion method:

☐ (1) The contractor may show a profit in one year, and a loss in another year, while the contract is still in the state of partial completion. Thus, the profit or loss picture for the interim years may be distorted and at complete variance with the overall net or loss profit realized on final completion of the contract.
☐ (2) The percentage of completion for any interim period cannot be accurately estimated in the case of long-term contracts, especially those involving subsurface work. Even where estimates are projected, the contractor may run into unexpected and unpredictable expenditures as happened in the case of *Sanford & Brooks Co.*, 282 US 359, 1931. In that case, a contractor, performing a contract for the dredging of the Delaware River, encountered entirely different bed material from that which was anticipated, with the result that actual expenses exceeded receipts on the contract price by approximately $160,000.

However, with improved and more refined methods of estimating and job cost accounting, the percentage of completion method is gaining increased recognition, largely because it reflects a more even and steady flow of reportable income.

[¶1307.2] Completed Contract Method

The entire contract price is taken into income in the year the contract is "finally completed and accepted." In other words, no profit or loss is reported before the year of completion. It is immaterial when the payments on the contract are received, whether before or after completion (*Rice, Barton & Fales, Inc.*, supra; OD 1147).

Expenses directly allocable to the contract are not deductible currently, but are deferred and deducted from the contract price in the year of completion. Thus, salaries of officers and employees to the extent their services and time are devoted to specific contracts should be allocated to the cost of such contracts.

Social Security taxes may be deferred along with the salaries and wages to which they pertain (IT 3434). Depreciation of equipment used exclusively on a specific contract job may be deferred until completion (ARR 8367). State franchise taxes directly allocable to an uncompleted contract may also be deferred until completion of the contract (*Patrick McGovern, Inc.*, 40 BTA 706).

However, general administrative expenses and overhead, which are not allocable to specific contracts, are deductible in the year paid or accrued. This applies, for example, to salaries of officers and employees whose services are not used on specific contracts but for the business as a whole.

Losses suffered in connection with the performance of the contract cannot be deducted in the year sustained but are deductible in the year the contract is completed (*Jones v. Smith*, 193 F.2d 381).

Advantages: Its major advantages are:

☐ (1) It is considered more conservative and accurate in reflecting true profit or loss from a long-term contract.
☐ (2) It avoids reporting of profit for interim years on the basis of partial completion during such years. Profit so reported for the earlier years may prove fictitious in the end; the final result may be a net loss to the contractor.

Disadvantages: As we have seen, postponement of income is not always an unmixed blessing. Here are the disadvantages that may crop up under the completed contract method:

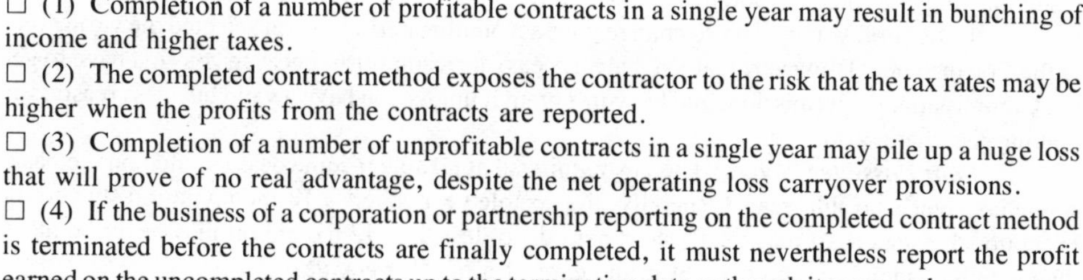

☐ (1) Completion of a number of profitable contracts in a single year may result in bunching of income and higher taxes.

☐ (2) The completed contract method exposes the contractor to the risk that the tax rates may be higher when the profits from the contracts are reported.

☐ (3) Completion of a number of unprofitable contracts in a single year may pile up a huge loss that will prove of no real advantage, despite the net operating loss carryover provisions.

☐ (4) If the business of a corporation or partnership reporting on the completed contract method is terminated before the contracts are finally completed, it must nevertheless report the profit earned on the uncompleted contracts up to the termination date as though it were on the percentage of completion basis. To avoid income from unduly piling up in this final period, continue the business if possible until the contracts are finally completed.

Substantial Completion vs. Final Completion: Since gross income under the completed contract method has to be reported for the taxable year in which the contract is "finally completed and accepted," fixing the date of final completion and acceptance becomes important. In long-term construction projects, there are frequently minor defects in workmanship that remain to be corrected or relatively small "extras" that still have to be furnished.

The Tax Court holds that "substantial completion" is all that is necessary (*Ehret-Day Co.*, 2 TC 25, 1943; *Ben C. Gerwick, Inc.*, 13 TCM 314, 1954). But the Ninth Circuit holds that "finally completed and accepted" means "what it plainly says" and that "substantial completion" will not suffice to fix the time for taxing the income from the contract (*E. E. Black, Ltd.*, 211 F.2d 879, CA-9, 1954; see also *Thompson-King-Tate, Inc.*, 296 F.2d 290, CA-6, 1962).

In the former case, a builder received $44,000 on a $44,500 construction contract, $500 being withheld until he completed the installation of certain thermostats for a fire alarm system. The court held that the contract was not "finally completed" until the following year when the thermostats were installed.

Who May Use the Long-Term Contract Methods: The long-term contract method is optional. A taxpayer can use the straight cash or accrual methods, if he so desires; or he may use the cash or accrual basis for other operations and the special methods just for the long-term contracts.

A taxpayer must adhere to the method of accounting that he initially adopts. Permission of the Commissioner must be obtained if he desires to change (1) from the cash or accrual method to either of the long-term contract methods, or vice versa, or (2) from one of the long-term contract methods to the other.

Steamship companies use a method of accounting similar to the completed contract method, which is commonly referred to as the "completed voyage and completed lay-up period method." All income and expenses are deferred to the year the voyage is completed or the lay-up period for repairs is ended. Here, too, general and administrative expenses must be deducted in the year paid or accrued (*Seas Shipping Co.*, 1 TC 30, 1942; *Planet Line, Inc.*, 34 BTA 253, 1936).

[¶1308] WHEN SHOULD YOUR TAX YEAR START?

Picking the right taxable year for your business pays off in substantial tax savings as well as in other ways. The initial choice of an accounting period is generally within the control of the taxpayer and does not require the permission of the Commissioner. However, many taxpayers forfeit this right of choice by giving the matter haphazard, last-minute consideration, with the result that they are forced to adopt an annual accounting period ill-suited to their business needs.

To be sure, you may try to change your accounting period, if you selected the wrong one in the first instance. However, that's not always easy to accomplish, because you first have to get the Commissioner's permission, and he won't grant it unless you have a valid business reason for making the change.

Four Possible Choices: The law requires that taxable income be computed on the basis of the taxpayer's taxable year. Generally, the taxable year covers a 12-month period. In certain exceptional instances, it may be a "short period" of less than 12 months. It may never be more than a full 12-month period, except in the case of a 52-53 week year.

Under the 1954 Code (§441), only four types of taxable years are recognized. They are (Reg. §1.441-1):

☐ (1) ***Calendar Year***—a 12-month period ending on Dec. 31 (§441(d)).

☐ (2) ***Fiscal Year***—a 12-month period ending on the last day of any month other than December (§441(e)).

☐ (3) ***52-53 Week Year***—a fiscal year, varying from 52 to 53 weeks in duration, which ends always on the same day of the week, which—

(a) occurs for the last time in a calendar month, or

(b) falls nearest the end of a calendar month (§441(f), Reg. §1.441-2).

☐ (4) ***Short Period***—a period of less than 12 months (allowed only in certain special situations such as initial return, final return, change in accounting period, and termination of taxable year by reason of jeopardy assessment) (§443(a)).

[¶1308.1] Factors Determining Choice of Accounting Period

The conditions for each type of annual accounting period may be summarized as follows:

Taxable Year	*Conditions*
(1) Calendar Year *must* be used by a taxpayer, if he . . .	(a) keeps no books, (b) has no annual accounting period, or (c) has an accounting period (other than a calendar year) that does not qualify as a fiscal year.
(2) Fiscal Year *may* be used by a taxpayer, if . . .	(a) he keeps books, (b) he has definitely established such fiscal year as his accounting period before the close of his first fiscal year, and (c) his books are kept in accordance with such fiscal year.
(3) 52-53 Week Taxable Year *may* be used by a taxpayer, if . . .	(a) he keeps books, (b) he regularly computes his income on a 52-53 week basis, and (c) his books are kept on such 52-53 week basis.

Checklist in Picking a Year

Consider	*Here's why*
Get a natural business year.	Your heavy income may come in the fall, but your expenses are not incurred until the following spring. You would not use a calendar year. Income would always be ahead of the expenses connected with it.
Close your year at a convenient time.	Inventories can be taken and financial statements prepared most conveniently when business activities are low. If the plant shuts down during vacation period—consider year end at that time.
Professional service.	Legal and auditing talent may also be less harried during the slack period. Better service and care will be given to your audit and tax return.
Several business interests; tax saving by the use of various fiscal years for different income sources	This gives rise to a postponing of a tax on income until subsequent years when the income might be lower and postpones paying the taxes to years where you might have losses to offset it.
Renewal of contracts.	Leases, labor contracts, and other renewals can be negotiated in the slack period where the pressure of the business will not cause hasty decisions.

[¶1308.2] Natural Business Year

You won't find the term "natural business year" in the tax law. However, the Internal Revenue Service looks upon it with favor and will readily grant permission to a taxpayer to change his established accounting period to conform with his natural business year.

What is the natural business year? It is an annual cycle of 12 consecutive months (or 52 to 53 weeks) that ends when the business activities of the enterprise are at their lowest point. At this point of the annual cycle, sales, and production activities are at their lowest level, inventories and accounts receivable are at a minimum, and the cash or liquid position of the enterprise is at its highest level.

The principal advantages ascribed to the natural business year are these:

☐ (1) Financial statements for your business, based on the natural business year, are apt to be more accurate than those prepared at the end of some other annual accounting period because, at the end of a natural business year, there are the fewest number of open transactions and unrealized operations, and necessary closing adjustments are at a minimum.

☐ (2) If your business operations fluctuate widely, with peak income concentrated in certain months of the year and heavy expenses incurred in other months, you will want to use a natural business year that embraces the peak periods of income and expenditures. You will then be in a better position to "match" the income with the related costs and expenses incurred in earning such income, thus presenting a more realistic picture of your true net income for the year.

□ (3) A financial statement of the close of a natural business year presents the best picture of your business for credit purposes. Your liquid position will normally be at its highest level then, with inventories and receivables low and cash high.
□ (4) You save considerable time, effort, and expense in taking physical inventories and in aging and verifying outstanding accounts receivable when they are at the lowest point of the year.
□ (5) You avoid the frenzied March 15th or April 15th tax return time by getting away from a December 31st closing of your books. Your office personnel is less harried. Your auditors and other professional advisors are under less pressure. It greatly facilitates the closing of your books and the preparation of your financial statements and tax returns when you have a ''natural'' fiscal year for your business.
□ (6) New tax laws are usually enacted in the spring or summer and are often made applicable to tax years beginning after the preceding December 31st. If you are on a fiscal year, you have more time than calendar-year taxpayers to figure out the impact of changes in the tax law.

Seasonal Business: Don't pick a year that splits your season into two different tax years or puts most of your receipts in one year and expenses in another. Avoid distortion of your annual income; spread it evenly over the years. In the long run, your tax burden will be lightest if you can show an even flow of annual income rather than peaks and valleys.

Starting a Business in the Middle of the Year: Here are a few tax-saving ideas to consider if you launch a new business enterprise in the middle of a year.

□ (1) ***Large Expenses or Losses at Beginning:*** A new business enterprise frequently runs into large expenses or losses at the beginning. If that is the case, and you start business in the middle of the year, it may be to your advantage to adopt a fiscal year instead of a calendar year. A fiscal year extended beyond December 31st may give you an opportunity to build up additional income to absorb the heavy opening expenses or losses.
□ (2) ***Large Seasonal Gain at Beginning:*** A new business started toward the end of the year may show a high seasonal gain for its first calendar year. If you expect such a result, you probably should adopt a fiscal year to enable the business to offset the high seasonal gain by expenses and losses incurred in subsequent slack months.
□ (3) ***Tax Deferment:*** You may want to adopt a fiscal year ending a month or so before your season starts. In this way, your anticipated high-income season will fall into your second fiscal year. This will enable you to postpone payment of taxes on the income derived from your first season's operations as long as possible. In the meantime, you can use these tax funds as working capital for your current business operations.
□ (4) ***Surtax Saving:*** A new corporation can save taxes by adopting a fiscal year ending when it expects its first few months' earnings to be approaching $25,000. It thus escapes the corporate surtax, which applies only to net income over $25,000. The corporation doesn't have to annualize the income reported in its first ''short period'' return.

[¶1308.3] 52-53 Week Tax Year

The Code lets a taxpayer elect to figure his income on the basis of an annual period varying from 52 to 53 weeks (§441(f)). The period must always end on the same day of the week; most taxpayers choose either Friday or Saturday, whichever is the last working day. Assuming, for example, the period ends on Friday, it must always end, too, on either: (1) the last Friday in the calendar month, or (2) the Friday nearest the last day of a calendar month.

[¶1309] WHAT TO WATCH OUT FOR IF YOU ARE GOING TO CHANGE YOUR ACCOUNTING METHOD OR TAX YEAR

There are many valid business reasons why you may want to change your accounting method or tax year. However, a change in either case can result in tax difficulties if you are not careful to comply strictly with IRS rules and procedures. Furthermore, even where you do comply with IRS requirements, you may have to make tax adjustments that could be costly and inconvenient. So, before you make the change, you will want to know exactly what to watch out for and what pitfalls to avoid.

[¶1309.1] Change of Accounting Method

Income, for tax purposes, must be computed under the same method of accounting regularly used by you in keeping your books. If you have not used a method regularly or if the method regularly used does not clearly reflect income, the Commissioner can compute your income under a method that he considers to clearly reflect your income.

Except for some special situations, you may not change your method of accounting without the prior consent of the Commissioner. If you make a change in your accounting method without prior consent, you will be required to make adjustments for pre-1954 Code years (in addition to adjustments for post-1954 Code years). Such adjustments are not required if the change was initiated by the Commissioner (§481).

Under the present procedure, application for permission to change an accounting method or practice is filed on Form 3115 within the first 180 days of the year to which the change is to apply.

Adjustments resulting from the change is taken ratably "over an appropriate period, prescribed by the Commissioner, generally ten years" beginning with the year of change. Applications generally receive favorable consideration if the taxpayer agrees to the ten-year spread or any other approach suggested by IRS.

Why Adjustments Are Required When a Change in Accounting Method Is Made: On the cash basis, we only included in income those amounts actually received (on accounts receivable) and deducted those amounts we actually paid out on inventory and accounts payable. So we didn't include our year-end uncollected accounts receivable as income; nor did we deduct our year-end unpaid accounts payable from income. On the other hand, we deducted amounts spent for inventory that we didn't sell yet, so this amount has to be added back into income. These are the adjustments necessary to convert from the cash to the accrual method, and they are cumulative—they affect all prior years' tax pictures. (If you pick up an inventory at the beginning of 1976, you should also show it as a closing inventory for 1975, and so on, going backwards. Similarly, the accounts receivable at the beginning of this year should have been reflected in last year's income—when they arose. That's the effect of these adjustments.)

What Adjustments Are Required When a Change in Accounting Method Is Made: A change in accounting method may be made by either the Commissioner or the taxpayer. If the Commissioner makes the change, §481 limits any change he can make to 1954 Code years. If *you* make the change of your own accord, you must make the same 1954 Code year adjustments *and, in addition* §481 says you must also make an adjustment for the pre-1954 Code years. The pre-1954 Code year adjustment is the adjustment that would have been required if the change had occurred in the first taxable year beginning after December 31, 1953, and ending after August 16, 1954 (in most cases that's the calendar year 1954). In the case of a calendar-year taxpayer changing from the cash to accrual basis, this would have been the sum of the accounts receivable and inventory on January 1, 1954, less accounts payable as of that date. The 1954 Code year adjustment is simply the difference between the adjustment made on the first day of the taxable year in which the change is made and the pre-1954 adjustment. Assuming a taxpayer, who should be on the accrual basis but has been reporting on the cash basis for many years (since he went into business), finally switches to the accrual basis in 1977, here is how these adjustments are computed:

	January 1, 1954	*January 1, 1977*
Accounts Receivable	$16,000	$32,000
Inventory	8,000	20,000
Total	24,000	52,000
Accounts Payable	6,000	10,000
Net Adjustment	$18,000	$42,000

The total adjustment for the year of change (1977) is $42,000. However, the pre-1954 adjustment is $18,000 and the 1954 Code year adjustment is $24,000 ($42,000 – $18,000).

If the Commissioner makes the change, he can only pick up $24,000 (1954 Code year adjustment) as additional income in 1977, the taxable year of the change. This is the difference between the $42,000 adjustment as of January 1, 1977 (the year of the change), and January 1, 1954, the pre-1954 adjustment of $18,000. If you make the change, you will have to pick up both the 1954 Code year adjustment of $24,000 and the pre-1954 Code year adjustment of $18,000 for a total of $42,000 of additional income in the year of the change.

Relief Provisions of §481(b): Because the adjustments the taxpayer has to make when he initiates the change may lump several years' income into one, there are relief provisions provided in §481 to soften the impact of this lumping. The purpose of these relief provisions is to permit the taxpayer to compute the tax deficiency resulting from the accounting change in the least costly way. In most of these options, the taxpayer is really after that method that will give him the lowest additional tax in 1977. *No amended returns are filed; there is no interest due on any underpayments of taxes.*

Pitfalls of an Involuntary Change of Method: Since, under the Regulations, no pre-1954 Code year involuntary adjustments are to be taken into account in the taxable year of change, there exists also the possibility of losing a favorable decrease in taxable income. For example, suppose these were the figures:

	January 1, 1954	*January 1, 1977*
Accounts Receivable	$ 5,000	$ 8,000
Inventory	3,000	14,000
Total	8,000	22,000
Accounts Payable	13,000	15,000
Net Adjustment	($5,000)	$ 7,000

If the change were involuntary, the $5,000 decrease in taxable income pertaining to pre-1954 Code years would not be taken into account. You'd have to pick up $7,000 in 1963, the year of change (see Reg. §1.481-1(c)(4)). In this case, it would pay to make a voluntary change of method.

Accounting Method Change Can Present a Tax Trap When Incorporating an Unincorporated Business: Assume a partnership, operating for a number of years, has been using the wrong accounting method. Say it should have used the accrual method because it had inventories, but it used the cash method. Now it wants to incorporate.

If it incorporates, it may be walking into a costly trap. IRS takes the approach that issuing the stock in exchange for the inventory and accounts receivable is the realization of income tied up in these assets. So the partners would have to pick up all that added income in the partnership's final return. Or IRS could force the new corporation to report on the accrual basis. Then the corporation would have to include the value of the partnership's closing accounts receivable and inventory in its taxable income. This can be done on the theory that these assets have a zero basis, having been received in a tax-free exchange. And to add to the injury, you couldn't get the relief provided by §481 because §481 only applies to a taxpayer's change in its own accounting, and the corporation is not the same taxpayer as the partnership (*Ezo Products*, 37 TC 385, 1961).

What to Do: One possibility (before incorporating) is for the partnership to request the change of accounting method. This should be done according to the Regulations. Then, you can take advantage of the relief provisions of §481. So, for example, if the pre-1954 adjustment is $30,000, you can spread the $30,000 equally over 10 years.

Another possibility is to have the corporation formed without acquiring the inventory or receivables of the partnership. The partnership continues in existence, and the corporation buys the partnership's inventory in dribs and drabs. In this way, the partnership would only pay tax on the receivables as they were collected and bunching of income would be avoided in both entities.

Cash to Accrual Method: IRS also permits a cash-basis taxpayer to switch to the accrual method without prior IRS approval. This automatic switching procedure, however, only applies to those whose *overall method* is the cash receipts and disbursements method. It doesn't apply where the installment method, long-term contract method, crop method, or any other special method is used. Also, this automatic method may not be used if a taxpayer's deduction or credit would not otherwise be allowed (e.g., carryovers of net operating losses, foreign tax credit, investment credit except for this switch to the accrual method) (Rev. Proc. 67-10, CB 1967-1, 585).

To get the automatic change, you must file Form 3115 and meet the following requirements:

☐ (1) Adjust the books at the end of the change year to reflect the accrual method. Here is an example of the type of adjustment:

Additions to income:	
Income accrued but unreported (e.g., Accounts Receivable)	$50,000
Inventory (cost at end of year preceding year of change)	15,000
Total	$65,000
Less:	
Expenses accrued but not deducted (e.g., Accounts Payable)	40,000
Net increase (decrease) (spread over ten years)	$25,000

☐ (2) After this adjustment, the accrual method is to be used for all items.

[¶1309.2] Change of Accounting Year

Once you adopt a tax year, you can't change to another accounting period without first getting the approval of IRS (§442).

However, blanket permission is given in the circumstances outlined below. If you come within the rule, you can make the change simply by filing a return for the short period and enclosing a statement. The filing date is three-and-a-half months after the close of the short period.

Shift of Tax Year—With Permission: If a taxpayer gets permission to change his accounting period, he has to file a return for the short period beginning on the day after the close of his old tax year and ending at the end of the day before the first day of the new tax year (§443). There are two ways of figuring the tax. Here's the usual way:

□ (1) Take your taxable income for the short period and put it on an annual basis. To do this, you multiply it by 12 and divide the result by the number of months in the short period. The result is the amount of income you would have earned if you'd been in business for a year and earned at the same rate you earned during the short period.

□ (2) Now figure the tax on this amount.

□ (3) Multiply the tax figured in step (2) by the number of months in the short period, and divide the result by twelve. The result is your tax for the short period, under the general rule.

There's another way to figure it if the general rule distorts income. Here's how this exception works:

Take your actual taxable income for the first 12 months you were in operation (or, if it's a closing short period, the last 12 months in operation), and figure the tax on it. Section 433 says the tax for the short period is reduced to the greater of the following:

(a) An amount that bears the same ratio to the tax computed on the taxable income for the 12-month period as the taxable income computed on the basis of the short period bears to the taxable income for the 12-month period; or

(b) The tax computed on the taxable income for the short period without placing the taxable income on an annual basis.

How to Get Permission: Application for permission to change must be made on Form 1128 not later than the last day of the month after the close of the short tax year resulting from the change. Motive can't be tax avoidance; there must be a business reason (Reg. §1.442-1(b)).

How to Change Without Permission: An existing corporation can change its tax year without prior IRS approval if: (1) it has not changed its accounting period within the previous ten years, (2) it does not have a net operating loss in the short year arising from the change, and (3) its income for the short year (on an annual basis) is at least 80% of its income for the previous year (Reg. §1.442-1(c)). If it is an electing small business (Subchapter S) corporation during the short period required to effect the change, it must get prior IRS approval.

As to an existing partnership, prior approval to change will not be necessary if all the principal partners have the same tax year or concurrently change to the year to which the partnership changes (Reg. §1.442-1(b)(2)).

SECTION XIV
INVENTORY METHODS

The term "inventory" is used to designate tangible personal property that is (1) held for sale in the ordinary course of business, (2) in the process of being produced for later sale, or (3) currently consumed in the production of goods or services to be available for sale. In a manufacturing firm, inventory is usually called "merchandise inventory."

Manufacturing firms have many types of inventory; for example, finished goods, work in process, raw materials, and manufacturing supplies. Finished goods of a manufacturing company are comparable to the merchandise of a nonmanufacturing company.

Depreciable fixed assets retired from regular use and held for sale should not be included in inventory. Raw materials and supplies that become part of a finished product, if used in sufficient quantities, become part of the inventory. Some supplies, however, used indirectly in the manufacturing process do not become part of the finished product; e.g., lubricants. Other supplies like paint, nails, screws do become part of the finished product; but it is usually impracticable to try to allocate their cost and include it in inventory.

In accounting for inventories we try to match appropriate costs against revenues. This gives us a proper determination of realized income. Another way of putting it is to say that by applying the best method of costing inventory, we are accurately measuring our "cost of goods sold."

Generally speaking, inventory accounting is required by the tax law wherever the production, purchase, or sale of merchandise is an income-producing factor. Only by inventories is income clearly reflected.

Inventory accounting may be prohibited in an industry where its use would prevent a clear reflection of the income or would not be necessary in making such a determination. Oyster culture and real estate dealing are two examples of businesses in which inventory accounting is not permitted.

Inventory accounting represents a means of deferring charges that are properly allocable against future business operations. A purchase of merchandise for future sale is not a current expense; you have merely exchanged one kind of value (money) for another (goods). Until you use the merchandise for the production of income, you cannot charge it against income. By using inventories you avoid income distortion.

A taxpayer who uses inventories is required to use the accrual method of accounting (Reg. §1.446-1). Since inventory accounting isn't based on actual intake and outgo of cash, the cash method wouldn't clearly reflect the income.

[¶1401] WHAT IS INVENTORY?

Inventory includes all goods held for sale in the ordinary course of business, as distinguished from goods held as an investment. For example, goods purchased for another party under arrangement for reimbursement when the goods are taken are not inventory goods (*Finance & Guaranty Co.*, 50 F.2d 1061, CA-4, 1931). These goods are not held for sale in the "ordinary" course of business.

Inventory includes raw materials, work (goods) in process, and finished goods. "Raw materials" are those materials that enter directly into the manufactured end product. "Work in process" constitutes those items that have passed the raw material stage, yet cannot be considered finished goods.

Inventories do not include: (1) raw materials and supplies, neither acquired for sale, nor to become part of merchandise intended for sale; (2) materials ordered for future delivery, title to which has not yet been transferred; (3) machinery, fixtures, land, buildings, accounts receivable, cash and similar capital; (4) goods received on consignment; (5) goods sold (or containers) when title has passed to your customer.

[¶1401.1] Treatment of Specific Inventory Items

The rule that you cannot inventory material unless title is vested in you may be important if you value your inventory at the lower of cost or market; failure to acquire title to goods that had declined in value would keep you from inventorying them and obtaining the tax benefit from the reduced market value. It may be important too if you value at LIFO (see ¶1404) because the amount of goods in inventory may affect the cost of sales, even without a decline in market value.

Passage of title is a matter of state law, but the intent of the parties (determined from the contract, their conduct, and the surrounding circumstances) is important too (*Brown Lumber Co.*, 35 F.2d 880, CA-D.C., 1929).

The mere physical acceptance of returned goods doesn't return title to the seller; latter doesn't regain title unless he either accepts them in cancellation of his claim against the purchaser or acknowledges his liability for them (*Perpetual Encyclopedia Corp.*, BTA Memo 1932).

Although the purchaser includes in his inventory goods to which he has acquired title, even though the goods are in transit, he shouldn't include goods ordered for future delivery where he hasn't yet received title. (Reg. §1.471-1.) Except for LIFO taxpayers, under certain conditions, future contracts aren't inventoriable (Reg. §1.472-1; *Elkan*, 2 TC 597, 1943).

Here is how certain specific inventory items are treated:

☐ (1) ***Operating Supplies:*** Need not be inventoried. Can be treated as a deferred expense, to be deducted as used or consumed.

☐ (2) ***Merchandise in Hands of Processor:*** Inventoried by the owner when the goods are to be returned in kind, such as paper for printing. But when a new product is to be returned, such as flour for wheat, it is not inventoried.

☐ (3) ***Goods Under Contract of Sale:*** Include in seller's inventory and exclude from buyer's, if the goods are not yet segregated and applied to the contract. However, if the contract is noncancellable and goods have been segregated and applied, they are to be included in the buyer's inventory and excluded from the seller's.

☐ (4) ***Merchandise:*** If title has passed to the buyer under local law, the merchandise is to be excluded from the seller's inventory and included in the buyer's inventory, even though the goods are in transit or the buyer does not have physical possession.

☐ (5) ***Goods Sent C.O.D.:*** Include in the seller's inventory until payment and delivery have been made (IT 1759).

☐ (6) ***Goods Shipped on Approval:*** Include in the seller's inventory until accepted.

☐ (7) ***Merchandise refused by the Buyer:*** Though shipped under contract; nevertheless, not includible in seller's inventory.

☐ (8) ***Goods Shipped on Consignment:*** Include in inventory until consignee sells them.

☐ (9) ***Goods Rejected Because of Defects:*** Include in seller's inventory, not buyer's, if the buyer is within his rights in rejecting (*Monroe Cotton Mills,* 6 BTA 172, 1946).

☐ (10) ***Sale by Sample:*** Where the goods are subject to inspection and rejection within a given time, include them in seller's inventory if promptly rejected by the buyer, even though not returned before the end of the year.

☐ (11) ***Foreign Money or Purchase Credits:*** Not inventoriable, as such, but a dealer in foreign exchange may inventory unconverted foreign money.

Goods subject to a contract to purchase aren't includible in the purchaser's inventory unless title has passed (*Barde Steel Products Corp.,* 14 BTA 209, 1928). The same applies to goods subject to a futures contract and to sellers with regard to goods subject to contract to repurchase.

[¶1402] INVENTORY VALUATION METHODS

Your choice of valuation method is limited to cost, or lower of cost or market.

☐ ***Cost:*** Although actual cost can be used for goods identifiable with specific invoices, this valuation is usually based on the cost of goods in inventory at the inventory date.

☐ ***Lower of Cost or Market:*** Goods in inventory are valued at the lower of their cost or their market value at the inventory date. This is the method most widely used. It produces lower values than does the cost method.

There are two ways to identify goods that have to be valued, the FIFO (first-in, first-out) method and the LIFO (last-in, first-out) method. Both these methods use a fiction in determining which goods were sold during the year and which remain in inventory.

☐ ***LIFO:*** This method assumes that the goods that were *last* bought were the *first* to be used; that the goods that were first bought are still in inventory. This method is beneficial taxwise in a rising market because you are able to charge against income the current "costs" of your merchandise; otherwise your income reflects an inventory profit that is caused by the rising market, not your product. See ¶1404.

☐ ***FIFO:*** This method assumes that the goods that were *first* bought were the *first* to be used; that the goods that were last bought are still in inventory. This method protects you from a falling market; there, lower profits are shown because the old (higher) costs are used in determining profit. This actually indicates an inventory loss rather than an operating loss. See ¶1403.
☐ ***Prohibited Methods:*** These inventory practices are prohibited (Reg. §1.471-2(f)): (1) Deducting reserve for price changes or estimate of depreciation in value; (2) Taking part of inventory at nominal or less than the actual value; (3) Omitting portions of stock; (4) Using constant price or nominal value for normal quantities of goods; (5) Including stock in transit without having title. Some of the advantages of (4) may be obtained by adopting LIFO when prices are low. See ¶1404.

[¶1402.1] Determining Cost

Cost depends upon your cost accounting system. Use that method, sanctioned by trade custom, that best reflects the true cost of the goods you use in your business. In complicated situations, you will have to accurately reflect burden and its distribution, cost of byproducts, supplies, shrinkage, competitive factors, volume changes, seasonal variations, and other factors in the realm of the cost accountant.

Here are the rules:

☐ (1) ***Merchandise on hand*** at the beginning of the year takes a cost equal to inventory price used at the beginning of the year.
☐ (2) ***Merchandise purchased*** since the beginning of the year is taken at invoice price less trade discounts, plus transportation or other necessary charges incurred in acquiring possession of the goods. You can add purchase commissions even if paid to your own employees. Deduction of interest discount for cash payment is optional, but you must be consistent (Reg. §1.471-3(b)).

Cash discounts should be used to reduce cost, this tending to defer their inclusion in income. An exception might arise with a new business if high early losses were anticipated, with a possibility they couldn't be all used up as carryovers. Then the thing to do would be to use up some of the losses currently by including the cash discounts in income.

Although you add transportation, etc., charges to cost where incurred in connection with acquiring the goods, don't add similar charges for moving the goods from place to place after acquisition, where value hasn't been increased.

We're talking about physical possession in your own facilities when we refer to goods already acquired. Mere passage of title wouldn't prevent your adding to costs subsequent freight and handling charges. You could probably include in costs transportation charges after acquisition if these added to value or use. Any carrying charges that add to the value of goods (for instance, cost of carrying liquor in bond) should be included in the inventory valuation (IT 3240).
☐ (3) ***Merchandise produced*** since the beginning of the year takes a cost based upon the cost system that best suits your operations. This should reflect cost of raw materials and supplies, expenditures for direct labor, indirect expenses incident to production including a reasonable proportion of management expenses, but not including any cost of selling.

The cost of raw materials and supplies should be determined the same way as cost of merchandise purchased. Direct labor includes payroll costs of those engaged directly in production, including bonuses and other extra compensation.

Indirect expenses include ordinary overhead. Accepted accounting practice permits inclusion of management expenses only as related to production, excluding general or administrative expenses. Includible indirect expenses are those ordinary and necessary to production under the conditions prevalent at the time. You would exclude expenses related more to other things, although they might not have been incurred except for the fact that you were in production. These might include costs incurred during strikes or losses from natural disasters (floods, earthquakes, and the like). Abnormal labor fluctuations and scrap losses, and possibly research expenses might be excludable, as not closely enough connected to production; but premium payments for scarce materials would be includible as common to production conditions at the time.

[¶1402.2] Determining Market Value

"Market" is the current bid price prevailing in the taxpayer's own market, at the inventory date for the particular merchandise, in the quantity usually purchased (Reg. §1.471-4). This value is applied to goods purchased and on hand, and the basic elements of cost (materials, labor, and burden) of goods in process of manufacture and of finished goods on hand. Not, however, to goods on hand or in process of manufacture for delivery upon noncancellable contracts at fixed price entered into before the date of the inventory. These goods must be inventoried at cost if they are under a contract that protects against loss.

When no current market exists or the quotations are nominal because the market is slow, the fair market price is determined by specific purchases or sales by you or others made in reasonable volume and in good faith at the dates nearest the inventory, or monetary consideration paid for cancellation of a contract for purchase commitments. Costs of replacement may be the best evidence of "market."

When, in the regular course of business, you offer merchandise for sale at prices lower than the current price, you can use these prices, less the direct cost of disposition. Here your value is based on actual sales and costs for a reasonable period before and after the date of inventory (Reg. §1.471-4(b)). However, in applying this method to goods in process, allow for cost of completion.

Don't use price lists published before the end of the year where the market has changed after publication and before the end of the year. The market after the end of the year shouldn't be reflected in closing inventory valuations. You needn't use quoted prices if you can show they were artifically pegged, or that transactions were completed outside the market at different prices and in volume equal to that for determining market prices; here you can use a weighted average of quoted and unquoted prices.

Apply the prevailing bid price both to goods purchased and to the basic cost elements of goods manufactured (Reg. §1.471-4(a)). The Treasury holds reproductive cost can be used only for manufactured goods for which there are no open market quotations or that haven't been processed to a stage where they are salable on the open market. Further, manufactured goods that are salable on the open market should be valued at the prevailing bid prices for such goods.

[¶1402.3] Determining Market—No Open Market

Where there is no open market, the taxpayer can use as evidence of fair market value the price of the nearest inventory purchase he has made. Here's an example.

Date Purchased	*No.*	*Price*	*Total Cost*
Jan. 10, 1974	10	$2.00	$ 20.00
March 10, 1974	20	2.10	42.00
May 10, 1974	30	1.90	57.00
July 10, 1974	40	2.00	80.00
Sept. 10, 1974	10	2.05	20.50
Nov. 10, 1974	10	2.10	21.00
Inventory on hand 1/1/74	25	2.00	50.00
	145		$290.50
There are on hand at 1/1/75	20		
Valued as follows			
10 units		$2.10	$ 21.00
10 units		2.05	20.50
			$ 41.50
Cost of units sold	125		$249.00

The procedure would apply where quotations were merely nominal. This means there is a lack of reality in prices; for example, prices published arbitrarily without the support of actual market transactions. "Nominal" doesn't include a mere decline in market prices; quoted prices should be used wherever they reflect actual transactions in reasonable volume (*Elder Mfg. Co.*, 10 F. Supp. 125).

With a usable market price, valuation is just a matter of proof. The nearest acceptable quotations before and after the inventory date can be used provided nothing has happened between inventory date and date of quotation to make the quotations inapplicable. The intention is to establish value at inventory date; so you won't be permitted to anticipate subsequent losses (*Cleveland Automobile Co.*, 70 F.2d 365, CA-6, 1934).

If usable quotations aren't available, you can refer to actual prices charged within a short time from the inventory date (*Franklin Mills*, 7 BTA 1290, 1927). Testimony of the principal supplier could be used to establish market prices (*Bloom Bros.*, 10 BTA 710, 1928). Your own judgment might be helpful if based on long experience; but it probably wouldn't be accepted (*True*, 6 BTA 1042, 1927; *Floyd*, 11 BTA 903, 1928; *Wickens*, 16 BTA 968, 1929).

Remember you can be required to prove market price when it is less than cost. Even orderly and systematic reproductions may not be accepted if not supported by proof (*Decline Mfg. Co.*, 6 BTA 711, 1927).

When it becomes necessary to reduce inventories to market, don't write down the inventory. Determine market by item before assembling the inventory totals, and keep the determinations as proof in case the examining agent raises a question.

[¶1402.4] Firm Sales Contracts

You can't value goods at market where manufactured or held for delivery on firm sales contracts at fixed prices protecting against actual loss, with neither party having the right to cancel and the contract having been made before the inventory date (Reg. §1.471-4(a)(2)). This means raw materials held to fill the contract, as well as goods finished or in process. Goods needn't have been segregated or allocated to the contract. Where inventory quantity is greater than needed to fill the contract, only as much as the contract calls for need be valued at cost. If the goods so needed can't be determined, market can be used if lower than cost.

Reduction in contract price after the inventory date doesn't relieve you from having to value at cost. However, cancellation before the inventory date does (*US Cartridge Co.*, 284 US 511, 1932). So, presumably, does an amendment before the inventory date. If you value inventories at lower of cost or market, therefore, and market has declined below cost and you know contract prices must be reduced, make your amendment before the inventory date.

[¶1402.5] Unsalable or Unusable Inventory

Inventory that is unsalable at normal prices, or unusable in the normal way, due to damage, style change, broken or odd lots, imperfection, shop-wear, etc., should be valued at estimated selling price, less direct cost of disposition. This covers also second-hand goods taken on trade-in. If the goods are raw materials or partly finished goods, held for use or consumption, value them at a reasonable basis considering their condition and usefulness; but valuation mustn't go below scrap (Reg. §1.471-2(c)).

This method of valuing unsalable or unusable goods can be used regardless of your regular method of valuing. Objective is to permit reduction of income for unrealized losses, due to the causes named above. Therefore, LIFO taxpayers can use it, too, notwithstanding the provision in the Regulations requiring valuation of LIFO at cost (§472(b)).

Selling price in this connection means actual offering price during a period ending not later than 30 days after the inventory date (Reg. §1.471-2(c)). Markdown was disallowed where offering at the reduced price wasn't made within 30 days and the evidence didn't show the basis for the adjustments (*Farmers Hardware Co.*, 2 BTA 90, 1925). Markdown by approximation has also been disallowed, even where supported by subsequently determined obsolescence.

However, there needn't be an offering if the goods are completely obsolete or worthless. Evidence of deterioration may be sufficient to justify the markdown, even without an offering at the reduced price (*May Lumber Co.*, 13 BTA 62, 1928).

The offering at reduced price may not always be practicable. For example, it may be sounder, in disposing of a lot of obsolete goods, to reduce the price gradually as the offering is made. Deduct the full loss from inventory when the estimate is backed by past experience; validity of loss determination gets more weight than immediate offering, particularly where the gradual technique is recognized in industry practice.

Markdown for unearned profit in inventories or a reserve for possible future losses is not permissible.

Taxpayer has the burden of proof that the goods qualify for the special valuation treatment as unsalable or unusable (Reg. §1.471-2(c)).

[¶1403] INVENTORY METHODS: FIFO

FIFO (or first-in, first-out) is probably the commonest inventory method. FIFO is, in fact, based completely on a very simple assumption—that the first goods taken into inventory are the first goods sold. To see how this works out, take a look at the following example:

Opening inventory (amount of goods on hand at beginning of year) and purchases each quarter are:

Opening Inventory	1,000 units @ $10	$10,000
1st quarter purchases	800 units @ $11	$ 8,800
2nd quarter purchases	500 units @ $14	$ 7,000
3rd quarter purchases	400 units @ $12	$ 4,800
4th quarter purchases	300 units @ $13	$ 3,900
Total	3,000	$34,500

At the end of the year, the closing inventory consists of 1,100 units. Since FIFO assumes that the first units taken into inventory were the first units to go out, the last units taken into inventory are the ones that make up the 1,100 units of closing inventory. Thus, all the 4th quarter units, all the 3rd quarter units, and 400 of the 2nd quarter units are left. These are valued as follows:

300 units @ $13 (4th quarter)	$ 3,900
400 units @ $12 (3rd quarter)	$ 4,800
400 units @ $14 (2nd quarter)	$ 5,600
Cost of 1,100 units closing inventory	$14,300

So, under FIFO, the cost of goods sold for the year in the example is $20,200, i.e., cost of opening inventory plus purchases ($34,500) less cost of closing inventory ($14,300). The average price, then, of the 1,900 units sold over the year is $10.63 per unit using FIFO.

Under the tax law, FIFO is a permissible inventory method and is used by many businesses. However, there is another method available, which is growing more popular all the time. This is LIFO, which will be explained in the next paragraph.

[¶1404] INVENTORY METHODS: LIFO

LIFO (or last-in, first-out) is designed to eliminate so-called ''inventory profits.'' It is the equivalent of an inventory reserve and is based on the theory that the charges for current operations should consist first of the cost of merchandise most recently purchased. Its chief advantage is that it directly links the current cost of merchandise to the current selling prices of the finished product.

[¶1404.1] How Goods on LIFO Are to Be Valued

Goods comprising the beginning inventory of the first year on LIFO must be valued at average cost. The average cost of units in each inventory class is obtained by dividing the aggregate cost of this inventory class, computed according to the inventory method previously employed by the taxpayer, by the number of units on hand. In effect, each unit is considered to have been acquired at the same time.

Goods of a specified type on hand at the close of a taxable year are treated as being: first, those included in the opening inventory of the taxable year in the order of acquisition, and, secondly, those acquired in the taxable year. The taxpayer is given permission to value any physical increment of goods of a specified type at costs determined as follows:

☐ (a) By reference to the actual cost of the goods most recently purchased or produced;

☐ (b) By reference to the actual cost of the goods purchased or produced during the taxable year in the order of acquisition;

☐ (c) By application of an average unit cost equal to the aggregate cost of all of the goods purchased or produced throughout the taxable year divided by the total number of units so purchased or produced, the goods reflected in such inventory increase being considered for the purposes of §472 as having been acquired all at the same time; or

☐ (d) Pursuant to any other proper method that, in the opinion of the Commissioner, clearly reflects income.

A survey found that most companies use option (b) for these reasons:

"In a steadily rising market the earliest goods purchased during the year usually will be acquired at lower prices than later purchases. Inventory increments built up on rising wartime markets, therefore, generally were found to be stated at lower values under option (b) than under option (a). Some managements experimented with all three options before filing their first LIFO return and formally elected the option which gave the lowest inventory valuation, and hence the smallest taxable income for the year.

"Another effect of the strict LIFO procedure is that it leaves management more flexibility in determining the amount of profits and taxable income reported in a given year. If prices have risen steadily during a year, for instance, profits can be reduced by building up inventory increments as of the year end. Such year-end purchases will be charged into cost of goods sold at their actual costs, but the inventory increments resulting from the purchases will be carried in the ending inventory at the costs of the first goods purchased during the year. Profits will be reduced by the excess of the costs of the year-end purchases over the cost of corresponding goods purchased at the beginning of each year."

Some companies deliberately build up inventories at the end of the year to reduce their taxable income. In years of falling prices, the building up of inventories will increase the income of the given year. Similarly, a reduction of inventory so that base stock is charged against current sales may increase taxable income. Thus, the adoption of LIFO places a premium on inventory control.

LIFO is designed particularly to charge increasing cost, in a period of rising prices, directly to operations. Under other systems of valuation, the increasing costs are charged to closing inventories. The effect is to reduce cost of sales and increase profits and taxes.

LIFO is the taxpayer's defense against an unrealistic tax on paper profits as distinguished from real profits. Here's an example that shows this unrealized profit.

Opening Inventory	*LIFO*	*FIFO*
100,000 at 30 cents	$ 30,000	$ 30,000
Add Purchases		
1,000,000 at 35 cents	350,000	350,000
100,000 at 45 cents	45,000	45,000
	425,000	425,000
Less Closing Inventory		
100,000 at 45 cents		45,000
100,000 at 30 cents	30,000	
Cost of Goods Sold	$395,000	$380,000

Thus, FIFO gives a lower cost and higher profits than LIFO. This example shows that once LIFO has been adopted, management must control its inventory quantities carefully, through purchasing procedures and production planning, in order to preserve the tax deferment for the longest possible time.

Naturally, LIFO will give a similar relative advantage for each succeeding year in which the cost of materials continues to rise; provided, however, closing inventory in terms of units doesn't drop below the quantity on hand at the beginning of the year in which LIFO was adopted. Taxpayers who refuse to adopt LIFO fear a decline in prices, but those who have adopted it have saved more than such a decline could cost.

LIFO valuation simply assumes that the most recent purchases are the first to be withdrawn, either for sale in the ordinary course of business or for the production of stock. Withdrawals from inventory are priced at the latest purchases.

Here are reasons why many corporations have adopted LIFO.

☐ (1) Determines income tax more accurately; profit and losses aren't exaggerated.
☐ (2) Gives a better correlation between current cost and selling prices.
☐ (3) Avoids wide fluctuations in periodic net income by the inflation of inventory values.
☐ (4) Eliminates paper profits, taxed as real profits.
☐ (5) Gives management better opportunity to determine its business course, profit and loss statements being more accurate.
☐ (6) A growing tendency to believe that, in a recession, the government will permit "cost or market" under LIFO.

[¶1404.2] Methods of Applying LIFO

There are three possible ways to compute LIFO: (1) under the individual quantity methods; (2) by the use of price indexes; (3) under the dollar-value method.

Under the quantity method, used where the principal products of a business consist of a single material, inventory is determined through the quantity group of materials. Under the retail price-index method, similar to the dollar-value method, the value of inventory will be determined by the price indexes put out by the Department of Commerce. The dollar-value method is based on the principle that all items in a related group can be expressed in dollar investment, physical identity of the goods being exchanged for dollars.

Under the dollar-value method, a manufacturer can group all inventory items of a "natural business unit" into a single pool or category, unless he elects a multiple grouping. See *Klein Chocolate Co.*, 32 TC 437, 1959. The advantage of grouping inventory into a single pool is to avoid "liquidation" of old inventory. That is, when the low-cost inventory on hand is reached, the taxpayer's profit will be higher because the lower "costs" are used in determining his profit. By pooling all his inventory items (raw materials, goods in process, and finished goods) he avoids liquidation to some extent because pooled inventory items are treated as a whole and the low-cost items of each category must be reached before a "liquidation" occurs (Reg. §1.472-8).

A taxpayer can change to the dollar-value method from a quantity method as long as he uses the same "pools." See *Harmon Manufacturing Co.*, 34 TC 316, 1960.

Note: Remember that when LIFO is adopted your inventory is either overstated or understated in the balance sheet. Creditors and banks are always interested in the ratio of current assets to current liabilities, and this factor should be considered during the year of a change of valuation. Although corporations don't always disclose in their balance sheets their methods of inventory valuation, the Treasury requires that in the year of the change to LIFO, LIFO must also be used in the annual report.

[¶1404.3] A Further Election Under LIFO

Where several types of raw materials are used, and inventory consists of these raw materials, work in process in various stages, and different types of finished goods, the application of LIFO requires more clerical work and stricter controls. Under the law, a taxpayer may elect LIFO with respect to any of its raw materials, limiting its use to these particular materials. It then becomes necessary to trace such raw materials or goods into the work in process and the finished goods. A manufacturer of steel, for example, might elect LIFO for ore, but not for the various chemicals and carbons that are added during the process of manufacture. The ore inventory covers not only the ore on hand that is not processed, but also the ore contents in work in process and the ore content in the steel on hand.

Or LIFO might be elected not only for raw materials, but also for labor in the work in process and finished goods. This means an even more complex cost control of purchasing and producing will be needed to avoid the hazards of LIFO.

The taxpayer may limit his election to a single raw material or single phase in the manufacturing process. To make this subelection, a written notice must be filed with the Commissioner of Internal Revenue. It must then be used for any previous year not closed and for all subsequent years.

Thus, in deciding whether to elect, the taxpayer must consider not only his present year, but all open years.

[¶1405] INVENTORY METHODS: RETAIL INVENTORY METHOD

Regulations permit department stores and other retailers to use LIFO in connection with the retail method of inventory, on the basis of the semiannual price indices prepared by the Department of Labor.

The retail method of inventory valuation is suitable for retail establishments and businesses where selling prices are very closely related to cost. It isn't suitable to a manufacturing concern. It has found favor because it is relatively easy to use in the control of merchandise inventories, especially those that involve numerous items.

Where records are kept of cost and selling prices, this method permits a sound valuation for inventories. Compared to other methods it is simple and inexpensive. Valuation is made by converting the current indicated retail values of an inventory into their related costs (*Hutzler*, 8 TC 14, 1947). Advantages are: (1) inventory for statement purposes can be obtained without a physical count; (2) the cost of each item of purchase is avoided; (3) ratios for merchandise turnover are more dependable because more inventory figures are available for ascertainment of average inventory methods.

This method is accepted by the Treasury when the taxpayer maintains accurate records of markup, markdown, markup cancellations, markdown cancellations, purchase cost, and sales. The National Dry Goods Association has given its official approval.

[¶1405.1] How the Retail Method of Inventory Works

The retail method involves the application of markups and markdowns. A markup represents the difference between cost and sales price. A markup may be divided into an initial markup and additional markups.

Markup cancellations are markup revocations, i.e., any decrease not below original selling price. Markdown is a reduction below original selling price. Markdown cancellations are markdown revocations, not above original selling price.

The retail method of inventory valuation (for one year) can be illustrated as follows:

		Cost	*Retail*
Jan. 1, 19—, Inventory		$ 62,000	$ 90,000
Purchases (Net)		140,000	230,000
Freight In		6,000	----------
Markup			52,000
Markup Cancellations			(32,000)
Total Merchandise to Be Accounted for		$208,000	$340,000
(Cost is 61.18% of retail price $= \frac{208}{340}$)			
Sales			$200,000
Markdowns			43,000
Markdown Cancellations			(23,000)
			$220,000
Dec. 31, 19—, Inventory at Retail	$120,000		
Dec. 31, 19—, Inventory at Cost 61.18% × $120,000	73,416		

In calculating the ratio of cost to retail price—61.18%—markups and markup cancellations were included, but markdowns and markdown cancellations were excluded. *Reason:* The ratio produces an inventory valuation under the principles of lower of cost or market. This would not be necessary under the FIFO basis.

Factory supplies and nonfactory supplies are ordinarily valued at last invoice cost unless the LIFO provisions are elected. Shopworn goods should be valued at expected sales value less gross profit, if any. Trade-ins and repossessions should be valued at selling price, less a deduction for gross profits.

[¶1405.2] LIFO and the Retail Inventory Method

The LIFO Regulations require that closing inventory at retail immediately preceding the first LIFO year must be reduced to cost. It must not be valued at the lower of cost or market. To accomplish this, it is necessary to use the net markup percent rather than the usual markup percent (CB 1948-1, 21). Although this is required in the first year, LIFO doesn't replace the retail inventory method. The retail inventory system is carried on in the LIFO store without alteration of the department store's stock ledgers. The necessary LIFO inventory adjustments are ascertained through simple accounting calculations made at the end of the year. Under the retail system, at year end the taxpayer is faced with the problem of converting to earliest cost his inventory investment stated in terms of latest cost, in order to value his inventory for LIFO. This is very easily determined by using the Department of Labor price indices. By applying these indices to your inventories the calculation is easily made, without affecting your books. It is required that the price indices be applied to each department separately since grouping is not permitted in using the indices. LIFO can be just as easily applied to Retail Inventory Method as the lower of cost or market.

[¶1406] INVENTORY METHODS: BOOK INVENTORIES

When book inventories are maintained, inventory accounts are charged with the cost of goods purchased or produced, and credited with the value of goods used, transferred, or sold, calculated upon the basis of cost of goods acquired during the year. Net value is the cost of goods on hand.

Balance shown by book inventories must be adjusted to physical inventories at reasonable intervals (Reg. §1.471-2(d)). Book inventory that is just an accumulation of costs, without reduction for goods used, transferred, or lost, isn't really an inventory and can't be used.

The best book inventory is one where the accounts are supported by records of quantities and values for each inventoried item. With the quantities available always for application of cost or other values, any method of valuation could be used.

The only requirement is that the books be kept on a sound accounting basis, with goods being charged or credited at cost; perpetual inventories of item quantities could be dispensed with so long as costs could be ascertained. However, without perpetual records, you probably won't be able to value at lower of cost or market; in the absence of quantity records, market values couldn't be applied.

Although verification of the book balances by physical inventory needn't be made annually, the Treasury may use the resulting adjustment to your disadvantage unless it is. Without proof that the beginning inventory was incorrect, an adjustment to reflect an increase in inventory accumulated in prior years can be added to income in the year the physical inventory is finally taken. If the opposite is the case and a physical inventory, taken after several years, shows an inventory shortage, the loss might be partly allocated to prior years or disallowed completely unless you can prove the actual year of loss.

Where an inventory based on actual count isn't possible, you can resort to estimating so long as you are accurate. However, once it is possible again to make actual count, the justification for estimating ceases.

Book inventories (which, in effect, are simply specific cost inventories) are used by many small businesses—not necessarily because the method offers any tax advantages, but rather because the small business often has no other way of knowing just where its inventories stand. This is a poor reason. Where inventories are properly accounted for under the other methods, an actual count can be taken from time to time to figure the losses due to spoilage, theft, or loss. There may still be substantial tax benefits from the use of another method, so all methods should be considered.

[¶1407] CHANGE OF INVENTORY METHOD

Except for LIFO, which the taxpayer adopts by election, change in inventory method is treated as a change of accounting method. See *Apco Valve Co.*, TC Memo 1962-304, where it was held that a change in computing the cost of inventory is "change in accounting method." The Commissioner's consent must be obtained; application must be filed within 90 days from the beginning of the year of change. Since tax saving isn't sufficient to warrant a change, state in your request the business objective you seek to accomplish.

Recomputation of the opening inventory according to your new method will ordinarily be required; the resulting adjustment should be included in determining the income for the year of change. If the increase in income exceeds $3,000, you may be able to spread the adjustment over the current and the preceding two years or possibly longer (§481(b)).

Statement of an inventory valuation basis in the first return is a binding election, even if there is no difference at that time between this method and some other method you try to use later. If permission to change is granted but you fail to make the change for the year approved, you must request permission again if you want to make it in a later year. However, the Commissioner can't take advantage of an oversight to force the use of an inconsistent method.

[¶1408] CHANGING TO LIFO—BASIC PROBLEMS

Inflation has a tremendous effect on corporate profits. Every time the inflation factor goes up 1%, the income taxes of some companies go up by about half that amount (assuming a 48% tax bracket). When you consider the recent increases in the inflation factor and the cumulative effect of these increases over the years, you can see the enormous drain on corporate profits.

You would think that because of these conditions almost every corporation would adopt the LIFO method of valuing inventories. LIFO has been considered an effective method of dealing with inflation, and its adoption has eliminated the overstatement of profits of many companies. However, LIFO has not been adopted by as many companies as you would expect. Many companies have hesitated because of the problems that such an election may cause. Here, we'll point out some of the problems that a company may run into in order to help a company decide whether or not it should take the leap.

☐ ***Binding Election:*** Unlike most tax elections, the company doesn't need the consent of IRS to adopt the LIFO method. The election can be made on Form 970 with a timely filed tax return. One condition to the use of LIFO, however, is that the company must agree to accept the adjustments required to clearly reflect income.

The difficulty comes when the company wants to get off LIFO. For this election, it needs IRS's consent, which in the past has been difficult to obtain.

☐ ***Disadvantages of Valuing Inventory at Cost:*** One of the requirements of using LIFO is that inventory for the year LIFO is adopted and for all subsequent years must be valued at cost, regardless of market value. This creates a number of problems.

One is with write-downs. The problem with the write-downs is that an adjustment of tax is likely with companies that are in an industry where these write-downs would be required. Having to ascertain the actual cost is another problem that arises where the company has used different cost techniques in allocating overhead expenses to inventory. A third problem is with the valuation of unsalable goods. How does the company value what becomes unusable or obsolete? A final point on the use of cost is the requirement that the first opening inventory be at "average cost" so as to avoid the possible application of LIFO benefits to years prior to the year of election.

☐ ***Expense and Complications of Conversion:*** Converting to the LIFO method, which requires, among other things, increasing inventories to full cost where they have been valued at market, is a complicated and very expensive proposition. The LIFO conversion calculations may be cut down by using probability sampling techniques. The work may also be cut down by computer programs. Once these programs are used, they can be used for later years without any substantial modification.

☐ ***Problems in Current Record Keeping:*** There are also complications in current record keeping, including, among others, pricing not only at current prices but also at base period prices all or a portion of an item; the development of price indices or of statistical methods to determine price levels; the fact that the method of cost or market, whichever is lower, that permitted the management a certain leeway in determining the profit for the period will now be replaced by a more rigid and inflexible method; and, finally, the requirement that if the LIFO method is adopted, no other method of valuing inventories can be used in the application to ascertain income profits or loss for the purpose of a report or statement to shareholders or other proprietors or for credit purposes.

What to Do: Here, we have merely touched on some of the very complicated problems of converting to LIFO. Our basic aim was to give you a flavor of the complications and some idea of what is involved in the changeover to LIFO.

There is no question that companies with very large inventories must give serious consideration, if they haven't already, to the conversion to LIFO. The regulations and the detail rules relating to LIFO do impose a substantial burden in terms of time and cost on management and on the staff of accountants and auditors, not to mention other tax consultants. However, with inflation showing no significant signs of slowing down and with the corresponding increase in the tax burden of companies that do not use the LIFO inventory method, the switch may not be a choice—it may be a necessity.

[¶1409] INVOLUNTARY LIQUIDATION OF LIFO INVENTORY

Section 1331 provides relief for LIFO taxpayers whose base stock inventory was liquidated involuntarily due to: (1) enemy capture or control of sources of supply; (2) shipping or other transportation shortages; (3) material shortage resulting from priorities or allocations; (4) labor shortages; (5) war conditions beyond the control of the taxpayer; (6) disruption of normal trade conditions between the countries.

The income of the year in which the inventories were involuntarily liquidated will be retroactively decreased by any excess of the aggregate replacement cost over the aggregate cost reflected in the opening inventory for the year of the involuntary liquidation. Conversely, an excess of inventory cost over replacement cost will increase income in the year of liquidation. The relief must be elected with the return, and you must give a detailed account of the inventory that was liquidated and the circumstances.

To Illustrate: Assume you had a television set in the base stock inventory as of 12/31/76, at a cost of $100; you sold the set in 1977, but you were unable to replace it until after its cost had risen to $125. The difference between the two prices, $25, is deductible as an expense in recomputing the tax for the year of liquidation. If the television set was replaced for $75, the difference would be an additional item of income in recomputing the tax for the year in which the liquidation occurred.

[¶1410] CHECKLIST OF INVENTORY ELECTIONS

As has been discussed, taxpayers have many inventory elections available. The following checklist is a summary of the most important of these elections under the tax law:

☐ (1) Taxpayer can elect, in the first return, the method of valuing inventory that conforms to the best accounting practice in the trade or business and that clearly reflects the income. The usual methods are (1) Cost, and (2) Cost or market, whichever is less.

☐ (2) Taxpayer can elect, in the first return, the method of measuring cost (by specific identification, first-in-first-out (FIFO), or average cost) (§471). Elections can be changed only with Commissioner's permission (Reg. §1.446-1).

☐ (3) Farmer can elect, in first return, to use farm price method (Reg. §1.471-6). A dealer in securities can elect to use market value (Reg. §1.471-5). Retailers can elect to use the retail inventory method (Reg. §1.471-8).

☐ (4) The last-in-first-out method (LIFO) can be elected with the Commissioner's approval (§472(a)). Application to use LIFO is made on Form 970, filed in triplicate with the return for the first year the method is to be used (Reg. §1.472-3). The election is irrevocable (Reg. §1.472-5).

☐ (5) A LIFO taxpayer who suffers an involuntary liquidation of "low cost" inventory can elect to apply the relief provisions of §1321(a). Election is irrevocable for the year for which made.

☐ (6) Miners and manufacturers can (with the Commissioner's consent) elect to use the "allocated cost" method of valuation when the inventory consists of several kinds, sizes, or grades (Reg. §1.471-7).

[¶1411] HOW IRS CHECKS ON INVENTORY

IRS has a policy of cracking down on inventory understatements. One of the methods of doing this is to ask some pointed questions on the tax returns:

☐ (1) Was inventory valued at—cost, lower of cost or market, or other method? If other, attach explanation.

☐ (2) Have write-downs been made to inventory? If "Yes," were the write-downs computed on the basis of: (a) Percentage reductions from parts of the inventory; (b) Percentage reductions from the total inventory; (c) Valuation of individual items. If "a" or "b," enter the percentage of write-downs. For "a," "b," or "c" enter the dollar amount of write-downs.

☐ (3) Was the inventory verified by physical count during the year? If "No," attach explanation of how the closing inventory was determined.
☐ (4) Was there any substantial change in the manner of determining quantities, costs, or valuations between the opening and closing inventories? If "Yes," attach explanation.

These questions are obviously designed to reveal any weak spots in your inventory valuation methods and raise red flags to revenue agents as to where further investigation might be fruitful. In fact, the Commissioner has stated that where the required information is not furnished, or where there are indications of inconsistent inventory valuations, or deviations from generally recognized inventory methods, these factors will be important considerations in the selection of a return for examination (TIR-354).

Inventories are getting close scrutiny on tax examinations. Gross profit tests, for example, may reveal that your inventory is way off, based on industry or your own usual markup percentages, and you may be called on to explain the discrepancy. Of course, you can have a perfectly legitimate explanation—unusually high percentage of sales at lower markup due to competition or general market conditions, for example.

Agents are also examining the purchases of the last few months of the year and comparing them with sales for the same period. Applying your usual markups, they determine how much of those purchases would still be left at year end. Your closing inventory should likely be larger than that figure since, presumably, you also had some stock on hand before you made those purchases.

Similarly, agents are examining sales and purchases for the first few months of the following year. Here, too, if the number of goods sold exceeds the number of goods purchased (taking your normal markups into consideration), your closing inventory for the previous year should at least account for the excess.

SECTION XV
EQUIPMENT

Tax factors play an important part in the decisions made in connection with plant and equipment. They affect the decision, for example, whether to buy or merely lease a plant or a particular piece of equipment, when to buy it, how to finance it, and how and when to replace it.

When equipment or a plant is acquired, there's the question of the cost—both initial cash outlay and overall outlay. Here, a company will want to make an analysis of the availability of cash and the cash flow that may be generated by depreciation deductions. This requires dealing with the complex rules and regulations that are fully discussed in Section X.

[¶1501] CHEAPER TO BUY OR LEASE?

This decision should not be made solely on the basis of the lowest net after-tax cost —although it is a significant factor. Other factors may tip the scale to another choice.

Before making the comparison, however, let's get straight just what we are comparing. On the one hand, we have a rental of a machine we do not own. On the other hand, we acquire ownership. What's more, we can acquire ownership by financing our purchase—a very large initial cash outlay may not be necessary (and most acquisitions today are made via financing). So, in a sense, in comparing rentals with purchases, we are comparing two different costs of money—the interest factor that's built into the rental structure and the interest that's paid for the equipment loan. Also, the tax factors have a considerable effect on determining the net cost.

[¶1501.1] Making the Comparison

When you lease, the rent paid is fully deductible. Thus, the net cost is the gross rent less the tax savings.

On the purchase side, the buyer is paying both purchase price and interest. The interest is tax deductible. In addition, he gets depreciation deductions. The depreciation deductions are made up of both the special first-year write-off (limited to 20% of a maximum cost of $10,000; $20,000 on a joint return) plus his annual depreciation on a straight-line basis or some accelerated basis (if he's eligible for it). Thus, his net cost is the total of purchase price plus interest reduced by the tax benefits derived from the investment credit, the interest deductions, and the depreciation deductions.

[¶1501.2] How to Set Up the Figures to Make the Comparison

There are a vast variety of rental arrangements available and numerous financing arrangements, as well. Rather than attempt to deal with a specific illustration that may or may not apply to the type of equipment you are likely to rent or buy, we have set forth below two worksheets. One is for determining the first-year, after-tax cash cost of renting, the other for determining the first-year, after-tax cash cost of buying. Similar worksheets (with modifications) can be used for determining after-tax cash costs in subsequent years. Thus, you can insert your own figures on the worksheets and come up with a comparison that has meaning for you.

Worksheet for Determining First-Year, After-Tax Cost of Renting

(1) Gross rent (enter it twice)	$_____	$_____
(2) Applicable tax rate	_____	
(3) Tax saved via rent deduction (line 1 × line 2)		$_____
(4) Net after-tax cost for first year (line 1 minus line 5 of following table)		$_____

Worksheet for Determining First-Year, After-Tax Cost of Buying

(1) Total cost of acquired assets[1]	$_____	
(2) Cash down payment in first year		$_____
(3) Other first-year installments paid		_____
(4) Interest paid on unpaid balance		_____
(5) Total cash outlay in first year (total of lines 2, 3, and 4)		$_____
(6) First-year write-off (20% of line 1) or $10,000 [$20,000 if joint return is filed], whichever is smaller	_____	
(7) Basis for depreciation (line 1 minus line 6)	$_____	
(8) Regular depreciation (figure depreciation on basis in line 7 using the particular method applicable and taking into account portion of year the asset is held)		$_____
(9) First year depreciation (same as line 6)		_____
(10) Interest paid (same as line 4)		_____
(11) Total deductible items (total of lines 8, 9, and 10)		$_____

Footnote:

[1] Normally, the total cost will be the contract price for the acquired assets. But if there is a trade-in, use adjusted basis—i.e., basis of the assets traded in plus balance paid or payable. If a trade-in is involved, substitute for the amount on line 1 (for the purposes of this computation) the amount paid or payable for the equipment over and above the amount allowed by the seller for the trade-in.

(12) Total tax saved by deductions
(line 11 × tax rate) .... $______

(13) Total tax saved (line 12 plus 13) .... $______

(14) Net after-tax, first-year cost
(line 5 minus line 14) .... $______

[¶1502] HOW TO GET NEW EQUIPMENT WITHOUT ANY CASH OUTLAY

In many instances, you will find it better to buy your new equipment rather than lease it. The availability of the 20% first-year depreciation writeoff and the accelerated depreciation methods discussed in Section X may sometimes equal or exceed the deduction for rental payments under a lease. In addition, new plant equipment having a useful life of over three years qualifies for a 7% investment credit against your tax.

With the 20% first-year write-off and the 7% credit, it may be possible in many cases to replace old machinery and equipment with new at little or no cash outlay. This would be true especially where a businessman has old equipment at a fairly high basis that is worth considerably less today. The tax savings arising from the combination of the loss to be realized on the sale of the old machine, the 20% first-year write-off, and accelerated depreciation plus the cash received on the sale of the old machine could pay for the new one.

For example, take a business with a machine having a book value of $10,000 and a market value of $5,000. It wants to buy a new $10,000 machine. On the sale of the old machine, it would realize a $5,000 loss. Add to that a $2,000 first-year writeoff, a $700 credit, and a $1,850 depreciation deduction (using 200%-declining-balance and assuming an 8-year life for the new machine). Depreciation deductions and loss add up to $9,000, which could give a cash benefit of $4,320 to a 48% bracket taxpayer. To that $4,320 add the $5,000 realized on the sale of the old machine and the $700 investment credit, and we have more than the full purchase price of the new machine.

[¶1503] WHEN IT'S BETTER TO SELL EQUIPMENT THAN TO TRADE IT IN FOR NEW

A number of tax factors enter into the considerations leading to a decision either to trade in old equipment or new purchases or to sell the old equipment or abandon it.

[¶1503.1] If There's a Loss

Suppose your tax basis for the old equipment is higher than its present value. That means you'd really have a loss on the trade-in. Since a trade-in is a tax-free exchange, you would not get any immediate tax benefit from that loss; the old basis would carry over and become part of the basis of the new property (that plus what you pay for the new property in addition to the trade-in allowance becomes the basis of the new property). On the other hand, if you sold the old equipment, you'd have an immediately deductible tax loss. You could then use the cash received on the sale plus the tax benefit from the loss to help pay for the new equipment. Don't sell it to the seller of the new equipment, however. IRS might treat the transaction as a trade-in instead of a sale, and the loss would be disallowed.

Where you can't find an outside customer for the property, you can still get a tax deduction for your basis by abandoning the old equipment; but here, of course, there's no sale price cash coming in—only the tax benefit of the loss deduction. You have to compare that with the amount of the trade-in allowance you'll be getting to see if the trade-in or the abandonment is better tax wise.

Example: You have an old machine with a $5,000 basis. You're offered $2,000 for it as a trade-in allowance. And you can't find an outside customer for it; however, you're in a 60% tax bracket. By abandoning it, you'll reduce your taxes by $3,000 (60% of your $5,000 basis). So, by abandoning it instead of trading it in, you're ahead by $1,000.

[¶1503.2] If There's a Profit

If you'd have a taxable profit were you to sell your old equipment, the temptation is to trade it in and avoid the tax. Time was when it might have made sense to sell and pick up the profit rather than trade in. *Reason:* The gain was taxable as capital gain with a maximum tax of 25%. The basis of the new property would then be stepped up to the current cost (if you traded in, your new basis would be your old basis plus additional amount paid over the trade-in allowance). This higher basis would then be recovered via depreciation deductions that would offset ordinary income. Thus, you'd be trading off capital gains against ordinary deductions. However, the 1962 tax law took most of the appeal out of this approach.

Under §1245, to the extent that your profit on the sale is a reflection of post-1961 depreciation, you have ordinary income on the sale. Consequently, especially as time goes on and the impact of §1245 becomes greater, there will be very little, if any, trading off of capital gain against ordinary income.

True, where you have a potential §1245 gain and you trade in, that potential §1245 gain carries over to the new property. But you don't realize that gain until you dispose of the new property, and you don't know what the tax situation will be at that future time. For example, if you hold the new property long enough, there may be no gain when you finally dispose of it; so §1245 will be academic at that point. Or you may trade in again in the future, again postponing the effect of §1245. So, where you can avoid §1245 now, you're likely to want to do so and not be too concerned over possible future application of that section.

[¶1503.3] First-Year Writeoff

The 20% first-year writeoff applies only to as much of the purchase price as is paid over the trade-in allowance. So, whether you trade in or sell to an outsider can make a difference in the amount of the first-year writeoff. The amount of acquisition eligible for the first-year writeoff in any one year is limited to $10,000 ($20,000 on a joint return), which makes the benefit rather limited. If a capital gains tax (or maybe even an ordinary income tax where §1245 applies) has to be paid on the gain on the old property as a price for the first-year writeoff, it is not likely to be worth picking up the gain—especially since whatever you can't pick up currently as a first-year writeoff is going to be picked up as a depreciation deduction in subsequent years anyhow.

[¶1503.4] Worksheet for Comparing Different Plans

The following example illustrates the type of arithmetic that should be done to arrive at an accurate decision. Let's assume that your corporation is in the 48% tax bracket. It has old equipment with a tax basis of $6,000 that it wants to replace. It's determined that the corporation could realize $9,000 on a sale to a third party or as a trade-in allowance with the supplier. If the equipment is sold, the $3,000 gain would consist of $2,500 of recapture income and $500 capital gains. The new equipment that is to be acquired has a ten-year useful life, and it's decided that the 200%-declining-balance method of depreciation will be used. Here's how the figures would shape up:

Trade-In v. Sale of Old Equipment to Third Party

	Sell Old Machinery				*Trade In Old Machinery*			
Price of new equipment				$45,000				$45,000
Trade-in allowance				—				9,000
Net price				$45,000				$36,000
After-tax proceeds from sale								
Sale of old machine		$ 9,000						
Gain on sale	$ 3,000							
Tax on gain:								
45% of $2,500	$ 1,200							
30% of $500	150	1,350						
Net after taxes			$7,650					
Tax benefits								
First-year depreciation		$ 2,000				$ 2,000		
Normal depreciation allowance:								
Cost	$45,000				$36,000			
Carryover basis of old equipment					6,000			
	$45,000				$42,000			
Less first-year depreciation	2,000				2,000			
Adjusted basis	$43,000				$40,000			
200%-declining-balance depreciation—20% of adjusted basis		8,600				8,000		
Total allowance		$10,600				$10,000		
Tax savings (48%)			$5,088				$5,000	
Total benefits				12,738				5,000
Initial cash requirements				$32,262				$31,000
Additional depreciation benefits				16,512				15,360
Total after-tax costs as of the end of the equipment's useful life				$15,750				$15,640

[¶1504] ADVANTAGES OF LEASING EQUIPMENT RATHER THAN BUYING IT

There are many excellent reasons why a business should think in terms of leasing rather than buying equipment. One of the more significant ones is that it gives the firm leverage. Leasing is a form of debt. Here is a quick rundown of some of the other reasons, tax and nontax, for leasing:

☐ (1) ***Conserves Cash:*** Leasing conserves capital, giving the lessee 90 to 100% financing as against a possible one-third or one-fourth down payment required on many purchases.

☐ (2) ***Hedge Against Obsolescence:*** On types of equipment that are subject to a high rate of obsolescence or uncertainty as to obsolescence, leasing can operate as a form of insurance against obsolescence. At the end of the term, lessee will be able to modernize his equipment and processes.

☐ (3) ***Cost Is Not Uncertain:*** On types of equipment not permanently needed, such as construction scaffolding, bulldozers, and cranes (where the lessee is not in the construction business), leasing offers a means of satisfying a temporary need at a definite cost in place of the uncertainty of buying and having to resell such equipment in an uncertain market.

☐ (4) ***Relieves Lessee of Maintenance Duties:*** On types of equipment where service and maintenance are important considerations, a lease of equipment to be serviced by the lessor will relieve the lessee of having to maintain his own service department or rely on independent contractors to provide maintenance and service.

☐ (5) ***Financial Statement Looks Better:*** Leasing may make for a better balance sheet. The lease won't appear on the liability side of the balance sheet. Hence, proponents say leasing makes for lower debt ratios, increased borrowing capacity, freedom from debt and budgetary limitations and restrictions and, as a side effect, increases the value of stock of the lessee corporation. However, sophisticated lenders will take account of leasing obligations, and accounting practice calls for footnoting such obligations. Also, debt and budgetary limitations or restrictions may be drafted so as to take in lease obligations. Further, if property was purchased on an installment contract, while the debt would be reflected on the liability side, the value of the equipment would appear on the asset side.

☐ (6) ***Avoids Management Problems:*** Leasing will not involve the control and supervision of operations that often attend traditional debt financing, won't threaten voting control as may equity financing, and won't involve the costs of underwriting a stock or bond issue.

☐ (7) ***Higher Current Deductions:*** Leasing often permits postponing taxes via higher current deductions than are obtainable with interest and depreciation deductions as in the case of installment purchases of equipment. Lease payments may be adjusted to match the declining-balance or sum-of-the-digits approach to depreciation.

☐ (8) ***No Recapture Problems:*** Leasing avoids the recapture of depreciation deductions and investment credit that arises in connection with the sale of equipment.

[¶1504.1] Types of Equipment That Should Be Leased

Certain types of equipment are more apt to be leased than others. Here are types where leasing may be called for:

☐ (1) Very intricate and complicated equipment.
☐ (2) Equipment subject to a high rate of obsolescence or uncertainty as to obsolescence.
☐ (3) Equipment with a high rate of depreciation, such as trucks and cars.
☐ (4) Equipment that it is impractical to buy, such as a railroad tank car.
☐ (5) Equipment for special use and not regularly used, such as construction equipment needed by a manufacturing company.
☐ (6) Equipment involving complicated servicing that the lessor is able to furnish and the lessee can't handle.
☐ (7) Equipment that the manufacturer prefers to lease rather than sell, such as some types of electronic computers and photocopying machines.

[¶1504.2] When a "Lease" Is Not a Lease

Although you may consider a transaction a lease, IRS might say it's not a lease but a sale. Obviously, the tax consequences of a lease are quite different from those of a sale. If a lease is regarded as a sale, for example, the payments made by the lessee will not be deductible as rent but will be treated as payments for the purchase of the equipment. The lessee would be allowed depreciation deductions, however. The lessor's picture is also different: The payments are not rental income; they are proceeds from the sale of assets. If the transaction does not qualify for installment reporting, he has to report the entire gain in the year of sale; that is, the year the transaction occurred. What's more, there may be imputed interest income under §483. The lessee would get an interest expense deduction to the extent of the imputed interest.

Numerous criteria have been established to distinguish a lease from a sale. Generally, a sale is indicated where the user has an "equity" interest in the property. This may arise, for example, where the user is granted an option to purchase the equipment or where the property is sold at the end of the term of the lease for a nominal price.

The courts generally rely on the criteria set forth in *Rev. Rul. 55-540,* CB 1955-2, 39. IRS says that in the absence of compelling persuasive factors to the contrary, the following conditions evidence a sale rather than a lease:

☐ (1) When portions of the periodic payments are made specifically applicable to the acquisition of an equity interest.
☐ (2) Where the lessee may acquire title upon payment of a stated amount of rentals and the payments are required under the contract.
☐ (3) Where the total amount that the lessee is required to pay for a relatively short period of use constitutes an excessively large portion of the total sum required to be paid to secure the transfer of the title.
☐ (4) Where the agreed rental payments materially exceed the current fair rental value. This may indicate that the payments include an element other than compensation for the use of the property.
☐ (5) Where property may be acquired under an option at a price that is nominal in relation to either the value of the property at the option date as determined at the time of entering into the original agreement or to the total payments required.
☐ (6) Where a portion of the periodic payments is specifically designated as interest or is readily recognizable as the equivalent of interest.

☐ (7) Where the total rental payments plus the option price approximate the price at which the property could have been purchased plus interest and carrying charges.

Installment Reporting: Where the lease is in fact a sale, the lessor should seek to cut his taxes by qualifying for installment reporting. See *Rev. Rul. 65-297,* CB 1965-2, 152, and *Scales,* 221 F.2d 133, CA-6, 1954.

With an installment sale, however, a portion of the payments is considered interest. Since the lease would not provide for interest, it would be computed by IRS at a rate of 5%. The interest is taxable as ordinary income to the seller, reducing capital gains, and is deductible as a current business expense by the user.

[¶1505] LEASING YOUR PROPERTY TO YOUR BUSINESS CAN CUT TAXES

When you own equipment or commercial real estate that will be used by your business, you have the choice of either transferring the property to the business or retaining it and leasing the property to your business. The big advantage of leasing your property is that you will be able to get the depreciation deductions while your business can deduct the rent it pays you for the use of the property.

[¶1505.1] Avoiding a Pitfall

If you lease to your controlled corporation at a bargain rent, you'll run into trouble. Depreciation deductions may be disallowed on the ground that the property is not held for the production of income because you agreed to forgo a profit. To avoid this pitfall, you should make sure to fix a fair rental for the property.

If your property is already in the business, you may consider the possibility of a sale-leaseback. The sale by the corporation may be to an individual shareholder or members of his family, either directly or in trust. The buyer then leases the property to the corporation. When the sale-leaseback is with a member of the family, the underlying objective is usually to save taxes by dividing income within the family. However, when a trust is used for this purpose, you should be sure that the seller has parted with all control over the property. The trust should have an independent trustee and the sales price and rental arrangement must be reasonable. See ¶1506.

[¶1505.2] Licensing Your Business to Use or Produce Your Patented Invention

If you own a patent, in many cases it will pay to sell it to your business because you will be eligible to treat the sales price as a capital gain on your personal tax return under one of three sections of the Code (§122, 1231, or 1235). However, if you own more than 80% of your company, any gain will result in ordinary income under Code §1239. Rather than realizing a large amount of ordinary income in any one year, it may pay you to license your business to produce and sell your invention over a period of years. The tax treatment is substantially the same as when you lease your plant or equipment to your business, except that none of the accelerated depreciation methods can be used to write off your patent. These methods can apply only to tangible property (§167(c)). However, even though the accelerated methods can't be used, the patent owner may be able to depreciate the cost of his patent over a comparatively shorter period. This would occur where technological advances made in the area of the patent render the patent commercially obsolete or shorten its useful life.

[¶1506] SELLING YOUR PLANT AND LEASING IT BACK INCREASES PROFITS

Sears, Roebuck was one of the pioneers of the sale-leaseback. When it switched from what was exclusively a mail order business to chain store retailing, it was faced with the problem of financing the sales outlets needed and the storage facilities servicing those outlets. It could have sold additional stock to the public; but since the retail stores would not return much income initially, that would have meant a substantial drop in the dividend policy consistently followed. Sale-leasebacks were suggested as an alternative.

Sears, Roebuck would put up the stores and warehouses, sell them to an insurance company at cost, and then lease them back at a good rent under a long-term lease.

[¶1506.1] How They Work

What's involved in a sale-leaseback is the sale of the property by the owner to an investor with an agreement to lease back the property to the seller.

Often, the sale-leaseback accomplishes the equivalent of mortgage financing; but the seller of the property, since he is in the position of a lessee, is entitled to tax deductions for the rental payments that he makes to his purchaser. As in the case of a mortgage, the seller-lessee keeps the use of the property (although he will lose it when his lease expires) and he pays a constant net rental, which can be conceived of as representing both interest and mortgage amortization. However, in the case of a mortgage, the owner only gets a tax deduction for the interest he pays, not for mortgage amortization.

In the sale-leaseback, since the rentals paid to the purchaser are, in effect, equivalent to interest and amortization on a mortgage, mortgage payments are now put on a tax-deductible basis. This may more than compensate for the loss of the depreciation deduction by the seller.

The investor-purchaser owns the building and is entitled to depreciate it. He is fully taxable on the rent he receives, and part of this rent represents amortization of his investment; but his depreciation of the property may provide enough of a tax deduction to make up for this. Nowadays, sale-leasebacks are often entered into with institutional, tax-exempt investors. Yet deals are still worked out even where the investor is not tax exempt, particularly where short-term leases and high building-to-land-valuation ratios exist. In this way, the investor shelters from taxation, by way of the depreciation deduction, most of the portion of his rent that represents amortization and recovers this amortization in a short period of time.

[¶1506.2] How the Arithmetic Works Out

Here is a hypothetical example of a typical sale-leaseback deal. By working it through, we can see how the figures affect both buyer and seller.

A corporation uses a plant in its business that it has owned for 15 years. Original cost was $1,000,000, of which $700,000 was allocated to the building and $300,000 to the land. It has taken $450,000 of depreciation, so its basis for the whole property is now $550,000. In the 16th year it decides to sell the property to an investor corporation if it can get a 15-year leaseback. The sale price is $750,000, with a net rental under the lease equivalent to a 15-year amortization of the $750,000 at a 6% return—or a rental of $77,225. Assume that the investor corporation can allocate $500,000 of its purchase price to the building for depreciation purposes.

The Seller: The seller corporation has a $200,000 gain on the sale and so pays a capital gains tax of $50,000. If it had borrowed $700,000 (the net amount it gets after the capital gains tax) at 5% interest payable over 15 years on a constant-payment basis, the yearly payment would have been $67,450. So, over the 15-year period the seller would have paid a total of some $1,012,000 instead of some $1,158,000 (15 times $77,225) that it pays on the sale-leaseback. But in the case of the mortgage, the seller only gets a tax deduction for the $312,000 interest that it pays. This together with the $250,000 depreciation that the seller had left on the property would have meant a total tax deduction of $562,000 at 48% corporate rates, a saving of $270,000. So, the mortgage would have cost the seller $742,000 ($1,012,000 minus the tax saving). But under the leaseback, the seller gets a tax deduction for the entire rental paid so there it would get a saving of $556,000 (48% of the entire 15-year rental), which would mean a cost to the seller for the leaseback of $602,000 ($1,158,000 minus $556,000). Therefore, the sale-leaseback costs the seller $140,000 less than what the mortgage would have cost.

The Buyer: The buyer under the sale-leaseback gets a deduction over the 15-year period of the lease, assuming that is the remaining life of the building, of $500,000, the amount that it allocated to the building. This means that $500,000 of the rent income is protected from tax. The tax on the remainder is $316,000. If the buyer had taken a mortgage position in this or similar property for $750,000 at 5% interest, it would have received $1,084,000 with $334,000, the interest, taxable to it (the remainder would have been mortgage amortization). This would have meant a total tax of about 160,500 or a net after taxes to the buyer of $923,500. This is almost $100,000 more than the buyer's net in the case of the leaseback.

[¶1506.3] What the Figures Mean to Both Parties

Figures don't always tell the whole story. Here are some additional factors that can mean a great deal to one or both parties.

To the Seller: The seller pays $140,000 less (net after tax deduction) than it would in the case of a mortgage. To get this, the seller has given up its ownership of the property at the end of the lease. At present, the land is valued at $250,000. So, the seller appears actually to lose some $110,000; but this is deceptive. Seller's building wears out at the end of the lease; and because of the favorable aspects of the deal to the buyer, the buyer would be able at the time of the sale-leaseback to give the seller an option to renew for, say, another 10 or 15 years at a very low rental. And any improvements constructed by the seller during the renewal term would be depreciated by the seller. Also, the sale-leaseback provides the seller with the maximum amount of financing, since with property worth $750,000 it would be hard, due to legal limitations on the amount of the mortgage in relation to market value in most states and to the desire by mortgagees for protection, to get a mortgage for the full market value.

To the Buyer: In effect, the buyer has $100,000 of his investment left in the property at the end of the original lease term, but the buyer has gotten out his yield plus the rest of his "principal" and will own property worth at least $250,000 if land values do not change. So, the buyer can afford to give the seller a renewal lease at a rental of only $8,000 a year and still get an 8% before tax return on its $100,000. By this method, during the renewal term, the seller will have the land on a tax-deductible basis. And if the renewal lease is set up properly, any improvements, such as a new building erected by the seller, will not be income to the buyer. If, at the end of the renewal term or the original lease, the seller does not renew, the buyer still owns the land.

[¶1506.4] Special Forms of Sale-Leasebacks

Besides the conventional sale-leaseback, there are some specialized ways of setting up this type of a transaction.

New Construction: Here a builder may arrange to finance a new plant that he is constructing for a business corporation by getting that corporation to agree to lease the property and by interesting an investor in the purchase of the property upon completion. In the meantime, the builder will obtain construction financing unless the investor is an insurance company or pension trust that can handle the financing from commencement of construction.

Pension Trusts: These trusts enjoy tax-exempt status. At one time, they were unwilling to enter into leasebacks. Now sale-leasebacks are being used not only where the pension trust is an outsider but also where a corporation sells its property to its own pension trust and takes back a lease. In order to satisfy IRS, the deal must be one that involves a fair sale price and reasonable rentals. If the seller corporation pays too much by way of rent, this will be treated as additional contributions to the pension trust. So, in a year where the maximum permissible amount of contributions for tax purposes was made to the pension trust, any deduction for the excess rent might be denied to the corporation. Also, rentals traced to borrowed funds of the pension trust will be treated, as in the case of charitable organizations, as unrelated business income not subject to the tax exemption.

The Use of the Family: Here you may want to set up a sale-leaseback with a relative or perhaps with a trust that you set up, say, for your children. In this way, by means of the rent deduction, you can shift the income from the property to lower tax brackets. Also, the trust gets a stepped-up basis for the property. However, you have to be careful about what type of arrangement you make. For example, if you enter into a sale-leaseback with a short-term trust in which you have a reversionary interest, you can lose the rent deduction because you will be considered as having an equity interest in the property; and you can't get a rent deduction when you have an equity interest in the leased property (§162(a)(3)). Other arrangements involving a trust have been approved where the seller-lessee was not the trustee and less than the entire amount transferred was leased back (*Skemp*, 168 F.2d 598, CA-7, 1948).

Avoiding the tax on the income in these deals is a lot easier than securing the rent deduction. IRS now has court backing (*Van Zandt*, 40 TC 824, 1963), for its position that the rent payments are not deductible in the absence of a showing of business purpose for the transfer of property to the trust.

Here's an Actual Case Involving a Family Foundation: Diana Stores wanted to sell its wholly owned hosiery mill in Bethel, N.C., and then lease it back; but always the buyer-landlord set too high a price. Finally, Diana made a satisfactory deal. Buyer: the Harry Greenburg Foundation, established by Diana's president and chief stockholder, directed by three of Diana's directors. Terms of leaseback: $14,000 a year for first 15 years, with 7 consecutive options of 5 years each at $6,000 a year.

Tax Advantages: Diana benefits because it can deduct the rent it pays. The foundation benefits because (as a charitable group) it doesn't have to pay any income tax on the rent received, except to the extent it borrows to swing the sale. Due to this tax break, the foundation can give Diana better terms than any ordinary buyer, who would have to pay tax on all rents received. Since both Diana and the foundation are controlled by the same people, relations should be smooth. Care must be taken to avoid abuse: Too good a deal for the company can deprive the foundation of its tax-exempt status.

[¶1506.5] Sale-Leaseback With Stockholders

Take a company that needs working capital. It has a plant that has appreciated considerably in value. One of its stockholders—rather than advance money as a loan—would be willing to buy the plant and lease it back to the company. That gives him a steady income via rent, enables the company to get its working capital, and puts the entire plant and land on a tax-deductible basis. Assuming reasonable rentals, the rent deal should stand up. One deal with a corporation controlled by lessee's stockholders' children and involving a percentage lease has IRS approval (*Southern Ford Tractor,* 29 TC 833, 1958). Watch these pitfalls:

☐ ***Look Out for Unexpected Dividends:*** If the stockholder does not pay full value for the property, he may very well end up with a taxable dividend equal to the difference between his purchase price and the full value of the land and buildings (see Reg. §1.301-1(j)).
☐ ***Don't Deal With 80% Stockholders:*** If the corporation is going to sell at a gain, it should avoid a sale to a stockholder who—together with his wife, minor children, and minor grandchildren —owns more than 80% of the corporation's stock. *Reason:* Gain on the sale on the buildings or other depreciable property will be ordinary income; gain on sale of land will still be capital gain (§1239).
☐ ***Look Out for 50% Stockholders If You Have a Loss:*** Sometimes a sale-leaseback will be worthwhile to establish a loss on the sale that can be used to offset other corporate income. But look out on a sale to a more-than-50% stockholder: Losses on such sales are disallowed (§267).

Note, too, that constructive ownership of stock in this case is much broader than under the 80%-rule above. Brothers', sisters', parents', trusts', partnerships', and other corporations' holdings of the selling corporation's stock can be attributed to the purchasing stockholder.

[¶1506.6] How to Get a Deductible Loss on Sale and Leaseback

Suppose you sell your plant at a loss and lease it back. You might go through the leaseback deal primarily to get the loss and offset other income; but if your leaseback is for more than 30 years, there's a good chance IRS will say your loss is not deductible. *Reason:* A 30-year lease, according to IRS, is equal to the ownership of the real estate (Reg. §1.1031(c)). So, says IRS, you've exchanged one property for a property of a like kind—a tax-free exchange under which a loss is not recognized even if you receive cash, too. The Tax Court and the Eighth Circuit have gone along with this argument (*Century Electric Co.,* 192 F.2d 155, CA-8, 1963), but the Second Circuit has put a twist on this interpretation that seems to open the way to deductible losses.

When You Can Get a Deductible Loss: First, says the Second Circuit, you look to the cash received on the sale portion of the sale-leaseback deal. Was the cash received equal to the value of the property sold? If it was, and if the rent under the leaseback was equal to the fair rental value of the property, then there was a sale here, not an exchange (*Jordan Marsh Co.*, 269 F.2d 453, CA-2, 1959).

This is an important decision, but keep in mind the need for firmly establishing values. If it can be shown that the cash received was less than the value of the property or that the rentals were particularly favorable, it may still be established that there was a tax-free exchange and no loss is recognized.

In *City Investing Company* (38 TC 1, 1962), a sale-leaseback deal was upheld where the lease was for 21 years at a stated rental with renewal options running for a total of 99 years and with rent to be fixed by arbitration or appraisal but in no event to be lower than the stated rent for the original 21-year term. The land was sold at not less than its fair market value, and the rental paid on the leaseback was the fair rental value of the land. So, there was no exchange—the sale was a bona fide sale even though it was made with tax considerations in mind, said the Court.

[¶1506.7] Recapture-of-Property Provisions in Leaseback Deals

One drawback in a leaseback arrangement is the fact that you will lose your property at the end of the lease term. To overcome this, either a recapture or a renewal provision is usually included. A recapture provision gives you the right to reacquire the property either at the end of the lease term or during it.

If the recapture price is nominal, the courts don't consider the original transaction a sale (*Jefferson Gas Coal Company*, 16 BTA 1135, 1929). Where the recapture price is substantial, it's more difficult to decide whether there has been a genuine sale. So, the option (recapture) price is compared with the value of the property at the time for exercising the option. The more nearly the option price approaches the fair market value of the property at the time the option is to be exercised, the more likely the courts are to consider the leaseback a genuine rental arrangement.

Usually the lease fixes either the option price or the value of the property at the beginning of the lease term and provides that this figure less the rentals paid shall be the option price.

Where the option price is stated in the lease, the court may look at the remaining useful life to determine value on the option date. For instance, the Tax Court disallowed deduction of the rentals on a five-year lease of property with useful life ranging from 12 to 16 years. To the Court, a low option price for the property useful for 7 to 11 more years meant the lessee had retained a substantial equity on the original sale (*Judson Mills*, 11 TC 25, 1948).

More frequently, the option price is determined by subtracting the rentals from the value of the property stated in the lease. A provision that the option can be exercised at any point over the life of the lease may bring a variable option price into the picture. Where the option price isn't stated in the lease, the total number of interim rental payments before the option is exercised becomes important.

Generally speaking, the deduction for rent can be supported if the rental payments are not materially larger than the depreciation charges. As the spread between the two becomes larger, it will be increasingly harder to sustain the rental deduction. When the rental payments substantially exceed depreciation, the inference is that the excess is being paid to acquire an equity that will be formally claimed by exercising the option (*Louis E. Whitham*, TC Memo 1951).

If you fix the option price in the lease agreement, you've done about all you can do to protect your rental deduction if your price is a reasonable estimate of what the value will be on the option date, based on the facts as you know them at the time. And if you've elected instead merely to fix the present value of the property, your best protection is to tie the rental figure as nearly to the depreciation as you can.

[¶1507] ADVANTAGES V. DISADVANTAGES OF SALE-LEASEBACKS

Although the sale-leaseback arrangement offers a variety of money-saving possibilities for the tax-conscious businessman, the disadvantages of this form of transaction can't be overlooked. In a nutshell, the following discussion summarizes both the advantages and the disadvantages of the sale-leaseback for both the buyer and the seller.

[¶1507.1] Advantages of the Sale-Leaseback to the Seller

☐ (1) Rent payments are put on a tax-deductible basis (land is now deductible).
☐ (2) Repair, maintenance, and capital alteration costs are now deductible over the life of the lease.
☐ (3) Maximum financing can be obtained.
☐ (4) Credit that otherwise would be tied up in ownership of the property is freed.
☐ (5) Credit is less directly tied up than in borrowing. The balance sheet looks more favorable.
☐ (6) Rent may be lower under the sale-leaseback, particularly during the renewal term; in an inflationary period, fixed rent is to the tenant's advantage.
☐ (7) Improvements erected during a lease can be deducted over the period of the lease or its useful life, whichever is shorter.

[¶1507.2] Advantages of the Sale-Leaseback to the Buyer

☐ (1) The sale-leaseback may return a higher profit yield than an ordinary financing deal.
☐ (2) Depreciation on the property makes part of the return tax free and helps cover ''amortization.''
☐ (3) Ownership of the property means safety of initial investment plus the chance of a rise in property values.
☐ (4) Leasing the property may mean the buyer is in the trade or business of leasing and so will be able to secure a capital gain on sale of its property used in that business.

[¶1507.3] Disadvantages of the Sale-Leaseback to the Seller

☐ (1) The seller is tied to the lease on the property.
☐ (2) An increase in value of the property will not accrue to the seller's benefit.
☐ (3) Fixed-charge rentals may be hard to meet in a time of economic decline.
☐ (4) The tenant-seller has to move at the end of the lease.

[¶1507.4] Disadvantages of the Sale-Leaseback to the Buyer

☐ (1) On bankruptcy of the tenant, the buyer-landlord's rights are restricted to those of a landlord, not those of a creditor for the amount of the purchase price.
☐ (2) If the tenant-seller defaults, the buyer will have to run the property.

[¶1508] HOW SOME MUNICIPALITIES PROVIDE YOU WITH TAX-FREE PLANTS

Many states permit their local governments to issue revenue bonds to finance the construction of industrial facilities for lease to private industry. The interest and amortization payments on these bonds can be met only with the revenue derived from the project.

Unlike general obligation bonds, the taxing power of the municipality cannot be used to secure and pay off the principal and interest due on the bonds. The lease guarantee insurance assures that the monthly rental payments due under the lease to the industrial company will be made. (The continuing ability of the company to make the payments due under the lease is the main form of security offered to the prospective bondholders.)

The financing provided makes it possible for the company to acquire the use of the facility it needs without the capital investment it would have to make if it put up its own facility. What's more, the rent it pays will reflect the fact that the property will usually be exempt from taxes and also the relatively low rate of interest paid on the bonds in view of the federal income tax exemption enjoyed.

[¶1508.1] How Lease-Guarantee Insurance Helps Sell Bonds, Reduces Industrial Company's Security Requirements, and Lowers Interest Rate

The underwriters of the bond issue may request lease-guarantee insurance to give the prospective investors in the bond issue greater security for their investment and thereby increase the marketability of the bonds.

Municipalities can issue tax-exempt bonds up to a specified limit provided the capital expenditures for the leased plant during a three-year period before and after the bond issue, combined with the issue, do not exceed the limit. While the ceiling was imposed to encourage the construction of small plants to be leased to small firms, the limited net worth of most of such companies makes it difficult to attract the interest of investors to this type of revenue bond. The lease-guarantee insurance overcomes this obstacle.

The industrial company gets an additional benefit in that the amount of security deposit required of it to assure its performance of the lease terms can be substantially reduced. As an extra bonus, the bonds may be marketable at a lower interest rate than without the support of the lease-guarantee insurance. (Of course, the industrial company will have to cover the cost of the insurance premiums.)

SECTION XVI
CAPITAL GAINS OPPORTUNITIES

One of the main reasons for the use of the corporate form is the tax-shelter potential it provides. In most cases, this potential is realized because of the laws governing capital gains. Then, the money which has been sheltered from tax by the corporation's lower bracket is eventually put into the hands of the shareholders, hopefully at low capital gains rates.

In this section, some of the various methods for getting capital gains treatment will be covered for both the corporate businessman and the noncorporate businessman or employee.

[¶1601] BASIC CAPITAL GAINS RULES

Capital gains are taxed at a considerably lower rate than ordinary income. Therefore, to the extent that ordinary income can be converted into capital gains, there will be tax shelter. To accomplish this favorable treatment, three elements are required:

☐ (1) A capital asset,
☐ (2) A sale or exchange of that asset,
☐ (3) A holding period or periods of ownership of the asset lasting more than six months.

When all three elements are satisfied, a long-term capital gain will result. However, these elements are not as simple as they appear. For example, the general rule that all property is a capital asset has the following exceptions:

☐ (1) Stock in trade or other inventory items.
☐ (2) Property held primarily for sale to customers in the ordinary course of business. ''Primarily'' means ''of first importance'' or ''principally'' (*Malat,* 383 US 569, 1966).
☐ (3) Depreciable property and real property used in trade or business, but this is a §1231 asset on which we can nevertheless enjoy capital gain treatment and on which we can get a fully deductible ordinary loss.
☐ (4) A copyright, literary, musical, or artistic composition held by an author or composer who created this property or by his donee.

☐ (5) Accounts and notes receivable acquired in the ordinary course of trade or business, for services rendered or from the sale of stock in trade, inventory items, or property held for sale to customers.
☐ (6) Obligations of the U.S., any of its possessions, a state, territory, or of any political subdivision, issued after March 1, 1941, on a discount basis and payable without interest at a fixed maturity date not exceeding one year from the date of issue (§1221).
☐ (7) If the seller is a dealer, real estate or securities that would be capital assets to other taxpayers are considered property held primarily for sale to customers in the ordinary course of business. In such case, any profit on the sale is ordinary income.

IRS contended that when a real estate investor purchased property, holding it for rental purposes (this connotes an investment motive) or sale depending on which course of action appeared most profitable, then the property *was* being held primarily for sale within the meaning of §1221(1). IRS's interpretation of the word "primarily" was that a purpose may be primary if it is a "substantial" one. But the Supreme Court says that "primarily" means "of importance" or "principally" (*Malat, supra*).

This rule as laid down by the Supreme Court would seem to permit favorable capital gain treatment in many instances where it was denied previously in "dual purpose" property. The Tax Court, however, appears to have taken a hardnose attitude in this area. Indeed, many tax men feel that the Tax Court is trying to reverse the Supreme Court on this issue. It is, therefore, helpful to make the following points based on *Scheuber*, 371 F.2d 996, CA-7, 1967, *rev'g* TC Memo 1966-107:

☐ (1) Both IRS and the courts concede that a real estate dealer may hold certain parcels not primarily for sale.
☐ (2) Such factors as frequency of sales, whether the property is improved or unimproved, length of holding period, substantiality of income, purpose of acquisition, extent of advertising are all important in determining whether (a) the property was held for sale and (b) the taxpayer is a dealer.
☐ (3) IRS contends that a dealer must sustain a heavier burden in proving that holding realty was not primarily for sale, but the Seventh Circuit has rejected a more stringent dealer test for advertising.
☐ (4) The realization of extraordinary gains on the sale of real estate is viewed by the Seventh Circuit as a strong investment factor.

Likewise, the definition of a sale or exchange is very complex. Generally, this means that there must be a final and unequivocal disposition of title or ownership in property. A lease, a loan, and a pledge of property as collateral for a loan are not sales or exchanges. We do not have a sale as long as the owner retains any interest in the property transferred or attaches any condition to a resale of the property that might bring him additional consideration in the future. Money received for loss in the value of property does not give rise to a sale if the property is retained. Thus, when the seller of property receives money damages for a default on the part of a buyer who has contracted to buy the property, he receives ordinary income if he keeps the property.

A compromise settlement of a claim or a judgment is not a sale or exchange. However, if there is a transfer of property in connection with a release of obligations, we may get capital gain or a combination of capital gain and ordinary income. Thus, when officers in a corporation sold their stock to other stockholders and, at the same time, renounced their claim to accrued salary, the Tax Court found that the sellers received more for their stock than they would otherwise have received, because the liability for their accrued and unpaid salaries was disregarded in computing the sale price of the stock. The sales price was found to be ordinary income to the extent of the accrued salaries that were renounced in the transaction. In another situation, a taxpayer exchanged notes of a bankrupt corporation for cash and release from liability as an indemnitor on outstanding surety bonds. This was done pursuant to a creditors' plan to continue operation. A sale was found so that the resulting loss was capital loss.

Surrender of property to satisfy a debt is a sale or exchange. Any excess of the amount credited in settlement of the debt over the basis of the property is capital gain provided the property surrendered is a capital asset. Where the credit is less than the basis of the property turned over, capital loss is realized.

This whole area is further complicated by the fact that in some cases, the tax law creates or finds a sale or exchange regardless of the actual existence of one. The following list illustrates some of the more important of these situations:

☐ (1) ***Retirement of Corporate Bonds:*** If the bond was issued before January 1, 1955, you get this result only if the bond is in registered form or has coupons attached. All corporate bonds issued after 1954 get the capital gain treatment on retirement except for discount bonds. If they were issued at a discount after 1954, the general rule is that the portion of the redemption or sale price (where you sell the bond prior to maturity) that covered the discount attributable to the period you held the bond is treated as ordinary income; the balance is capital gain. If you sell at a loss, you have a capital loss (§1232).

☐ (2) ***Corporate Liquidations:*** Gain or loss on the complete liquidation of a corporation is treated as capital gain or loss (i.e., the amounts received in liquidation are in exchange for your stock). The same rule applies to partial liquidations.

☐ (3) ***Corporate Redemptions:*** Certain partial or complete redemptions of stock by a corporation are treated as sales or exchanges giving rise to capital gains.

☐ (4) ***Distributorship and Lease Cancellations:*** The payments received are treated as received in exchange for the distributorship or lease and can therefore result in capital gain.

☐ (5) ***Patents:*** Sale of patents by the inventor or someone who got an interest in the patent before the invention was reduced to practice gives long-term capital gain regardless of the holding period, the professional status of the seller, or the method of payment (i.e., the payment can be in the form of royalties).

☐ (6) ***Options:*** The sale or exchange of an option or allowing an option to go unexercised can give capital gain, if the sale or exchange of the property on which you hold the option would also result in a capital gain.

☐ (7) ***Lump-Sum Payouts From Qualified Pension or Profit-Sharing Trusts:*** If the total payout from a qualified pension or profit-sharing trust is in one year, a portion of the gain on the transaction may be treated as if received in a sale or exchange of property held more than six months—in other words, long-term capital gain.

By the same token, certain transactions, although similar to those discussed above, are *not* treated as sales or exchanges and so give rise to ordinary income or loss. Here is a rundown of these items:

☐ (1) ***Building and Loan Association Distributions:*** Such distributions on maturity of the installments are not gain from the sale of exchange of a capital asset but are dividends.

☐ (2) ***Breach of Contract Damages:*** Even where contract is for sale of a capital asset, an amount received as liquidated damages for failure to complete the contract is not capital gain.

☐ (3) ***Arbitration Damages:*** Damages received under an arbitration award are taxable as ordinary income to the extent the award was intended to compensate the taxpayer for lost profits. To the extent the award was to compensate for impairment of the value of an interest in a partnership, it is taxable as capital gain.

☐ (4) ***Accounts or Notes Receivable:*** Income from collection of such items is ordinary income even where the receivables or notes are capital assets since there is no sale or exchange. If you originally got such notes for goods or services you supplied, sale at a discount generates ordinary loss, and sale at a premium generates ordinary income.

☐ (5) ***Employment Contract Settlement:*** Amounts received in a lump sum in cancellation of an employment contract, if actually for past services, are taxed compensation. This is true whether the termination is because of age, ill health, dismissal for cause, dissolution of the employer, or surrender of the employment contract (*Rev. Rul. 58-301*, CB 1958-1, 23).

☐ (6) ***Contract Settlements Generally:*** Payment received for terminating a contract is ordinary income, but amounts received on settlement of a contract for the sale or transfer may be entitled to capital gains treatment. The deciding factor is whether the underlying nature of the transaction comes closest to an extinguishment of rights or to a sale or transfer. If more in the nature of an extinguishment, the amount received will be ordinary income.

☐ (7) ***Sale of Note:*** Weiner held a demand note of a corporation that he controlled. Instead of letting his corporation redeem the note (giving him ordinary income), he transferred the note to a factor; 90 days later, the factor collected the note from the corporation. The Court says his gain was ordinary income. The substance of the deal indicates that there was no business purpose behind it (the corporation was solvent at the time of the transfer). The only purpose was tax avoidance; and under the facts, it did not constitute a bona fide sale (*Weiner*, TC Memo 1962-44).

☐ (8) ***Sales and Exchanges Between Spouses and Stockholder and Close Corporations:*** One situation in which a sale or exchange generates ordinary income is where it involves the transfer of depreciable property between spouses or between an individual and his controlled corporation (§1239). The gain from these sales or exchanges is treated as ordinary income whether the sale or exchange is made directly or indirectly.

The same rule applies to the sale between two corporations controlled by the same individual, says IRS. Capital gains can't be obtained by merely substituting a controlled corporation for the individual owner (*Rev. Rul. 69-109*, CB 1969-1, 202).

For this purpose, an individual is considered to be in control of a corporation if more than 80% in value of the outstanding stock is beneficially owned by him, his spouse, his minor children and minor grandchildren. This includes legally adopted children and their children (Reg. §1.1239-1). However, the Fourth Circuit disagrees with the Tax Court and IRS as far as "beneficial ownership" is concerned. It has held that stock held in trust by a father for his minor children does not count in determining whether the 80% test has been met (*Mitchell*, 300 F.2d 533, CA-4, 1962, *rev'g* 35 TC 550). So, under the Mitchell case, by the judicious use of trusts, you can avoid the 80% rule and transfer appreciated property to your corporation at capital gain rates.

However, in spite of all these rules, numerous opportunities for converting ordinary income into capital gains do exist, and these will be examined in the following paragraphs.

[¶1602] COMPENSATION INTO CAPITAL GAINS

Your salary or other earnings from your job are normally treated as ordinary income; however, you can convert some of this income into capital gains through the use of stock options (assuming you work for or own a corporation). A stock option is simply the right to buy stock of your employer at some future time at a given price. The key is that if the stock appreciates (in which case you would exercise the option), the appreciation will result in capital gains for you when you sell the stock. Note that you are taxed when you *sell* the stock—not when you exercise the option.

However, there are two important limitations to this plan. The first is that the option must be a ''qualified'' option. This means generally that the option must be granted by the employer corporation to an employee pursuant to a plan lasting for only ten years, and the price at which the option is offered must not be less than the fair market value of the stock at the time the option is granted. In addition, the option must expire after five years and cannot be exercised before prior qualified options to the same employee are exercised, unless the prior options can be exercised at a lower price than the later options. Finally, a qualified option cannot be granted to a stockholder who owns more than 10% of a small corporation or 5% of a large corporation (equity capital more than $2,000,000).

The other limitation is the possible application of Rule 16(b) of the Securities Exchange Act dealing with insider profits. This rule, however, can only be an issue if the option is exercised, and the stock sold, within a six-month period.

Stock options, however, are not the only way that the employee can convert his salary into capital gains. He can also use outright purchases of his employer's stock, under an agreement with the employer to redeem the stock later. Or, he can have a part of his compensation paid tax free into an employee benefit plan set up as a profit-sharing trust. If paid as a lump sum upon retirement, a portion of the money may qualify for capital gains treatment. Payments made to such a plan after 1975 will not qualify for capital gains when distributed, but they will qualify for ten-year income averaging, which may well work out to be taxed at an even lower rate than capital gains.

This special averaging also applies to lump-sum distributions from Keogh or HR-10 Plans, so employees of noncorporate businesses (or self-employed persons) may also take advantage of these special low rates of tax.

[¶1603] INTEREST INTO CAPITAL GAINS

Interest in most cases is deductible and to that extent can be used to offset ordinary income. For example, the interest you pay on a mortgage is deductible, and if you later sell the property at a profit, this is converted into capital gains, since without paying the interest, you would not have the appreciated property for the gain or the reduced income for the deduction.

What you may not know is that the other side of the coin—interest received—may also qualify for capital gains treatment. What's more, it may be completely nontaxable, although this is rare.

Interest is nontaxable when it is received on the obligations of states or municipalities, the obvious example of which is interest on tax-free municipal bonds. But interest paid by a state or municipality to finance ordinary purchases, such as of supplies or equipment, is also tax free since it fits within the statutory definition. So, if your business sells anything to a state or a municipality, there is a possible tax exemption for you in the financing.

More common, although also overlooked, are the opportunities to convert interest received into capital gains. These opportunities lie in the four following situations:

□ (1) ***Installment Sales:*** The practice had been to lump interest with the sale price without any interest stated and thereby pick up interest as capital gain. Section 483 outlaws this practice by "imputing interest" where no interest—or too low an interest rate—is stated. But you can get the most possible capital gain by stating the lowest rate okayed by IRS—i.e., 4% simple interest (subject to change by later IRS announcements).

□ (2) ***Mortgages, etc., Nearing Maturity:*** By selling before the maturity date, anything that would have been taxable as ordinary income will become capital gain. But look out for items with built-in increments—e.g., annuity policies. Gain on sale is treated as realization of the built-in interest in the policy.

□ (3) ***Retirement of Bonds:*** If purchased at a discount (other than original-issue discount), capital gain is realized on retirement.

□ (4) ***Time Sales:*** Since interest will necessarily be an element of any time sale, the actual agreed rate need not be stated as interest but rather can be stated as a minimum rate, such as 4%, with the rest allocated to other capital assets. So, where the seller is concerned, he will use a normal rate of interest to arrive at the total time-sale cost and then try to get as much of the increment allocated to capital assets as he can. The buyer, on the other hand, will try to get as much of the cost allocated to interest as he can, since this will be deductible by him. Where either party to the transaction is not tax wise, the other can reap a substantial benefit; since once the agreement is formalized, neither party will be able to claim that it does not accurately reflect the transaction absent fraud, duress, or undue influence.

[¶1604] DEPRECIATION INTO CAPITAL GAINS

As you will recall, the various methods of depreciation were discussed at length in Section X. With the advent of depreciation recapture under Code §1245 and 1250, it became very difficult, if not impossible, to get capital gains treatment for depreciation deductions. However, certain kinds of real estate covered by §1250 are notable exceptions, including §236 housing constructed before 1976, property subject to the 60-month writeoff of Code §167(k), and, to a lesser extent, all residential rental property.

The reason that these kinds of property are exceptions is that the recapture phases out at a rate of 1% per month after a period of either 20 or 100 months; so it is possible, if you hold this kind of property long enough, to avoid recapture entirely. If you do, you can convert all the depreciation deductions you have taken against ordinary income into capital gains.

Even if your real estate is not of the kind mentioned above, you still get a break if you hold the property for more than one year. Section 1250 recapture applies only to *excess* depreciation, which is defined as depreciation greater than that allowed under the straight-line method. So, if you hold the property at least a year, you can convert all the straight-line depreciation you have taken into capital gains, since only the excess will be recaptured.

For both real and personal property, recapture works out better than it sounds, even if you don't get capital gains treatment. The depreciation will always be deductible, offsetting your other ordinary income; if it is later recaptured, the amount of tax due is in effect equivalent to an interest-free loan. If you put the proceeds of the loan (the ordinary income you shelter each year with the deduction) into tax-free municipals, for example, you can make back the money to pay the tax later at no cost to yourself. Note that although this works out to a loan from the government in practice, it is not a loan within the meaning of the tax law. So you don't have to worry about any of the rules about having to carry a tax-free investment, even though you borrow money to buy the depreciable property.

Finally, if you time your sale of the property carefully or use the installment method, you can further reduce the tax bite of recapture. So it is not really any reason not to invest in depreciable property.

[¶1605] RENTS AND ROYALTIES INTO CAPITAL GAINS

Rents and royalties are normally treated as ordinary income to the recipient, but there are various ways in which this unfavorable treatment can be avoided. The following list is a useful summary of some of the most common methods:

□ (1) ***Sale of Lease:*** If you have a good lease and want to cash in on it, you can sublet. However, if you do this, the income will be ordinary income. If, instead, you sell your leasehold, you should qualify for capital gains treatment.

This method can be useful where you have a very profitable business due in part to the low rent you pay. Since your business profits are probably taxable as ordinary income, both you and your landlord may profit from a saleback of the lease to him: You get capital gains treatment, and he gets more rent. If you then lease other property at a more reasonable rent, you will have a better deduction, which could help to keep your taxable business income down. This would be a good move if you wanted to move to a better location with a higher sales potential (justifying greater salary deductions if you are incorporated) at little or no after-tax cost.

□ (2) ***Patents:*** If you are in a business where you own patents, you should know that if you sell licenses, the income you get will be ordinary income. You might be better off to sell the patent outright, retaining or taking back a license, so that the gain on the sale will be a capital gain and the payments you later make will be deductible expenses. In order to have a sale of a patent, you must transfer either all substantial rights to the patent or an undivided interest in all such rights. Under the tax law, those rights are the right to make, use, and sell the device or article covered by the patent.

□ (3) ***Copyrights:*** Like patents, the royalty income from copyrights is ordinary income. However, if you own a copyright, even the outright sale of it will result in ordinary income because of the rule that a copyright cannot be a capital asset if held by the person who created or was the author of the copyrighted works.

But all is not lost. If the copyright is transferred to a corporation for a nominal consideration, the earnings of the copyright may later be converted into capital gains upon the liquidation of the corporation. You must, however, watch out for the collapsible corporation provisions, as well as the personal holding company rules.

Another approach is to trade copyrights with another author. Then, each copyright will be a capital asset in the hands of the authors, since neither produced the one he holds, and each can get capital gains on the later sale.

□ (4) ***Improvements to Rental Property:*** Rent, as you know, is normally ordinary income to the recipient. Since a portion of the rent received by a landlord actually reflects his costs for current and anticipated improvements, he can convert some of this ordinary income into capital gains by agreeing to a lower rental cost under a new lease where the tenant undertakes to make the improvements. This is usually not too tough on the tenant, since he can amortize the improvements over the life of the leasehold and so get full deductions. When the landlord later sells the property, all this increment will become capital gains.

□ (5) ***Sale and Leaseback:*** If you own a piece of real estate that you use in your business, you are entitled to deduct the depreciation. However, when the depreciation is used up (or when the annual amount is very low), you should consider a sale and leaseback. Under such an arrangement, you pay capital gains tax (in most cases) on the gain from the sale of the property, and your later rent payments on the lease from the new owner offset your other income.

One example of this arrangement is the sale of your real estate to an elderly parent. The parent is guaranteed an income via the provisions of the lease, and you can deduct all your rental payments, provided that they are reasonable. When the parent eventually dies, you get the property back, subject only to the estate tax. Since the basis in the estate will be the fair market value, you will be entitled to depreciate the property all over again.

[¶1606] STOCK DEALS FOR CAPITAL GAINS

Stock, which represents the ownership of corporate assets, can provide many capital gains opportunities. Since corporate earnings are taxed at a lower rate than those of a sole proprietor or individual businessman, a stockholder can sell his stock (in effect selling the business) at a higher price which reflects the accumulated income, and realize greater capital gain on the sale. The following paragraphs deal with some of the ins and outs of capital gains deals using stock and some special capital gains strategies.

[¶1606.1] Dividends Into Capital Gains

As you know, when a corporation pays dividends, it gets no deduction, and the shareholder who receives the dividends pays tax on them at ordinary income rates. However, ownership of stock gives you rights—particularly if you are the controlling stockholder—that can be used to make capital gains out of dividend income. Here are some possible courses of action:

□ (1) ***Sale Before Stock Goes Ex-Dividend:*** Announcement of a dividend often increases the price of stock; after the record date, the price goes down again. A sale before the record date means that the dividend is reflected in the proceeds of sale and is therefore taxable as capital gain. If you wait until the dividend is paid, the same money will be taxed as ordinary income.

Of course, there are other considerations in the handling of investments besides tax savings. But where the dividends are substantial, the tax consideration may outweigh the others.

In that case, a sale before the stock goes ex-dividend (so that title passes to the buyer before the record date) may well be advisable.

If you want to retain the stock as an investment, you can repurchase it immediately after it goes ex-dividend (acquiring title to the stock after the vend date). This achieves the tax saving without the offsetting disadvantage of possible upward fluctuations in price that might occur if you waited any amount of time before making the repurchase. If you have a paper loss on the stock, the advantage of selling before the stock goes ex-dividend may be even greater. Here, there isn't even a capital gains tax to pay. The proceeds of sale will still reflect the dividend.

Note: With closely held corporations, you had better transfer the stock before the dividend is declared. The courts distinguish this type of situation from the usual rule that the owner as of the record date picks up the income and have taxed the transferor who transferred the stock between the declaration date and the dividend date.

You will have to be careful about losing the benefit of the loss through the wash sale provisions. If you wait the required 31 days before repurchasing in order to protect your deduction, market fluctuations may result in your paying a higher price for the stock.

☐ (2) ***How Corporation Uses Ex-Dividend Rule:*** A corporation would get the best breaks by reversing the dates—i.e., buying the stock before it goes ex-dividend and selling it immediately afterward. This will have the effect of turning what would be capital gain into ordinary income. The advantage in this comes from the fact that a corporation pays tax on only 15% of its dividends from other domestic corporations. With the corporation rate of 22% or 48%, that means a tax of only 3.3% or 7.2% on this dividend money. This is better than the 25% capital gains maximum rate.

This method of picking up lightly taxed dividends is not necessarily attractive in many cases. Reason: The corporation doesn't get the dividend deduction (i.e., reduction of the taxable dividend to 15% of the dividend) unless it holds the stock for at least 16 days (91 days in the case of accumulated preferred dividends covering a period of more than 366 days) (§246(c)). In many cases, 16 days may be longer than the corporation may care to hold the stock—especially with a volatile stock.

☐ (3) ***Have Corporation Hold Stock:*** The fact that a corporation pays tax on only 15% of the dividends it receives from a domestic corporation is an argument in favor of having your corporation hold your stock. Dividend income of $20,000 taxed in a 70% personal income tax bracket will net you only $6,000. The same amount of dividends taxed at the 48% corporate rate and subject to the 85% dividend received deduction will net the corporation $18,560. A sale of stock or a liquidation will get this money out of the corporation at the capital gain rate, leaving you with $13,920 net.

Care would have to be used to make sure that holding the stock in the corporation didn't invoke either the personal holding company surtax or the penalty for unreasonable accumulation of earnings. These penalties can often be avoided, however.

☐ (4) ***Sale of Unpaid Dividends:*** Unpaid dividends on preferred stock become taxable as capital gain if, instead of declaring the dividend, the corporation includes it in the price of a redemption. This plan is practical only where different stockholders own the common and preferred and the corporation is planning a redemption for business reasons. Anything that appeared to be a bailout of earnings would have to be carefully avoided.

Suppose a corporation has outstanding 100,000 preferred shares, with $20 par value and 6% cumulative dividend rate. The shares are redeemable at par with accumulated dividends upon

30 days' notice. If the corporation decides to redeem the preferred, it may declare a dividend that will be taxable to the stockholders as ordinary income. This would amount to $120,000 (6% of total par value of $2,000,000). The stock would then be redeemed at par. Or the corporation could notify the stockholders it was redeeming the preferred stock at $21.20 a share. The stockholders would receive the same money this way, but the dividend would be taxed as capital gain instead of as ordinary income.

Where the big stockholders are corporations, it may be better to make the distribution as a dividend rather than as part of a redemption. A corporation is taxed on only 15% of its domestic dividends, as we have already pointed out, the equivalent of a tax rate of only 7.2%, which is better than the maximum capital gain rate of 30%.

Where the preferred stock was originally received in a tax-free transaction, the redemption may be taxed as a dividend (§302 and 306).

□ (5) ***Corporation Without Current Profits:*** Distributions by a corporation without current or accumulated earnings are taxable at the capital gain rate, at most. To the extent the distribution doesn't exceed the basis of the stock, it merely reduces that basis and there is no tax at all. Once the basis has been reduced to zero, further distributions are capital gain.

Reduction of the basis means that more of the proceeds of sale of the stock will be taxed as capital gain than if the basis hadn't been reduced by nontaxable distributions. But this merely changes the time when the gain will be realized; it doesn't alter the fact that the tax will be at the capital gain rate. Stock held until death, however, will be received by the beneficiaries at its stepped-up (appreciated) basis.

Here's how the capital gain angle works: Assume a corporation that has been operating successfully and distributing earnings regularly runs into a bad loss year. Without accumulated earnings and with a loss for the year, a dividend distribution will be nontaxable or, at the worst, taxable as capital gain. If sufficient cash isn't available to pay a large dividend, the money can be borrowed for this purpose.

There is no objection to borrowing; and since a generally successful company's credit will be good, it should have no trouble raising the loan. Assuming that operations return to profitable, the borrowed money can be repaid out of future earnings. If money wasn't borrowed to pay the dividend in the loss year, the same dividend paid in later years would be taxable as ordinary income.

□ (6) ***Company With Accumulated Deficit and Current Earnings:*** If your corporation has an accumulated deficit from the past few years but is currently making money, you may still be in a good position to pick up some tax-free corporate distributions. Reason: A corporate distribution is only taxable to the extent of its accumulated earnings and profits (plus its current year's earnings and profits) for the year the payout is made. So, by timing these distributions to occur in a year when earnings and profits are low, any excess over this amount will first be treated as a return of capital; then, as capital gains.

Example: As of January 1, 1975, your corporation showed a deficit of $20,000. But 1975 looks like a $10,000 profit year and so does 1976. And you want to pay out a $10,000 dividend this year. Strategy: Hold off on any distribution in 1975. Instead, distribute $20,000 in 1976. There will be no accumulated earnings or profits at the end of 1976 (the $20,000 deficit will offset 1975 and 1976 profits). Any 1976 distribution is only taxable up to $10,000 (the 1976 earnings). If you distribute $10,000 in 1975 and $10,000 in 1976, you will have $20,000 of taxable dividends because there were $10,000 of current earnings each year.

☐ (7) ***Other Dividend Opportunities:*** The following list is a brief summary of some of the other capital gain opportunities using dividends:

(a) *Mutual Funds:* Dividends are taxed as capital gains to the extent they arise from corporate capital gains.

(b) *Low-Dividend Stocks:* If you're in a high bracket, buy into corporations with a policy of plowing back earnings rather than distributing them; the increase in value will be capital gain when you sell the stock.

(c) *Preferred Stock:* Unpaid preferred dividends, included in the redemption price, are taxed at the capital gains rate instead of at the ordinary income rate.

(d) *Dividends in Kind:* If property has appreciated in value, the corporate tax on the appreciation is avoided by distributing the property itself rather than selling it and distributing the proceeds. But here the corporation may realize ordinary income via depreciation recapture if it distributes depreciable personal property or real estate.

(e) *Paper Losses:* If your stock is quoted at less than you paid for it, sell it to realize capital loss rather than take the dividend. This reflects the dividend as capital gain instead of ordinary income.

[¶1606.2] Capital Gains Through Stock Syndicates

Members of investment syndicates are able to get capital gains even though the syndicate is controlled and organized by one or more securities specialists. The Tax Court says that even though the securities specialist might have the intention to sell securities held by the syndicate to his customers in the ordinary course of his business, and even assuming arguendo that this intention should be imputed to the members of the syndicate, this doesn't mean that the members may not be entitled to capital gains treatment on the sale of these securities. If it can be shown that the members of the syndicate are traders in securities rather than dealers or merchants in securities there is no statutory authority that would deny them the benefit of capital gains.

For 1962, a group of investors formed a syndicate for the purpose of acquiring, holding, and eventually selling at a profit the common stock of "Northwestern," a stock and mutual life insurance company. At that time, the syndicate acquired from another syndicate (with the same members) an option to buy the stock.

Both syndicates were organized and controlled by James C. Bradford, who had over 35 years of experience in the securities industry and numerous connections and dealings with persons and companies in the life insurance industry and was the controlling partner of a securities firm specializing in life insurance stock. In mid-1963 (more than six months after the acquisition of the stock), the syndicate sold some of the securities to a group of underwriters who, in turn, disposed of the stock in a public offering. The syndicate was then liquidated.

The Tax Court ruled that the sale of the Northwestern stock by the syndicate to the underwriters did not constitute the sale of property held by any of the members for sale to customers in the ordinary course of business. The sale to the underwriters constituted the liquidation of investments made by the members of the selling syndicate who were traders in securities rather than dealers in securities, said the Court. The members were clearly engaged in a speculation in stock for their own accounts. In purchasing, holding, and selling the securities, the syndicate acted no differently from any other stock speculator trading on its own account (*Francis C. Currie*, 53 TC 185, 1969).

[¶1607] LIQUIDATIONS

Generally, a distribution in complete liquidation is treated as a sale of stock by the stockholder to the corporation in exchange for his share of the corporation's assets; the excess of the value of the property (including cash) received over the stockholder's basis for his stock is taxed to him as capital gain (§331 and 1001). "Collapsible" corporations are an exception, the proceeds being taxed as ordinary income (§341) (see ¶1609).

The main types of liquidations recognized under the tax law are:

□ (1) An ordinary, complete liquidation of the corporate business, which may be made in a series of distributions and which produces capital gain to the stockholders on the difference between the cost of their stock and the values received in liquidation.
□ (2) A one-month liquidation in which the shareholders can avoid tax on unrealized appreciation of corporate assets at the price of paying the ordinary income tax on accumulated earnings received in liquidation. (¶1607.3.)
□ (3) A 12-month liquidation in which double tax is avoided on the sale of a corporate business. If the rules are met, the corporation sells its assets and pays no tax. Only one tax is paid (capital gain) when the corporation makes distributions in liquidation after the sale of its assets. (¶1607.2.)
□ (4) A partial liquidation in which distributions may be received at capital gain rates provided statutory conditions are met or a bona fide contraction of the business can be demonstrated. (¶1607.4.)
□ (5) Complete liquidation of a subsidiary. (¶1607.5.)

A complete liquidation takes place when a corporation winds up its affairs and distributes its assets (in one or a series of distributions) to its stockholders. Generally, these steps are involved in a complete liquidation: (1) a resolution of stockholders authorizes dissolution, and a plan of liquidation is adopted; (2) information return (Form 966) is filed with the Commissioner within 30 days; (3) corporate affairs are wound up, debts paid, assets distributed, the corporation dissolved; and (4) income tax returns are filed, request is made for assessment within 18 months, information returns (Forms 1096 and 1099L) for $600 or more liquidating dividends paid any stockholder are filed by February 28 of the following year.

[¶1607.1] Tax Effect of Liquidating Distribution on Corporation

Normally, a corporation realizes no gain or loss as a result of a distribution in partial or complete liquidation (§336). There are exceptions to this rule, however:

□ (1) Generally, if the corporation distributes installment obligations, it will realize the same type of gain it would realize from the sale of the property for which the installment obligations were given. The gain is the difference between the basis for the installment obligations and their fair market value (§453(d)).
□ (2) The rule in (1) does not apply to the liquidation of a subsidiary under §332 (where no gain or loss is recognized on the liquidation). But where the liquidation results in a step-up in basis of the distributed items in liquidation under §334(b)(2), then the provisions in (1) above apply to distributions of installment obligations after November 13, 1966 (§453(d)(4)(A); amended by

P.L. 89-809). In such a case, the subsidiary will realize gain as if it sold the notes and distributed cash to its parent.

☐ (3) The rule in (1) also does not apply where there is a §337, 12-month liquidation if the corporation would not have realized any gain or loss had it sold the installment obligation to an outsider on the day of liquidation. Here, too, however, the rule in (1) would apply to the extent the corporation would have had a §1245 or §1250 gain had it sold the obligations (see item (4) below).

☐ (4) In all liquidations except the tax-free liquidation of a subsidiary under §332, if the corporation distributes depreciable property, it may realize ordinary income to the extent of all or part of the previously deducted depreciation that is reflected in the difference between the basis of the property distributed and the fair market value of that property at the time of distribution.

[¶1607.2] Twelve-Month Liquidations (§337)

Under §337, if a corporation in complete liquidation distributes all its property (except assets—cash or other assets—retained to meet claims) within 12 months after adoption of a plan of liquidation, gain or loss on sales or exchanges of property by the corporation during that period will not be recognized or taxed to the corporation (§337). By eliminating the tax on the corporate level, the double tax is avoided.

This permits a liquidating corporation to sell—without taxable gain or loss—its noninventory items or make bulk sales of inventory. The tax-free treatment is limited to sales of property (which is carefully defined), so as to eliminate double taxation of corporate earnings only where sales are incident to liquidation.

If you liquidate under §337, you have to follow its rules. So if assets have appreciated, the corporation (in order to avoid tax on gain) should adopt a plan of liquidation before making any sales and then liquidate within a 12-month period. If assets have depreciated, the corporation (in order to obtain deductible loss) should sell the property before adopting a plan or delay completion of the liquidation for more than 12 months after the date of adoption of the plan.

Section 337 requires that there be a plan of complete liquidation and that the tax-free corporate sales take place within the 12-month period beginning on the date of adoption of the plan. (Of course, there has to be a complete liquidation within that 12-month period, too.) While the usual procedure is to adopt the plan of liquidation and then go through with the sale, the Regulations concede that if the sale occurs earlier, but on the same day as the adoption of the plan of liquidation, §337 will apply (Reg. §1.337-1).

You cannot use the 12-month liquidation route where you have a collapsible corporation, a one-month (§333) liquidation, or a tax-free liquidation under §332. Nor does it apply where all the assets are distributed to creditors. Furthermore, where the property disposed of by the corporation is depreciable property, part of the benefit of §337 can be lost. This is because the recapture provisions of §1245 and §1250 supersede §337 and create ordinary income.

Timing Distributions: Just because §337 requires that all assets (other than those held back to pay corporate debts) must be distributed within 12 months of the adoption of your liquidation plan doesn't mean you have to rush into making the distributions as soon as the assets are available for distribution. As long as you get the assets out of the corporation to the stockholders within the 12 months, you avoid double taxation on the sale of the corporation's property. So, the next step is to look over the stockholders' tax picture.

Where the 12-month period after adoption of the plan of liquidation cuts across two taxable years of the stockholders (which it will do unless the plan of liquidation is adopted as of the first day of the stockholders' taxable year), you can have the corporation split its distribution over the two taxable years. In the first year, an amount equal to the stockholders' basis for their stock can be distributed to them without tax. After that, any additional distribution will result in capital gain.

How you want to split the capital gain over the two years will depend on the stockholders' personal tax pictures. Do they have any capital losses this year? Or do they expect any next year? Distributions in the year of loss will let them offset the gains on distributions with the losses.

In some cases, a change in personal tax brackets between the stockholders' two taxable years can dictate the year in which they would want most or all of the capital gain. That is so because the capital gain rate is not automatically 25% in all cases; it can be less. Where the stockholder's ordinary income bracket is less than 50%, his capital gain bracket is half of that. So, timing the liquidation distribution to throw most of the gain in a year when he's below the 50% mark can cut his taxes.

[¶1607.3] One-Month Liquidations (§333)

If you meet the requirements of §333, you can avoid any tax on the liquidation of a corporation. What happens is that the basis of the stockholder's stock becomes the basis of the property received in the liquidation. So, where the property is appreciated property—i.e., worth more than basis of the stock—the tax on the gain is postponed until the stockholder disposes of the property.

One big advantage of a §333 liquidation is that the stockholders can turn around and make an installment sale and use the installment method of reporting the gain—i.e., spreading the tax out over the period of collection. This approach is not available in other situations where the corporation has to be liquidated to avoid a double tax on the transaction (i.e., either the 12-month, §337 liquidation or liquidation followed by resale under §331).

The big problem with §333 is that it is only useful where the corporation has no accumulated earnings or profits to speak of and little or no cash or stock and securities acquired after 1953. Where earnings and profits are present, there will be ordinary income to the distributees in the liquidation. And where the cash and post-1953 stock and securities are distributed, there can be capital gain. So, the advantage of §333 is really restricted to those cases where the corporation has highly appreciated property other than stocks and securities acquired after 1953 but has had little or no income.

To have the provisions of §333 apply, you need the adoption of a plan of liquidation, written consent of the stockholders within 30 days of the adoption of the plan, and a distribution in complete redemption of all the stock interests that takes place within one calendar month.

Section 333 applies only to those stockholders who file consents. But, in the case of noncorporate stockholders, 80% of the voting power (other than stock held by corporations) have to consent. In the case of corporate stockholders, 80% of the corporate stockholdings have to consent (stock held by a corporation owning 50% or more of the combined voting power at any time after 1953 is not counted in this calculation).

The election to come within §333 is made on Form 964, which must be filed in duplicate with the District Director. A copy of the form must be attached to the shareholder's return for the year of liquidation (Reg. §1.333-3).

Failure to file the election turns the liquidation into a standard §331 liquidation. Neither the Treasury nor the courts can waive the election requirement. Also, keep in mind that you usually cannot change your mind once you choose the one-month liquidation route, though you subsequently discover you made a mistake and, as a result, wind up with a higher tax.

The stockholder in a §333 liquidation figures his tax in the following way. First, he determines the amount of the gain (i.e., the difference between his basis for the stock in the liquidated corporation and the total fair market value of everything received in the liquidation distribution). Then he determines the portion of the gain that is taxable. That amount is the larger of the following two amounts: (1) His ratable share of the corporation's accumulated earnings and profits through the end of the month of the distribution; (2) The total of cash and the value of stock and securities acquired after 1953 distributed to him.

If the stockholder is a corporation, the larger of (1) or (2) is taxable to it as a capital gain (long- or short-term depending on the holding period). The remainder of the gain is not taxed.

If the stockholder is other than a corporation and the larger amount is (1), then the entire amount is treated as a dividend. Where, however, the amount in (2) is larger than (1), then to the extent of the total arrived at in (1), the gain is taxable as a dividend. The excess of the amount in (2) over the amount in (1) is treated as capital gain (long- or short-term depending on the holding period). Any gain in excess of the larger of (1) or (2) is, of course, not taxable.

Example: Three stockholders (two individuals and one corporation) each own one-third of the stock of corporation X for more than six months. Each stockholder has a basis of $100 for his stock. The corporation has accumulated earnings and profits of $90; cash, stock, and securities acquired after 1954 valued at $210; and other property with a value of $600. In a liquidation qualifying under §333, the total distribution of cash, stock, securities, and other property comes to $810. Each stockholder gets a distribution valued at $270 and so has a gain of $170. Since each stockholder's share of the cash, stock, and securities comes to $70 and that is more than each stockholder's share of the earnings and profits ($30), $70 is the taxable amount to each stockholder. The corporate stockholder reports the entire $70 as long-term capital gain. Each individual stockholder reports $30 (his share of the earnings and profits) as a dividend and $40 as a long-term capital gain.

The basis for the property received in a §333 liquidation is the basis of the redeemed stock, decreased by the amount of cash received and increased by the amount of the recognized gain. Basis is allocated among the assets received in proportion to their net fair market values (Reg. §1.334-2).

On a §333 liquidation, additional unanticipated income may be created that increases earnings and profits. Since the optimum §333 situation calls for as little earnings and profits as possible, preliquidation planning to avoid ordinary income situations is important.

The first thing you must do is analyze and determine the amount of earnings and profits. Earnings and profits for book purposes are not the same as earnings and profits for tax purposes. Where a corporation determines that its distributions are partly or wholly nontaxable as dividends, computations and data supporting such determination, as prescribed in *Rev. Proc. 65-10,* CB 1965-1, 738, modified by *Rev. Proc. 67-12,* CB 1967-1, 589, must be filed with IRS.

The next step is to try to avoid items that may increase earnings and profits. The following is a list of the type of items that you should pay close attention to:

☐ ***Disposition of Installment Obligations:*** The distribution of an installment obligation is considered a "disposition," and income is realized by the corporation to the extent market value exceeds basis (§336).

☐ ***Reserve for Bad Debts:*** The disposition of accounts receivable makes the balance in the reserve for bad debts no longer necessary, and IRS and some courts say that it must be restored to income.

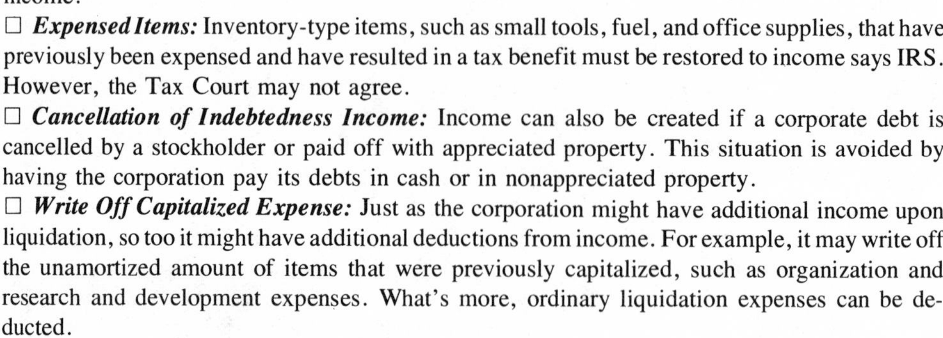

☐ ***Expensed Items:*** Inventory-type items, such as small tools, fuel, and office supplies, that have previously been expensed and have resulted in a tax benefit must be restored to income says IRS. However, the Tax Court may not agree.

☐ ***Cancellation of Indebtedness Income:*** Income can also be created if a corporate debt is cancelled by a stockholder or paid off with appreciated property. This situation is avoided by having the corporation pay its debts in cash or in nonappreciated property.

☐ ***Write Off Capitalized Expense:*** Just as the corporation might have additional income upon liquidation, so too it might have additional deductions from income. For example, it may write off the unamortized amount of items that were previously capitalized, such as organization and research and development expenses. What's more, ordinary liquidation expenses can be deducted.

[¶1607.4] Partial Liquidations (§346)

A distribution of property to a stockholder by a corporation with respect to his stock generally must be treated as a dividend to the extent of the earnings and profits of the corporation. One exception to this general rule is found in §331. Under that section, amounts received by a stockholder as the result of a partial liquidation of a corporation under §346 are treated not as a dividend but as the proceeds of a sale of his stock.

Any gain that a stockholder recognizes as a result of the distribution in a §346 partial liquidation will be capital gain and not ordinary income if the stock was a capital asset in his hands. Recognized gain or loss is measured by the difference between the basis of the stock surrendered and the fair market value of the property received (§1001 and 1002). Moreover, a corporation that distributes property in partial liquidation under §346 does not recognize gain, even though such property has a value in excess of its adjusted basis (§302 and 346(c)).

The idea underlying partial liquidations is that since a corporation will continue in business after the partial liquidation, it will distribute only that part of the property it no longer needs to redeem a portion of the outstanding stock. In effect, this means the stock is redeemed out of funds made available because part of the business operations must be ended. By way of contrast, a complete liquidation envisages the termination of the entire business in corporate form. *Note:* The rules governing partial liquidations are equally applicable to Subchapter S corporations (Reg. §1.1372-1(c)).

Distributions in partial liquidation may occur in one of three forms.

☐ (1) One distribution in a series in complete liquidation under §346(a)(1). IRS is inclined to class this category with other complete liquidations (see, for instance, *Rev. Rul. 74-89*). The partial liquidation must be pursuant to a plan of complete liquidation. This usually means you have to have a formal plan of complete liquidation, as well as timely action in fact.

☐ (2) Contractions of a corporate business under §346(a)(2). This provision, enacted by the 1954 Code, reflects a concept crystallized by the courts under the 1939 Code. A distribution will qualify as a partial liquidation under §346(a)(2) if it (a) is not essentially equivalent to a dividend; (b) is in redemption of part of the stock of the corporation pursuant to a plan; and (c) occurs within the taxable year in which the plan is adopted or within the succeeding taxable year (§346(a)(2); Reg. §1.346-1).

Elements (b) and (c) of the above test are basically mechanical in that an examination of the corporate records will generally reveal whether or not the taxpayer has satisfied them. However, the question of whether a distribution is "not essentially equivalent to a dividend" is far more bothersome. Ordinarily, it is closely connected with a genuine or bona fide contraction of the corporate business. In reaching a conclusion, a drastic reduction in capital requirements and the distribution or sale of the old business is usually considered determiniative (*Rev. Rul. 59-20*, CB 1959-1, 472).

Stripped to its core, a partial liquidation under §346(a)(2) must constitute a genuine or bona fide contraction of the corporate business, whether voluntary or involuntary. This partial liquidation is measured solely at the corporate level. In essence, the question will be whether the sale of assets in a corporate contraction was accompanied by a significant reduction in the corporation's net worth and a substantial reduction in its business activities. What's contemplated is a significant event in the life of the corporation as opposed to a mere sale of unwanted assets.

While the question of whether or not there has been a contraction of corporate business is the foremost consideration in determining qualification under §346(a)(2), it is not the only factor. For instance, a distribution that contracts the size of a corporation may yet fail to qualify under §346(a)(2) and thus be treated as a dividend.

Therefore, after determining whether or not a corporate contraction has taken place, IRS and the courts will also examine the following factors:

(a) The net effect of the transaction;

(b) The presence or absence of a bona fide corporate business purpose;

(c) Whether the action was initiated by the stockholders or by the corporation;

(d) The size of the corporate earned surplus;

(e) The amounts, frequency, and significance of the dividends paid by the corporation in the past;

(f) Whether there were any special circumstances relating to the distribution;

(g) Whether at the time of sale in partial liquidation the corporation had comparatively large amounts of accumulated earnings and profits; and,

(h) Whether the corporation had been paying low dividends in comparison with its earnings.

These factors will be carefully scrutinized to prevent tax avoidance, particularly in the case of purported partial liquidations by closely held family corporations. Moreover, the problem will be compounded where distributions are pro rata and do not meaningfully reduce any stockholder's proportionate interest in the corporation (see *Davis*, 397 US 30, 1970).

☐ (3) Termination of one of a number of businesses conducted by the distributing corporation (§346(b)). This form of liquidation was a new concept when enacted by the 1954 Code. The main requirement of this provision is known generally as the "five-year business requirement." It contemplates that the distributing corporation must be engaged in the active conduct of at least two businesses that have been actively conducted (whether or not by the corporation) for the five-year period ending on the date of distribution. The distribution of one of these businesses will automatically qualify as a partial liquidation (§346(b)), as long as the corporation is actively engaged in the conduct of business afterwards.

[¶1607.5] Tax-Free Liquidation of a Subsidiary (§332)

The complete liquidation of a subsidiary under §332 results in nonrecognition of gain or loss to the parent and a carryover to the parent of the subsidiary's basis of the distributed assets.

(The parent takes over the subsidiary's adjusted basis for the distributed assets, without regard to the cost basis of the subsidiary's stock held by the parent and cancelled; thus, a surplus or deficit in the dissolved corporation would be reflected in increased gain or loss upon liquidation of the transferee corporation.) To effect a tax-free liquidation of a subsidiary, the parent must comply with the following requirements:

□ (1) Adoption of a plan of liquidation. The plan need not be formal; but since a certified copy must be filed with the parent's return (Reg. §1.332-6), it is advisable to prepare a plan at the outset.

□ (2) From the date of the adoption of the plan until the receipt of the property, the parent must own at least 80% of the voting stock of the liquidating subsidiary and at least 80% of all other classes of stock (except nonvoting stock that is limited and preferred as to dividends).

□ (3) All property under the liquidation must be distributed and all stock must be cancelled either within the taxable year or within three years from the close of the taxable year in which the first liquidating distribution is made, in order for any distribution under the plan to be considered a distribution in complete liquidation. If liquidation is not completed within the taxable year the parent must waive the statute of limitations and post a bond (Reg. §1.332-4).

□ (4) If the subsidiary is a foreign corporation, gain is recognized unless the Commissioner is satisfied that the purpose of the plan is not the avoidance of taxes (§367). Loss is ordinarily recognized if the requirements of §332 are not met.

□ (5) Where a liquidating subsidiary is indebted to the parent, no gain or loss is recognized to the subsidiary on the transfer of property in satisfaction of the debt (§332(c)). (If a subsidiary is indebted to its parent, and has assets which have appreciated, a tax-free liquidation will help wipe out the debt without tax consequences.)

[¶1608] OTHER CAPITAL GAINS OPPORTUNITIES

The following paragraphs cover a few other capital gains opportunities, which are more limited since they depend upon special circumstances. If any of these apply to you, you may find that you qualify for a big tax break.

[¶1608.1] Trust Income Into Capital Gains

Normally, the life beneficiary of a trust receives ordinary income—his share of the interest, dividends, rents, etc., that the trust earns. He has a basis for his interest (usually based on a proportionate part of date-of-death value where the trust was set up by will or of the donor's basis where the trust was set up by gift). Each year, as the life beneficiary's life expectancy decreases, his basis, according to the Regs also decreases (see Reg. §1.1014-5; 1.1015-1(b)). But he cannot offset the decrease in his basis against the ordinary income that he receives from the trust.

Suppose, however, he sells his interest. Then, to the extent the sale price is more than his basis, he's entitled to capital gain. However, this arrangement, while giving the seller capital gain, wouldn't normally be feasible if the buyer couldn't offset his cost of the life income interest against the income received. Otherwise, the buyer wouldn't be willing to pay much for the interest and the life tenant wouldn't benefit from the sale (if he got too little for his interest, he.could be better off continuing to pay tax on ordinary income).

Luckily, the courts have ruled that the buyer does get a deduction. He can spread his cost (i.e., what he pays the seller) over the life expectancy of the seller (the life beneficiary from whom he bought the life interest). And this is true even if the buyer is the remainderman (the one who would get the property when the trust ends—i.e., when the life beneficiary dies).

Here are two examples of how substantial tax savings can be had under these arrangements:

☐ (1) Smith owns a substantial block of income-producing stock. He transfers these securities to two trusts. The income from trust #1 is payable to his son John for life, with the remainder to his other son, Tom. The income from trust #2 is payable for life to Tom, with the remainder to John. Tom later buys John's life interest in trust #1, and John buys Tom's life interest in trust #2. Then each begins to amortize part of his cost over the other brother's life expectancy. Thus, part of the dividend income each receives is now a return of capital. If the two brothers are close in age, each paid the other approximately the same amount for his life interest. So, on a net basis, little if anything changed hands for the two life interests.

☐ (2) Arnold owns an apartment house. The annual net rent it throws off is $6,000. He transfers the building to a trust, naming himself life beneficiary and his son as the remainderman. Arnold's life expectancy is 20 years. The son buys Arnold's life interest for $90,000, payable $4,500 a year. The son writes off $4,500 (5% per year straight-line method) each year. Net result, considering father and son part of one family unit, is that $6,000 of net income from the apartment house still stays in the family, but now only $1,500 is taxable each year.

[¶1608.2] Private Annuities

A private annuity arrangement is almost always between family members. It consists of a transfer of property (usually appreciated in value) by one family member (also called the transferor or annuitant) to a second family member (known as the obligor or annuitor) in return for a promise to make periodic payments to the annuitant for the remainder of the annuitant's life.

A private annuity may be used to carry out any of the following objectives:

☐ (1) To retire with a good income while leaving the business in the control of sons or key employees;

☐ (2) To remove property from the estate and turn it into present cash without prohibitive tax costs;

☐ (3) To exempt marital deduction property from tax in the survivor's estate;

☐ (4) To generate charitable deductions and exemptions;

☐ (5) To provide an investment opportunity with extraordinary rewards.

As an example of the tax treatment of a private annuity, assume that a widow, 74 years of age, has stock and securities valued at $300,000. Her cost for these securities (acquired in 1950) is $150,000. So, there is a potential long-term capital gain of $150,000 which would be realized on a sale of these securities. She transfers these securities to her daughter in exchange for the daughter's unsecured promise to pay her an annuity for the rest of her life.

Tax Benefits to Widow: On an outright sale of such securities, there would be $150,000 of long-term capital gains realized. The maximum income tax would be $47,500 (25% on the first $50,000 and 35% on the excess) all incurred in the year of sale.

By transferring the securities to her daughter, any tax on the gain is deferred until the widow first recovers her cost ($150,000); then, the tax is spread over a number of years instead of being payable in one year. This subjects the gain to lower tax brackets. The transfer of appreciated property for an *unsecured promise* to pay an annuity has been held not to be a "closed" transaction because the value of the annuity payments cannot be determined. Where property has decreased in value, it should first be sold so that a deductible loss will be realized. Transfer of depreciated property may result in disallowance of the loss. In addition, the annuity arrangement shifts the burden of any income tax on dividends or interest earned on these securities from the widow to the daughter (in this respect, an annuity differs from a transfer with a retained life estate). Assuming these securities throw off an annual yield of 5%, the $15,000 of annual income would be taxed to the daughter at her lower income tax bracket and permits the added utilization of the daughter's dividend exclusion and applicable deductions and exemptions.

Another key advantage of this arrangement is that the $300,000 of securities are removed from the widow's taxable estate. Assuming that the net estate (after the $60,000 flat exemption), including the $300,000 of securities, would amount to $500,000, the estate tax saved due to the annuity arrangement comes to $95,000.

If the widow transferred the $300,000 of securities to her daughter in one year as a lifetime gift, assuming that no part of the $30,000 lifetime exemption had been used, the taxable portion of the gift would be $267,000 ($300,000 minus $30,000 lifetime exemption, minus $3,000 annual exclusion), and the gift tax payable would come to over $53,000. In order to pay this gift tax, additional sales of securities might be necessary. This, too, could create an immediate tax on any capital gains.

It had been generally accepted that a taxpayer could recover the cost of his investment before reporting capital gains when he swapped appreciated property for a private annuity. But IRS now says that this is not the right way to report the gain from a private annuity transaction.

According to IRS, the gain should be reported ratably over the years of the annuity payments. Although this rule lessens the tax appeal of the private annuity, it is not expected to lessen its use (*Rev. Rul. 69-74*, CB 1969-1, 43).

The tax effects of a private annuity to the annuitor can be more varied and complicated than to the annuitant.

The basis of the property received may vary from year to year as annuity payments are made during the life of the annuitant. Only upon the annuitant's death does the basis of the property become fixed. If the annuitor sells the property after making several payments, his basis is determined by adding the present value of the annuity payments which still have to be made to the annuitant to the amount already paid to him.

The rules for determining losses, however, are different. The loss is determined only as it is actually incurred. Therefore, in the year of sale, the loss would be determined on the basis of only the payments that have been made; the future payments do not come into play until they are actually made.

[¶1608.3] Sales at a Contingent Price

Suppose an individual sells a piece of property (gain on which would give him capital gain) which had a basis to him of $25,000 for $5,000 cash and 1% of the buyer's gross receipts for the next 10 years. Our seller argues that he cannot value the right to get 1% of the buyer's gross receipts for the next 10 years, so that the contract has an unascertainable value. That being the case, he has an "open" transaction. Until he recoups his $25,000 basis, he has no gain or loss. Thereafter, any amounts he receives are part of this open transaction and are taxable as capital gains in the years received.

This argument is based on the Supreme Court decision in *Burnett v. Logan*, 283 US 404. IRS goes along with this argument of the seller's, but it insists that it is a rare case where value is not ascertainable (*Rev. Rul. 58-402*, CB 1958-2, 15).

On the other hand, if the contract received has an ascertainable value (even if that value is a flat zero), we have a closed transaction. Gain or loss is figured at that time by comparing basis with the value of what has been received (e.g., cash plus the ascertainable value of the contract). Thereafter, if more than the total value taken into account in determining the gain or loss is received, the excess is treated as ordinary income in the year received. *Reason:* The excess is not received by reason of a sale or exchange.

Note that even where you have an unascertainable value and thereby postpone the capital gains tax until you receive payments in the future, the imputed interest rules can make part of those payments ordinary income.

Since subsequent capital gain depends on whether you have an ascertainable or unascertainable value when the contract or other promise is received, it becomes important to determine just which you have. IRS takes the position that a contract or claim would almost always have an ascertainable value. Only in rare and extraordinary cases would value be unascertainable.

Here are examples of the extraordinary situations in which IRS would concede that a contract's value is unascertainable: (1) where there is a contingent reversionary remainder involved (*Robinette*, 318 US 184, 1943), (2) where greatly disturbed and uncertain conditions in an oil field make it greatly uncertain that wells drilled in the field on contracts would pay out (*Edwards Drilling*, 35 BTA 341, 1936), and (3) where it was not ascertainable whether land company stockholders would ever recover their capital investments out of payments made by the Mexican Government (*Brant*, 13 TC 712, 1949).

The courts, however, take a more liberal view than IRS. For example, in one case, the Tax Court found that a contract calling for payments totalling $160,000, payable at the rate of 10% of the purchaser's gross sales of a product (the rights to which product were the subject of the sale in question) did not have an ascertainable value (*Altorfer*, TC Memo 1961-48).

Here is a rundown of court decisions where it was found that there was *no ascertainable value:*

☐ Oil brokerage contracts received in liquidation (*Carter*, 170 F.2d 911, CA-2, 1948).
☐ Royalty contracts received in liquidation.
☐ Stock redemption agreement under which the stockholder received 20% of the corporation's proceeds from sales (*Bradford*, 22 TC 1057, 1954).
☐ Insurance claim by corporation (denied by insurer) distributed to stockholders in liquidation (*Burnett*, TC Memo 1956-210).
☐ Mortgage commission claims (which depended on the closing of certain real estate transactions) distributed in liquidation (*Lentz*, 28 TC 1157, 1957).
☐ Royalties contingent on future production and sales of a company which the taxpayer did not control (*Hoy*, TC Memo 1958-28).

[¶1608.4] When Contract Sales Give Capital Gains

Certain types of contract sales give capital gains—and the rights to the capital gains are spelled out in the tax law. The most important of these situations are sales or cancellations of distributorship agreements, and sales of option contracts.

(1) ***Distributorships:*** Under §1241, where a distributor has a substantial capital invest-

ment in his distributorship, the receipt of money for the cancellation of a distributorship of goods is treated as an *exchange* for the distributorship agreement. Hence, we get a capital gain. Even under these rules, however, it is important to show that the money received was solely for cancellation of the distributorship agreement and that no nonexclusive agency was retained nor a new agency granted. If the Commissioner can show that the payment was only for the release of certain rights, the granting of certain concessions or the modification of a distributorship, the rules of §1241 might not produce capital gain.

Considerable stress is laid on the fact that there must be a substantial capital investment in the distributorship, and it must be one for the distribution of goods. An agency to represent theatrical people would thus not come under these rules.

(2) ***Option Contracts:*** The person having the right to buy the property under the option can realize capital gain by selling his option, as long as the underlying asset is a capital asset or a §1231 asset (§1234). The period for which the option has been held prior to sale determines whether the capital gain or loss is short term or long term. A payment received for surrendering the right to exercise the option should be treated as a gain from the sale of the option. If the option holder fails to exercise the option, he is treated as having sold it on the day it expired.

If you are looking to pick up a long-term gain from the sale of an option, make sure you don't take title to the property before you sell. Nor should you undertake to deliver the property. You should assign the option and then let your assignee pay the purchase price to the seller of the property. What he pays you is your option cost and your profit. You may agree in your assignment that if he is unable to obtain marketable title from the seller, the assignment is void and he gets his money back. Such a clause in the assignment will not cause you to be held to have exercised the option.

Don't take any action that adds up to the equivalent of an exercise of the option by you with an immediate retransfer of the property to your assignee. Even though the net result (from the point of view of who got the property eventually and who made what profit) may be the same, the tax result is entirely different. If you exercise the option, you get a new holding period for the property acquired. And if you then resell it immediately, you have a short-term gain.

[¶1609] TAX PITFALLS OF CAPITAL GAINS

There are three main areas where taxpayers get into trouble in their search for capital gains. These are the Personal Holding Company, Accumulated Earnings and Collapsible Corporation provisions of the Code. The first two of these provisions have already been discussed in Section I. Now, we turn to the Collapsible Corporation rules.

The attempt to convert ordinary income into capital gains via a corporate structure is thwarted to a great extent by the "collapsible corporation" rules (§341). Under these rules, the capital gain that would otherwise result from the sale of corporate stock, the liquidation of a corporation or the distribution from a corporation in excess of its earnings and profits becomes ordinary income.

Keep in mind that if you fall within the collapsible corporation rules of §341, you have ordinary income even if you can show that you could have gotten capital gains in the first place had you never incorporated. That's what the Supreme Court said when it had that contention put before it (*Braunstein,* 374 US 65, 1963). So, you have to watch the technical rules of §341 carefully and then plan accordingly to avoid getting caught in the snare they create for the unwary.

[¶1609.1] How the Collapsible Rules Work

Section 341 defines a "collapsible corporation" as a corporation which is formed or availed of principally to:

☐ (1) Manufacture, construct, or produce property; or
☐ (2) Purchase property which (in the corporation's hands) is inventory, stock in trade, property held primarily for sale to customers, unrealized receivables or fees or §1231(b) assets (trade or business property, see ¶2511) and hold this purchased property for less than 3 years; or
☐ (3) Hold stock in a corporation so formed or availed of, with a view to:

(a) Having the shareholders sell or exchange the stock (in liquidation or otherwise) or having a distribution made to the shareholders before the corporation realizes a substantial part of the taxable income to be derived from the property and

(b) Having the shareholders realize gain attributable to the property.

There is a presumption that a corporation is collapsible if at the time of the sale, exchange or distribution the fair market value of its §341 assets (set forth in (2) above) is:

(1) 50% or more of the fair market value of its total assets, excluding cash, obligations which are capital assets (includes government obligations described in §1221(5)) and stock in another corporation and

(2) 120% or more of the adjusted basis of its §341 assets. But the absence of these conditions will not give rise to a presumption that the corporation was not collapsible.

Gain realized by a shareholder with respect to his stock in a collapsible corporation won't be subjected to the ordinary income rates by reason of §341 unless:

(1) The shareholder owned (directly or indirectly) more than 5% in value of the outstanding stock of the corporation at any time after the commencement of the manufacture, construction or production of the property or at any time after the purchase of the property. For this purpose, the constructive ownership rules apply: Taxpayer is treated as owning the stock owned by his family, including his or her spouse, lineal descendants; their spouses, ancestors, brothers and sisters of whole or half blood and their spouses.

(2) More than 70% of the gain is attributable to the property so manufactured, constructed, produced or purchased.

(3) The gain is realized within three years following the completion of such manufacture, construction, production, or purchase.

[¶1609.2] Relief Provisions—Section 341(e)

Section 341(e) was added to the collapsible provisions in 1958 to take out of the reach of the collapsible rules those cases where insubstantial amounts of ordinary income would be converted to capital gain.

For example, in the simple situation where the only property held by the corporation would qualify for capital gains treatment if sold by the company (i.e., an apartment house it built and on which it was now collecting rent from tenants), Congress decided there was no point in applying the collapsible rules and permitted the stockholders to cash in on any appreciation on the building at capital gain rates by either selling their stock or liquidating the corporation. But special provisions were tacked on to these §341(e) "relief" provisions to prevent dealers in property from using this provision to pick up capital gain on items held by a corporation, which, if held by the dealers, would be property on which they'd realize ordinary income.

Under §341(e), if the unrealized appreciation of "ordinary income" assets of the corporation is not more than 15% of the corporation's net worth (on a market value basis), you can collapse the corporation and get capital gain. You can either (1) sell your stock, (2) have a complete liquidation, (3) have the corporation sell assets followed by a liquidation and avoid double taxation under §337 or (4) have a one-month liquidation under §333 (avoiding recognition of gain except as to earnings and profits and cash and securities).

"Ordinary income" assets are those assets which, if sold at a gain by the corporation, would result in ordinary income to the corporation. If a shareholder owns more than 20% of the corporation's stock, ordinary income assets of the corporation also include those corporate assets which, if held by that shareholder and sold by him, would result in ordinary income to him. This provision is aimed at dealers who use separate corporations.

But as to securities held by a corporation, they do not become ordinary income assets merely because a securities dealer is a more-than-20% stockholder. If the dealer holds his stock in the corporation in his investment account as provided in §1236(a) (which lets dealers in securities segregate securities held for investment and treat those segregated securities as investments), then the securities held by the corporation do not become ordinary income assets.

In some cases, the corporation will not qualify for the special rule if transactions in similar corporations are carried out by stockholders owning more than 5% of the corporation's stock.

[¶1609.3] Relief Provisions—Section 341(f)

A stockholder selling stock in what would otherwise be a collapsible corporation can get capital gains if the corporation consents to pick up taxable income when it disposes of its "Subsection (f) assets." These assets, which are not capital assets, are owned by the corporation on the date the stock is sold (or on which the corporation has an option at that date). Included here too, however, are land and any other interest in real estate (except a security interest) and unrealized receivables and fees.

For the provision to apply, the corporation has to file a consent with IRS to be taxed when it disposes of the Subsection (f) property. And the stock has to be sold within six months of that consent. (Where the corporation owns 5% of the value of stock in another corporation, or there is a chain of corporations connected by the 5%-ownership requirement, all the corporations have to file consents within the six-month period.)

The gain taxable as ordinary income to the corporation is the difference between (1) the sale price (if there's a sale or exchange) or the market value (on any other disposition) and (2) the adjusted basis of the asset.

Normally when a corporation makes a distribution in liquidation—partial or full—it realizes no income even though the property distributed is worth more than its basis (except to the extent that depreciation recapture applies), see §336. Now, if the consent was filed, the corporation will have to pick up the gain (ordinary income if the asset distributed is held for sale to customers, for example, capital gain if it is a depreciable asset used in the business—i.e., a §1231 asset). Where there is a §1231 asset distributed and say §1245 (depreciation recapture) applies too, first, so much of the gain that §1245 applies to will be taxable as ordinary income and then any remaining gain will be taxable as capital gain under §341(f).

Just as in the case of a distribution in liquidation, gain will also be recognized on distributions of in-kind dividends of property owned by the corporation when a consent was filed under §341(f).

Corporate consent is made by means of a statement, signed by any officer duly authorized to act on behalf of the corporation. The statement must contain the names, addresses and taxpayer account numbers of any corporations coming within the 5%-stock-ownership rule referred to above. The statement is to be filed with the District Director with whom the corporation files its tax return. The stockholder who sells his stock should attach a copy of the corporate consent to his tax return on which he claims capital gain treatment on the sale of the stock (TIR-621).

Buyer Better Beware: When a buyer acquires stock in a corporation, he should keep in mind that a consent may have been filed under §341(f). Apparently, it could be filed without the buyer's knowing it. In the usual case, presumably he'll know that, as part of the transaction, the corporation is filing a consent. But in some cases, if he doesn't ask, he may not be told. Then, some years later, he may be in for a big, unpleasant surprise.

[¶1609.4] Getting Around the Collapsible Corporation Trap

Here is a rundown on some of the moves that can be taken to avoid collapsibility and get capital gain treatment.

□ ***Stock Ownership Not High Enough:*** The rules do not apply if after commencement of construction, you do not own more than 5% of the value of the corporation's stock. This defense by itself should exempt most shareholders of widely held corporations.

□ ***Gain Attributable to Noncollapsible Property:*** If at least 30% of the recognized gain is attributable to noncollapsible property, collapsible status may be avoided (§341(d)(2)). This rule is most useful because collapsibility may be avoided where the corporation has more than one property and a substantial amount of income is realized from one of them. Here are two examples of how this works:

Example (1): A corporation owning two commercial buildings on separate tracts is collapsed at a time when $80,000 out of a possible $200,000 total rental income is realized from one building and nothing (out of a possible $300,000) is received on the other which was just completed. If 40% constitutes a "substantial" realization of income, the first building constitutes a noncollapsible asset. And if a sale of the stock yields a gain of $475,000, with $175,000 (after expenses) attributable to the noncollapsible asset, then the 30% rule is satisfied.

Example (2): If, however, the two buildings in example (1) were physically connected, on a single tract and were rented to a single commercial tenant, they might constitute an integrated property so that with only 16% of the total income recognized ($80,000/$500,000) the entire property would probably be deemed "collapsible," and the 30% rule would have no application.

Note: IRS has held that land and the improvements thereon are a single property so that in most cases involving land and buildings, the 30% rule would not help (*Rev. Rul. 68-476,* CB 1968-2, 139).

□ ***Right Timing:*** The rules do not apply if gain is realized by the shareholder after the expiration of three years following the completion of construction of the property.

Note: While routine repairs would not constitute "construction" for purposes of §341

(*Rev. Rul. 63-114*, CB 1963-1, 74), substantial improvements would prolong completion of the activity and thus the running of the three-year waiting period.

☐ ***Sale of Assets:*** Where the corporation is thought to be collapsible, it may be best to have the corporation sell its assets and then liquidate. If the corporation is in fact collapsible, the corporation will presumably pay a capital gains tax on the sale, and you will have to pay a capital gains tax on the liquidation on the amount that's left.

☐ ***Tax-Free Reorganization:*** The adverse results of a collapsible situation can also be avoided by a tax-free reorganization, since the collapsible rules do not extend to transactions in which there is no recognized gain.

☐ ***Multiple Entities:*** When you intend to develop more than one property, it may be advantageous to incorporate each property separately. In this way, the favorable three-year rule can be applied on an individual basis. What's more, if an unfavorable determination is made with regard to one property, it will not infect other properties. However, a single corporation may be preferable where you want to keep the gain above the 30% limit so as to come within this exception.

☐ ***Subchapter S Election:*** If a potentially collapsible corporation has an office building or other §1231 asset as its principal asset, electing Subchapter S treatment may avoid §341 consequences. If the corporation sells the assets and distributes the proceeds to the shareholders in liquidation, the gain on the sale passes through to the shareholders as a long-term capital gain.

☐ ***Using Two Holding Companies to Avoid Collapsible Rules:*** You can't avoid the collapsible rules by using a corporation (other than the corporation manufacturing, constructing, producing or purchasing collapsible assets) to hold the stock of a collapsible corporation. Section 341 provides that such a holding company is also a collapsible corporation. However, since the Section only speaks of one such holding company, it might be possible to avoid it by the use of two holding companies—the first holding company holds the stock of the collapsible corporation, and the second holding company holds the stock of the first holding company. Note that where the collapsible rules have been applied to the liquidated subsidiary, they won't be again applied upon liquidation of the parent (*Rev. Rul., 56-50,* CB 1956-1, 174).

[¶1610] HOW TO AVOID OR DEFER CAPITAL GAINS TAX

If you own property which has increased in value, you might get money without selling and save taxes at the same time. If you do sell, the transaction may be arranged to minimize or postpone the tax burden.

You must move with caution, but there are these possibilities: (1) borrow money on your property and then incorporate; (2) place property under option agreement which defers realization of gain; (3) use escrow arrangement; (4) lease property instead of selling it; (5) work out a tax-free exchange; (6) use installment and deferred payment sales.

[¶1610.1] Borrow Money on Your Property

This can usually be done by executing a bond or note secured by a mortgage; the funds you receive from the mortgagee will not create any tax liability.

Where property has appreciated in value after purchase, this is a good way of acquiring monies which represent a portion of the appreciation without tax consequence. For example, assume the real estate cost $20,000 but is now worth $100,000. If a mortgage loan is negotiated for $80,000, nothing has occurred to create any tax liability; and, at the same time, you have received much of the benefit of this appreciation.

After placing a mortgage on the property, you can form a corporation and transfer the property to the corporation for its stock in a tax-free transfer (§351). The basis of the stock received will be the basis of the property transferred reduced by the amount of the mortgage indebtedness (§358(a), 358(c)). Of course, gain will be recognized on a later sale or exchange of stock.

Note: Where the mortgage indebtedness is in excess of the basis of the property, caution must be observed since you will have taxable gain on the excess of the mortgage loan over your basis (§357(a), 357(c)).

Assume that real estate or other property cost $10,000 but has appreciated to a value of $15,000. You can borrow up to $10,000 against the property and transfer the property to the corporation subject to the mortgage without paying any tax. If you borrow $15,000, you have a $5,000 gain to report on the transfer. The nature of the gain will depend on whether the property was a capital or noncapital asset. Note that your basis for the stock will be zero since your original basis of $10,000 is first increased by your gain of $5,000 and then decreased by the mortgage of $15,000 on the property (§358).

Suppose the mortgage debt is less than the basis of the property. The corporation's acquisition of the property subject to that liability (or the assumption of the mortgage by the corporation) will *not* be treated as money received by the transferor stockholder. So, he will not ordinarily have any income on the transfer. But he *can* have income if the principal purpose of the corporate acquisition or assumption is avoidance of federal income tax or was not for a bona fide business purpose (§357(a)(b)).

[¶1610.2] Placing the Property Under Option

There are several methods frequently used to sell and postpone tax. You might get an option payment. Usually, this provides for forfeiture of the option price if the option is not exercised. If the option is exercised, the option price is credited to the purchase price. Options are practically a down payment. But there is no income when they are received. Unless the option period expires, you do not know how it will finally be applied. If it is forfeited, you then have ordinary income. If it is exercised, it is added to the sale price. But a word of caution: You want to be sure the option contract states what will happen if it is forfeited and if it is exercised. Otherwise, you will be taxed as soon as you receive the option payment (Reg. §1.1234-1).

Or, you can lease properties with an option to buy. You start out by leasing the property to the buyer. Also, you agree on a purchase price if and when there is a sale. Then, give the lessee an option either to buy after a period of time or to extend the lease term. To get that option, the lessee has to pay a stated amount. But the amount he pays for the option will be applied to the purchase price if he finally agrees to buy before the lease term ends.

You get the payment for the option and have the use of the money. But until the lessee agrees to buy and pays the balance of the purchase price or until the extended lease period runs out, you don't know whether you have received payment for extending the lease term (ordinary income) or partial payment of the purchase price of the property (capital gain after recovery of basis). And until you know, say the Tax Court and the 3rd Circuit, there is no income to report (*Dill*, 294 F.2d 291, CA-3, 1961).

If you try this approach, however, be prepared for a fight from IRS because it announced that it would not follow the Tax Court decision.

Also keep in mind that the courts will treat as sales some forms of leases with options to buy, e.g., where the option price is only nominal or the rental price is larger than normal rentals for the type and value of the property involved. But note that in a situation where a lease did not contain an option to buy—even where the industry practice was to offer the equipment for sale—and the lessee *did in fact* buy the equipment, the Eighth Circuit still held it was a lease (*Western Contracting Corp.*, 271 F.2d 694, CA-8, 1959, rev'g TC Memo 1958-77).

[¶1610.3] Use an Escrow Arrangement

You can intentionally postpone delivery of title. Thus, each side must still perform his side of the contract. In the case of real property, the sale usually occurs on the closing or settlement date. Receiving a down payment or earnest money does not of itself fix the date of sale. So, you will not be taxed at that time if title or possession does not pass. A true escrow arrangement with some of the purchase price set aside to be paid to the seller together with the balance of consideration at the closing date provided seller furnishes a marketable title and otherwise complies with the contract will defer the tax on the entire transaction until the closing or settlement date. But if you give possession to the buyer before title passes, chances are the sale, for tax purposes, will be treated as having taken place at the time you gave possession.

You might use this arrangement where your buyer wants to settle the deal now, but you don't want the gain this year. Although the buyer doesn't get possession, he gets peace of mind, and you get the gain in the year you want. In this situation you can also consider an installment sale (see ¶1610.6).

[¶1610.4] Long-Term Leases of Depreciable Property

If you lease rather than sell, you preserve your right to take depreciation deductions. That may often give you a better tax position than a sale of your property. For example, the depreciation deduction may offset rental income in full. That means a nontaxable return. If you sell at a gain, you'll have to pay an immediate tax on the net proceeds. Before selling, work out the mathematics of your particular case. (See also, Sections X and XV.)

[¶1610.5] Exchange as a Substitute for Sale and Purchase

If an asset has gained value and you sell to buy something else, your capital is impaired by capital gain tax. But an exchange is tax free, if both before and after the swap, we have property of like kind held for productive use in business or for investment (§1031).

You can have tax freedom (avoid tax on gain if desired) if you fit into the following:

(1) The property is business or investment property but is not part of your stock in trade, inventory property or securities.

(2) The property received is property of a like kind.

(3) The property received is held for business use or investment.

Remember: Not only is the tax on gain postponed when you have an exchange, but a loss is not recognized either. So, if you want a current loss deduction, *avoid* a tax-free exchange; make an outright sale. The tax-free exchange provisions of §1031 are *not* elective. If you don't want them to apply, make sure you avoid the elements of an exchange—e.g., don't take back like-kind property.

Although you need a like-kind exchange to avoid a tax, you can have an exchange that is partly tax free and partly taxable. For example, if you take back like-kind property plus cash, you'll be taxed on only the portion of the gain that does not exceed the cash received. Here's how that works:

To be tax free, the exchange must be even; that is, no boot (such as cash) involved. If boot is taken, then the gain, up to the amount of the boot, is taxable. The gain beyond boot would not be taxed. If boot is given, no loss can be taken for the boot. This is regarded simply as additional investment in property of the kind exchanged (§1031(b)(c)).

Finally, where boot is involved, don't forget to consider the effect of depreciation recapture under §1245 or §1250 (which will also apply to the boot). (See also Section X.)

[¶1610.6] Installment Sales

On casual sales of personal property for more than $1,000 or the sale of any real property, the sale price may be received over a period of years. If not more than 30% of the selling price is received in the year of sale, the income from the sale can be spread over the period of collection by electing the installment method of reporting income. And if the gain on the sale is capital gain, the installment sale method of reporting will preserve the capital gain treatment of the portion of each installment that is treated as taxable gain. (See also, Section XII.)

SECTION XVII

GETTING PROFITS OUT OF THE CORPORATION

As we have seen, one of the key reasons for doing business in the corporate form is to accumulate corporate profits in the business at a lower tax rate than an individual businessman would have to pay. For most purposes, leaving the profits in the business will do no harm, since that is where they will be most useful; in time, however, every shareholder will face the problem of getting these profits out of the business and into his own pocket. Of course, he will want to do this at the lowest possible tax cost. He will be faced, then, with several alternatives. The most obvious is simply to sell out the business, either by selling his stock or liquidating and then selling the assets. Liquidations, you will remember, were discussed in Section XVI; selling a business will be discussed in the next section.

In this section, then, the other alternatives for taking out profits are discussed: they are, primarily, redemptions and dividends. (The other main alternative, which is the use of compensation payments, has already been discussed in Section VII.)

[¶1701] REDEMPTION OF STOCK

A redemption of stock is simply the repurchase of the stock of a shareholder by the corporation. A redemption may or may not constitute a dividend, depending on the facts and circumstances of a particular case. In almost every case it is desirable to have the redemption *not* constitute a dividend, since a dividend is normally taxable to the shareholder as ordinary income.

When stock is redeemed, short of a complete liquidation, dividend treatment may be avoided if the distribution falls into one of the following categories:

□ (1) It is not essentially equivalent to a taxable dividend (§302(b)(1)).
□ (2) It reduces by 20% the interest of a person who is not the controlling shareholder after the distribution—the ''disproportionate'' redemption (§302(b)(2)).
□ (3) It terminates the interest of a shareholder (§302(b)(3)).
□ (4) It does not exceed death charges of an estate whose holdings meet the prescribed percentage of the net or gross estate (§303).

☐ (5) It is not in redemption of §306 stock.
☐ (6) It qualifies as a distribution in partial liquidation (§346).

If the redemption falls into any of the above categories, the shareholder will realize capital gain on the transaction.

[¶1701.1] Distributions Not Essentially Equivalent to a Dividend

The Regulations, §1.302-2, say that whether a distribution is essentially equivalent to a dividend depends on all the facts and circumstances of each case. All pro rata distributions when there is only one class of stock add up to dividends.

Most of the criteria for determining this question were established under the 1939 Code. The courts still rely on many of them, since they take the position that Congress intended the same criteria to be applied under the 1954 Code. Here are some of the criteria relied on by the courts:

☐ Did the corporation adopt a plan of contraction of its business and did the transaction actually result in a contraction? (Section 346 now specifically addresses itself to that problem.)
☐ Did the initiative for the distribution come from the corporation or the stockholders?
☐ Was the proportionate ownership of stock changed? (Two sections now address themselves to that point: §302(b)(2), the disproportionate redemption rule; §302(b)(3), the total redemption rule.)
☐ What is the dividend-paying history of the corporation?
☐ Was the distribution out of accumulated earnings,or all, or part, from capital? Of course, when distributions exceed accumulated earnings, the excess cannot be taxable as a dividend.
☐ Was there a bona fide business purpose for the distribution?
☐ Is the net effect of the dividend the distribution of earnings to the shareholders?

It is useful to examine some specific distribution situations to see when they were considered to be essentially equivalent to a dividend and when they were not.

Not Equivalent to a Dividend

☐ *Redemption of part of nonvoting stock*, limited and preferred as to dividends and liquidation, owned by a stockholder who owns no other stock in the corporation (Reg. §1.302-2(a)).
☐ *Redemption of sole stockholder's preferred stock* followed by a tax-free "B" reorganization (stock for stock) under §368(a)(1)(B). The combined effect of the redemption and reorganization resulted in a substantial change of interest and redemption was not the equivalent of a dividend.
☐ *Pro rata redemption of 20% of preferred stock* with large dividend arrearages and voting rights (because of the arrearages) when 50 of the 54 stockholders also owned common stock. Those who owned both classes of stock had widely varying proportions of each class. And no one person or family group had more than 25% voting power of the corporation (*Rev. Rul. 56-485*, CB 1956-2, 176.) Compare (*Rev. Rul. 59-258*, CB 1959-1, 105).
☐ *Redemption of estate's stock* still left the estate the constructive owner of substantial stock through attribution of its beneficiaries. But, as a practical matter, the estate lost control of the corporation since the executor and the beneficiaries through whom the estate had constructive ownership did not see eye to eye on the conduct of the business (*Squier*, 35 TC 950, 1961).
☐ *Redemption of a large portion of father's stock* still left him constructive owner of 97% of the stock because his son owned the rest. But the purpose of redeeming the father's stock was to

transfer control of the corporation to the son since the two could not agree on running the business (*Parker*, TC Memo 1961-176).

□ *Pro rata redemption of part of the two stockholders' stock* was first step in complete redemption of one stockholder's stock. After the pro rata redemption, the capital of the corporation was sufficiently reduced so that an outsider who was to buy a half interest in the business could afford to buy the remaining shares of one of the stockholders (*Carey*, 289 F.2d 531, CA-8, 1961).

Equivalent to a Dividend

□ *Transfer of Stock in Exchange for Cash and Stock of Second Corporation:* The taxpayer owned 55% of White Corporation stock and 70% of Grey Corporation stock. He transferred all the White stock (cost, $50,000) to Grey Corporation for $50,000 in cash plus $50,000 of Grey stock. After the transaction, he held 80% of Grey's stock. It was held that there was no meaningful change in shareholder position because he had effective control of a majority of the shares of both corporations. Neither was it a legitimate business purpose (*Haserot*, 399 F. 2d 828, CA-6, 1968, *aff'g* 46 TC 864, 1966).

□ *Failure to reduce proportionate ownership substantially*—directly or constructively—made the distributions essentially equivalent to a dividend even though the following business purposes for the redemption were present:

□ *Redemption plan to improve the corporation's credit status* (*Sorem*, 40 TC 206).

□ *To qualify for consolidated returns* by having one buy the stock of the other from the stockholder who controlled both companies (*Kerr*, 326 F.2d 255, CA-9, 1964, *aff'g* 38 TC 723, 1962).

□ *To eliminate cumulative dividends at high rate* by redeeming the preferred no longer needed (since preferred was originally issued to accommodate needs of one stockholder and that stockholder was no longer a stockholder) (*Ballenger*, 301 F.2d 192, CA-4, 1962).

□ *To "clean up" open account indebtedness* owed to the corporation by stockholder (*Bradbury*, 298 F.2d 111, CA-1, 1962).

□ *To redeem stock held by estate* to give it needed liquidity (*Lewis*, 35 TC 71, 1960) even if pursuant to a buy-sell agreement between the deceased and the corporation (*Rev. Rul. 56-103*, CB 1956-1, 159).

□ *To give the stockholders sufficient funds* to pay for stock they bought from a stockholder who left the business because of disagreements as to management policies (*Rev. Rul. 57-353*, CB 1957-2, 223).

Note: Redemption by One-Man Corporation Is a Dividend Despite Business Purpose. When a corporation wants to borrow money it's quite common for the lender to require additional capital contributions by the stockholders. The stockholders are usually reluctant to put in more capital because they may not be able to take it out at a later date without being taxed. Some courts have allowed a subsequent tax-free redemption where the capital contribution was principally for business reasons. (See *Morris Comess*, 309 F. Supp. 1215, DC Va., 1970, and the cases cited therein.)

However, the Supreme Court says that a business purpose is not enough in some cases. Where the net effect of the redemption is in effect a pro rata distribution the business purpose does not remove the dividend taint, says the Supreme Court. To qualify for preferred treatment under §302, says the Court, a redemption must result in a meaningful reduction of the shareholder's proportionate interest in the corporation (*Davis*, 397 U.S. 301, 1970, *rev'g* 408 F.2d 1138, CA-6, 1969).

[¶1701.2] Disproportionate Redemptions

The disproportionate redemption test (§302(b)(2)) is tricky, and it's important to understand clearly the rules and make accurate computations. The redemption does not constitute a dividend if it comes within the following rules:

☐ (1) After the redemption, you own less than 50% of the combined voting power of all classes of voting stock (even if you meet the 80% rules in (2), the redemption doesn't qualify unless you meet this 50% rule, too).

☐ (2) After the redemption, the ratio of your voting stock to all the voting stock of the corporation is less than 80% of the ratio of your voting stock to all the voting stock of the corporation before the redemption. In addition, if you own any nonvoting common stock, the 80% rule applies to it, too (and if there's more than one class of common, the 80% rule is figured on the basis of fair market value).

The constructive ownership rules apply in determining stock ownership before and after the redemption.

To illustrate how the 80% rule works, assume that Green owns 40 shares in the G-W Corporation. There are 100 shares outstanding. That means Green owns 40% of the stock. After the redemption, he has to own less than 32% of the outstanding stock (80% of 40% is 32%; and he has to end up owning less than 80%).

Here's a formula to find how many shares must be redeemed to leave Green with less than 32% of the outstanding stock after redemption.

Assume: A is the number of shares owned by Green;
B is the number of shares outstanding before the redemption;
C is the percentage of the outstanding stock that is 80% of the percentage owned by Green before the redemption (if this percentage is more than 50%, then reduce this figure to 50%), and X is the number of shares to be redeemed.

Then, our formula would be: $A - X = C\ (B - X)$.

Applying our own figures, we get: $40 - X = .32\ (100 - X)$.

$$X = 11.76$$

(11.76 was only carried out to two decimal places. If necessary, you may have to carry it several more places.) Since redemption of 11.76 shares would leave Green with a shade over 32% and he must have less than 32%, we must redeem something more than 11.76 shares. Assume we redeem whole shares. So, Green will have 12 shares redeemed.

Proof of the Computation: If Green has 12 shares redeemed, the outstanding shares of the corporation are reduced to 88. Thirty-two percent of 88 shares is 28.16. Since Green will have only 28 shares left after the 12 shares are redeemed, he will have less than 32% of the outstanding voting shares of the company, and he will meet the disproportionate redemption test.

Note: Watch Out for Constructive Ownership! In determining the stockholder's ownership for purposes of the 80%-50% test, stock of which he is deemed to be constructively the owner must be attributed to him. These rules can't be circumvented by arranging the redemptions for related stockholders in different years or by redemptions and reissuances as part of a plan.

There are five classes of persons or entities whose holdings will be attributed to a shareholder whose stock is retired (§318):

☐ (1) *Members of the family:* These include spouse, children, grandchildren, and parents but do not include brothers and sisters.
☐ (2) *Partnerships and estates:* Stock owned directly or indirectly by or for a partnership or estate is considered as being owned directly and proportionately by the partners and beneficiaries. Stock owned directly or indirectly by or for a partner or beneficiary of an estate is considered as being owned by the partnership or estate.
☐ (3) *Trusts:* Stock owned, directly or indirectly by or for a trust is considered as being owned proportionately by the beneficiaries and stock owned directly or indirectly by or for a beneficiary is considered as being owned by the trust. Stock owned by a beneficiary who has less than a 5% interest in the trust will not be attributed to the trust. The grantor of a reversionary trust owns the stock owned by the trust and vice versa.
☐ (4) *Corporations:* If 50% or more in value of the stock of a corporation is owned, directly or indirectly, by or for any person, then that person is considered as owning the stock owned, directly or indirectly, by or for that corporation in the ratio of the value of his stock to that of all the outstanding stock and the corporation is considered as owning the stock by or for that person.
☐ (5) *Options:* If a person has an option, he will be considered as owning the stock.

An entity is considered as owning all the stock of the beneficiary, while the individual is considered as owning his proportionate share of the stock held by the entity.

Family ownership rules are not piled on each other. That is, a wife's holdings will be attributed to the husband but not to her husband's father. All other constructive ownerships are cumulative.

Example: The stock of X Corporation is owned as follows: 50% by A; 30% by A's wife; 10% by A's son; 10% by A's father. A is considered as owning all the stock.

Let us assume that ABC partnership owns 30% of the stock of Y corporation. A, B, and C each have a one-third interest in the partnership. Thus, A is considered as owning 10% of the stock of Y corporation. Let us assume that A individually owns 20% of the stock of the corporation. Under the rules, the partnership would be considered as owning 50% of the stock of the corporation, and A, 30% of the stock.

When stock is attributed to a partnership, estate, trust, or corporation from a partner, beneficiary, or 50%-or-more shareholder, the stock is not again attributed to another partner, beneficiary, or 50%-or-more shareholder (§318(a)(5)).

[¶1701.3] Complete Termination of Interest

The redemption of stock will not result in a taxable dividend if it retires all the stock owned by a taxpayer (§302(b)(3); 302(c)(2)). In this situation, a redemption of a shareholder's entire interest is treated as a capital gain even though there is a family attribution if: (1) The retired stockholder retains no interest in the corporation other than as a creditor (but he is not a creditor if payment of his obligations depends upon amount or certainty of the corporation's earnings (Reg. §1.302-4(d)). An interest includes remaining as an officer, director, or employee or having an agent on the board of directors to see that the payout agreement is carried out. (2) He does not acquire an interest except by bequest or inheritance within ten years from the date of redemption. (3) He files an agreement to notify the Treasury of any such acquisition.

Despite complete retirement of a stock interest, however, we may have a taxable dividend if:

☐ (1) Any part of the stock redeemed was acquired from a person whose ownership can be attributed to the distributee under the constructive ownership rule. This rule is intended to close the loophole where a husband gives his wife half of his stock and then the wife's stock is redeemed.
☐ (2) Any person owns (at the time of distribution) stock, the ownership of which is attributable under rules of constructive ownership to the distributee, and such person acquired the stock directly or indirectly from the distributee within the last ten years unless the stock acquired is also redeemed in the same transaction. This closes the loophole of the husband giving his wife some stock and causing his stock to be redeemed while his wife's remains outstanding.

These so-called look-back rules do not apply if the previous acquisition or disposition of stock did not have tax avoidance as one of its principal purposes.

If a husband and wife own all the stock of a company, we cannot get a capital gain redemption by reducing the ownership of one of them by 20% in a disproportionate redemption discussed in ¶1801.2. This is because the constructive ownership rules will still give them 100% ownership. We can sell some stock to outsiders and make it possible to reduce the family ownership by 20%, but we will still have to reduce the family ownership to less than 50% of the voting control. We can keep voting control in the family by selling stock to a brother or someone else who is not a lineal descendant and then redeeming enough stock to bring the combined ownership of husband and wife down by 20% and below a 50% voting power. This approach seems likely to achieve practical objectives in only a limited number of situations.

Either the husband or the wife can be bought out at capital gain rates if this procedure is followed:

☐ (1) Redeem all the stock owned by either the husband or wife.
☐ (2) Have the retired stockholder sever all connections with the company as an officer, employee, or director.
☐ (3) A creditor relationship may be retained; and, thus, the stock may be redeemed with notes, debentures, or bonds.
☐ (4) Don't have any of these corporate obligations convertible into stock.
☐ (5) Don't have any security provisions in the stock retirement deal that might return the stock to the retired party. If the stock did not come back within 10 years, we'd stand to lose the capital gain treatment.
☐ (6) See that the retired party does not reacquire any stock in the company during the 10 years after the redemption except by bequest or inheritance.
☐ (7) If, within 10 years prior to the redemption, the retired party made any gifts of stock to a spouse or ancestors or descendants, redeem that stock, too.
☐ (8) The retired party must not have received any gifts from the remaining related stockholders within 10 years prior to redemption.

We may carry through a complete stock retirement without being concerned about these prior gifts if it can be shown that income tax avoidance was not the principal purpose of the gift. The shifting of stock to members of the family in order to get lower income tax rates will not make a complete redemption taxable as a dividend. Nor will transfers aimed at death tax savings. It would appear that the only gifts that would make a complete redemption taxable as a dividend would be those intended to distribute holdings in a way that will facilitate a capital gain distribution from the corporation.

[¶1701.4] Redemptions of Stock to Pay Death Taxes

Where a good portion of an estate consists of stock in a closely held corporation, redemption of the stock may often be necessary to raise money to pay the estate tax. Notwithstanding the fact that there is a buy-sell agreement calling for the redemption of the stock by the company, the redemption can still be a distribution essentially equivalent to a dividend where the disproportionate redemption or complete redemption requirements are not met.

In these cases, §303 can come to the rescue. Where §303 applies, the redemption is not treated as a dividend. And since the basis of the decedent's stock is stepped up to date-of-death value, there is likely to be no gain at all on the redemption.

To qualify under this section, the stock of a corporation must: (1) be included in the decedent's estate; (2) constitute either more than 35% of the value of the gross estate or 50% of the value of the taxable estate; (3) be redeemed for an amount not in excess of the total estate tax liability plus funeral and administration expenses. The redemption has to be made within 3 years and 90 days of the due date of the estate tax return or when the return is filed if it is filed after the due date (*Rev. Rul. 73-204*, CB 1973-1, 170), or within 60 days after a Tax Court decision fixing the death tax obligation becomes final. The Tax Court proceeding must be bona fide. A petition for a redetermination that is entered solely for the purpose of extending the period will not suffice.

Note that while the intention of §303 was to provide a method of acquiring funds from the corporation to pay death taxes and funeral and administrative expenses, it is not limited for those purposes. Under the provisions of §303, redemptions can be made of stock held by specific legatees, donees of gifts in contemplation of death, trustees of inter vivos trusts, and any others holding in such manner that the stock was included in the gross estate (Reg. §1.303-2(f)). Where, however, the holder of the stock acquired it as a transferee from a qualified person, the Regs say redemptions from him do not qualify for §303.

Sometimes an estate will have stock in two corporations. Neither stockholding may meet the 35% or 50% test; but taken together, they can meet the test. The law provides that stock of two or more corporations is treated as stock of one corporation if more than 75% in value of the outstanding stock of each corporation is included in the gross estate (Reg. §1.303-2(a)). Here's an example:

Estate of decedent presents the following facts:
Gross Estate — $1,500,000
Net Estate — $750,000

Stock of Corporation Includible in Gross Estate

	Value of Stock	*Percentage of Ownership of Stock Includible*
Corporation A	$300,000	50
Corporation B	300,000	100
Corporation C	250,000	100

Corporations B and C but not corporation A would, for the purposes of §303, be treated as stock of a single corporation. In consequence, a redemption of the stock of corporation A would not qualify under §303 since the value of the stock of corporations includible in the gross estate is less than 35% of the gross estate ($525,000) and also less than 50% of the net estate ($375,000). In the case of corporations B and C, a redemption of the stock of either would qualify since the value of both corporations, treated as a single corporation includible in the gross estate ($550,000), exceeds 35% of the gross estate ($525,000) and also since such value exceeds 50% of the net estate ($375,000).

For the purpose of the 75% requirement, stock that represents the surviving spouse's interest in community property is treated as having been included in the decedent's estate.

A §303 redemption is usually a much better arrangement than a sale of the same stock to an outsider, since using a redemption will decrease the proportional ownership less. For example, assume Brown owned 8,000 of the 10,000 shares of a close corporation; the other 2,000 shares are owned equally by Black and White. Assume also that Brown's estate must sell 2,000 shares to pay federal estate taxes and funeral and administration expenses. Here's the effect of the sale of these shares to the named buyers:

Stock Owned by	*Before Sale*	*After Sale to Outsider*	*After Sale to Black & White*	*After Sale to Corporation*
Brown	8,000 – 80%	6,000 – 60%	6,000 – 60%	6,000 – 75%
Black	1,000 – 10%	1,000 – 10%	2,000 – 20%	1,000 – 12½%
White	1,000 – 10%	1,000 – 10%	2,000 – 20%	1,000 – 12½%
Outsider		2,000 – 20%		

From this, we can see that redemption by the corporation preserves for the decedent's family a greater proportionate interest in the business.

For the taxable year in which a stockholder died or any taxable year thereafter, a corporation may accumulate earnings for purposes of redeeming a stockholder's shares to pay death taxes. This means that many small corporations can accumulate earnings with less pressure from IRS or minority stockholders to make dividend distributions.

Here is a checklist of some of the considerations to keep in mind in planning for §303 redemptions:

☐ (1) We may want to recapitalize so that the redemption of stock to meet estate tax obligations does not result in loss of control over the corporation. Thus if the person whose estate is being planned owns only 51% of the voting common stock, we may want to create a preferred class that can be redeemed without resulting in a loss of voting control. This can be done during life or the executor can effect a recapitalization after death, and still redeem the new stock free of tax as a dividend. However, the determination of whether a distribution is essentially equivalent to a dividend is made without regard to §303.

☐ (2) We no longer need be concerned about splitting corporations, lest we thereby fail to qualify for a tax-free redemption, as long as 75% ownership of the stock in each corporation is retained.

☐ (3) If we find that the stock of no one corporation is likely to meet the percentage requirements and the person whose estate is being planned owns bonds in the corporation or a less-than-75% interest in another corporation, we may be able to qualify the estate by converting the bonds to stock, by increasing the ownership of one corporation to 75%, or by consolidating the two corporations. The conversion of bonds to stock should be a last resort, because the corporation can pay off the bonds tax free just as well as it can redeem stock. However, if the conversion of bonds to stock will make possible a larger tax-free receipt of cash by the executor than the retirement of the bonds, it may be a wise thing to do.

☐ (4) We may be able to qualify the stock for tax-free redemption by transferring insurance and other property out of the estate by lifetime transfer in order to bring the stock up to the required percentage.

☐ (5) Where there is doubt as to values or the size of the estate tax liability, we will have to defer redemption until it can be determined whether the stock exists in the estate in the required percentages. Where we are not sure about the ultimate estate tax liability, we should take steps to build up sufficient liquidity in the corporation so that it can distribute cash in redemption of stock to meet death tax obligations. This can be done most effectively by carrying insurance on the life of the owner; we can do this if the owner is active in the business and can qualify as a key man.

☐ (6) We should clear away legal and balance sheet restrictions and disabilities to permit a redemption.

☐ (7) We should consider the need for an agreement in which the corporation is committed to redeem stock of a deceased stockholder.

[¶1701.5] Redemptions of §306 Stock

Section 306 stock is stock falling into one of the three following categories:

☐ (1) ***Stock Received as a Dividend:*** Ordinarily, this means preferred stock distributed as a tax-free dividend on common stock and distributed at a time when the corporation had earnings and profits.

☐ (2) ***Stocks Received in a Corporate Reorganization or Division:*** This means stock other than common stock that was distributed in a tax-free reorganization, where the effect of the transaction was the receipt of a stock dividend or where other §306 stock was exchanged in such a transaction.

☐ (3) ***Stock With a Transferred or Substituted Basis:*** This is basically designed to insure that stock that was §306 stock in the hands of a transferor will remain §306 stock in the hands of a transferee who computes his basis by reference to the transferor's basis. Thus, §306 stock included in the estate of a decedent transferor would not be §306 stock in the hands of the legatee, since the legatee gets a new basis under §1014.

In most cases, §306 will apply only to preferred stock issued as a tax-free dividend on common stock, in the so-called ''preferred stock bailout.''

The problem with §306 stock in redemptions is that the proceeds will be taxed as ordinary income, rather than capital gains. In the following cases, a redemption of §306 stock will not produce ordinary income:

☐ (1) If there is a complete redemption of all the stock held in the corporation by a shareholder—a termination of his interest. The rules in ¶1701.3 apply.

☐ (2) If it is redeemed in a partial or complete liquidation of the corporation. The liquidation must meet the requirements discussed in Section XVI.

☐ (3) If the government is satisfied that the distribution or redemption was not in pursuance of a plan having as its principal purpose the avoidance of income tax (*Rev. Rul. 56-116*, CB 1956-1, 164). Since §306 is aimed only at preventing tax avoidance, preferred stock dividends can still be safely declared and the preferred stock later safely redeemed, provided we can prove a legitimate motive. Here are three examples:

(a) Issuance of preferred stock in a merger was held free of the §306 taint where good business reasons for the issuance existed and issuance was not in anticipation of redemption except as required by certain sinking fund provisions (*Rev. Rul. 56-116, supra.*).

(b) Sales of preferred stock issued in a recapitalization were held not subject to the ordinary dividend rates; the transactions were made pursuant to prior agreement with the selling shareholders, who were retiring employees. Here was a consideration other than tax avoidance (*Rev. Rul. 56-223,* CB 1956-1, 162).

(c) A disposition of a fraction of a shareholder's §306 stock together with an equal fraction of his original shares would probably be all right, since tax avoidance would not ordinarily be a feature of such a transaction. However, there are no cases on this point, so it cannot be considered as certain as (a) and (b).

[¶1702] OTHER TAX CONSIDERATIONS IN REDEMPTIONS

Once you have decided to use a redemption, there are certain points you should keep in mind. The following paragraphs discuss some of the better-known considerations and techniques that may prove valuable in a particular case.

[¶1702.1] Using Appreciated Property for Redemption

Under prior law, in general, gain or loss was not recognized to a corporation if it distributed property with respect to its stock. Congress sought to prohibit large corporations from attempting to avoid tax on appreciated property (such as investments, inventory, and business property) by distributing their large portfolios of investments acquired some time ago at prices appreciably below present values.

Now, if a corporation distributes property to a shareholder in redemption of part or all of the shareholder's stock and the property distributed has appreciated in value in the hands of the distributing corporation, gain is to be recognized to the extent of this appreciation (§311).

This rule is inapplicable to distributions made before April 1, 1970, under binding contracts in existence on November 30, 1969, and written offers that were made before December 1, 1969, or are made pursuant to a ruling request filed with IRS or a registration statement filed with the Securities and Exchange Commission before that date. Such offers must not be revocable by their express terms.

The rule is inapplicable also in the following cases:

☐ (1) ***Complete Redemption of Interest:*** A distribution in complete termination of the interest of a shareholder owning at least 10% of the stock.

☐ (2) ***Stock Distribution of Related Corporation:*** A distribution of stock of a business corporation that has not received a substantial part of its assets from the distributing corporation in a §351 transaction and at least 50% or more is owned by the distributing corporation.

☐ (3) ***Stock Distribution Before 12/1/74:*** A distribution made before December 1, 1974, of stock of a business corporation whose assets were acquired on or before November 30, 1969.

☐ (4) ***Distribution Pursuant to Antitrust Laws:*** A distribution of stock or securities made pursuant to a final judgment relating to the antitrust laws.

☐ (5) ***Section 303 Redemption:*** A distribution made in redemption of stock to pay death taxes.

☐ (6) ***Distribution to Private Foundations:*** A redemption of stock described in §537(b)(2)(A) and (B) from private foundations.
☐ (7) ***Mutual Funds and REITs:*** A distribution by these if the distribution in redemption of stock is made on the demand of the stockholders.

[¶1702.2] Installment Payments on Corporate Redemptions

Very often, the payout from the corporation in a complete redemption is made over a period of years. It is understood that IRS insists on the following arrangements in these cases before agreeing that a redemption qualifies under §302(b)(3):

☐ (1) There is a contract, note, or other evidence of indebtedness to the retiring shareholders. Just an account payable on the corporate book apparently is not enough.
☐ (2) The stockholder whose interest is being redeemed must surrender all his shares at the time of the redemption. He can't hold his shares as collateral.
☐ (3) The deal can't be arranged to permit a retired stockholder to recover his stock upon a default of the redemption payments. The debt may be secured, however, by a mortgage on the property of the corporation.
☐ (4) After the redemption, the retiring stockholder may be a creditor of the corporation only as a consequence of the redemption. He may not lend money to the corporation nor become a creditor for any other reason.

Imputed Interest on Installment Payments: Where the payout is to take more than one year, if interest is not called for in the contract (or if called for but at a rate that is too low), interest will be imputed so that part of each installment will consist of interest income (and the corporation will be entitled to an interest deduction). For a complete discussion of the imputed interest rule, see Section XII.

[¶1702.3] Timing the Redemption

Timing can be important when we are dealing with stock redemptions. Suppose, for example, you are sure the redemption will result in a capital gain. Timing the gain to fall in a year when the stockholder has offsetting capital losses can cut or even eliminate your tax altogether. Or suppose you have some doubts about the redemption; you think it should qualify for capital gain treatment but there's a possibility it may be deemed essentially equivalent to a dividend. Timing the redemption to fall in a year of low or no corporate earnings (assuming there's no accumulated income) can cut the dividend or completely eliminate it.

Regardless of when the resolutions and other preliminary actions are taken in connection with the redemption, don't endorse the stock certificates and turn them over to the corporation until the year in which you want the redemption to fall. The Tax Court has ruled that when the certificates are endorsed and turned in is the time the redemption occurs (*Moore,* TC Memo 1961-257).

[¶1702.4] How to Handle Stock Redemption Where It Results in Loss

How does a corporation handle the situation where the redemption results in a loss and it wants the loss to be recognized? A recent case suggests how to do it.

Owens Machinery Co., engaged in the business of selling and servicing heavy construction equipment, was owned by two principal stockholders. When the stockholders had a falling out, it was decided that the stock of Owens's subsidiary (worth about $100,000) plus $25,000 in cash would be distributed to one stockholder for his Owens stock and that Owens would sell particular real estate to the stockholder for $150,000. Owens realized a loss on the redemption and a gain on the sale of the real property. It offset the gain by the loss. IRS said no good: Only that part of the loss attributed to the redemption of stock for cash could be offset against the gain.

The Tax Court allowed the offset of the entire loss. It used a theory, however, that was different from Owens's. Owens had contended that the two transactions—the redemption and the sale of the property—should be treated as a single transaction. The Court said that although each transaction was part of an overall plan designed to separate the two businesses and the interests of the conflicting stockholders, it doesn't follow that the tax consequences should be lumped together. In determining whether there is any gain or loss, each transaction should be treated separately.

When you examine the redemption, however, you can't fragment the stock transaction into a redemption of stock for stock and an exchange of stock for cash. It must be treated as a single exchange of stock for stock and cash. As such, it does not come under §311, said the Court.

Section 311 applies to "distributions with respect to stock." It is used only to refer to distributions without consideration, not to sales for cash and consideration. Since the exchange in this case included both stock and cash, it did not constitute a distribution within §311 (*Owens Machinery Co.,* 54 TC 877, 1970).

What to Do: On the basis of this decision, it seems that any time you have a redemption that would result in a loss, the way to have the loss recognized and to avoid §311 is to use cash in addition to the stock. The cash part of the Owens redemption was substantial, about 25% of the consideration involved in the transaction. The cash used in your deals should be a substantial part of the deal, too.

[¶1703] DIVIDENDS

The payment of dividends is usually considered only as a last resort by shareholders who want to get money out of the corporation. This is because, under the tax law, dividends are doubly damned—the corporation gets no deduction, and the shareholder gets ordinary income treatment. So, dividends are really taxed twice—once at the corporate level, as corporate income, and again at the shareholder level, as ordinary income.

However, dividend payments do not always work out so badly. For example, if the shareholder is incorporated, he will be entitled to deduct 85% of the dividends received in most cases under §243. If the corporation paying the dividends has no earnings and profits, then the dividends will be taxed as a return of capital up to the shareholder's basis, and the excess will be capital gains. To the extent the dividends exceed the corporation's earnings and profits, they will be taxed to the shareholder in the same way. Also, in many cases, stock dividends will not be taxable to the shareholder when he receives them, and if he later sells the stock he will receive capital gains treatment.

The following paragraphs discuss the basic rules involving dividends, some strategies for achieving the best tax treatment, and some pitfalls to avoid.

[¶1703.1] Earnings and Profits

"Earnings and profits" as used in the Code is a term of art. Its main importance is in relation to corporate distributions, since the tax treatment of the distributions depends on the corporation's earnings and profits. There are two kinds—current earnings and profits, and earnings and profits accumulated since 1913.

[¶1703.2] Current Earnings and Profits

Current earnings and profits are determined as of the close of the current year; the amount of earnings and profits on the date of distribution is immaterial (§316).

Suppose, for example, a corporation with no accumulated earnings at the beginning of the year has a deficit of $150,000 at the halfway mark. Nevertheless, it pays a dividend of that amount. If the deficit is wiped out by the end of the year and a surplus of at least $150,000 rolled up, the midyear distribution is a taxable dividend, even though there was a deficit when made. And the earnings at the year end are $150,000, despite the distribution.

A deficit for prior years doesn't reduce the earnings and profits for the current year. Thus, a corporation with $350,000 deficit for prior years but $100,000 earnings in the current year has $100,000 of earnings available for dividends.

If the corporation has earnings, every distribution is deemed made out of them and from the most recent earnings first. Corporations can't arbitrarily allocate a distribution to capital in order to save taxes for the stockholders.

Earnings and profits are computed in accordance with accepted accounting principles. However, there are some exceptions (see Reg. §1.312-6).

To determine current earnings available for dividend payments, start with the taxable net income for the year (the corporation's regular method of accounting—i.e., cash, accrual, or installment—is followed to calculate this) and then make the following adjustments:

☐ (1) Deduct federal income taxes paid or accrued.
☐ (2) Deduct net capital loss, if any.
☐ (3) Add back 85% of dividends received from other corporations (for dividends in kind, §243 and 301(b)(1)(B) would limit the adjustment to the distributing corporation's adjusted basis).
☐ (4) Add back net operating loss carryovers and carrybacks from other years.

These are the major adjustments, but other adjustments may be required, for example:

☐ (1) Add exempt interest, such as that from municipal bonds. (Amortizable bond premiums, although not deductible, must be taken into account.)
☐ (2) Add life insurance proceeds received by reason of death.
☐ (3) Deduct premiums on life insurance carried on an officer or employee.
☐ (4) Deduct charitable contributions in excess of the amount allowed.
☐ (5) Deduct special assessments that aren't deductible as taxes.
☐ (6) Add back excess of percentage depletion over cost depletion. (Excess doesn't reduce earnings, even though allowed as a deduction to mining and oil corporations.)
☐ (7) For taxable years beginning after June 30, 1972, add back depreciation in excess of straight line.

☐ (8) Add corporation debt to stockholder, collection of which is barred by the statute of limitations. (But a debt gratuitously forgiven would be a contribution to surplus, not an addition to earnings.)

Earnings and profits are not increased by items whose taxable recognition is merely postponed (e.g., §108 income). What happens here is that the basis of the assets is reduced so that taxable income will be realized when these assets are subsequently disposed of. At that time, earnings and profits are increased.

Nonrecognition of gain or loss is never permanent: It is merely a postponement. On an exchange, the basis is carried over to the new property; the postponed gain or loss is recognized on disposition of the new property. The same is true on a wash sale. In either case, the adjustment to earnings is made on the subsequent disposition. This rule doesn't extend to losses on sales to controlling stockholders, disallowed by §267. These losses are charged to earnings, even though they don't reduce taxable income.

Appreciation or depreciation in the value of the corporation's assets doesn't increase or decrease earnings and profits. And gain or loss on the sale of exchange of corporate assets is taken into account only to the extent recognized for tax purposes (§312). Unrecognized gains and losses include those realized in reorganization exchanges and involuntary conversions; also disallowed are wash sale losses.

When the corporation holds property acquired from a stockholder in a nontaxable exchange, the stockholder's basis must be used on sale of the property in calculating the gain or loss to be taken into the earnings and profits account (§312). For instance, if a stockholder contributes to the corporation property worth $5,000, the stockholder's basis being only $1,000, and the corporation sells the property for $8,000, the amount to be taken into earnings is the full gain, $7,000.

A corporation may inherit earnings from another corporation in a nontaxable exchange (§381(c)(2)). A deficit, on the other hand, can be used to offset only the earnings accumulated after the date of transfer (§381(c)(2)).

From these adjustments, it is plain that the object is to conform taxable income to economic income.

[¶1703.3] Accumulated or Retained Earnings

Earnings that aren't distributed go into the accumulated earnings account, becoming part of the amount available for distribution of taxable dividends in future years. To find the amount of undistributed earnings at the close of the year, deduct dividends paid to stockholders during the year. If paid in cash, deduct the amount of money; if paid in obligations of the corporation, deduct the principal amount; if paid in other property (except certain inventory assets), deduct the adjusted basis (§312(a)). It has been held that a mere declaration of a dividend reduces earnings, even if the dividend isn't paid or taxed to the stockholders until a later year.

If inventory assets (defined in §312(b)(2)) with a fair market value exceeding adjusted basis are distributed as a dividend, the excess increases the earnings account; but the account is then decreased by the lesser of the fair market value of the distributed inventory assets or the earnings as so increased (§312(b)(1)).

If distributions for the year exceed the current earnings, the excess is charged to the accumulated earnings at the beginning of the year. This reduces the accumulation to be carried forward to subsequent years. Only taxable dividends are chargeable to earnings. Distributions from capital, capital surplus, valuation writeups, pre-1913 earnings, and other nontaxable sources don't reduce earnings (§312(d) and (e)).

[¶1704] DECLARING AND PAYING DIVIDENDS

A corporation has three general methods of distributing assets to its stockholders in the form of a dividend: (1) It may sell the assets and then pay out the proceeds as a cash dividend, (2) it may declare a dividend in the amount of the fair market value of the assets and then use the assets to satisfy the dividend obligation, or (3) it may declare a dividend simply of the assets it wants to distribute to its stockholders. Whether you want to use this method sometimes depends on whether the distribution results in a paper profit or a paper loss:

☐ (1) Sale of the property by the corporation followed by a declaration and payment of a cash dividend will lead to a taxable gain or loss to the corporation. Thus, if the property has depreciated in value, the corporation has a device to offset other gains if it desires. The stockholder is treated in the same manner as for any other cash distribution.

☐ (2) When a corporation declares a dividend of a definite amount and then satisfies the resulting obligation by a property distribution, it will generally realize a taxable gain or a loss equal to the difference between the corporation's basis for the property and the amount of indebtedness discharged. This method may be used, therefore, as an alternative to the first when the property has depreciated in value. This procedure must be carefully spelled out, however, or the Commissioner may claim that it is a distribution in kind for which no loss may be taken.

☐ (3) The method of both declaring and paying a dividend in kind is used primarily when there are appreciated assets.

As an example of the difference that the method of paying a dividend can make, take the following case. A corporation paid $100,000 for a piece of land that is now worth $200,000. The corporation has ample earnings and profits to cover a dividend, and its sole shareholder is in the 70% bracket.

Sale and Distribution of Proceeds (Method 1 or 2)	
Corporation's gain	$100,000
Tax	30,000
Net proceeds distributed	170,000
Tax on shareholder	119,000
Net dividend after taxes	51,000

Distribution and Sale by Shareholder (Method 3)	
Dividend (value of property)	$200,000
Tax	140,000
Net dividend	60,000

By eliminating tax on the gain at the corporate level, the shareholder winds up with an extra $9,000. The savings will increase as his tax rate decreases.

The cut in total taxes becomes more dramatic when the corporation doesn't have anything in its earnings and profits account.

If a deficit corporation sells appreciated property, it immediately generates current earnings and profits equal to the net after-tax gain. This amount will be a dividend when the corporation passes it on to the shareholder. On the other hand, if it distributes its property, the distribution will not be a dividend. Instead the distribution will reduce the shareholder's basis for the stock and any excess will be taxed as capital gain. Thus:

Sale and Distribution (1 or 2)	
Corporate gain	$100,000
Tax	30,000
Net proceeds	170,000
Taxable dividend	70,000
Tax	49,000
Net after taxes	121,000
Distribution and Sale by Shareholder (3)	
Dividend	0
Gain on resale	0
Decrease in basis for stock	$200,000

Watch Out for Corporate Shareholders. When the shareholder is a corporation, it usually is better to sell the property and distribute the proceeds. Basically this is because of the interaction of the dividends-received deduction and the way of computing the amount of the dividend on property distributions to corporate shareholders.

The corporate shareholder's dividend only equals the distributor's basis on the property. This preserves the gain on resale. But the shareholder has already paid a tax, albeit at a very low rate, on the basis.

Sale and Distribution (1 or 2)	
Gain	$100,000
Tax	30,000
Net distribution	170,000
Tax at 7.2%	12,240
Net	167,760
Distribution and Sale by Shareholder (3)	
Dividend	$100,000
Tax	7,200
Gain	100,000
Tax	30,000
Net	162,800

However, if the distributing corporation has no earnings and profits, it is better to pay out the property rather than the proceeds from the sale.

Sale and Distribution (1 or 2)

Gain	$100,000
Tax	30,000
Net distribution	170,000
Taxable dividend	70,000
Tax at 7.2%	5,040
Net after taxes	164,960

Distribution and Sale by Shareholder (3)

Dividend	0
Gain on resale	$100,000
Tax on gain	30,000
Net	170,000

To use method 3 to save taxes, the planner must be sure that the distributing corporation won't realize a gain as a result of the distribution. The first step is a careful selection of the property it is going to transfer to its shareholders. Certain kinds of property can trigger a tax at the corporate level. These include:

☐ ***LIFO Inventory:*** If LIFO (last-in, first-out) accounting produces a smaller profit than a nonLIFO method, such as FIFO (first-in, first-out), a company that has used LIFO must report the difference.
☐ ***Liability Bigger Than Basis:*** If the property is mortgaged for more than its basis, the excess is income to the distributor. However, if the shareholder doesn't assume the mortgage, the ceiling on the distributor's gain is the value of the property.
☐ ***Installment Obligations:*** A corporation can't transfer to its shareholders notes from installment sales without paying tax. It made the sale; it has to pay tax on the gain.
☐ ***Recapture:*** When a company has claimed accelerated depreciation or investment credit on property, the planner has to tread carefully. A premature distribution can trigger recapture.
☐ ***Collapsible Assets:*** If §341(f)(2) describes the assets, the company will recognize gain on a distribution.

The essence of this strategy is that the corporation doesn't pay tax on the appreciation. For savings the planner must confine the tax to the shareholder level. Therefore, he must also be sure to:

☐ ***Keep the Corporation Out of the Sale Negotiations:*** If the company finds a buyer, irons out a deal, sets up a contract, and then turns the property over to the shareholder just before the closing, it will probably be the seller for tax purposes and it will have to pay tax on the gain.

Can it play any role in the selling process? Ideally it shouldn't. When the planner becomes aware that the company has property it should unload through an in-kind distribution, he should put high barriers between it and potential buyers until the dividend is complete. Certainly if serious negotiations between the corporation and one buyer have started, the tax saving is in jeopardy.

☐ ***Don't Use Written-Off Property:*** Suppose a company has notes that it considered worthless and for which it has already claimed a deduction. The debtor has a comeback and the company turns the notes over to its shareholders for collection. It may have income equal to the earlier deduction. The reasoning is similar to the rationale for recapture provisions. It got the benefit of a deduction on certain assumptions. If the final facts are different, then it can't avoid income by transferring the notes. It took the deduction and it has to account for the later upsurge in value.

☐ ***Watch Out for Depreciation Recapture:*** A corporation has a piece of depreciable personal property with an adjusted basis of $10,000. The property is subject to a $12,000 mortgage. It has a recomputed basis of $15,000 (i.e., the adjusted basis plus post-1961 depreciation). The fair market value of the property is $20,000. The property is distributed to the shareholders as a dividend.

Under §311(a), a corporation normally realizes no income on the distribution of appreciated property with respect to its stock. But §311(c) provides that where the property distributed is subject to a liability in excess of its basis, the excess is taxable to the corporation. Here, the mortgage exceeds the basis by $2,000. So, that excess would seem to be taxable.

Code §1245 and 1250 make the difference between the basis and the lower of the recomputed basis or fair market value taxable to the corporation as ordinary income—here, $5,000. Here, too, even though §311(a) exempts corporations from tax on distributions in respect of their stock, §1245 and 1250 supersede all sections of the Code unless otherwise specified; and §311 is not otherwise specified.

Furthermore, both §311(c) and 1245 apply here to make a total of $7,000 taxable to the corporation; the $2,000 taxable under §311(c) is not included in the $5,000 taxable under §1245.

[¶1705] STOCK DIVIDENDS

The normal rule is that stock dividends are not dividends in the sense that they are not distributions of the corporation's earnings and profits. However, this rule has three basic exceptions:

☐ (1) Stock dividends that can be received by the shareholder either in stock or in cash or other property at his election;

☐ (2) Stock dividends that were paid in discharge of preference dividends;

☐ (3) Stock dividends that have the effect of the receipt of cash or other property by some shareholders and an increase in the proportional interest or ownership of other shareholders in the earnings and profits or the assets of the corporation.

Of the above exceptions, only (3), which was added to the Code fairly recently, requires special explanation. The key to the operation of this exception is that the distribution of stock be disproportionate, i.e., at the end of the transaction, some shareholders end up with a bigger or smaller interest in the corporation than they had before.

In determining whether there is a disproportionate distribution, any security convertible into stock or any right to acquire stock is treated as outstanding stock. For example, if a corporation has common stock and convertible debentures and stock dividends are issued on the common stock, there is a disproportionate distribution.

In determining whether there is a disproportionate distribution with respect to a shareholder, each class of stock is considered separately:

☐ (1) ***Distribution of Common and Preferred Stock:*** If a distribution or series of distributions has the result of the receipt of preferred stock by some common shareholders and the receipt of common stock by other common shareholders, all the shareholders are taxable (under §305(b)(3)) on the receipt of the stock.

□ (2) ***Distributions of Preferred Stock:*** The distribution is also taxable if it is with respect to preferred stock, other than an increase in the conversion ratio of convertible preferred stock made solely to take account of a stock dividend or stock split with respect to the stock into which such convertible stock is convertible (§305(b)(4)).

□ (3) ***Distribution of Convertible Preferred:*** A distribution of convertible preferred stock is taxable (under §301) unless it is established that it will not have the result of a disproportionate distribution (§305(b)(5)).

Example: If a corporation makes a pro rata distribution on its common stock of preferred stock convertible into common stock at a price slightly higher than the market price of the common stock on the date of distribution and the period during which the stock must be converted is four months, it is likely that a distribution would result in a disproportionate distribution. Those stockholders who wish to increase their interests in the corporation would convert their stock into common stock at the end of the four-month period, and those stockholders who wish to receive cash would sell their stock or have it redeemed.

On the other hand, if the stock were convertible for a period of 20 years from the date of issuance, there would be a likelihood that substantially all the stock would be converted into common stock, and there would be no change in the proportionate interest of the common shareholders.

In addition IRS has authority to issue regulations to deal with transactions that have the effect of distributions but in which stock is not actually distributed. A change in conversion ratio, a change in redemption price, a difference between redemption price and issue price, a redemption treated as a §305 distribution, or any transaction (including a recapitalization) having a similar effect on the interest of any shareholder is to be treated as a distribution with respect to each shareholder whose proportionate interest is thereby increased.

However, the changes made by the Revenue Act of 1969 do not apply to disproportionate distributions (or deemed distributions) as provided under §305(b)(2) made before January 1, 1991, with respect to stock outstanding on January 10, 1969, or issued pursuant to a contract binding on January 10, 1969, on the distributing corporation. (The September 7, 1968, date in the transitional rule of the regulations is changed to January 10, 1969, so that there is no gap between the transitional rule of the regulations and the transitional rule of the new rule.)

The transitional rule applies only where the corporation's dividend policy and capital structure on January 10, 1969, were such that stock dividends paid by it would be taxable under the new rules. The transitional rule does not apply unless the stock as to which there is a receipt of property was also outstanding on January 10, 1969 (or was issued pursuant to a contract binding on that date). But only if the corporation made on or before January 10, 1969, a distribution of property with respect to the stock and a distribution (or deemed distribution) of stock with respect to the stock to which the transitional rule applies.

Shareholders of corporations to which the transitional rule applies are taxable on stock dividends paid on stock issued after January 10, 1969, even if the new stock was issued as a dividend on stock to which the transitional rule applies. The transitional rule also applies to additional stock, whether sold or distributed as stock dividends, if the new stock is of the class of stock having the largest fair market value of all the classes of stock subject to the transitional rule. (This would normally be common stock of the corporation.) It also applies to stock received as dividends on stock to which the transitional rule applies.

The transitional rule ceases to apply if at any time after October 9, 1969, the corporation issues any stock (other than in a distribution with respect to stock of the same class) which is not:

☐ (a) Nonconvertible preferred stock;
☐ (b) Additional stock of the class of stock having the largest fair market value of the classes of stock subject to the transitional rule;
☐ (c) Preferred stock convertible into the class of stock referred to in (b) if it has full antidilution protection.

Increases in the conversion ratio of convertible stock made before January 1, 1991, are not taxable if they are made pursuant to the terms relating to its issuance that were in effect on January 10, 1969.

Note: Don't Forget §306. Stock received as a stock dividend may be classified as §306 stock, which produces ordinary income when disposed. If you get common stock as a dividend on common stock, §306 will not apply; but in any other case, it might. For example, a dividend of common on preferred, or preferred on common, would be §306 stock, if the corporation had earnings and profits. (See also ¶1701.5.)

[¶1706] TAXABILITY OF CORPORATION ON DISTRIBUTIONS

As a general rule, a corporation realizes no taxable gain or loss from distributions to its stockholders, whether in cash, stock, or property (§311). But there are four exceptions:

☐ (1) ***LIFO Inventory:*** If the corporation, inventorying goods under the LIFO method provided in §472, distributes inventory assets, it has a gain in the amount by which the inventory valued by a method other than LIFO (see §471) exceeds the inventory valued by the LIFO method (§311(b)).
☐ (2) ***Assumption of Liability:*** If the corporation distributes property subject to a liability or the stockholder assumes a liability of the corporation in connection with the distribution, it has a gain in the amount, if any, by which the liability exceeds the corporation's adjusted basis for the property. The gain will be capital or noncapital as the asset distributed was capital or noncapital; the holding period will be determined as if the property were sold on the date of distribution (§311(c)).
☐ (3) ***Installment Obligations:*** If the corporation distributes an installment obligation, it has a gain in the amount by which the fair market value of the obligation exceeds its basis (§453(d)).
☐ (4) ***Appreciated Property:*** If a corporation distributes property other than its own obligation in redemption of its stock, it realizes taxable gain to the extent that the fair market value exceeds the amount that would have been received had the property been sold at the time of distribution (§311(d)). (See also ¶1702.1.)

[¶1707] CONSTRUCTIVE DIVIDENDS

Any corporation with earnings and profits has to beware of "constructive dividends." By this we mean corporate payouts that are ostensibly something other than dividends but wind up being taxed like dividends because that's what they really are. Constructive dividends take several and varied forms, the most usual of which is the payment of excessive and unreasonable salaries to stockholder-employees. Note that no formal declaration is necessary for any distribution to be a dividend. The following material represents a comprehensive analysis of important cases on the subject and has been classified according to the form of the payment. In every item there was a finding of a constructive dividend unless otherwise noted.

Debts

□ Pays or assumes debts of its stockholders (*Iverson*, 29 BTA 863, 1934; IT 1279).
□ Cancels stockholders' debts (*Shephard*, TC Memo 1963-294; *Pliner*, TC Memo 1961-218; *Natwick*, 36 BTA 866, 1937; *Muller*, 16 BTA 1015, 1929; *Wilson*, 27 TC 976, *aff'd* 255 F.2d 702, CA-5, 1958).
□ Pays the sole stockholder's income taxes that were incurred before incorporation (*Silverstein*, 36 TC 438, 1961; see also *Ruben*, 97 F.2d 926, CA-8, 1938, where no dividend resulted when a corporation paid damages in litigation brought against its stockholders personally).
□ Account book debits and credits prove validity of loan (*Harris*, 370 F.2d 887, CA-4, 1967).

Fines or Penalties

□ Pays officer-stockholder's fine (*Sachs*, 277 F.2d 879, CA-8, 1960).

Interest

□ Pays interest on corporate obligations held by stockholders. Where the ratio of debt to equity is high [''thin incorporation''], there may be danger that debt securities are really stock masquerading as debt. This, of course, is the decisive factor on whether or not interest deductions by a corporation will be allowed.
□ Pays interest on bonds where debt securities have been issued for equity securities and the interest rate is variable (*Kelley*, 326 US 521, 1946).

Leasehold Improvements

□ Makes improvements on property it rents from a stockholder under a lease that can be terminated on 30 days' notice (*Jaeger Motor Car Co.*, 284 F.2d 127, CA-7, 1960).

Life Insurance Premiums

□ Pays the premiums on insurance on officer-stockholders' lives where the stockholders are the beneficiaries (TIR-321, 6/9/61; OD 659, but see *Prunier*, 248 F.2d 818, CA-1, 1957; *Casale*, 247 F.2d 440, CA-2, 1957; and *Sanders*, 253 F.2d 855, CA-10, 1958, discussed at ¶1807.2, for contrary view).

Loans

(See ¶1707.1.)

Personal or Living Expenses

□ Contributes toward living expenses of stockholder's family (*Lengsfield*, 241 F.2d 508).
□ Constructs and operates racing boats that were the personal hobby of the sole stockholder and these expenses were not related to the corporation's business (*American Properties, Inc.*, 262 F.2d 150; *W.D. Gale, Inc.*, TC Memo 1960-191).
□ Pays stockholders' personal expenses (*Koyl*, TC Memo 1957-130; *Western Supply & Furnace Co.*, TC Memo 1959-57; *Clarke Fashions, Inc.*, TC Memo 1969-121; see also *Cummins Diesel Sales of Oregon*, 321 F.2d 503, CA-9, 1963).
□ Permits funds or other moneys due it to be diverted to stockholders' personal uses (*Carter*, TC Memo 1960-205; *Cruser*, TC Memo 1961-60).
□ Purchases property for the personal use of a corporate officer (*Von Hessert*, TC Memo 1961-226; *Gaddy Motor Co., Inc.*, TC Memo 1958-189; see also *Briggs*, TC Memo 1956-86).

Tax in these situations is measured by the value of the personal use rather than by the cost of the corporate property (*Greenspon*, 23 TC 138, *acq.; Rodgers Dairy Company*, 14 TC 66, 1950).
☐ Permits officer-stockholders to use company cars for their personal use. But there is no tax to the extent the car is used for corporate business (*Rosania*, TC Memo 1956-116).
☐ Your corporation can't pay your "club" expenses (*Riss, Sr.*, 374 F.2d 161, CA-8, 1971).
☐ Disallowed corporate expenses were dividends to sole stockholder (*Accessory Fashions, Ltd.*, TC Memo 1967-108; but see *Long Chevrolet Company*, TC Memo 1967-212).

Property Distributions

☐ Distributes a tract of mineral land, that it owns and leases to others, to stockholders (*Rev. Rul. 56-512*, CB 1956-2, 173).
☐ Transfers a patent to its stockholders (*Stearns Magnetic Mfg. Co.*, 208 F.2d 849, CA-7, 1954).

Purchases

☐ Buys real estate from a stockholder for an excessive price in exchange for bonds (*Castle*, 9 BTA 931, 1928). You may be able to show the price wasn't excessive by showing that an amount was for goodwill or for some other intangible property (*Staab*, 20 TC 834, 1953).

An arrangement to make payments out of profits may create an anticipatory dividend for the excess paid over value (*Crabtree*, 21 TC 841, 1954; but see *William E. Lamble*, TC Memo 1967-185).

Rent

☐ Pays excessive rents to stockholders (*Limericks*, 165 F.2d 483, CA-5, 1948; *Floridian Hotel Operators, Inc.*, TC Memo 1953; *Jolly's Motor Livery Co.*, TC Memo 1957-231).

Determination of what constitutes excessive rent also hangs upon a factual determination of what's reasonable. In a closed corporation, the Treasury is almost certain to require some proof that the arrangement was at arm's length. Formal, documented dealings would, of course, be important. However, just to keep any disallowance as small as possible, it would be wise to have available a record of the going rent for comparable property.
☐ Rents property to a stockholder at a rent substantially less than fair rental value. The excess of the fair rental value may be a dividend (*Rev. Rul. 58-1*, CB 1958-1, 173; but see *Peacock*, 256 F.2d 160, CA-5, 1958).

One possible way of turning a potential dividend into a corporate deduction would be to perform sufficient services to turn the inadequate rent by the stockholder into compensation for stockholder's services (*Dean*, 9 TC 256, 1947).
☐ Reimburses a stockholder for excess of rent paid by him for the corporation (*Maloney*, TC Memo 1958-39; but see *Riss, Sr.*, 374 F.2d 161, CA-8, 1973).

Royalties

☐ Pays excessive royalties to stockholders (*Peterson & Pegau Baking Co.*, 2 BTA 637, 1925).
☐ Liquidates, followed by the organization of a new corporation with royalty payments to be paid to stockholders who had also been stockholders of the old company (*Ingle Coal Corp.*, 127 F. Supp. 503, CA-7, 1949).

Salaries

☐ Pays excessive salaries to stockholder-employees.

In these situations, the amount of dividend (not deductible by the corporation) is that amount in excess of a reasonable salary (cases are too numerous to cite, but *Botany Worsted Mills*, 278 US 282, 1930, is the leading one). The stockholder-employee's position may actually improve; as a dividend, the dividend credit will reduce his tax liability. Bonuses in proportion to stock ownership are usually dividends; but see *Safety Engineering*, 374 F.2d 885, CA-5, 1967.

Sales to Related Persons

The proceeds received by a father from the sale of stock in a corporation controlled by him to a realty company controlled by his son are a dividend. Although the father owned no stock in the realty company, he had 100% control by virtue of the fact that all his son's stock is attributable to him (*George L. Coyle, Jr., rev'd* 415 F.2d 488, CA-4, 1968).

Bargain Sales to Stockholders

☐ Sells property to a stockholder for less than the fair market value of the property, the dividend being equal to the difference between the fair market value of the property distributed and the amount paid for the property (Reg. §1.301-1(j); *Riss, Sr.*, 374 F.2d 161, CA-8, 1973).

So, where a stockholder bought lots from his corporation at bargain prices, the difference between the fair market value and what he paid was a dividend—even where the corporation didn't have sufficient earnings and profits to cover the distribution. Artificial profits were created to the extent of the appreciation of the property in the corporation's hands since the property was inventory under §312(b)(1) (*Dellinger*, 32 TC 1178, 1959).

In a close corporation, watch out for sales of property made at book value. If no attempt is made to fix the price at fair market value, an unintended dividend may result for the excess of fair market value of the property over book value. Bargain sales to shareholders are dividends (*Goodling*, 395 F.2d 938, CA-5, 1968).

Stockholders' Services

☐ Pays the stockholders for services rendered where those services are unusual (e.g., finder's fee) (*Darco Realty Corp.*, 301 F.2d 190, CA-2, 1962).

Liquidations, Redemptions, Reorganizations

☐ A genuine stock redemption is taxed at the capital gain rate. But a dividend disguised as a redemption will be taxed at ordinary income rates. The transaction must meet certain specific requirements of §302. In a complete liquidation of either the corporation's or of the stockholder's interest in the corporation, there won't be any question; the capital gain rate will apply (§302(b)(3)).

Where the redemption of a shareholder's stock is "substantially disproportionate" (§302(b)(2)), the capital gain rates will also apply. But where the redemption is only partial and does not meet either of these tests, there is danger of ordinary income rates being assessed unless it can be shown that the facts of the situation meet the "not essentially equivalent to a dividend" test of §302(b)(1).

Corporate reorganizations, including spin-offs, are governed by technical requirements (§355 and 356). Genuine business motives or accomplishments are also important.

If the reorganization doesn't qualify for tax-free treatment under the rules, any profits on the various exchanges will be taxed to the receiving stockholders as dividends. These profits are what we mean by "boot."

Charitable Contributions

☐ Some IRS agents have been trying to hit stockholders of closely held corporations with dividends when their corporations contributed to charities in excess of the 5%-of-taxable-income limit on corporate charitable contributions. If there's a charitable contribution allowed to the individual, there's a washout (dividend income is offset by the deduction—or perhaps the dividend credit can permit the stockholder to even come out ahead). But if the individual has already used his maximum contribution deduction for that year, he may be hurt. Further, there's no carryover for individuals as there is for corporations. IRS's latest word on this subject is that unless there is suspicion that the true tenor of the transaction is a gift by the stockholder, the corporate contribution will not be attributed to the stockholder (TIR-457, 3/4/63).

Distribution of property to a "grandparent" corporation may be an indirect dividend (*First National Industries, Inc.*, TC Memo 1967-136).

[¶1707.1] Loans as Constructive Dividends

Not every withdrawal of funds by a stockholder is classified as a dividend. A corporation may, for example, validly lend money to a stockholder. However, "loans" of this type are examined very closely by IRS—especially in the case of corporations not publicly held, since they may really represent a disguised distribution of corporate profits. The determination of loan or dividend is based upon the fact situation. Courts differ in the weight given to any one particular test, but generally these facts are considered: the degree of control the borrower-stockholder has over the company; the interest to be paid for the loan; whether notes or other evidence of debt are executed; the existence of earnings and profits; how handled on the corporate records. These purely factual tests are used to shed light on two tests of intent: whether repayment was intended and whether the parties regard these withdrawals as true loans.

Here is a rundown of cases on this issue, showing the type of business involved and the principal fact or factors that influenced the Court's decision.

Loans

☐ ***Import and Export:*** Corporation organized in 1946. Sole stockholder withdrew money for himself and wife (a director) from time to time for three years. Treated as loans in corporate books although no interest was paid. Notes were executed. Amount of withdrawals did not support dividend distribution (*Shaken*, 21 TC 785, 1954).

☐ ***Real Estate:*** A 50% stockholder paid no interest to corporation on note which he executed for advance. Loan authorized by stockholders and board. Note never repayed. Facts showed intent to repay a bona fide loan. The fact that no interest was paid was not controlling (*Perkins*, TC Memo 1957-128).

☐ ***Stock Brokerage:*** Corporation organized in 1931 with wife of taxpayer owning all but 2 of the company's 2340 shares of outstanding stock from inception. For a period of five years—1943 to 1948—the corporation bought securities for the taxpayer, his wife (the chief stockholder), and their minor son. The corporation advanced the money and held the securities as collateral. When stock was sold, gain or loss was set up on taxpayer's account. Fact pattern taken as a whole showed bona fide loan (*Bass & Co.*, TC Memo 1957-208).

☐ ***Real Estate:*** Fifty-percent stockholders withdrew large sums from corporation in 1932 and for several years prior thereto. Record silent as to how many years money was withdrawn. These were all treated as loans on the books. No notes, no interest, and no evidence of repayment. Since earnings and profits were insufficient for a taxable dividend, the amounts received by shareholders should be applied against and reduce the basis of their stock. Any excess constitutes income taxable as gain (*Kinnear*, 36 BTA 153, 1936).

☐ ***Service Business:*** Family corporation. Shareholder owned about 25% and withdrew $15,000, which was evidenced by a note and treated on the books as a loan. Shareholder planned to repay loan but held off pending this tax litigation (*Callan Court Co.*, 274 F.2d 532, CA-5, 1960).

☐ ***Wholly Owned Corporation:*** Taxpayer and wife borrowed $2 million from their corporation, giving their noninterest bearing notes. IRS tried to impose tax on the $2 million they would have had to pay if they borrowed from outside sources, but the Tax Court okayed the loans. If they were charged with interest income, they'd get an offsetting deduction for interest paid (a washout) (*Dean*, 35 TC 1083, 1961).

Dividends

☐ ***Oil Field Supplies:*** Husband owned 40 shares, wife owned 40 shares, and corporation held remaining 40 shares. Withdrawals lasted over nine-year period. No note or security was given, nor were dividends ever paid to stockholders. The withdrawals were used for personal expenses (*Kountz*, TC Memo 1962-29).

☐ ***Oyster Shell Products:*** Two shareholders owned 100% of stock. Withdrawals running over a 10-year period treated by the parties as a loan. But no interest was ever paid and no notes executed, nor was there a fixed time for repayment. Corporation never paid dividends since its organization some 35 years before (*Oyster Shell Products, Inc.*, 313 F.2d 449, CA-2, 1963).

☐ ***Merchandise Brokerage:*** Family corporation—200 shares issued, 1 share each to two husbands and 198 divided between their respective wives. Corporation organized in 1928. No dividend paid since 1931. Throughout the corporate existence, husbands withdrew funds for personal use that were not proportionate to shareholdings since wives owned almost all stock. Husbands had complete control of amounts withdrawn. These were not loans but informal distribution of dividends (*Baird*, 25 TC 387, 1955).

☐ ***Lumber and Coal:*** Family corporation controlled by shareholder and his wife. Sums withdrawn for personal use. Handled as loans on company's books but facts showed no intent to repay. Repayment occurred only after dispute arose (*Anketell Lumber & Coal Co.*, 1 F. Supp. 724, Ct. Cl., 1935).

☐ ***Department Store:*** Taxpayer owned 467 shares, balance of 190 shares owned by his children. Taxpayer withdrew sums for two years and gave notes that were later cancelled as uncollectible. No dividends declared. Facts show the moneys could have been repaid. Taxpayer and his children simply helped themselves to corporate earnings whenever they saw fit (*Hunt*, 6 BTA 558, 1946).

☐ ***Entertainers:*** One hundred shares divided equally among four shareholders. Officer and wife together owned 50 shares. Withdrew funds from time to time for at least five years. No notes executed. No real intent to repay. No interest charged or paid. No evidence of indebtedness from corporation to shareholders (*Levy*, 30 TC 1315, 1958).

☐ ***Movie Theatre:*** Five hundred shares divided equally among taxpayer and two brothers-in-law. Sums withdrawn for personal use over four-year period. Withdrawals treated as loans on books. No notes executed. No interest charged or paid. Taxpayer had complete control of corporation (*Spheeris*, 284 F.2d 928, CA-7, 1961, *aff'g* TC Memo 1959-225).

☐ ***Hotels:*** Several hotel corporations with total stock of 2,134 shares were controlled by taxpayer and wife who held 1,796 shares after death of principal stockholder. There were withdrawals for personal use over five years. The withdrawals were not in proportion to stock. No notes were executed. No interest charged or paid. No security given. No set time for repayment. Few dividends ever declared. From the facts, there was no intent to repay (*Roschuni*, 271 F.2d 267, CA-5, 1959, *aff'g* 29 TC 1193, 1958).

☐ ***Automobile Sales Agency:*** Two stockholders—each owned 50% of stock. Corporation formed in 1942. Dividends were declared for years 1948 to 1953. During these years, corporation paid no salaries as such to two principals but paid them monthly or weekly amounts. These were treated as loans on the books. From the facts, there was no intent to repay. There was no restriction in the use of the funds (*Carter,* TC Memo, 1960-205).

☐ ***Automobile Sales Agency:*** One hundred shares of stock issued in 1946; 90 shares held by taxpayer, 9 shares held by his wife, and 1 share held by an employee (and brother-in-law). In 1947, some of controlling stockholder's stock was put in trust for his minor children. Controlling stockholder at all times ran the business. Dividends were paid out on several occasions over the years. In 1952, a $10,000 check was issued to taxpayer, which he agreed to repay "if and when" needed. There was no note, interest, or security. Although the transaction was set up on books as a loan, stockholder never repaid the $10,000 although he had the funds. Held to be a taxable dividend (*Hamer,* DC Ill., 1960).

[¶1707.2] Stockholder Life Insurance as Constructive Dividend

The cost of stockholder life insurance is a dividend to the stockholder where purchased solely for his benefit; for instance, where the stockholder names the beneficiary and the proceeds are to be used to adjust the purchase price of a stock purchase agreement between the two people who owned all of the stock (*Paramount-Richards Theatres, Inc.*, 153 F.2d 602, CA-5, 1946).

The employer gets no deduction in any case except where the premium constitutes additional compensation (§264; GCM 8432).

As a result of a series of court decisions that IRS has agreed to follow, you can have the corporation take out insurance on the stockholders' lives without having a dividend (*Rev. Rul. 59-184,* CB 1959-1, 65).

The stockholders and the corporation can enter into a buyout agreement under which the corporation will buy the stock of a deceased stockholder at a price determined by the terms of the agreement. The corporation can then take out insurance on the lives of the stockholders. The contract or agreement between the corporation and the stockholders can require the insurance. The insurance proceeds will then make funds available to buy the deceased stockholder's stock.

The corporation can be the beneficiary, collect the proceeds, and then use them to make the stock purchase. Or, says IRS, each stockholder can name the beneficiary of his policy. But in such case, the right of the beneficiary to receive the proceeds must be conditioned on the transfer of the deceased stockholder's stock to the corporation. In other words, it must be clear that the insurance proceeds are part or all of the purchase price of the stock. You could also set up a trust to collect the proceeds and pay them over to a beneficiary. Again, the result is the same if receipt of the proceeds is conditioned on transferring the stock to the corporation.

Caution: In the above situations, payment by the corporation of the premiums on the policies insuring the stockholders' lives will not be treated as a dividend to them. But, if the original agreements are between the stockholders (i.e., each stockholder agrees to buy out the other) and then the corporation assumes the obligations for the buyouts, the corporate buyouts could be dividends to the stockholders (see, however, *Decker,* 32 TC 326, 1959, where the Tax Court said there was no dividend where there was a good corporate purpose for the corporation's assumption of the stockholders' obligations).

SECTION XVIII
BUYING AND SELLING A BUSINESS

Whenever a businessman buys or sells a business in an arm's-length transaction, the question of primary importance to him is usually: What is the business worth? However, the question of valuation is not very important in the tax law, except in relation to goodwill. This is because in most cases, a tax benefit to one party to the transaction (for instance, large capital gain on the sale of stock) will be offset by a tax disadvantage to the other party (for instance, low depreciable basis in the assets). So the tax law is primarily concerned with the structure of the sale; that is, how much is being paid for various assets, what form the payment will take, and, finally, the timing of the transaction. These questions are important in that various provisions of the tax law provide special benefits, either to the buyer or the seller, depending on the answer: Benefits ranging from the transaction being almost wholly taxable as ordinary income all the way to its being almost completely tax free, with various degrees of deferral or reduction of tax in between.

These issues, then, are the ones considered in this section, along with various strategies that provide the most tax benefit in a given circumstance. They will be considered generally from the point of view of the seller; in most cases the point of view of the buyer will be exactly the opposite, and this fact will be regularly noted. Although it seems surprising, in many sales of businesses neither party fully understands the tax consequences in advance. With careful tax planning, the very worst that can happen is a fair deal carefully negotiated, and the best may turn out to be a tax bonanza.

[¶1801] VALUATION OF A BUSINESS

Although it is not the primary tax consideration, the valuation of a business is an important starting point in any sale. Even if you already have a rough idea, you will have to justify your opinion with some facts. There are various ways of valuing a going business, but most focus on one of two factors—the assets of the business or the stream of earnings the business generates.

[¶1801.1] Asset Valuation

The beginning point of any asset valuation is the basic source of these values—the books. However, since book value is adjusted for depreciation and is not adjusted for inflation, it will be too low in almost every case. So, book value can be seen as a bare minimum—the rock bottom price for any successful business.

The main thing to remember in using asset valuation is that you must include all the assets—insurance prepayments and prepaid expenses of every sort, reserves, tax refunds—anything that will pass with the sale of the business and add value to it. You should also try to value the goodwill, i.e., the past satisfaction you have given to your customers that would make them likely to bring you repeat business. Goodwill is, in effect, your good business reputation, which will pass to the buyer with a sale of the business.

After you have figured goodwill, you should estimate the appreciation of the other assets over their book value. For example, if you use FIFO, your inventory value will not have to be adjusted too much; but if you use LIFO, it will be, in most cases, grossly undervalued. Likewise, your real estate has probably appreciated substantially over your basis on the books. Your accountant can help you in reevaluating these assets; nevertheless you should be aware that many will be worth far more than their book value.

After you have arrived at a reasonable value for all your assets, including goodwill, you should add the value of any covenants not to compete that you plan to give as a part of the deal. You should now have a reasonable value of the business based on its assets. For negotiation, you can adjust some of these figures upward (such as goodwill) with a view towards reducing them later. Somewhere between this top figure and the rock bottom figure for actual book value is the actual economic value of your business. As a seller, you want to hit as close to the top as you can. A buyer, of course, will want to get you down as close as possible to book value. But that's the name of the game.

[¶1801.2] Capitalization of Earnings

Under this second method of valuation, you estimate the annual earnings that your business can sustain and then discount this stream of earnings to present value. You must remember, however, that if this method of valuation produces a figure equal to or lower than book value, it does not mean that the business is worth less. Since you should be able to liquidate and get at least book value (not counting goodwill), your rock bottom selling figure should still be not less than book value.

When you capitalize earnings, you are looking at the income potential of the business. Thus, the steadier the income stream in your business, the more accurate this method will be. You should also be sure to include the value of your salary. To the person buying the business, this will presumably be income; although to an investor who did not intend to operate the business, it would merely be an expense that would reduce the net earnings.

Once you have the annual earnings figure, you can capitalize it in either of two ways. The first way is to figure what is a normal return on assets in that line of business (e.g., 12½% might be normal) and divide the earnings stream by the normal percentage of return. For example, if your average earnings were $25,000, the value of the business would be $200,000 ($25,000 ÷ .125 = $200,000).

The other way is to figure the risk factor of the business, which can run anywhere from 4% for a very secure business to 25 or 30% for high-risk businesses with a high proportion of annual failures and short business lives. For example, if the risk factor were a discount rate of 20% and the average earnings were $25,000, the value of the business would be $125,000 ($25,000 ÷

.20 = $125,000). As you can see, this is merely a variation of the first equation. Both attempt to calculate the present worth of a stream of future payments at an interest rate that either reflects the return on a comparable investment or discounts a comparable risk.

You should note that both the rate of return and the risk discount factor will vary not only with the peculiar facts of your own business compared to similar businesses, but also with the going rate of return for risk-free investments, such as government bonds. This simply reflects the fact that an investor will demand a better rate of return on an investment with risk, such as a business, than he will on a risk-free investment. Put another way, your business will be worth more when interest rates are low than when they are high, if you value it by capitalizing your earnings. Therefore, in times of high interest rates, you should also value your business using the asset method to back up your demands for a higher price; but don't forget that you can afford to take less for your business, since you can reinvest the money you receive for a higher return. The point is simply that whatever method of valuation you use, it does not exist in a vacuum but is relative to other outside factors like the cost of money. Your main job is to have reasonable evidence of the value you seek, with an eye to the fact that you can always just liquidate, which will establish your base minimum price. Other than that, the sky is the limit—depending on how well you present your case and how effectively you negotiate.

A buyer will of course do everything he can to beat down the basic price, and to do this he also will need evidence. He can use, for example, evidence of failures in the line of business, high rates of return on similar investments, and, if applicable, tight money that would make for a buyer's market. It will help him if he also knows the liquidation value of the business, since he will probably not get a final figure lower than this and should be wary if he does. He should also be prepared initially to dispense with any padding of assets or the like that he thinks the seller has done for negotiation purposes. As far as he is concerned, this is not real negotiation, since the seller intended all along to give this up. He will want to begin, in terms of asset value, with his top estimate of adjusted book value and work down as close to liquidation value (or somewhere near actual book value) as he can.

[¶1802] FORM OF THE SALE

As already mentioned, the structure of the sale is a very important question in the tax law. Basically, the sale of a small business can take on one of three forms: sale of assets of an unincorporated business, sale of stock of an incorporated business, or sale of assets of an incorporated business. The following paragraphs examine the differences in these kinds of sales.

[¶1802.1] Sale of Assets of Unincorporated Business (Sole Proprietorship)

If an unincorporated proprietorship is sold for a lump-sum consideration, the sale proceeds must be allocated among the individual assets of the business and the gain or loss computed accordingly. The owner is not permitted to treat the sale of his business as the sale of a single capital asset (*Williams*, 152 F.2d 570, CA-2, 1946). Moreover, the burden of proving that any portion of the sales proceeds is attributable to the goodwill and other capital assets of the business is upon the vendor. The problem may be eased by drafting the contract of sale or bill of sale to provide for specific prices for each individual asset in the business (*Wilson Athletic Goods*, 222 F.2d 355, CA-7, 1955).

Great care is necessary in allocating the sales price among the various assets, both to obtain the capital gain rate for as much of the proceeds as possible and to arrive at an overall result that will be fair to each party.

If you don't make the allocation, the Treasury will make it for you; or if you make an allocation you can't support, the Treasury will reallocate. Both of these are to be avoided. For example, just because nothing is allocated to goodwill or going-business value does not mean the Commissioner or the courts will accept it if they are convinced that the parties recognized the existence of that value.

The allocation of the price usually entails some clash of interest between the buyer and seller, and a party without adequate understanding of the issues involved is at a great disadvantage.

For this reason, the tax consequences resulting from the sale of various types of assets are summarized in the list below:

☐ (1) ***Receivables:*** In the allocation of the price, receivables are generally discounted to reflect the reserve for bad debts and the cost of collection. The discount is an ordinary loss to the seller. If the buyer is fortunate enough to collect more than he paid, the excess is ordinary income to him. Costs of collection will wipe out some—perhaps all—of the buyer's gain. Thus, this is a good tax result on the whole. The seller has an immediate deduction, and the buyer pays no tax until he collects income.

☐ (2) ***Installment Receivables:*** Gain on unpaid installments becomes taxable as of the date of sale. The gain will be capital gain or ordinary income depending on whether the property sold was a capital or noncapital asset. As a practical matter, most of the installment accounts will be trade accounts, to which the ordinary income rates will apply. Allowance for bad debt and expense of collection will raise the same questions we discussed in connection with the regular receivables.

☐ (3) ***Inventory:*** The proceeds of sale are ordinary income even though sold in bulk and not in the course of business. Therefore, gain or loss on transfer of the business will be ordinary income or loss. Payments allocated to inventory will be recovered quickly by the purchaser since he can deduct them as costs of goods sold. The more generous the allocation, the bigger will be his deduction. So, he will try for a substantial allocation. The seller, on the other hand, will want a limited allocation. The smaller the allocation, the smaller will be the amount taxable to him as ordinary income.

☐ (4) ***Prepaid Expenses:*** These are capital assets. Expenses for such things as insurance, supplies, etc., are often prepaid. Prepaid expenses won't be of much interest to the seller; they are usually transferred on the basis of unexpired cost, and there is little or no gain or loss to him. But as expenses deductible from future operating income, they are of interest to the purchaser.

☐ (5) ***Land and Leaseholds:*** Land and leaseholds used in a trade or business are not capital assets. Both are §1231 assets, net long-term gain being taxed as capital gain, while net loss is fully deductible as ordinary loss. But there is one important difference between them—land isn't depreciable, while leaseholds are.

The seller will want a big part of his gain allocated to land: He will pay only the limited capital gain rate on it. The purchaser, on the other hand, will want a small allocation: He can't recover the cost of land through depreciation deductions, so a small cost will suit him best.

There may be room for compromise here. A low enough valuation for the land would leave the seller with a loss, which he could fully deduct. This would offset larger allocations that would have to be made to other assets. It would also give the buyer the low investment in nondepreciable land he wants. As a practical matter, however, it would be difficult to prove that the site of a profitable business had depreciated in value unless special circumstances could be shown.

The purchaser wouldn't have the same objection to a high valuation for leasehold interests. It would give him larger depreciation deductions to offset operating profits over the years.

□ (6) ***Buildings, Machinery, Furniture, and Equipment:*** There are also §1231 assets, taxable upon sale as capital gain or ordinary loss. Being depreciable, the purchaser can recover amounts allocated to them by depreciation deductions. Therefore, it would at first appear that both buyer and seller will be served by high valuations.

But there are other considerations that also enter into the picture. There's depreciation recapture that can turn part or all of the capital gain on the sale of these items into ordinary income. Where there is a large potential recapture, the seller will want a lower value allocated to these assets. On the other hand, the buyer may want a substantial value assigned to machinery and equipment.

□ (7) ***Goodwill:*** Goodwill is a nondepreciable capital asset, producing capital gain for the seller and a capital asset that cannot be written off for the buyer. So, normally the seller looks to assign a large portion of the payment to his goodwill, and the buyer wants to assign less.

[¶1802.2] Sale of Stock of Incorporated Business

The tax consequences of this method of sale depend upon what is received. If the seller receives cash or other property, he has capital gains. If he receives stock of the purchaser for his stock, he will also get capital gains treatment, but not until he sells the stock he receives. So, in the latter case, there will be no tax consequences at the time of the exchange unless he also receives other property in addition to the stock, which will be taxed to the extent that the seller recognizes gains.

It is very unusual for a seller to receive cash or other property for his stock, since the buyer will be stuck with the basis on the corporate books for the assets of the corporation. If, however, a *corporation* has bought the seller's stock, and the seller's stock was representative of 80% or more of the corporation he is selling, then the buyer corporation can later get a stepped-up basis in the assets.

More common is the situation where the seller receives stock of the buyer corporation in one of the various ''reorganization'' transactions recognized under the tax law. Special rules apply in these cases that generally give tax benefits to both buyer and seller; these rules will be discussed in detail in ¶2207.

[¶1802.3] Sale of Assets of Incorporated Business

This is by far the most common method of selling a small business. The reason is that a buyer will always want as much of the price as possible allocated to depreciable assets, since this will give him a later tax benefit. In addition, he may be very hesitant to take some of the assets of the seller, for any number of reasons. Through liquidation, the seller can sell some or all of the assets, separately or in bulk, thus tailoring the deal to the wishes of both parties.

The following chart summarizes the various tax consequences of different methods of selling incorporated businesses. Specific details and strategies of these methods will be discussed in subsequent paragraphs.

Type of Transaction	*Tax Consequence to Seller*	*Tax Consequence to Buyer*
Sale of assets by the corporation	Corporation realizes gain or loss in same manner as proprietorship. If proceeds are then distributed to the stockholders in liquidation, a second tax (capital gain) is paid by them.	Purchase price is allocated in same manner as in purchase of sole proprietorship.
Sale by corporation after adopting a liquidation resolution and distribution within 12 months (§337)	Corporation pays no tax on its gain—stockholders pay a tax on liquidation. But corporation has income to the extent of the recapture of depreciation or investment credit.	Same as above.
Liquidation and subsequent sale of the assets by stockholders	Stockholders pay a capital gains tax on liquidation (unless corporation is collapsible); basis for assets received is fair market value. (Corporation can also be taxed on liquidation if there's depreciation recapture.) So, they have no gain or loss on the resale. But make sure corporation didn't enter into sales negotiations before liquidation; otherwise, the double tax won't be avoided.	Buyer's basis is what he pays for the assets—allocated in same manner as on purchase of sole proprietorship.
Liquidation by corporation within one month (§333)	No gain or loss recognized on liquidation. (Here, too, depreciation recapture creates income to corporation.) Basis for assets received is basis for stock. Gain is then recognized on subsequent resale—with nature of the gain on each item dependent on the nature of the asset in the hands of the selling stockholder. Warning: if corporation has	Same as above.

Type of Transaction	Tax Consequence to Seller	Tax Consequence to Buyer
	earnings and profits, there is a dividend on liquidation. And cash and securities distributed are immediately taxable, too.	
Sale of stock in the corporation	Seller generally gets capital gain unless the corporation is "collapsible."	Buyer has a basis for his stock equal to what he paid for it; the corporation retains the same basis for its assets as before the sale. But if the assets have appreciated in value and 80% or more of the stock was purchased by a corporation within a 12-month period, the purchased corporation can be liquidated within two years and the basis stepped up to the purchase price of the stock (§334(b)(2)). Depreciation recapture is taxable to corporation being liquidated.
Tax-free acquisitions via one of several types of reorganizations	Seller usually acquires stock in the buying corporation, and there is no gain or loss on the transaction recognized for tax purposes. Where "boot" (cash or property other than the permitted stock) is received, however, it is taxable to the extent it represents a gain (§356). Seller's basis for his new stock is same as his basis for his old, increased by any recognized gain and decreased by the amount of boot received (§358).	The buyer's basis for the property acquired is generally the same as the basis of the property to the transferor prior to the transfer. But if there was any recognized gain to the transferor on the exchange, then the buyer's basis is increased by that gain (§362(b)).

[¶1803] SALE OF ASSETS AND LIQUIDATION UNDER §337

Where assets are to be sold, usually the simplest and most satisfactory way to effect the sale of a profitable corporate business for both the seller and buyer is to proceed under §337. The selling corporation adopts a plan of complete liquidation, sells its depreciated assets within a 12-month period beginning on the date of the adoption of the plan, and distributes the sales proceeds and all its other assets (except those retained to meet claims) within that 12-month period. Gain realized from the sale of assets by the corporation after the adoption of the plan of complete liquidation escapes taxation to the corporation. Likewise, any loss from the sale of assets in that period is not recognized. There is capital gains tax on distribution of the proceeds of sale to the stockholders.

The biggest advantage to the seller is that §337 offers a simple, straightforward method of avoiding double taxation on the sale of a corporate business; that is why it is so widely used. On the minus side, however, keep in mind that you cannot pass along installment obligations to the stockholders on liquidation without their picking up the market value of these obligations. This removes any advantage of selling the corporate assets in an installment sale.

As for the buyer, a §337 liquidation approach offers him these advantages:

☐ (1) He can buy the assets he wants without also having to take other assets that would go along with the corporate stock. This can also have the effect of using the company's own assets to help pay for it. When the buyer does not take the cash and other assets in a company, the seller keeps those assets.

☐ (2) He can step up the newly acquired assets to a tax basis equal to his cost without effecting a corporate liquidation following the purchase of stock.

☐ (3) He can set up his own corporate structure to carry on the business, and this will usually give him a chance to get a larger part of his investment out tax free by employing debt in the corporation that buys the assets.

☐ (4) He has less problems with possible contingent, unknown, or contested liabilities.

☐ (5) He doesn't have to deal with minority shareholders.

☐ (6) He can more definitely allocate the purchase price among the acquired assets along lines agreed on with the seller.

[¶1803.1] Sale of Corporation Where Assets Have Lost Value

Where corporate assets have depreciated in value, both parties to the sale of the corporation will want the maximum tax mileage made available by this loss of value. Here are the points they will want to keep in mind:

If the selling corporation has not realized any taxable income in the year of sale or in the two preceding years, it will derive no tax benefit from the loss resulting from a sale of the assets.

If the selling corporation does have operating income in the year of sale and for the preceding two years so that tax benefit might be derived from its realization of losses on the sale, the seller must be careful not to adopt a plan of liquidation prior to the sale. If it adopts such a plan, then sells the assets at a loss and distributes the assets in liquidation within 12 months following the adoption of the plan, the loss would be disallowed, since *neither gains nor losses* are recognized under §337. Note, too, that §337 is not elective; if you meet the rules, it applies. It is possible that the loss would be disallowed even if the sale precedes the formal adoption of a plan of liquidation, since the plan of liquidation might be deemed to have been adopted at the time it was determined to sell all the assets and dissolve the corporation (Reg. §1.337). Under these circumstances, discretion would indicate that a comfortable period of time beyond the 12 months should elapse before the distribution in liquidation. Then §337 could not apply.

Where there has been a loss of value in some assets and a gain in others, we have a different problem. If it is possible to segregate the loss assets from the gain assets and sell them to different purchasers, a possible approach would be to have the corporation sell all loss assets, continue the business in corporate form, negotiate for sale of the gain assets, adopt the plan of liquidation, and then sell the gain assets under §337.

If the selling corporation has income in its taxable year or the immediately preceding two years but the purchaser insists upon the acquisition of stock, the loss of the tax benefit can frequently be compensated for by an increase in the purchase price. This is a question of arm's-length negotiation.

From the buyer's point of view, if he desires to preserve the benefits of tax losses in the selling corporation or other valuable tax attributes, he must purchase the stock and retain the corporation in existence for a minimum period of time. The period of time will depend on the application of various sections of the tax law. These include §381, relating to carryover of acquired losses, and §382(a), relating to the time of liquidation. Since losses are involved, the buyer (if a corporation) must also avoid §334(b)(2), which means, in effect, that the buyer must continue the seller corporation's existence for at least two years.

[¶1804] SALE OF ASSETS AND RETENTION OF PERSONAL HOLDING COMPANY

Owners of a successful corporate business that has substantially appreciated are often reluctant to sell it because of the large capital gains tax they will have to pay on its sale. This is why some turn to selling only the working assets of the business, retaining the corporation and converting it into a personal holding company. In the right situation, this approach can cut the owners' tax bite. Here's an example of how it works.

Assume the stockholders' cost of stock in the corporation is $50,000. The corporate basis of assets is $1,000,000, and the fair market value of the assets is $1,050,000. If the stockholders either sold stock in the corporation for $1,050,000 or had the corporation sell its assets for $1,050,000 followed by a liquidation under §337, only one tax would be incurred. But it would be a capital gains tax of $250,000. Suppose, instead, the corporation sold its assets at a gain of $50,000 and then continued as a personal holding company. The tax liability on the sale would be only $12,500. The stockholders and their corporation would have additional capital of $237,500.

Retaining the corporation as a personal holding company is not as costly as some people believe. While the stockholders might have to have all of the corporate earnings distributed to avoid personal holding company penalties, they'd have had to pay the tax on those earnings anyhow if they personally reinvested the funds received in liquidation. Although there's double taxation on the distributed corporation earnings, the maximum corporate tax on dividends is only 7.2% (15% × 48% tax bracket).

For example, if the $237,500 of retained capital is invested in stock of domestic corporations showing an average dividend yield of 5%, the selling corporation has increased its annual income by $11,875 each year. This income is subject to a corporate tax of a maximum of 7.2%, the intercorporate dividend rate on net income in excess of $25,000 (§243). This tax amounts to $855, leaving a balance for distribution as a dividend to the stockholder of $11,020. (If the only income is from dividends, then only a 3.3% rate applies to approximately the first $166,000 of dividend income. This is because a deduction of 85% of the dividend is allowed, resulting in net income of not more than $25,000.) Further, the income tax on liquidation of the selling corporation may be eliminated forever if the selling stockholder continues to hold the stock until his death. The corporation can then be liquidated, and the selling stockholder's family would be richer by $237,500 less estate taxes.

The personal holding company plan is especially applicable where the stockholders of the selling corporation are advanced in years. Its application, however, is not limited to this type of situation. It can be used even where the stockholders are younger, provided the stockholders are willing to live only on the income from the capital and will not require any substantial capital distributions from the corporation.

[¶1805] SALE OF BUSINESS WITH LONG-TERM PAYMENT

Frequently, owners of a business will want to sell out but find that they are not able to get a buyer who will have the same confidence in the future of the business as they have. To get the price they want, the owners may have to sell for a down payment and payments over a period of years. Moreover, the payments may be made contingent on future earnings and other variables.

[¶1805.1] Sale Where Price Depends on Future Earnings and Other Variables

It often happens that the final amount to be paid for stock is not determined at the time of the sale but depends on such variables as future earnings of the stock of the corporation being sold or the future production and sale of certain specified units by the corporation.

The tax results of this arrangement to the seller have been clear since *Burnet v. Logan*, 283 US 404, 1931, in which the Supreme Court held that the gain on the amounts received under such an arrangement are realized only as the amounts become fixed in the case of an accrual-basis taxpayer or as the amounts are actually received by a cash-basis taxpayer. To get this result, however, you must be able to sustain your claim that the value of the consideration received for your business is unascertainable. IRS will give you a fight on this; it maintains that values are rarely unascertainable.

An obligation of the seller with such a variable character has been held not to be subject to valuation, and thus no gain can arise with respect to it at the time the obligation is created and no loss can arise at the time of the sale because the existence and amount of the loss cannot then be established. This rule has been applied where the variable consisted of the amount of the dividend paid on the stock in a specified period after the sale.

[¶1805.2] Installment Sales

While the purchase price for the business may be ascertainable, the payout period may still be long. It is not always necessary to pick up the entire gain in the year of sale: Installment sale reporting may be available.

If not more than 30% of the sales price is taken in the year of sale, the sale can qualify for installment reporting. In that case, only a proportionate part of the gain is reported each year as the installments are collected. If the gain on the sale would result in a capital gain if the entire gain were reported in the year of sale, then the proportionate part of the gain reported each year under the installment method would also be capital gain. However, if interest is not separately called for in the agreement or if enough interest is not called for, then part of each installment payment will be treated as interest income under the "imputed interest" rule.

One problem with using installment reporting on the sale of a business is that this method is generally feasible only when stock is sold or where the corporation sells its assets but does not liquidate. Where a liquidation is required as part of the arrangement, installment reporting is not feasible.

If the §337 (12-month) liquidation approach is used, the stockholders will have to pick up the market value of the installment obligations when they are distributed to them in liquidation. So, they end up paying an immediate tax on that value although they collect on the installment obligations over a period of years.

If the corporation liquidates first and then the stockholders sell the assets, the stockholders can make an installment sale; but they are taxed on the full value of the assets received in the liquidation and there's little, if any, gain to be realized on the sale of the assets. So, again, the tax has to be paid before the installments are collected.

There is one situation where a liquidation followed by an installment sale can be used without an immediate tax on the stockholders. That's where a one-month (§333) liquidation is used. Here, there is no tax on the liquidation if the requirements of §333 are met. The stockholders do not step up their basis to market value of the assets received (they use the basis of their stock as the basis of the assets). So, they realize their gain when they sell the assets, and that sale can be an installment sale. The trouble is, of course, that §333 is only useful in a limited area. You would only use it where the company had property that had appreciated in value but had no appreciable earnings and profits, cash, or securities. Otherwise, there could be a lot of ordinary income on the liquidation.

[¶1805.3] Deferred Payment Sales

Where a sale may not qualify for installment reporting (as where more than 30% of the sales price is received in the year of sale), there may still be a means of deferring some of the tax. This entails valuing the notes or other evidence of indebtedness received from the buyer. If the market value of these evidences of indebtedness is less than face, you pick up only the market value in the year of sale. The balance of the gain (represented by the difference between the value you picked up and the face value) is reported only when the notes or other evidences of indebtedness are paid off.

There are a number of drawbacks to the use of this method. For one thing, accrual-basis taxpayers can use this method only on the sale of real property, not personal property. That may not be too bad, since most stockholders are on the cash basis.

A bigger drawback, however, is the fact that to the extent that the reporting of the gain is deferred, capital gain may be converted into ordinary income. Here's why: When you pick up the market value of the purchaser's obligations, you have a closed transaction; that is, you compute the full amount of your gain or loss by comparing your basis with the value of what you receive.

Thereafter, when you collect on the purchaser's obligation in excess of that value your collections do not arise from a sale or exchange. Hence, you have ordinary income. However, the redemption of corporate obligations is treated as a sale or exchange (§1232(a)); so, you should get capital gain where there is a corporate purchaser. (If it can be shown that the face amount of the obligations were actually greater than the value of the business transferred, it might be said there is an "original issue discount"; then there would still be ordinary income on the redemption—see §1232(a)(2).) In any case, where capital gain could result, the "imputed interest" rule could convert part of that gain to ordinary interest income.

[¶1806] BUYER'S STRATEGY: HOW TO BUY A COMPANY WITH ITS OWN ASSETS OR EARNINGS

The buyer's planning will often include an attempt to use the acquired company's own funds or future earnings to help pay for the company.

Several different techniques are available, and the choice of method will usually depend on the fact situation in a particular case. Among these methods are redemptions and §337 liquidations, which have already been discussed. The following paragraphs will cover some of the other more common alternatives.

[¶1806.1] New Company Organized to Buy the Assets

Where buyer wants to use the company's future earnings as well as its assets to help swing the deal instead of purchasing the stock personally, he can organize a new corporation, have that corporation buy the stock, and execute notes for the purchase price. The new corporation then completely liquidates the old corporation and takes over all its assets. The new corporation will then owe the purchase price and will have all the assets of the old corporation, including its future earnings, to apply on the indebtedness for the purchase price. The new corporation will realize no taxable gain or loss on the receipt of the assets in complete liquidation, and the basis of the assets will be stepped up to market value (§334(b)(2)). The old corporation also realizes no taxable gain on the liquidation of the transfer of its assets to the new corporation—except to the extent of any depreciation recapture under §1245 or 1250.

In addition, since the debt is an obligation of the new corporation that will own and operate the business, the interest on the debt will be deductible against the income of the business.

Example: Let's assume that you are interested in buying 100% of the outstanding stock of Close, Inc., a small, closely held corporation. The asking price for the stock is $475,000, and you can raise $125,000. You can personally borrow the remaining $350,000 from relatives; however, that would require a dividend payout by your new corporation in order to pay interest and principal on these debts. Since in your tax bracket you only wind up with 50 cents of every dollar, it could turn out to be a losing proposition after taxes; but by organizing a new company to buy the stock you may be able to swing the deal. Here's how it was done in one case.

Arthur Kobacker entered into a contract with Reiner's, a small department store, in which he agreed to buy all Reiner's stock for $475,000. Since he only had a small portion of the necessary cash, he formed the Alfred Investment Company, and Alfred raised the remainder of the cash needed by issuing bonds and a note to various relatives. Then Kobacker assigned his personal contract with Reiner's to Alfred Company, and Alfred bought out Reiner's. Later, Alfred was merged into Reiner's, Reiner's stock was retired, and new shares were issued. Reiner's assumed all Alfred's debts, and interest was paid as it became due.

In 1955, Reiner's repaid $90,000 on its note to Jerome Kobacker, Arthur's uncle. IRS determined that this constituted constructive dividends to Reiner's sole shareholder (i.e., Arthur) based on the shareholdings, since (1) it had been held that payment by a corporation of a liability representing part of the consideration for the purchase of its stock constitutes a constructive dividend to the purchasing shareholder, and (2) IRS contended that these related obligors were in reality the purchasers, since Alfred Investment Company was a sham and the loans in reality were loans to Arthur personally.

In upholding the genuineness of these transactions, the Tax Court stated that a taxpayer has a legal right to conduct his dealings so as to avoid or minimize his taxes by lawful means. Further, said the court, the formation of Alfred Company was not a sham, but a legal business entity formed for a legitimate reason. It complied with all state laws and engaged in substantive business activity (Alfred ran one of the departments in the Reiner's store under a lease agreement before the merger). It is true that the discharge of the corporation's debts would enhance the value of the stockholder's stock, but this appreciation in stock value would not be taxable until the stock was sold or disposed of (*Kobacker*, 37 TC 882, 1962).

[¶1806.2] Using Mortgage Money to Buy a Company

Where real estate is owned by the purchased company, the borrowing can take the form of a mortgage on the property. Here's how it was done in one case:

Murphy and Kuckenberg wanted to buy the Medical-Dental Building in Portland, Oregon. The building was owned by a corporation, and the stockholders were willing to sell only their stock. So, Murphy and Kuckenberg borrowed most of the purchase price and paid $942,000 for the stock. A month after they bought the stock, the corporation was able to get an $800,000 mortgage on the property. A few days later, the corporation was liquidated, and Murphy and Kuckenberg each got a half-interest in the building and half the mortgage proceeds. The proceeds were used to pay back the bulk of their loans, but Murphy continued to owe some part of the loan.

Then Murphy decided that he'd rather have his interest in the building in a corporation. So, he formed Murco, Inc., transferred his half interest in the building to it, and took back all its stock plus a $50,000 promissory note.

That's when he ended up in the Tax Court. IRS argued that the amount Murco paid Murphy on his note was not a repayment of debt; it was, said the government, a dividend. However, the Tax Court disagreed. This was a bona fide debt, it said, because:

☐ (1) A negotiable promissory note was used.

☐ (2) It was treated on the books as a debt and, although unsecured, was not subordinated to any other unsecured debts.

☐ (3) The debt was actually paid off—even before it was due—and the interest called for was paid.

☐ (4) Murco was not undercapitalized. Taking into account the mortgage debt, too, and looking at the market value of the equity in the building transferred to the corporation (not its lower basis), the ratio of debt to capital was approximately 2.6 to 1. This, said the court, was not excessive.

☐ (5) There was a good business purpose for the debt—to allow Murphy to extract money from the corporation so he could pay off the debt he incurred when he first bought the stock in the corporation that owned the Medical-Dental Building (*Murphy*, TC Memo 1962-219).

Net Result: Murphy used the building's earnings to help pay for the building, and he was able to use a corporate form of ownership while doing so.

[¶1806.3] Buying Some of the Assets and Leasing Others

By buying only some of the assets and leasing the rest, the future earnings of the company are used to pay the rent. One way to do this is to have a third party buy the assets, sell some to the ultimate buyers, and rent the rest to the buyers. Where the stock must be bought in the first place, partial liquidation of the corporation may be required. To avoid any tax on a partial liquidation, the third party can be a tax-exempt organization. Here's an actual case:

Max Bliss and Fred Vogel, owners of two paper companies, wanted to acquire the stock of the Ryegate Paper Company, a New Hampshire paper manufacturer. The asking price for the stock of Ryegate was $1,200,000. This was a lot more than Vogel and Bliss were ready to pay, so they entered into a deal with the Rhode Island Charities Trust.

The Trust arranged to buy the Ryegate stock for $1,075,000. Immediately after the purchase, the fixed assets of Ryegate were paid out to the Trust as a dividend. (Since the Trust was tax exempt, a dividend distribution to it created no tax problems.) This left only inventory, automobiles, and trucks in the corporation. Then, Bliss and Vogel bought the Ryegate stock from the Trust for $375,000 and had Ryegate lease the fixed assets from the Trust. Thus, after the deal was completed, Vogel and Bliss had the Ryegate Company for a much smaller cash outlay and had the use of the fixed assets on a tax-deductible basis to the corporation (the corporation deducted the rent paid to the Trust). So, the money needed for the fixed assets came from the future earnings of the business.

The rental arrangement called for $250,000 the first year, $225,000 a year for the next three years, and then 5% of net sales, with a minimum of $50,000 a year. IRS tried to disallow about 56% of the first year's rent and 65% of the second year's rent as not being ordinary and necessary expenses. It argued that under the rent schedule, the Trust would recover the full cost to it of the assets rented to Ryegate in three years. This type of arrangement, said the government, did not serve any business purpose of Ryegate. What's more, said IRS, the lease agreement was merely a device to help Vogel and Bliss get the Ryegate stock.

The Tax Court, however, allowed the full rent deductions. The fact that this was an arrangement to help Vogel and Bliss get the stock was beside the point. The important fact here was that all negotiations were between strangers and at arm's length, including the determination of the amount of the rent. The fact that it may have been a bad bargain for Ryegate does not change the nature of the payment—it was a payment for the use of assets needed in the business and therefore deductible as rent.

Note, too, that a few years later, the corporation found it difficult to pay the rent. So Vogel and Bliss negotiated with the Trust to have the corporation buy the leased assets for $687,500, payable partly in cash and partly with notes. But this later purchase, said the Court, did not prove the corporation could have used the assets in the prior years without paying rent. So, the rent deduction for those years was valid (*Ryegate Paper Company*, TC Memo 1961-193).

[¶1806.4] How to Use Tax Money to Buy a Corporation

There are several possibilities along these lines. Their use meets with resistance, but they deserve consideration because substantial companies have attempted to employ them. One approach is to buy assets at less than their book value. The seller realizes cash by using the operating loss carryback, charging the resulting loss against income taxed in earlier years. Other approaches involve allocating a large part of the purchase price to assets that can be very quickly charged off against the buyer's income. This frees dollars, which would otherwise become taxable to the buyer, to pay for the acquired business. Here is another way to buy a business with tax money: The purchase of a business may be effected by renting the assets and allowing the seller to keep liquid assets and to convert inventory into cash. This approach may have these advantages:

☐ (1) The seller avoids capital gains tax on appreciation in physical assets.
☐ (2) Depreciation offsets rental income for the seller.
☐ (3) The buyer's rental payments may exceed depreciation deductions otherwise available to him.

[¶1807] STATUTORY REORGANIZATIONS

The tax law recognizes six different transactions involving businesses as "reorganizations." These are called A, B, C, D, E, and F reorganizations, depending on which subsection of §368 is involved. The rules for these reorganizations are extremely complex, and where they are employed, the parties should always seek the service of a competent tax advisor. The following paragraphs summarize some of the simpler rules and principles and provide an outline of the possibilities they present.

The commonest reorganizations are the A-, B- and C-types. Type A is the acquisition by a statutory merger; type C, the acquisition in exchange for voting stock; and type B, the acquisition of stock in exchange for voting stock. Besides these three, there are the D-type (transfer to a controlled corporation) E-type (a recapitalization) and F-type (change in identity, form, or location).

Where the requirements of any of these statutory reorganizations are met, the transaction will be wholly or partially tax free.

[¶1807.1] Statutory Merger or Consolidation—Type A

This means a merger or consolidation effected in accordance with the corporation laws of the U.S., a state or a Territory, or the District of Columbia. The merger may combine a parent and its subsidiary or may involve two previously disassociated companies.

Although a statutory merger has an advantage over the other types of reorganization allowed by §368 in the sense that specific restrictions aren't placed on the exchanges necessary to carry out the merger, this advantage isn't as valuable as it looks. The state itself will impose restrictions, and you may not be able to meet these state law requirements. In that case, you would resort to one of the other types of reorganization authorized by §368—probably the C-type, which is the alternate way to acquire assets.

Another serious drawback to this A-type reorganization lies in the fact that the surviving corporation assumes all of the obligations of the transferor corporation by operation of law.

One important difference between the exchange of stock requirements for an A-type transaction and those for B- and C-type transactions (discussed below) should be noted. In a B- or C-type reorganization, the acquiring corporation must issue nothing except voting stock in exchange for the stock or property it acquires. Unless this limitation is observed, the reorganization won't qualify for tax-free treatment. No such limitation is imposed with respect to a statutory merger. Nonvoting common or preferred stock may be issued.

In practice, preferred stock isn't likely to be issued in exchange for common stock, although it may be issued in exchange for other preferred. An exchange of preferred stock for common might result in tax as an ordinary dividend under the provision of §306 on the later sale or redemption of this preferred stock.

[¶1807.2] Acquisition of Stock for Stock—Type B

This is described as the acquisition by one corporation, in exchange solely for all or a part of its voting stock (or all or a part of the voting stock of a corporation that controls the acquiring corporation), of stock of another corporation if, immediately after the acquisition, the acquiring corporation has control of the other corporation ("regardless of whether or not it had control before"). The acquiring corporation can transfer all or a part of the stock acquired to its subsidiary. "Control" means ownership of stock possessing at least 80% of the total combined voting power of all classes of stock entitled to vote and at least 80% of the total number of shares of all other classes of outstanding stock.

A unique feature of the B-type reorganization is that it is either fully taxable or fully nontaxable. A- and C-type transactions can be partially taxable.

The definition of a B-type reorganization has a parenthetical qualification, which we have paraphrased above as "regardless of whether or not it had control before." The actual wording is "whether or not such acquiring corporation had control immediately before the acquisition."

This parenthetical clause has become known as the "creeping control" amendment. Its effect is to treat as acquired in exchange for voting stock, for B-type reorganization purposes, any stock of the acquired corporations that was acquired by the acquiring corporation before the transaction that resulted in the latter acquiring enough additional shares of the former to give it "control." For example, an acquiring corporation buys 20% of the stock of the acquired corporation for cash; one year later, it acquires 60% more solely in exchange for some of its own voting stock. The second transaction is a tax-free B-type reorganization exchange under the creeping control amendment. This is because the acquiring corporation had control after the second transaction, and the status before this transaction is immaterial.

According to the Regs, the creeping control amendment is to be strictly applied according to its literal language; exchange of anything in addition to voting stock in a single transaction would disqualify the reorganization for tax-free treatment, even though it could be established that the "control" was actually acquired for the voting stock and the "other property" included was for additional assets (Reg. §1.368-2(c)). Thus, if voting stock was exchanged for 80% of the acquired corporation's stock and in the same transaction the remaining 20% was acquired for nonvoting preferred stock and bonds, the entire reorganization would be taxed.

Giving heed to the Regs, it would be advisable for the acquiring corporation to give absolutely nothing but voting stock in the big exchange. Subsidiary exchanges might be arranged to take place either before or after the big exchange. Section 368(a)(1)(B) specifically authorizes a prior exchange; a subsequent exchange would have no bearing on the tax-free status of the main exchange unless immediate enough for it to constitute a part of the main plan. The Regs seem to suggest that exchanges over a 12-month period would be considered one exchange.

In other words, a cash purchase of stock from the minority holders, 13 months after and apart from the exchange pursuant to plan that resulted in acquisition of the controlling interest, would not likely be held to have cost the planned exchange its tax-free status.

[¶1807.3] Acquisition of the Assets for Stock—Type C

This is described as the acquisition by one corporation, in exchange solely for all or a part of its voting stock (or of voting stock of a corporation that controls the acquiring corporation), of substantially all the properties of another corporation (but assumption of liabilities in connection with such acquisition or the fact that property acquired is subject to a liability shall be disregarded in determining whether an acquisition was solely for stock). However, if the acquiring corporation issues anything other than its own voting stock in the exchange, the assumed liabilities are treated as cash paid by that corporation. If the assumed liabilities plus the property or securities issued in addition to voting stock exceed 20% of the value of the assets acquired, the transaction is disqualified as a C-type reorganization.

A selling corporation does not have to liquidate after a C-type reorganization. For example, Corporation X transferred all its assets subject to liabilities to Corporation Y, an unrelated preexisting corporation, in exchange for shares of the voting common stock of Y. After the transaction, X owned approximately 43% of Y's common and none of its preferred (the 43% constituting more than 20% of the fair market value of all the outstanding stock of Y). X was not dissolved immediately but was kept in existence solely to hold the stock of Y.

IRS says that the transaction qualifies as a C reorganization (§368(a)(1)(c)), provided the principal purpose of the reorganization is not evasion of income tax under §269. What's more, since all the assets were transferred, Y will take into account all the tax attributes of X as described in §381 (carryovers).

What constitutes "substantially all" the property of the acquired corporation in a C-type reorganization isn't defined in the law. The Tax Court says the facts and circumstances, rather than an arbitrary percentage, should be the test.

The 80%–20% Rule: In a C-type reorganization, as long as voting stock is given for property with a market value of at least 80% of the market value of all the property of the acquired corporation, the remaining consideration may be paid in money or other property.

Furthermore, this consideration other than voting stock need not be distributed pro rata to the stockholders of the acquired corporation. The "continuity of interest" requirements wouldn't be violated even if one group of stockholders received only voting stock and another group only cash—as long, of course, as the cash didn't exceed the 20% restriction.

As an example of how the 80%–20% rule works, let's assume we have an acquired corporation with assets worth $250,000 and liabilities of $30,000. The acquiring corporation obtains the assets, subject to the liabilities, in exchange for its voting stock plus $15,000 cash. Since the liabilities plus cash ($45,000 total) don't exceed 20% of the value of the assets ($250,000), this qualifies as a C-type reorganization.

The difficulty in successfully bringing off a C-type reorganization under the 80%–20% rule may come in determining the amount of assumed liabilities. If only a fixed amount of liabilities is assumed, there is no problem. We can add this amount to the "other property" the acquiring corporation is giving (in addition to voting stock) to make sure we are not exceeding the 20% limitation. When all of the liabilities are assumed, we may have no way of finding out until later whether or not we have met the 80%–20% test. By that time, it will be too late.

[¶1807.4] Transfer to Controlled Corporation—Type D

This is described as a transfer by a corporation of all or a part of its assets to another corporation if immediately after the transfer the transferor or one or more of its stockholders (including those who were shareholders immediately before the transfer) or any combination thereof are in "control" of the corporation to which the assets are transferred. In pursuance of the plan, stock or securities of the corporation to which the assets are transferred must be distributed in a tax-free corporate division or other tax-free statutory exchange (§354, 355 and 356). "Control" means at least 80% of the total combined voting power of all classes of stock entitled to vote and at least 80% of the total number of shares of all other classes of outstanding stock. There's no requirement that distribution of the acquired stock be in proportion to the interests of transferors in the transferred assets.

Note that the transaction doesn't meet the D reorganization requirements unless "substantially all" the assets are transferred (§354(b)(1)(A)). The purpose of this restriction is to prevent avoidance of the "active business" requirement of the "spin-off" provisions by casting the spin-off in the form of a reorganization. However, the Treasury will permit retention of enough assets to satisfy existing business liabilities not represented by securities (Reg. §1.354-1(a)(2)). Sometimes you will find that a particular transaction fits both the C reorganization and D reorganization definitions. In that case, the transaction will be treated as a D reorganization only (§368(a)(2)(A)).

[¶1807.5] A Recapitalization—Type E

This is described as an arrangement whereby the stocks and bonds of the corporation are readjusted as to amount, income, or priority or an agreement of all stockholders and creditors to change and increase or decrease the capitalization or debts of the corporation or both.

[¶1807.6] Nominal Changes—Type F

This exempts from tax a mere change in identity, form, or place of organization, however effected. For purposes of offsetting losses against premerger profits, the courts have recognized an F-type reorganization even though two or more operating corporations were involved. IRS protested in vain (*Rev. Rul. 69-185*, CB 1969-1, 108).

Color was a wholly owned Subsidiary of Movielab. In 1967, Color was merged into Movielab, but Color's business continued as before, and the same shareholders as before owned Movielab. In 1969, Movielab incurred a net operating loss of nearly $4 million, of which over $3 million was incurred with respect to the business acquired from Color. In 1966, Color had taxable income of $2 million, and Movielab carried back its 1969 $3-million loss to 1966, offsetting the loss against Color's income for that year. The carryback allowed Movielab to obtain a refund of nearly $1 million (*Movielab*, 494 F.2d 693, Ct. Cl., 1974).

A shell-home business operated in the form of 123 separate corporations, all of which were later consolidated into a single corporation. The new corporation ran into financial trouble but could offset losses against earlier earnings of its predecessor corporations (*Home Construction Corp.*, 439 F.2d 1165, CA-5, 1971).

Three successful companies owned by the same interests merged into one. After the merger, the surviving corporation incurred losses, which it could offset against premerger profits of the three corporations (*Est. Stauffer*, 403 F.3d 611, CA-9, 1968).

[¶1807.7] Illustration of Practical Application of Reorganization Rules

To help translate the complex reorganization rules into everyday terms of a typical business situation, the following example considers the various problems that can arise among the interested parties (some of whose interests conflict with the others) when one corporation is seeking to acquire another and the various methods that can be used to solve these problems.

Suppose the following situation arises: Black Corporation, a metal parts manufacturer, all of whose stock is held by one stockholder and whose net assets are $200,000, wants to acquire White Corporation, a machine tool business worth $100,000. White's stock is owned 70% by Jones, the operator, and 30% by Smith, the investor.

Three tax-free choices are: (1) The A-type merger or consolidation, (2) the B-type stock-for-stock acquisition and (3) the C-type stock-for-assets acquisition.

□ (1) ***Statutory Merger or Consolidation—A-Type:*** Suppose a merger is the plan and Smith doesn't like the idea. He does not get along with Jones and is not happy about the expansion. He wants to be paid for his interest in cash or some other property. Jones, on the other hand, is looking forward to the merger and is all for it.

Would the cash or other property given to Smith make the merger taxable? No. A sufficient continuity of interest exists in Jones. Reg. §1.368-1(b) requires a continuity of interest on the part of persons who directly or indirectly were the owners of the enterprise prior to the reorganization. Jones's 70% interest in the assets of White Corporation is probably sufficient, as a 69% interest was approved by the Tax Court (*Murrin*, 24 TC 502). Smith, on the other hand, will be subject to a capital gains tax for the difference between his basis in the stock and the cash or other property received.

In addition, the receipt of boot would not invalidate the tax-free status of the merger but would only result in the boot being taxed (§356(a)).

Could Smith take back securities, such as long-term bonds, for his interest and not be taxed? No. This would be tantamount to receiving boot, and Smith would be taxed at capital gain rates to the extent of the fair market value of the bonds (§354(a)(2), 356(d)).

Could Jones and Smith each be given part stock and part boot for their interest in White Corporation? Yes. But both could realize capital gains to the extent the boot didn't exceed gain (§356(a)). They could also be subject to possible ordinary income treatment as a dividend if White Corporation has earnings and profits and the distribution of the boot is on a pro rata basis or has the effect of a distribution of a dividend (§356(a)(2)).

Could Jones and Smith be given preferred stock in addition to voting stock for their interest in White Corporation? If the preferred stock is distributed pro rata to Jones and Smith, the answer could be "no" because then the transaction could be substantially equivalent to a dividend and the preferred stock would become tainted "§306 stock" (§306(c)(1)(B)). Upon a subsequent sale or redemption of such stock, Jones and Smith would realize ordinary dividends to the extent of the amount that would have been a dividend if money had been distributed instead of the preferred stock. Gain in excess of these dividends plus the basis of the "§306 stock" would be taxed as capital gains (§306(a)(1)(B)).

Could Jones and Smith immediately sell the stock received in the exchange? It may be risky. If they did, then the entire transaction could be considered by IRS to be, in effect, a plan to extract ordinary dividends from White Corporation at capital gain rates; and they may wind up with unintended dividends (*Heintz*, 25 TC 132).

Would an A-type reorganization result in less expense and payout than a B- or C-type? That depends on the size of the merger and the applicable state law. The use of the statutory merger eliminates the necessity of drawing up various title documents for the transfer of assets as the filing of the merger agreement automatically vests title. On the other side of the coin, however, state law may give dissenting stockholders the power to demand an appraisal and payment for their shares that would subject the surviving and merged corporation to a substantial cash payout.

□ (2) ***Stock-for-Stock—B-Type:*** Suppose a statutory merger or consolidation is not feasible or practical for some of the reasons mentioned above. A stock-for-stock acquisition might be used.

Could Smith, the investor, block the entire reorganization by demanding cash, bonds, or preferred stock for his interest in White Corporation? Yes. Since he owns 30% of the stock of White Corporation, he could prevent the acquiring corporation, Black, from obtaining the necessary 80% control immediately after the reorganization (§368(c)).

Could Smith be paid for his 30% interest partly in stock to comply with the 80% control requirement and partly in cash? Not if there is only one transaction. The transaction to qualify for a B reorganization must be solely for voting stock (*Turnbow*, 368 US 337). However, if 20% of the stock were picked up for cash first and after a period of time the other 80% were picked up for the voting stock, it would seem that the requirements of the B reorganization would be met.

Could Black Corporation transfer part or all of the White stock to its controlled subsidiary? Yes. This is now permitted under §368(a)(2)(C).

□ (3) ***Stock-for-Assets—C-Type:*** Suppose Black Corporation doesn't want to acquire White's stock as it wants to avoid being responsible for any of White's possible contingent liabilities or other pitfalls. The stock-for-substantially-all-the-assets transaction could be the answer.

Could Black Corporation, in addition to giving all or part of its voting stock, assume White's liabilities or take property subject to a liability? Yes; but if consideration other than voting stock is given, the total of liabilities and the other consideration cannot exceed 20% of the value of the acquired assets.

Could Black Corporation acquire 80% of the value of White's total properties solely for voting stock and the remaining 20% for cash or other property? Yes. Code §368(a)(2)(B) and Reg. §1.368-2(d)(2) specifically allow this. Caution should be used in this kind of transaction to make sure that Black doesn't assume or take property subject to any liability of White. If so, the liabilities would be considered to be cash, the 80%-value rule would be violated, and the entire reorganization would be voided.

Could White Corporation in the previous transaction distribute the cash and some stock to Smith for his 30% interest and all stock to Jones for his 70% interest? Yes, but Smith would be subject to tax at capital gain rates to the extent of the cash received (§356(a)).

Could Black Corporation transfer part or all of the assets received from White to Black's controlled subsidiary? Yes. Code §368(a)(2)(C) specifically allows this. However, if voting stock of *both* Black and its subsidiary is given in exchange for the assets, the transaction will not constitute a reorganization (Reg. §1.368-2(d)(1)).

Could White arrange for the redemption of Smith's 30% stock interest before initiating the reorganization? It depends on the time between the redemption and the reorganization. If one follows closely on the other, IRS may treat the consideration to Smith as coming from Black Corporation and void the reorganization as not being an exchange of 80% of the value of White's property solely for Black's voting stock (*Westfir Lumber Co.*, 7 TC 1014).

□ (4) ***Transfer of Part of Assets to Controlled Corporation—D-Type:*** Suppose White Corporation wanted to retain some of its assets, say a building that was not useful to the business any more, and only transfer the remaining business assets to Black Corporation in return for Black stock. This would not qualify as a reorganization.

Could White Corporation transfer the assets desired, less the retained building, to a new controlled subsidiary? Yes. The plan here would be subsequently to distribute the subsidiary stock to Jones and Smith. Such a transfer would be tax exempt under §351, but the subsequent distribution would be taxable unless the spin-off requirements under §355 are met: the assets transferred constituted a trade or business actively conducted for five years (§355(d)(2)). If the subsidiary's stock and building were subsequently distributed to Jones and Smith, they would be taxed at capital gain or ordinary income rates on the transaction, depending on whether the distribution was in the nature of a liquidation or a dividend. In brief, in order to avoid tax, White Corporation must transfer substantially all its assets (§368(a)(1)(D)). If it transfers part of its assets, it must either liquidate under §337 or come within the spin-off requirements of §355.

Can the building not used in the machine tool business be spun-off by itself? Probably not. It is not considered an active trade or business even if it is held for rental (Reg. §1.355-1(d)). If it spun-off with the machine tool business, it would probably be considered "boot," if no longer used in the business, and taxed (§356(a)(1)).

□ (5) ***Split-Ups, Split-Offs, and Spin-Offs—D-Type:*** Suppose Black and White Corporation consolidated by means of A-type reorganization into a new corporation, Grey, with all stockholders receiving common stock in proportion to the book value of their respective corporations. Wilson, the sole stockholder of Black Corporation with net assets of $200,000, would receive 100 shares; Jones and Smith, owning respectively 70% and 30% of the stock of White Corporation with net assets of $100,000, would receive 35 and 15shares respectively. After operating for some time, the stockholders find that they conflict with each other. They decide to divide the business.

Could the machine tool business assets be separated from the metal parts business? Yes; but only if, at the time of separation, the machine tool business was actively conducted by White, or Grey as a successor, or both for at least a five-year period ending on the distribution date and is continued immediately after the distribution (§355(b)). The remaining metal parts business would have to be conducted by Grey, by Black or by both for a similar five-year period and be continued after the separation. Furthermore, the transaction must not be a device for the distribution of earnings and profits (§355(a)(1)). If negotiations were entered into before the distribution took place for the sale of part or all of the stock, such acts would be evidence that the transaction was principally to distribute earnings and profits (Reg. §1.355-2(b)). Even if there was only one business and it was divided into two via a split-off or spin-off, you could still have a tax-free transaction if the five-year provision is met.

Note: Just because a reorganization is wholly or largely tax free does not mean that it is necessarily advantageous. There may be numerous instances when it is *not* desirable to have a tax-free transaction. For example, the basis of assets for purposes of depreciation is often an important consideration. If assets are acquired in a tax-free reorganization, their depreciation basis is unchanged. If most of their cost has already been depreciated, deductions after the acquisition will be small. If they have appreciated in value, there will be a substantial tax to pay if they are subsequently sold.

If the assets are acquired in a taxable transaction, there will still be the tax to pay. But the depreciation basis will have been stepped up to the new cost, meaning larger depreciation deductions to offset future income.

Even where stock is acquired instead of the underlying assets, the basis can be stepped up. This is accomplished by liquidating the company within two years (§334(b)(2)). The basis is increased to the extent the purchase price exceeded the predecessor's basis or decreased to the extent it was less than the predecessor's basis.

No rule covers all cases; but, generally speaking, a taxable transaction that steps up the basis of assets is considered preferable to a tax-exempt transaction. A tax-exempt transaction is considered better where a taxable transaction will decrease the basis.

This general rule may not apply in the case of a taxable acquisition where the cost of properties acquired is allocable to various assets in an unfavorable manner. Oil leases offer a good illustration. Assume that a corporation wants to purchase the assets of another corporation producing oil. The property consists mainly of producing leases for which full tax depletion has been taken, undeveloped leases mostly valueless, and depreciable leasehold equipment. The price to be paid is substantially higher than the basis.

A great part of the price to be paid for the assets will be allocated to the producing leases, which will result in a higher basis; but assuming that percentage depletion equals or exceeds cost depletion, allowable on such higher basis, stepping up the basis here will be wasted (§611, 613). Many of the unproductive leases will be abandoned. Decrease in the basis of these will mean smaller loss deductions.

Where a change in basis will bring an overall unfavorable tax result, as in this hypothetical illustration, it will be better to preserve the existing bases either by casting the transaction in the form of a tax-free reorganization or by buying the other company's stock rather than its assets.

[¶1808] SALE OF PART OF A BUSINESS

There can be many situations when you might consider selling only part of a business. The corporation may have a carryover loss that you still want to use up, and so you don't want to sell the entire corporation. Perhaps the corporation has a pension or profit-sharing plan that has been approved, and you doubt you could get such a beneficial plan approved again. There, too, you might want to hold on to the corporation. Or you might have a corporation holding a very large tract of undeveloped land. You don't want to sell it all now but would like to sell part.

When we want to sell only part of a business we generally have these alternatives:

☐ (1) Incorporate one of the businesses and either spin it off and sell the stock (the spin-off will be tax free and the subsequent sale effected at capital gain rates if the sale was not prearranged, the two businesses have been conducted for five years, and the other requirements of §355 are met) or attempt to cast the deal as a tax-free reorganization. A drawback in proceeding under §355 stems from the Regulations that provide that if part of the stock or securities of either corporation is sold or exchanged after the distribution (as is intended in this instance), such sale or exchange will be evidence that the transaction was primarily a device for the distribution of earnings and profits (Reg. §1.355-2(b)).

☐ (2) Effect a partial liquidation of the corporation by distributing the assets of the business to be sold to stockholders. If the partial liquidation meets the requirements of §346(b), the sale can be worked out at a single capital gains tax.

☐ (3) Arrange a corporate sale of assets. This leaves the proceeds in the corporation, with the result that there will be a second tax cost in distributing the proceeds to stockholders.

☐ (4) Arrange for sale of stock and redemption with assets. The stockholders sell part of their stock to purchasers who really want to buy some of the corporation's assets. Immediately thereafter, the corporation redeems the stock acquired by the purchasers and pays out the assets the purchasers wanted. *Net result:* The old stockholders get a capital gain on the sale of their stock; the corporation has no gain or loss on the transfer out of the purchased assets (the Tax Court refuses to treat the transaction as if a sale of the assets has been made by the corporation with a subsequent distribution of the sale proceeds to the old stockholders). So, the old stockholders end up owning the corporation and what's left in it and realize the appreciation on the portion of the business sold at the cost of a single capital gain tax.

SECTION XIX

KEEPING RECORDS TO PROTECT YOU FROM TAX TROUBLE

There is nothing in the Code specifically dealing with the retention period for books and records. The Regulations and the IRS Guide to Record Retention Requirements generally deal with the problem, however. In most cases, the directive is simply that the taxpayer "retain his books and records for so long as the contents thereof may become material in the administration of any internal revenue law." This is construed to mean a time within which IRS may make an assessment for a deficiency on tax in a subsequent audit.

There are several rules and specific requirements concerning what records you must keep in the course of your business and personal activities. In this section we outline exactly what records you should keep, how you should keep them, and the factors that you should consider in determining how long they should be kept.

[¶1901] RECORD KEEPING IN GENERAL

If your income tax return is audited by IRS, you may be asked to explain the items reported. Thus you should keep records that support the items of income or deductions that appear on your return until the statute of limitations expires for that return. Usually, this will be three years from the date the return is due or filed or two years from the date that tax was paid, whichever occurs later.

However, the statute of limitations will be six years where IRS suspects an understatement of income of at least 25%. In addition, no limitation statute applies to fraudulent returns.

What Records Should Be Kept? Until the appropriate statute of limitations expires, a taxpayer should keep any records necessary to substantiate his return. These will include (but not be limited to) sales slips, invoices, receipts, cancelled checks, and other documents that explain financial transactions.

[¶1901.1] Additional Items to Keep

Tax Returns: Although IRS doesn't require taxpayers to keep their earlier returns, it will usually be advantageous to do so. For one thing, it may prove to be necessary in preparing a current year's returns, as where there are capital loss carryforwards or the income-averaging election is used. In addition, it will prove helpful if IRS ever questions whether a return was filed.

What If an Old Return Is Lost? You can get a copy of your old returns for any of the past six years by filing Form 4506, Request for Copy of Tax Return.

Proof of Tax Payments: It is very important to keep all canceled checks for tax payments. These represent proof not only that you paid your tax liability for a given year but also that you filed a return. If IRS has no record, the statute of limitations would never begin to run without such a showing.

Bequests: If you inherit property, your basis will be its fair market value either at death or at an alternate valuation date. You should maintain records to substantiate this value and keep them until you eventually dispose of the property.

Gifts: If you receive a gift, your basis will be the same as that of the donor, increased by any gift tax paid. You should ascertain your donor's basis and maintain that record in your files as well as a copy of any gift tax return with respect to the property.

Stock Records: You should keep brokerage records, receipts, or other detailed substantiation concerning your stock trades. You will need these to determine gain or loss whenever you sell or otherwise dispose of your holdings.

House Records: You should keep all records that pertain to your basis in your house —proof for what you paid; receipts for improvements, repairs, landscaping, etc.; and records of any depreciation deductions, such as for a home office. These records will prove of value when the house is eventually sold.

[¶1901.2] Keeping Business Records

Professionals or businessmen must keep permanent records to substantiate items appearing on their income tax, employment tax, excise tax, or other returns. Records must clearly show income, deductions, and credits; employees' names, addresses, and Social Security numbers; inventories; sales of items subject to excise taxes; and other information pertinent to the return required to be filed.

□ ***Microfilm:*** Reproductions of general books of account (cash books, journals, vouchers, ledgers, etc.) are not acceptable. However, microfilm copies of supporting records (payroll, cancelled checks, invoices, etc.) will suffice only if you provide appropriate facilities for the preservation and ready inspection of the records, and you can readily make transcriptions of any required information.

□ ***Automatic Data Processing:*** Punch cards, magnetic tapes, disks, etc., are adequate for record-keeping requirements if the system includes a method for producing visible and legible records that will provide information for the verification of tax liability.

□ ***Bank Accounts:*** Taxpayers should deposit all business receipts in a special bank account and establish a petty cash fund for small expenses. All business expenses paid by cash should be clearly shown to be for business purposes.

☐ ***Disbursements:*** If possible, taxpayers should pay by check to document business expenses. Checks payable to cash should be avoided; where they must be drawn to pay a business expense, taxpayers should include receipts or an adequate contemporaneous explanation in their records.
☐ ***Classification:*** Taxpayers should classify accounts in groups relating to income, expenses, assets, liabilities, and equity. Asset accounts should be classified as current or fixed and should record detailed dates of acquisition, depreciation, depletion, and other entries affecting basis.
☐ ***Depreciation:*** The depreciation method used for tax purposes may be different from that used for keeping books. However, taxpayers must keep a permanent auxiliary depreciation record to permit reconciliation of book depreciation with tax depreciation. Without a record of the cost and other information concerning assets, depreciation allowances cannot be determined. If the assets are sold, become fully depreciated, or capital improvements are made to them, only a permanent record will reflect their unrecovered cost.
☐ ***Travel and Entertainment:*** These business expenses must be justified and well documented. Employee statements should show the business nature and the total of the expenses (including those charged directly or indirectly to the employer through credit cards or otherwise) broken down into such broad categories as transportation, meals and lodging while away from home overnight, entertainment expenses, and other business expenses. Adequate controls must insure that employees are paid for only those expenses that are ordinary and necessary and incurred in the conduct of the business.
☐ ***Employment Taxes:*** The employer is responsible for payment of all F.I.C.A. and F.U.T.A. taxes, as well as for withholding part of the F.I.C.A. taxes from his employees' wages. Records should be detailed enough to determine the wages paid and the income tax and Social Security tax withheld. These records should be kept for at least four years.

[¶1902] RECORD KEEPING IN DETAIL

In many cases, it is difficult to determine exactly what information should be kept. To assist the taxpayer, the Record Retention Guide contains IRS guidelines relating to the keeping of records in a variety of situations. While the Guide does not have the effect of law, regulation, or ruling, it is the prime source of information on the subject. The material that follows is excerpted from the Guide.

Income Tax

Except for farmers and wage earners, records must be retained in the following situations by persons subject to income tax as long as the contents may become material in the administration of any Internal Revenue law.

Section 38 Property: Computation of Investment Credit and Qualified Investment:

☐ (a) Members of an affiliated group must keep as part of their records a copy of the consent of the common parent (or a copy of the statement containing all the required consents) to the apportionment of the maximum limitation of $25,000 among them.
☐ (b) Persons computing qualified investment in certain depreciable property must maintain sufficient records to determine whether §47 of the IRC, relating to certain early dispositions of §38 property, applies with respect to any asset.
☐ (c) For recomputation of credit and qualified investment, maintain records which will

establish with respect to each item of §38 property the following facts: (1) date the property is disposed of or otherwise ceases to be §38 property, (2) estimated useful life which was assigned to the property for computing qualified investment, (3) month and the taxable year in which property was placed in service, and (4) basis (or cost), actually or reasonably determined, of the property.

Taxpayers who for purposes of determining qualified investment do not use a mortality dispersion table with respect to §38 assets similar in kind but consistently assign to such assets separate lives based on the estimated range of years taken into consideration in establishing the average useful life of such assets, must, in addition to the above, maintain records which will establish to the satisfaction of the district director that such asset has not previously been considered as having been disposed of.

☐ (d) Disposition or cessation of §38 property by any taxpayer who seeks to establish his interest in a trade or business, a former electing small business corporation, an estate or trust, or a partnership must maintain adequate records to demonstrate his indirect interest after any such transfer or transfers.

☐ (e) For used §38 property, ($50,000 cost limitation) records must be maintained which permit specific identification of any item of such property, placed in service by the person selecting the property. Each member of an affiliated group must maintain as part of its records a copy of the statement containing the apportionment schedule which was attached to the common parent's return.

☐ (f) Where the lessor of new §38 property elects to treat lessee as purchaser, both the lessor and the lessee must keep as a part of their records the statement of the election filed with the lessee and signed by the lessor. The statements must include the written consent of the lessee.

Persons paying travel or other business expenses incurred by an employee in connection with the performance of his services must maintain detailed records of ordinary and necessary travel, transportation, entertainment, and other similar business expenses, including amount and nature of the expenditures, and keep supporting documents, especially in connection with large or exceptional expenditures.

Persons claiming allowance for depreciation of property used in trade or business or property held for the production of income must keep records and accounts with respect to the basis of property, depreciation rates, reserves, salvage, retirements, adjustments, elections, cost of repair, maintenance or improvement of property, agreements with respect to estimated useful life, rates, salvage, and other factors.

Persons changing method of depreciation of §1245 property must maintain records which permit specific identification of the property in the account with respect to which the election is made.

Persons claiming a deduction for amounts expended in maintaining certain students as members of households must keep adequate records of amounts actually paid.

Persons electing additional first-year depreciation allowance for §179 property must maintain records which permit specific identification of each piece of "§179 property" and show how and from whom such property was acquired.

Persons receiving any class of exempt income or holding property or engaging in activities, the income from which is exempt must keep records of expenses otherwise allowable as deductions which are directly allocable to any class or classes of exempt income and the amounts or parts of items allocated to each class.

Taxpayer substantiation of expenses for travel, entertainment, and gifts related to active conduct of trade or business must include each element of an expenditure and by adequate records or sufficient evidence to corroborate the taxpayer's own statements.

Corporations receiving distributions in complete liquidation of subsidiaries must keep records of the plan of liquidation and its adoption.

Qualified electing shareholders receiving distributions in complete liquidation of domestic corporations other than collapsible corporations must keep substantial records showing all facts pertinent to the recognition and treatment of gain realized on shares of stock owned at the time of the adoption of the plan of liquidation.

Persons who participate in a transfer of property to a corporation controlled by the transferor must keep substantial records containing the information necessary to facilitate the determination of gain or loss from a subsequent disposition of stock or securities and other property, if any, received in the exchange.

Persons who participate in a tax-free exchange in connection with a corporate reorganization must maintain substantial records showing the cost or other basis of the transferred property and the amount of stock or securities and other property or money received (including any liabilities assumed on the exchange or to which any of the properties received were subject), in order to facilitate the determination of gain or loss from a subsequent disposition of such stock or securities and other property received from the exchange.

Persons who exchange stock and securities in corporations in accordance with plans of reorganizations approved by the courts in receivership, foreclosure, or similar proceedings or in proceedings under Chapter X of the Bankruptcy Act must keep substantial records showing the cost or other basis of the transferred property and the amount of stock or securities and other property or money received (including any liabilities assumed on the exchange), in order to facilitate the determination of gain or loss from a subsequent disposition of such stock or securities and other property received from the exchange.

Corporations which are parties to reorganizations in pursuance of court orders in receivership, foreclosure, or similar proceedings or in proceedings under Chapter X of the Bankruptcy Act must keep substantial records in showing the cost or other basis of the transferred property and the amount of stock or securities and other property or money received (including any liabilities assumed on the exchange), in order to facilitate the determination of gain or loss from a subsequent disposition of such stock or securities and other property received from the exchange.

Records required in computing depreciation allowance carryovers of acquiring corporations in certain corporate acquisitions must be maintained in sufficient detail to identify any depreciable property to which §1.381(c)(6)-1 of the regulations applies and to establish its basis.

Corporations and shareholders for whom elections are filed with respect to the tax treatment of corporate reorganizations must keep permanent records of all relevant data in order to facilitate the determination of gain or loss from a subsequent disposition of stock or securities or other property acquired in the transaction in respect of which the election was filed.

Qualified pension or annuity plans with provisions for certain medical benefits must keep a separate account for record-keeping purposes with respect to contributions received to fund medical benefits described in §401(h) of the IRC.

Employers claiming deductions for contributions to an employee's trust or annuity plan or compensating an employee under a deferred-payment plan must keep records substantiating all data and information required to be filed with respect to each plan and the deductions claimed thereunder. These records must be kept available for inspection at all times.

Persons required to seek the approval of the commissioner in order to change their accounting period must keep adequate and accurate records of their taxable income for the short period involved in the change and for the fiscal year proposed.

Persons selling by the installment method must maintain such records as are necessary to clearly reflect income. With a *revolving credit plan* the percentage of charges which will be treated as sales on the installment plan must be computed by making an actual segregation of charges in a probability sample of the revolving credit accounts in order to determine what percentage of charges in the sample is to be treated as sales on the installment plan. The taxpayer must maintain records in sufficient detail to show the method of computing and applying the sample.

Prepaid Dues Income: An accrual-basis taxpayer who makes the election to spread out prepaid dues income to subsequent years shall maintain books and records in sufficient detail to enable the district director to determine upon audit that additional amounts were included in the taxpayer's gross income for any of the three taxable years preceding such first taxable year.

Persons engaged in the production, purchase, or sale of merchandise must keep a record of inventory, conforming to the best accounting practice, which clearly reflects income and is consistent from year to year.

Supplemental unemployment benefit trusts must maintain records indicating the amount of employment separation benefits and sickness and accident benefits which have been provided to each employee. If a plan is financed in whole or in part by employee contributions, records must be maintained of each employee's total contributions allocable to employment separation benefits.

Farmer's cooperative marketing and purchasing associations must keep permanent records of the business done with both members and nonmembers. The records must show that the association was operating during the taxable year on a cooperative basis in the distribution of patronage dividends to all producers.

Controlled entities arm's length charges must be verified by maintaining adequate books and records showing costs or deductions which were a factor in determining the charge for services rendered to other members of a controlled group.

Corporations claiming deduction for dividends paid must keep permanent records necessary (a) to establish that dividends with respect to which the deduction is claimed were actually paid during the taxable year and (b) to supply the information required to be filed with the income tax return of the corporation as well as cancelled dividend checks and receipts obtained from shareholders acknowledging payment.

Mutual savings banks, etc., maintaining reserves for bad debts must maintain as a permanent part of the regular books of account, an account for (1) a reserve for losses on nonqualifying loans, (2) a reserve for losses on qualifying real property loans, and (3), if required, a supplemental reserve for losses on loans. A permanent subsidiary ledger containing an account for each of such reserves may be maintained.

Mutual savings banks, etc., making capital improvements on land acquired by foreclosure must maintain the records necessary to reflect clearly, with respect to each particular acquired property, the cost of each capital improvement and whether the taxpayer treated minor capital improvements with respect to such property in the same manner as the acquired property.

Persons claiming allowance for cost depletion of natural gas property without reference to discovery value or percentage depletion must keep accurate records of periodical pressure determinations where the annual production is not metered.

Persons claiming an allowance for depletion and depreciation of mineral property, oil and gas wells, and other natural deposits must keep a separate account in which the cost or other basis of such property together with subsequent allowable capital additions to each account and all other required adjustments are accurate. They must also assemble, segregate, and have readily available at a principal place of business, all the supporting data used in compiling certain summary statements required to be attached to returns.

For taxable income, computation, and allocation of §1245 gain for mineral property, the taxpayer must have available permanent records of all the facts necessary to determine with reasonable accuracy the portion of any gain recognized under §1245(a)(1) of the Code which is properly allocable to the mineral property in respect of which the taxable income is being computed. In the absence of such records, none of the gain recognized under §1245(a)(1) will be allocable to such mineral property.

Persons claiming an allowance for depletion of timber property must keep accurate ledger accounts in which are recorded the cost or other basis of the property and land together with subsequent allowable capital additions in each account and all other adjustments.

Persons electing to aggregate separate operating mineral interests must maintain adequate records and maps that contain a description of the aggregation and the operating mineral interests within the operating unit which are to be treated as separate properties apart from the aggregation.

Regulated investment companies must maintain records showing the information relative to the actual owners of its stock contained in the written statements to be demanded from the shareholders. For the purposes of determining whether a domestic corporation claiming to be a regulated investment company is a personal holding company, the records of the company must show the maximum number of shares of the corporation (including the number and face value of securities convertible into stock of the corporation) to be considered as actually or constructively owned by each of the actual owners of any of its stock at any time during the last half of the corporation's taxable year and maintain a list of the persons failing or refusing to comply with the demand for statements respecting ownership of shares.

Real estate investment trusts:

☐ (a) A REIT must maintain in the district in which it is required to file its income tax return permanent records which disclose the actual ownership of its outstanding stock.

☐ (b) Shareholders of record may not be the actual owners of the stock; accordingly, the REIT must demand a written statement from shareholders of record disclosing the actual owner of the stock (§1.856-6(d)). A list of the persons failing or refusing to comply in whole or in part with the trust's demand for such statement must be maintained as a part of the trust's records.

☐ (c) For the purpose of determining whether a trust claiming to be a REIT is a personal holding company, the permanent records of the trust must show the maximum number of shares of the trust (including the number and face value of securities convertible into stock of the trust) to be considered as actually or constructively owned by each of the actual owners of any of its stock at any time during the last half of the trust's taxable year, as provided in §544 of the Code.

Persons claiming credit for taxes paid or accrued to foreign countries and possessions of the United States must keep readily available for comparison on request the original receipt for each such tax payment, or the original return on which each such accrued tax was based, or a duplicate original, or a duly certified or authenticated copy, in case only a sworn copy of a receipt or return is submitted.

A Western Hemisphere Trade Corporation must keep records substantiating income tax statement showing that its entire business is done within the Western Hemisphere. If any purchases are made outside the Western Hemisphere, the amount of such purchases, the amount of its gross receipts from all sources, and any other pertinent information must be retained.

United States shareholders of controlled foreign corporations must provide permanent books of account or records which are sufficient to verify for the taxable year Subpart F, export trade, and certain other classes of income and the increase in earnings invested in United States property.

Election to use the average basis method for certain regulated investment company stock (added) must be backed by such records as are necessary to substantiate the average basis (or bases) used on an income tax return in reporting gain or loss from the sale or transfer of shares.

Executors or other legal representatives of decedents, fiduciaries of trusts under wills, life tenants and other persons to whom a uniform basis with respect to property transmitted at death is applicable must make and maintain records showing in detail all deductions, distributions, or other items for which adjustment to basis is required to be made.

Persons making or receiving gifts of property acquired by gift after December 31, 1920 must preserve and keep accessible a record of the facts necessary to determine the cost of the property and, if pertinent, its fair market value as of March 1, 1913, or its fair market value as of the date of the gift, to insure a fair and adequate determination of the proper basis.

Persons participating in exchanges or distributions made in obedience to orders of the Securities and Exchange Commission must keep substantial records showing the cost or other basis of the property transferred and the amount of stock or securities and other property (including money) received.

Gain on sale or exchange of obligations issued at an original issue discount after December 31, 1954 must be backed by taxpayer records of the issue price and issue date on or with each such obligation if known or reasonably ascertainable by him. If the obligation held is an obligation of the United States received from the United States in an exchange on which gain or loss is not recognized because of §1037(a) of the Code (or as much of §1031(b) or (c) as relates to §1037(a)) the taxpayer must keep sufficient records to determine the issue price of such obligations for purposes of applying §1.1037-1 of the Regulations on the disposition or redemption of such obligations.

Record retention requirements for corporations and shareholders with respect to the substantiation of ordinary loss deductions on small business corporation stock are as follows:

☐ (a) *Corporations:* The plan to issue stock which qualifies under §1244 of the IRC must appear on the records of the corporation. In addition, in order to substantiate an ordinary loss deduction claimed by its shareholders, the corporation should maintain records showing the following: (1) The persons to whom stock was issued pursuant to the plan, the date of issuance to each, and a description of the amount and type of consideration received from each ; (2) if the consideration received is property, the basis in the hands of the shareholders and the fair market value of such property when received by the corporation; (3) which certificates represent stock issued pursuant to the plan; (4) the amount of money and the basis in the hands of the corporation of other property received after June 30, 1958, and before the adoption of the plan for its stock as a contribution to capital and as paid-in surplus; (5) the equity capital of the corporation on the date of adoption of the plan; and (6) information relating to any tax-free stock dividend made with respect to stock issued pursuant to the plan and any reorganization in which stock is transferred by the corporation in exchange for stock issued pursuant to the plan.

☐ (b) *Shareholders:* Any person who claims a deduction for an ordinary loss on stock under §1244 of the Code must file with his income tax return for the year in which a deduction for the loss is claimed a statement setting forth: (1) the address of the corporation that issued the stock; (2) the manner in which the stock was acquired by such person and the nature and amount of the consideration paid, and (3) if the stock was acquired in a nontaxable transaction in exchange for property other than money, the type of property, its fair market value on the date of transfer to the corporation, and its adjusted basis on such date.

In addition, a person who owns "§1244 stock" in a corporation must maintain records sufficient to distinguish such stock from any other stock he may own in the corporation.

Foreign investment companies must maintain and preserve such permanent books of account, records, and other documents as are sufficient to establish what its taxable income would be if it were a domestic corporation. Generally, if the books and records are maintained in the manner prescribed by regulations under §30 of the Investment Company Act of 1940, the requirements will be considered satisfied.

Recomputed basis of §1245 property and additional depreciation adjustments to §1250 property when such property is sold, exchanged, transferred, or involuntarily converted must be backed by permanent records which include (1) the date and manner in which the property was acquired, (2) the basis on the date the property was acquired and the manner in which it was determined, (3) the amount and date of all adjustments to basis, and (4) similar information with respect to other property having an adjusted basis reflecting depreciation or amortization adjustments by the taxpayer or by another taxpayer on the same or other property.

Persons involved in the liquidation and replacement of LIFO inventories must keep detailed records so as to enable the Commissioner, in his examination of the taxpayer's return for the year of replacement, readily to verify the extent of the inventory decrease claimed to be involuntary in character and the facts on which such claim is based, all subsequent inventory increases and decreases, and all other facts material to the replacement adjustment authorized.

Records by small business corporations of (1) distributions of previously taxed income and (2) undistributed taxable income must be kept of (a) distributions of the net share of the previously taxed income of each shareholder and (b) each person's share of undistributed taxable income. In addition, each shareholder of such corporation must keep a record of his own net share of previously taxed income and undistributed taxable income and make such record available to the corporation for its information.

Persons required to withhold tax on nonresident aliens, foreign corporations, and tax-free covenant bonds on payments of income made on and after January 1, 1975 must keep copies of Forms 1042 and 1042S.

Affiliated groups accounting for deferred gain or loss in intercompany transactions must maintain permanent records, including work papers, which will properly reflect the amount of deferred gain or loss and enable the group to identify the character and source of the deferred gain or loss to the selling member and apply the applicable restoration rules.

Affiliated groups electing allocation of federal income tax liability under §1.1502-33(d)(2)(i) of the regulations must maintain specific records to substantiate the tax liability of each member on a separate return basis for purposes of paragraphs (a)(1) and (b)(1) of subdivision (i). In addition, allocation of tax liability may be made in accordance with any other method approved by the Commissioner, but a condition of such approval must be that the group maintain specific records to substantiate its computations pursuant to such method.

Tax-exempt organizations generally must keep records and books of account pertaining to information included in the annual return, including items of gross income, receipts, disbursements, and contributions and gifts received, and other pertinent information which will enable the district director to inquire into the organization's exempt status. An organization claiming an exception from the filing of an information return must maintain adequate records to substantiate such claim.

☐ (a) Employees' trust must keep as a part of their records written notification from an employer to the trustee that the employer has or will timely file the information required under §404.
☐ (b) For group returns, the central organization must retain the certified statements of those local organizations authorizing their inclusion in a group return.

Retention periods are as follows, for taxable years prior to January 1, 1970, permanent; for taxable years after December 31, 1969, until the expiration of six years after the last taxable year for which a group return includes the local organization.

Withholding agents making payment to nonresident aliens, foreign partnerships, or foreign corporations after December 31, 1971, which are subject to a reduced rate or an exemption from tax pursuant to a tax treaty must keep Form 1001, Ownership, Exemption or Reduced Rate Certificate.

The retention period. For coupon bond interest is at least four years after the close of the calendar year in which the interest is paid; for income other than coupon bond interest or dividends, at least four years after the close of the calendar year in which the interest is paid.

Gift Tax

Persons making transfers of property by gift must maintain such books of account or records as are necessary to establish the amount of the total gifts, together with the deductions allowable in determining the amount of taxable gifts and other information required to be shown in their gift tax returns. The records must be retained *permanently*.

Employment Tax

General record retention requirements are as follows:

☐ (a) *Form of Records:* Records must be kept accurately, but no particular form is required. Keep such forms and systems of accounting as will enable the district director to ascertain whether liability for tax is incurred and, if so, the amount.
☐ (b) *Copies of Returns, Schedules, and Statements:* Every person who is required to keep any copy of any return, schedule, statement or other document, must keep such copy as a part of his records.
☐ (c) *Records of Claimants:* Any person (including an employee) who claims a refund, credit, or abatement must keep a complete and detailed record with respect to the tax, interest, addition to

the tax, additional amount, or assessable penalty to which the claim relates. Such record must include any records required of the claimant by paragraph (b) relating to the claim.

☐ (d) *Records of Employees:* While not mandatory except in the case of claims, it is advisable for each employee to keep permanent, accurate records showing the name and address of each employer for whom he performs services as an employee, the dates of beginning and termination of such services, the information with respect to himself that is required to be kept by employers, and all receipts furnished by employers.

☐ (e) *Place for Keeping Records:* All records required must be kept, by the person required to keep them, at one or more convenient and safe locations accessible to internal revenue officers, and must at all times be available for inspection by such officers.

Retention period is four years after the due date of the tax for the return period to which the records relate or the date such tax is paid, whichever is later. The records of claimants required by paragraph (c) must be maintained for a period of at least four years after the date the claim is filed.

[¶1903] YOUR METHOD OF REPORTING INCOME

The tax consequences of your business transactions are usually determined by their legal status, the accounting treatment of such items, or both. It therefore becomes imperative to plan your accounting and legal techniques *before* entering into any transactions.

Once the transaction has occurred and the book entry has been made, it is usually too late to worry about the tax consequences. Even minor issues should be worked out in advance via proper procedures. For example, proper wording of purchase orders will often insure proper description on invoices, so that portions of work done that are deductible as repairs are properly described and billed separately from work done on installations, improvements, etc., that are required to be capitalized.

In order to plan properly, you must know the accounting techniques available to you. Here are the broad choices:

☐ (1) The cash method
☐ (2) The accrual method
☐ (3) The "hybrid" method
☐ (4) The installment method
☐ (5) The deferred payment sales method
☐ (6) The long-term contract method
☐ (7) The completed contract method

These methods of accounting are explained in detail at Section XIII.

[¶1903.1] What the Tax Law Does and Doesn't Require

The law specifies only that you compute taxable income in accordance with the method of accounting you regularly employ in keeping your books; however, such method must clearly reflect your income (§446(a)).

Each taxpayer is authorized to adopt such forms and systems of accounting as in his judgment are best suited to his purpose (Reg. §1.446-1). No uniform method is prescribed for all taxpayers.

Nevertheless, the Regulations (Reg. §1.446-1) do provide that:

☐ (1) All items of gross income and deductions must be treated with reasonable consistency.
☐ (2) In all cases in which the production, purchase, or sale of merchandise is an income-producing factor, an accrual method is necessary, and inventories of merchandise on hand (including finished goods, work in process, raw materials and supplies) must be taken at the beginning and end of the accounting period and used in computing taxable income of the period.
☐ (3) Expenditures made during the year should be properly classified as between capital and expense; expenditures for items such as plant and equipment that have a useful life extending substantially beyond the end of the year must be charged to capital rather than to expense.
☐ (4) Where capital costs are being recovered through deductions for wear and tear, depletion, or obsolescence, expenditures (other than ordinary repairs) made to restore the property or prolong its useful life should be added to the property account or charged against the appropriate reserve, not to current expense.

Those who neither produce nor sell goods, and consequently have no inventories, can use either of the two regular methods of accounting, the cash or accrual. This includes artists; authors; artisans, such as carpenters and masons who either use their customers' materials or buy materials for specific jobs only; professionals, such as accountants, architects, attorneys, dentists, physicians, and engineers; and brokers and agents rendering services of various kinds.
☐ (5) Special methods of accounting are also prescribed in the Code. Such methods include the installment method (§453) and the long-term contract method (§451). There are also special methods of accounting for particular items of income and expense.
☐ (6) A combination of methods (hybrid system) of accounting may also be used in connection with a trade or business if consistently used.
☐ (7) The fact that books are kept in accordance with the requirements of a supervisory agency does not mean that income for tax purposes must be computed in the same manner (*Barretville Bank & Trust Co.*, TC Memo 1958-148).

[¶1904] CONFLICTS BETWEEN TAX AND BUSINESS ACCOUNTING

The conflicts between tax accounting and generally accepted business accounting center around the questions: (1) *when* is it income, and (2) *when* is it deductible? To illustrate the differences that have existed in these two areas, we include the following list that was submitted by the American Institute of Accountants to the House Committee on Ways and Means in connection with the Hearings on the 1954 Code. The important areas of conflict are discussed in the paragraphs that follow the list.

Divergences Involving the Time of Recognition of Revenues

(A) Revenues, deferred for generally accounting purposes until earned, but reportable for tax purposes when received:
   (1) Revenues susceptible of proration on a fixed-time basis or on a service-rendered basis: Rentals.

Commissions.
Revenues from maintenance and similar service contracts covering a specified period.
Warehousing and trucking fees.
Advertising revenues.
Advance royalties on patents or copyrights.
Transportation ticket and token sales.
Sales of coupon books entitling purchaser to services.
Theatre ticket sales.
Membership fees.
Tuition fees.
Laboratory fees.

(2) Revenues susceptible of proration over average duration of demand:
Life memberships.
Revenues from service contracts extending over life of article serviced or period of ownership by original owner.

(B) Revenues deferred for general accounting purposes until right to retain them is substantially assured, but reportable for tax purposes when received:

(1) Receipts under claim of right.

(C) Revenues accrued for general accounting purposes, but not reportable for tax purposes until collected:

(1) Dividends declared.
(2) Increase in withdrawal value of savings and loan shares.

Divergences Involving the Time of Allowance of Deductions

(A) Costs and expenses, recognized for general accounting purposes, on basis of reasonable estimates, in period of related revenues; but not deductible for tax purposes until established with certainty by specific transactions:

(1) Sales returns and allowances.
(2) Freight allowances.
(3) Quantity discounts.
(4) Cash discounts allowable to customers.
(5) Allowances for customers' advertising.
(6) Provisions for return of commissions resulting from cancellations of related contracts.
(7) Costs of product guarantees.
(8) Deferred management compensation and incentive bonuses.
(9) Vacation pay.
(10) Pending injury and damage claims.
(11) Rentals on percentage lease with minimum.
(12) Provisions for major repairs and maintenance regularly done at intervals of more than a year.
(13) Professional services rendered but unbilled.
(14) Social security taxes on unpaid wages.
(15) Retailers' occupation taxes on credit sales.
(16) Costs of restoration of property by lessee at termination of lease.
(17) Contractors' provisions for restoration of property damaged during construction.

(18) Costs of handling, packing, shipping, installing, etc., of merchandise already sold.
(19) Provisions for future costs to be incurred in collection of accounts receivable arising from installment sales, where profit is reported in the year of sale.
(20) Provisions for losses on foreign exchange.
(21) Allowances for perpetual care of cemetery (where not actually segregated from receipts).

(B) Expenses, deferred for generally accounting purposes to period of related benefit, but deducted for tax purposes in year of payment or incurrence of liability:
(1) Advertising expenses from which benefit has not yet been obtained, including costs of preparation of catalogues not yet put into use.

(C) Property taxes recognized for general accounting purposes ratably over the year for which they are levied, but deductible in toto for tax purposes on a certain critical date.

The foregoing differences do not include conflicts that result from Congressional policy decisions. These include, on the *income side*, tax-exempt interest, tax-free exchanges, exemption of life insurance proceeds, capital gains, etc., and, on the *deduction side*, percentage depletion, amortization of emergency facilities, loss carryovers, and the disallowance of excess charitable contributions, losses on wash sales, losses on sales between certain relatives or related business interests, capital losses, etc.

The special treatment accorded to these items originates from social, economic, and revenue considerations that, in the main, are unrelated to accounting principles.

[¶1904.1] Income Received in Advance

Frequently, a taxpayer receives payment for services he has not yet performed (e.g., club membership dues, magazine subscriptions). The question then is in what year does the taxpayer have to report these payments as income.

Accounting Rule: The accountant says that you have no income until it is actually *earned;* that the mere receipt of cash or property does not result in a realization of income. The accountant treats the prepayment as a liability that obligates the recipient to perform services before he can be said to have *earned* the payment. (This problem applies to accrual-basis taxpayers; cash-basis taxpayers are considered to have *earned* a prepayment when it is received.)

Tax Rule: You have income when you have the *right to receive* it, even though it is not earned. Thus, cash payments received in advance, negotiable notes received as advance payments, and contract installments due and payable are taxable to the recipient as advance income, even though these payments are for services to be provided by the taxpayer in a subsequent tax year (*American Automobile Association,* 367 US 687, 1961; *Schlude,* 372 US 128, 1963). Here is a composite tax picture:

Type of Income	*Basis*	*Extent Taxable*	*Authority*
Cash Receipts	Cash or Accrual	Full Amount	*American Automobile Association,* 367 US 687; *Schlude,* 372 US 128.
Negotiable Notes	Cash	Fair Market Value	*Pinellas Ice Co.,* 287 US 462; Reg. §1.61-2(d)(4).

Type of Income	*Basis*	*Extent Taxable*	*Authority*
	Accrual	Face Value	*Schlude,* 372 US 128; *Schlude,* TC Memo 1963-307; see *Spring City Foundry Co.*, 292 US 182.
Unpaid Contractual Payments Due and Payable Under Terms of the Contract	Cash	None—no fair market value	*Est. of Ennis,* 23 TC 799; *nonacq.*, 1956-2 CB 10; *Ennis,* 17 TC 465.
Unpaid Contractual Installments Neither Due Under the Contract nor Evidenced by Notes	Cash	None	*Schlude,* 372 US 128.
	Accrual	None	*Schlude,* 372 US 128.

The tendency of the courts seems to be to require reporting prepaid receipts. A furrier was required to include in income advance payments for fur coat orders and was not allowed to estimate the cost of goods sold for the year receipts were included in income. See *Hagen Advertising Displays, Inc.*, 47 TC 139, 1966; *Boyce*, 405 F.2d 526 Ct. Cl., 1968. But see *Artnell Co.*, 400 F.2d 981, CA-7, 1968, where a baseball team deferred preseason sales receipts.

Special Relief Provisions: Sections 455 and 456 of IRC were enacted to provide special relief from the results of *Schlude*.

☐ (1) ***Accrual-basis taxpayers*** may elect to defer prepaid income from service contracts or from the sale of goods. See *Rev. Proc. 71-21* and Regs. §1.451-5.
☐ (2) ***Publishers*** may elect to spread prepaid subscription income, §455.
☐ (3) ***Membership organizations*** organized without capital stock, which do not distribute earnings to any members and do not report income by the cash receipts and disbursements method, may spread their prepaid dues income ratably over the period (not to exceed 36 months) during which they are under a liability to render services.

[¶1904.2] Repayment of Income Received Under Claim of Right

Since the tax law requires the accrual-basis taxpayer to include payments received (although not yet earned) in taxable income when received, it obviously disagrees with good accounting practice on how to treat such payments if they must be repaid.

If the payments are properly handled so that unearned payments are not picked up as income, repayments of unearned accounts pose no problem. They merely reduce the liability that the prepayments imposed. The income statements for the year of receipt and year of repayment are therefore not affected.

However, says the accountant, the tax rule is unrealistic and inequitable. The inclusion of disputed income in year of receipt and the allowance of a deduction in the year of repayment result in a distortion of taxpayer's income in two years. It can also result in higher tax liability (for example, where taxpayer is in a higher tax bracket in the year of receipt than in the year of repayment, the tax rates are higher in the year of receipt than in the year of repayment).

Tax Rule: If you are required to repay money received under a claim of right, the tax law says you can deduct it in the year of repayment (*Lewis,* 340 US 590, 1951).

Relief Provisions: Section 1341 eliminates the inequity if the amount of repayment exceeds $3,000; the taxpayer may reduce his tax for the year of repayment by the amount of tax he would have saved in the year of receipt had he been permitted to exclude the subsequent repayment from the original amount received. Alternatively, he may deduct the amount repaid in the year of repayment if that will result in a smaller tax to him.

The relief provision does not apply to refunds, allowances, bad debts, etc., applicable to sales of inventory or stock in trade.

Section 1341 provides relief to a *recipient* of income who is required to repay all or part of such income in a later year. Section 1342 affords similar relief to a *payor* who makes payments to a third party because of a court judgment in a patent infringement suit and in a later year recovers all or part of such payments (which were deducted in the previous year) because of a subsequent reversal of the court decision on the ground that it was induced by fraud or undue influence.

If the recovery exceeds $3,000, the taxpayer is given the option of computing the additional tax for the year of recovery in one of two ways: (a) including the amount recovered as income in the year of recovery; (b) decreasing the deduction taken for the amount paid in the earlier year by the amount of the subsequent recovery and paying the additional tax (plus interest) recomputed for such earlier year.

Prepaid interest is not income received under "claim of right" (*Rev. Rul. 58-226*, CB 1958-1, 318). But §1341 applies to F.H.A. windfall involuntarily repaid by shareholders to corporation (*Rev. Rul. 58-456*, CB 1958-2, 415).

[¶1904.3] Containers

Many companies sell merchandise in returnable containers, the customer being charged for the container at the time of sale and receiving a refund or credit therefor upon the return of the container. Typical are bottles, cases, kegs, barrels, and reels in which beverage companies, brewers, and manufacturers of wire and cable sell and ship their products. The question arises: When is the charge for the container reportable as income?

Accounting Rule: The accountant says no income results from the shipment of the container to the customer. It is not a real "sale" but a "conditional sale" burdened with an obligation on the part of the seller to repurchase the container on demand by the customer. Accordingly, the amount received for the container should be treated as a "deposit liability"; it should be credited to a reserve account computed upon the reasonable expectancy of repurchases.

Tax Rule: If title to the container *passes* to the customer, the transaction is treated as a sale and the amount billed for the container is taken into income by the seller. When the container is returned, the seller treats the refund or credit made to the customer as a repurchase of the container (*Okonite Co.*, 155 F.2d 248, CA-3, 1946). If title *does not pass*, then the amount charged for the container is treated as a "deposit liability." Refund of the container deposit merely cancels the liability.

However, unclaimed deposits may be converted into taxable income if they build up to an excessive amount or if the seller, by a bookkeeping entry, transfers any part of the "deposit liability" account to his surplus account (*Fort Pitt Brewing Co.*, 92 F.2d 825, CA-3, 1954; *Nehi Beverage Co.*, 16 TC 1114, 1951).

[¶1904.4] Reserves for Estimated Costs and Expenses

The general rule is that an expense is deductible by a cash-basis taxpayer when he pays it and by an accrual-basis taxpayer when his liability is fixed (Reg. §1.446-1).

Where a taxpayer receives income for services he is to perform in the future, the question arises as to when he may deduct the expenses attributable to such income. (This question is the other side of the question: When are prepaid receipts income?)

Accounting Rule: An accrual-basis taxpayer should be allowed to estimate future expenses that are attributable to current income, provided the estimate can be made with a reasonable degree of accuracy. In this way he can match his costs with his income and have an accurate picture of his income for a particular period.

Tax Rule: For an accrual-basis taxpayer, deductions are allowed for the year in which "all events" have occurred to fix the *fact* and the *amount* of the liability (*Anderson*, 269 US 422; *Dixie Pine Products Company*, 320 US 516). The fact that a company may have a reasonable basis for its estimate does not change the result. In *Milwaukee and Suburban Transport Company*, 368 US 976, it was held that a common carrier could not deduct the estimated amount of personal injury and property damage liability even though it had a reasonable basis for its estimate. See also *Simplified Tax Records, Inc.*, 41 TC 75, where the taxpayer was not allowed to set up a reserve for estimated costs of future accounting services that it sought to charge against prepaid fees.

[¶1904.5] Contested Liabilities—When Deductible?

Contested liabilities present a special case among deductible business expenses, since they may never be paid and, even if paid, may be returned if the contest is successful. Under present law, a contested liability is handled in the following manner:

(1) If payment is not made until *after* the contest is settled, an accrual-basis taxpayer must accrue the deduction in the year of settlement, and a cash-basis taxpayer must take the deduction in the year paid.

(2) If payment is made in full *before* the contest is settled, both cash- and accrual-basis taxpayers take the deduction in the year paid. Then, when the contest is later settled, if there is a refund, the cash-basis taxpayer includes the refund in the year he receives it (or constructively receives it), and the accrual-basis taxpayer includes the refund in the year of final settlement, regardless of when it is paid (see Code §461(f)).

(3) If a taxpayer received no tax benefit from the deduction for the original payment of the contested liability, the later recovery of the payment in whole or in part when the contest is settled will not be taxable under §111.

In order to get the deduction in (2), above, a taxpayer must actually transfer money or other property in satisfaction of the liability in such a manner that he no longer has control of the funds. This can be done by actually paying the claimant asserting the liability or by transferring the funds into an escrow account, provided the escrow agent is not under the control of the taxpayer and provided the taxpayer gives up all rights to the funds except the right to a refund if the claim is settled for less than the full amount. Further, the escrow account can even be secret, in that the claimant need not know about it (*Poirer and McLane Corporation*, 63 TC No. 55, 1975).

Although the Regulations (§1.461-2(c)) specifically require the written agreement of the claimant to such an arrangement, the Tax Court chose to ignore this as impractical in the cited case.

Note, however, that §461 relates only to the timing of the deduction. Thus, the expense must still be a deductible expense under some other provision, such as §162. What §461 does, then, is allow the deduction of the full amount paid or put into escrow in the year transferred and determine the year in which the refund, if any, is to be included in gross income.

[¶1904.6] Prepaid Expenses and Real Estate Taxes

For both the accountant and the tax collector, an accrual-basis taxpayer must generally deduct prepaid expenses ratably over the years to which they relate (unlike the accrual of prepaid income). One exception is prepaid advertising expenses. These expenses are deductible in the year they accrue, although the benefits from such expense may extend over a period of years (*A. Finkenberg's Sons, Inc.*, 17 TC 973, 1952). The accountant would rather prorate the expense.

Accounting Rule: A cash-basis taxpayer should deduct prepaid expenses when paid; in this manner he obtains, to some extent, a matching of income with expenses, since he is also required to report prepaid income when received.

Tax Rule: The Treasury, whenever possible, requires cash-basis taxpayers to defer specific types of prepaid expenses. For example, a cash-basis taxpayer must ratably deduct prepaid rent (Reg. §1.461-1). The Treasury usually justifies deferral on the grounds the prepayment constitutes a capital asset that should be amortized (''useful life'' test, see Reg. §1.461) or merely a ''deposit.''

Prepaid Interest: One area of conflict is the prepayment of interest. Back in 1945, IRS okayed a deduction by a cash-basis taxpayer for interest paid for five years in advance. IRS, however, now says that if interest is prepaid for a period extending more than 13 months beyond the end of the current taxable year, it will consider the deduction of such interest in the year of payment as materially distorting income.

Insurance Expense: Another area of conflict is the prepayment of insurance premiums. The First Circuit (*Boylston Market Association,* 131 F.2d 966, CA-1, 1942), has denied an immediate deduction for payment of prepaid insurance premiums, while the Eighth Circuit (*Waldheim Realty,* 245 F.2d 823, CA-8, 1957) has allowed it on the grounds that prepaid insurance premiums are not a capital asset.

Real Estate Taxes: While the accountant and the tax collector used to differ here the areas of difference have been largely eliminated.

Accounting Rule: The accountant holds that real estate taxes should be spread ratably over the year for which they are levied. Thus, if a real estate tax is imposed for the calendar year 1974, the entire tax would be considered as an expense of that year. If the tax is imposed for a fiscal year beginning October 1, 1973, and ending September 30, 1974, $^{3}/_{12}$ of the tax would be treated as an expense for 1973 and the remaining $^{9}/_{12}$ as an expense for 1974.

Tax Rule: Accrual-basis taxpayers can deduct real estate taxes on the date they accrue, i.e., the lien date. Thus, for example, if the taxpayer was on a calendar-year basis and the taxes for the year accrued on December 1, the taxpayer would be entitled to deduct the entire amount although the taxes may relate to the next calendar year. However, a taxpayer who wishes to use the business accounting method may elect under a special provision (§461(c)) to prorate the taxes over the period to which they relate.

Where the taxpayer uses the accrual date for deducting real estate taxes, he is prevented from deducting the taxes twice; this might occur where there is a change in state or local law (see Reg. §1.461-1) or a change in taxpayer's accounting period.

SECTION XX
THE TAX AUDIT

There is no question but that one of the more disturbing elements of business, professional, or personal life is the discovery that IRS wants to audit or otherwise examine your income tax return. Even for those who have nothing to hide and whose returns have been prepared in all good conscience, there is still a reaction ranging from rage and infuriation to sheer panic. To most businessmen and professionals, the mysteries of an income tax audit are exactly that—mysteries. Even the careful and conscientious taxpayer has that sinking feeling where he just *knows* that he is going to come out on the short end of the stick.

The reason for this is that, by and large, the average taxpayer doesn't know what an audit is, what it involves, what the rights and obligations of either side are, and what procedures are involved. This section covers these points and helps banish the mystery from the nuisance called the tax audit.

[¶2001] WHAT HAPPENS AFTER YOU FILE YOUR TAX RETURNS?

When IRS receives your tax return it is checked for accuracy and completeness in two ways:

The first check is manual for clearly unallowable items, e.g., duplicate deductions. Returns are verified from W-2 Forms.

The second check is by computer to detect mistakes that escaped manual scanning, e.g., mathematical errors, computation floors and ceilings, say, failure to take 3% of adjusted gross income from medical deductions. The process is known as DIF (Discriminate Function System).

DIF crosschecks as many as 15 or 20 items on a return and involves thousands of comparisons. Returns scoring high have a high probability of error and go to experienced IRS "screeners." Their job is to combine computer scoring with human judgment in deciding whether or not to audit. These audits are in addition to certain other audits.

[¶2002] WHAT ARE YOUR CHANCES OF BEING AUDITED?

There is no practical way of determining the odds or probabilities of your tax return being audited, for the simple reason that not only do many varied criteria apply, but these criteria are also differently applied in various districts throughout the country. Often this depends on the district's past experience combined with its assigned workload in areas other than audit. But there are a few general rules that can serve as at least tentative guidelines. Here they are, in detail.

[¶2002.1] Tax Bracket as a Factor

By and large, taxpayers in lower brackets have the least probability of being audited. Up to the $10,000 bracket, only about 2% face scrutiny. However, as the bracket increases, so does the percentage. Those with nonbusiness incomes in the $50,000 bracket or higher have an audit rate of about 12% or higher.

On the corporate front (and this can include professional corporations as well), the audit rate tends to depend on the amount of corporate assets. A corporation with $50,000 to $100,000 in assets can usually count on a nominal 4% audit rate. But, in the case of a corporation showing $500,000 to $1,000,000 or more, the rate jumps to 20% or better. It should be noted that the increase in audit rate for those in higher brackets does not mean that IRS is implying that wealthier taxpayers tend to cheat. Rather, IRS points out that where large sums are involved, both the transactions and the tax treatment are more likely to be subject to different interpretations.

[¶2002.2] Type of Business or Source of Income as a Factor

There are certain businesses and occupations that attract IRS audit like a sugar cube attracts flies. The reason for this is not any special grudge that IRS has against any business or profession. Rather it is the result of findings made by the Taxpayer Compliance Measurement Program, usually known as TCMP.

Under TCMP, IRS carefully scrutinizes individuals and corporations in a random fashion and then tabulates results into business and professional categories. If one of these categories should indicate what IRS feels is less than adequate compliance, the audit rate for that category rises sharply.

Based on TCMP findings, emphasis is presently being placed on contractors and subcontractors in the construction industry, managers in direct selling activities, insurance salesmen, and attorneys. There is some indication that both the jewelry industry and the medical profession may soon make the TCMP list.

Obviously, any taxpayer fitting within a TCMP category is going to have a greater likelihood of an audit than one belonging to a category in which TCMP has found substantial compliance. This is a factor to be considered not only when actually faced with an audit, but also in the preparation of the return.

[¶2002.3] Informants as a Factor

Informants provide a huge source of audit cases that go straight to the Intelligence Division of IRS. The usual result is an audit contact from a "special agent" (see ¶2005).

Informants are motivated by any number of reasons, although most can be placed into one of three categories: love, hate, or greed.

Love: These are citizens who love their country, and who for one reason or another suspect a taxpayer of not meeting his fair share.

Hate: This is by far the largest group, whose reasons for tipping off IRS as to suspected taxpayer misfeasance all fall under the heading of envy or revenge. Here you might find: fired employees, jilted mistresses (or wives); competitors; jealous neighbors. IRS is very democratic in whom it listens to.

Greed: Here you'll chiefly find the "ten-percenters." Contrary to public opinion, IRS does not *have* to reward informants whose leads prove accurate. However, the Treasury usually *will* do so—turning over 10% of the taxes and penalties collected in most instances.

[¶2002.4] Organized Crime as a Factor

Odds are if you're an organized crime chieftain you won't be reading this book. But organized (and sometimes un- or dis-organized) crime figures highly in the question of IRS audits. Basically, IRS compares notes with the Department of Justice and the Bureau of Narcotics and Dangerous Drugs to obtain information about individuals who might have violated the revenue laws. Virtually every one who is a target of another agency will be audited. So, too, with the smaller fish: Statistics show that persons convicted of crimes get audited far more often than their more law-abiding counterparts.

[¶2002.5] Large Transactions as a Factor

IRS personnel regularly scan records of mortgage transactions and other business deals, read newspaper reports of business promotions, and monitor large stock or currency transfers to draw leads for audits. Treasury regulations require banking institutions to report large cash deposits, for instance. These are currently defined as deposits of $2,500 or more made in bills of $100 or more, or cash deposits of $10,000 made in any denominations (T.D. Release No. A-590, 8/3/59). An audit will often automatically result from a lead derived from one of these sources.

[¶2002.6] Geography and Workloads as Factors

The taxpayer's geographic location is another strong factor in assessing the probability of an IRS audit. Some illustrative figures show that roughly 1 of 37 returns faces audit in New York City, 1 of 59 in San Francisco, 1 of 33 in Reno, and 1 of 52 in New Orleans.

The principal reason for this, oddly enough, has little or nothing to do with any belief in the taxpayer's honesty or accuracy in preparation. For the most part, it is a question of district office workload combined with the number of qualified personnel available.

Selection of a return for an audit is becoming less and less a human function. It is now handled, for the most part, by computers. At first, in 1969, only personal returns were computer selected. Commencing in 1973, small businesses are also being processed by means of the computer. However, the fact that the computer has selected a particular return for audit does not necessarily mean that the return will be audited. The computer may well have selected far more audit candidates than can be conveniently processed by the district office.

The TCMP, discussed earlier, was actually conceived as a partial solution to this problem. When a district office is faced with more audit possibilities than it can physically handle, common sense alone suggests that more emphasis will be placed on "red flag" TCMP categories. Thus, while this may result in fewer audits overall, those audits actually undertaken will be more productive.

[¶2002.7] Time as a Factor

Generally speaking, IRS has a three-year time limit in which to audit a return (Code §6501(a)). This time period commences on the April 15 on which the return is due or on the date actually filed if the taxpayer secured an extension or simply was late in filing. For corporate returns, the same rules apply to a March 15 deadline. This three-year rule also applies to carryback situations. For example, if you elect to take a five-year carryback in 1974 (thus, in effect, amending all returns filed up to five years prior to that date), the time limit on any one of the amended returns is still governed by the three-year rule.

There are, however, exceptions to the time rule. For example, if IRS can prove that a taxpayer omitted 25% or more of his gross income for the year in question, the time limit is expanded to six years (§6501(e)(1)). Of course, the burden of proof is on IRS and not on the taxpayer. Here, though, an exception to the exception helps taxpayers. Where such an omission occurs but the principal facts of the pertinent transaction appear in the return or an attached schedule, the normal three-year limit applies (§6501(e)(1)(A)(ii)). Example: Your boss provides you with a $10,000 year-end "gift." You note the item on your return, along with your explanation that it is not taxable. Although your explanation may be faulty, and the "gift" should properly be included in your income, IRS will have to say so within three years.

Another exception is the presence of any element of fraud. If IRS suspects fraud in any way, such as willful failure to report income, there is no time limit, and the Government can go back to any year (§6501(c)(1)(2)). As with our previous example, the burden of proof rests with IRS.

One last exception occurs when the taxpayer waives the usual IRS limitations by agreeing to an extension of time for assessment (§6501(e)(4)). Sometimes IRS can apply pressure on a taxpayer to extend the limit (see ¶2006.6).

These time limits are for what is termed "civil fraud." If IRS proves its case, the penalty is the amount of the original tax due, plus a 50% surcharge or penalty, and 9% interest per annum on the total amount (6% for periods prior to July 1, 1975).

The other side of the coin is "criminal fraud," which carries the penalty of a fine, a prison term, or both. Further, if IRS elects to proceed under criminal fraud and proves a case, it will almost inevitably next proceed on civil fraud to recover the unpaid tax, plus surcharge, plus interest.

For all practical purposes, the three-year rule is a matter of government procedure and convenience. In actuality, the auditing cycle usually takes 26 months in the case of individuals and 27 months in the case of corporations. To IRS, this time cycle doesn't mean starting the audit, but rather starting it and *completing* it.

Now, with modern technology, such as specialized computers, IRS is hopeful of reducing even that cycle time to 20 months for individuals and 21 months for corporations. This has already been accomplished in a majority of audit investigations, and the coming decade may see even shorter cycle times.

[¶2002.8] A Summing Up of Audit Possibilities

The trend toward random auditing has gone down to a great extent. In the early 1960s, an average of 5.8% of all income, estate, and gift returns were audited. By 1972, this rate had dropped to 1.9%. While a certain amount of this drop can be attributed to increased work assignments for IRS as a whole, the real reason is the approach of selectivity.

At one time, audit decisions were made on a shotgun basis. Today, a rifle is used. Research tools such as TCMP, computer selection of returns to be audited, and other technological advances have shifted the IRS approach to one of identifying "red flag" areas and concentrating on those rather than simply picking returns at random. The results have proven startlingly effective and set the pattern for all future auditing activities.

Thus, while ratewise (1.9% today as against 5.8% ten years ago) it would seem that the odds are increasing in favor of the taxpayer, the truth of the matter is that they are increasing only in favor of the taxpayer who never had to be concerned with an audit in the first place. But for the taxpayer in the high-income bracket, filing in an area of high audit rate and within a TCMP "red flag" category, the exact reverse is true. His or her chances of facing an audit are directly proportional to these factors—and there is no way in which they can presently be projected in mathematical terms.

[¶2002.9] Key IRS Criteria for Determining Whether Your Return Will Be Audited

In determining whether a particular return is to be singled out for audit, IRS screeners are instructed to scan each return for certain specific characteristics. A return is most likely to be audited where:

☐ (1) The income seems to be insufficient to support the claimed exemptions.

☐ (2) The refund appears to be out of line considering the gross income and exemptions.

☐ (3) The taxpayer's occupation or business is one that is normally considered to be more profitable than reflected by the return. Also, where he may have other income not subject to withholding tax, such as tips.

☐ (4) The profit on a reported investment is less than what could have been realized by depositing the same amount in a savings account.

☐ (5) The return reports a high gross but a low net income, and the standard deduction is used.

[¶2003] HOW THE AUDIT PROCEDURE BEGINS

Once a return has been selected by IRS for audit, the taxpayer is notified either by mail or telephone. The person making the contact on behalf of IRS is a revenue agent and will be the person conducting the audit. The object of this communication is not only to notify the taxpayer but also to set up a firm time and place for a meeting.

The time is usually at the convenience of the taxpayer and is often quite flexible. The agent readily understands that the taxpayer will need some time to gather together all the receipts, books, records, and other evidence that may be needed. The place of the audit can be either at the IRS office or the taxpayer's place of business.

[¶2003.1] When Is an "Audit" Really an "Audit"?

The first reaction on the part of most taxpayers receiving a notice of audit is something akin to panic, and they not infrequently have visions of some detailed search or inquiry into their entire financial and tax affairs. While this may be true in some cases (and those taxpayers are well aware that they have reason to be apprehensive), it is more likely than not that the so-called "audit" is not a true audit in the strict sense of the word but merely a desire on the part of IRS to see some tangible substantiation for deductions. As such, the scope of the audit is limited to this narrow area, and IRS will be satisfied with some measure of documentary proof of the claim. However, if the taxpayer cannot produce the necessary supporting evidence, then the inquiry might take on more aspects of a true audit. IRS reasoning is simply that if you can't provide backup for essentially minor deductions, there is enough smoke to justify looking for a possible fire.

Although such a procedure is not really a true audit, should the IRS agent disallow certain deductions and propose a reassessment involving the payment of additional taxes, the taxpayer still has the right of appeal just as if the proceeding were a full-blown audit.

[¶2003.2] Should You Represent Yourself or Seek Outside Professional Assistance Such as a CPA or Tax Attorney?

This is probably the single most difficult decision that the taxpayer will face in the early stages of an audit. There is no hard-and-fast rule that can be applied to all situations. But there are some guidelines that can prove helpful in reaching that decision. Here are some of them:

(1) As a starting point, ask yourself just how complex the matter is. If you have reason to believe that it is simply a question of providing receipts or cancelled checks, you might very well be able to handle the situation yourself. If, however, more complex issues are involved or if the position you have taken in the preparation of the return involves such things as new concepts in tax liability or is based on relatively new Revenue Rulings or Tax Court decisions, you are far better off being represented by either a CPA or a tax attorney. Ideally, one or more of these individuals should have had a hand in the preparation of the return under audit, but this is not strictly necessary.

If you elect to represent yourself and things take an adverse turn, all is not lost. At any stage of the proceeding and where the water begins to deepen, you can always turn to the agent and say, in effect, "I'm afraid this is beginning to get a little over my head. If it's all right with you, I'd like to come to a stop at this point and secure some outside representation. Do you have any objection?" The agent will automatically adjourn the meeting at this point and set up another interview date, giving you adequate time to consult with, and be represented by, the attorney or accountant of your choice. The only danger in this technique is that by the time you stop the interview and turn to outside assistance, you may have already said too much. Unless you are a practicing professional in this area, you are probably unfamiliar with the rules of disclosure. As a result, you may have, in all innocence and candor, opened a whole new can of worms and made more difficult the job of your representative.

(2) Before you decide to represent yourself, take a good long look at your own

personality and candidly weigh your ability to handle this type of negotiation situation. If, for example, you are outraged at IRS for even questioning what you know to be a legitimate deduction, that outrage may manifest itself in an overly aggressive or antagonistic attitude. If you are possessed of the ''I'll fight this to the Supreme Court'' syndrome and make this quite evident, the revenue agent might very well give you all the grounds you need by denying virtually everything and assessing a whopping deficiency. On the other hand, if you attempt to be too charming or too smooth, the agent may very well wonder if you are not happy to concede these few points as long as the rest of the rug is not lifted up.

Agents, after all, are human, and they have human reactions in encounter situations. Albeit implied, the relationship is still one very akin to accuser versus accused. Further, since the revenue agent is doing this merely as a job function and you are there because of your personal interests, no peer relationship is established.

This situation radically changes when the taxpayer is represented by another professional. A peer relationship is quickly established because neither side has any personal interest in the matter and the business at hand is conducted on a professional level. For these reasons, outside representation is always to be preferred. In fact, in some situations, your representative will prefer to conduct the matter entirely on his own without your even being present during the actual audit. This is one effective way of eliminating the possibility that you may interrupt the audit and unknowingly (and often in an attempt to be helpful) blurt out the wrong thing at the wrong time.

(3) Choosing your representative depends largely on the problems expected to be encountered in the audit. There are three basic types of representatives, each serving a slightly different function and having limits as to the extent of how far he or she can carry the representation.

The first is the *enrollee,* who may or may not be a CPA but is nevertheless licensed to practice before IRS. The limitation on the enrollee is that he or she cannot represent you beyond the level of an administrative appeal. Should the matter come to actual litigation, you will need a tax attorney.

The second category is the *CPA*. CPAs are automatically licensed to appear before IRS but are limited in litigation appearances to practice before the U.S. Tax Court. If the matter justifies an appeal from the Tax Court to a higher court, you will need an attorney.

The third category is the *attorney*. Attorneys are usually specialists in tax matters and can represent you at any stage of the proceeding, from the initial audit through the level of the appellate courts.

It is for these reasons that great care must be made in picking your representative. If there is a probability, or even strong possibility, of any form of litigation, you are better off with an attorney brought in during the very first stages. This is especially true where there is the possibility of litigation even at the relatively low level of the U.S. Tax Court. While CPAs are authorized to practice there, most prefer not to become involved in litigation of any type.

Keep in mind that there is no reason why you cannot put together a ''team'' to handle your problems. For example, you could be represented by an enrollee or CPA during the actual audit and subsequent administrative appeals, with an attorney in the background who can provide not only legal guidance but also be prepared to step in and take charge should the matter reach the stage of actual litigation. This is often the best technique where major issues or substantial money is involved.

[¶2004] WHAT IRS WANTS YOU TO PROVE

Let's assume that you have been notified by IRS that your return will be audited. Whether you elect to appear yourself or be represented, there are certain preparations that must be made and that you alone can make. For the most part, this consists of bringing together whatever records you have that can be applicable to the audit. The list is endless; it should include receipts, cancelled checks, papers and documents relative to certain transactions, stock purchase and sales records, W-2 Forms, 1099 Forms, various schedules, rough working papers if available—in short, anything and everything that may in any way relate to the subject matter of the audit.

Don't be disturbed by the quantity of material you may put together. It is always safer to have too much than too little; the time to be selective is after you have all the material at hand, not while deciding what to include and what to omit. This process may involve a certain amount of extra effort on your part. For example, to establish your cost basis in property (real or personal) that you may have held for a lengthy period of time, it may be necessary to contact other parties for copies of their records. Take the time and effort to do this; it may be critical at some stage of the proceeding.

[¶2004.1] How to Evaluate Your Raw Material

It is at this stage of the proceeding that you should decide whether you will appear yourself or be represented. If you are going to be represented, all you need do is take all of your material to your representative (together, of course, with the questioned return) and make yourself available to explain the material or answer any questions. If your return was prepared by a CPA or enrollee, he or she will at least have a passing familiarity with the material and be in a position to evaluate it more quickly. If you elect this course of action, still contact your regular attorney. He can then keep track of the progress and, when the time comes, either enter the case himself or recommend a tax specialist.

If you decide to represent yourself, the process of evaluating your raw material should begin with the return itself. Go over it with a fine-tooth comb and make a mental note as to every possible questionable area. This, in effect, is what your representative would do. However, he has the advantage over you of knowing from experience the areas most likely to be IRS targets.

Having done this, put your material into various categories as they are applicable to various parts of the return. If possible, use separate file folders to prevent later confusion. With this done, you can then sort the contents of each file folder and rank them in degree of relevancy and importance.

After completing this, make photostatic copies of all your documents or at least the most important ones. The reason for this is that a revenue agent will frequently ask you for supporting documents to attach to the report of his findings. Although he will probably not tell you (and, in fact, sometimes implies to the contrary), you do *not* have to furnish the originals. Copies are quite sufficient for IRS audit purposes, and the originals should always remain in your files.

This is quite important since original files not infrequently somehow get lost while in the possession of IRS. Reconstructing those files could require a lot of work on your part. Rather than face that task, you might just want to settle the whole thing on the basis of the revenue agent's findings and reassessment. Another reason is that should the matter ultimately go to litigation, you will want to introduce originals and not copies that may not even be admissible as evidence unless properly certified—another time- and expense-consuming process.

Another reason for not turning over files will become apparent if an IRS "special agent" comes into your audit (see ¶2005). Ordinarily, you will politely cease all cooperation with IRS at this point and contact a competent tax attorney. He'll handle matters from there. Suppose that the special agent has been conducting a net worth study of you because of suspicion of tax fraud. Suppose, further, that IRS has lost your original return and any copies. (Admittedly, this is unlikely because all tax records for 13 years are kept; still, it sometimes happens.) To prove a tax fraud on your part, the agent will need your returns, since he must prove (among other things) that you underpaid your true tax. Here the alert practitioner, if asked for *your* copies of your returns for the year in question, will refuse. If pressed, he should merely tell the agent that it's IRS's responsibility to keep copies of returns and his responsibility to defend you.

[¶2004.2] Count on the Revenue Agent's Being Fully Prepared

If there is one thing certain in any audit investigation, it is that the revenue agent handling the case will usually be fully and completely prepared. For one thing, he is a professional and knows how to prepare himself. Secondly, he keeps up to date on Revenue Rulings and Tax Court decisions. He may not be an attorney himself, but he has a very firm grasp of general tax law and the IRS interpretation of the Internal Revenue Code. He will not argue a point of law with you, because that is not his function.

This is not to say that if your return was prepared reflecting a new approach or "loophole" in the existing law, the revenue agent will not listen to your explanation of the "hows" of that approach and the "whys" for taking it. If you can explain these in a manner understandable to him, it will give him the opportunity to thrash this out with others in the District Office who may be more familiar with the points involved. Needless to say, though, variant approaches and interpretations presented by CPAs or attorneys are usually given more credence than the same point presented by the taxpayer.

Another thing you can be certain of is that if you have had any audits or tax problems in the past, the agent assigned to this audit will have all records of past encounters. For this reason, you should maintain complete files of any previously audited returns. It may very well be that a past audit has given birth to the present one and that the agent is again going over once-plowed ground but as reflected in the present return.

[¶2004.3] Why the Revenue Agent Is So Well Prepared

The Internal Revenue agent, like any other professional, is motivated by a desire for advancement, which is based on performance. Since the basic function of IRS is to collect as much as legally allowable in the way of taxes, surcharge penalties, and interest, it would be rather naive to assume that this is not a strong factor in the approach any revenue agent takes toward any return under audit, notwithstanding the official protestations of IRS that this is not a criterion in measuring agent productivity.

This, of course, is not the only factor. Others may include the amount of workload completed during a given period, the amount of audits returned as "no change" items, etc. The "no change" items are of particular interest since this is the IRS way of presenting an agent with a classic "Catch-22" situation. It works in this manner:

Any return (usually computer selected) forwarded to the District Director for possible audit is presumed to have some potential for producing an "adjustment," which is usually a euphemism for a "reassessment." These returns are then given to the revenue agents, who have broad powers of judgment and discretion. As each agent examines each return, he may either list it for audit or merely "survey" it. The term "survey" is "governmentalese" for either "I can't find anything wrong with this one" or "We can get something out of this one, but it's not worth the time and effort." In short, a "survey" means no audit.

But what if the return is put on the audit list? Here is where the "Catch-22" situation arises. If the return is selected for audit, it is presumed that the selection was made because the agent, in his judgment and discretion, felt it needed an adjustment. This, as noted, usually means an upward reassessment. If an audit fails to turn up any reassessment, it means that in terms of productivity the agent failed to pick the right return or, having picked it, could not make a reassessment case out of it. Either way, his record will reflect less than maximum productivity, and that will be a factor in further promotion. With this in mind, you can be certain that in any full audit, the agent is going to do his best to find that reassessment. To do that he will prepare his case down to the last detail.

[¶2005] HOW TO PROTECT YOUR RIGHTS IF YOUR TAX RETURN IS QUESTIONED

Let's assume that you are going to handle your own audit. An appointment has been set up in your place of business, you have prepared your files, and your books and records are at hand. What is the first step? Facetious as it may sound, the first step is to examine the agent's credentials. This is extremely important for this reason: There are two classes of Internal Revenue agents, "revenue agents" and "special agents." A revenue agent conducts the normal and usual audit, and his objective is to determine whether or not some adjustment and/or reassessment is necessary. A "special agent," on the other hand, is concerned with matters of tax fraud, and his objective is to determine whether or not there is possible criminal charge.

A special agent is supposed to make his role known to you by reading you a short statement (similar to a "Miranda" warning) outlining his function and advising you that anything you say may be used against you, that you cannot be forced to incriminate yourself by answering any questions or producing any documents, and that you have the right to seek legal advice before responding (*IR No. 949*). The actual warning agents are supposed to give reads: " . . . I cannot compel you to answer any questions or to submit any information if such answers or information might tend to incriminate you in any way" (*IRS Intelligence Division Manual*, ¶9384.2).

However, special agents sometimes like to keep their presence as low-profile as possible, and the technique of merely flashing an I.D. card in front of the taxpayer in hopes that the special agent designation will not be noticed is not at all uncommon. Unless you are careful and examine the identification offered, you might find yourself dealing with an agent whose interest is in criminal charges rather than civil settlement. The courts usually look dimly upon such subterfuge, and many cases have resulted in fraud charges being dismissed because a special agent failed to deliver his prescribed warning (*Haffner*, 420 F. 2d 809, CA-4, 1969; *Leahey*, 434 F. 2d 7, CA-1, 1970). Not all courts have agreed, though, so care is your best weapon.

Should you discover the agent to be a special agent, immediately terminate the interview and advise the agent that you will not produce any material or discuss the matter in any way until you have had the opportunity to seek legal counsel. Under no circumstances should you attempt to handle your own case when a special agent is involved.

Also, be on the alert when more than one agent appears. Special agents sometimes work in teams with revenue agents, and the revenue agent uses his credentials to get entry for both of them. Sometimes the revenue agent will imply that the other agent is either his assistant or a new man being field trained. Don't buy this. Demand to see each man's identification; and if one turns out to be a special agent, terminate the interview.

Let's assume, though, that you are now representing yourself, and the man with whom you are dealing is a revenue agent. Here are some things to take into consideration.

[¶2005.1] Defining and Limiting the Scope of the Audit

Begin the process by a polite discussion with the agent, asking him to define the scope of his audit investigation and what books and records he might want to see. Do this in a friendly way, conveying the idea that you are trying to be helpful and to expedite the inquiry. Assure him at the same time that any additional material he may want to see will be made available.

A request to define the scope of the audit is one that the agent can hardly refuse. After all, it's to help him. Actually, the real object is to prevent, as far as possible, giving the agent an opportunity to casually browse through all of the books and records. Presenting this will be helpful in avoiding the possible accidental discovery of adverse material.

[¶2005.2] Cooperation With the Revenue Agent

Normally, full cooperation with the agent will produce the best results, both in terms of getting the audit over with and achieving the desired results. The agent is a technically qualified auditor whose job it is to ascertain from the taxpayer's books and records that all taxable income has been reported and that only proper deductions are claimed. He has the right—and the duty—to examine all relevant documents.

Lack of cooperation will slow the audit, and refusal to produce any document will at the very least engender suspicion and may result in a summons. Refusal or resistance to the production of documents usually produces an extremely unsatisfactory atmosphere for settlement. Adopting the attitude that the agent can see anything he asks for tends to engender the healthy feeling that the taxpayer has nothing to hide.

However, there is a fine line that must be drawn between cooperation and the volunteering of too much information. When an agent asks a question, that question should be answered in a factually correct manner and exactly on point. A rambling or overdetailed answer not only impedes the progress of the audit but can also open the proverbial new can of worms.

While the truth must be told, it need not necessarily be the "whole truth" unless the nature of the question requires it. There's a fine line here. If your answers are evasive or obviously incomplete, this may stimulate some agents to a more detailed audit than would be produced by complete candor. But, on the whole, you are better off saying as little as possible.

[¶2006] HOW TO MAKE SETTLEMENTS

When the audit is completed and before the Revenue Agent's Report (known as the "RAR") is completed, you will have an opportunity to discuss the proposed adjustments and reach a settlement. Where the audit has disclosed obvious errors, you would be well advised to acknowledge them promptly and, if necessary, provide any data required to make revised tax computations. In these black-and-white situations, there isn't very much you can do. You were wrong, and the error has been pointed out to you.

This, however, does not necessarily hold true in the grey areas, e.g., those areas in which the data are inconclusive or the tax liability interpretation is open to some question. For the purposes of this section, we will be concerned only with the grey areas. The guidelines that we suggest are applicable to those situations only and not to the clear-cut, black-and-white areas.

[¶2006.1] Don't Be too Quick to Accept an Adjustment

As you may suspect, the first proposal for settlement made by the auditing agent is going to be the most favorable possible to IRS. Every grey area is going to be interpreted as a black-and-white area. There are two strong reasons why you should not accept this proposed adjustment immediately.

The first is that any quick acceptance might be construed by some agents as an indication that you might have a lot to hide and are willing to settle for this reassessment just to get off the hook. Your eagerness might well lead to audit of earlier returns and a possible "red flag" situation on those yet to be filed. It can even lead to a special agent situation.

The second reason is that the revenue agent is usually "shooting high." In short, he knows that some of his points are weak, but he's going to try for the best he can do anyway.

When you encounter the second situation, that of unwarranted adjustments, it will be necessary for you to politely, knowledgeably, persuasively, and discreetly demolish the agent's position. If the disagreement turns on an issue of fact, your carefully prepared files should produce the documentary evidence needed to support your position. Make it clear to the agent that while you are obviously willing to cooperate (you can stress your acceptance of the black-and-white findings), you will not tolerate being required to pay more tax than is actually due. If the agent's proposed adjustment on the point in question was made on a somewhat casual basis (and a surprising number are), he can often be persuaded to your view with an avalanche of data and supporting evidence.

If, however, the proposed adjustment turns on a point of law or an interpretation of the Code, you will need professional assistance. It may be necessary for your legal representative to explain your position in technical terms and cite appropriate references. When this situation presents itself, simply tell the agent that you are not prepared to accept the adjustment as he proposes it and you want to consult with an attorney before proceeding any further on that point.

[¶2006.2] Don't Try "Horse Trading" on Your Own

"Horse trading" is an accepted part of the art and science of successfully negotiating settlements. What it amounts to is this: If there are two grey areas in controversy, each with roughly the same amount of tax liability and otherwise similar in the sense that the position taken by either side can logically be advanced and defended, a good settlement solution would be for each side to concede one area in exchange for the adjustment proposed for the other. In short, split it down the middle.

The problem for you is that such a solution is almost always accomplished as a result of the peer-group relationship as between professionals who represent other parties. When a revenue agent hears such an offer from an attorney, the immediate gut reaction is that this is a serious attempt to expedite the matter through a compromise based on each side knowing the other's relative strength. But when such an offer comes from the taxpayer, the agent's reaction is often that the taxpayer believes he is caught on both and is simply trying to buy his way out as cheaply as possible. This may boomerang on the taxpayer by making the agent press his point even harder. For this reason, make sure that any "horse trading" is strictly in the hands of your representative.

[¶2006.3] Resolving Technical or Difficult Issues

Let's assume your return presents a problem in that it turns on a technical or difficult issue. Nevertheless, you feel your background is sufficient to challenge the agent with regard to the resolution or interpretation of that point. However, you are unable to convince him or budge him from his position.

One thing you can do is to request that the agent submit the matter to the National Office in Washington, D.C. This will first require clearance and approval by the agent's supervisor. Assuming that this is granted, the agent and the taxpayer then prepare and submit written statements of their respective positions to the National Office.

If the agent or his supervisor refuses your request, you may then appeal to the Chief, Audit Division. The agent will then be required to forward to Washington a notice to the effect that you did request the technical advice, a thumbnail reference to the issue involved, and a statement that your request has been refused. On the basis of this, the National Office may order that a technical advice request be submitted. If so, this advice will be binding on the agent and on the district conferee. It will not be binding on the Appellate Division.

Should the advice not sustain your position, you will then have to litigate to get it overturned. For this reason, a request for advice should be submitted only when you are sure of your ground and have plenty of supporting law behind you. Otherwise, it could boomerang.

[¶2006.4] Completing the Audit

When the audit is completed, the agent will prepare a Revenue Agent's Report ("RAR"). This report will list all proposed adjustments and state, in summary form, the reasons for the proposed adjustment. One of three possibilities will occur. In some cases, the report will recommend "no change," and the return is left as filed. In some (albeit rare) instances, the agent may actually propose a refund for overpaid taxes. The third, and most common, recommends an assessment for underpaid taxes. Obviously, this is the one with which we will be concerned.

Keep in mind that the agent's proposed assessment is nothing more than a recommendation to his superiors. However, he will ask you to sign a waiver (Form 870) if you agree to the assessment. (A copy of Form 870 can be found in the appendix at p. 439.) Then the RAR, together with the waiver, is sent to his superiors for approval. As a matter of practice, this approval is routinely given and the matter is brought to a conclusion.

Execution of the waiver doesn't summarily close the case. Additional assessments can be made by the Commissioner within the allowable statute of limitations. The signing of the waiver and its acceptance by the Commissioner bar a proceeding before the Tax Court. (The interplay of these rules makes possible the use of a tactical maneuver that may prove valuable. See ¶2007.2.) In the event it is desired to file a claim for refund after payment of the tax and the claim is disallowed, the proceedings must go before the U.S. District Court or the U.S. Court of Claims. Only these courts have jurisdiction to handle refund claims.

[¶2006.5] Why You Should or Should Not Sign the Waiver

You should sign the waiver if the assessment is based on obvious errors you have made in the return. If you are demonstrably in the wrong, you are better off agreeing to payment of the additional tax plus interest at the rate of 9% per annum. The interest charge, incidentally, stops running 30 days after you sign the waiver. Further, the interest you will pay, plus legal and other advisory fees incurred as a result of the audit, are all deductible items on the following year's return.

Another reason for signing the waiver is that, despite the fact that you personally do not agree with the agent's findings, the amount in controversy doesn't warrant your time and effort in taking the matter up on appeal. If it is a small sum, you just might want to get the matter over and done with and not face extended litigation and additional expenses. Essentially it is a question of personal economics.

You should *not* sign the waiver if you feel the agent has seriously overassessed any possible deficiency, refused to take any of your supported points or positions into consideration, or misinterpreted the applicable law. In this case, just refuse to sign the waiver and the appellate or post-audit procedure will commence.

]¶2006.6] The Statute of Limitations

As discussed earlier, the Internal Revenue Code places definite time restrictions on IRS's ability to assess a tax deficiency (see ¶2002.7). If settlement negotiations at either the audit stage or one of the post-audit procedures (discussed at ¶2007) have become protracted to the point where the statute of limitations may run before agreement is reached, IRS usually asks the taxpayer to extend the statute by executing Form 872. This form, technically known as a "Consent Fixing Period of Limitations upon Assessment of Income and Profits Tax," is illustrated in the appendix at p. 440. Execution of the consent extends the statute of limitations for assessment of the taxes under examination to the time specified in the form.

The Pros and Cons of Signing Form 872: If the taxpayer refuses to execute the form, IRS will issue a statutory notice of deficiency requiring payment of the tax or the filing of a petition to the Tax Court within 90 days (see ¶2007.5). Form 872 should be executed to avoid these alternatives if they would prematurely terminate settlement negotiations. On the other hand, if further negotiations seem unpromising, it may be desirable to precipitate IRS action by refusing to execute the form. Even though the request to execute the form is complied with, it is not necessarily advisable to extend the statute to the date requested. For example, if a request is made in January for an extension of the statute that will expire in April, it is generally not necessary to agree to an extension to the April of the following year. Extension to December should suffice and may encourage the Service to carry on negotiations more expeditiously.

It is Service policy to keep requests for consents to a minimum. However, they serve a useful function not only in prolonging the period for negotiation but also in permitting extended examinations where an arbitrary and excessive determination might otherwise have to be made. They may also be used to permit suspension of action on a case until important litigation is concluded.

Execution of the Form: Form 872 must be executed before the statute expires. However, it may be executed after the expiration of the normal limitation period where the statute has previously been extended. The form is not effective unless executed by both the taxpayer and the government. The instructions on the form contain directions for its execution. Two signed copies are sent to the government and a copy signed on behalf of the government will be returned to the taxpayer.

One Last Note: It should be stressed that, unlike the execution of Form 870, a taxpayer's signing of Form 872 is not an agreement with IRS as to his liability. By executing the extension, he has preserved all the rights of administrative appeal and judicial review he may wish to utilize.

[¶2006.7] Overview: The Desirability of Early Settlement

Most seasoned tax practitioners agree that a case should be settled at the lowest possible level. Early settlement saves time and expense and eliminates the possibility that new issues will be raised on review. Moreover, at the audit stage, there is usually freer trading of issues, less emphasis on technicalities, and a lower standard of proof. And the agent may consider certain issues weak that his superiors conducting a conference further up the ladder might consider strong. Thus settlement with the agent is desirable if his proposed adjustments are within a reasonable range. Indeed, there are circumstances where it may be desirable for the taxpayer to tolerate a little unreasonableness as the price for a prompt and final exit of the agent. If the unreasonableness produces a substantial deficiency, a refund claim may recoup it. On the other hand, some agents may seek an unfair settlement and let it be known that unless the taxpayer gives in they will "throw the book at him." Such an attitude normally should not be tolerated and administrative appeal should be taken.

[¶2007] HOW TO HANDLE APPELLATE AND POST-AUDIT PROCEDURE

Although you may have handled the audit situation yourself with little or no professional representation, appellate procedure is an entirely different matter. For one thing, there are two types of appellate review, one termed "administrative," the other, "judicial." The decision as to which course to pursue, or whether to exhaust one (administrative) before proceeding to the other (judicial), is often a matter of strategy and should be evaluated by a tax attorney. Let's now examine these two kinds of review on a step-by-step basis, commencing with the administrative review.

[¶2007.1] 30- and 90-Day Letters

If you do not accept the agent's proposed assessment findings and refuse to sign a waiver, you will shortly thereafter receive a copy of the RAR along with a form-like letter of transmittal. This will advise you of your right to appeal and note that you have 30 days in which to file that appeal. For obvious reasons, this is called the "30-Day Letter." Form RSC-564 is used for this purpose. Attached to this will be Form 1902-E (Report of Individual Income Tax Audit Changes) and Form 3547 (Explanation of Adjustments). Also included in the package will be Publication 5 (Appeal Rights and Preparation of Protests for Unagreed Cases). Copies of these four documents can be found in the appendix at p.444. At this point in the process, you can avail yourself of the administrative appeals (which we shall describe) or simply ignore the 30-Day

Letter. If you choose to ignore the 30-Day Letter, IRS will issue a second letter and deficiency notice. This is the "90-Day Letter" (Notice of Deficiency) and is so termed because no effort at collection will be made until 90 days after the date of the letter. A copy of this form is found in the appendix at p.441. The 90-Day-Letter does not terminate your right of appeal. In fact, there may be good reason for you to request the immediate issuance of a 90-Day Letter rather than the 30-Day Letter and pursue the judicial appeal rather than the administrative.

[¶2007.2] The District Conference

If you choose to file an administrative appeal after receiving the 30-Day Letter but prior to receiving the 90-Day Letter, you may request a "district conference." The district conference, held before an IRS officer known as the "district conferee," is an opportunity for the taxpayer to attempt to resolve factual issues that he was not able to resolve in meetings with the revenue agent.

The district conferee is wholly independent of either the revenue agent or the agent's supervisor. He has broad discretionary powers to resolve factual issues, but not legal issues unless the tax involved is not more than $2,500 for the year in question and the legal issue has been resolved at the next higher administrative appeals level.

There are several good reasons why the district conference is a popular form of appeal. Here are some of them:

☐ (1) You may have had the unfortunate experience of encountering a very "gung-ho" revenue agent who was somewhat overzealous in his interpretation of the facts, thus materially increasing the proposed tax assessment. The district conferee, on the other hand, is more likely to take a practical and realistic approach and understand that it is sometimes unreasonable to demand that every "i" be dotted and every "t" crossed. You might find that the compromise rejected by the revenue agent is, at least in part, acceptable to the district conferee.

☐ (2) The costs and expenses of an appeal before the district conferee are minimal as compared with the costs in a formal judicial appeal. You can appear for yourself or be represented by either an enrollee or a CPA.

☐ (3) The issue that is at the heart of the controversy may be a recurring one; for example, a particular interpretation and application of tax law to a transaction spread over several years. If so, this problem is likely to be challenged again, and you would like to raise the same defenses. If you elect judicial appeal rather than administrative appeal and the court holds against you, you are precluded from again raising this defense in a subsequent audit.

☐ (4) As previously indicated, it is usually considered preferable to attempt to settle a case at the lowest level. This is true because at lower levels there is less exposure to new issues, proceedings are less formal, and processing is more rapid. Experience indicates that the less complicated cases involving relatively small amounts are most likely to be settled at the district conference. Cases involving complex issues or large sums tend to be shunned at the district level. Indeed, the Service has encouraged taxpayers to request district conferences because they usually result in the more expeditious disposition of cases than appellate division conferences.

When to Use a District Conference: Generally, if the amount involved in the dispute is relatively small or the issues presented not extremely complex, a district conference would seem well advised in terms of potential time savings alone. Where the amount involved is great, going directly to an Appellate Division conference might be wise, especially when you consider that settlement percentages are generally favorable at the upper level.

There are several other points to consider in deciding whether to ask for a district conference. First, remember that you use Form 870 for settlements at the district level and Form 870-AD at the Appellate Division level. Form 870 doesn't preclude a subsequent claim for refund but 870-AD may. See page 359. Thus settlement at the Appellate Division is final; a district conference settlement isn't. Second, an adverse decision at the district conference puts you at a disadvantage in an Appellate Division conference that you wouldn't have suffered if you had gone directly to the Appellate Division. If a district conference approves the agent's position, the appellate conferee will normally be less inclined to reverse his findings. Therefore, unless the chances are good for a favorable settlement at the district conference, avoid it. Finally, you should evaluate the settlement record at the district conference level. More than half the cases that go to district conference are settled. This record of success suggests that in borderline cases perhaps you should decide in favor of a district conference.

Procedure at Conference: After you ask for a conference, the case is assigned to a conferee for hearing. The conferee reviews the revenue agent's report and the protest, if you filed one, and arranges a conference date.

The conference usually begins with a review of the adjustments proposed in the revenue agent's report. The findings in the RAR are deemed to be correct by the conferee and the burden is on the taxpayer to show that they are wrong. The taxpayer will then be given an opportunity to submit factual data, including documents and affidavits, to support his position. He is also afforded an opportunity to present legal arguments or to further explain the legal arguments presented in the protest.

Changes in the agent's report will be reflected in a Conference Audit Statement that will be forwarded to the taxpayer. If the taxpayer agrees with the proposed settlement, Form 870 will be furnished to him and the case will be closed upon execution of this form. If agreement is not reached, the taxpayer can ask that the file be forwarded to the Appellate Division. The taxpayer must also file a written protest in order to obtain a hearing at the Appellate Division.

Successful Negotiation Tactics: The district conference is designed to be informal, and you should make an effort to maintain a friendly atmosphere. Tactics for negotiation at this level are not essentially different from those discussed in handling conferences with the Appellate Division. However, remember that the level of technical expertise is not as high at the district level as at the Appellate Division. While conferees may have had considerable experience in the field as revenue agents, they are not necessarily experts on the intricacies of complex questions of tax law. Thus, legal arguments should be simple and, if possible, you should rely only on favorable regulations and rulings, and cases in which the Commissioner has acquiesced.

The conferee is duty bound to give the taxpayer a fair and impartial hearing. If you present factual data supporting your position in a firm but friendly manner, there is a strong possibility that the issues will be favorably resolved. Remember that the conferee *wants* to settle the case and will do so if he is given facts and law that justify a settlement. If the "correct" result is not clear or the issue is unusual and complex and there is a lack of uniformity among district offices, you can and should ask for technical advice on the issue from the National Office in Washington, D.C. 20224.

Seizing a Valuable Tactical Advantage: Sometimes this situation presents the taxpayer with a valuable tactical advantage. If you can't reach a satisfactory settlement at the district level, and don't want an Appellate Conference because of the possibility that new issues may be raised, then it may be prudent to agree to the proposed deficiency, execute the Form 870, and then file a claim for refund *after* the period of limitations on the assessment of further deficiencies has expired and within two years of the deficiency payment. This approach prevents the government from asserting an increased deficiency while you try to recover the amount of the former deficiency through the refund procedure. While it is possible that the government may raise new issues in the refund proceeding as a setoff against the refund claim, it will not be possible for the government to assert an increased deficiency as it could at the Appellate Division or even in the Tax Court. This tactic not only limits the amount in dispute but also thrusts the burden of proof on the government as to any new issues.

Look Before You Sign: Ordinarily the district director sends the filled-in Form 870 in duplicate to the taxpayer's representative with the request that he have the original executed by the taxpayer. Make sure that the amounts entered in the form actually reflect the agreed settlement. Sign the waiver in accordance with the instructions contained on the form.

[¶2007.3] What If You Lose in the District Conference?

You may find that the district conferee agrees with the revenue agent's recommendations. This leaves you with several choices. These are:

(1) Pay the assessment plus interest and close the case on the revenue agent's recommendations. You do so by executing a waiver on Form 870.

(2) File an appeal with the Appellate Division, requesting a hearing before the Appellate Division conferee. Generally, this course is followed where the key issue is a legal rather than factual point.

(3) Sign a waiver, pay the tax, and then immediately file a claim for refund with IRS. If IRS refuses (and it generally will), sue for a refund in either the U.S. District Court or the U.S. Court of Claims. This is not, strictly speaking, an appeal. Rather it is a new suit that you have filed against the U.S. Government for a refund of money improperly collected.

How to Decide Whether to Appeal to Appellate Division: Since the Appellate Division settles more than two out of three cases appealed to it, the decision to bypass the Appellate Division should not be taken lightly. Nevertheless, appeal to the Appellate Division unquestionably presents hazards.

Perhaps the greatest hazard presented arises from the special skill of the conferees themselves. They are tax law specialists who are well equipped to ferret out issues overlooked by the revenue agent.

Before appeal is taken, counsel should not only evaluate the known issues but should make an investigation to determine if there are other potential issues that the conferee might discover during the course of settlement negotiations. The entire file is before the conferee and if he discovers an issue that might result in an increased deficiency he may request the revenue agent to conduct a supplemental investigation. As a result, the taxpayer may be confronted with a considerably larger deficiency than if he had bypassed the Appellate Division and allowed the issues to become "frozen" by the issuance of a notice of deficiency.

After issuance of the notice, the government has the burden of proof with respect to new issues it raises. This not only makes the raising of new issues less likely, but also makes them easier to handle if raised.

On the other hand, if prospects for settlement are strong, particularly in less complex cases, the Appellate Conference is probably desirable. This is especially true if all the taxpayer's evidence has already been revealed. Of course, the time and expense involved in a Tax Court petition are always factors that must be considered.

If it is believed that settlement is unlikely with the Appellate Division and that the case must be taken to the Tax Court before settlement can be reached, it is probably advisable to refrain from filing a protest and to bypass the Appellate Division. There will be an opportunity to negotiate a settlement with the Appellate Division after the case is docketed in the Tax Court and many practitioners believe that a protest before the case is docketed merely serves to expose their evidence, offer an opportunity to the government to raise new issues, and cause needless delay and expense. Moreover, after docketing, the Regional Counsel's office has concurrent jurisdiction in settlement negotiations and often the presence of the attorney from Counsel's office who will handle the litigation creates a more realistic atmosphere for settlement on the basis of litigation hazards. If a conference with the Appellate Division is not desired, the taxpayer should merely wait for or request the 90-day letter or statutory notice of deficiency.

[¶2007.4] The Appellate Division Conference

The Appellate Division is wholly and completely separate from the District Director. It will hear a matter either as an appeal from a district conference or, if you choose, can be the first step in an appeal from the revenue agent's recommendations. In short, you have the option of bypassing the district conference and going directly to the Appellate Division conference. This is a technique often used when the issue is legal rather than factual.

If the total disputed tax plus penalty does not exceed $2,500 and you have gone through the stage of the district conference, no written statement of your position need be filed, although the request for the conference itself must be in writing. Despite this, it is still a good idea to sum up your legal position and arguments and attach it to the request.

The appellate conference is a little more formal than the district conference, and the conferee has the power to decide legal issues. In fact, unless there is a legal issue to be resolved, it may be a better idea to bypass the appellate conference and proceed directly to judicial review.

Successful Negotiation Tactics: Several points concerning negotiation technique should be kept in mind. It is important to approach the Appellate Division conferee in an open, friendly manner and to present factual and legal arguments persuasively. Negotiations should not be regarded as a debate where one party can "win," but as a technique for resolving issues where the virtues of both parties' cases are professionally evaluated. The range of settlement figures should be known in advance. A flexible attitude should be maintained with a view toward trading or splitting issues where this will facilitate the desired settlement.

Standing on "principle" is not conducive to settlement, and the client is usually less interested in the niceties of tax law than in how much the settlement will cost him.

Generally, the taxpayer's representative should politely make it clear that if a reasonable settlement cannot be reached, then the taxpayer will not hesitate to litigate. And the taxpayer's representative must be prepared to demonstrate his conviction by actual litigation if a reasonable settlement cannot be reached.

The "friendly but firm" atmosphere is probably the most conducive to settlement. In this atmosphere the legal and factual issues should be fully developed and settlement possibilities should be patiently and persistently explored without ultimatums. When an offer to dispose of an issue is made, the taxpayer's representative should know what it will cost the taxpayer and that it is acceptable to the taxpayer.

Agreement with Appellate Division: Agreed cases at the Appellate Division are normally closed by execution of Form 870-AD, "Offer of Waiver of Restrictions on Assessment and Collection of Deficiency in Tax and of Acceptance of Overassessment" (See appendix p.440). This form is prepared by the Appellate Division and submitted to the taxpayer for signature. By signing the form the taxpayer offers to waive the normal statutory restrictions on assessment and collection of the tax. The "offer" is then returned to the Appellate Division and if it is accepted by the Commissioner, then the case will not be reopened except in the case of fraud or other specified extraordinary circumstances, "and no claim for refund or credit shall be filed or prosecuted." The form is not effective until it is signed on behalf of the Commissioner. However, even though the offer must be reviewed by the Appellate conferee's superior before it is accepted on behalf of the Commissioner, such offers are rarely refused because the experienced conferee normally irons out any problems with his superior before the form is submitted to the taxpayer.

[¶2007.5] Judicial Review

You can, if you choose, completely eliminate the entire process of administrative appeal. This is accomplished by requesting a 90-Day Letter immediately after the completion of the audit and then filing a petition to the U.S. Tax Court. One advantage in this technique is that a new issue raised by the government carries with it the burden of proof by the government. This is the exact reverse of what happens when new issues are raised during the course of administrative appeals. As we noted a few moments ago, the burden of proof in those situations is on the taxpayer.

Another advantage of judicial review is that your case can be initiated by merely filing a petition setting forth the basic facts. No legal arguments need be presented at that time, and the government will have to go to trial without knowing your legal reasoning and support until the case is actually heard.

Still another advantage is the fact that once you decide on this approach, you or your representatives can hold regular conferences with the attorney from the Regional Counsel's office. After all, since he is the one who must try the case and has the power to effect a pretrial settlement, you might just find him a little more reasonable than the revenue agent or the conferees.

[¶2007.6] Where Do the Best Settlement Opportunities Lie?

Since there are two tiers at which to settle prior to litigation—and a third opportunity to settle with IRS's regional counsel if the Tax Court is chosen as a forum—the question often arises at what level the practitioner is apt to be able to settle on terms most favorable to his client. An examination of the nearly 50,000 cases that went beyond audit in 1972 provides some interesting data bearing on the question of where to settle.

District Conference: In 1972, taxpayers settled with IRS in 67% of the district conferences, agreeing to settlements that averaged about 41¢ for every dollar of deficiency claimed originally by the revenue agent.

Appellate Division: At this level more than 77% of all disputes with IRS were settled by taxpayers in 1972. The average settlement came to about 37¢ per dollar of asserted deficiency. Part of the favorable settlement rate at this level comes from the willingness of Appellate Conferees to waive such items as 25% penalties and 6% interest charges in order to avoid litigation.

Tax Court: Settlement may still be reached with IRS after a taxpayer has petitioned the Tax Court for trial of his dispute. Of the cases docketed in the Tax Court in 1972, about 78% were settled without trial. Taxpayers were able to settle at a favorable rate of about 30¢ for each dollar of deficiency initially asserted by the revenue agent.

In the aggregate, then, it would seem that a taxpayer is more likely to settle with IRS on favorable terms as he climbs up the ladder. Bear in mind, though, that these are only *average* figures on a nationwide basis. The average figures within the various IRS regions vary greatly: for example, taxpayers in one IRS region may have averaged district conference settlements amounting to, say, 27¢ per dollar of deficiency while taxpayers within another region have had to pay as much as 65¢ per deficiency dollar in order to settle. Clearly, then, any determination a practitioner may make as to his chances for gaining favorable settlement at the various levels should take into account the experience within his region. The figures showing this regional breakdown may be found in the most recent Commissioner's Annual Report.

[¶2007.7] When Should You Litigate?

After settlement negotiations have come to a point where each party's ''final'' offer has been made and it appears that the government's offer is too small, the moment of truth has arrived. It is now that the always difficult decision about litigation must be made. In most cases this decision is not unlike deciding about an investment in a speculative security: It is necessary to weigh the potential for gain against the risks of loss. When the anticipated recovery after deduction of litigation costs substantially exceeds the government's offer and the likelihood of recovery is strong, litigation is indicated.

Weighing the Cost Against the Gain: First, it is necessary to estimate the amount that will be recovered on each issue where recovery is likely. From this amount the cost of litigation should be subtracted. This cost includes lawyer's fees and related expenses such as the cost of accountant's services and expert witnesses. The cost estimate for litigation should also take into account the possibility of appeal and the fact that tax litigation costs are deductible for tax purposes. The resulting net recovery is the maximum benefit that may be expected unless the case involves a recurring issue. It is then necessary to estimate the chances of winning. This difficult estimate involves a careful evaluation of the strength of the taxpayer's case in view of both the facts and the law. If the taxpayer has the burden of proof, as is usually the case, particular care should be taken to determine whether sufficient evidence is available to carry that burden.

Chances of Winning: If the chances for winning are even or better than even, then if the amount to be won substantially exceeds the cost of litigation, the taxpayer should normally go to court. At least in smaller cases, if the chances are not better than even, or if the costs of litigation are high in relation to the amount to be recovered, the taxpayer should be counseled that discretion is the better part of valor.

Intangible Costs: The intangible costs of litigation should also be taken into account. Some taxpayers enjoy a fight with the government. But most find trial preparation and trial both time consuming and a drain on energies that might be spent more profitably in another pursuit. Many also develop a sense of frustration with the inevitable delays and uncertainties associated with litigation. These factors assume particular importance in marginal cases.

Risk of New Issues: It is also necessary to evaluate the fact that litigation in the Tax Court opens the possibility that new issues will be raised. Even though the government has the burden of proof on new issues, this danger may be severe. An issue not perceived at lower levels may be discovered by the Regional Counsel attorney. He has authority to request a supplemental investigation and is fully capable of developing a strong affirmative case. Where a potential issue involving a substantial amount is resting quietly under the rug, the most prudent course is to sign a Form 870 and sue for a refund.

Win-Loss Percentages: In deciding whether to litigate and in choosing the proper forum, statistics are of little value in any particular case. Nevertheless, the results in the various courts may aid the taxpayer's representative to develop a feel for the proper recommendation. The win-loss statistics, generally, are as follows:

Court	*Percentage for Government*	*Percentage for Taxpayer*
Tax Court	75	25
District Courts	68	32
Court of Claims	48	52

In evaluating these percentages it is important to bear in mind that they do not reflect the substantial number of cases where each party obtains a partial victory.

More important, even, than the won-loss percentages after litigation are the average amounts all taxpayers had to end up paying, expressed as a percentage of the deficiency originally assessed against the taxpayer. This figure for 1972 came to about 42% for all taxpayers in Tax Court and 64% for all taxpayers in the Court of Claims. The following table compares the Tax Court results of taxpayers who settled prior to trial with the results of those who litigated:

	Taxpayer Liability as % of Service Claim				
	1968	*1969*	*1970*	*1971*	*1972*
Settlement before trial	29%	36%	30%	32%	30%
Result after trial	48%	38%	50%	41%	42%

The conclusion seems inescapable that IRS settlement offers are for the most part generous compared to the risks taxpayers may have to face in Tax Court. Although figures are not as readily available, the same holds true for taxpayers facing litigation in either the Court of Claims or one of the district courts.

[¶2008] CHECKLIST FOR AVOIDING AUDIT OF TAX RETURN

As we've seen, an audit can be a pretty unhappy experience, even when you've made the best of it. Clearly a solution not to be overlooked is simply that of not being audited in the first place. While it's true that there's no way you can make absolutely sure that any tax return you file won't be audited, you can cut down the chances by observing the points in this checklist:

☐ (1) ***Meeting the ADP Requirements:*** Your return may be the target of an audit merely because it doesn't pass muster with the IRS Automatic Data Processing (ADP). The ADP screens tax returns for mathematical errors, discrepancies, and other significant changes in income or deductions. The most likely candidates for audit are returns of businesses, of individuals with income of $25,000 or more, those with mathematical errors, those with discrepancies between the amounts of income reported on the return and the amounts indicated on information returns, those showing significant changes in income or expense items, when total expenses are large in relation to income, when a lot of big round numbers are used, those involving issues currently receiving special attention by IRS, and those returns that are not accompanied by required detailed schedules.

☐ (2) ***Include All Income:*** All income, no matter how small, should be included in the return. If an item covered by withholding or an information return is missed, it will be spotted by ADP and you'll get an audit.

☐ (3) ***Verify All Returns:*** Get copies of all withholding and information returns filed by employers, banks, clients, and other payers of income. Verify their accuracy and be sure to report the same amount they report to IRS. If an information return should be wrong, have it corrected.

☐ (4) ***Check Details and Math:*** Double-check the math. Make sure the return is correct in all other details, especially those that might trigger a reaction from the computer. For example, these basic points are important:

(a) Attach W-2 forms;

(b) Check the right blocks on personal exemptions and filing status;

(c) Get the numbers on the right line; and,

(d) Give complete address and social security number.

☐ (5) ***Support Unusual Items:*** Supplement the return with a fully documented explanation of any unusual deductions or legal position reflected on your return. For example, explain the nature of casualty or theft losses and how you figured the amount of the deduction. Use exact amounts, rounded to the nearest dollar.

☐ (6) ***Follow IRS Guidelines:*** Don't exceed any guidelines IRS has established for estimates and unsupported expenses. Make contributions by check whenever at all practical and specify the donee on each contribution. Bracketing several religious beneficiaries under "church" or "missions" merely invites scrutiny.

☐ (7) ***Reasonable Allocation:*** If you use your car or home partly for business, make a reasonable allocation based on time or values between business and personal use.

☐ (8) ***Supporting Schedules or Statements:*** Some expenses, such as business expenses of an employee, require a detailed statement supporting the deduction. For example, if you deduct expenses for travel away from home, attach to the return either:

(a) A statement showing the following information: The number of days away from home during the year on business; the total expense incident to meals and lodging while absent from home on business during the year; the total other expenses incident to travel and entertainment claimed as a deduction; or

(b) Form 2106, "Statement of Employee Business Expenses."

☐ (9) ***Substantiate Expenses or Deductions:*** Keep any deduction of entertainment expenses reasonable and be ready to substantiate any expenses that haven't been cleared by the employee's company. If you claim a bad debt deduction, IRS requires a statement be attached giving these details: The nature of the bad debt; name of the debtor and his relationship to the creditor; when the debt was due; the efforts made to collect it; why it became worthless this year rather than another year. If the loan was made to a relative, strong evidence to support the claim is needed to show a bona fide loan. You also have to be ready to support other representations made in connection with the debt.

SECTION XXI

TWELVE TAX KEYS TO WEALTH

Investments involve the commitment of savings or disposable income with the dual goals of recovering the initial deposit or investment in full, plus enjoying either regular income or a profit when the investment is liquidated. The value of an investment depends on the safety of the principal, the certainty and size of the prospective income, and a variety of other factors.

Taxes affect the net return on an investment in these ways:

□ (1) Income taxes reduce the real or spendable income that the investor can expect and reduce the real value of the investment proportionately.
□ (2) When an investment produces a loss, there may be restrictions on deducting the loss from taxable income to the full extent of the monetary loss.
□ (3) It may be difficult to replace capital already accumulated if it should be lost, so safety becomes relatively more important than potential income.
□ (4) As taxes reduce income and make capital more difficult to accumulate, the appeal of any investment that promises a steady growth of capital is enhanced.

[¶2101] TWELVE KEY TAX SHELTERS

There are twelve key routes used to shelter income from tax:

□ (1) Tax-free income; e.g., the yield from tax-exempt bonds or notes.
□ (2) Deduction from income that has no relationship to real cost; e.g., percentage depletion.
□ (3) Tax-free return of capital while investment yield is maintained and the money value of the property may be maintained; e.g., income-producing buildings where cost is returned tax free via depreciation, while inflation and deductible repairs enhance the value.
□ (4) Assured buildup in value that can be realized tax free; e.g., life insurance proceeds.
□ (5) Assured buildup in value that may be realized at favored capital gain rates or used to produce income based on matured values; e.g., a citrus grove or timber tract in which natural growth enhances value but those higher values cannot be taxed until the property is sold.

☐ (6) Definite buildup in value that can be indefinitely deferred; e.g., building up a cattle herd whose value is enhanced by both growth and propagation.
☐ (7) Capital value acquired with substantially deductible expenses; e.g., oil drilling, where intangible drilling expenses and dry holes can be charged off against other income so that oil strikes constitute capital largely financed by tax money.
☐ (8) Investments with a high degree of security against loss and also a potential for sizable capital gain; e.g., convertible bonds with equity participation benefits.
☐ (9) Investments in which 50% of the capital loss can be deducted against ordinary income ($1,000 a year) and in which the prospect of capital gain is high in relation to the impact of possible loss; e.g., common stock warrant.
☐ (10) Investment yields have special protection; e.g., dividends received by a corporation, the $100 exclusion for individuals, and the 85% dividends-received deduction for corporations.
☐ (11) Income received from its source at capital gain rates; e.g., mutual fund distributions and some sales of timber and breeding cattle.
☐ (12) Income that can be taken or reported currently or postponed; e.g., interest on E bonds.

(***Note:*** Tax-oriented investments are under scrutiny. The main target is the writing off of expenses before income is realized. This may take some glamour from routes (2), (3), and (7).)

[¶2102] WHAT TAX SHELTER CAN DO FOR FAMILY SECURITY

Before the imposition of the income tax, a dollar of income was worth a dollar. Today, the answer is not so simple. It depends on what tax bracket the investor is in and whether the income involved is tax free, ordinary income, or capital gains. There are many different answers for many different individuals. The table set out on the following page shows how much $1 of additional income is worth after taxes from:

Tax-Free Income (includes municipal bonds, life insurance return, special return, special income earned abroad, etc.).

Ordinary Income (includes interest on taxable bonds, dividends [not considering the $100 exclusion], royalties, net rental income, etc.).

Earned Income (includes wages, salaries, commissions, and professional fees and other compensation from personal services).

Capital Gains (includes sales and exchanges of capital items, dividends on stock where company has no earnings and profits, etc.).

This table does not take into account the 10% minimum tax on tax preferences in excess of $30,000 plus the amount of regular income taxes paid nor the reduction of earned income eligible for the earned income ceiling by the amount of tax preferences in excess of $30,000.

The table shows that tax-free income is the only kind of income worth one hundred cents on a dollar right down the line. What this means in terms of ability to accumulate capital is dramatically shown in our "Wealth-Injector Chart" on page 366. The chart assumes a man in the 50% tax bracket has two sources of income, one tax free, the other fully taxable, each in the amount of $2,000 annually. The chart shows the comparative results when the amount is invested at different rates of interest (4, 6, 8, and 10%) over a span of 35 years. Thus, assuming a return of

Taxable Income (thousands of dollars) Joint Return	Tax-Free Income	"A" Ordinary Income	"B" Earned Income	"C" Capital Gains (up to $50,000)	"D" Capital Gains Over $50,000	Net of "C" Over "A"	Net of "C" Over "B"	Net of "D" Over "A"	Net of "D" Over "B"
$ 4-8	$1.00	$.81	$.81	$.905		12%	12%		
8-12	1.00	.78	.78	.89		14	14		
12-16	1.00	.75	.75	.875		17	17		
16-20	1.00	.72	.72	.86		19	19		
20-24	1.00	.68	.68	.84		24	24		
24-28	1.00	.64	.64	.82		28	28		
28-32	1.00	.61	.61	.805		32	32		
32-36	1.00	.58	.58	.79		36	36		
36-40	1.00	.55	.55	.775		41	41		
40-44	1.00	.52	.52	.76		46	46		
44-52	1.00	.50	.50	.75		50	50		
52-64	1.00	.47	.50	.75	.735	60	50	56%	47%
64-76	1.00	.45	.50	.75	.725	67	50	61	45
76-88	1.00	.42	.50	.75	.71	79	50	69	42
88-100	1.00	.40	.50	.75	.70	88	50	75	40
100-120	1.00	.38	.50	.75	.69	97	50	82	38
120-140	1.00	.36	.50	.75	.68	108	50	88	36
140-160	1.00	.34	.50	.75	.67	121	50	97	34
160-180	1.00	.32	.50	.75	.66	134	50	103	32
180-200	1.00	.31	.50	.75	.655	142	50	111	31
200-300	1.00	.30	.50	.75	.65	150	50	116	30
300-400	1.00	.30	.50	.75	.65	150	50	116	30
400 and over	1.00	.30	.50	.75	.65	150	50	116	30

10%, the figures in the lower right-hand corner of the chart show that at the end of 35 years there will be $596,213 under a tax-free arrangement as against a mere $94,336 under a taxable setup. The results would be better for a man in a higher bracket and less for a man in a lower bracket.

Wealth-Injector Chart

Number of Years	4%		6%		8%		10%	
	Tax-Free	Taxable	Tax-Free	Taxable	Tax-Free	Taxable	Tax-Free	Taxable
5	$ 11,266	$ 5,308	$ 11,950	$ 5,468	$ 12,672	$ 5,633	$ 13,431	$ 5,802
10	24,970	11,169	27,943	11,808	31,211	12,486	35,061	13,207
15	41,645	17,639	49,578	19,157	58,531	20,825	69,897	22,657
20	61,935	24,783	78,297	27,676	98,673	30,969	126,003	34,719
25	86,618	32,671	116,730	37,553	156,287	43,312	216,348	50,113
30	116,648	41,379	168,139	49,003	242,319	58,328	361,862	69,761
35	154,311	50,994	236,958	62,276	368,720	76,598	596,213	94,336

[¶2104] A RATING OF INVESTMENT OPPORTUNITIES

There are several specific investments that are subject to some degree of tax shelter. The small businessman with extra cash on hand may be wise to make a tax-sheltered investment; just what form that investment should take will depend on his particular circumstances. The following detailed discussion of each major sheltered investment should aid the investor in making up his mind as to which shelter is best for him.

[¶2104.1] Tax-Exempt Bonds

Tax-free bonds have long been a favorite tax shelter. Although there have been efforts to tax interest on municipal bonds, the law still favors them over other forms of tax shelter.

There are six major types of tax-exempt bonds available for investment. They are:

☐ (1) ***General Obligation Bonds:*** These bonds usually get and deserve the highest tax-exempt rating since they are backed by the full power of the governmental body issuing the bond.

☐ (2) ***Limited Tax Bonds:*** A step down the scale, these issues are not backed by full taxing powers but only by the "full faith and credit" of the issuing body or by receipts from a particular tax.

☐ (3) ***Revenue Bonds:*** Receipts from particular facilities or projects built or maintained for public use by local political units are pledged to secure these issues.

☐ (4) ***Special Assessment Bonds:*** These are financial arrangements on local improvement projects, such as sewers, secured by levies imposed on taxpayers obtaining immediate benefits therefrom.

☐ (5) ***Housing Authority Bonds:*** These are either type (1) or (3) or a combination of both issued by local housing authorities and backed by the Federal Public Housing Administration.

☐ (6) ***Industrial Development Bonds:*** With these bonds, there are limits on the exemption. Only issues for $5,000 or less can qualify and then only under certain conditions. If the issue has a face of $1,000,000 or less, the conditions are almost completely relaxed. They are used by local authorities to finance construction of privately owned or operated projects to attract industry. A contract is entered into between the governmental entity and a private company; for example, the local authorities offer a community-built project in return for rental payments.

How to Find Good Buys: The best buys in tax exempts are found at dealers in tax-exempt bonds, in large brokerage firms handling this type of security, or in the investment department of a bank or other investment adviser. It is advisable to seek out someone who has special bond expertise. There are also tax-exempt bond funds analogous to mutual funds that can place your money in the market by investment in their diversified portfolio of municipal bonds. In this way, the investor gets a "safer" and wider choice than is normally available with new series offerings.

Yield Bonds: The biggest yields among tax exempts are found in a group called "yield bonds." They are usually at the low end of the quality scale. They're considered safer than a corporate debenture but riskier than a first mortgage corporate bond secured by specific tangible property rather than forecasted revenue.

Investment Pitfalls of Tax Exempts: Before an investor jumps into tax exempts as "sure things," remember that they involve two risks: price fluctuation and unmarketability. While defaults in tax exempts are extremely rare, their prices nevertheless will fluctuate in accordance with changes in the prevailing interest rates. This will not matter if the bond is held until maturity; if not, care must be exercised in choosing the time to buy.

Unmarketability is a common problem of bonds issued by small taxing districts. If an investor has to sell such bonds, the bond dealer may impose an extra charge because of the risk that he may not be able to resell them. Conversely, an investor often can pick up these same bonds at a discount—but he should be prepared to hold them indefinitely.

If the prospect of a net yield reduced by a fee to unload the bonds frightens an investor, he should take comfort in the fact that even if he turns in other "safe" investments, such as certificates of deposit before maturity, he will forfeit some of the high stated interest rate.

Insurance Protection for Investors in Tax Exempts: With the financial difficulties some municipalities have been having, the prudent investor might legitimately ask, "Are municipals safe?" He may also ask, "Can I count on interest being paid regularly and on time?"

To reassure the investor, insurance protection is offered by an insurance company called the American Municipal Bond Assurance Corporation (AMBAC).

AMBAC will insure relatively small issues (par value of from $300,000 to $3,000,000 to begin with) considered to be of medium investment quality. The municipality pays the premium. Standard & Poor's Corporation, which rates municipals, has indicated its recognition of the value of AMBAC insurance by assigning an "AA" rating to AMBAC-insured issues.

The investor who holds an insured bond gets the assurance that interest and principal will be paid promptly and without question. The insurance also reduces the risk of substantial depreciation in the market value of his bond if the issuer defaults. Both factors, in turn, increase the marketability of his bond(s) if it is ever necessary to sell before maturity.

Bond Ratings: Leading services (Moody's and Standard & Poor's) rate all types of bonds—tax exempts as well as others. Included are statistical data and current quotations resulting in an alphabetical grading of triple-A to D, based on estimated adequacy of revenues behind the bond, including the issuer's credit rating. The popular *Bond Buyer's Index of 20 Municipal Bonds* is another rating aid.

[¶2104.2] Tax Shelters in Real Estate Investments

Real estate offers an attractive investment. The favorable cash flow coupled with the depreciation and interest deductions available from real estate investments makes them profitable for individuals in high-tax brackets. As an investment, real estate has one disadvantage for the investor: Generally, it requires more time than other forms of investments since real estate must be managed. Of course, a busy investor may employ a real estate man to manage his property. Even if a professional manager is engaged, the owner generally has to spend more time managing his investment than he would had he invested in municipal bonds, mutual funds, or corporate stock.

Frequently, investments are made in real estate through real estate investment trusts (REITs) or syndications. Investors in REITs or syndications are not required to participate in the business of the venture. The investor's role is like that of an investor in a mutual fund or a corporation.

Investing via Real Estate Investment Trusts (REITs): As noted, a REIT puts the real estate investor in the same position as investors who purchase shares in mutual funds. By pooling his funds with those of others, the investor in a REIT may (1) reduce his risk by means of diversification of investment, (2) gain the benefit of expert investment counsel, and (3) get into projects that are too big for him to undertake singly.

A mutual fund, if it qualifies under the law, avoids double taxation: The only tax is paid at the shareholder level. All investors, small and large, are put in a position of equality, at least as far as opportunity is concerned. In the case of a REIT, 90% or more of its ordinary income must be distributed to its beneficiaries (i.e., its investors). Capital gains may be distributed or reinvested. The trust pays no tax on the distributed income, so that, in the last analysis, only one tax may be paid.

Real Estate Syndicates: Real estate syndicates also provide a convenient means for busy individuals to invest in real estate. Syndications are generally in the form of a partnership for two reasons: (1) During the period of construction and in the early years when there are "losses" they are passed through to the limited partners who can use them to offset other income. (2) When the loss period is over, the partnership form avoids the double taxation inherent in the corporate form.

Rental Housing Provides Special Tax Breaks: Limited partnership interests in residential properties enjoying special tax benefits under the federal tax and housing laws offer prospective investors opportunities for earning as much as a 16 to 20% annual after-tax return on the unrecovered balance of their investment over its life.

New rental housing of all types is favored over all other types of income-producing real estate under our present tax laws. The fastest methods of depreciation are available (200%-declining-balance and sum-of-the-digits).

The depreciation on nonresidential real estate in excess of that permitted by straight line is subject to recapture when the real estate is sold. However, with federally assisted low- and moderate-income housing built under §221(d)(3) and 236 of the Housing Act, there's no recapture when a sale is made after the property has been held for ten years. With all other rental housing the accelerated depreciation taken and subject to recapture on sale is reduced at the rate of 1% per month after the property has been held for 100 months. In other words, after the property has been held 200 months (16⅔ years) there's no more recapture. This can be a long time, but it's not an indefinite period as with nonresidential real estate where there's recapture until straight line catches up with faster writeoffs.

Rollover Benefit: A special "rollover" provision permits the investor to elect to sell the project without recognizing any capital gain provided the proceeds are reinvested in a similar project within a specified time. The tax basis of the second project is reduced by the amount of gain not recognized, so that the capital gain not recognized earlier may eventually have to be paid.

Tax Planning in Real Estate: Real estate enjoys some unique tax advantages, so that with careful planning an otherwise bad deal can be made acceptable and a good deal, exceptional.

Depreciation deductions have always played an extremely important part in real estate calculations. Depreciation deductions, especially those provided by accelerated depreciation, produce large tax-free returns. For this reason, sophisticated real estate investors always carefully scrutinize the relationship between various methods of depreciation open to them and other elements of a proposed transaction—particularly amortization payments required under the mortgage—in order to derive the greatest possible advantages. In structuring a real estate transaction, whether setting up financing, building, or leasing, the choice of the most advantageous depreciation method has always been important. The relationship between deductible depreciation and nondeductible mortgage amortization should be projected over the full term of the mortgage or at least until the mortgage has been reduced to the level where it can be refinanced. A reduced amortization can be weighed against depreciation and projected investment return.

Real Estate Profits May Qualify for Capital Gain Treatment: It is possible to build up the value of real property and eventually realize it in the form of capital gain by tax-deductible repair expenditures and by tax-free improvements made by tenants. These methods of creating value are generally unavailable in other forms of investment.

Tax-free Exchanges of Real Estate: Another advantage which real estate has over stocks and bonds and other investments is its potential for exchanging and pyramiding without the need to pay taxes.

Favorable Treatment of Costs for Carrying Real Estate: Great leverage is obtainable in real estate investments either by leasing or mortgaging the property. For a small equity, the investor gets the full benefit of any increase in value and tax deductions for his costs for carrying the property.

Delayed Realization of Gains From the Sale of Real Estate: Tax on the sale of real estate may be postponed by techniques such as installment sale, deferred sale, option agreements, etc. While these may be used for other investments, they are customary in real estate.

Ordinary Loss Treatment: This is available for losses realized on the sale of business property. If depreciable business property is sold at a loss, a deduction against ordinary income is available even though a gain would have been subject only to capital gain rates.

Investment in Residential Property: When a piece of real estate is purchased with the sole purpose of renting it to others all year round, all the items of expense including interest on the mortgage, real estate taxes, casualty losses, and depreciation are fully deductible even though they exceed the income from the property. A taxpayer with other income can take advantage of these deductions against other income.

However, if the residential property is the taxpayer's home (that is, he occupies it part time and rents it out part time), the hobby loss rules may affect the amount of the deduction available (§183). If a taxpayer engages in personal (rather than business) activity, his deductions cannot exceed the gross income from that activity.

[¶2104.3] How Depreciation Makes Real Estate an Attractive Investment

Depreciation makes real estate an attractive investment because it permits the development of highly favorable cash flow while providing substantial income tax deductions.

What is Depreciation? Depreciation for tax or accounting purposes is a reasonable allowance for the exhaustion, wear, and tear (including a reasonable allowance for obsolescence) of property—a sum set aside each year in order that, at the end of the property's useful life, the aggregate of the sums set aside will (with salvage value) be sufficient to provide an amount that's equal to the original cost.

Thus, tax depreciation permits an investor to recover the cost or other basis of the property over the period of its useful life. He gets an ordinary business deduction for the amount of the annual depreciation. This deduction requires no cash outlay. Since its effect is to increase the accumulation of cash, we say his ''cash flow'' is increased.

What Is Depreciable Property? As a general rule, depreciation can be taken only on property used in a trade or business or held for the production of income. If the personal residence is also used for a business purpose, as in the case of the physician who maintains his office in his home, depreciation can be taken for the portion of the house that is used for business. Land is not depreciable as it is not subject to physical decay or obsolescence nor does it have a definite useful life. To be depreciable, property must be subject to physical decay or obsolescence and must have a definite useful life.

Who Can Take Depreciation Deductions? As a general rule, the person who takes the economic loss because of the decrease in value is the one who is entitled to the depreciation deductions. In most cases, this is the owner of the property. To qualify for the depreciation deduction, however, the owner must have a real investment interest in the property. His investment or basis may be the purchase price, or he may acquire a special basis in the case of bequests or gifts.

What Depreciation Methods Are Available? Under the IRC, the methods of depreciation available to a taxpayer for real property are dependent upon the nature of the property. Different methods are applied to new and used property. Residential property is subject to a more liberal set of depreciation methods.

New Real Property: A reasonable allowance for depreciation in the case of new real property other than new residential properties includes an allowance figured under (1) the straight-line method, (2) the declining-balance method (using a maximum rate of 150% of the straight-line rate), and (3) any other consistent method that will produce an annual allowance that, when added to all allowances for the period beginning with the taxpayer's use of the property and including the taxable year, won't, during the first two-thirds of the property's useful life, exceed the total of such allowances that would have been used if such allowances were figured under the 150%-declining-balance method.

New Residential Real Property: The depreciation deduction on new residential real property may be determined by any of the following:

(a) The straight-line method;
(b) The declining-balance method (up to double straight line);

(c) The sum-of-the-years-digits method (Rate is a fraction. The numerator is the remaining useful life. The denominator equals the sum of each year of life: If the property had a five-year life it would be 15 [1 + 2 + 3 + 4 + 5].);

(d) Any other consistent method that during the first two-thirds of the property's useful life does not give greater depreciation than the declining-balance method.

Used Real Property (Other Than Residential): With used real estate other than used residential rental property with a remaining useful life of 20 years or more, depreciation is limited to an amount figured under (1) the straight-line method or (2) another method determined by the Treasury to result in a reasonable allowance but not including any declining-balance method, the sum-of-the-years-digits method, or any other method allowable solely by reason of the application of IRC §167(b)(4) or 167(j)(1)(C), which permit methods that produce fast writeoffs equivalent to those produced under the 200%- and 150%-declining-balance methods. With used residential rental property having a useful life of 20 years or more, the 125%-declining-balance method or its equivalent or the straight-line method can be used.

Rehabilitated housing expenditures can be written off in five years if the tests set out in the IRC and regulations are met. This program is designed for rehabilitated housing for low- and moderate-income tenants.

Depreciation May Be Recaptured If the Property Is Sold: Although some forms of accelerated depreciation are still available to real estate investors, the Government has developed a rule to recapture accelerated depreciation if the property is sold. Accelerated depreciation taken in excess of allowable straight-line depreciation with respect to all forms of depreciable real estate except residential rental property is subject to recapture as ordinary income to the extent of gain resulting from the sale. As to residential rental property, a 1% per month reduction in the amount subject to recapture is allowed after the property has been held for 100 full months.

Commercial, Industrial, and Office Buildings: One hundred percent of the excess of accelerated over straight-line depreciation is subject to recapture with respect to all properties other than residential rental properties, including commercial, industrial and office buildings. This applies to depreciation for periods subsequent to December 31, 1969, with respect to properties acquired before that date as well as to properties acquired after that date.

Residential Rental Properties: The entire excess of accelerated over straight-line depreciation as to new residential properties is recaptured as ordinary income if the property is disposed of within 100 months. Thereafter, the amount recaptured as ordinary income is reduced by 1% for each month. The result is that if the property is sold after a holding period of 16 years and 8 months, the entire gain on the sale will be long-term capital gain. The same rule applies in the case of rehabilitated expenditures for low- and moderate-income rental housing. In the case of housing covered by §221(a)(3) or 236 of the National Housing Act, there's no recapture after 10 years.

[¶2104.4] Sale-Leasebacks for the Small Businessman

Sale-leaseback transactions often make sense as a means of raising capital or investing funds built up through years of successful practice.

A sale-leaseback involves the sale of property by its owner to an investor with an agreement to lease it back to the seller. In this way the capital tied up in the real estate is freed for other purposes. The cost of the freed capital is the loss of the depreciation deduction formerly available to the owner plus the net cost of the deductible rent. (Generally, there is a capital gain tax liability at the time of the transaction.)

You can often accomplish more by transacting sale-leaseback than by mortgaging the property. Since the seller becomes the lessee under a sale-leaseback, he is entitled to deduct his entire rental payment instead of merely the interest he would be obliged to pay if he had mortgaged the property. In effect, the sale-leaseback makes the cost of the land depreciable. Under a mortgage, the mortgagor can neither depreciate the land himself nor can he deduct the amortization payments to the mortgagee. In other words, the rent paid to the purchaser in a sale-leaseback transaction is, in effect, equivalent to interest and amortization on a mortgage. Mortgage payments are thus put on a tax-deductible basis. In this way, the seller may be more than compensated for the loss of depreciation deduction.

The investor-purchaser owns the building and is entitled to depreciate it. He is fully taxable on the rent he receives, and part of this rent represents the amortization of his investment. However, his depreciation of the property may provide enough of a tax deduction to make up for this.

Sale-leasebacks are entered into with institutional tax-exempt investors and also with investors that are not tax exempt, especially where short-term leases and high building-to-land valuation ratios exist. In this way, the investor shelters from taxation, by way of the depreciation deduction, most of the portion of his rent that represents amortization and recovers this amortization in a short period of time.

[¶2104.5] The Tax-Sheltered Joy of Farming

Many investors look to farmland, using one building on the farm as a vacation home and employing a farmer to work the rest of the property. In this way they are able to hold the farmland as an investment while it appreciates. (Department of Agriculture figures indicate that farmlands are appreciating at a record pace.)

Special Tax Benefits for Farmers: While most farm expenses are governed by the general rules that apply to all business expenses, special treatment is provided in certain areas. In order to be treated as a farmer for tax purposes, the investor must be a person (an individual, corporation, or partnership) engaged either as owner or tenant in the operation or management of a farm for gain or profit. ''Farming'' includes the cultivation, raising, and harvesting of any agricultural or horticultural commodity and the raising, shearing, feeding, caring for, training, and management of livestock, bees, poultry, and fur-bearing animals and wildlife. A ''farm'' as used in its ordinary, accepted sense includes stock, dairy, poultry, fruit, fur-bearing animal and truck farms, plantations, ranches, nurseries, ranges, greenhouses, or other similar structures used primarily for the raising of agricultural or horticultural commodities and orchards.

☐ (1) ***Soil and Water Conservation Expenditures:*** A taxpayer engaged in the business of farming enjoys a special election to expense (rather than capitalize) money spent on land for soil and water conservation and for the prevention of land erosion. The deductible amount in any year may not exceed 25% of gross income from farming for that year. However, any excess can be carried over, but only to the extent of the 25% limit per year. The option applies to expenses for the treatment or moving of earth on land actually used in farming, either before or during the time the expenditures are made. The land must be used for the production of crops, fruits, or other agricultural products or for the sustenance of livestock. It does not apply to money spent on depreciable facilities or structures. Such items must be capitalized.

This deduction can be added to an operating loss and carried over as a part of an operating loss. Where the expenditures exceed 25% of gross income, the excess can be carried over and deducted until it has all been deducted, but only against income from farming. However, with the election in operation, the excess can't be added to the basis of the improved land. Thus, when the land is sold, the capital gain is not reduced by the portion of the expenses not deducted because they were in excess of the 25% limit. But even though the land has been sold, these expenses can be deducted against subsequently realized farm income.

This special deduction affords an opportunity to convert ordinary income into capital gain. A person buying a piece of farmland can deduct 25% of his expenses for leveling, grading, clearing brush, building drainage ditches, etc., against ordinary (farm) income. When the property is sold, it will bring a higher price because of the work, and the gain will be taxed at more favorable capital gain rates.

☐ (2) ***Development Expenses:*** The farmer also has an election to capitalize or deduct expenses such as taxes, labor, seed, fertilizer, insurance, interest, etc., during the period of development. Once the productive state is reached, however, he must deduct them currently. There is no option to deduct currently capital expenditures, such as wells, irrigation pipes, drain tile, masonry or concrete tanks, reservoirs or dams, and roads. Capital expenditures in connection with soil and water conservation are an exception.

☐ (3) ***Casualty Losses:*** Farmers (as other taxpayers) can deduct casualty losses resulting from, for example, hurricane, tornado, heavy rains, freezing, lightning, floods, storm, drought, cyclone, landslides, avalanches, dust storms, sinking of land, ice pressure, cave-ins, thaws, severe blizzard and cold, and other such natural causes.

☐ (4) ***Expenses of Clearing Land:*** Farmers can elect to deduct currently the expense of clearing land if the purpose is to make the land suitable for farming. Expenditures that are for the purchase, construction, installation, or improvement of structures or facilities subject to depreciation are excluded. So are expenses that are deductible under any other section of the tax law. However, depreciation of property, such as tractors, that will be used in farming as well as in the actual clearing of land is allowed.

The deduction is limited to the lesser of $5,000 or 25% of taxable income from a farming business. Usually, there won't be any taxable income from farming during the preparatory period; but if the taxpayer has income from farming operations other than the operation in the preparatory period of development, he can apparently use the deduction to offset income from the other farming operation.

Farmers' Excess Deduction Account: If an individual with a farm loses money from his farming operation, he is required to maintain an excess deduction account that is increased annually by the amount of farm losses in excess of $25,000 claimed by the taxpayer. This rule applies only in years in which the taxpayer had nonfarm income in excess of $50,000. In years when there is farm income, the excess deduction account is reduced. If the farm property is sold, it is subject to recapture to the extent of the excess deduction account.

In addition, there is a recapture provision covering losses on the sale of land to the extent of allowable soil and water conservation expenditures and land clearing expenditures incurred in the current year and the prior four years. If the sale occurs six to ten years after the expenditure occurs, the amount recaptured is reduced by 20% a year with no recapture after ten years. Gain on the sale of depreciable property such as buildings, barns, etc., is subject to the recapture rules applicable to depreciable real property.

Farm Must Not Be a Hobby Farm: In order to get a tax shelter for nonfarming income from the development of farm property, the farming operation must be a business and not a hobby. Loss deductions for farming undertaken primarily for recreation are not allowed. If it is a hobby, whatever deductions an investor gets are limited to the gross income from the farming operation exclusive of interest and property taxes. To be classified as a business, the profit motive must be the dominant factor.

[¶2104.6] The Tax Shelter in Citrus Groves

Investing in a citrus grove especially fits the career and tax position of the person who will be at peak income for a 5- to 15-year stretch while he is carrying expenses and building the grove and who is looking for capital values of a regular income for his retirement years.

The initial investment can be small, a good part of the expenses can be defrayed by what would otherwise be tax dollars, and the payoff by sale or annual crop income can be anywhere from 5 to 15 years away and should become larger the longer it's deferred. Then, by adding more holdings, the citrus income can build additional values. The investor may lay out $300 to $1,500 an acre for land. How much he spends will depend on when and where he buys, how good the land is, how much clearing it needs, and whether or not some planting has been done. At $1,200 to $1,500 an acre, he should be able to purchase a young grove. At $300 to $500, he'll get only raw land. The cost of clearing the land should run $120 to $150 an acre, $140 an acre to buy young trees at $2 each, $23 an acre for planting, $30 to water an acre, and $5 an acre to plant cover grass. All these will be nondeductible capital costs; so that, one way or another, he'll have an investment of about $1,500 an acre. He may also pay for each acre $50 for labor and equipment, $10 for fertilizer, $10 for miscellaneous taxes, and about $500 a year to carry, manage, and care for it. Those costs subject to limitations together with the interest he paid on money borrowed to buy or improve the land will produce tax savings. Or he may buy a grove that has been started. Fruit-bearing groves can be found in Florida for $2,000 to $4,000 an acre.

Grove Management: Management is important and can usually be arranged for on a satisfactory basis. Professional organizations that care for groves will undertake to develop the grove and handle the harvesting and marketing of the fruit. Even investors living in the citrus areas usually use this type of service, which includes spraying, cultivating, marketing, and presentation of financial statements to owners. Ten acres is considered the minimum-sized grove that can be operated economically. With full financing, an investor will need a few thousand dollars of his own money to acquire this kind of a grove for future growth.

Tax Protection Elements: Citrus growers in the four growing states of Florida, Texas, Arizona, and California have six elements of tax protection going for them.

☐ (1) In starting a new grove or in buying a young one, time and nature add value that cannot be taxed until the grove is sold, at which time the profit on the sale is capital gain.

☐ (2) Expenditures incurred for cultivating or maintaining a grove that was planted prior to December 30, 1969, are currently deductible. Such expenses include fertilizer, management charges, water charges, and spraying and cultivation of the trees. As to groves planted on or after December 30, 1969, such expenses if incurred before the end of the fourth year after the planting of the grove must be capitalized. After the four-year period, they are currently deductible.

☐ (3) Taxes and interest paid (see the discussion of financing below) are, of course, currently deductible at all times.

☐ (4) The cost of plantings and trees must be capitalized but may be depreciated over a life expectancy of from 35 to 50 years. As the depreciation guidelines note, due consideration must be given to the geographic, climatic, genetic, and other factors that determine depreciable life of trees and vines. Some groves may in fact produce for longer periods than their depreciable lives. Thus, a grove being depreciated on the assumption of a 50-year life expectancy may in fact produce for 75 years.

☐ (5) By election, soil and water conservation expenses can be deducted to the extent of 25% of farm income, as well as leveling, terracing, grading, building drainage ditches, and eradication of brush. However such expenses are "recaptured" as ordinary income on sale of the grove within five years of acquisition and slide off in 20% increments for each year longer the grove is held until the tenth year, when there is no more recapture.

☐ (6) When a grove is sold, the owner realizes his profit as capital gain, except as noted in the preceding paragraph. Any loss on sale is fully deductible.

Financing: If an investor doesn't want to risk a bundle of cash in the venture, he'll probably be able to arrange purchase money loans up to 72% of the cost of a grove. Top-production groves can be had for a down payment of 28%, while newer groves require more capital outlay.

The interest payments are not within range of the 50% limitation on the deduction of excess investment interest insofar as the operation is conducted as a trade or business. However, if the investor occupies a purely passive role, it could be argued that the limitation applies. The line between an investment and a trade or business may be difficult to draw in some cases.

Loans can be arranged through banks and insurance companies in the growing areas. The amount of money involved and the terms available will depend on the particular property to be purchased, including the age of the grove, fruit prices, and the type of fruit under cultivation or contemplated. Banks may offer up to 50% of the cost of a producing grove, charge the going rate of interest, and schedule repayments over four to five years. Some insurance companies may lend as much as 60% over a 10- to 12-year period.

Four Investment Alternatives: An investor has these basic choices:

☐ (1) Buying a mature grove, which means putting maximum capital at risk and enjoying immediate income;

☐ (2) Buying a grove just beginning to yield that requires less capital, returns a modest income at once, and promises capital growth;

☐ (3) Buying a newly planted grove that defers income but maximizes capital growth; or

☐ (4) Buying raw land and building a grove.

Groves may be bought when full bearing—18 to 25 years old—or as young plantings just set out, or at any intermediate age. Each age category serves a different investment purpose. A full-bearing grove provides maximum immediate income but no capital gain. A newly planted grove provides maximum capital gain. Income is deferred during the first years but ultimately equals and exceeds the income from a grove bought when full bearing. Intermediate grove stages may be found to suit individual investment purposes.

Let's see what $25,000 invested in each type of grove may be able to accomplish in 20 years. The figures used are approximations that may vary with locale and time, and the projections of future values take no account of inflation or deflation.

Age at time of purchase	20 yrs	10 yrs	5 yrs	1 yr
Price per acre	$2,500	$1,650	$1,150	$500
Number of acres $25,000 will buy	10	15.1	21.7	50
Total market value in 20 years	$25,000	$37,800	$54,400	$125,000
Capital gain	None	$12,800	$29,400	$100,000
Earned income	$80,000	$110,000	$130,000	$203,000
Total increment (gain plus income)	$80,000	$122,800	$159,400	$303,000
Ratio increment to cost	3.2 to 1	4.9 to 1	6.4 to 1	12 to 1
Average yearly yield	16%	22%	26%	40%

The younger the grove at the time of purchase, the higher the ultimate and average yield and the greater the growth of capital. Young plantings have another advantage: They can be had in small units of 10 acres and up and can be handled for as little as $5,000 cash or $2,500 on terms.

Building a Grove: Despite the fact that the tax law bars the current deduction of the expense of maintaining, cultivating, and developing a grove for the first four years after planting, building a grove still offers profit potential, and by the sixth year the grove should be developed to the point where income covers expenses.

[¶2104.7] Oil and Gas Investments Offer Tax Shelter

Investments in oil drilling exploration funds will normally in the year of investment provide the investor with a tax deduction equal to 70 or 80% of the amount of the investment. A taxpayer in the 50% tax bracket can recover 40% of his investment in the first year of the investment.

Of course, oil exploration is a risky business. There is no guarantee that an oil exploration fund will find oil. The risks, however, are rewarded by the tax shelter available. The following deductions are available:

☐ ***Costs That Can Be Charged Off as Incurred:*** This category includes:

(1) Intangible drilling costs, that is, all costs of drilling except for the cost of depreciable property used in drilling. This charge-off is allowed whether the hole is dry or producing.

(2) Lease rentals.

(3) Costs of general exploration not related to an area of interest.

☐ ***Costs Capitalized but Charged Off When Property Is Abandoned:*** Lease acquisition costs and exploration costs, including such items as geological and geophysical studies, on nonproductive properties.

☐ ***Costs Capitalized and Taken as Depreciation:*** Costs of drilling equipment.

☐ ***Costs Capitalized and Taken as Cost Depletion Unless Percentage Depletion Is Used:*** Exploration costs and lease acquisition costs on productive properties.

☐ ***Depletion:*** The investor or operator can deduct each year the greater of cost depletion or percentage depletion. Percentage depletion is computed as the lesser of 22% of the gross value of the oil or gas at the well or 50% of the net income from the property. Cost depletion is computed by combining the capitalized cost of the property, that is, the lease acquisition cost, plus the specific property exploration costs less prior depletion, cost or percentage, and taking the portion of this each year equivalent to the ratio of oil or gas extracted to the estimated recoverable reserve on the property.

How to Make Oil and Gas Investments: There are several ways to get into oil and gas investments. The principal alternatives are:

☐ (1) Drilling under a lease or sublease on either wildcat or proven ground.
☐ (2) Purchase of an already producing working interest, partly or fully developed. The working interest may be acquired by purchase or discovery. It is usually held under a lease giving the lessee the right to develop the property for oil, subject to landowner's royalties and possibly to other overriding royalties. The holder of the landowner's royalty is usually entitled to a one-eighth interest in the oil produced out of the ground and bears none of the burden of development and lifting costs. The owner of the working interest keeps seven-eighths of the oil, less overriding royalties, which are seldom more than one-eighth. Out of this he must carry the burden of development and lifting costs.
☐ (3) Investment in limited partnerships for exploration or drilling.
☐ (4) Purchase of a royalty interest.
☐ (5) Purchase of stock in an oil and gas company.

How Wildcatting Pays Off: Investing in a wildcatting operation is the most risky means of investing in oil and gas. It is also the type of investment that has the highest potential for substantial profit.

Only in the oil business and other natural resource businesses is the operator's or investor's deduction for wasting capital permitted to exceed his actual unrecovered capital cost. This arises because such a large part of capital cost is permitted to be deducted as incurred, and then depletion is allowed as a percentage of receipts without regard to the remaining unrecovered cost. An example will clarify this:

In wildcatting, a ratio of ten dry wells to one producing well is not uncommon. Let's say a group of investors forms a drilling partnership consisting of 11 partners with each contributing $10,000. Eleven wells are drilled—ten are dry and one is productive—at a cost of $10,000 each or a total cost of $110,000. The productive well has a value of $220,000 based on an estimate of the value of the oil in the ground on discovery and over a lifetime produces $800,000 in gross income. The cost of raising the oil to the surface over the life of the well is $200,000. Here's how the investment shapes up taxwise:

		Tax Treatment
10 Dry Wells	$100,000 Cost	$ 70,000 Currently Deductible
		30,000 Deductible as Depreciation
1 Productive Well	$ 10,000 Cost	5,000 Currently Deductible
		5,000 Lease Cost Not Deductible
		176,000 Deductible as % Depletion
		200,000 Deductible as Lifting Cost
Total Tax Deductions		$481,000

Our investors will have enjoyed net income of $490,000 by the time the productive well is exhausted: $800,000 gross income less $110,000 exploration and drilling cost and $200,000 in lifting costs. However, their taxable income would amount to only $319,000 because of the $481,000 in tax deductions permitted. It is worth noting that the percentage depletion deduction in the example amounts to 176% of the initial investment.

High Profit Potential for the Individual Investor: How would the individual investors fare? The answer depends on their tax brackets and might vary for individual partners from year to year, whether or not all of the drilling costs were incurred in the initial year, the period of productivity, and the evenness of the flow. Assume that the investor is in the 50% tax bracket ($44,000 to $52,000 in taxable income on a joint return) at all times, all drilling costs are incurred in the first year, and the well produces for six years at an even rate. The picture for the investor who stayed with the program would look like this:

Net Income, 1/11 of $490,000 or	$44,545
Taxable Income, 1/11 of $319,000 or	$29,000
Taxes on Taxable Income (50%)	$14,500
After-Tax Return	$30,045

The return includes a return of capital so that the after-tax profits are $20,045 or roughly 33% per year, using a six-year base. This, of course, would be the equivalent of a 66% before-tax return. The after-tax return might be even better on a continuing series of annual investments in drilling programs. In the first year of a drilling program the investor can get a deduction for his intangible drilling costs, and these amount to 70 to 80% (higher if the partnership is leveraged and borrows outside money for drilling costs) of the total investment. These high deductions would be used to offset the income from the producing well(s).

Effect of the Mimimum Tax: There is a minimum tax of 10% on tax-preference income over a $30,000 exemption plus a credit for regular federal income taxes paid. To the extent that depletion exceeds the cost or other basis of the property involved, it is treated as tax-preference income. The cost or other basis on which the tax preference is based does not include intangible drilling and development costs. Because of the $30,000 exemption, few professionals will be faced with the tax on tax-preference income. Applying the figures in the above example, the $5,000 lease cost would appear to be the sole cost or basis of the property involved. The percentage depletion would total $176,000, leaving $171,000 in tax-preference income over the life of the well. In the example we assumed that the life of the well was six years and that there was even production over the six-year period. If the $171,000 in tax-preference income is divided by six years and then divided among the 11 partners, each would have less than $2,500 in tax-preference income, substantially under the $30,000-plus-actual-taxes-paid exemption from the minimum tax.

How to Choose an Oil Program: The following is a checklist of factors to be considered in selecting an oil program:

☐ (1) ***Liability:*** Programs may be cast as either joint ventures or limited partnerships. The former involve unlimited liability; hence, only the limited partnership-type program should be considered.

☐ (2) ***Assessability:*** Consider only programs that limit total assessability. Avoid unlimited commitments. This is the only way an investor can be sure he can "afford" the investment.

☐ (3) ***Diversification:*** All programs offer diversification among several wells. The more money raised, the more wells drilled, the greater the diversification. But unless an investor gets in on the tail end of an offering, he can only know about potential, not the actual diversification of the program he's investing in.

However, too much diversification can operate to reduce marketability. For example, an individual who has a $10,000 investment in a $100 million program will have only a 1/10,000 interest in each well, and it will be hard to sell such a small interest. Many administrative costs are apt to be of a fixed nature, not varying with the size of the program; but if the program is too big, with too many investors—e.g., a $100 million program with 10,000 investors—a certain loss in efficiency of administration can be expected.

To avoid too much or too little diversification and excessive administrative costs, avoid the extremes in program size.

□ (4) ***Liquidity:*** An investor should not get into a drilling program if he thinks he might be forced to sell in an emergency. Drilling programs should be considered permanent investments for all practical purposes. If he's in doubt or he's in a borderline situation and decides to invest, he should look for a program that promises a buy-back at any time, but he can expect that the discount on the buy-back will be steep enough to discourage practical exercise.

□ (5) ***Risk:*** Some programs concentrate on wildcatting, e.g., drilling and development of unproven prospects, others on development wells, e.g., drilling in areas immediately next to proven fields, and others undertake a program balanced between wildcatting and development drilling. Still others offer investments in producing properties where the risk will be low but so will the returns. This type of program should be avoided. Only the investor in the 70% top tax bracket should consider a pure wildcat program. All others should consider a development or balanced program.

□ (6) ***Sharing Agreement:*** Three income/expense categories are usually covered: (a) management fees, (b) the sharing of drilling costs and (c) the sharing of income. There are five basic ways of handling (b) and (c): overriding royalty, carried interest, net profits interest, disproportionate ratio, and tangible-intangible expense method.

Under the last, investors pay all intangible drilling costs and drilling program management pays for tangible equipment. Oil production income is shared according to specified percentages. The tangible-intangible sharing method may be the only viable arrangement because it allows immediate writeoff of total drilling investment and so reduces risk by lowering the after-tax investment base. It does not penalize future production income and increases the rate of return per dollar of income.

The agreement should provide that no purchase of existing production will be undertaken because such purchases afford no tax shelter and the investment return is apt to be low.

The key factors in comparing drilling programs are (a) maximum tax benefits and (b) maximum potential income.

Income potential is calculated by multiplying (a) the amount available for drilling (gross investment less all loading charges, e.g., commissions, management fees, underwriting charges, etc.) by (b) the after-tax rate of return, computed by dividing the net after-tax investment from the investor's share of $100 drilling costs. The resulting figure is basically a "made-up number" based on the assumption that each $100 of drilling cost will recover only $100 in revenue but is useful in comparing sharing arrangements.

□ (7) ***Conflicts of Interest:*** There will be potential conflicts of interest in virtually every drilling prospectus. Watch for management fees that permit the operator to collect twice for the same service such as a payment of a percentage of the fund for management fees on top of a payment of general overhead expense. Scrutinize so-called turnkey drilling contracts. The idea of this type of contract is to assure a stated drilling price for a well. If management has total discretion to set turnkey prices, there is an obvious potential conflict of interest. Look to an earlier prospectus or income statement to get an idea of how much management has been making on these turnkey contracts. Such an investigation may show that the bulk of the operator's profit has been derived from turnkey operations, not the production of oil and gas. Look carefully also at "well-operating charges." Sometimes the program may permit a monthly charge without regard to actual expenses. This may operate as an incentive to continue operation of a well even though production has declined to below the breakeven point.

☐ (8) ***Management:*** Look at organization, experience, record, and ability to spend program funds. There are two basic types of operators: (a) independent oil companies that generate their own drilling prospects and (b) companies that rely on outsiders for drilling ideas and then buy what they consider the best investment, similar to mutual funds. The latter "double dip" the investor by paying the originator of the prospect for finding it and then paying itself for acquiring the prospect. More important, perhaps, the investor has no means of evaluating the skills of those who are to generate drilling prospects.

Evaluating experience is difficult. One approach might be to select only established programs, but the trouble with this approach is that the older programs often don't have the liberal sharing arrangements of newer, more competitive programs. A capable management group, even though lacking experience in administering drilling programs, may be preferred to a more experienced crew with a less liberal sharing arrangement. Evaluating track records in producing oil is also difficult. You should look at (a) the wildcat success ratios of management as an indication of pure geographical skill and (b) oil and gas revenues adjusted for price changes. If revenues have remained constant or declined over a period of years this may be more significant than overall drilling success ratios.

Ability to spend program funds also deserves attention. A group may be able to raise more money than it can spend judiciously. Here the number of wells drilled in the past should be taken into account. If management has been able to drill five to ten net wells for each $1 million raised without a major drop in success ratio, the picture appears good. If more than $10 million is to be spent in one year, check the prospectus for some indication on how the funds are to be spent. If a company plans to double or better the amount spent in the past, the deal should be avoided unless the prospectus shows how this is possible.

Opportunities for Small Investors in Proven or Semiproven Leases: There are now varying types of limited partnerships designed to enable a modest investor to get into oil with a small monthly investment. These plans sometimes require no more than a $1,500 lump-sum investment, which may be even further eased by the monthly payment plan.

The capital contributed to each of these partnerships is usually invested in proven and semiproven leases, although investments in other producing oil properties may sometimes be made. Proven leases are leases situated near enough to known oil deposits that are reasonably sure to yield oil in profitable quantities. "Semiproven leases" are those usually located further away from proven wells, so that there is not the same degree of certainty of profitable oil yield. Voluntary withdrawals are usually permitted at any time during the life of the partnership, but when the cash surrender value of an interest is calculated, an investor may take an out-of-pocket loss. Before investing in this type of lease partnership, then, the prospectus must be analyzed thoroughly to find out just what will happen if an interest was liquidated early in the venture.

Tax Impact of Monthly Investment Plans: Each investor is taxed on his distributive share of the partnership income, whether or not it is actually distributed to him during that taxable year. In addition, each investor may claim his share of partnership deductions for intangible drilling and development costs (as discussed above), tangible equipment, leasing equipment costs, costs of oil and gas leases, and depletion allowance, provided the total deduction doesn't exceed his cost or basis. Limited partnerships may give a substantial tax break.

The Attraction of Royalty Investments: Investment in oil royalties can afford many of the opportunities available to investors in working interests. A full royalty interest is almost always one-eighth of the oil produced. It is free of all development and lifting costs. Fractional interests are sold off. They are initially purchased from the landowner. The selection of a good royalty depends on knowledge of the property and its productive potential. Royalties are available through dealers in oil securities and the standards of value run roughly this way:

☐ (1) The price of the royalty should be about one-third the value of the oil in the ground that will go to the royalty interest.

☐ (2) The royalty should return 12 to 14% of its cost each year. Out of this 12 to 14% the investor will have to recover his investment and get his income yield.

☐ (3) The royalty interest should pay out in seven to eight years. That is, the investor should receive gross proceeds in the amount of his capital cost over a seven- to eight-year period. Of these gross proceeds, under the 1969 Tax Law, 22% will be fully applicable to recovering his capital, and the balance will be applicable only after income tax is paid on 78% of the proceeds.

☐ (4) A well should be figured to have a life of no more than 20 years. Many of them run to 40 years or beyond, but that should be considered as a dividend and not part of the basic investment.

How Even Small Investors Can Get High Tax-Sheltered Returns From Low-Risk Investments in Oil and Gas: With direct investment in producing oil and gas wells, an investor doesn't get the same high degree of tax shelter that he does in drilling-exploration investments, although there is a good deal of shelter from the depletion allowance and depreciation deductions. However, he doesn't have the risk that he has with exploratory operations either.

How to Get Into Oil and Gas With a Relatively Small Investment: Investments in producing wells were once the exclusive preserve of the super rich. But now, under programs being developed by those already in the field, an investor doesn't have to be super rich or even rich to get an injection of black gold in his family income flow. The oil industry has a constant need for fresh exploration capital. Only part of that capital need can be supplied with drilling-exploration funds. Then, if a strike is made, the bigger part of the profits will likely go to the outside investors. To provide their capital requirements, those in the oil industry will often sell producing properties at prices considerably less than the projected ultimate cash return.

This type of program may be sold on an installment basis. The investor benefits not only because he can pay in installments, but also because the program provides diversification so that all his investment dollars are not riding on a single well. Investors may get into this type of program with an investment of $8,000 of which only $3,000 is paid immediately as a down payment. The balance is payable in quarterly installments of $1,000 each. The investor becomes a limited partner in six separate oil ventures and gets the benefit of diversification, which can be a safety factor in most any type of investment.

Leverage Potential: The investor can liquidate his interest after six months. His shares are considered good collateral by lenders. While enjoying a continued return on a series of rollover oil management programs, he can also put his shares to work securing loans whose proceeds he can invest in other tax-sheltered opportunities.

Tax-Favored Distributions to Pyramid Returns: In a particular oil income program, some of the distributions will be tax free because they represent a return of capital. Reinvestment of capital rather than receipt of cash is encouraged. However, an investor must act quickly to get cash, for the manager automatically reinvests (to boost working capital) unless an affirmative act demanding cash is made.

Timing: Knowing when to get out of an oil deal is crucial. Sudden spurts of productivity interlaced with poor production usually are indicative of a well that is almost bled to death. Of course, the periodic reports on the various producing wells held by the partnership should be analyzed by an impartial geologist to see whether it is time to pull out of the deal.

[¶2104.8] Cattle as a Tax-Sheltered Investment

Many high-bracket men and women invest in cattle programs because of the available tax shelter. Traditionally, cattle have been used to build up capital in two ways; by breeding and by feeding.

☐ (1) ***By Breeding:*** Cows are capital assets that multiply at a predictable rate. They have calves from January to April, and the calves are weaned at about 7 to 8 months of age. Bull calves can be traded for heifers, which can be bred when they are 15 months old. Since the gestation period is 9 months, the heifer will have her first calf when she is 24 months old, at which point she becomes a cow. Cows will normally produce a calf each year until they are 10 or 12 years of age.

In a breeding program an investor is permitted to use his expenses to offset ordinary income while the herd is being built up. When the herd is sold the taxpayer can get capital gains.

☐ (2) ***By Feeding:*** A calf grows from 75 pounds at birth to 350 to 450 pounds at 6 months, 625 as a yearling, 850 to 900 at 2, and 1,000 at 3 years. More than two-thirds of our beef production is grain-fed on feeder lots for five or six months before slaughter.

In a feeding program, the key tax advantage was that the taxpayer could defer his income. The investor could get into a feeder program at the tail end of his tax year and prepay the fully deductible food and interest costs, thus offsetting his ordinary income for that year. However, IRS has recently taken the might out of this investment strategy by announcing that the tax break will not be available where it materially distorts a taxpayer's income (TIR 1261 1973). The IRS position has been upheld by the Court in *Cattle Feeders Tax Committee* (CA-10 12/13/73). In light of these recent developments only the tax treatment of the breeding program will be discussed in detail in this chapter.

How to Invest in a Breeding Program: An investor can get into the breeding business with as little as 10% equity. In the cattle belt, ranchers and institutional lenders are willing to provide 90% financing for cattle investments.

If an animal is purchased for $200 in the fall, an investor would pay as little as $20 down. The rancher would take back a $180 nonrecourse mortgage at about 8% and would be prepaid approximately $60 per head as an advance against the maintenance contract. Also, the rancher would be prepaid interest on the loan. So, in dollars, approximately $75 per head would be prepaid and be available as a deduction in the first tax year.

When an investor purchases a herd or a partnership interest in a herd, the seller usually includes an annual management and maintenance contract as part of the transaction. The manager assumes the active responsibility for overseeing the herd. He acts as the investor's agent and is usually authorized to handle all aspects of the transaction, including the sale of the cattle and the bookkeeping. Periodic reports are submitted to the investor.

There are a number of ways an investor can profit from his breeding cattle herd.

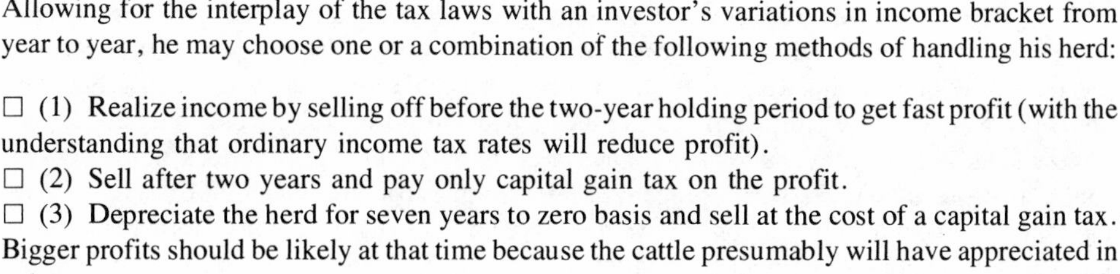

Allowing for the interplay of the tax laws with an investor's variations in income bracket from year to year, he may choose one or a combination of the following methods of handling his herd:

☐ (1) Realize income by selling off before the two-year holding period to get fast profit (with the understanding that ordinary income tax rates will reduce profit).
☐ (2) Sell after two years and pay only capital gain tax on the profit.
☐ (3) Depreciate the herd for seven years to zero basis and sell at the cost of a capital gain tax. Bigger profits should be likely at that time because the cattle presumably will have appreciated in value.
☐ (4) Leave the herd alone except for periodic culls and bequeath it to children or grandchildren. In the estate, the herd will get a stepped-up basis and sale will generate an estate tax lower than a tax on sale during lifetime.
☐ (5) Defer income by not selling off and allowing the herd to increase in value and numbers, meeting the annual cash expenses out of other income.
☐ (6) Sell enough of the herd so that current expenses are covered and the operation is not a drain on outside income.
☐ (7) Liquidate the entire investment all at once or over a period of years and get capital gains either way.
☐ (8) Manage the property for annual income by selling enough each year to defray expenses and realize additional income without liquidating the herd.

Investment Credit Offers Additional Tax Incentive: The investment tax credit offers additional incentives for investments in breeding cattle. Livestock acquired for breeding, dairy, or work purposes qualifies for the investment credit.

If substantially identical livestock has been sold or otherwise disposed of by the taxpayer during a one-year period beginning six months before he acquires other livestock, the cost of the acquired livestock is to be reduced by the amount realized on the sale of the substantially identical livestock. This rule is not applicable, however, if there is an investment credit recapture on the disposition of the substantially identical livestock or if the replacement is due to an involuntary conversion—even if resulting from drought or disease.

"Excess Deduction Account" Must Be Maintained: Although a farm (or cattle breeding) loss is deductible in full for the current year against nonfarm income, heavy losses may ultimately affect capital gain treatment on sales of cattle (breeding and feeding). A taxpayer with net farm losses exceeding $25,000 in one taxable year is required to keep a record of that excess in an "excess deduction account" (EDA). Each year's farm loss exceeding $25,000 is put into the EDA. Farm income in any later year reduces the amount of losses in the account. Any gains taxed as ordinary income (such as sale of cattle not held two years) are also used to reduce the EDA, on a dollar-for-dollar basis. Losses and gains now subject to recapture are not counted in computing loss for EDA purposes. Recapture is provided for in IRC §1245. Gain on the disposition of a recaptured asset will ordinarily be the difference between the amount realized and its adjusted basis.

The EDA does not apply unless nonfarm taxable income exceeds $50,000 (on a joint return), nor does it apply if the cattle owner uses accrual rather than cash accounting. EDA rules apply ratably at the partner's level in a cattle breeding partnership. There is also a passthrough to shareholders of Subchapter S corporations.

Depreciation as Tax Deferral Device: The tax advantages of depreciating breeding cattle consist mainly of deductions during the years an investor holds the cattle. However, new recapture rules impose added tax on the disposition of the cattle, whether by sale or gift. Better tax benefits are obtained by selling only part of the herd and disposing of the remainder during later lower income years at favorable capital gain rates. Only the original livestock in the herd are subject to depreciation. The herd's progeny, whose feeding costs are deductible expenses, are not themselves subject to depreciation. Since they were born to animals the investor already owns, they cost him nothing out-of-pocket when acquired and have no basis. Thus, even though his herd increases, depreciation deductions do not keep pace after the first few years.

Accelerated depreciation may be used by the owner for animals as to which he is the first user.

Depreciation Recapture: Gain on eventual sale of a herd is subject to recapture or taxation as ordinary income to the extent of depreciation taken on the breeding cattle bought after 1969.

Business Deductions: Annual deductions that help carry the cost of holding a breeding herd include:

☐ (1) Interest on the cattle mortgage (as long as it is not prepaid more than one year in advance);
☐ (2) State and local property taxes;
☐ (3) Feed or maintenance bill;
☐ (4) Operating losses incurred during the year.

CROSS REFERENCE TABLE

The following cross reference table should be used to locate:

(1) corresponding paragraph or page references in other IBP services, and

(2) fuller and more detailed treatment of specific items in which you may be interested.

Simply locate the appropriate paragraph number in the column headed "Tax Desk Book for the Small Business" and follow this number across to the column which bears the heading of the IBP service with which you are concerned.

Tax Desk Book for the Small Business	Tax Planning	Professional Corporations	Financial Planning	Pay Planning	Real Estate Investments	Closely Held Corporations
¶	¶	¶	¶	¶	¶	Page #
101	1101.8,.9	5001			56,500	
102	1101.3,.8	5036			56,500	507
103.1	1101.4	5001.1				
103.2	1101.10					
103.3	1101.10	5031.3			56,605.7	712
103.4	1101.10	5031.4			56,605.2	706.6
103.5	1101.10	5516				909
103.6	1101.10					
104	1301	5276			56,604	
104.1	1301.2				56,605.3	
104.2	1301.1	5301				
104.3	1301.1	5301				
104.4	1301.3					
104.5	1301.5					
104.6	1301.6					
104.7	1301.7					
104.8	1301.8					
104.9	1311.2	5301.3				
105	1611.12	5306				320A
105.1	1611.12	5306.1				
106						507
201	3806	5926	1056		56,607	533

Tax Desk Book for the Small Business	Tax Planning	Professional Corporations	Financial Planning	Pay Planning	Real Estate Investments	Closely Held Corporations
¶	¶	¶	¶	¶	¶	Page #
202	3806.1	5926.1	1056		56,609	534A
203	3806.10	5926			56,611	534A
203.2	3806.5	5926.1			56,610	538
203.3	3806.8					
203.4	3806.9	5926.1				535
204	3806.11	5926	1056			533
205	3806.15	5926.14				534
205.1	3806.15	5926.14				534
205.2	3806.12	5926.7				534
205.3	3806.16	5926.14				533
206	3806.13	5926.10				533
206.1		5926.12				
206.2	3806.13	5926.11				533
206.4	3806.13	5926.13				533
206.5	3806.13	5926.14				534
207	3806.12	5926.5				534
208	3806.12	5926.5				534
208.1	3806.12	5926.8				534
209			1056.1			
210	3806.7	5926.16				
211	3806.20	5926.2				533
212	3806.23					
213	3806.25	5926.18				538
301	3811.2	5001				
302	3811.15	5001.2				
304	3811.1					
304.1	3811.1	5756				308
304.2	3811.1	5761				
305	3811.1	5766				944A
305.1		5766.2				944A
305.2		5766.3				
305.3		5766.4				944A
305.4		5766.5				
306						978A
307	3811.5	5001.2				
307.1	3811.5	5011				
307.2		5016				
401	3601.1	5066			56,530	
402	3601.2	5071				
403	3606				56,531	
403.1	3606.1					
403.2	3606.2					
403.3	3606.3				56,533	
403.4	3606.4				56,532	
403.5	3606.5					
403.6	3606.6					
403.7	3606.7					
403.8	3606.8					
403.9	3606.9					
403.10	3606.10					

Tax Desk Book for the Small Business	Tax Planning	Professional Corporations	Financial Planning	Pay Planning	Real Estate Investments	Closely Held Corporations
¶	¶	¶	¶	¶	¶	Page #
403.11	3606.11					
403.12	3606.12					
404	3611					
404.1	3611.1					
404.2	3611.2				56,537	
404.3	3611.4					
404.4	3611.4				56,546	
405	3626				56,545	
405.1	3626.1					
405.2	3626.2					
405.3	3626.3					
405.4	3626.4					
405.5	3626.5					
405.6	3626.6					
405.7	3631.2					
406	3651				56,866	
406.1	3651.1				56,560	
407	3656					
501	3461	5066.1	1046		56,560	311
502	3461		1046			
502.1	1121					
502.2	1121					
502.3	1121					
502.4	3436.5					312
503	1121					
503.1	1121					313
602.1		5211				
602.2		5000				
603			1506.1	11,201		
603.1	1619	6001				
604			3300			
605.2			1941.3			
701.1	2111.3	5031.4				
701.2	2121	5516				
701.3	1708	5506				
701.4	1731	5506.1				
702		5521				
702.1	1706	5521				
702.2	1706.3	5521.4				
702.3	1746					
703	1603					
703.1	1605	5986				
703.2	1605.1	5986				
703.3	1607	5991				
703.4	1609	5996				
704	1611					
704.1	1611.1					
704.2	1611.2	5996				
704.3	1611.3					
704.4	1611.4	5996				

Tax Desk Book for the Small Business	Tax Planning	Professional Corporations	Financial Planning	Pay Planning	Real Estate Investments	Closely Held Corporations
¶	¶	¶	¶	¶	¶	Page #
704.5	1611.5					
704.6	1611.6					
704.7	1611.7					
704.8	1611.8					
704.9	1611.9					
704.10	1611.10					
704.11	1611.11					
704.12	1611.12					
704.13	1611.13					
704.14	1611.14					
704.15	1611.15					
704.16	1611.16					
705	1105.2					
705.1	1105.3					
800	1756					
801	1756.1	5546	1596	9201		
801.1	1756.1	5546.1	1596.1	9201.1		
801.2		5546.3	1596.3	9201.3		
802		5551	1606	9207		
802.1		5556	1606	9207		
802.2	1791.4	5556.1	1606.1	9207.1		
802.3	1791.4	5556.7	1616.2	9216.2		
802.4		5556.3				
803	1756	5551.3				
804	1831		1536	8612		
804.1	1831.4		1545.1	8621.1		
804.2	1831.5					
804.3	1831.1			8621.1		
804.4				8621		
804.5	1831.7		1545.2	8621.2		
804.6	1831.8					
804.7	1841		1561	8656		
805		5761				
805.1	3491.12	5761.2	1076.12	11,414.3		
805.2	3491.12	5761.2				
805.3		5761.2				
806	3201					
806.1	3215	5756	1991	10,726		
806.2	3225		2001,2006			
901	2876				55,620	552
901.1	2876.1				55,621	
901.2	2876.2				55,622	
901.3					50,402.7	539
901.4	2876.6				55,625	553
901.5					50,402.9	548-D
902.1	1615	6001				
902.2	1617	6001.2				
903	1619	6006-6011		11,286		
903.1	1621	6007		11,286.5		964
903.2	1621.3	6007		11,286.7		

Tax Desk Book for the Small Business	Tax Planning	Professional Corporations	Financial Planning	Pay Planning	Real Estate Investments	Closely Held Corporations
¶	¶	¶	¶	¶	¶	Page #
903.3	1621.3	6007.1		11,286.8		
903.4	1621.8	6007		11,286.10		
903.5	1621.11	6007.3		11,286.12		
904	1625	6010		11,286		969
904.1	1625.1	6010.1				970
904.2	1625.2	6010.2				970
904.3	1625.3	6010.3				
905	1627	6011		11,268.1		964
905.1	1627.1	6011				
905.2	1627.1	6011.1				964
905.3	1627.2	6011.2				964
905.4	1629	6011.6				964
906	1637					556
906.1	1637.6					
907	1639					557
907.1	1639.1					
907.2	1639.3					
908	1641	6021				560
909	1643	6026				
910	1645	6031				557
911	1647					
912	1649	6011.1				
912.1	1649.2					
912.2	1649.3			11,404		
1001	1906	6312.1	2306		55,900	539
1002	1916				55,930	
1002.1	1916.1					
1002.2	1916.6				55,931	
1003	1926	6312.4			55,911	539
1003.1	1926.1				55,913	539
1003.2	1926.2				55,914	539
1003.3	1926.3				55,915	540
1003.4	1926.6					
1003.5	1926.7					
1004	1931				55,940	
1004.1	1907		2306.2			
1004.2	1931					
1004.3	1907.2					
1004.4	1907.7					
1004.5	1907.8					
1004.6	1907.9					
1004.7	1907.11					
1004.9	1907.10					
1004.10	1946					
1005	1911					541
1006	1991		2306.2		56,150	323
1006.2		6312.6			56,151	544
1101						569
1101.1	1669					570
1101.2	1669.1	5301				573

Tax Desk Book for the Small Business	Tax Planning	Professional Corporations	Financial Planning	Pay Planning	Real Estate Investments	Closely Held Corporations
¶	¶	¶	¶	¶	¶	Page #
1101.3	1669.1					
1101.4	1667.1					574
1102	1665	5946				574
1102.1	1665.1					575
1102.2	1665.1					575
1103	1663					571
1104	1681					
1105	1671					
1106	1675					
1107	1679					
1108	1673					
1201	1683.1					568
1202	1683.2					
1203	1683.4					
1204	1683.5					569
1205	1683.6					569
1206	1683.7					
1207	1683.8					
1208	1683.10					568
1209	1683.11					
1210	1683.12					
1211	1683.13					
1212	1685					
1213	3806.5	5426.14				
1300	1525					
1301	1525.1	5956			56,297	
1302	1527	5961				
1302.1	1527.1	5961.1				
1302.2	1527.2	5961.2				
1302.3	1527.3	5961.3				
1302.4	1527.4	5961.4				
1302.5	1527.5	5961.5				
1302.6	1527.6	5961.6				
1303	1529	5966				
1303.1	1529.1	5966.1				
1303.2	1529.2					
1303.3	1529.4					
1304	1529.5					
1305	1531		1276		50,301	
1305.1	1531.1					
1305.2	1531.2					
1305.3	1531.2A					
1305.4	1531.2B					
1305.5	1531.3					
1305.6	1531.7					
1305.7	1531.8					
1305.8	1531.9					
1306	1537				50,301	
1306.1	1537.1					
1306.2	1537.3					

Tax Desk Book for the Small Business	Tax Planning	Professional Corporations	Financial Planning	Pay Planning	Real Estate Investments	Closely Held Corporations
¶	¶	¶	¶	¶	¶	Page #
1306.3	1537.4					
1307	1541					
1307.1	1543					
1307.2	1545					
1308	1549	5976				
1308.1	1551	5981				
1308.2	1551.2	5981.1				
1308.3	1553					
1309.1	1547	1371				
1309.2	1557					
1401	1573					509
1401.1	1575					509
1402	1583					510
1402.1	1585					510
1402.2	1587					510
1402.3	1587.1					510
1402.4	1587.2					
1402.5	1587.3					
1403						511
1404	1591					511
1404.1	1591.1					512
1404.2	1591.2					
1404.3	1591.3					
1405	1593					512
1405.1	1593.1					
1405.2	1593.2					
1406	1571					
1407	1589					513
1408	1597.2					512
1409	1595					
1501	1976					
1501.1	1976.1					
1501.2	1976.2					
1502	1976.5					
1503	1981					
1503.1	1981.1					
1503.2	1981.2					
1503.3	1981.3					
1503.4	1981.4					
1504	1976.3					
1504.1	1976.4					
1504.2	1976.6					
1505.2	2591					
1506	2001		2361			
1506.1	2001.1		2361.1			
1506.2	2001.2		2361.3			
1506.3	2001.3					
1506.4	2001.4		2361.8			
1506.5	2001.5		2361.9			
1506.6	2001.6					

Tax Desk Book for the Small Business	Tax Planning	Professional Corporations	Financial Planning	Pay Planning	Real Estate Investments	Closely Held Corporations
¶	¶	¶	¶	¶	¶	Page #
1506.7	2001.7		2361.6			
1507.1			2361.4		55,154	
1507.2			2361.4		55,154.1	
1507.3			2361.5		55,155	
1507.4			2361.5		55,155.1	
1508					57,306.4A	
1601	2501.1		2791			347
1602	2506.1					342
1603	2506.4					344
1604	1906	6312				
1605	2506.5					344
1606						344
1606.1	2506.2					344
1607	2166	6525				750
1607.1	2166.1	6525.1				
1607.2	2171	6525.3				750
1607.3	2181	6525.1				750
1607.4	2191					751
1607.5	2186					751
1608.1	2506.6					
1608.2	2521		1286			
1608.3	2526					
1608.4	2536	6525.17				
1609	2556	6515				
1609.1	2561.1	6515.1				1721
1609.2	2561.4					
1609.3	2561.5					
1609.4	2566	6515.4				
1610	2516					
1610.1	2516.1					
1610.2	2516.3					
1610.3	2516.4					529
1610.4	2516.5					554
1610.5	2516.6					
1610.6	2516.7	6525.7				525
1701	2141	6521	1945.1			741
1701.1	2141.2	6521.2				742
1701.2	2146	6521.5				742
1701.3	2151	6523				
1701.4	2211	6527				747
1701.5	2206					
1702						743
1702.1	2156	6523.5				
1702.2	2151.5	6523.4				
1702.3	2141.1	6521.1				
1702.4	2141.6					
1703	2106	5506.1				727
1703.1	2111					
1703.2	2111.1					
1703.3	2111.3					

Tax Desk Book for the Small Business	Tax Planning	Professional Corporations	Financial Planning	Pay Planning	Real Estate Investments	Closely Held Corporations
¶	¶	¶	¶	¶	¶	Page #
1704	2116					729
1705	2121					729
1706	2126					728
1707	2131	5301				731
1707.1	2131.2	5301				731
1707.2	2131.3					737
1801						759
1801.1						760
1801.2						760A
1802	2316					
1802.1	2446					
1802.2		6517.2				
1802.3	2316.7					750
1803	2321	6525				757
1803.1	2321.1					
1804	2331					1748
1805	2341					
1805.1	2341.1					
1805.2	2341.2	6525.7				523
1805.3	2341.4					
1806	2336					
1806.1	2336.2					1316D
1806.2	2336.4					
1806.3	2336.5					
1806.4	2336.7					
1807	2381.2	6525.5				1720
1807.1	2386.1					
1807.2	2386.3					1322
1807.3	2386.4					
1807.4	2386.6	6525.5				
1807.5	2386.7	6525.5				
1807.6	2386.8	6525.5				
1807.7	2411					
1808	2356					753
1901.1	1060.11					
1901.2	1060.11					
1903	1525	5956				518
1904	1501					
1904.1	1513	5936				
1904.2	1515	5941				
1904.3	1517					517
1904.4	1519	5946				
1904.5	1521	5951				
1904.6	1523					
2001	1065.3					
2002	1065.2					
2003	1065.3					
2006.5	1065.8					
2006.6	1065.8					
2007	1065.4					

Tax Desk Book for the Small Business	Tax Planning	Professional Corporations	Financial Planning	Pay Planning	Real Estate Investments	Closely Held Corporations
¶	¶	¶	¶	¶	¶	Page #
2007.1	1065.3					
2007.4	1065.4					
2007.5	1065.5					
2101		6303	3306			335
2102		6304.3	3301			338
2103		6304.4	3311.1			338
2104.1	3086	6306	3316			335
2104.2	2801	6311	3321			318A
2104.3	2806.3	6311.4	3323			319
2104.4	2001	6313	3325			322
2104.5	4301	6314	3327			328
2104.6	4361	6315	3329			
2104.7	4201	6316	3336			
2104.8	4356	6317	3341			317

INDEX

A

B

R

S

U

V

W

Y

APPENDIX

Federal Income Tax Rates for Individuals

Single Person		Head of Household	
Taxable Income	Rate on Excess	Taxable Income	Rate on Excess
$ – $ 500	$ 14%	$ – $ 1,000	$ 14%
500 – 1,000	70 15%	1,000 – 2,000	140 16%
1,000 – 1,500	145 16%	2,000 – 4,000	300 18%
1,500 – 2,000	225 17%	4,000 – 6,000	660 19%
2,000 – 4,000	310 19%	6,000 – 8,000	1,040 22%
4,000 – 6,000	690 21%	8,000 – 10,000	1,480 23%
6,000 – 8,000	1,110 24%	10,000 – 12,000	1,940 25%
8,000 – 10,000	1,590 25%	12,000 – 14,000	2,440 27%
10,000 – 12,000	2,090 27%	14,000 – 16,000	2,980 28%
12,000 – 14,000	2,630 29%	16,000 – 18,000	3,540 31%
14,000 – 16,000	3,210 31%	18,000 – 20,000	4,160 32%
16,000 – 18,000	3,830 34%	20,000 – 22,000	4,800 35%
18,000 – 20,000	4,510 36%	22,000 – 24,000	5,500 36%
20,000 – 22,000	5,230 38%	24,000 – 26,000	6,220 38%
22,000 – 26,000	5,990 40%	26,000 – 28,000	6,980 41%
26,000 – 32,000	7,590 45%	28,000 – 32,000	7,800 42%
32,000 – 38,000	10,290 50%	32,000 – 36,000	9,480 45%
38,000 – 44,000	13,290 55%	36,000 – 38,000	11,280 48%
44,000 – 50,000	16,590 60%	38,000 – 40,000	12,240 51%
50,000 – 60,000	20,190 62%	40,000 – 44,000	13,260 52%
60,000 – 70,000	26,390 64%	44,000 – 50,000	15,340 55%
70,000 – 80,000	32,790 66%	50,000 – 52,000	18,640 56%
80,000 – 90,000	39,390 68%	52,000 – 64,000	19,760 58%
90,000 – 100,000	46,190 69%	64,000 – 70,000	26,720 59%
Over $100,000	53,090 70%	70,000 – 76,000	30,260 61%
		76,000 – 80,000	33,920 62%
		80,000 – 88,000	36,400 63%
		88,000 – 100,000	41,440 64%
		100,000 – 120,000	49,120 66%
		120,000 – 140,000	62,320 67%
		140,000 – 160,000	75,720 68%
		160,000 – 180,000	89,320 69%
		Over $180,000	103,120 70%

Federal Income Tax (continued)

Married Filing Joint Return; Surviving Spouse		Married Individuals Filing Separately and Estates and Trusts	
Taxable Income	Rate on Excess	Taxable Income	Rate on Excess
$ – $ 1,000	$ 14%	Not over – $ 500	$ 14%
1,000 – 2,000	140 15%	$ 500 – 1,000	70 15%
2,000 – 3,000	290 16%	1,000 – 1,500	145 16%
3,000 – 4,000	450 17%	1,500 – 2,000	225 17%
4,000 – 8,000	620 19%	2,000 – 4,000	310 19%
8,000 – 12,000	1,380 22%	4,000 – 6,000	690 22%
12,000 – 16,000	2,260 25%	6,000 – 8,000	1,130 25%
16,000 – 20,000	3,260 28%	8,000 – 10,000	1,630 28%
20,000 – 24,000	4,380 32%	10,000 – 12,000	2,190 32%
24,000 – 28,000	5,660 36%	12,000 – 14,000	2,830 36%
28,000 – 32,000	7,100 39%	14,000 – 16,000	3,550 39%
32,000 – 36,000	8,660 42%	16,000 – 18,000	4,330 42%
36,000 – 40,000	10,340 45%	18,000 – 20,000	5,170 45%
40,000 – 44,000	12,140 48%	20,000 – 22,000	6,070 48%
44,000 – 52,000	14,060 50%	22,000 – 26,000	7,030 50%
52,000 – 64,000	18,060 53%	26,000 – 32,000	9,030 53%
64,000 – 76,000	24,420 55%	32,000 – 38,000	12,210 55%
76,000 – 88,000	31,020 58%	38,000 – 44,000	15,510 58%
88,000 – 100,000	37,980 60%	44,000 – 50,000	18,990 60%
100,000 – 120,000	45,180 62%	50,000 – 60,000	22,590 62%
120,000 – 140,000	57,580 64%	60,000 – 70,000	28,970 64%
140,000 – 160,000	70,380 66%	70,000 – 80,000	35,190 66%
160,000 – 180,000	83,580 68%	80,000 – 90,000	41,790 68%
180,000 – 200,000	97,180 69%	90,000 – 100,000	48,590 69%
Over $200,000	110,980 70%	Over $100,000	55,490 70%

Federal Income Tax Rates for Corporations

The tax rate for corporations is computed as indicated by the table below. However, for 1975 only, the first $25,000 is taxed at the rate of 20%, the next $25,000 at 22%, and the remainder at 48%.

Taxable Income	*Tax Rate*
$0 – $25,000	22%
Over $25,000	48%

Estimated Tax Payments for Corporations

Every corporation whose estimated tax liability is expected to be $40 or more is required to make estimated tax payments (Code §6154(a)). The estimated tax is the corporate income tax liability less either 40% of such liability or $2,200, whichever is less. So, any corporation whose expected tax liability is greater than $66.67 in any year will be required to make these payments, which can be deposited in any authorized bank if accompanied by a properly filled-out Form 503.

Payments of estimated tax must be made in accordance with the following schedule:

		The following percentages of the estimated tax shall be deposited on or before the 15th day of the—			
If the $40 requirement is first met—	*The number of installments to be deposited is—*	*4th month*	*6th month*	*9th month*	*12th month*
Before the 1st day of the 4th month of the taxable year	4	25	25	25	25
After the last day of the 3d month and before the 1st day of the 6th month of the taxable year . . .	3	. . . .	33⅓	33⅓	33⅓
After the last day of the 5th month and before the 1st day of the 9th month of the taxable year . . .	2	. . . .	. . . .	50	50
After the last day of the 8th month and before the 1st day of the 12th month of the taxable year . .	1	. . . .	. . . .	. . . .	100

Income Averaging

Income averaging is an elective method of computing income tax for individuals who have unusually large amounts of taxable income in any given year. Income averaging will provide tax benefit whenever current taxable income is at least $3,000 more than 120% of the average taxable income in the last four years. The amount by which current taxable income exceeds 120% of the average taxable income for the last four years is the "averageable income." The tax on this "averageable income" is determined by dividing it by five and adding the amount you get to 120% of the average taxable income for the last four years. Then, you figure the tax on this additional amount, and multiply it by five, as in the example below:

Example: Jones, a single taxpayer, has a 1975 taxable income of $50,000. His taxable income was $12,000 in 1971, $13,000 in 1972, $19,000 in 1973, and $17,000 in 1974. So, his average base period income was $15,250 ($12,000 + $13,000 + $19,000 + $17,000 = $61,000 ÷ 4 = $15,250) and 120% of this amount is $18,300. Since his 1975 taxable income is $50,000, which is more than 120% of his average base period income plus $3,000, he will benefit from income averaging. He computes his tax, using income averaging, as follows:

(1) 120% of average base period income	$18,300
(2) 1/5 of averageable income ($50,000 − 18,300 = $31,700 ÷ 5 = $6,340)	6,340
(3) Sum of (1) and (2)	24,640
(4) Tax on (3)	7,046
(5) Tax on (1)	4,618
(6) (4) − (3)	2,428
(7) (6) × 4	9,712
(8) Tax for 1975 ((4) + (7))	$16,758

If Jones had *not* used income averaging, his 1975 tax would have been $20,190, so he saves $3,432.

(Note that the above example is computed without reference to any changes made by the Tax Reduction Bill of 1975.)

Before you decide to elect income averaging, remember that there are two basic limitations:

(1) You can't use the alternative capital gains tax, and

(2) You can't use the maximum tax on earned income.

You should also note that there are special rules for computing taxable income in base period years for married taxpayers who have not been married to the same spouse or who have not filed jointly with the same spouse for any base period year, or for single taxpayers who have been married in any base period year. In any of these cases, you should consult the regulations.

Maximum Tax on Earned Income

The Code provides for a 50% ceiling on the tax on earned income. Earned income generally includes wages, salaries, professional fees or compensation for personal services, and, in the case of a taxpayer engaged in a trade or business where both personal services and capital are a material income-producing factor, a reasonable amount but not more than 30% of his share of the net profits of the business.

The 50% limit is applicable to earned income reduced by tax preferences in excess of $30,000 in the current year or the average tax preferences in excess of $30,000 for the current year and the prior four years, whichever is greater. Tax preferences for this purpose are the same as those applicable to individuals under the minimum tax.

Earned taxable income is defined as that proportion of total taxable income which is in the same ratio (but not in excess of 100%) as the ratio of earned income to adjusted gross income. Thus, if 40% of an individual's adjusted gross income is earned income, then 40% of this taxable income is considered earned taxable income.

If, during a taxable year, a taxpayer has earned taxable income which exceeds the 50% tax bracket, he figures his tax as follows:

(1) Takes the lowest amount of taxable income that is taxed over 50%. Computes the tax on this amount.

(2) Takes 50% of the amount by which earned taxable income (as defined above) exceeds the taxable income used in step (1).

(3) Computes the regular tax on the entire taxable income and deducts the tax computed on only the earned taxable income.

(4) Adds the amounts under steps (1), (2), and (3).

How the Tax Is Computed—The following example shows how the tax on earned income is calculated.

In 1972, Jones, married and filing a joint return, has $90,000 salary and bonus, $10,000 dividends on stock, $5,000 unreimbursed travel expenses, and $10,000 itemized deductions and personal exemptions. He has no capital gains, lump-sum pension distribution, or tax-preferred income. His tax is calculated as follows:

Salary and bonus	$ 90,000
Dividends	10,000
Gross income	$100,000
Unreimbursed travel and entertainment expenses	5,000
Adjusted gross income	$ 95,000
Itemized deductions and personal exemptions	10,000
Taxable income	$ 85,000

The computation is:

(1) Tax on $52,000 (the highest amount on which the tax rate is 50%) $18,060

(2) Earned taxable income.

$$\frac{\$90{,}000 \text{ (salary)}}{\$95{,}000 \text{ (adjusted gross income)}} \times \$85{,}000 \text{ (taxable income)} = \$80{,}530$$

Minus income taxed in step (1)	52,000
Balance	$28,530

50% of balance = ... $14,265

(3) Tax on $85,000 of total taxable income	$36,547	
Tax on $80,530 of earned taxable income ..	33,647	
Balance		2,850
(4) Total tax (sum of (1), (2), and (3))		$35,177

The total tax without the special earned-income tax limit would be $36,547. Thus, there is a $1,370 saving by using the special limit.

Minimum Tax on Tax-Preference Income

The Code imposes a minimum tax, in addition to any regular tax, on income defined as "tax-preference income." This income includes:

(1) The excess of investment interests over net investment income. This applies to individuals, Subchapter S corporations, and personal holding companies. It does not apply to regular business corporations because its interest is business rather than investment interest. Beginning in 1972, excess investment interest is not treated as tax-preference income. Instead, the deduction of such interest is limited to 50%.

(2) Accelerated depreciation on real estate.

(3) Accelerated depreciation on personal property subject to a net lease.

(4) Excess depreciation over straight-line for housing rehabilitation expenditures.

(5) Amortization over accelerated depreciation on pollution control equipment.

(6) Amortization over accelerated depreciation on railroad rolling stock.

(7) For executives, the amount by which the fair market value exceeds the option price on the exercise of a qualified stock option.

(8) Bad debt deductions of financial institutions.

(9) The excess of percentage over cost depletion.

(10) Corporate capital gains, but only to the extent of the ratio of the regular corporate tax rate minus the special capital gains rate to the regular corporate rate. In other words, assuming the corporation pays the maximum capital gains rate of 30% (effective beginning in 1972), it would include three-eighths of its long-term capital gains (in excess of net short-term capital losses) as tax-preference income; that is, 48% minus 30% divided by 48%. In the case of individuals, one-half of net long-term capital gain in excess of net short-term capital losses is included as tax-preference income.

The tax is imposed at a rate of 10% on all tax-preference income which exceeds $30,000 plus the amount of regular taxes paid. For example, suppose a corporation has $200,000 of tax-preference income and has a regular tax bill of $50,000. To determine the amount of tax on the tax-preference income, you would subtract the $30,000 exemption plus the $50,000 regular tax. This would leave a balance of $120,000. Applying the 10% rate, the tax on preference income would be $12,000, and the total tax bill would come to $62,000 instead of $50,000.

Agreement to Repay Excess Compensation—"Oswald" Bylaw

In compensating an employee, the corporation is entitled to take a tax deduction for the amount of his compensation, provided that it is not ruled unreasonable by IRS. If part of the compensation is ruled by IRS to be unreasonable and excessive, it can result in a double tax—the corporation doesn't get its deduction, yet it remains as taxable income to the employee. However, if the parties have agreed that the employee will reimburse the corporation for any part of the compensation that is disallowed as a deduction to the corporation, the tax on the employee level can be eliminated.

If the employee's employment is subject to his acceptance of an agreement to repay that part of his salary deemed excessive and unreasonable by the IRS, the repayment will be deemed ordinary and necessary and an allowable deductible expense incurred in connection with his business of being a corporate officer.

Repayment of such amounts by the executive-officer in compliance with the requirement is deductible in the year of repayment.

The agreement must be a legally enforceable commitment entered into by the corporation with the employee requiring him to reimburse the company for any part of the salary paid to the employee which IRS disallows as excessive and unreasonable.

The following provisions have been passed on by the Tax Court and agreed to by IRS. They establish the necessary obligation upon the executive-officer to repay amounts of salary deemed excessive.

At (1), below, a proviso is set forth that can be used in the compensation clause of an employment contract. At (2), below, a bylaw mandating repayment is set forth. A corporate resolution directing such repayment follows at (3), below.

(1) *Agreement to Repay Excessive Compensation*

PROVIDED, HOWEVER, in the event that the deduction for federal income tax purposes of any part of the aforesaid compensation shall be disallowed and the Company shall be required to pay a deficiency on account of such disallowance, employee shall pay to the Company an amount equal to the amount of the said deficiency, such payment to be made by certified check at the principal office of the Company within one year from the day on which the Company paid the deficiency with respect to such compensation.

(2) *Bylaw Providing for Repayment by Corporate Officer of Excess Compensation Disallowed by IRS* (This bylaw is taken from a case in which the Tax Court approved a deduction in year of repayment by the executive (*Oswald,* 49 TC 645 1968; *Rev. Rul. 69-115*).)

Any payments made to an officer of the Corporation such as a salary, commission, bonus, interest, or rent or entertainment expense incurred by him, which shall be disallowed in whole or in part as a deductible expense by the Internal Revenue Service, shall be reimbursable by such officer to the Corporation to the full extent of such disallowance. It shall be the duty of the Directors, as a Board, to enforce payment of each such amount disallowed. In lieu of payment by the officer, subject to the determination of the Directors, proportionate amounts may be withheld from his future compensation payments until the amount owed to the Corporation has been recovered.

(3) *Resolution Mandating Repayment of Excessive Compensation*

Salary payments made to an officer of the Corporation that shall be disallowed in whole or in part as a deductible expense for federal income tax purposes shall be reimbursed by such officer to the corporation to the full extent of the disallowance. It shall be the duty of the Board of Directors to enforce payment of such amount disallowed.

Table of ADR Classes

(Rev. Proc. 72-10 as amended and supplemented)

Asset guide-line class	Description of assets included	Asset depreciation range (in years) Lower limit	Asset guide-line period	Upper limit	Annual asset guide-line repair allow-ance percent-age
00.0	DEPRECIABLE ASSETS USED IN ALL BUSINESS ACTIVITIES, EXCEPT AS NOTED:				
00.2	Transportation Equipment:				
00.21	Aircraft (airframes and engines) except aircraft of air transportation companies	5	6	7	14.0
00.22	Automobiles, taxis	2.5	3	3.5	16.5
00.23	Buses	7	9	11.0	11.5
00.24	General purpose trucks, including concrete ready-mix trucks and ore trucks for use over-the-road:				
00.241	Light (actual unloaded weight less than 13,000 pounds)	3	4	5	16.5
00.242	Heavy (actual unloaded weight 13,000 pounds or more)	5	6	7	10.0
00.25	Railroad cars and locomotives, except those owned by railroad transportation companies	12	15	18	8.0
00.26	Tractor units used over-the-road	3	4	5	16.5
00.27	Trailers and trailer-mounted containers	5	6	7	10.0
00.28	Vessels, barges, tugs and similar water transportation equipment, except those used in marine contract construction	14.5	18	21.5	6.0
00.3	Land Improvements:[1]				
	Improvements directly to or added to land that are more often than not directly related to one or another of the specific classes of economic activity specified below. Includes only those depreciable land improvements which have a limited period of use in the trade or business, the length of which can be reasonably estimated for the particular improvement. That is, general grading of land such as in the case of cemeteries, golf courses and general site grading and leveling costs not directly related to buildings or other structural improvements to be added, are not depreciable or included in this class but such costs are added to the cost basis of the land.				
	Includes paved surfaces such as sidewalks and roads, canals, waterways, drainage and sewers; wharves and docks; bridges; all fences except those included in specific classes described below (i.e., farm and railroad fences); landscaping, shrubbery and similar improve-				

Asset guide-line class	Description of assets included	Asset depreciation range (in years) Lower limit	Asset guide-line period	Upper limit	Annual asset guide-line repair allow-ance percent-age
	ments; radio and television transmitting towers, and other inherently permanent physical structures added to land except buildings and their structural components. Excludes land improvements of electric, gas, steam and water utilities; telephone and telegraph companies; and pipeline, water and rail carriers which are assets covered by asset guideline classes specific to their respective classes of economic activity		20		
01.0	Agriculture: Includes only such assets as are identified below and that are used in the production of crops or plants, vines and trees (including forestry); the keeping, grazing, or feeding of livestock for animal products (including serums), for animals increase, or value increase; the operation of dry lot or farm dairies, nurseries, greenhouses, sod farms, mushroom cellars, cranberry bogs, apiaries, and fur farms; the production of bulb, flower, and vegetable seed crops; and the performance of agricultural, animal husbandry and horticultural services.				
01.1	Machinery and equipment, including grain bins and fences but no other land improvements	8	10	12	11.0
01.2	Animals:				
01.21	Cattle, breeding or dairy	5.5	7	8.5	
01.22	Horses, breeding or work	8	10	12	
01.23	Hogs, breeding	2.5	3	3.5	
01.24	Sheep and goats, breeding	4	5	6	
01.3	Farm buildings	20	25	30.0	5.0
10.0	Mining: Includes assets used in the mining and quarrying of metallic and non-metallic minerals (including sand, gravel, stone, and clay) and the milling beneficiation and other primary preparation of such materials	8	10	12	6.5
13.0	Petroleum and natural gas production and related activities:				
13.1	Drilling of oil and gas wells: Includes assets used in the drilling of onshore oil and gas wells on a contract, fee or other basis and the provision of geophysical and other exploration services; and the provision of such oil and gas field services as chemical treatment, plugging and abandoning of wells and cementing or perforating well casings; but not including assets used in the performance of any of these activities and services by integrated				

Asset guide-line class	Description of assets included	Asset depreciation range (in years)			Annual asset guide-line repair allow-ance percent-age
		Lower limit	Asset guide-line period	Upper limit	
	petroleum and natural gas producers for their own account	5	6	7	10.0
13.2	Exploration for petroleum and natural gas deposits: Includes assets used for drilling of wells and production of petroleum and natural gas, including gathering pipelines and related storage facilities, when these are related activities undertaken by petroleum and natural gas producers	11	14	17	4.5
13.3	Petroleum refining: Includes assets used for the distillation, fractionation, and catalytic cracking of crude petroleum into gasoline and its other components	13	16	19	7.0
13.4	Marketing of petroleum and petroleum products: Includes assets used in marketing, such as related storage facilities and complete service stations, but not including any of these facilities related to petroleum and natural gas trunk pipelines	13	16	19	4.0
15.0	Contract construction: Includes such assets used by general building, special trade, heavy construction and marine contractors; does not include assets used by companies in performing construction services on their own account.				
15.1	Contract construction other than marine	4	5	6	12.5
15.2	Marine contract construction . . . . Includes floating, self-propelled and other drilling platforms used in offshore drilling for oil and gas.	9.5	12	14.5	5.0
20.0	Manufacture of foods and beverages for human consumption, and certain related products, such as manufactured ice, chewing gum, vegetable and animal fats and oils, and prepared feeds for animals and fowls:				
20.1	Grain and grain mill products: Includes assets used in the production of flours, cereals, livestock feeds, and other grain and grain mill products	13.5	17	20.5	6.0
20.2	Sugar and sugar products: Includes assets used in the production of raw sugar, syrup or finished sugar from sugar cane or sugar beets	14.5	18	21.5	4.5
20.3	Vegetable oils and vegetable oil products: Includes assets used in the production of oil from vegetable materials and the manufacture of related vegetable oil products	14.5	18	21.5	3.5

Asset guide-line class	Description of assets included	Asset depreciation range (in years)			Annual asset guide-line repair allow-ance percent-age
		Lower limit	Asset guide-line period	Upper limit	
20.4	All other food and kindred products: Includes assets used in the production of foods, beverages and related production not included in classes 20.1, 20.2 and 20.3	9.5	12	14.5	5.5
20.5	Manufacture of food and beverages—special handling devices:[5] Includes assets defined as specialized materials handling devices such as returnable pellets, pelletized containers, and fish processing equipment including boxes, baskets, carts, and flaking trays used in activities as defined in classes 20.1, 20.2, 20.3, 20.4. Special handling devices are specifically designed for the handling of particular products and have no significant utilitarian value and cannot be adapted to further or different use after changes or improvements are made in the design of the particular product handled by the special devices. Does not include general purpose small tools such as wrenches and drills, both hand and power-driven, and other general purpose equipment such as conveyors, transfer equipment, and materials handling devices	3	4	5	20.0
21.0	Manufacture of tobacco and tobacco products: Includes assets used in the production of cigarettes, cigars, smoking and chewing tobacco, snuff and other tobacco products	12	15	18	5.0
22.0	Manufacture of textile mill products:				
22.1	Knitwear and knit products: Includes assets used in the production of knit fabrics, knit apparel, and yarns processed for knitting, such as boarding machines, dryers, knitting machines, loopers, warpers, winders, seaming machines, twisting machines, twist setting machines, texturizing machines, and collection system equipment	7	9	11	7.0
22.2	Textile mill products, except knitwear: Includes assets used in the production of spun yarn and woven or non-woven fabrics, mattresses, carpets, rugs, pads, sheets, and of other products of natural or synthetic fibers, such as preparatory equipment for fibers, and machinery for carding, combing, drawing, roving, spinning, twisting, warping, winding, slashing, and weaving	11	14	17	4.5

Asset guide-line class	Description of assets included	Asset depreciation range (in years) Lower limit	Asset guide-line period	Upper limit	Annual asset guide-line repair allow-ance percent-age
22.3	Finishing and dyeing: Includes assets used in the finishing and dyeing of natural and synthetic fibers, yarns, fabrics including knit materials, and knit apparel, such as assets used for washing, bleaching, finishing, printing and dyeing, and drying	9.5	12	14.5	5.5
23.0	Manufacture of apparel and other finished products: Includes assets used in the production of clothing and fabricated textile products by the cutting and sewing of woven fabrics, other textile products and furs; but does not include assets used in the manufacture of apparel from rubber and leather..................	7	9	11	7.0
24.0	Manufacture of lumber and wood products:				
24.1	Cutting of Timber: Includes logging machinery and equipment and road building equipment used by logging and sawmill operators and pulp manufacturers on their own account	5	6	7	10.0
24.2	Sawing of dimensional stock from logs: Includes machinery and equipment installed in permanent or well-established sawmills	8	10	12	6.5
24.3	Sawing of dimensional stock from logs: Includes machinery and equipment installed in sawmills characterized by temporary foundations and a lack, or minimum amount, of lumber-handling, drying, and residue disposal equipment and facilities	5	6	7	10.0
24.4	Manufacture of lumber, wood products, and furniture: Includes assets used in the production of plywood, hardboard, flooring, veneers, furniture and other wood products, including the treatment of poles and timber	8	10	12	6.5
26.0	Manufacture of paper and allied products:				
26.1	Manufacture of pulps from wood and other cellulose fibers and rags: Includes assets used in the manufacture of paper and paperboard, but does not include the assets used in pulpwood logging nor the manufacture of hardboard	13	16	19	4.5
26.2	Manufacture of paper and paperboard: Includes assets used in the production of converted products such as paper coated off the paper machines, paper bags, paper boxes, and envelopes	9.5	12	14.5	5.5

Asset guide-line class	Description of assets included	Asset depreciation range (in years) Lower limit	Asset guide-line period	Upper limit	Annual asset guide-line repair allow-ance percent-age
27.0	Printing, publishing and allied industries:				
	Includes assets used in printing by one or more of the common processes, such as letterpress, lithography, gravure, or screen; the performance of services for the printing trade, such as bookbinding, typesetting, engraving, photoengraving, and electrotyping; and the publication of newspapers, books, and periodicals, whether or not carried out in conjunction with printing	9	11	13	5.5
28.0	Manufacture of chemicals and allied products:				
	Includes assets used in the manufacture of basis chemicals such as acids, alkalies, salts, and organic and inorganic chemicals; chemical products to be used in further manufacture, such as synthetic fibers and plastics materials, including petro-chemical processing beyond that which is ordinarily a part of petroleum refining; and finished chemical products, such as pharmaceuticals, cosmetics, soaps, fertilizers, paints and varnishes, explosives, and compressed and liquefied gases. Does not include assets used in the manufacture of finished rubber and plastic products or in the production of natural gas products, butane, propane, and byproducts of natural gas production plants	9	11	13	5.5
30.0	Manufacture of rubber and plastics products:				
30.1	Manufacture of rubber products:				
	Includes assets used for the production of products from natural, synthetic, or reclaimed rubber, gutta percha, balata, or gutta siak, such as tires, tubes, rubber footwear, mechanical rubber goods, heels and soles, flooring, and rubber sundries; and in the recapping, retreading, and rebuilding of tires	11	14	17	5.0
30.11	Manufacture of rubber products—special tools and devices:[5]				
	Includes assets defined as special tools, such as jigs, dies, mandrels, molds, lasts, patterns, specialty containers, pallets, shells and tire molds and accessory parts such as rings and insert plates used in activities as defined in Class 30.1.				
	Does not include tire building drums and accessory parts and general purpose small tools such as wrenches and drills, both power and hand-driven, and other general purpose equipment such as conveyors and transfer equipment	3	4	5	—

Asset guide-line class	Description of assets included	Asset depreciation range (in years) Lower limit	Asset guide-line period	Upper limit	Annual asset guide-line repair allow-ance percent-age
30.2	Manufacture of miscellaneous finished plastics products: Includes assets used in the manufacture of plastics products and the molding of primary plastics for the trade. Does not include assets used in the manufacture of basic plastics materials nor the manufacture of phonograph records	9	11	13	5.5
30.21	Manufacture of miscellaneous finished plastic products—special tools:[5] Includes assets defined as special tools such as jigs, dies, fixtures, molds, patterns, gauges, and specialty transfer and shipping devices, used in activities as defined in Class 30.2. Special tools are specifically designed for the production or processing of particular parts and have no significant utilitarian value and cannot be adapted to further or different use after changes or improvements are made in the model design of the particular part produced by the special tools. Does not include general purpose small tools, such as wrenches and drills, both hand and power-driven, and other general purpose equipment such as conveyors, transfer equipment, and materials handling devices	3	3.5	4	5.5
31.0	Manufacture of leather: Includes assets used in the tanning, currying, and finishing of hides and skins; the processing of fur pelts; and the manufacture of finished leather products, such as footwear, belting, apparel, luggage and similar leather goods	9	11	13	5.5
32.0	Manufacture of stone, clay, glass, and concrete products:				
32.1	Manufacture of glass products: Includes assets used in the production of flat, blown, or pressed products of glass, such as float and window and window glass, glass containers, glassware, and fiberglass. Does not include assets used in the manufacture of lenses	11	14	17	12.0[6]
32.11	Manufacture of glass products—special tools:[5] Includes assets defined as special tools such as molds, patterns, pallets, and specialty transfer and shipping devices such as steel racks to transport automotive glass, used in activities as defined in Class 32.1. Special tools are specifically designed for the production or process-				

Asset guide-line class	Description of assets included	Asset depreciation range (in years)			Annual asset guide-line repair allow-ance percent-age
		Lower limit	Asset guide-line period	Upper limit	
	ing of particular parts and have no significant utilitarian value and cannot be adapted to further or different use after changes or improvements are made in the model design of the particular part produced by the special tools. Does not include general purpose small tools such as wrenches and drills, both hand and power-driven, and other general purpose equipment such as conveyors, transfer equipment, and materials handling devices	2	2.5	3	10.0
32.2	Manufacture of cement: Includes assets used in the production of cement, but does not include any assets used in the manufacture of concrete and concrete products nor in any mining or extraction process	16	20	24	3.0
32.3	Manufacture of other stone and clay products: Includes assets used in the manufacture of products from materials in the form of clay and stone, such as brick, tile and pipe; pottery and related products, such as vitreous-china, plumbing fixtures, earthenware and ceramic insulating materials; and also includes assets used in manufacture of concrete and concrete products. Does not include assets used in any mining or extraction processes	12	15	18	4.5
33.0	Manufacture of primary metals: Includes assets used in the smelting and refining of ferrous and nonferrous metals from ore, pig, or scrap, the rolling, drawing, and alloying of ferrous and nonferrous metals; the manufacture of castings, forgings, and other basic products of ferrous and nonferrous metals; and the manufacture of nails, spikes, structural shapes, tubing, and wire and cable:				
33.1	Ferrous metals	14.5	18	21.5	8.0
33.11	Ferrous metals—special tools:[5] Includes assets defined as special tools such as dies, jigs, molds, patterns, fixtures, gauges, and drawings concerning such special tools used in the activities as defined in Class 33.1, Ferrous metals. Special tools are specifically designed for the production or processing of particular products or parts and have no significant utilitarian value and cannot be adapted to further or different use				

Asset guide-line class	Description of assets included	Asset depreciation range (in years) Lower limit	Asset guide-line period	Upper limit	Annual asset guide-line repair allow-ance percent-age
	after changes or improvements are made in the model design of the particular part produced by the special tools. Does not include general purpose small tools, such as wrenches and drills, both hand and power-driven, and other general purpose equipment such as conveyors, transfer equipment, and materials handling devices.				
	Rolls, mandrels and refractories are not included in Class 33.11 but are included in Class 33.1 . .	5	6.5	8	4.0
33.2	Nonferrous metals	11	14	17	4.5
33.21	Nonferrous metals—special tools:[5]				
	Includes assets defined as special tools such as dies, jigs, molds, patterns, fixtures, gauges, and drawings concerning such special tools used in the activities as defined in Class 33.2, Nonferrous Metals. Special tools are specifically designed for the production or processing of particular products or parts and have no significant utilitarian value and cannot be adapted to further or different use after changes or improvements are made in the model design of the particular part produced by the special tools. Does not include general purpose small tools such as wrenches and drills, both hand and power-driven, and other general purpose equipment such as conveyors, transfer equipment, and materials handling devices.				
	Rolls, mandrels and refractories are not included in Class 33.21 but are included in Class 33.2	5	6.5	8	4
34.0	Manufacture of fabricated metal products:				
	Includes assets used in the production of metal cans, tinware, nonelectric heating apparatus, fabricated structural metal products, metal stampings and other ferrous and nonferrous metal and wire products not elsewhere classified	9.5	12	14.5	6.0
34.01	Manufacture of fabricated metal products—special tools:[5]				
	Includes assets defined as special tools such as dies, jigs, molds, patterns, fixtures, gauges, and returnable containers and drawings concerning such special tools used in the activities as defined in Class 34.0. Special tools are specifically designed for the production or processing of particular machine com-				

Asset guide-line class	Description of assets included	Asset depreciation range (in years)			Annual asset guide-line repair allow-ance percent-age
		Lower limit	Asset guide-line period	Upper limit	
	ponents, products or parts, and have no significant utilitarian value and cannot be adapted to further or different use after changes or improvements are made in the model design of the particular part produced by the special tools. Does not include general purpose small tools such as wrenches and drills, both hand and power-driven, and other general purpose equipment such as conveyors, transfer equipment, and materials handling devices	2.5	3.0	3.5	3.5
35.0	Manufacture of machinery, except electrical and transportation equipment:				
35.1	Manufacture of metalworking machinery: Includes assets used in the production of metal cutting and forming machines, special dies, tools, jigs, and fixtures, and machine tool accessories	9.5	12	14.5	5.5
35.11	Manufacture of metalworking machinery—special tools:[5] Includes assets defined as special tools, such as jigs, dies, fixtures, molds, patterns, gauges, and specialty transfer and shipping devices, used in activities as defined in Class 35.1. Special tools are specifically designed for the production or processing of particular machine components and have no significant utilitarian value and cannot be adapted to further or different use after changes or improvements are made in the model design of the particular part produced by the special tools. Does not include general purpose small tools such as wrenches and drills, both hand and power-driven, and other general purpose equipment such as conveyors, transfer equipment, and materials handling devices	5	6	7	12.5
35.2	Manufacture of other machines: Includes assets used in the production of such machinery as engines and turbines; farm machinery, construction, and mining machinery; general and special industrial machines including office machines and non-electronic computing equipment; miscellaneous machines except electrical equipment and transportation equipment	9.5	12	14.5	5.5

Asset guideline class	Description of assets included	Asset depreciation range (in years): Lower limit	Asset depreciation range (in years): Asset guideline period	Asset depreciation range (in years): Upper limit	Annual asset guideline repair allowance percentage
35.21	Manufacture of other machines—special tools:[5] Includes assets defined as special tools, such as jigs, dies, fixtures, molds, patterns, gauges, and specialty transfer and shipping devices, used in activities as defined in Class 35.2. Special tools are specifically designed for the production or processing of particular machine components and have no significant utilitarian value and cannot be adapted to further or different use after changes or improvements are made in the model design or the particular part produced by the special tools. Does not include general purpose small tools such as wrenches and drills, both hand and power-driven, and other general purpose equipment such as conveyors, transfer equipment, and materials handling devices	5	6.5	8	12.5
36.0	Manufacture of electrical machinery, equipment, and supplies: Includes assets used in the production of machinery, apparatus, and supplies for the generation, storage, transmission, transformation, and utilization of electrical energy.				
36.1	Manufacture of electrical equipment: Includes assets used in the production of such machinery as electric test and distributing equipment, electrical industrial apparatus, household appliances, electric lighting and wiring equipment; electronic components and accessories, phonograph records, storage batteries and ignition systems	9.5	12	14.5	5.5
36.11	Manufacture of electrical equipment—special tools:[5] Includes assets defined as special tools such as jigs, dies, molds, patterns, fixtures, gauges, returnable containers, and specialty transfer devices used in activities as defined in Class 36.1. Special tools are specifically designed for the production or processing of particular machine components, products or parts, and have no significant utilitarian value and cannot be adapted to further or different use after changes or improvements are made in the model design of the particular part produced by the special				

Asset guide-line class	Description of assets included	Asset depreciation range (in years): Lower limit	Asset depreciation range (in years): Asset guide-line period	Asset depreciation range (in years): Upper limit	Annual asset guide-line repair allow-ance percent-age
	tools. Does not include general purpose small tools such as wrenches and drills, both hand and power-driven and other general purpose equipment such as conveyors, transfer equipment, and materials handling devices	4	5	6	—
36.2	Manufacture of electronic products: Includes assets used in the production of electronic detection, guidance, control, radiation, computation, test and navigation equipment and the components thereof. Does not include the assets of manufacturers engaged only in the purchase and assembly of components	6.5	8	9.5	7.5
37.0	Manufacture of transportation equipment: Includes assets used in the production of such machinery as vehicles and equipment for the transportation of passengers and cargo.				
37.1	Manufacture of Motor Vehicles:				
37.11	Motor vehicle manufacturing assets: Includes assets used in the manufacture and assembly of finished automobiles, trucks, trailers, motor homes, and buses. Does not include assets used in mining, printing and publishing, production of primary metals, electricity, or steam, or the manufacture of glass, industrial chemicals, batteries, or rubber products, which are classified elsewhere. Includes assets used in manufacturing activities elsewhere classified other than those excluded above,[4] where such activities are incidental to and an integral part of the manufacture and assembly of finished motor vehicles such as the manufacture of parts and subassemblies of fabricated metal products, electrical equipment, textiles, plastics, leather, and foundry and forging operations	9.5	12	14.5	9.5
	Activities will be considered incidental to the manufacture and assembly of finished motor vehicles only if 75 percent or more of the value of the products produced under one roof are used for the manufacture and assembly of finished motor vehicles. Parts which are produced as a normal replacement stock complement in connection with				

Asset guide-line class	Description of assets included	Asset depreciation range (in years)			Annual asset guide-line repair allow-ance percent-age
		Lower limit	Asset guide-line period	Upper limit	
	the manufacture and assembly of finished motor vehicles are considered used for the manufacture and assembly of finished motor vehicles. Does not include assets used in the manufacture of component parts if these assets are used by taxpayers not engaged in the assembly of finished motor vehicles.				
37.12	Motor vehicle manufacturing subsidiary assets:[5] Includes assets defined as special tools, such as jigs, dies, fixtures, molds, patterns, gauges, and specialty transfer and shipping devices, owned by manufacturers of finished motor vehicles and used in qualified activities as defined in Class 37.11. Special tools are specifically designed for the production or processing of particular motor vehicle components and have no significant utilitarian value and cannot be adapted to further or different use after changes or improvements are made in the model design of the particular part produced by the special tools. Does not include general purpose small tools such as wrenches and drills, both hand and power-driven, and other general purpose equipment such as conveyors, transfer equipment, and materials handling devices	2.5	3	3.5	12.5
37.2	Manufacture of aerospace products: Includes assets used in the manufacture and repair spacecraft, rockets, missiles and their component parts	6.5	8	9.5	7.5
37.3	Ship and boat building:				
37.31	Ship and boat building machinery and equipment: Includes assets used in the manufacture and repair of ships, boats, caissons, drilling rigs and special fabrications not included in asset guideline class 37.32. Specifically includes all manufacturing and repairing machinery and equipment, including machinery and equipment used in the operation of assets included in asset guideline 37.32. Excludes buildings and their structural components	9.5	12	14.5	8.5
37.32	Ship and boat building dry docks and land improvements: Includes assets used in the manufacture and repair of ships, boats, caissons, drilling rigs and special fabrications not included in asset guideline class 37.31. Specifically includes floating and fixed dry docks, ship basins, graving docks, shipways, piers and all other land improvements such as water,				

Asset guide-line class	Description of assets included	Asset depreciation range (in years) Lower limit	Asset guide-line period	Upper limit	Annual asset guide-line repair allow-ance percent-age
	sewer, and electric systems. Excludes buildings and their structural components	13	16	19	2.5
37.33	Ships and boat building—special tools:[5] Includes assets defined as special tools such as dies, jigs, molds, patterns, fixtures, gauges, and drawings concerning such special tools used in the activities as defined in Classes 37.31 and 37.32. Special tools are specifically designed for the production or processing of particular machine components, products or parts, and have no significant utilitarian value and cannot be adopted to further or different use after changes or improvements are made in the model design of the particular part produced by the special tools. Does not include general purpose small tools such as wrenches and drills, both hand and power-driven, and other general purpose equipment such as conveyors, transfer equipment, and materials handling devices	5	6.5	8	0.5
37.4	Manufacture of railroad transportation equipment:				
37.41	Manufacture of locomotives: Includes assets used in building or rebuilding railroad locomotives (including mining and industrial locomotives). Does not include assets of railroad transportation companies or assets of companies which manufacture components of locomotives but do not manufacture finished locomotives	9	11.5	14	7.5
37.42	Manufacture of railroad cars: Includes assets used in building or rebuilding railroad freight or passengers cars (including rail transit cars). Does not include assets of railroad transportation companies or assets of companies which manufacture components of railroad cars but do not manufacture finished railroad cars	9.5	12	14.5	5.5
38.0	Manufacture of professional, scientific, and controlling instruments; photographic and optical goods, watches and clocks: Includes assets used in the manufacture of mechanical measuring, engineering, laboratory and scientific research instruments, optical instruments and lenses; surgical, medical and dental instruments, equipment and supplies; ophthalmic goods, photographic equipment and supplies; and watches and clocks	9.5	12	14.5	5.5
39.0	Manufacture of products not elsewhere classified: Includes assets used in the production of jewelry; musical instruments; toys and sporting goods; pens,				

Asset guide-line class	Description of assets included	Asset depreciation range (in years) Lower limit	Asset guide-line period	Upper limit	Annual asset guide-line repair allow-ance percent-age
	pencils, office and art supplies. Also includes assets used in production of motion picture and television films and tapes; as waste reduction plants; and in the ginning of cotton	9.5	12	14.5	5.5
40.0	Railroad Transportation:				
	Includes the assets identified below and which are used in the commercial and contract carrying of passengers and freight by rail. Excludes any nondepreciable assets included in Interstate Commerce Commission accounts enumerated for this class. Excludes the transportation assets included in class 00.2 above.				
40.1	Railroad machinery and equipment	11	14	17	10.5
	Includes assets classified in the following Interstate Commerce Commission accounts:				
	Road accounts:				
	(16) Station and office buildings (freight handling machinery and equipment only)				
	(25) TOFC/COFC terminals (freight handling machinery and equipment only)				
	(26) Communication systems				
	(27) Signals and interlockers				
	(37) Roadway machines				
	(44) Shop machinery				
	Equipment accounts:				
	(52) Locomotives				
	(53) Freight train cars				
	(54) Passenger train cars				
	(55) Highway revenue equipment				
	(57) Work equipment				
	(58) Miscellaneous equipment				
40.2	Railroad structures and similar improvements	24	30	36	5.0
	Includes assets classified in the following Interstate Commerce Commission road accounts:				
	(6) Bridges, trestles, and culverts				
	(7) Elevated structure				
	(13) Fences, snowsheds, and signs				
	(16) Station and office buildings (stations and other operating structures only)				
	(17) Roadway buildings				
	(18) Water stations				
	(19) Fuel stations				
	(20) Shops and enginehouses				

Asset guide-line class	Description of assets included	Asset depreciation range (in years): Lower limit	Asset guide-line period	Upper limit	Annual asset guide-line repair allow-ance percent-age
	(25) TOFC/COFC terminals (operating structures only)				
	(31) Power transmission systems				
	(35) Miscellaneous structures				
	(39) Public improvements construction				
40.3	Railroad wharves and docks	16	20	24	5.5
	(23) Wharves and docks				
	(24) Coal and ore wharves				
40.5	Railroad power plant and equipment:				
	Electric generating equipment:				
40.51	Hydraulic	40	50	60	1.5
40.52	Nuclear	16	20	24	3.0
40.53	Steam	22.5	28	33.5	2.5
40.54	Steam, compressed air, and other power plant equipment	22.5	28	33.5	7.5
41.0	Motor transport-passengers: Includes assets used in the urban and interurban commercial and contract carrying of passengers by road, except the transportation assets included in class 00.2 above	6.5	8	9.5	11.5
42.0	Motor transport-freight: Includes assets used in the commercial and contract carrying of freight by road, except the transportation assets included in class 00.2 above	6.5	8	9.5	11.0
44.0	Water transportation: Includes assets used in the commercial and contract carrying of freight and passengers by water except the transportation assets included in class 00.2 above	16	20	24	8.0
45.0	Air transport: Includes assets used in the commercial and contract carrying of passengers and freight by air	5	6	7	14.0
46.0	Pipeline transportation: Includes assets used in the private, commercial, and contract carrying of petroleum, gas, and other products by means of pipes conveyors. The trunk lines related storage facilities of integrated petroleum and natural gas producers are included in this class	17.5	22	26.5	3.0
48.0	Communication: Includes assets used in the furnishing of point-to-point communication services by wire or radio, whether intended to be received aurally or visually; and radio broadcasting and television.				

Asset guide-line class	Description of assets included	Asset depreciation range (in years) Lower limit	Asset guide-line period	Upper limit	Annual asset guide-line repair allow-ance percent-age
48.1	Telephone: Includes the assets identified below and which are used in the provision of commercial and contract telephonic services:				
48.11	Central office buildings: Assets intended to house central office equipment as defined in Federal Communications Commission Part 31 Account No. 212 whether section 1245 or section 1250 property	36	45	54	1.5
48.12	Central office equipment: Includes central office switching and related equipment as defined in Federal Communications Commission Part 31 Account No. 221 ...	16	20	24	6.0
48.13	Station equipment: Includes such station apparatus and connections as teletypewriters, telephones, booths, private exchanges and comparable equipment as defined in Federal Communications Commission Part 31 Account Nos. 231, 232, and 234	8	10	12	10.0
48.14	Distribution plant: Includes such assets as pole lines, cable, aerial wire and underground conduits as are classified in underground conduits, and comparable equipment as defined in Federal Communications Commission Part 31 Account Nos. 241, 242.1, 242.2, 242.3, 242.4, 243, and 244 .	28	35	42	2.0
48.2	Radio and television broadcasting	5	6	7	10.0
48.3	Telegraph, Ocean Cable, and Satellite Communications: Includes communications-related assets used to provide domestic and international radio-telegraph, wire-telegraph, ocean-cable, and satellite communications services.				
48.31	Electric Power Generating and Distribution Systems .. Includes assets used in the provision of electric power by generation, modulation, rectification, channelization, control, and distribution. Does not include these assets when they are installed on customers' premises..	15.0	19.0	23.0	—
48.32	High Frequency Radio and Microwave Systems ...... Includes assets such as transmitters and receivers, antenna supporting structures, antennas, transmission lines from equipment to antenna, transmitter cooling systems, and control and amplification	10.5	13.0	15.5	—

Asset guide-line class	Description of assets included	Asset depreciation range (in years)			Annual asset guide-line repair allow-ance percent-age
		Lower limit	Asset guide-line period	Upper limit	
	equipment. Does not include cable and long-line systems.				
48.33	Cable and Long-line Systems	21.0	26.5	32.0	—
	Includes assets such as transmission lines, pole lines, ocean cables, buried cable and conduit, repeaters, repeater stations, and other related assets. Does not include high frequency radio or microwave systems.				
48.34	Central Office Control Equipment	13.0	16.5	20.0	—
	Includes assets for general control, switching, and monitoring of communications signals including electromechanical switching and channeling apparatus, multiplexing equipment, patching and monitoring facilities, in-house cabling, teleprinter equipment, and associated site improvements.				
48.35	Computerized Switching, Channeling, and Associated Control Equipment	8.5	10.5	12.5	—
	Includes central office switching computers, interfacing computers, other associated specialized control equipment, and site improvements.				
48.36	Satellite Ground Segment Property	8.0	10.0	12.0	—
	Includes assets such as fixed earth station equipment, antennas, satellite communications equipment, and interface equipment. Does not include general purpose equipment or equipment used in satellite space segment property.				
48.37	Satellite Space Segment Property	6.5	8.0	9.5	—
	Includes satellites and equipment used for telemetry, tracking, control, and monitoring.				
48.38	Equipment Installed on Customer's Premises	8.0	10.0	12.0	—
	Includes assets installed on customer's premises, such as computers, terminal equipment, power generation and distribution systems, private switching center, teleprinters, facsimile equipment, and other associated and related equipment.				
48.39	Support and Service Equipment	11.0	13.5	16.0	—
	Includes assets used to support but not engage in communications. Includes store, warehouse, shop, tools, and test and laboratory assets.				
48.4	Cable television:				
	Includes communications—related assets used to provide cable television (community antenna television) services. Does not include assets used to				

Asset guide-line class	Description of assets included	Asset depreciation range (in years) Lower limit	Asset guide-line period	Upper limit	Annual asset guide-line repair allow-ance percent-age
	provide subscribers with two-way communications services.				
48.41	Headend	9	11	13	5
	Includes assets such as towers, antennas, preamplifiers, converters, modulation equipment, and program non-duplication systems. Does not include headend buildings and program origination assets.				
48.42	Subscriber connection and distribution systems	8	10	12	5
	Includes assets such as trunk and feeder cable, connecting hardware, amplifiers, power equipment, passive devices, directional taps, pedestals, pressure taps, drop cables, matching transformers, multiple set connecter equipment, and converters.				
48.43	Program origination	7	9	11	9
	Includes assets such as cameras, film chains, video tape recorders, lighting, and remote location equipment excluding vehicles. Does not include buildings and their structural components.				
48.44	Service and test	7	8.5	10	2.5
	Includes assets such as oscilloscopes, field strength meters, spectrum analyzers, and cable testing equipment, but does not include vehicles.				
48.45	Microwave systems	7.5	9.5	11.5	2
	Includes assets such as towers, antennas, transmitting and receiving equipment and broad band microwave assets if used in the provision of cable television services. Does not include assets used in the provision of common carrier services.				
49.0	Electric, gas and sanitary services:				
49.11	Electric utility hydraulic production plant:				
	Includes assets used in the hydraulic power production of electricity for sale, related land improvements, dams, flumes, canals, and waterways	40	50	60	1.5
49.12	Electric utility nuclear production plant:				
	Includes assets used in the nuclear power production of electricity for sale and related land improvements	16	20	24	3.0
49.121	Nuclear fuel assemblies:				
	Includes initial core and replacement core nuclear fuel assemblies (i.e., the composite of fabricated nuclear fuel and container) when used in a boiling water, pressurized water, or high				

Asset guide-line class	Description of assets included	Asset depreciation range (in years)			Annual asset guide-line repair allow-ance percent-age
		Lower limit	Asset guide-line period	Upper limit	
	temperature gas reactor used in the production of electricity. Does not include nuclear fuel assemblies used in breeder reactors	4.0	5.0	6.0	—
49.13	Electric utility steam production plant: Includes assets used in the steam power production of electricity for sale, combustion turbines operated in a combined cycle with a conventional steam unit, and related land improvements	22.5	28	33.5	2.5
49.14	Electric utility transmission and distribution plant: Includes assets used in the transmission and distribution of electricity for sale and related land improvements	24	30	36	2.0
49.15	Electric utility combustion turbine production plant: Includes assets used in the production of electricity for sale by the use of such prime movers as jet engines, combustion turbines, diesel engines, gasoline engines and other internal combustion engines, their associated power turbines and/or generators, and related land improvements. Does not include combustion turbines operated in a combined cycle with a conventional steam unit	16	20	24	4.0
49.2	Gas Utilities: Includes assets used in the production, transmission, and distribution of natural and manufactured gas for sale, including related land improvements and identified as:				
49.21	Distribution facilities: Including gas water heaters and gas conversion equipment installed by utility on customers' premises on a rental basis	28	35	42	2.0
49.22	Gas making facilities:				
49.221	Manufactured gas production plant: Includes assets used in the manufacture of gas having chemical and/or physical properties which do not permit complete interchangeability with domestic natural gas	24	30	36	2.0
49.222	Substitute natural gas (SNG) production plant (naphtha or lighter hydrocarbon feedstocks): Includes assets used in the catalytic conversion of feedstocks of naphtha or lighter hydrocarbons to a gaseous fuel which is completely interchangeable with domestic natural gas	11	14	17	4.5

Asset guide-line class	Description of assets included	Asset depreciation range (in years) Lower limit	Asset guide-line period	Upper limit	Annual asset guide-line repair allow-ance percent-age
49.23	Natural gas production plant	11	14	17	4.5
49.24	Trunk pipelines and related storage facilities	17.5	22	26.5	3.0
49.3	Water utilities: Includes assets used in the gathering, treatment, and commercial distribution of water	40	50	60	1.5
49.4	Central steam production and distribution: Includes assets used in the production and distribution of steam for sale	22.5	28	33.5	2.5
49.5	Industrial steam and electric generation and distribution systems:[5] Includes assets used in the production and distribution of electricity with rated total capacity in excess of 500 Kilowatts and/or assets used in the production and distribution of steam with rated total capacity in excess of 12,500 pounds per hour, for use by the taxpayer in his industrial manufacturing process or plant activity and not ordinarily available for sale to others. Assets used to generate or distribute electricity or steam of the type described above of lesser rated capacity are not included, but are included in the appropriate manufacturing equipment classes elsewhere specified	22.5	28	33.5	2.5
50.0	Wholesale and retail trade: Includes assets used in carrying out the activities of purchasing, assembling, sorting, grading, and selling of goods at both the wholesale and retail level. Also includes assets used in such activities as the operation of restaurants, cafes, coin-operated dispensing machines, and in brokerage of scrap metal	8	10	12	6.5
50.1	Wholesale and retail trade service assets: Includes assets such as glassware, silverware (including kitchen utensils), crockery (usually china) and linens (generally napkins, tablecloths and towels) used in qualified activities as defined in class 50.0 . .	2	2.5	3	—
65.0	Building Services[3] Provision of the services of buildings, whether for use by others or for taxpayer's own account. Assets in the classes listed below include the structural shells of buildings and all integral parts thereof; equipment that services normal heating, plumbing, air conditioning, illumination, fire prevention, and power requirements; equipment for the movement of passengers and freight within the building; and any additions to buildings or their components, capitalized remodeling costs, and				

Asset guide-line class	Description of assets included	Asset depreciation range (in years) Lower limit	Asset guide-line period	Upper limit	Annual asset guide-line repair allow-ance percent-age
	partitions both permanent and semipermanent. Structures, closely related to the equipment they house, which are section 38 property are not included. See section 1.48-1(e)(1) of the regulations. Such structures are included in asset guideline classes appropriate to the equipment to which they are related. Depreciation periods for assets used in the provision of the services of buildings and which are not specified below shall be determined according to the facts and circumstances pertinent to each asset, except in the case of farm buildings and other building structures for which a class has otherwise been designated.				
65.1	Shelter, space, and related building services for manufacturing and for machinery and equipment repair activities:				
65.11	Factories		45		
65.12	Garages		45		
65.13	Machine shops		45		
65.14	Loft buildings		50		
65.2	Building services for the conduct of wholesale and retail trade, includes stores and similar structures		50		
65.3	Building services for residential purposes:				
65.31	Apartments		40		
65.32	Dwellings		45		
65.4	Building services relating to the provision of miscellaneous services to businesses and consumers:				
65.41	Office buildings		45		
65.42	Storage:				
65.421	Warehouses		60		
65.422	Grain elevators		60		
65.43	Banks		50		
65.44	Hotels		40		
65.45	Theaters		40		
70.0	Services:				
70.1	Administrative Services:				
	Includes assets used in administering normal business transactions and the maintenance of business records, their retrieval and analysis, whether these services are performed for others or for taxpayer's own account and whether the assets are located in a single location or widely dispersed.				
70.11	Office furniture, fixtures, and equipment:				
	Includes furniture and fixtures which are not a structural component of a building. Includes				

Asset guide-line class	Description of assets included	Asset depreciation range (in years) Lower limit	Asset guide-line period	Upper limit	Annual asset guide-line repair allow-ance percent-age
	such assets as desks, files, safes, and communications equipment (not to include communications equipment which is included in other ADR classes)	8.0	10.0	12.0	2.0
70.12	Information systems:				
	Includes computers and their peripheral equipment (does not include equipment that is an integral part of other capital equipment and which is included in other ADR classes of economic activity, i.e., computers used primarily for process or production control, switching and channeling)	5.0	6.0	7.0	7.5
	Information systems defined:				
	1) Computers: A computer is an electronically activated device capable of accepting information, applying prescribed processes to the information and supplying the results of these processes with or without human intervention. It usually consists of a central processing unit containing extensive storage, logic, arithmetic and control capabilities. Excluded from this category are adding machines, electronic desk calculators, etc.				
	2) Peripheral equipment consists of the auxiliary machines which may be placed under control of the central processing unit. Nonlimiting examples are				
	Card readers, card punches, magnetic tape fees, high speed printers, optical character readers, tape cassettes, mass storage units, paper tape equipment, keypunches, data entry devices, teleprinters, terminals, tape drives, disc drives, disc files, disc packs, visual image projector tubes, card sorters, plotters, collators.				
	Peripheral equipment may be used on-line or off-line.				
70.13	Data Handling Equipment, except Computers:				
	Includes typewriters, calculators, adding and accounting machines, copiers and duplicating equipment	5.0	6.0	7.0	15.0
70.2	Personal and Professional Services:				
	Includes assets used in the provision of personal services such as those offered by hotels and motels, laundry and dry cleaning establishments, beauty and barber shops, photographic studios and mortuaries. Includes assets used in the provision of professional services such as those offered by doctors, dentists, lawyers, accoun-				

Asset guide-line class	Description of assets included	Asset depreciation range (in years) Lower limit	Asset guide-line period	Upper limit	Annual asset guide-line repair allow-ance percent-age
	tants, architects, engineers, and veterinarians and which are not classified in other ADR classes. Includes assets used in the provision of repair and maintenance services and those assets used in providing fire and burglary protection services and which are not classified in other ADR classes. Includes equipment or facilities used by cemetery organizations, news agencies, teletype wire services, plumbing contractors, frozen food lockers, research laboratories, hotels, and motels and which are not classified in other ADR classes	8	10	12	6.5
70.21	Personal and professional services—service assets: Includes assets such as glassware, silverware, crockery, and linens (generally sheets, pillowcases and bath towels) used in qualified activities as defined in class 70.2	2	2.5	3	—
79.0	Recreation: Includes assets used in the provision of entertainment services on payment of a fee or admission charge, as in the operation of bowling alleys, billiard and pool establishments, theaters, concert halls, and miniature golf courses. Does not include amusement and theme parks and assets which consist primarily of specialized land improvements or structures, such as golf courses, sports stadia, race tracks, ski slopes, and buildings which house the assets used in entertainment services	8	10	12	6.5
80.0	Theme and amusement parks: Includes assets used in the provision of rides, attractions, and amusements in activities defined as theme and amusement parks, and includes appurtenances associated with a ride, attraction, amusement or theme setting within the park such as ticket booths, facades, shop interiors, and props, special purpose structures, and buildings other than warehouses, administration buildings, hotels, and motels. Includes all land improvements for or in support of park activities, (e.g., parking lots, sidewalks, waterways, bridges, fences, landscaping, etc.) and support functions (e.g., food and beverage retailing, souvenir vending, and other non-lodging accommodations) if owned by the park and provided exclusively for the benefit of park patrons. Theme and amusement parks are defined as combinations of amusements, rides, and attractions which are permanently situated on park land and open to				

Asset guide-line class	Description of assets included	Asset depreciation range (in years) Lower limit	Asset guide-line period	Upper limit	Annual asset guide-line repair allow-ance percent-age
	the public for the price of admission. This guideline class is a composite of all assets used in this industry except transportation equipment (general purpose trucks, cars, airplanes, etc. which are included in asset guideline classes with the prefix 00.2), assets used in the provision of administrative services in asset guideline classes with the prefix 70.1, and warehouses, administration buildings, hotels, and motels	10	12.5	15	12.5

1. This class is established for a three-year transition period in accordance with section 109(e)(1) of the Revenue Act of 1971 (P.L. 92–178, I.R.B. 1972–3, 14) and will be in effect for the period beginning January 1, 1971 and ending January 1, 1974 or at such earlier date as of which asset classes incorporating the assets herein described are represcribed or modified.
2. All asset classes defined below include subsidiary assets within the meaning of Section 109(e)(2) of the Revenue Act of 1971 whenever such assets are used in the economic activities specified. However, in accordance with the provisions of that section of the Act, during the period beginning on January 1, 1971 and ending January 1, 1974 or such earlier date as of which asset classes incorporating the subsidiary assets are represcribed or modified, taxpayers may exclude from an election all subsidiary assets in a specified class provided that at least 3 percent of all the assets placed in service in the class during the taxable year subsidiary assets. See section 1.167(a)-11(b)(5)(vii) for application of 3 percent test.
3. This class is established for a three-year transition period in accordance with Section 109(e)(1) of the Revenue Act of 1971 (P.L. 92–178, CB 1972-1, 443) and will be in effect for the period beginning January 1, 1971 and ending January 1, 1974 or at such earlier date as of which asset classes incorporating the assets herein described are represcribed or modified. See Sections 1.167(a)-11(b)(3)(ii), 1.167(a)-11(b)(4)(i)(a), and 1.167(a)-11(b)(5)(vi) of the regulations for special rules relating to real property.
4. Does not include any assets not classified in manufacturing activity classes, e.g., does not include assets classified in asset guideline classes 00.1 through 00.3, 70.11 through 70.13 or 65.1 through 65.45.
5. This is subclass and is treated as an addition to and part of the appropriate class to which it relates for purposes of the Regs. §1.167(a)-11(b)(5)(v) rule concerning property depreciated or amortized by special methods.
6. Rev. Proc. 74-37 says that if the ADR repair allowance deduction is elected, "cold tank repairs," including refractory relining expenditures to glass furnaces, must be treated as Regs. §1.167(a)-11 (d)(2(iv) (a) deductible repairs.

Waiver of Restrictions on Assessment and Collection of Deficiency in Tax and Acceptance of Overassessment (Form 870)

Pursuant to section 6213(d) of the Internal Revenue Code of 1954, or corresponding provisions of prior internal revenue laws, the undersigned waives the restrictions provided in section 6213(a) of the Internal Revenue Code of 1954, or corresponding provisions of prior internal revenue laws, and consents to the assessment and collection of the following deficiencies with interest as provided by law. The undersigned also accepts the following overassessments as correct:

DEFICIENCIES

YEAR ENDED	KIND OF TAX	AMOUNT OF TAX	PENALTY	

OVERASSESSMENTS

YEAR ENDED	KIND OF TAX	AMOUNT OF TAX	PENALTY	

NAME AND ADDRESS OF TAXPAYER(S) *(Number, street, city or town, State, ZIP Code)*

(The Internal Revenue Service does not require a seal on this form, but if one is used, please place it here.)

Signature(s)		DATE
		DATE
BY	TITLE	DATE

NOTE: The execution and filing of this waiver will expedite the adjustment of your tax liability. It is not, however, a final closing agreement under section 7121 of the Internal Revenue Code and does not preclude assertion of a further deficiency in the manner provided by law if it is later determined that additional tax is due; nor does it extend the statutory period of limitation for refund, assessment, or collection of the tax.

Furthermore, execution and filing of this waiver will not preclude the taxpayer's filing under section 6511 of the Code a timely claim for refund or credit, on which (if disallowed by the Service) suit may be brought in the appropriate District Court or the U.S. Court of Claims.

If this waiver is for a year for which a JOINT RETURN was filed, it must be signed by both husband and wife unless one, acting under a power of attorney, signs as agent for the other.

If the taxpayer is a corporation, this waiver must be signed with the corporate name followed by the signature and title of the officer(s) duly authorized to sign.

This waiver may be signed by the taxpayer's attorney or agent provided his action is specifically authorized by a power of attorney which, if not previously filed, must accompany the form.

If this waiver is signed by a person acting in a fiduciary capacity (such as executor, administrator, trustee, etc.), Form 56, "Notice of Fiduciary Relationship," should, unless previously filed, accompany this form.

U.S. GOVERNMENT PRINTING OFFICE : 1969 O—108-033

FORM 870 (REV. 6-69)

Offer of Waiver of Restrictions on Assessment and Collection of Deficiency in Tax and of Acceptance of Overassessment (Form 870-AD)

Pursuant to the provisions of section 6213(d) of the Internal Revenue Code of 1954, or corresponding provisions of prior internal revenue laws, the undersigned offers to waive the restrictions provided in section 6213(a) of the Internal Revenue Code of 1954, or corresponding provisions of prior internal revenue laws, and to consent to the assessment and collection of the following deficiencies with interest as provided by law. The undersigned offers also to accept the following overassessments as correct:

DEFICIENCIES

YEAR ENDED	KIND OF TAX	TAX				

OVERASSESSMENTS

YEAR ENDED	KIND OF TAX	TAX				

This offer is subject to acceptance for the Commissioner of Internal Revenue. It shall take effect as a waiver of restrictions on the date it is accepted. Unless and until it is accepted, it shall have no force or effect.

If this offer is accepted for the Commissioner, the case shall not be reopened in the absence of fraud, malfeasance, concealment or misrepresentation of material fact, an important mistake in mathematical calculation, or excessive tentative allowances of carrybacks provided by law; and no claim for refund or credit shall be filed or prosecuted for the year(s) stated above other than for amounts attributed to carrybacks provided by law.

SIGNATURE OF TAXPAYER		DATE	(The Internal Revenue Service does not require a seal on this form, but if one is used, please place it here.)
SIGNATURE OF TAXPAYER		DATE	
BY	TITLE	DATE	

NOTE.—The execution and filing of this offer will expedite the above adjustment of tax liability. This offer, when executed and timely submitted, will be considered a claim for refund for the above overassessments, as provided in Revenue Ruling 68-65, C.B. 1968-1, 555. It will not, however, constitute a closing agreement under section 7121 of the Internal Revenue Code.

If this offer is executed with respect to a year for which a **JOINT RETURN OF A HUSBAND AND WIFE** was filed, it must be signed by both spouses unless one spouse, acting under a power of attorney, signs as agent for the other.

If the taxpayer is a corporation, the offer shall be signed with the corporate name followed by the signature and title of the officers authorized to sign.

This offer may be executed by the taxpayer's attorney or agent provided his action is specifically authorized by a power of attorney which, if not previously filed, must accompany the form.

FOR INTERNAL REVENUE USE ONLY	DATE ACCEPTED FOR COMMISSIONER	SIGNATURE
	OFFICE	TITLE

U. S. GOVERNMENT PRINTING OFFICE : 1970 O - 100-212

FORM **870-AD** (REV. 4-70)

90-Day Letter (Notice of Deficiency—Form RSC-531)

Date:

Tax Year Ended:

Deficiency:

Information Copy Only

Person to Contact:

▷ Supersedes RSC-531 (Rev. 2-74)
Destroy Present Stock

Contact Telephone Number:

This letter is a NOTICE OF DEFICIENCY--as required by law--that we have determined the income tax deficiency shown above. We regret we have been unable to reach a satisfactory agreement in your case. The enclosed statement shows how the deficiency was computed.

If you do not intend to contest this determination in the United States Tax Court, please sign and return the enclosed Short-Form Statutory Notice Statement. This will permit an early assessment of the deficiency and limit the accumulation of interest. The enclosed self-addressed envelope is for your convenience.

If you decide not to sign and return the statement, the law requires that after 90 days from the date of mailing this letter (150 days if this letter is addressed to you outside the United States) we assess and bill you for the deficiency. However, if within the time stated you contest this determination by filing a petition with the United States Tax Court, 400 Second Street, N.W., Washington, D.C. 20217 we may not assess any deficiency and bill you until after the Tax Court has decided your case. The time in which you may file a petition with the Court (90 or 150 days, as the case may be) is fixed by law, and the Court cannot consider your case if your petition is filed late.

The United States Tax Court has a simplified procedure for handling cases where the disputed portion of the deficiency does not exceed $1,500. You can obtain information on this special procedure, as well as a copy of the rules for filing a petition with the Tax Court, by writing to the Clerk of the Tax Court at the address shown in the third paragraph of this letter.

If you have any questions, please contact the person whose name and telephone number are shown above.

Sincerely yours,

Commissioner
By

Director, Service Center

Enclosures:
Statement
Envelope

Strip in "P.O. Box, City, State, ZIP Code" of Service Center Audit Div., in bottom left corner (face only) aligned with form number (½" left, ⅜" bottom margin). (10 pt News Gothic Bold)

Form RSC–531 (Rev. 11–74)

30-Day Letter (Form RSC-564)

Address any reply to: P.O. Box 450, Holtsville, N.Y. 11742

Department of the Treasury

Internal Revenue Service Center

North-Atlantic Region

Date: JAN 27 1975 | In reply refer to: Dif

Tax Year Ended:

Dear Taxpayer:

Enclosed are two copies of our report explaining why we believe adjustments should be made in the amount of your income tax. Please look this report over and let us know whether you agree with our findings.

If you agree with our findings, please sign the consent on one copy of the report and mail it to this office within 15 days from the date of this letter. If additional tax is due, you may send your payment with a copy of the report; otherwise, we will bill you. (See the enclosed publication for payment details.)

If you do not agree with our findings, you may do one of the following within 15 days from the date of this letter:

1. Mail us any additional evidence or information you would like us to consider.

2. Request a meeting with a tax auditor at one of our local district offices. Please write or phone us and we will transfer your case to your district office. They will contact you to arrange a convenient time and place. During this informal discussion, you may submit any additional evidence or information you would like considered.

3. Request a conference with a conferee at one of our district offices. Please write or phone us and we will transfer your case to the conference staff in your district office and they will contact you. The conferee will not be the person who examined your return. However, since the examination was conducted entirely by correspondence, we would appreciate your first discussing our findings with a tax auditor, as in item 2, above.

The enclosed publication concerning unagreed cases explains your appeal rights.

Form **RSC-564** (8-72)

If we do not hear from you within 30 days, we will have no alternative but to process your case on the basis of the adjustment shown in the enclosed examination report. If you write us about your case, please refer to the symbols on the front of this letter. A self-addressed envelope is enclosed for your convenience.

Thank you for your cooperation.

Sincerely yours,

Charles De Marco Jr.

Chief, Service Center Audit Division

Enclosures:
Examination Report (2)
Publication 5
Envelope

If you need to call us, our telephone number is 516-654-6367

Report of Individual Income Tax Audit Changes (Form 1092-E)

Name of Taxpayer	Year	Form	Filing Status	In Reply Refer To:
	73	1040	JOINT	AU:CA:DIF
Name And Title of Person With Whom Audit Changes Were Discussed	Date of Report		Social Security No.	Examining District
	1-27-75			19

INCOME AND DEDUCTION AMOUNTS ADJUSTED

Explanation No. (See Attached)	Items Changed	Amount Shown on Return or As Previously Adjusted	Corrected Amount of Income And Deduction	Adjustments Increase or (Decrease)
21.04	CONTRIBUTIONS	470.00	.00	470.00
21.04	MEDICAL & DENTAL EXPENSES	1485.11	.00	1485.11
	If you agree with this determination, please sign and return this copy.			

A. Adjustment in Income--Increase or (Decrease)--(See Explanation of Adjustments Attached)			1955.11
B. Total Income or Taxable Income Reported or as Previously Adjusted			4391.27
C. Corrected Total Income or Taxable Income			6346.38
D. Tax Computed With Exemptions 3	.190	140.00	1065.81
E. Tax Surcharge			.00
F. Tax Credits (Retirement Income, Investment, Foreign, or Other Allowable Credits) (If Adjusted, See Explanation Attached)			
G. Self-Employment Tax, Tax From Recomputing Prior Year Investment Credit (If Adjusted, See Explanation Attached)			
H. Corrected Tax (Line D Plus Line E Plus Line G Less Line F)			1065.81
I. Tax Shown on Return or as Previously Adjusted			694.34
J. Statutory Deficiency (Additional Tax Before Credits, Line H Less Line I)			371.47
K. Overassessment (Overpayment Before Credits, Line I Less Line H)			
L. Net Prepayment Credits, Excess FICA, Non-Highway Gasoline Tax Credit, Regulated Investment Company Undistributed Capital Gain Credit, Previous Assessments, Refunds, And Credits (If Adjusted, See Schedule Attached)			694.34
M. Additional Tax (Line H Less Line L)			371.47
N. Overpayment (Line L Less Line H)			
O. Penalties, If Any (See Explanation Attached)			

Although this report is subject to review you may consider it as your written notice that your case is closed if you are not notified of an exception to these findings within 30 days after a signed copy of this report or a signed waiver, Form 870, is received by the District Director. If you agree, please sign one copy and return it in the enclosed return envelope. Keep the other copy with your records.

Consent To Assessment And Collection.. I Do Not Wish To Exercise My Appeal Rights With The Internal Revenue Service or To Contest in The United States Tax Court The Findings in This Report: Therefore, I Give My Consent To Either:
(1) The Immediate Assessment And Collection of The Additional Tax Shown on Line M. Plus Any Interest Due on This Tax, And Also Any Penalties Shown on Line O. or
(2) The Overpayment Shown on Line N. Plus Any Interest And Adjusted By Any Penalties Shown on Line O.

Signature of Taxpayer	Date	Signature of Spouse, if Joint Return	Date

FORM **1902-E** CONTINUOUS (REV. 8–70)

Explanation of Adjustments (Form 3547)

SINCE YOU HAVE NOT ESTABLISHED THAT YOU ARE
ENTITLED TO CERTAIN ITEMIZED DEDUCTIONS
LISTED IN THE REPORT,THE DEDUCTION IS DIS-
ALLOWED AND YOUR INCOME TAX HAS BEEN RECOMPUTED
ACCORDINGLY.

```
*****   SINCE YOU HAVE NOT ESTABLISHED THAT YOU ARE
*   *   ENTITLED TO CERTAIN ITEMIZED DEDUCTIONS
*   *   LISTED IN THE REPORT,THE DEDUCTION IS DIS-
*****   ALLOWED. IN RECOMPUTING YOUR INCOME TAX, THE
        MINIMUM STANDARD, OR THE 15 PERCENT STANDARD
        DEDUCTION, WHICHEVER IS GREATER, HAS BEEN
        ALLOWED.
```

Form 3547 (2-63)

Appeal Rights and Preparation of Protests For Unagreed Cases (Publication 5)

INSTRUCTIONS

IF YOU AGREE

If you decide to agree with the findings of the examiner in the enclosed examination report, please sign and return to that officer the agreement form enclosed with our transmittal letter. By signing you will indicate your agreement to the amount shown on the form; and if you owe additional tax, you will stop a six percent interest charge 30 days after filing the form. No further interest (or penalties) will be charged unless you fail to pay the amount you owe within ten days after you receive a notice of such amount. However, if you pay the tax when you sign the agreement form, interest stops immediately.

If you wish to pay, make your check or money order payable to the Internal Revenue Service. Include interest on the additional tax (but not on penalties) at six percent a year from the due date of the return to the date of payment. Please do not send cash through the mail. If the examination results in a refund, the Internal Revenue Service can refund your money more promptly if you sign the agreement form. You will receive interest at the rate of six percent per year on the amount of the refund.

IF YOU DON'T AGREE

If you decide not to agree with the examiner's findings, we urge you to first appeal your case to higher levels within the Service before you go to court.

Because people sometimes disagree on tax matters, the Service maintains a system of appeals. Most differences can be settled in these appeals without expensive and time-consuming court trials.

If you do not want to appeal your case in the Service, however, you can take it directly to court.

The following general rules tell you how to appeal your case.

APPEAL WITHIN THE SERVICE

We have two levels of appeal: The District Conference Staff and the Appellate Division.

Your first level of appeal from the findings of the examiner is the District Conference Staff. If you want a District conference, ask for it in accordance with our letter to you enclosing these instructions. We will then arrange a meeting at a convenient time and place, and a conferee from the Staff will discuss the disputed issues fully with you or your representative. You or your representative should be prepared to discuss all disputed issues and present your views at this meeting, in order to save the time and expense of additional conferences. Most differences are resolved at this level.

If you and the conferee don't reach agreement at your District conference, however, you may appeal your case to the second level—the Appellate Division in the Regional Commissioner's office. Or, if you do not want a District conference, you may appeal directly to the Appellate Division.

If you want an Appellate Division hearing, address your request to your District Director in accordance with our letter to you enclosing these instructions. Your District Director will forward your request to the Appellate Division, which will arrange for a hearing at a convenient time and place.

If agreement is not reached at your District conference or your Appellate Division hearing, you may, at any stage of these procedures, take your case to court. See the last headings in this publication concerning appeals to the courts.

WRITTEN PROTESTS

So that your case may get prompt and full consideration by the District or Appellate conferee, you need to file a written protest with the District Director. You don't have to file a written protest, however, if you are appealing to the District Conference Staff, and

(1) the proposed increase or decrease in tax, or claimed refund, does not exceed $2,500 for any of the tax periods involved; or

(2) your examination was conducted by correspondence or by an interview at our office.

A written protest is required for an Appellate Division hearing in all cases except those (1) where the amount involved does not exceed the $2,500 limit described above and (2) you appealed to the District Conference Staff first. If you filed a protest for your District conference, you don't have to file another for the Appellate Division hearing.

If a written protest is required, it should be submitted in duplicate within the 30-day period granted in the letter transmitting the report of examination and should contain:

1. A statement that you want to appeal the findings of the examining officer to the District Conference Staff or to the Appellate Division, as the case may be;
2. Your name and address;

3. The date and symbols from the letter transmitting the proposed adjustments and findings you are protesting;
4. The tax periods or years involved;
5. An itemized schedule of the adjustments with which you do not agree;
6. A statement of facts supporting your position in any contested factual issue; and
7. A statement outlining the law or other authority upon which you rely.

A statement of facts, under 6 above, must be declared true under penalties of perjury. This may be done by adding to the protest the following signed declaration:

"Under the penalties of perjury, I declare that I have examined the statement of facts presented in this protest and in any accompanying schedules and statements and, to the best of my knowledge and belief, they are true, correct, and complete."

If your representative submits the protest for you, he may substitute a declaration stating:

(1) That he prepared the protest and accompanying documents; and
(2) Whether he knows personally that the statements of fact contained in the protest and accompanying documents are true and correct.

REPRESENTATION

You may represent yourself at your District conference or Appellate Division hearing, or you may be represented by an attorney, certified public accountant, or an individual enrolled to practice before the Internal Revenue Service. Your representative must be qualified to practice before the Internal Revenue Service. If he attends a conference without you, he must file a power of attorney or a tax information authorization before he may receive or inspect confidential information. Form 2848, Power of Attorney, or Form 2848-D, "Authorization and Declaration" (or any other properly written power of attorney or authorization) may be used for this purpose. Copies of these forms may be obtained from any Internal Revenue Service office.

You may also bring witnesses to support your position.

APPEALS TO THE COURTS

If you and the Service disagree after your conference or hearing, or if you skipped our appeals system, you may take your case to the United States Tax Court, the United States Court of Claims, or your United States District Court. These courts are independent judicial bodies and have no connection with the Internal Revenue Service.

TAX COURT

If your case involves a disagreement over whether you owe additional income tax, estate or gift tax, or excise tax of a private foundation, you may go to the United States Tax Court. To do this, ask the Service to issue a formal letter, called a statutory notice of deficiency. You have 90 days from the date this notice is mailed to you to file a petition with the Tax Court (150 days if addressed to you outside the United States).

The Court will schedule your case for trial at a location convenient to you. You may represent yourself before the Tax Court, or you may be represented by anyone admitted to practice before that Court.

In cases involving tax disputes of $1,000 or less for any year ($1,500 or less beginning January 1, 1974), there are simplified procedures. Information regarding these procedures and other matters relating to the Court may be obtained from the Clerk of the Tax Court, Box 70, Washington, D. C. 20044.

DISTRICT COURT AND COURT OF CLAIMS

You may take your case to your United States District Court or to the United States Court of Claims. Certain types of cases, such as those involving manufacturers' excise taxes, can be heard only by these courts. Generally, your District Court and the Court of Claims hear tax cases only after you have paid the tax and have filed a claim for refund. You can obtain information about procedures for filing suit in either court by contacting the Clerk of your District Court; or the Clerk of the Court of Claims, 717 Madison Place, N.W., Washington, D. C. 20005. If we haven't acted on your claim within six months from the date you filed it, you can then file suit for refund, and you can also file suit for refund at any time within two years after we have disallowed your claim.

☆U.S. GOVERNMENT PRINTING OFFICE: 1973-733-297/3434